C000109157

edited by
Daniel Naegele

the letters of
Colin Rowe five decades of
correspondence

Artifice
books on architecture

For Pavleena.

And in memory of Dorothy Rowe.

———

Generously supported by The Graham Foundation for Advanced Studies in Fine Arts.
Also supported by Iowa State University and Paul Mellon Centre for British Art.

Contents

List of Recipients

Acknowledgements

In 1987, when I was a student at the Architectural Association in London, at my request Dorothy Rowe wrote for me a three-page biography of her famous brother-in-law. Four days later, at Colin Rowe's insistence, she rescinded it; but for many years my bootlegged copy of her biography remained the only reliable information I had on Colin Rowe, this despite much searching of London libraries. Were it not for Dorothy Rowe, I would not have written at all about Colin Rowe. Her enthusiasm and love for her brother-in-law were infectious, and most fortunately her significant presence is evident in Colin's many letters to her in this collection. Dorothy died in 1996, but it is she who I would like to thank most. This book is dedicated to her memory.

In May 2009, when I first began to collect material for this book, I requested letters from, among many others, Alan Colquhoun, David Rowe, and Paul Zygas. Their unbridled enthusiasm for the subject and their insistence on its importance overwhelmed me. I am most grateful to all three, especially to David Rowe who provided many of the letters and many of the photographs for this collection. He hosted me in London and Oxford and coached me through trips to Bolton-on-Dearne, Castle Howard, and the Yorkshire countryside. For his exceptional generosity as well as for his wonderful insights about and profound affection for his brother, I am very, very thankful.

Robert Maxwell was Colin Rowe's friend and colleague from 1940 until Rowe's death in 1999 and knew him longer and perhaps better than did anyone except Colin's brother, David. Maxwell graciously talked with me at length in Oxford and in Liverpool. He wrote on my behalf for funding and for years he has answered my many email questions—this in addition to his own wonderful writings on Rowe. He has contributed more than he will ever know to the making of this book and I am most grateful.

John Miller, Michael Spens, Judith DiMaio, Steven Peterson and Simon Rowe have added tremendously to my understanding of Rowe. I owe special thanks to them for their many letters and photographs, of course, and for their extreme kindness and patience in answering my questions, but mostly for their unique knowledge and love of Colin Rowe.

I am very grateful for the many observations, suggestions and wonderful stories offered to me by Bruce Abbey, Stanford Anderson, George Baird, Richard Becherer, Matt Bell, Julia Bloomfield, Nicholas Boyarsky, Lisa Germany, Charles Graves Jr, Maddy and Phil Handler, Mark Hinchman, Marco Iuliano, Brian Kelly, Tom Muirhead, Werner Oechslin, and Mary Stirling. All kindly and patiently answered my many questions and their insights have greatly enriched both this book and my understanding of Colin Rowe.

The Graham Foundation, Iowa State University, and the Paul Mellon Centre for British Arts financially supported the development and publication of this collection. Without their help it would not have been possible to do this work. I am very indebted to them and to Mary McLeod, Joan Ockman, and Robert Maxwell who wrote to these institutions in support of this project.

I owe a special debt of gratitude to Tony Eardley, at one time co-editor of this book, and to his son Dominic, whose technical support was invaluable to me. I am also very grateful to Debra Wheeler for her months of editorial assistance and to Maddy Handler who helped—indeed, managed—the writing of biographical notes and who, together with her husband, Phil, assisted me time and again locating photographs for the book. I thank Joy Kestenbaum in New York City who enthusiastically served as genealogist to this project, unearthing much valuable information on Rowe's parents and grandparents and rescuing me often when finishing seemed all but impossible.

Most especially I thank Patricia DeMartino in Rome who tirelessly and generously advised me on all things Italian, editing both Rowe's use of foreign languages and my translations of these foreign phrases. Her tremendous knowledge of Italy and Italian language, as well as French, German and Latin, brought rigor and substance to my notes. Her kind, methodical and thorough attention bettered the book enormously.

At Iowa State University, Gregory Palermo secured funding for me to travel to Lexington and to Austin. More importantly, he talked to me often about the project, offering valuable insights and making remarkable connections that never would have occurred to me otherwise. Mira Engler and Gaye Simonson were instrumental in obtaining an Iowa State Book Subvention Grant for this project. Numerous Iowa State University librarians assisted my long-distance research, Carlota Guttierez being especially helpful. Samantha Krukowski gave much-needed advice on publishing and Deborah Hauptmann's interest in Colin Rowe's writing inspired me to completion. I thank all of them.

Many others deserve very special thanks for their help in the making of this book. They include: Valerie Bennett, Barry Bergdoll, Philip Bess, Guglielmo ('Billi') Bilancioni, Andre Brown, Glenn Brown, Brenda Canniff, Robert Davis, Heather Dean, Michael Dennis, Diane Dorney, Elaine Engst, Marcie Farwell, Kenneth Frampton, Jose Gelabert-Navia, Michelle Ghaffari, Lorna Goudie, Renata Hejduk, Mui Ho, Zhengyang Hua, Marco Iuliano, Iain Jackson, Ruixue Jia, Edward Jones, Kevin Keim, Brian Kelly, Deborah Koshinsky, Peter Land, Kristyn Leinen, Roberta Marcaccio, Igor Marjanovic, Rick Mather, Daniel Myers, Eisha Neely, Hannah Newell, Janet Parks, Rachel Pfleger, Will Plambeck, Elizabeth Plater-Zyberk, James Rowe, Pat Sachs, William Saunders, Denise Scott Brown, Margie Shackleford, Graham Shane, Roger Sherwood, Howard Shubert, Dale Smith, Sue Taylor, Jorge and Luis Trellis, Jesse Turpen, Wilvan Van Campen, Anthony Vidler, Victoria Watson, Jerry A Wells, Bill Whitaker, Iain Boyd White, Glenn Williams, Judith Wolin and Hilary Wong. To all, I am most grateful.

Abbreviations

A.A.	Architectural Association	M.P.	Member of Parliament
A.D.	*Architectural Design*	MoMA	Museum of Modern Art
A.R.	*The Architectural Review*	mon	money
apt.	apartment	N.B.	*Nota Bene*, Italian: note well
B.O.D.	Bolton-on-Dearne	N.Y.	New York
BRF	British Royal Family	NYT	*The New York Times*
C.U.	Cornell University	P. of W.	Prince of Wales
D.	David Rowe	P.O.W.	Prince of Wales
D. & D.	David and Dorothy Rowe	Pce	Prince
E.E.C.	European Economic Community	Pcesse	Princess
fac	faculty	Q. of E.	Queen of England
G.B.	Great Britain	Q.V.	Queen Victoria
Geo. V	King George V	Qu.V.	Queen Victoria
GSD	Graduate School of Design	R.F.	Royal Family
H.B.M.	Her Britannic Majesty	R.G.M.	Royal Gold Medal
H.R.H.	Her Royal Highness	S.	Simon Rowe
I.	Ireland	SMR	St Margaret's Road
J.	James Rowe (mostly)	U.D.	Urban Design
J. & S.	James and Simon Rowe	v.	very
J.S.	James Stirling		
lec	lecture		
lib.	library		

Un abbraccio, Italian: a hug, an embrace

Colin Rowe
a brief biography

This book is a collection of letters, a sometimes-uneven portrait of Rowe written over a 56-year period by Rowe himself. It is not a biography. However, because the letters offer much previously unknown information about Rowe, a revised biography is needed. Revision is especially necessary for the years from 1938—the year Rowe entered the University of Liverpool—to 1980—a time shortly after the publication of his first and most influential books, *The Mathematics of the Ideal Villa and Other Essays* and *Collage City*. This sketch focuses on that time. It follows Rowe through his years of study at Liverpool; his military service; and the time he spent at the Warburg Institute with Rudolf Wittkower.* It details his movements from Liverpool to the United States; his teaching in Texas, in New York City, and in Ithaca; his return to England to teach at Cambridge; and his subsequent return to the US to teach for 30 years at Cornell. It examines his concerns for staying in the US, his need to return to England, and his desire in the mid-1950s to secure a permanent teaching position in either one country or the other. Additionally, it gives an account of his early essays—the first essay that he wrote in 1947, and the essays he later wrote in the US in the 1950s—and discusses the two books mentioned above and the circumstances under which they were written.

Perhaps the greatest architectural theorist of the late twentieth century, Colin Frederick Rowe was born on 27 March 1920 to Frederick W* and Helena (née Beaumont) Rowe* in Rotherham, England, just eight miles south of Bolton-on-Dearne, the South Yorkshire coal-mining community where he lived for the first 18 years of his life. His father was a schoolteacher and his only sibling, David,* was born in October 1928. As a child, Rowe excelled at English and history, winning scholarships to the nearby Wath-on-Dearne grammar school and later a West Riding Scholarship to the University of Liverpool, 85 miles west of his hometown.[1] At the age of 18, in the fall of 1938, he began to study architecture there.[2]

Less than a year after Rowe began his studies in Liverpool, Britain declared war on Germany. In early December 1942, he was "called up" and after completing basic military training he enlisted in the British Royal Air Force later that month, volunteering for the paratroopers.[3] In early July 1943, in a practice parachute jump in England, he sustained a severe injury to his spine. Placed in a cast from his neck to his hips, he was hospitalized for more than six months. The first and oldest letter in this collection was written at that time, on 20 August 1943, to a University of Liverpool colleague, Ursula Mercer.* It describes in detail both the accident and the hospital life that followed it.[4]

In January 1944, Rowe was discharged from hospital and from military service and returned to the University of Liverpool to complete his studies. The Polish School of Architecture had moved to Liverpool in 1942 to escape Germany's occupation of Warsaw, bringing to the largely neo-classical English school an interest in Modern architecture, particularly the work of Le Corbusier,* though Rowe's thesis project, completed in 1945, did not reflect this interest.[5] A design for "Pump Rooms and Baths for Cheltenham", the thesis, his colleague Robert Maxwell* remembered, was "sort of classical [with] a number of axes, that terminated on niches containing statues".[6]

In 1946, Rowe moved from Liverpool to London, to a basement apartment in Chelsea to begin graduate studies in Art History at the Warburg Institute under

the supervision of Rudolf Wittkower.[7] Wittkower, a German Jew and renowned scholar of Italian Renaissance and Baroque art and architecture, had fled Germany for London in 1933 and in 1934 had begun teaching at the University of London's Warburg Institute. It was while he was a student of Wittkower's, at the age of 26, that Rowe wrote what would prove to be his most famous essay, "The Mathematics of the Ideal Villa".[8] Published in the blue pages of the March 1947 issue of *The Architectural Review*, the essay related contemporary architecture to the architecture of the Renaissance through the medium of proportional numbers. It employed the villas of Le Corbusier and Andrea Palladio* as examples. An authority on mathematics and proportions in Renaissance architecture, Wittkower was "not amused, in fact he was horrified" by the essay, Rowe wrote in the mid-1990s. "Apparently I had not, as I hoped […], made Palladio in any way accessible to a twentieth century sensibility [and], almost as bad as this, I had damaged modern architecture's myth of absolute uniqueness."[9] Eight months after the publication of the essay, Rowe submitted to Wittkower his Warburg thesis "Theoretical Drawings of Inigo Jones: Their Sources and Scope".[10] Unlike "The Mathematics of the Ideal Villa", this writing apparently pleased Wittkower and in 1953 he, himself, took up the subject of Inigo Jones.[11]*

Even before Rowe had completed his Warburg studies, he began teaching architecture at the University of Liverpool, overseeing the thesis of Robert Maxwell first in 1947–1948 and then again in 1948–1949.[12] In 1950, he supervised the thesis of James Stirling* who would later become a world-renowned architect and Rowe's best friend. Neither Maxwell's nor Stirling's theses, however, showed evidence of the classicizing tendencies apparent in Rowe's own 1945 thesis. Rather the published work of Le Corbusier was the obvious influence on both.[13]

After three years of teaching at Liverpool, in late summer 1951, Rowe moved to the US, to New Haven, Connecticut to study for a year at Yale on a combined Smith-Mundt fellowship and Fulbright Scholarship. There, together with his Liverpool friend Brian Richards,* he attended lectures by the renowned architectural critic and historian Henry-Russell Hitchcock.* Hitchcock later befriended the two and ultimately had a profound influence on Rowe with whom he corresponded regularly for the next three years.[14]

In June 1952, Rowe and Richards purchased Bill Jordy's Willys Jeep and, despite the University of Liverpool's expectation that Rowe would return there to teach, the two set off across North America on a year-long tour. As documented in the letters to his parents and to Hitchcock, the tour included a trip to Mexico and visits to numerous recently completed buildings, among them Ludwig Mies van der Rohe's* Farnsworth House; the architecture of the 'Chicago School'; and Frank Lloyd Wright's* Johnson Wax Headquarters, Taliesin, Taliesin West, and numerous Usonian houses. Also visited were works by Bruce Goff and Frank Lloyd Wright in Oklahoma; by Philip Johnson* in Houston; and by Richard Neutra in Southern California. During the trip, Rowe and Richards supported themselves financially by working for brief periods in architectural offices in Vancouver and in Bakersfield, California.[15]

Returning from Mexico in April 1953, Rowe met Jean Harris* in Norman, Oklahoma, where Bruce Goff chaired the university's department of architecture. Her husband, Harwell Hamilton Harris,* was completing his inaugural year as chair of the newly established Department of Architecture at the University of Texas at Austin. She suggested Rowe apply to teach at Texas. Uncertain about both the US and Texas, and concerned about beginning his career so far from the established centers of architectural education, in May Rowe wrote to Hitchcock from Houston for advice. "After the real west", he said, he now found Texas "rather depressing". However, he now was weary of the nomadic life he had been living, a life that left him with a "complete inability to take any more travel". America had had "a delightfully expanding effect" on him; indeed, before coming to America, he was "beginning to feel like a gramophone record caught in a Corbu groove". But after 18 months in the US, "I've at least discovered that the groove is of no absolute significance", he wrote. Still, he told Hitchcock, he could not decide "as to whether to go back to England, whether to work down here for some time longer and return at a leisurely rate to New York, or whether to attach myself once again to some university."[16]

Over the next nine months, he did all three. After a brief stay in Houston, he moved to New York City. From there, a few months later, he telephoned Harwell Hamilton Harris in California to secure a teaching position in Austin, one that would begin in January 1954. He then left for England to visit his parents to whom he had been promising his return for nearly two years. Two days before sailing from New York to visit them, though, on 7 September 1953, he wrote them, telling them that he had decided to return to America after the first of the year, a decision he rationalized in economic terms. "I don't know what you would have one do", he reasoned. "Stick around in Liverpool? Or live in London […] and not have money left for anything. You know $120 is rather better than £12 as a weekly salary." He then reassured them: "I would never dream of staying in this country nor on this side of the Atlantic, but one may as well make the best of it while one can."[17]

Despite the distance of Texas from England and from the US East Coast, and despite the brevity and turbulence of his teaching engagement there, teaching in Texas proved of great importance. It offered Rowe stability and intelligent companionship as well as an opportunity to initiate a way of teaching aligned with his innate intelligence and talents. Robert Slutzky,* Bernhard Hoesli,* Werner Seligmann,* John Hejduk,* Lee Hodgden,* and Lee Hirsche* were new faculty. Like Rowe, all believed in the formal values of European Modernism. As with the Warsaw Poles in Liverpool a decade earlier, they brought news of Modern architecture to a provincial state giving Rowe the opportunity to couple his extensive knowledge of past architectures with contemporary architectural theory and concerns.

Teaching at Texas was intimately tied to a social scene that was often dramatic and that more often than not seemed to delight Rowe. In a lengthy letter to Hitchcock dated 23 September 1955, he cast the architecture faculty as characters in a satirical play, first recognizing that teaching in Austin "has been a most illuminating experience and I know that I could have only experienced it with such devastating charity in Texas", and then speculating that, "It has I think something to do with the light and something to do with geography. H.H.H. miscalculated Texas […] He did not understand that the Texans, because of geographical accident, will always prefer order to expression. That Texas is the predestined colony of Chicago and not that of the Bay Region." Though Rowe later described Austin as his "forty days in the desert", in 1998, writing nostalgically of his Texas years, he entertained the idea of establishing an archive of his furniture, rugs, prints and papers in Austin at the Charles Moore Foundation, "an 'in my beginning is my end' affair […] a little tribute to Texas which, after all is said and done, does remain my favorite state".[18]

During the years between 1953 and 1957, including the Texas years, Rowe wrote some of his best-known essays though many were not published until much later and are known only in their amended forms. Before coming to America, he had published two essays in *The Architectural Review*, Britain's premier professional journal. During his initial seven-year stay in the US, however, he published only two short reviews and two essays: the 1956 essay "Chicago Frame" in *The Architectural*

Review; and the 1957 essay "Lockhart, Texas" in the American *Architectural Record*, co-authored by John Hejduk with whom he had taught in Austin.[19] In 1953 and 1954, before Texas and prodded by Henry-Russell Hitchcock, Rowe had written "Character and Composition", but the essay was published only in 1974 when Rowe's former student and friend Peter Eisenman* featured it in *Oppositions*. A year earlier, in 1973, Eisenman and *Oppositions* had published "Neo-'Classicism' and Modern Architecture" parts 1 and 2 written in New York City the year after he left Texas.[20] In 1963, the Yale journal *Perspecta* published for the first time "Transparency: Literal and Phenomenal, Part I", an important essay Rowe had written with Robert Slutzky when the two were teaching together in Texas between 1955 and 1966.

Rowe taught at Austin for five semesters only, from January 1954 to June 1956. The first three of these semesters were taught under Harwell Hamilton Harris who resigned as chair of the department in June 1955. A year later, Rowe returned to the East Coast to live in New York City and teach at Cooper Union before moving to Ithaca in fall 1957 to teach at Cornell. After an academic year at Cornell, in fall 1958, he returned to England to begin teaching at the University of Cambridge where he remained for four years, though, as the letters show, he quickly recognized the return as a mistake, "the great folly of my life" as he wrote to Joan Ockman* in 1999.[21] In fall 1962, with the consent of Leslie Martin,* Director of Architecture at Cambridge, he returned to Cornell with the intent to teach as visiting professor for one semester only. On arriving in Ithaca, however, he was offered a three-year position as Associate Professor, and though Cornell ranked only third on his list of preferred institutions in which to teach in the US, he readily accepted the job.[22]

At Cornell in 1963, Rowe initiated an Urban Design Program that attracted students from across the US as well as from Europe, Asia and the Caribbean. Though the program was a great success and the students some of the finest that Rowe would ever teach, and though Rowe had time and again expressed his dislike of life in England, in spring 1966 he interviewed for the position of Chair of the Architectural Association in London and later that year expressed interest in the possibility of teaching permanently at Princeton. No position was offered him at either institution, however, and he remained at Cornell for the next three decades, occasionally considering the prospects of teaching at Yale, Harvard, Princeton or Columbia.

In the mid- and late-1960s, seemingly unaffected by either the tremendous social unrest or rapid rise in popular culture that defined these years, Rowe dedicated his efforts to resolving the difficult urban design issues that plagued American cities. In 1965–1966, he led his Cornell Urban Design studio in a project for improving the waterfront of Buffalo, New York. Shortly after, with a different group of Cornell students, he completed a competition entry for the urban renewal of Harlem. During this time, too, he wrote a joint review for *The New York Times* of Robert Venturi's *Complexity and Contradiction in Architecture* and Reyner Banham's* *The New Brutalism*, two books seminal to architectural theory in the years following the death of Modern architecture's master, Le Corbusier.[23]

In 1969, Oswald Matthias Ungers,* a German colleague concerned with urban design issues in Europe, assumed the chairmanship of Cornell's Department of Architecture. In 1967, Ungers had asked Rowe to chair the Free University of Berlin. Rowe declined. Less than two years later, when Ungers was being considered for chairmanship at Cornell, Rowe enthusiastically supported the nomination.

Ungers began at Cornell in fall 1969, a semester when Rowe was at the American Academy in Rome. Rowe had believed Ungers would be sympathetic to his Urban Design Program, but this was not the case. Writing in 1971 to his friend John Miller* in London, he noted, "You liked Ithaca in '66 because I had made a scene here. But this scene, apparently, aroused jealousy, so every attempt has been made to smash it by that insufferable [Ungers]".[24]

In December 1972, Ungers fired Fred Koetter,* Alan Chimacoff, and Roger Sherwood, three young professors who Rowe had taught in his Urban Design Program in the 1960s. Exasperated, Rowe turned his attention to his own personal development, focusing on both writing and publishing his previously written essays and lectures as books. "The catastrophes which have fallen on this place have resulted in at least one good", he wrote to Robert Slutzky in August 1973. "One can say 'forget it' and, forgetting the lack of education which the students are now about to receive, one can concentrate upon the, personally, more advantageous."[25]

A year before writing to Slutzky, Rowe had written an introduction to *Five Architects: Eisenman, Graves, Gwathmey, Hejduk, Meier*, broaching the subject of a legitimate Modern architecture. Immediately after, from August to December 1973, he and Fred Koetter wrote *Collage City*. At the same time, he published two essays written in the 1950s, "Neo-'Classicism' and Modern Architecture" and "Character and Composition"[26] and in fall 1976, he published an essay he had written several years earlier, "Robert Venturi and the Yale Mathematics Building".[27]

At this time, too, Rowe published his first book in English, *The Mathematics of the Ideal Villa and Other Essays*, a collection of essays he had written more than 15 years earlier.[28] The book took its title from the 1947 "The Mathematics of the Ideal Villa" that Rudolf Wittkower had so disliked at the time of its publication. According to Rowe, in 1947 Wittkower had found the essay "trivial and frivolous", thought that it "made an impossible comparison", and that its "findings could only be irrelevant". Rowe regarded Wittkower's harsh dismissal of this, his first published work, as "the most devastating criticism" he had ever received.[29] For the re-publication, he made small but significant changes to the wording of the 1947 edition of the essay and provided it with a new illustrative text. The alterations made the comparisons universal, investing the essay with a special vocabulary and relieving it of the triviality that Wittkower had condemned.

The subtle changes made manifest a new critical position, one that Rowe had developed and refined during the intervening three decades. Five of the other eight essays in the book were not published at the time of their completion in the 1950s. This heightened their mystique and allowed time for amendments. For the book, Rowe revised their illustrative texts, and gave two dates for each essay: the date when the essay was written and the date when it was first published. In the end, Rowe's selection, alignment, and careful editing of both verbal and illustrative texts in *The Mathematics of the Ideal Villa and Other Essays* allowed him to present in 1976 his critical position in essays he had written before 1961. Published a decade after Robert Venturi's *Complexity and Contradiction* and a year before Charles Jencks'* *The Language of Post-Modern Architecture*, *The Mathematics of the Ideal Villa and Other Essays* predated by two years the publication of the already-written *Collage City*.[30]

Co-authored by Fred Koetter in the latter half of 1973, *Collage City* was intended as an essay to be published in *The Architecture Review* as early as 1974, but it proved too long. Consequently, it was sent to Rowe's friend, Michael Spens,* for publication as a 'slim book'. After years of delays, publication was reassigned to MIT Press. The lag time proved important. The book came out at a time more favorable to its reception. In addition, as urban theory, *Collage City* seems logically to follow the critical position established in *The Mathematics of the Ideal Villa and Other Essays*. But *The Mathematics of the Ideal Villa and Other Essays*, though published first, was edited and organized after *Collage City* had been written. The essays in *The Mathematics of the Ideal Villa and Other Essays* are not arranged chronologically, but in an order that progresses from the individual to the collective, from singular buildings to urban design.[31] "The Mathematics of the Ideal Villa" opens the collection; "The Architecture of Utopia" closes it, establishing a trajectory that anticipates the already-written *Collage City*. In other words, Rowe could construe *The Mathematics of the Ideal Villa and Other Essays* to lead logically to *Collage City*.

Collage City found Modern architecture, contemporary urban design, and the theories on which both were based to be lacking. Its proposed remedies championed the past over the present. While some regarded this as heresy, others understood it as an ingenious assessment of the contemporary urban situation and admired the temporal depth of its suggested solutions. Famous or infamous, *Collage City* was immensely popular and Rowe's renown spread. More and more he was called away from Ithaca to teach and to lecture: at Notre Dame in Indiana; at Rice in Texas; at the University of Virginia; in Germany, Switzerland, and England; and most frequently in Rome and Florence.

In 1984, Bernhard Hoesli, Rowe's friend and colleague who had translated *Collage City* to German, died unexpectedly at the age of 62. Rowe wrote to Dorothy, his sister-in-law in England, of the "most violent extremities of grief" he was experiencing. Surprised by the depth of this emotion, he explained it as brought on by the loss of two aspects of life he loved dearly. "One grieves for people because they are no longer available for dinner", he told her, "because one had planned little dinners for them and little drives around places in Toscana".[32] At the age of 64, he was confronted with his own mortality.

In 1985, Cornell named Rowe the Andrew Dixon White Professor of Architecture. In the same year, the American Institute of Architects awarded him the Topaz Medal for Excellence in Education for his "seminal influence on architecture in this country". In October 1985, he underwent successful hip surgery in Boston. And in 1986 and 1987 he worked to further establish the Cornell programs in architecture and urban studies in Rome.

But in late October 1987, in Ithaca he was again confronted with mortality when his friend and Cornell colleague, JO Mahoney,* died. His concern for his own legacy began to grow, manifesting itself in his assessment of his personal wealth and in anxiety over the fate of his library—a collection he regarded "in a minor way [...] 'Warburgian'."[33] By the late-1980s, he wanted to leave Ithaca permanently but made no move to do so. Still living there in 1990, having retired from Cornell and with his students now 50 years his junior, he felt alienated. "People come from Boston and Miami and New York and Los Angeles; but this isn't exactly like Voltaire at Ferney", he wrote to his brother, David. "People ring up from Rome and Bilbao; but never, never have I received a phone call from any colleague here. Nor, do I think, will."[34] He began to regard Ithaca not as a small, remote college town, but as a tiny fraction of a larger geographic area that he likened to areas of nineteenth-century Russia described in the novels of Ivan Turgenev, an area he called "Upstate".

In early 1992, Rowe moved from Ithaca to Rome where he taught for the last time for Cornell before moving to London, to an apartment his brother David had prepared for him. In June 1992 his best friend, James Stirling, died suddenly and tragically in a British hospital after undergoing minor surgery. Devastated, Rowe remained in London only through the summer after which time he returned to Ithaca. In early 1993, he underwent back surgery in Boston, and in September 1993 he moved back to London again.

Rowe planned on writing extensively during his retirement. In the 15 years since the 1978 publication of *Collage City*, he had published many essays, but no books though clearly he had expected to. In 1973, 20 years earlier, he had written to Robert Slutzky of his ambitions to publish four books: *The Mathematics of the Ideal Villa and Other Essays*; *Collage City*; a book to be titled *The Architecture of Good Intentions: Towards a Critical Retrospect* (designating a 1975 publication date); and, *The Theoretical Drawings of Inigo Jones and John Webb*.[35] And in 1979, he had written to Roger Conover★ at MIT Press of his plans to write an "anthology of Disraeli pieces [...] concerning houses, people, politics" to be called *The Disraeli Book*, as well of plans to write *The Architecture of Good Intentions*, a book "for which notes and text [existed] in abundance" including "bits of which I have, for years and years, thrown away as items in casual lectures". Though the books on Inigo Jones★ and on Benjamin Disraeli★ were never realized, in 1993 he contracted with Academy Editions in England to publish *The Architecture of Good Intentions*, which came out the following year while he was living in London. In addition to *The Architecture of Good Intentions*, and also while living in London and with much editorial assistance from Alex Caragonne,★ Rowe assembled a three-volume collection of essays, memoirs, and eulogies that he titled *As I Was Saying* and ultimately published in the US in 1996.

Finding London expensive, lacking in stimulation, and without the friendships he had anticipated—Alvin Boyarsky★ had died in 1990; Douglas Stephen and James Stirling in 1992—in fall 1994, Rowe returned to the US, to Washington, DC, where several of his closest friends and former students were teaching at the University of Maryland. There he wrote a handful of essays intended for a book to be called *Footprints and Footnotes*, a collection of short writings he described as "a sort of inferior, contracted and architectural version of William Hazlitt's *The Spirit of the Age*, 1825".[36] In 1995, with Leon Satkowski★ he began to write a definitive history of the architecture he most admired, *Italian Architecture of the 16th Century*. In the same year, in recognition of his lifelong achievements in teaching and writing—the "most significant architectural teacher of the second half of the 20th century" and "one of modern architecture's most consistent and inspired critics"—Rowe received the Royal Institute of British Architect's gold medal, the highest honor of its kind.

Around this time, in 1995, in a remarkable 'in anticipation' auto-obituary, Rowe wrote of himself, "For all his obvious happiness in the United States, he remained very English." Like his beloved WH Auden★ or a character in a Henry James★ novel, his identity was intimately linked to his displacement. Born and educated in England, he never married and he had no children. He lived in the US for 44 of his 79 years often returning to Western Europe for lengthy stays in England and in Italy and to lecture in Germany and Switzerland. Still, in 1987, he became a US citizen. Five years later, he retired to England only to return to America again in 1994.

A professor and architectural theorist of the highest order, Rowe combined his special understanding of the history of politics and high society with an extensive knowledge of six hundred years of the history of Western architecture, first-hand observations of Western architecture and landscapes, and an understanding of contemporary philosophies of science and liberty to arrive at a critical view of twentieth-century architecture. His writings reflected this understanding and could often be obscure. Typically—with the exception of *Italian Architecture of the 16th Century* published posthumously by co-author Leon Satkowski—they were either long essays or collections of essays and talks. He was an extraordinary 're-presenter', an essayist of great genius who delighted in opportunities to adjust, renovate, and reorder. Like Hadrian's villa or the poems of WH Auden, his writings are verbal bricolage, his words 'carefully careless'.

Much of Rowe's best writing is found in his letters. Convinced in 1977 that his influence belonged "not so much to the area of the printed word, as to the areas of, apparently, casual speech and suggestive, provocative drawing", in the 20 years following the publication of *Collage City*, he assumed a style of writing that spoke as he spoke, a fireside chat style of relaxed conversation first cultivated in the letters written in the last two decades of his life.[37] Uninhibited by the printed page, given structure and space by the typewriter and colored paper, these letters had Rowe's voice. They *talked*, and as such proved the perfect medium for a man so utterly adept at saying what he thought, telling us what we would never know otherwise. "In a man's letters, you know, Madam", Dr Johnson wrote to Hester Thrale in 1777, "his soul lies naked, his letters are only the mirror of his breast, whatever passes within him is shown undisguised in its natural process. Nothing is inverted, nothing distorted, you see systems in their elements, you discover actions in their motives."[38]

Rowe died on 5 November 1999, having suffered a stroke earlier that year. The following spring, his ashes were scattered in Yorkshire, England at Castle Howard's Temple of the Four Winds, the pavilion that in 1726 Sir John Vanbrugh had modeled after Palladio's sixteenth-century Villa Rotonda.

---

1   Dorothy Rowe,★ in a three-page biography of Colin Rowe she wrote for Daniel Naegele★ in 1987.
2   To her 10 September 2014 email reply to my enquiry regarding Rowe and the University of Liverpool, Lorna Goudie, Library Assistant in the Special Collections and Archives at the University of Liverpool Library, attached a scan of an index card, the University's primary record of Rowe. The card lists Rowe's "Date of Entry" to the University as "October, 1938"; his dormitory as "Derby Hall"; his thesis as "Pump Rooms and Baths for Cheltenham"; and under "Subsequent Career" it notes, among much else, "Called up 3.12.42"; "injured paratrooper discharged Jan 1944 retd to school"; and "October 1948 Appointed Lecturer and Studio Instructor, Liverpool School of Architecture". In addition, Goudie wrote of a second index card in the library's holdings that describes Rowe's graduation. It reads: "ROWE, COLIN FREDERICK / B.Arch (II) 7th July 1945". She notes that the words "Honours" and "Class" are crossed out.
3   See note 2 above. According to Robert Maxwell,★ "called up" was the British equivalent of the American "drafted".
4   Letter to Ursula Mercer★ dated 20 August 1943 (see p 29 in this volume).
5   Rowe's own account of his time at the University of Liverpool and of the Polish School there in the 1940s can be found in Rowe, Colin, "James Stirling: A Highly Personal and Very Disjointed Memoir", *James Stirling: Buildings and Projects*, Peter Arnell and Ted Bickford ed, New York: Rizzoli, 1984, pp 10–13. For the Polish School, see both Szmidt, Boleslaw, ed, *The Polish School of Architecture, 1942–1945*, Liverpool: Charles Birchall and Sons, Ltd, 1945, and proceedings from the symposium on the Polish School held at the University of Liverpool, 28 November, 2013.
6   Robert Maxwell,★ in an email to Daniel Naegele,★ 30 August 2014. The email continues: "That was a feature that he borrowed from David Crowe. Crowe was an Englishman who lived a couple of years in Paris. It was a pretty awful design, but Liverpool wasn't high on design at this time. Colin wasn't either. He could talk, he knew just about everything, but he was no good as a designer." Regarding the title to Rowe's thesis, see note 2 above.
7   From an unpublished, untitled, undated paper written by Rowe around 1997.
8   Rowe, Colin, "The Mathematics of the Ideal Villa: Palladio and Le Corbusier Compared", *The Architectural Review* 101, March 1947, pp 101–104.
9   See note 29.
10 Rowe, Colin, "Theoretical Drawings of Inigo Jones: Their Sources and Scope", MA thesis, University of London, November 1947.
11 Wittkower, Rudolf, "Inigo Jones, Architect and Man of Letters", *Journal of the Royal Institute of British Architects*, LX 1953, pp 83–90.
12 In an email to the editor on 1 August 2014, Robert Maxwell★ wrote: "I returned to Liverpool in September 1947 to do my final year, and Colin was my tutor. I couldn't work, I suppose from wartime stress, and withdrew at Easter, returning in September, again with Colin as tutor. So he started work as Fifth Year master in 1947." The University of Liverpool's index card record of Rowe (see note 2 above) states: "October 1948 Appointed Lecturer and Studio Instructor, Liverpool School of Architecture".

13 By 1947, Le Corbusier* had published the first three volumes of his *Œuvre Complète*. For Stirling's* thesis project, see Arnell, Peter and Ted Bickford eds, *James Stirling Buildings and Projects*, New York: Rizzoli, 1984, pp 28–29.

14 For more on Hitchcock,* see Rowe's 1988 essay "Henry-Russell Hitchcock" in Rowe, Colin, *As I Was Saying: Recollections and Miscellaneous Essays*, Alexander Caragonne ed, 3 vols, Cambridge, MA: MIT Press, 1996, vol 1, pp 11–23.

15 For the Vancouver firm of Sharp Thompson Berwick & Platt, Rowe and Richards* designed the Seamans Institute in 1952, described in detail in a 21 March 1996 letter to Phyllis Lambert* and in a 6 August 1998 letter to Joan Ockman* (see p 473 and p 530 in this volume). For the Bakersfield California firm of Wright, Metcalf & Parsons, they designed the Bakersfield College in September, 1952 described in the September, 1952 letter to Henry-Russell Hitchcock* (see p 58 this volume).

16 Letter to Henry-Russell Hitchcock* dated 6 May 1953 (see p 77 in this volume).

17 Letter to Mr* and Mrs Frederick Rowe* dated 17 September 1953 (see p 85 in this volume).

18 Letter to Irving Phillips* dated 20 May 1998 (see p 528 in this volume). Rowe's library, a small collection of his papers, and few of his personal possessions are held at the Charles Moore Foundation located in Moore's former home and studio, in Austin, Texas. "In my beginning is my end" is the opening line of TS Eliot's 1940 poem, "East Coker".

19 The illustrative text of the 1976 republished "Chicago Frame" featured images of Wright's* Mrs Thomas Gale House, Jenney's Second Leiter Building, and Burnham's Reliance Building, all buildings Rowe might have seen on his visit to Chicago in 1952. It also featured Wright's St Mark's Towers project, later built as the Price Tower in 1953, a building Rowe had seen in Oklahoma. Ostensibly concerned with the steel frame as manifestation of both the ideal and the real, indirectly "Chicago Frame" questions the *zeitgeist*-motivated history of Sigfried Giedion's *Space, Time and Architecture*. A third of the illustrations for Rowe's "Chicago Frame", as republished in 1976 in *The Mathematics of the Ideal Villa and Other Essays*, are the same as those in Giedion's *Space, Time and Architecture*.

20 As well as "Chicago Frame", "Lockhart, Texas" and the two "Neo-'Classicism' and Modern Architecture" essays make ample use of buildings Rowe and Richards* had visited on their travels across North America: American architecture, not Italian; Mies* and Wright,* not Le Corbusier.*

21 Letter to Joan Ockman* dated 7 January 1999 (see p 538 in this volume).

22 Letter to Alvin* and Elizabeth Boyarsky* dated 25 September 1961 (see p 130 in this volume). Rowe closes the letter by noting: "My preference would run: i. M.I.T, Princeton. ii. Columbia, iii. Cornell. But my possibilities of *entrée* would run i. Cornell, ii. M.I.T. iii. Princeton, Columbia."

23 "Waiting for Utopia" (review of Venturi, Robert, *Complexity and Contradiction in Architecture,* and Banham, Reyner *The New Brutalism), The New York Times Book Review,* 10 September 1967, p 351.

24 Letter to John Miller* dated 11 August 1971 (see p 186 in this volume).

25 Letter to Robert Slutzky* dated 21 August 1973 (see p 189 in this volume).

26 "Neo-'Classicism' and Modern Architecture", parts 1 and 2, *Oppositions,* no 1, September 1973, pp 1–26. "Character and Composition; or, Some Vicissitudes of Architectural Vocabulary in the Nineteenth Century", *Oppositions,* no 2, January 1974, pp 41–60.

27 "Robert Venturi and the Yale Mathematics Building", *Oppositions,* no 6, fall 1976, pp 1–23.

28 See bibliography. Typically considered Rowe's first book, *The Mathematics of the Ideal Villa and Other Essays* might also be thought of as his second. *Tranparenz,* a German translation of Rowe and Slutzky's* 1963 "Transparency: Literal and Phenomenal, Part I", was published in Basel by Birkhäuser in 1968.

29 English original to Rowe, Colin, "Vorwort", *Die Mathematik der idealen Villa und ander Essays,* Basel: Birkhäuser, 1998, p 9. Published only in German, this "foreword" introduces the unknown Lilian Priuli-Bon, a figure whose influence on Rowe he compares to that of Wittkower and Hitchcock. Rowe wrote a longer essay on Priuli-Bon intended for *Footprints and Footnotes,* a collection of essays unpublished on his death. Regarding this book, see the letters dated 4 January 1996 to George Baird* (p 459 in this volume); 8 March 1996 to Tom Schumacher* (p 468 in this volume); 24 March 1996 to Alexander Caragonne* (p 474 in this volume); and the mid-October 1994 memo to Cynthia Davidson* (p 415 in this volume).

30 Though the language and imagery of Jencks'* seminal book seem insincere, its account of contemporary architecture in the late-1970s is intelligent and incisive and offers a critique of Rowe and Koetter's* *Collage City* that deserves consideration.

31 For elaboration on Rowe's changes, see my unpublished thesis, "Delights of the Oblique View: A Study of Aesthetic Form and Style in the Writing of Colin Rowe", London: The Architectural Association, 1988.

32 Letter to Dorothy Rowe* dated 5 September 1984 (see p 245 in this volume).

33 Letter to David* and Dorothy Rowe* dated 11 November 1988 (see p 312 in this volume).

34 Letter to David Rowe* dated 17 November 1990 (see p 350 in this volume).

35 Letter to Robert Slutzky* dated 21 August 1973 (see p 189 in this volume). In this letter, after writing of his plans for *The Architecture of Good Intentions*, Rowe notes parenthetically that "so much of this exists […] the hold up, you know has been the inhibition about doing a demo-job on modern architecture; but, by now, the poor thing has been so demolished that a further attrition may be the only hope for salvation; and probably this book would include an excursus to be called "The Present Predicament of Architectural Education!""" He then explains his desire to publish: "You say: How funny, and I do too. It's called going public and I have always had inhibitions about its vulgarity. But, if nasty, I suppose it may be necessary; and the joke of it is that, were I to stay at Cornell—or if I don't succeed in getting out, they would/will pay me far more for a neglect of my academic duties than for any strict attention to them."

36 Letter to George Baird* dated 4 January 1996 (see p 459 in this volume).

37 Colin Rowe, in an unpublished, undated autobiographical sketch written after the 1976 publication of *The Mathematics of the Ideal Villa and Other Essays* but before the 1978 publication of *Collage City* (see pp 24–25 in this volume).

38 *The Works of Samuel Johnson*, 2 vols, New York: Alexander V Blake, 1846.

Preface

In 1991, if the telephone rang in the middle of the night and I was sleeping, it woke me and I left my bed and went to the kitchen of my Philadelphia apartment to answer it. This happened one November night at 3 am. It was, the voice on the telephone said, Colin Rowe calling.

I was not fully awake when I answered but certainly, I thought, the call was a prank. No remotely considerate person would phone at such an hour, and so I moaned into the phone, "Who is this *really*?" Undeterred, the caller said calmly, "I have received your thesis and have written you a letter regarding its content. I shall read it to you now."

I had never met Colin Rowe, though I had heard him read many years earlier. I remembered he swayed back and forth as he read a lecture, gripping the lectern firmly with both hands. The lectern rocked with his swaying causing a rhythmic, syncopated tapping that kept time as he described Italian hillside towns, "Bumpy on the outside, smooth on the inside; smooth on the inside, bumpy on the outside." The effect was mesmerizing and the memory of it that night led me to remember that I *had* sent him a paper just a few weeks before this call, a thesis unabashedly titled "Rowe's Erection: A Private Proscenium and the Elliptic Illustrations of *Collage City*". I had called it this because when said quickly and with a Midwestern habit of gluing words together, "Rowe's erection" becomes "resurrection" and the sexually suggestive blossoms into an uplift only a god might accomplish.

I wanted a title that would change itself when spoken, that would metamorphose. I wanted this because my thesis conjectured that the illustrative text of *Collage City* was replete with meaningful duplicity, that many of its images could and should be read two ways and that this conscious ambiguity visually presented the dialectical condition that Rowe and co-author Fred Koetter* championed. I liked the title and imagined that Rowe liked it, too, but he said nothing about it on the phone. Rather he proceeded to read his letter and by the time he reached the final page I knew that it *was* him. A few days later, the letter arrived by mail. It was on pink paper.

More than 17 years later, in the spring of 2009, not looking for it, I came across Rowe's letter in a box with other letters—in its original envelope with my name and a Philadelphia address typed on the front and a 29¢ red tulip stamp in its corner. I remembered some things about it. I remembered first that I hadn't expected a reply and was surprised to receive it, even after the phone call. I remembered that it was three pages long and was written on pink paper, and that the paper was heavy and the typewritten words sometimes smeared. I opened the envelope, cautiously unfolded the letter, and re-read it. Its re-reading brought back more memories: of the small Philadelphia apartment where I lived when I received the letter; of the long staircase to its front door; of the blue telephone that hung on its kitchen wall.

Though I vividly recollected the image of the letter, I remembered little of its content. Reading it again, I was astounded by the beauty of its prose. Effortlessly, it blended the off-the-cuff, intimate and contemporary with hints of English formality, nineteenth-century grammar, and exotic, sometimes foreign vocabulary. It was extravagant and expansive in an age of immediacy and curt, frugal communication. Unapologetically it presented, with exquisite prose, letter-writing as an art. I reasoned then that if Rowe had sent such a letter to me, surely he must have sent letters of a similar sort to many others—better letters written to special people, regarding special topics.

Which is the story of <u>Collage City</u> about the ikkustrations of
which you have made so many ingenious surmises. Both Fred and
myself óbjected to the pseudo chi-chi format which reduced our
text to a coffee table book; but, after five years of frustration
, just what can you do ?

Hence do not attribute this pics in C.C. either to me or to Fred.
They are the result of a <u>force majeure</u>. As part of the American
take over of this book. MIT felt obligated to accept the work of
the English compositor alrea dy appointed by Studio International.

~~Then about other things.~~

<u>Transparency</u> was written in Austin, Texas in late '55 and early '56
and was sent to the A.R. where it was conceived by Nikolaus Pevsner
to be sacréligious and, hence, it was rejected--not to see the light
of day until eyars later in <u>Perspecta</u>. And the two pieces, <u>N.C. and
M.A.</u>, were both written at a small apt. which I had in N.Y.C. on
East 9oth between Madison and Park. It was in a brownstone, now demolished for a large new apt building on Madisón, at the center of
what developers now like to call Carnegie Hill; but it wasn't called
that in my time. And my time there <u>was</u> '56-'57. But where to publish ?

Pevsner,and perhaps Banham too, had deprived me of the resource of
the A.R. and these two pieces, slight though they may be, were <u>un P⊗
troppos intellectuale</u> for the American architectural press of that
period. So,yet again, they languished in darkness, only to see the
light of day after P.D.E. set up <u>Oppositions</u>.

And now a quote from Alexander Pope:
    Oh let me flap this bug with gilded wings
    This painted thing of dirt that stinks and stings.
So my bug during these years was, primarily, Peter Reyner Banham,
that populist (I think card carrying) Marxist about whom I could
say so much--not susceptible to publication. But just one thing:
aesthetic <u>nerve</u> or aesthetic <u>verve</u> ? But <u>very</u> different implications ?
And don't you just turn a letter upside down to make the point ? But
this is exactly what happened in the Mumford article of way back. <u>My</u>
text, which said <u>nerve</u>, was sent for my correction as <u>verve</u>; and I
wrote a special letter back to insist on <u>n</u> rather than <u>v.</u> However,
no matter, it still came out as <u>v.</u> And, in this as in much else, I
feel enitled to perceive the manipulations of P.R,B. Because <u>verve</u>

But before 2009, I had seen only one Rowe letter other than mine: a black and white copy of the 1956 letter he had written to the famous architect Louis Kahn.* His letter to me was very different. Personal, informal, and humorous, it had no point to argue but seemed instead to want to ruminate, to set the record straight. When he had read it on the phone, it was flat and officious; when I read it silently to myself, it seemed personal and talkative. In it Rowe recalled the conditions under which his own writings had been made. He expressed his extreme dislike of a contemporary British critic—a "populist (I think card-carrying) Marxist"—who he was certain regarded him, Colin Rowe, as "erudite, *sans gene*, presumably rich […] like someone escaped from a late Henry James novel".[1] And he ended the letter by questioning the English "sincerely", preferring instead the Italian *un abbraccio fervente per tu*. But after ending the letter, after having signed it, he opened it anew with a P.S. that questioned its necessity:

But, having gotten so far, I rang up Fred and Fred (pseudo cowboy from Montana) said to me: <u>But why are you being so protractedly nineteenth century, your sort of letters were gone away long ago. Just ring the bastard up</u>. Not what Fred exactly said but what he intimated; and, therefore, my phone call.

"Just ring the bastard up." But one imagines that Rowe wrote this letter, as he must have written many other letters, not simply to communicate efficiently with another person, but to give voice in written form to what he was thinking, to *see* what he was saying—and without needing to concern himself with the person to whom he was speaking. "*Écrirer, c'est une façon de parler sans être interrompu.*"[2] Rowe's phone call was not a substitute for his written words, it was a *voice* for them. By speaking the letter, he transformed it. "Fred said"; "so protractedly nineteenth century". Its rhyming was made to be read aloud. The letters were uninterrupted conversations and eventually Rowe's essays became like that, too. In 1996 he titled his final collection of them *As I Was Saying*.

For years I believed Rowe's middle-of-the-night phone call and the eccentricities of his letter unique to me. The call, the casualness of the letter, made it personal and inimitable. Only when I collected hundreds of Rowe's letters did I know otherwise. Colored paper, gossip, ambiguity, innuendo and multiple postscripts are found in many Rowe letters from the 1980s and 1990s. To learn they were not unique to my letter altered my understanding of the nature of Rowe's letters in general. I had believed the form spontaneous and unconsidered, I now thought it intentional, calculated, evolved to be both object and event simultaneously. The phone call facilitated this.

The publication of the letters as a collection cannot convey the letter as event. This book records Rowe's words, but alters the image of those words. The colored paper, the typewriter rhythm, the smudges and texture of handwriting are gone. Letters once unique are reproduced here as similar in size and identical in shape, color, and texture. Once specific to a time and place, the private letter is now arranged chronologically and placed in the context of other letters. The original form of the letter adopts another order, that of the printed page.

And yet the collection has many advantages. A collection of letters makes letter writing evident as a medium. Through comparison and contrast its characteristics become apparent. What is written in a letter and the manner in which it was written, gains significance by association with the facts in other letters. Perceptions expressed in a single letter are modified, enlarged, made more evident when expressed in different circumstances, at different times. Things are rendered differently when told from different points of view. We see how Rowe's style of writing, his construction of his own perceptions changes over the course of decades; how as a means of expression it creates and re-creates that which it talks about. With each letter we know something that we had not known before about Rowe and one imagines Rowe himself would have applauded this way of knowing him. "You see I believe in the reading of memoirs, diaries, autobiographies, biographies and the like", he wrote to a former student in 1996. "That is because, like Disraeli, I conceive these to be the stuff out of which history is made. Then, also, it's because I do like a bit o' gossip...."[3]

The letter was an ideal medium for Rowe and he wrote a better letter than almost anyone. Informal and casual, the letter encouraged immediate, uninhibited recording of thought—expression structured by grammar and tempered by the cadence of type writing. It allowed him to write his voice, to invest the written word with oral quality. It allowed him to present his impressions; express his emotions; talk without fear of repercussions; to gossip; to ruminate; to assemble many thoughts as one; and to exercise his love of writing English language. Are the letters merely a postscript to 'Rowe writing'? To me, the letters are more than just 'merely'. Their after-the-fact presentation is a Colin Rowe postscript that casually calls into question—even as it qualifies and explains—much of what he wrote in his life. It illuminates Colin Rowe. More importantly, it illuminates the art of writing.

Editorial Remarks

The book favors the famous Colin of the later years over the unknown Colin of earlier years. Only 40 of the letters in this collection are from 1943 to 1958, while more than half are from the last 15 years of Rowe's life, 1984 to 1999. There were far fewer letters available from the early years. David Rowe,* Colin's brother, provided most of these, many of them letters to Rowe's parents in England. Others came from the Henry-Russell Hitchcock* archive; two came from the Louis Kahn archive. Most of the letters from the late 1950s, the 1960s and the 1970s are to Alvin* and Elizabeth Boyarsky* or to John* and Pat Miller.* By the 1980s, Rowe's fame was firmly established and his letter writing style far more extravagant than in earlier years. Letters from these years, prized by their many and varied recipients, were saved and made available to this collection.

A Rowe letter written before 1975 assumes the conventional five-part letter format of heading, salutation, body, closing, and signature. Almost all the letters were typed. Smudges, closed o's and e's, and much underlining punctuate each page. An address in all capital letters and a date on the same line create a border paralleling the upper edge of the first page. The right margin is regularly violated. Write-overs, strikeouts, marginal notes, page numbers and multiple signatures are penciled in by hand.

All of this is typical of most typewritten letters of the time, not just Rowe's. Slight eccentricities become evident in Rowe's letters from the mid-1970s. At that time, Rowe began to write not on conventional typing paper but on rough-hewn colored copy paper. Pink, pumpkin, and gray were preferred colors. Occasionally on completing a letter, often in the middle of the night as described above, he telephoned the intended recipient to read the letter aloud before posting it. Multiple afterthoughts were often added to the end of a letter with a typical P.S. followed by a P.P.S.; and this P.P.S. sometimes followed by a P.P.P.S.—an accumulation of postscripts that leaves the letter without a definite ending.

This book groups the letters into ten chapters, each introduced with a brief biography of Rowe relevant to the period covered and to the letters featured. Introducing and concluding this ten-chapter body of letters are short autobiographical sketches, summaries of Rowe's life written by Rowe himself. The opening account is from 1977, the concluding from 1997.

The book features only letters from Rowe, never letters to Rowe, the vast majority of these having been lost. He kept very few of the letters he received and only rarely did those who wrote him keep copies of their letters to him. On the rare occasions that I had copies of the correspondent's reply to a Rowe letter, when this reply assisted in the understanding of the letter, I summarized it in my annotations. These include summaries of letters from his parents, his brother David, Henry-Russell Hitchcock,* Ernst Gombrich,* Lisa Germany,* and Werner Oechslin.*

In addition to letters, there are several memos and a eulogy in this collection. Three of the memos are letters to individuals; others are letters to groups of people, often to Cornell faculty, addressing with wit and insight public concerns such as proposals for Cornell's Urban Design and Rome Programs and proposals for lecture series. The eulogy, too, is letter-like—Rowe's intimate, touching portrayal of his sister-in-law Dorothy.

I have made no changes to the grammar of any of the letters. Rowe prided himself on his writing style, repeatedly likening his way of writing to that of Henry James. He loathed by-the-book editing, regarding the application of *The Chicago Manual of Style* as "destructive of <u>nuance</u> and the possibilities of irony". He recognized that the rules of grammar change periodically and understood that an insistence on correct contemporary grammatical form could only undermine the integrity and range of his James-like expression. His grammar and his style are inseparable.

Typewriting did not allow for italicized emphasis in the letters. Rowe sometimes used all capital letters for emphasis, but mostly he underlined. Like musical notation, this underlining of stressed words gives the letter voice. Rowe, however, used underlining for more than just emphasis. He underlined to indicate paraphrased speech, to denote titles of books and paintings, and to distinguish foreign words. Where Rowe used all capital letters for emphasis, I also use all capital letters; but to alleviate unintentional ambiguity, I underline only where Rowe used underlining for emphasis. Where his underlining denotes paraphrased speech, I use quotation marks. Where it indicates titles or foreign words, I use italics.

Typewriting also did not allow for the addition of diacritical marks. Occasionally Rowe penciled these in by hand. More often, he left the typed word without marks. In the body of the letter, I have left the words as Rowe wrote them, with or without diacritical marks. In the notes, I use diacritical marks.

A few letters in this collection were handwritten—the earliest in cursive; the later ones in block printing. Neither was easily deciphered. Handwritten letters are recorded here using both upper and lower case even when they were printed in upper case letters only. All are designated as "handwritten" in the heading.

Transcriptions of letters in this book are from copies of letters, never from originals. In some cases, I traveled to personal and public archives—in Oxford, Washington DC, Austin—and made copies of originals myself. Most often though I relied on others to send copied letters by post as photocopies or by email as scans. In one instance only, several letters were sent to me already digitally reproduced. Most copies were in black and white, but some were in color, revealing the vivid paper on which Rowe wrote in his later years.

The copies I received were seldom perfect, almost always requiring a degree of interpretation. Edges of the letters were often truncated when copied and parts of words were sometimes missing. Occasionally, entire lines were left out of the copy.

Rowe's spelling was generally excellent. The few errors that were made were typographic or involved foreign names or the names of obscure towns or people. I corrected these without noting that corrections had been made. I left British spellings that differ from American spellings and left the misspelling of proper names only when this misspelling seemed it might be intentional on Rowe's part: "Poundsbury" for "Poundbury", for instance. I also left Rowe's probably unintentional misspelling of the proper names of certain friends—"Rudolfo" for "Rodolfo"—in the body of the letter, amending it in my notes. Occasional errors in Rowe's use of foreign words or phrases have either been corrected in the notes or otherwise noted if the meaning is unclear.

Rowe put dates on nearly all of his letters. Occasionally, these were indirect such as "the second Sunday in April" and in such cases I substituted a more direct date. In those rare instances in which he did not date a letter, an approximate date was determined based on the content of the letter. My interpretation is always noted as such.

Rowe typically indicated the recipient of a letter in the salutation on the first page. He did not, however, note the location to which the letter was sent. Only rarely were envelopes with this information kept. Through inquiries and deduction, nearly all of these locations were determined and are shown in my heading to the letter. When no convincing location could be ascertained, no location is indicated.

Omissions were made for a variety of reasons. Sometimes words and phrases were illegible. Occasionally words, phrases or entire lines were cut off in the copies and could not be recovered. In some cases, the recipient or owner of the letter censored parts of it prior to copying it to me. In a few instances I was given uncensored letters and asked to remove certain parts. Regardless of the reason, all omissions are indicated in the same way, with a bracketed ellipsis: '[…]'.

In his letters, Rowe sometimes enclosed photocopies of pages from books and clippings from newspapers and magazines. Many of these enclosures have been lost and of those that exist, many are in poor condition. No attempt has been made to reproduce enclosures as images. Rather I note the source of the clipping, summarizing it if the content of the clipping is vital to the understanding of the letter.

A table of contents, foreword, introduction, biographical notes and various listings and credits—all common to a collection of this sort—support the letters which are introduced and annotated in a manner that favors factual explanation over interpretation, though some degree of interpretation was necessary. The notes resist extensive cross-referencing. Most of the many foreign words and phrases that Rowe employs are translated into English. Not translated are words and phrases that occur regularly in the letters, often as closings—*Un abbraccio*, for instance—and foreign words or phrases common in English usage—*déjà vu*, for example. For effect as much as for efficiency, Rowe often abbreviated names and words. Frequently used abbreviations are explained in an appendix (see p 7); those less frequently used are explained in the notes. The biographical notes provide basic, very limited information on recipients of letters and on persons repeatedly referenced in the letters. An asterisk after the person's name indicates an entry in these notes. All letter recipients are listed with the exception of those few who asked that they not be included.

The collection is not comprehensive, but representative. It contains less than ten per cent of the letters written by Rowe in his lifetime. In addition to these letters, as noted above, the book features several letter-like memos, a eulogy for Dorothy Rowe,* and two short autobiographical sketches written 20 years apart. These articles were selected from over 500 collected. The letters not selected for inclusion were written in a matter-of-fact manner not representative of Rowe's 'style' and typically are of four kinds: business-like transmittals; short perfunctory letters of gratitude; redundant letters; and longer letters concerned with money matters, investments, and the details of wills and travel.

Letters came from many sources. Some were found in archives, libraries and personal collections in Washington DC, Phoenix, Austin, Ithaca, Montreal and New York City. Most were given to me directly by the recipients. An overwhelming number of letters came from David Rowe. These include not only letters to David himself but to his former wife, Dorothy; to his sons, James and Simon; to his and Colin's parents; to Ursula Mercer,* Robert Maxwell,* Michael Spens;* and a few of the many letters in this collection written to Judith DiMaio.* Alex Caragonne* had begun a "Rowe letters project" in 2002. In 2011, he sent me copies of the letters he had collected for nearly a decade. Judith DiMaio graciously contributed numerous letters and patiently assisted me in annotating them. Rowe's friends in England, especially John Miller, Nicholas Boyarsky, and Mary Stirling, provided large numbers of letters as did Matt Bell* in Washington DC. Smaller caches—some with detailed descriptions of the circumstances under which they were received—came from Paul Zygas,* Tom Muirhead,* Mark Hinchman,* and Joan Ockman. Of particular importance to me is the first letter I collected, a 1990 hand-printed letter to Alan Colquhoun* who, in three drafts, 'translated' the letter for me, deciphering Colin's handwriting while explaining the more obscure parts of the sometimes cryptic letter.

Regrettably, no letters from Rowe were found in the archives of Rudolf Wittkower* or Philip Johnson* and the collection features only two letters to Peter Eisenman and only one to Jim Stirling.* And though numerous attempts were made, no letters were collected from Fred Koetter, Susie Kim,* Michael Dennis,* Michael Graves,* John Hejduk or Sam Stevens.

Though letters are the focus of the book, it features an assortment of photographs of Rowe, images intended to enhance, not complete the verbal text. I had found surprisingly few photographs of Rowe who is said to have been camera shy. But in May 2014, Simon Rowe* astounded me with his discovery of remarkable pictures of his uncle from his infancy to his seventieth birthday party. Other exceptional photographs were provided by Matt Bell, Valerie Bennet, Judith DiMaio, Sandra Lousada, Joan Ockman and Judith Wolin.

---

1 See 9 November 1991 letter to Daniel Naegele* (see p 368 in this volume).
2 "Writing is a way to talk without being interrupted." Renard, Jules, *Lessons of Writing and Reading*, 1895, p 52.
3 Memorandum to Mark Hinchman* dated 21 January 1996 (see p 462 in this volume).

Rowe on Rowe I
written by Colin Rowe, c 1977[1]

Colin Rowe was born in England on 27 March 1920 and received his architectural education at the University of Liverpool during the years 1938–1942 and 1944–1945. The years 1942–1944 were spent in not very effective military service and terminated in a fractured spine sustained on the occasion of his eighteenth parachute jump. In some ways this was fortuitous—for <u>him</u>; otherwise he might very well have been killed in the allied landings in Normandy—if not before. However, in other ways, it was less than agreeable. A fractured spine, with some residual paraplegia, rendered the drawing board the reverse of easy and, consequently, an invitation from the Warburg Institute of the University of London to accept a Junior Research Fellowship could only be regarded as an attractive proposition. And the result was his working for two years as, at that date, the only student of the late Rudolf Wittkower* in the preparation of a thesis "The Theoretical Drawings of Inigo Jones and John Webb" and, extracurricular, involvement (which did <u>not</u> meet with approval) in the comparison of certain aspects of Le Corbusier* and Palladio.[2]*

He followed this by a three year teaching period at the University of Liverpool; and then, in 1951, he came to the United States to study under Henry-Russell Hitchcock* who was at that time teaching at Yale. The year 1952–1953 was spent mostly in travel throughout the United States, parts of Canada and most of Mexico; and, following this, by another three year teaching period at the Austin campus of the University of Texas which, for him, proved to be a highly stimulating and formative experience and where he would have been happy to continue.

But the situation promoted by Harwell Hamilton Harris,* to all intents and purposes, came to an end in 1955; and accordingly, Rowe proceeded to spend the next two years, one in New York serving as visiting critic at Cooper Union and the other in a similar capacity at Cornell, before an invitation from Professor Sir Leslie Martin* attracted him once more to England and to the School of Architecture at Cambridge.

It might be imagined that the confrontation of the memories of Texas and the realities of Cambridge was, to say the least, severely jolting; but, since there was much to be said for both sides of the experience, Rowe remained at Cambridge, somewhat seduced but never wholly convinced, until 1962 when, deciding that King's College by itself was not a sufficient pretext for a more protracted sojourn, he returned definitively to the United States and to Ithaca, NY.

Rowe has been full Professor at Cornell since 1966 and, since 1963, he has been in charge of Cornell's Urban Design Program which is no way to be confused with Cornell's Department of City and Regional Planning.

So much for a, sometimes, jumpy and spasmodic chronology and now for a characterization. Rowe is something of a straddler. He is not completely an architect, not completely an historian, not exactly a private personality, not wholly a public one. He is, conceivably a teacher rather than a scholar and relatively happy to be so; but, though his published writings have been few, they have enjoyed a reputation and an alleged influence far in excess of their quantity.[3] Indeed, it might almost be said that what is sometimes spoken of as 'the new literacy in American architecture' (a 'literacy' which may begin to be excessive) is to be regarded as a primary result of Rowe's conversations with his students, both past and present. Rowe who is often regarded as simply a formalist critic and a proponent of the positions of Le

Corbusier has always been extremely open to any questioning and highly accessible to his students; but he has also conducted almost every project which has involved him with exemplary rigor, little regard for personal gain, and a conspicuous regard for student ingenuousness and passion.

Like the late Louis Kahn,* Rowe is a late developer and, probably, always regarded himself as such; but, if his interests and the components of his background have been rather widespread—modern architecture, Italian *maniera*, and critical theory; Liverpool, London, and New York; Texas and Italy—there are now all the indications of some sort of a symbiosis/synthesis occurring, as witness the recent *Mathematics of the Ideal Villa* and the forthcoming *Collage City*.[4]

However, in spite of these and other publications, it must still be recognized that Rowe's influence belongs not so much to the area of the printed word as to the areas of, apparently, casual speech and suggestive, provocative drawing. For, in a curious, impressionist, nervous and often agitated way, Rowe is perhaps a not unimportant draughtsman who is rapidly able to condense issue after issue into a series of laconic sketches which are likely to be partly over cerebral and partly from the gut; and it is, possibly in this way, with no words uttered, that he is most able to communicate with students.

In any case, Rowe's particular conception of urban design is likely to become of increasing importance. To a large extent based upon gestalt theory, it has always been anti-Corbusian, contextualist (a Cornell word), and eclectic. French gardens, pre-Columbian sites, Alvar Aalto, Gunnar Asplund, Parisian *hôtels particuliers*, the Villa Adriana at Tivoli, and an inordinate number of pieces implicating ideas of accommodation, have always been part of its stock-in-trade; and it has never shown any favor towards allegedly, 'neutral' research. Indeed and to the contrary, it has always assumed that the making of cities is a process not wholly unlike cooking where, while ideal recipes may, no doubt, be entertained, these are always likely to be defeated by what the market offers and, then, only to be salvaged by what *bricolage* may invent.

---

1 Not a letter, this autobiographical sketch was written by Rowe after the publication of his first book, *The Mathematics of the Ideal Villa and Other Essays*, Cambridge, MA: MIT Press, 1976, and before the publication of *Collage City*, Cambridge, MA: MIT Press, 1978, a book he co-authored with Fred Koetter.*

2 Rowe, Colin, "The Mathematics of the Ideal Villa: Palladio and Le Corbusier Compared", *The Architectural Review* 101, March 1947, pp 101–104.

3 Rowe, *The Mathematics of the Ideal Villa and Other Essays*.

4 Rowe and Koetter,* *Collage City*.

Class photo (detail), University of Liverpool, c 1941. Rowe is in the fourth row, sixth from left.

1
Injury

When Britain declared war on Germany in 1939, Colin Rowe was 19 years old and studying architecture at the University of Liverpool. In December 1942, he was 'called up', served in basic military training, and later that month he joined the British Royal Air Force. The following summer he trained as a parachutist in a camp just south of Manchester where— in an early July 1943 practice jump from 700 feet—he severely injured his back, crushing two spinal vertebrae. Hospitalized for nearly six months, he was placed in a plaster cast from his shoulders to his hips. The injury affected him for the rest of his life.

From his hospital bed, Rowe printed a letter by hand on 17 small sheets of paper to Ursula Mercer,* a friend and fellow architecture student at Liverpool. The letter tells of visits to the hospital from friends Bob Maxwell,* Sam Biggins and Bill Kidd, and from the Duchess and Duke of Gloucester. "'Hef you been abwoad?' he said. He is very Hanoverian." In the letter Rowe poetically describes the sensations of parachuting—the "green striking up from below, and an immensity of blue above… a vast three-dimensional ballet"—and recounts the accident in detail. The letter ends with Rowe telling Mercer of the "very eclectic selection" of books on architecture that he has ordered and with an apologetic wish that he "didn't run to such long letters. It's excess I think really, but I find that I can't stop myself."

[handwritten]¹

To **Ursula M. Mercer,** ℅ Theodore Tulley, Prince of Wales Drive, Battersea, London   20 August 1943   **001**

Davyhulme Military Hospital, Manchester

My Dear Ursula,²

Thank you very much indeed for your elegant letter—I really must start writing in black ink. Also thank you very much for your efforts at the R.I.B.A. and the Holfords on my behalf.³ I've had letters from both Holford and the Library.⁴

Your account of the Yorke-Rosenberg menage—Kay and Eugene is charming.⁵ The rotting architectural paraphernalia in the pink concrete courtyard, Yorke's pyjamas, the fuchsias and Mrs. Holford—how very lucky you are!

How, do you get on with Mrs. Holford? I send you a copy of George du Maurier's *Trilby* which I think might amuse.⁶ Miss Trewerey, who was at Bedford Street when I was, thought the resemblances between Trilby and Mrs. H. very striking.⁷ Do observe from close range.

As for things here. On Wednesday I received the Duke and Duchess of Gloucester⁸ and also Sam Biggins,⁹ a most stimulating day.

Sam Biggins rolled in unheralded and unexpected. The Duke and Duchess, who came about an hour later, arrived with an enormous suite and said nice things. The Duchess, in a sort of apricot-to-pink edge-to-edge coat, white straw hat and veil, in manner and style of graciousness rather like an actress. I succeeded in making persiflage.

He, the Duke—much more portentous. One felt as he came in, that half the Blood in the Almanach de Gotha had surged in with him, a vast integral sea, propagated by a thousand serene highnesses. The effect was almost sacramental, one understood the idea of being washed in the blood of the lamb—it must have the same sort of soothing effect as being mollified by the blood of the Royal Family, tapped and flowing into a hospital ward for you—genuine thick Coburg blood.

"Hef you been abwoad?" he said. He is very Hanoverian.

———

Your parcel, you know, I thought was some interesting chemicals. I thought at first that someone was perhaps sending me morphia or some sort of sleeping draught—I like the shape as it is, it's rather like coral. I think it would be almost a pity to do anything with it?

Where, by the way, is Godstowe?[10]

And where is Vincent Square?[11]

Do you Know Smith Square, Westminster? It's towards the end of Abingdon Street. A charming early Georgian district, in the early thick manner. The square is occupied by a full-blooded baroque church of Phillip Archer's. I get the impression that you might be somewhere near this. Are you?

———

To go on to my accident.

Ringway where one trains is twelve miles to the South of Manchester.[12] Tatton Park, where one jumps, a short distance from Knutsford. Ringway is an immense dynamic affair, an assortment of temporary huts and huge hangars and neo Georgian round a field, where everything is perpetual movement on concrete runways. Tatton Park is one of the show places of Cheshire complete with lakes, Georgian stables, walled kitchen gardens, a fine avenue of elms, a Doric lodge, several temples of love, and so on.

The contrast is rather amusing—a sort of perpetual merry-go-round goes on, out in aeroplanes, down in parachutes, and back again in buses. It can be very stimulating.

The Georgian park whirling below, the austerely classical stables, the avenue and lake all swinging about, and oneself floating down under a huge silk canopy to drop into a pastoral scene, where sheep grace the middle distance as seen from the house.

At first one goes up in balloons. A light canvas cage is suspended below a barrage balloon, and then one goes up attached to a winch. The first evening we did this was perfect, with a beautiful view over towards Altrincham and Bowdon Hill. Five of us climbed in, the balloon goes up 700 feet. The primary sensations are an immense vacancy, poised in air at the end of a gently humming wire, and two colours that one receives vividly, green striking up from below, and an immensity of blue above.

You fall about 200 feet before the chute [...opens] and then you float down—it's most buoyant—into the world of sheep, and sandy parkland, and instructors directing you through megaphones.

It was so exquisite an evening that the smell of the pinewoods was blown up.

We did two jumps, and the next time the air was so light that I didn't know when I touched the ground. Only the gentlest transition from vertical to horizontal motion.

After that you seem to be jumping all the time, you become terribly casual and even blasé about it. It seems silly I suppose to say that, but really, Ursula, it is so. If you could translate its very simple technique into terms of art, create a vast three-dimensional ballet, complete with the most elaborate pyrotechnics, then the thrill might be perpetuated. As it is, once acquired, interest I'm afraid vanishes. There is only splendid raw material and one longs to do something coherent with it.

I'd just forgotten that I saw you after making the first three jumps. That was on the Saturday.[13] (Weren't Sybil, Hilda etc. titilated by the idea of it, by the way? Robert was amused and devastated by their reactions as we'd just talked ourselves into sheer misery—thank you for the supper—I didn't get to Manchester until 12 o'clock, and had to evade the M.P.s at the Central).[14]

On Sunday we jumped again twice, and on Monday once more. Tuesday was too wet and windy, but on Wednesday morning we jumped.

I was fed up, uninterested, my chute was caught in the most wild oscillation which I wasn't able to get under control. In spite of that I made quite a soft sort of grounding, but the wind took my chute, blew it backwards, my legs slipped on the wet ground and I fell and tore my back............................ [...] which is a square, very hard box. The two movements, falling and being taken backwards, are so instantaneous as to be inseparable really—but I think that that must have been the process.

My first reaction, shameful to say, was that I shouldn't have to carry the Bren round the scheme that we were supposed to be doing, my next was surprise that I could neither feel nor move my legs.[15] So I remained prostrate, and feebly waving till they brought an ambulance and a Polish M.O. and then I came here.

If nothing else, Ursula, I've left a mark on history—the Parachute Regiment no longer carries the respirator in the middle of the back—all this because of me.[16]

I wish I didn't run to such long letters. Here I've covered 14 pages, it's excess I think really, but I find that I can't stop myself.

I expect a visit from Robert and Elizabeth, either tomorrow, Saturday, or Sunday.[17] The last time they came they traveled First Class, and brought me a box of nectarines. My people were with me at the time, and as Bill Kidd had only just left I felt rather like a French king <u>receiving</u> in bed.[18]

With regard to other things. Please <u>do</u> keep my library card. You may as well as I can't do anything with it. The librarian wrote asking me what I wanted. I ordered Worringer's *Form in Gothic*, Anthony Blunt's *François Mansart*................... and the second volume of the *Œuvre Complète*—a very eclectic selection I'm afraid.[19]

    Colin

No. 14366798
Spr Rowe C.F.[20]
Ward 9, Military Hospital,
Davyhulme, Manchester

P.S. Is Prince of Wales Drive very Prince's Parky?[21]
Was the P.O.W. Edward VII?[22]

1 Written by hand in ink on 17, 4 x 6 inch sheets of paper.
2 Ursula Margaret Mercer* (b 1923) completed a degree in architecture from Liverpool University in 1945. She was a classmate of Robert Maxwell* (b 1922), in the year behind Rowe. At the time of this letter, she was a student intern employed in the office of Yorke and Rosenberg, and lived with her elder sister, Alice, and Alice's husband, Theodore James Tulley. After graduating from Liverpool in 1945, she returned to London and spent most of her professional life working as an architect for the National Health Service.
3 William Graham Holford (1907–1975), Liverpool architect who designed depots, factories, hostels, barracks, and prisoner of war camps for the Ministry of Supply and the War Office during the first half of the Second World War. Both Yorke and Rosenberg, for whom Mercer* worked, had at one time worked for Holford.
4 The Royal Institute of British Architects (RIBA) library where EJ Carter (1902–1982) was the librarian. Carter was also editor of RIBA's journal.
5 Francis Reginald "Kay" Yorke (1906–1962); Eugene Rosenberg (1907–1990).
6 du Maurier, George, *Trilby*, London: Osgood, McIlvaine, and Co, 1894, a Gothic horror novel.
7 "Bedford Street" was the familiar name for the Civic Design annex to the School of Architecture, Liverpool.
8 Prince Henry, Duke of Gloucester (1900–1974), and Princess Alice, Duchess of Gloucester (1901–2004).
9 Samuel Biggins was a Liverpool classmate of Rowe and Mercer.*
10 Godstowe School, a preparatory school for girls in High Wycombe, Buckinghamshire.
11 Vincent Square, Westminster.
12 From June 1940, RAF Ringway (now Manchester International Airport) became the wartime base for the No 1 Parachute Training School, providing initial training for allied paratroopers.
13 Saturday, 3 July 1943.
14 Sybil, Hilda, and Robert Maxwell,* Liverpool architecture classmates attending a supper party hosted by Ursula Mercer.* "M.P.": Military Police. "The Central": Manchester Central, one of the city's major rail terminals, where Rowe changed trains.
15 The "Bren" was a light machine gun adopted by the British Army in the mid-1930s. Though Rowe's handwriting is nearly undecipherable here, the "square, very hard box" which he notes in the preceding paragraph was the respirator that all parachutists carried "in the middle of the back".
16 In emails dated 8 January and 7 February 2012, David Rowe* recalled that his brother's accident occurred in the first week of July 1943. Two spinal vertebrae were crushed and he was in a plaster cast from his shoulders to his hips for six months. "The top bit", David wrote, "looked like the top of a strapless ball gown and his party trick, once he started becoming mobile, was to wrap his lower half in the bedspread, ballooning it out, and do a catwalk thing". On 25 January 1944, Rowe was honorably discharged with a modest disability pension. The crushed vertebrae left him with partial paraplegia in his left leg. As he grew older, a painful spinal stenosis developed.
17 Robert Maxwell* and Elizabeth Tilbury.
18 William Kidd was a classmate of Rowe who had enlisted with him at the Queens Barracks, Perth, in early December 1942.
19 Worringer, Wilhelm, *Form in Gothic*, Munich: R Piper & Co, 1911; Blunt, Anthony, *François Mansart and the Origins of French Classical Architecture*, London: Warburg Institute, 1941; Le Corbusier and Pierre Jeanneret, *Œuvre Complète de 1929–1934*, vol 2, Willi Boesiger ed, Zurich: Editions H Girsberger, 1935.
20 "Spr" is the Royal Engineers' abbreviation for "Sapper", the designation applied to Rowe on his assignment to a Field Company of the Royal Engineers after basic training in early 1943.
21 Cyril Mansions (1894), where Ursula was staying with her elder sister, Alice, is one of the earliest structures in a row of eight grand apartment buildings (1893–1897), which line the Prince of Wales Drive for two-thirds of one mile.
22 Rowe wants to know if Prince of Wales Drive was named for Edward VII.

2
America and Austin

1951–1958

By summer 1951, Rowe had completed his studies in architecture both at the University of Liverpool and at the Warburg Institute in London, and had taught three years at Liverpool where Robert Maxwell* and James Stirling* had been his students. In fall 1951, with combined Smith-Mundt and Fulbright scholarships, he left England and traveled to the United States to study at Yale University. Although he did not receive a degree from Yale, he attended the lectures of architectural historian Henry-Russell Hitchcock* who later became his friend and with whom he corresponded regularly for the next five years.

In summer 1952 Rowe set out on a road trip across North America with Brian Richards,* his roommate in New Haven, a fellow Englishman and classmate at Yale, a 1950 graduate from Liverpool. The two visited cities and architecture in the Midwest, California, Texas, Arizona, Mexico, Canada and elsewhere, supporting themselves by working in architectural offices in Vancouver and Bakersfield, California. In spring 1953, as the trip wound down, Rowe met Mrs Harwell Hamilton Harris in Norman, Oklahoma. The wife of the newly appointed dean of the school of architecture at the University of Texas at Austin, Mrs Harris suggested Rowe might teach for her husband, a suggestion Rowe pursued with telephone calls to Harris himself from New York City that summer. After Harris hired him by phone, Rowe returned to Europe in fall 1953, visiting his parents in Yorkshire, England, before traveling on to London and Paris.

In January 1954 he returned to the US and began teaching at Austin, where, he wrote, "quite frequently it is like waiting for the top of Krakatoa to blow off". With a host of talented new faculty—many of who later were labeled "The Texas Rangers" and became Rowe's lifelong friends—Rowe introduced Modern architecture to the American West. After only five semesters, however, the department collapsed. Rowe left Texas for New York City, where he taught at Cooper Union for a year while negotiating a position at Cornell University. At this time, while in New York City in January 1957, Rowe learned of his mother's death.

Rowe moved to Ithaca, New York, in fall 1957, to teach at Cornell for a single academic year. Fulfilling a promise to his parents, he then moved back to England, where he taught for four years under the direction of Leslie Martin* at the University of Cambridge.

The letters from the first five years of this period, 1951–1956, to his parents and to Henry-Russell Hitchcock, describe in detail his impressions of Yale, of Mexico, of the many renowned American buildings that he visited, and especially of America and Americans and the effect his travels had on him. "Before coming here", he wrote to Hitchcock in 1953, "I was beginning to feel like a gramophone record caught in a Corbu* groove. Now, I've at least discovered that the groove is of no absolute significance."

To his parents and to Hitchcock, Rowe wrote—in a different voice to each—of his experiences working in architectural firms, of the drama of teaching in Austin, of his concerns for establishing himself in architectural education, and of the possibility of returning to England. Repeatedly, he advises his parents to move from their Yorkshire home in Bolton-on-Dearne to London, taking special interest in their attempt to find a house appropriate to their situation.

After teaching in Ithaca for six months, in April 1958, Rowe wrote to his friend Sandy Wilson* at Cambridge that he feels Cornell "breeds indifference" and that in the US "one lives the full horror of American relativism". He had applied for a teaching position at Cambridge and in this letter confided in Wilson that he is "consumed with curiosity and various anxiety neuroses as to how my little cause is proceeding in your part of the world".

To Mr & Mrs Frederick Rowe,
Highgate Lane, Bolton-on-Dearne, Yorkshire, England   *31 October 1951*   **002**

131 Westwood Road, New Haven, Connecticut[1]

Dear Parents,

The largo from Dvorak's *New World Symphony* was Mr Edward Harkness's favourite piece of music. Mr Harkness was Standard Oil, and he was the Pennsylvania State Railroad, and during the 1920's he was (since he provided the money) the arbiter of the physical form which this university should take. He stamped upon it his expensive passion for small Cotswold manor houses, and in the Harkness Tower his architect celebrated his taste for fifteenth century English Gothic.[2] The result is a tower more superb, more overwhelming, more convincing in its spuriousness than almost any genuine English fifteenth century tower. Parts of it had to be pulled down because they weren't expensive enough. The result is heartrending, admirable, but sparing of neither private sentiment nor public feeling.

Every day at 12 noon the Harkness Tower emits chimes and always cloying the air is the largo from the favourite symphony. It's a sort of systematic bereavement [...] a repeated nostalgia for Europe and a warming by the false, throbbing fires of sentimentality. You will agree that this is a harrowing experience [...] daily, before lunch to be forcibly, morbidly obliged to mourn the impossible, and at the same time to be obliged to accept canned consolation. And all this in commemoration of a commercial dignity [...] I mention it because I think it a typical American experience [...] they don't entirely realise its angst-provoking possibilities.

I've been going to write for about ten days or so [...] but to send a letter across so many miles of water seems to require at least some mildly portentous content [...] and I simply haven't been able to think of the content [...] so I've been exploring the American mind and trying to think of something to say about it.

Brian Richards* of course, thinks that the American mind is hell. And also America. The poor man, however, has had sinus trouble from the moment of landing about six weeks ago [...] and perhaps suffering of this kind rather vitiates judgement. It's interesting how many Europeans do develop sinus trouble over here (Marilyn Marston for instance).[3] It's something in the climate I believe, and is basically responsible for the American accent. When one thinks about it American speech isn't nasal at all [...] but the English way is. The thing about the Americans is that they don't speak through their noses [...] because they have a tradition of sinus trouble and they can't [...] American speech is consequently flat, un-accentuated. The English speak through their noses (just try) and they use their noses to produce that resonance which is lacking in American speech [...] this amused me quite a lot when I realised it the other day.

To return to the American mind. They are of course sentimental. They are in a lot of ways like sentimental children (if that were possible). I experienced this to the full last Saturday going to the first and last football match which I shall ever attend on this side of the Atlantic. It took place in an enormous arena, rather larger than the Colosseum, and one imagines just as solid [...] looking externally rather like the fortifications of Verona. This is called the Yale Bowl. The teams were probably Yale and Cornell, and Cornell won (which is by the way, because the game itself was very, very boring). It was the rest of the show which was so incredible and which represented such an idealisation of infantility on the part of people who should know better. There were two brass bands [...] one for each team. And two teams of cheer-leaders dressed in white and carrying large, elegant white megaphones, and performing acrobatic ballets on the edge of the field throughout the proceedings. If some catch had been particularly brilliant, one knew all about it, because the cheer-leaders began to perform cartwheels, and entrechats and double somersaults in the air, so as to illustrate their enthusiasm and arouse that of the crowd. And at the same time one or the other of the bands would burst out into a few appropriately expressive bars of music. The brass bands marched around in the most disciplined fashion, making a great deal of noise and spelling with extraordinary precision C. O. R. N. E. L. L. and Y. A. L. E., and all the time a performing bear and a large bulldog were dragged around as emblems of the two universities. All, as you perceive, incredible.

Afterwards I went to three parties which were rather more real. They were all architects' parties and consequently not seriously interested in the ball game because American architects affect the same hypercritical standards about popular taste and public entertainment as the English ones do.

The Philip Johnson* evening was rather entertaining. Besides Hitchcock* and self there was a David Pleydell-Bouverie and wife.[4] He was an architect in England about fifteen years ago... married an Astor and leads the life of a country gentleman in California. The Johnson house is more impressive than I had imagined.[5] The Chinese servant performed all the cooking in the living room while we drank Martinis in front of the Poussin, and outside, the woods were suggestively illuminated by spotlights. The walls are entirely window from floor to ceiling; the floor, polished brick; the carpet, defining a small sitting area, white; the chairs, stainless steel and leather (costing 500 dollars each); the occasional table, armour plate glass an inch thick; [...] a few other casually disposed works of art;.... the kitchen, rather like a long low buffet; and a dining table about fifty feet away, comprised the entire living room.

After dinner we drove back again to New Haven [...] about sixty miles [...] and then Hitchcock insisted on talking. He'd already been talking since about three in the afternoon almost without stopping but now, stimulated by a bottle of whiskey, a present from David Bouverie, he was able to go on talking throughout the night. At eight o'clock in the morning, after seventeen hours of continuous conversation, when we went to breakfast he was showing no signs of exhaustion. This, I think, is an instance of American enthusiasm. Everything was reviewed, and the occasional word edgeways, which was all that one could get in, merely stimulated him to fresh efforts.

Will write again soon.

Colin

---

1   This is the first of 19 letters written by Rowe to his parents in Bolton-on-Dearne, England between 1951 and 1956, and in 1963. Though nearly all other letters in this collection were transcribed from photocopies or are scans of the original letter, these 19 were provided to me already in a digital format and with omissions indicated. Rowe had typewritten all 19 of the original letters.

2 James Gamble Rogers (1867–1947) designed the Harkness Tower, financed in 1917 by a donation from Anna M Harkness to memorialize her son, Charles William Harkness (graduated from Yale University in 1883), who had died suddenly the year before.

3 Marilyn Marston was a contemporary of Brian Richards* (1928–2004), a graduate of the University of Liverpool who had lived with Rowe in New Haven and had attended classes with him at Yale. For a year, beginning in June 1952, Rowe and Richards traveled together across North America.

4 By 1951, Hitchcock* and Johnson* had been Harvard College friends, travel companions, and exhibition and publishing colleagues for almost 30 years. David Pleydell-Bouverie (1911–1994), a founding member of the Modern Architectural Research Group (MARS) in 1933, migrated to the US and married Ava Alice Muriel Astor (1902–1956), daughter of John Jacob Astor IV, in 1946.

5 Philip Johnson's* Glass House of 1950 in New Canaan, Connecticut.

To *Mr & Mrs Frederick Rowe,*
Highgate Lane, Bolton-on-Dearne, Yorkshire, England   *14 December 1951*   **003**

131 Westwood Road, New Haven, Connecticut

Dear Parents,

It's so long since I wrote that I feel I must have been carried away by the tide of events, but looking back over the last three weeks I'm not really aware of any very memorable things happening.

Went up to Boston one weekend. Perhaps one had entertained extravagant ideas about Boston, but I found it rather a disappointing town, [...] although perhaps it's unfair to judge a place on the experience of a Saturday afternoon and Sunday. It's more metropolitan than any English provincial town [...] has rather a cold, chilly, refined sort of atmosphere which a little suggests Edinburgh done over in brick and brownstone rather than in granite. But most of its architecture is neither quaint in a provincial sense, nor refined in an international one, and somehow one had expected it to be both. Harvard too failed to excite. It lacks the concentration of this place.

The landscape on the way has its Scottish moments, and also, according to Brian Richards* who also went up, its reminiscences of Southern Sweden. It's untidy, big, uncultivated, scrappily forested and very geographical-looking with big outcrops of rock. How in the world this part of the country got the name New England is rather a complete mystery. Few landscapes could be less similar. All the way [...] and that is more than 170 miles, we didn't see a single cow… and the same goes for the landscape between here and New York [...] nor is there any more than the merest trace of any other agricultural activity. That is because it couldn't be done on a scale big enough to make it pay [...] so that one drives through miles of territory which looks today wilder than it did 150 years ago [...] where the milk comes from, God knows, the fruit possibly from Florida, meat and bread etc., apparently from the Mid West. Everything is very probably frozen, and nothing comes from the locality.

You buy all these things in super-markets, which are rather delightful shops in which, as one enters, one takes a small sort of wire perambulator and pushes it around, taking up things as they occur and finally ending up at one of a series of cash desks where you pay a bill. And of course, absolutely everything is packaged, and pasteurised and homogenised and all the rest of it. The meat has probably been dead for years and the vegetables frozen for months. Sometimes you get these shops miles out in the country. There's one we stopped to look at near Boston that had just been opened about four days before. Parking for four thousand cars, a cinema, an enormous domed market, etc., etc.[1] All life at more than a mile radius from the centre of a town is based on the idea of two cars to a family [...] the husband goes to work in one and the wife goes shopping in another [...] the Americans will probably soon lose the capacity to walk because they do so little of it. Lots of banks have a porte-cochere up to which you drive, pass in your cheque and get paid without ever having to get out of the car. Also there are lots of open air cinemas where the same thing happens [...] you drive up in a car, into the enclosure and watch the show without ever having to stretch your legs [...] Out west, I gather there are bars and restaurants upon the same principle [...] so you see how mass production and physical ease contrive to destroy any idea of society.

You can see the same results in the organisation of this university here, which is the second wealthiest in the country. The different colleges can neither afford service in their dining halls nor cleaners for any other than the public rooms [...] so the dining rooms are completely self-service and if you live in a college you have to clean your own room. Privation doesn't end here because you eat [...] and this goes for everybody [...] in a way which even in the British Army would be considered crude [...] out of big trays with six divisions stamped in them. They put different parts of the meal into different parts of the tray [...] and then you stagger away with it, and everybody appears to consider this completely normal. This is the sort of thing that logically developed mass production brings you to [...] you can't afford servants [...] most things are cheap except labour. But you point out to them [...] that this, in England, would be considered the depths of privation, that poor as the English are, they have never descended to this, that on the whole the English would prefer to have the food badly cooked and decently served etc. [...] they say something about its being democratic that way [...] and since they're adaptable and the frontier is close behind them they don't seem to sense that anything has been lost.

This is all to do with mass production, obviously [...] but apart from that, Americans seem to have a weakness for things which are too big to cope with. The Sunday *New York Times* weighs 2½ pounds, it contains 100's of pages of newsprint and is very exhausting to carry and too big to read. Nobody ever seems to give a small party for about 5–10 people where conversation might conceivably flourish, but nothing less than 50 will do, where noise makes conversation impossible (conversation of course isn't practised anyway [...] just as soon as it's got going they tend all to run away [...] with the exception of course of people like Hitchcock★ who monopolise it for about 15 hours or so). They also have a weakness for huge masses of statistics which no mind can possibly digest [...] and also for enormous steaks which are too big to eat.

Food, of course, is much better cooked than in England, but at the same time almost monotonously the same [...] because all rather too rich and lacking in piquancy.

There are a lot of rather curious Indian remains, like waffles and wheat cakes and griddle cakes and maple syrup, which all rather go together and which one can eat for breakfast, involving maple syrup with bacon if one wants. There are also rather a dreary collection of pies [...] lemon meringue, blueberry, cranberry, huckleberry, Boston cream and pumpkin. Pumpkin is quite the worst [...] I never want to eat another as long as I live. There are curious indefinable vegetables with names like succotash, coccotash etc. Most vegetables are spoiled by having been deep frozen. Fried potatoes are always called 'French fries'. There are a series of other exotics called after various nationalities, towns, etc. Thus:- English muffins, London crumpets (neither what you think), French toast (a delicious sort of toast fried in a mixture of batter and raw egg, and served with maple syrup and butter) and of course PIZZA. Pizza is Italian but you can't get a decent pizza anywhere in Italy north of Naples, whereas in this part of the world it's almost a national dish, consisting of a sort of pancake baked in a special oven with tomatoes, mushrooms, bacon etc. and eaten with one's fingers. It's almost embarrassing to order ice cream. There are so many varieties, including some with names like pecan, that ice cream is obviously a miracle which will never be solved. In all its infinite varieties, however, American ice cream is nothing more than adequate [...] one would never miss anything by not eating it [...] it has nothing to compare with Italian *granite*, or torte, or cassata.[2] There are also things like a local soup called Clam Chowder which is sometimes good, and fried oysters which give one an interesting sensation of luxury and conspicuous consumption. The coffee is banal. There are no teapots to be bought. Nor are kettles in general use. The natives use what they call tea bags. Chicken or turkey is generally rather cheaper than steak but becomes, after a time, a little boring with its continuously over-rich accessories. The natives seem to like to drink coffee quite often throughout a meal [...] like the English lower orders drinking tea. Beer is rather more desperate than English beer and has nothing like the quality of the best French or German [...] so people drink things with names like Old Fashioned and Total Collapse. At all parties they serve very elaborate and potent punches, and appalling Martinis which are made rather worse by having singularly unpleasant little onions dropped into them [...] I think these are called 'Gibson's'. Sherry is considered a privation. At a party you tend to drink out of a paper carton.

In most restaurants you find television or juke-boxes or both. You can drop in a nickel or a dime and have 5 to 10 minutes of gooey, highly coloured, saccharine orchestration to such titles as "Sin", "Temptation", "Kisses Sweeter than Wine", "Ave Maria", etc. I suspect that all Americans quite like these things, but the more sophisticated ones get a cultural inferiority complex about it.

Being English, one is received with mixed feelings of contempt, admiration and curiosity. In the more remote sections one becomes an ethnographical specimen, or even a sort of *'objet d'art'* [...] of a kind which hasn't been seen much for the last 170 years. One has to accept the fact that the English are stuffy, that's even a national myth, often that they're rampantly imperialist or not completely serious, or too suave to be really true. All this is very amusing. There is a morbid interest in the British Royal family, and a belief that the English are similarly interested. One sees captions like this:- "Safe, Sound and Sexless: Elizabeth" (or possibly, "England's Queen") at the cinema. One plunges into the following article with interest and agitation, only to discover that the first part of the caption applies to the film and not to the Queen of England.

As you see, one is being subjected to a continuous bombardment of impressions which it is a little difficult to sort out and put into any kind of coherent letter. One scarcely experiences spasms of acute pleasure, one is never violently irritated, one achieves a fairly continuous state of moderate animation and amusement. Sometimes it's convulsively funny.

    Colin

P.S. Am going up to Toronto for Christmas—but have also been invited by Hitchcock* to drive down to Canada with him. If I can put him off for a few days or so—I hope I'll do both.

    Colin

1 'Shoppers' World' in Framingham, Massachusetts, one of the earliest shopping malls in the US.
2 *granite,* Italian: granuled ice with lemon, coffee or other syrup.

004 *To Mr & Mrs Frederick Rowe,*
        37 Highgate Lane, Bolton-on-Dearne, Yorkshire, England   *17 December 1951*

131 Westwood Road, New Haven, Connecticut

Monday

Dear Parents,

    Am writing this before leaving for New York the day after tomorrow, and up on to Toronto.

It's suddenly begun to get quite cold here. It was pretty cold about a month ago and then it became rather like an English June. Ten days ago in New York it was so hot that one was able to promenade in the evening almost like an Italian town in the late summer. There's been snow for about a month a hundred miles or so to the north but it came here last Friday. It began very gently at about 4 in the afternoon, and by five everything was covered and pretty thick. By Saturday lunchtime, the streets and pavements were immaculately swept, and the snow was all frozen into position with a beautifully swept and smooth-polished sort of surface. The light is brilliant, I've never seen such pleasant snow, the sun shines, the sky is excessively blue— outside it's very cold—about 20° below freezing point. Inside it's subtropical—so that one doesn't feel the winter to anything like the extent one does in England. It's rather pleasant getting up in the morning in an overheated room and looking outside across the roofs of the houses to the West Rock—an enormous sandstone lump—where three of the judges of Charles I hid to escape capture in 1661—I never look at the thing without thinking of them—after that they disappeared, went west somewhere and were never heard of again—probably eaten by Indians or something of that kind.[1]

New Haven is rather too Christmassy—New York even more so. Christmas trees sprout all over the place—on the steps of churches, on New Haven Green, at prominent cross roads, everything is tricked out in fairy lights, they all sing carols on the slightest provocation, lights are left on in skyscrapers so as to suggest stars and crosses, all the churches have electric candles burning in the windows—and on New Haven Green again, the Italian community have set up a most elaborate stable full of rather sixteenth century shepherds, virgins, prophets—which emits gramophone music. What "the company of English Christians led by John Davenport", who founded this town in 1638, would have said if they could have seen this last thing, I don't know. Rome established on <u>their</u> Green.[2]

I imagine, anyway, that it will be rather a relief to escape all this—although conceivably Canada may be even more so. I'll write and tell you all about that anyway. Possibly the train journey may be interesting—although all the railway carriages are too big to be anything but oppressive. I think that I shall get off at Niagara Falls on the way, to have a look at the marvels of nature. I believe one goes through Albany, Syracuse, Rochester and Buffalo—I can't wait to see the latter—am quite sure it's crammed with cow boys—or how did it get its name. Will probably go from Toronto, through Ottawa to Montreal, and come back with some people who are going skiing about a hundred miles north of Montreal.

It will be a great relief to have <u>done</u> Canada. It means one doesn't have to go there again. You can always say—'Canada! But I've been <u>there</u>'!

Was going to send you a lot of tins of ham in a parcel—but was told last week that I had left it rather late—and at the moment haven't got any money until I come back again—so will send you some early in January.

Would you like some Neapolitan wafers?

Dried fruit?

Tinned Butter?

NYLONS?—these can be sent inside letters—if so what size?

Have recently been entertained by the English colony. They are nearly all Cambridge, and tend to presume that Cambridge is the only place on earth where civilization flourishes. A rather patronising, heavy, roaring type from Clare;[3] a pleasant drama student who has just spent a year in Spain, which is apparently entirely crowded with fiercely Fascist, anti-British, Catholic Irishmen (and Irishwomen who say 'when I hear an Englishman speak it makes me <u>ill</u> for a week'—this story never fails to delight Americans); a pleasant man who was a master at Eton last year and is writing a book on American History—he is ex-Guards and all that and is sure to go down well with Ian MacKenzie, who is coming here in January.[4]

Have discovered a feeling for cold snowy countries, and think that I might rather like to go to Sweden.

This letter makes no pretence to any arrangement or sequence—and I think had better stop now.

Do have a nice Christmas and give my love to people.

    Colin

1 West Rock, a rock cliff that defines an edge of New Haven, served as the hideout for Edward Whalley and his son-in-law, General William Goffe, who were two of the three "regicide judges".
2 John Davenport (1597–1670), Puritan clergyman and cofounder of New Haven.
3 Clare College, Cambridge.
4 Ian MacKenzie, a native of Edinburgh, on the administrative staff at Liverpool University where he became a friend of Rowe before joining the publishing house of McMillan & Company in London. MacKenzie transferred to New York in 1952 as managing director and president of St Martin's Press, a McMillan subsidiary.

To **Mr & Mrs Frederick Rowe,**
Highgate Lane, Bolton-on-Dearne, Yorkshire, England   *8 January 1952*   **005**

332 George Street, New Haven, Connecticut

Dear Parents,

    I got back here from Canada about four days ago. As you see, the address is changed.[1] I also found on arrival the slides which you had posted in October (thank you very much) and which had just arrived, after, I should say, having been rather over-examined by the F.B.I. or something of that kind.

Somehow Christmas in Canada was not conducive to making the extensive tour including Ottawa and Montreal, so that I contented myself with Toronto and trips to Niagara Falls and to Lake Simcoe.

Last time, when I wrote rather over-dramatically about snow I was really wrong, because now it's all melted again... in fact it melted a day or so before I left for Canada. Rather horrible melting and freezing at the same time, so that in some of the streets one could scarcely remain standing. The day before I left I saw a dead man in a seat on New Haven Green, who had probably expired of cold and not having had anything to eat. Against the luxurious background of Yale, this made the perfect Russian propaganda photograph.

The lower part of the Hudson, going north from New York, is very magnificent (once one gets over the rather unpleasant brown rock). It's an extremely wide gorge with very steep cliffs and the bottom of the valley almost completely occupied by the river. In places, from time to time, there have been definite attempts by means of elaborate castellated country houses to turn the whole scene into the American version of the Rhine. This sort of scenery goes on for a couple of hours or so, until you reach Albany, where it is replaced by lower hills, rather open landscape and slower rivers with canals. There is a sort of international canal scene which one appears to find throughout the world, and it is perhaps the presence of this sort of landscape which makes the country between Albany and Syracuse so familiar. In Buffalo, one had to wait for hours but since there was a terrific blizzard blowing one had to wait all the time in the station. This was grim because the whole place was so overheated that it was hardly possible to breathe. One's first view of Canada was an enormous neon advertisement seen across the St. Lawrence. saying 'ESSO ESSO ESSO CANADA WELCOMES YOU WITH ESSO'. Then because it was quite dark one saw no more until finally the train arrived in Toronto.

Toronto is rather a meagre, sprawling, frontier kind of town where Scottish caution has been too deeply ingrained for so long that it is extremely unlikely that anything very splendid will ever happen. Imagine the late nineteenth century suburbs of London, add a twentieth century suburbia, make no allowance for any centre to the town, provide narrow streets with tram cars and overhead telegraph wires, and you have something like Toronto. The shopkeepers, for the most part, have no comprehension that anything visual matters, nor have they any confidence that they will ever be very much of a financial success. So lacking the wholesome American extravagance, for a very long time nothing has happened. However, one gathers lately that Toronto has struck a boom, which will result in its complete Americanisation.

As it is, visiting Toronto at the moment is rather like going to the Mid-West to get halfway to England, because however much it may be a frontier town, in half its sympathies it is excessively English. They talk about London even if they actually go to New York. This allows one to feel like the principal personage of a royal tour all the time. Also the Canadians are on the whole quieter, less aggressive and more polite than the Americans. In some ways this is very restful, but in other ways rather a bore, since it makes things, if easier, a little less stimulating.

It wasn't as cold in Toronto as down here in New England, and indoors of course one never noticed the cold at all, but the Keys had arranged so many things for me to do that it was quite impossible to go on to Montreal.[2] There appeared to be at least one party every night, sometimes two or three, and by the time the end of my fortnight was finished I sank back into the New York train in a state of complete exhaustion. One had discovered that Toronto, socially, was a much more complicated sort of town than it might appear on first observation. Most interesting people were perhaps a Frenchwoman called Mrs Zacks, who's just settled there, and has developed round herself rather a fabulous small collection of modern paintings [...] one or two early Picasso's, Matisse, Chagall, Renoir, several Klee's, some Modigliani drawings etc. etc. etc.[3] Another Frenchwoman married to a White Russian sculptor [...] is selling paintings like mad [...] I went there to tea, or at least, I had expected that it was going to be tea [...] instead it was a white Bordeaux with caviar and truffled *foie gras* on slices of pumpernickel, followed by meringues [...] afterwards, in spite of feeling slightly sick one did feel that one was floating on air (I should like to reproduce this kind of tea as soon as possible).[4] There was also rather an expansive sort of dowager who had a dining room lined with Dufy's and who talked about nothing but architecture and Victorian furniture [...] all of which seems rather strange and exotic in Toronto.[5]

Niagara Falls is one of the most amusing of anti-climaxes. It might be impressive if, after having gone out for a walk in the woods one day you'd discovered it all for yourself, but as it is, it completely fails to look big. The Southern Ontario country through which you approach it is dead flat and reminds one a little of Lincolnshire. Then you climb an escarpment and get into another dead flat country. After going through that for some miles you arrive at the Falls, which is really a sort of residential resort, half in America, half in Canada, with a waterfall and rather a wide river in between. You approach it all through a little landscape park with gate lodges and places where you get picture postcards, you buy tickets and go down in an elevator to a room where a man dresses you up in rubber boots, capes, sou'westers and things, after which you go down still further, to emerge into an artificial tunnel rather like a London tube. From time to time in here, you get occasional glimpses of the reverse side of the Falls, which allow you to see that, after all, there is quite a lot of water going over. The river below the Falls was frozen all over and so were the edges of the waterfall. It was excessively icy, cold and damp. Afterwards, one retires to the dining room on the twelfth floor of the General Brock Hotel, which one soon realises gives one quite the most impressive view... but I think that at Niagara one has to be very imaginative indeed to be in any way moved by the thing. Afterwards, one drove to a rather delightful late eighteenth century village in the flat Dutch Ontario country, called Niagara-by-the-Lake. It was then just about time to dash back along the beautifully swept roads to Toronto.

The main roads are immediately swept and cleaned after any fall of snow by a whole range of snow-ploughs, sweeping machines and things, so that there is absolutely no trouble in driving at sixty miles an hour through an otherwise snowbound landscape. And since the cars and the houses are all warmed, one really does feel the cold far less than in England.

Colin

---

1 Rowe had moved to 333 George Street, in the center of New Haven, two blocks from the Yale campus.
2 Sydney James Key* (1918–1956), a Canadian art historian and museologist, spent 1946 and 1947 in England studying the paintings of John Constable (1776–1837). Rowe attended lectures given by Key at the Courtauld, and Key accompanied Rowe on his first Italian tour in summer 1947. In 1948 Key became curator of the Art Gallery of Toronto. See Rowe, Colin *As I Was Saying: Recollections and Miscellaneous Essays*, Alexander Caragonne ed, 3 vols, Cambridge, MA: MIT Press, 1995, vol 1, pp 3–6; Rowe, *As I Was Saying*, vol 3, pp 335–336.
3 Ayala Zacks (1912–2011) and her husband Sam (1904–1970) were internationally known Toronto art collectors.
4 Marthe Rakine (b 1905) was married to the painter and sculptor, Boris Rakine (1905–1970).
5 Probably Constance Matthews.

To Mr & Mrs Frederick W. Rowe,
Highgate Lane, Bolton-on-Dearne, Yorkshire, England   *5 February 1952*

333 George Street, New Haven, Connecticut

Tuesday

Dear Parents,

Haven't had a reply to my last letter so I assume, and it seems quite probable to me, that I sent you the wrong address. Sorry.

However, we have been so busy decorating this place and going off to New York, etc., to buy things that there really hasn't been time. The confusion began to subside at the beginning of last week, since when I've caught up on an awful lot of letters that I should have written since last October.

Since arriving here last month we have: built a wall [...] made a cupboard [...] two tables with metal legs [...] completely redecorated two rooms [...] caused a tribe of girls to come and make curtains (they bring the most delightful little sewing machines you've ever seen with them) [...] so this place which was nothing about a month ago, really begins to look quite elegant [...] everybody wildly impressed at fantastic display of energy, etc.

Spent rather an amusing day with Bill Osmun in New York about a week ago.[1] He was looking excessively English and being rather nostalgic about Europe generally. All his clothes are English, and since Locks, Huntsmans, Tremletts and all the other right firms have been left his sizes in gloves, hats, shoes, suits, shirts, etc., will continue to be so.[2] I was extremely amused at all this. He is going to work in a Museum downtown some time soon, and will live at home [...] because he appears to believe (which is not the case) that furniture and things are fabulously expensive over here.

Went one day last week with Hitchcock★ up to Farmington and Middletown, which are some way north of here, where things begin to get slightly hilly.[3] Farmington is an extraordinarily elegant place. Imagine a village which consists of almost nothing but the most distinguished <u>large</u>, late Georgian houses [...] all so scrupulously immaculate that they must be painted at least once every six months. There had been snow and the whiteness of everything was startling. We went to lunch with the Soby's,★ who live there or rather with Mrs Soby, since it appeared that after 20 years of marriage, she and her husband were getting divorced.[4] I can just imagine how galling this would be, since I'm sure that he would insist on the house <u>and</u> on the pictures [...] and it is one of the very best private collections of modern paintings in the U.S. You know, a drawing room about 20′ by 50′ with three enormous Picasso's, a piece of Henry Moore sculpture, and so on.[5]

The dining room rather more eclectic, with Venetian eighteenth century furniture and decoration, and a superb French Gothic birdcage which had artificial birds in it, done by Calder, and which stood between the windows [...] Don't think that I've ever before been in such an immaculate, precise house [...] very little there, but everything, glasses, trays, drinks, food, pictures, servants etc. [...] the best that could be bought.

The landscape outside the house has been redone quite recently by Christopher Tunnard,★ who is a delightful person who is Professor of Town Planning over here.[6] He was in England before the war [...] was a Canadian citizen [...] Mrs T.

was also Canadian by birth, became American by accident [...] spent months getting Canadian citizenship again, and then married him just as he'd become naturalised American. He is Montreal, she Boston. She is very proper Boston [...] which means that she calls the town Boorston (as opposed to the New Yorkers, who call it Barston) but otherwise speaks English, and presumably like other Bostonians considers that only two cities in the English-speaking world are worth her notice [...] London and Boston [...] New York is apparently beneath contempt [...] she is a second cousin of Hitchcock's and has all that family's volubility and physical presence, which I think her poor dear husband finds a little trying. She is his third wife since he came over here 12 years ago [...] which is extraordinary since he's so mild and easy going and quiet [...] in a sort of super English way [...] but I think she has him for good. They of course, do not entertain in the grand Soby manner [...] instead, you're taken into the kitchen at the end of dinner to see the dishwasher in operation.

American houses are all completely en-suite on the ground floor with no doors [...] and this tradition goes back for more than a hundred years [...] they tend to have one or two small rooms... and perhaps one or two large ones [...] but you usually are able to sit in one and look into two others at the same time [...] the floors are always superb... and they tend to have loose mats. The Tunnard's drawing room was, again, enormous, about 20′ by 36′ and rather low [...] the reason why I think she had won hands down, was that what was obviously her furniture [...] had conquered what was obviously his (the modern) in this room, so that rather a curious mixture had resulted. But I can't tell you how pleasant it is to sit in a room this size [...] with no doors separating you from the other rooms [...] just big 10′ openings [...] and not to feel in the slightest bit cold. There are no draughts, the central heating always works [...] it's always impossible to wear a pullover and a jacket [...] and even when it's cold, to have more than two blankets on a bed is unendurable. It was the same in Canada too.

Not, of course, that it's cold at the moment. It's so warm that really one is very often obliged to go out without an overcoat [...] it's almost like a mild May in England at the moment [...] except that from time to time it gets very cold for a day or so [...] then snows [...] but in New Haven immediately melts. The light is always brilliant [...] it only rains for about one morning every week [...] and then it's a deluge with the rain falling perfectly vertically, [...] which is apparently always so along this coast [...] (it happens like this in Halifax, Nova Scotia) [...] so you see that in spite of what people say the New England winter is mildness in itself.

A curious thing is the amount of electricity that there seems to be in the atmosphere over here, you get electric shocks from handrails, from coins, even from touching other people. This can be very embarrassing [...] they won't believe it doesn't happen in Europe.

    Colin

1   William Osmun (1910–2012), educated at Yale University in art history, met Rowe in 1947 at the Courtauld Institute where he earned a PhD in decorative arts. Osmun became Curator at the Cooper-Hewitt Museum for the Arts of Decoration, and in 1957 he was named Senior Curator for the Los Angeles County Museum of Art.
2   James Lock & Co, hatters, St James' Street, London; Henry Huntsman & Sons, tailors, Savile Row, London; and Washington Tremlett, tailors and shirtmakers, Savile Row, London.
3   Henry-Russell Hitchcock;★ Farmington, Massachusetts and Middletown, Connecticut.
4   James Thrall Soby★ (1906–1979), was an author, critic, collector, patron of the arts, and a member of the Acquisitions and Photography committees at New York's Museum of Modern Art (MoMA). Soby wrote a monthly art column for *The Saturday Review of Literature*, edited the *Magazine of Art*, and wrote many monographs on twentieth-century artists. He married Eleanor ("Nellie") Howland, his second wife, in 1938, and Melissa Wadley Childs, his third wife, in April 1952.

5 This room was designed for Soby* by Henry-Russell Hitchcock.* See Rowe, Colin,
   As I Was Saying: Recollections and Miscellaneous Essays, Alexander Caragonne ed, 3 vols,
   Cambridge, MA: MIT Press, 1995, vol 1, p 18.
6 Christopher Tunnard* (1910–1978), a Canadian landscape architect and city planner. At
   the invitation of Walter Gropius, he taught at Harvard from 1939 until he was drafted into
   the Royal Canadian Air Force in 1943. After the war he taught city planning at Yale.

007   *To Mr & Mrs Frederick Rowe,*
          Highgate Lane, Bolton-on-Dearne, Yorkshire, England   *21 March 1952*

333 George Street, New Haven, Connecticut

Dear Parents,

   Sorry not to have written for so long. Would have written about a week ago
but have been ill. Went to a party and everyone there, almost, got a particularly
violent form of American cough and cold. It leaves you quite palsied. They call
it 'Virus Pneumonia' which sounds quite terrifying... however it's slight, and
apparently a natural feature of the American spring, like New England Sinus. Both
Brian and myself had it, which made life complicated [...] but we were able to
encourage sympathetic people to come and bring us things like jellied consommé,
tinned pineapple juice and what not [...] to be consumed in vast quantities [...]
very agreeable.[1]

The light here is getting stronger and stronger every day [...] the angle of the sun
brilliantly acute. One tends to forget, because most of the vegetation is Scandinavian,
that the place is about the latitude of Rome, and so one is always surprised by this
extreme lighting. Also it doesn't improve the look of things. One expects with that
sort of Mediterranean lighting, a Mediterranean solidity about the buildings, which
of course there just isn't. One doesn't quite expect the folksy, woody, New England
flimsiness, while the chromium plate merely suggests that one has got into Tel Aviv
by mistake. Really, the chromium has taken to glittering lately in a way that it never
did during the winter. Cold air, gasoline smells, bright sunlight and shining chromium
are so characteristic of urban America. All these things mixed up with telegraph
wires and neon tubes begin to get just a bit messy [...] and the scene becomes only
redeemable because of its obviously extreme prosperity. Although of course the
same messiness runs through that too. Downtown New Haven on Saturday tends to
become rather like an overcrowded third-class Italian railway carriage [...] so much
in America is addressed to the European peasant [...] it's quite alarming [...] one
sees why America has been the big success, and why it has quite destroyed Europe.
The mere existence of the American frontier in the nineteenth century destroyed
any European social pattern which had escaped Napoleon. It's only recently of
course, that the Europeans have become conscious of this [...] but the American
frontier (which also destroyed what there was of American aristocracy) absolutely
completed the European debacle [...] more so, I think, really, than the two wars. It
created a new social order, and if you consumed Chicago's tinned meat it meant
you ultimately would have to accept the new standards [...] you wouldn't be able to
survive otherwise [...] it's just no question of right or wrong [...] because obviously
Europe and the older America were right.

By abandoning an old social order based on certain ritual observances, by seeing
things directly rather than symbolically, the Americans were able to create mass

production [...] unexampled comfort and prosperity if only you threw over the old system. Naturally it wasn't surprising that all the peasants in Europe should do so [...] that New York should become the peasant Mecca, the third Rome. Just as the system required peasant labourers to work, in its beginnings it needed peasant consumers, and all American manufacturers really assume a market only one generation removed from the peasant [...] consequently the gaudy packaging, the tins, the artificiality of the deep freezes [...] consequently the fact that except in delicatessens you can't buy a crusty loaf in the whole of this town [...] they're all soft, or almost like cake.

There's nothing really very metropolitan about America [...] all its towns are provincial [...] New York [...] in Paris or London terms, certainly is [...] but the question of being provincial doesn't enter into it. A provincial town which has struck a boom doesn't become a capital city [...] but it can, depending on the scale of its boom [...] buy up the capital. In some ways this is precisely America.

Bill Osmun is very amusing about New York, but I quite forget the sort of things he says.[2] However, he is very amusing on the English selling themselves out to the U.S. Do you know that the Royal Family own a block in the best part of Fifth Avenue? Bill's father knows the agent who looks after it [...] otherwise it's a wildly secret thing, apparently. But Bill is better on things like the occasion in Newport in the late eighties, when society was all arranged, and determined to boycott Mrs Vanderbilt for her divorce [...] the Vanderbilt's until then having been such a quiet family. Mrs V. was just back from Europe [...] it was Sunday morning [...] the showdown was to be after church [...] but at church there was not only Consuela, but the Duke of Marlborough too [...] and disgrace was turned into triumph.[3] Bill makes this sort of thing hysterically funny [...] but of course, if the Duke saved her face [...] he was bought to do it [...] and the long sell-out had really begun. All very depressing.

The death of George VI was enormous news over here. I saved some papers for you but I've so far forgotten to send them. Americans are apt to get very emotional about such things. Like the Italian shopkeeper who said "What do yer mean, Good morning...." And you say that you mean precisely that [...] and he says "Not a good morning, the King's dead" [...] you are then expected to throw a faint, burst into hysterical weeping, or something of that kind [...] a chair is put forward for you to do all these things in [...] great disappointment is registered that one doesn't. Persistently Geo. VI is referred to as the king rather than the king of England. All very touching.[4] Typical piece of reporting says how Princess Elizabeth received the news in a remote African colony, part of 'the now rapidly crumbling Empire' [...] one has a picture of the poor girl sitting in a Zulu kraal.[5] Actually, the most amusing thing was told me by a man here who attends a series of lectures on Anglo-American affairs. The lecture at 9.10 was a bit of a strain anyway and nobody liked it [...] the Professor said [...] 'Gentlemen, the King is dead [...] under these circumstances I don't think that it would be fitting for me to speak to you today!' Where in England would you have found such exaggeratedly exhibited mourning? It became positively embarrassing to go out [...] one didn't possess enough platitudes to go around [...] that's not apropos of the Yalies, who have all been to Europe, but the Greek shopkeepers and waiters and people were all most touchingly solicitous.

That's about all, unless I make this letter cost 30 cents, which I can't really afford at the moment.

Colin

1   Brian Richards.*
2   For William Osmun, see 5 February 1952 letter (p 44 in this volume).

3 Alva Vanderbilt (1853–1933) divorced William Kissam Vanderbilt for alleged adultery in March 1895, scandalizing polite society and receiving a substantial settlement that included several estates.
4 George VI (1895–1952), died on 6 February at the age of 56, having reigned since 11 December 1936.
5 The Duke and Duchess of Edinburgh were at Sagana Lodge, the royal residence in Kiganjo, in the foothills of Mount Kenya, when they learned of the king's death.

008 *To Mr & Mrs Frederick Rowe,*
Highgate Lane, Bolton-on-Dearne, Yorkshire, England   *11 May 1952*

333 George Street, New Haven, Connecticut

Sunday

Dear Parents,

I'm so glad that you are not going to live at Springwell Farm, but do tell me precisely what is happening, as obviously Grandma can't spend half the week down Highgate Lane and anyone retain any sanity at the end of it. It seems to me that either arrangement is equally disastrous. I suspect that by default of anything positive on your part, the situation is working itself out negatively and for the worst. I do hope that you are being firm enough.

I've just been for three days or so to Newport, Rhode Island. It was rather a charming excursion to stay with Bill Jordy (who lectures here) and his wife, at a summer cottage which they have.[1] Between 1880 and 1929 Newport was the summer foyer of American society, and to put in an appearance there was more or less essential for social survival. There are so many summer palaces that the natives have been reduced to a state of complete servility. It's like paying a visit to Europe, there's none of the American rudeness, all the European respect. The scale of Newport and of Rhode Island is quite European too, small and intricate, so that Newport is rather like a small Devonshire seaside place with a most opulent Edwardian suburb added to it. You feel that by historical accident, Newport should have been left out of the U.S. altogether, so as to be a minute independent state, probably under the personal sovereignty of the President and the Bishop of Quebec. Everything is luxuriant and everything is in decay. Elderly gardeners mow the lawns and clip the bushes... you feel that the gardens will reach a final immaculacy just as the architecture is about to collapse. The paint flakes off the houses, the windows are boarded up, wood lice run out of the shingles and vines cover the floors of the piazzas [...] it's all decaying while the inhabitants discuss the quality of the detail which has perhaps just fallen off the gable. The more baroque and the more outrageous palaces now seem all to be Catholic institutions, and in the ballrooms designed by Richard Morris Hunt or Stanford White there are nuns by the score engaged in perpetual devotion.[2] All round them are mirrors, silver gilt, sconces, chandeliers, improper goddesses on the ceiling, and a rather ineffective veneer of religious art which they have superimposed. A very famous house of 1884 which had been abandoned for 10 years was in a state of complete decay. We climbed in through a broken shutter. Inside, everything had just been left for 10 years when, presumably, the front door had been locked for the last time. Outside, enormous Sycamores, which had sprouted like weeds, had broken up the paving, the driveway had disappeared, the boards of the verandas were beginning gently to rot away [...] it was quite astonishing [...] the end of an epoch feeling.

Christopher Tunnard* told me to go and look at a garden he'd designed for another rather charming town house.[3] Here everything was scrupulous, and after all the

Catholicism and rot it was an immense relief. He'd installed a little modern garden with 4 fountains which led out of another French garden made fifty years ago by a Monsieur Greber, who was rather good.[4] Inside, the house, which was Georgian, had been Frenchified about fifty years ago, and then modernised by the woman who lived there now. Everything perfect. The woman was called Warren, and since Mr W was upstairs in bed, having just broken his hip, and the son was in Europe doing postgraduate research, she had nothing to do except to take the second Cadillac out of the four-car garage, and we went out to spend a delightful afternoon looking at more decaying houses and people.[5] I met Mr Landsberg, who owns Malcontenta outside Venice, and who I was sure must be dead [...] but he was merely in Newport instead.[6] We went to another house which had Tiepolo ceilings brought over from Vicenza, to the vulgar Vanderbilt house, now a museum, called The Breakers, to a replica of the Petit Trianon where no expense had been spared [...] and even when people can afford it, no one can bear to live in these places [...] so the garden ornaments fall to bits and the real estate men rip out the fireplaces and sell them in New York, and in another ten years, except for the Catholic institutions there'll be nothing left.[7]

Brian and myself have just been discharging our social obligations in a series of three parties, and feel that by now we have entertained all the wit and talent of the East Coast. Not exactly true, but a pardonable exaggeration. The first was the most complete surprise, since uninvited and separately there arrived Christopher Tunnard which was nice, Pietro Belluschi* who is Professor of Architecture at M.I.T., and William Holford, who just breezed in through the kitchen and was very expert, elegant and urbane.[8] Ostensibly, he is a visiting critic at Harvard, but Hitchcock* thinks that he is hanging around to be in at the death. That is Gropius's metaphorical death, since he's due to retire next year.[9] So all the boys are collecting around in a rather ghoulish way, just to see if they can get the position, to remind the Harvard committee that they still exist, and to cut each others' throats or serve each other poison if they believe it to be necessary. However, will probably go up to Boston and see the Holfords before they leave [...] I think that it would be judicious, and one could also call on Gropius too. The second party was more or less a Hitchcock request, as an entertainment for a man from A.A. who turned out to be awful. However, since we suspected this might be so, we had adequate buffers, but of all people, Philip Johnson* arrived, looking a little sheepish. The third party was entirely a student affair and comprised our swan song to New Haven.

Last weekend Ken White, the man I came over on the boat with (architect from Leeds) was up from Princeton with a rather naïve and very Americanised Australian called Geoff. Summerhayes, also a Princeton architect.[10] The Australians are very directed towards this country [...] take anything American as God's gift to man, and think that they have nothing at all to get from Europe. He was perpetually shocked by our anti-American conversation, undemocratic sentiments, and all the rest of it. Ken is very good at this sort of thing, since he has a variety of R.A.F.[11] approaches which are guaranteed to be extremely funny, and also to make the standard American answer impossible [...] a great deal of "well let's face it" and all that sort of thing. We made rather a caustic little tour of Yale, and also some houses in Connecticut, with Geoff getting more and more hot under the collar [...] all very amusing.

For all these reasons it's been rather difficult to write. Also, since I've been finishing off the Hitchcock paper, which I shall send to Nikolaus in a week or two for him to put in the *Arch. Rev.*[12] Also, I've been writing a long review of a new book called *Forms and Functions of Twentieth Century Architecture* which is to be put in a periodical called *The Art Bulletin*.[13] I shall be able to sell the book (four volumes of it, for 50 dollars) but the review is really too good for where it's going. Also, I'm writing another article for Nikolaus which should be more exciting, and which will be a good thing in about September or so.[14]

So as you see, things here have become finally quite stimulating, and we are hoping to get some money to travel to Chicago with.

Please write and tell me what you are doing and how things have worked out [...] or as I rather suspect, how they are not working out. Please don't get caught.

Love,

Colin

1 William H Jordy (1917–1997) and Sarah Stoughton Spock. Jordy, an art and architectural historian educated at Yale, published *Henry Adams: Scientific Historian*, New Haven, CT: Yale University Press, 1952.
2 Richard Morris Hunt (1827–1895), architect; Stanford White (1853–1906) of McKim, Mead, and White.
3 The garden was located at the Warren Residence, a Georgian house built in 1810, located at 118 Mill Street in Newport.
4 Jacques-Henri-Auguste Gréber (1882–1962), French architect specializing in landscape architecture and urban design. Gréber designed many private gardens in the US.
5 Katherine Urquhart Warren (1897–1976), art collector and historic preservationist.
6 Albert Clinton Landsberg (1889–1965).
7 The Marble House, designed by Richard Morris Hunt for William K Vanderbilt.
8 Pietro Belluschi* (1899–1994), Italian American architect, dean of the MIT School of Architecture and Planning from 1951 to 1965.
9 Walter Gropius (1883–1969), director of the Bauhaus in 1919, chair of Harvard's Department of Architecture from 1938 to 1953.
10 Geoffrey Edwin Summerhayes (1928–2010), architect from Perth, Western Australia.
11 "R.A.F.": Royal Air Force.
12 This "Hitchcock paper" was probably an early version of Rowe's "Character and Composition; or Some Vicissitudes of Architectural Vocabulary in the Nineteenth Century". Nikolaus Pevsner* did not publish it in *The Architectural Review*. It was first published in *Oppositions*, no 2, January 1974, pp 41–60.
13 "Reply to Talbot Hamlyn's Recent Book", *The Art Bulletin* 35, no 2, June 1953, pp 169–174.
14 "Roots of American Architecture: An Answer to Mumford's Analysis", *The Architectural Review* 116, August 1954, pp 75–78.

009 *To Mr & Mrs Frederick Rowe,*
Highgate Lane, Bolton-on-Dearne, Yorkshire, England   *20 May 1952*

333 George Street, New Haven, Connecticut

Dear Parents,

The heat in this place has become appalling, so that one perceives that only with summer does America become specifically American. All one's resistance collapses, so that one is <u>obliged</u> to buy seersucker, nylon socks and all the rest of it. (Actually nylon socks are rather a good thing and never wear out or require mending—they probably suddenly dissolve.)

Last week, Bill came up to see an exhibition of Italian pictures in the gallery here, and we introduced him to Hitchcock,* who was at the reception for the opening of the exhibition.[1] As soon as Hitchcock realised that Bill came from London, he was on to ways as to how he was to get to Balmoral,[2] which at the moment appears to be the apex of his ambition. Blunt, Sir Eric Maclagan, Osbert Sitwell,[3] have all failed him [...] or been lacking in the necessary influence [...] but as soon as he realised that Bill knew Martin Charteris, who is the Queen's Private Secretary, hope dawned.[4] The hope was so violent and extreme [...] that Hitchcock went on talking until one in the morning, took us to dinner, drank two bottles of wine and innumerable liqueurs, all the while Bill was whispering that he would by no means introduce this man [...] etc. It was all very diverting, and ended by arrangements for Hitchcock's going to have dinner with Sam Stevens, who would have the Turkish girl, Velia there, who would later give a dinner for Hitchcock and Martin Charteris, etc.[5] All this because Hitchcock is quite crazy to find out what sort of an architect the Prince Consort really was [...] and more so, one really suspects, to have a succession of Balmoral anecdotes.

I've been slaving for the last two days on the thesis of a man here, Vincent Milone.[6] It has been, as they say here... traumatic... (traumatic, very much used, is a psycho-analytical term for harrowing). Vincent can't make up his mind, requires help, flaps at all suggestions, we can't do this and then perhaps we can. All this in the School of Architecture here, a Gothic building, against a perpetual background of Italian operatic records from the other end of the studio. Yesterday was the worst of all, a perpetual noise of Hitchcock bellowing from the garden down below, a girl who spent most of the day climbing the ivy so that she was able to get in two floors up by a variety of unusual means, another man sobbing with George Howe,* the Professor,[7] because he thought his marks weren't high enough, Lees Brown, the First Year Tutor, lurching around in an obese and faintly drunk condition throughout the day, two Russians arguing with Wu[8] (Charles Chen's friend, who instructs Third Year) because they thought they had been unjustly criticised, and all the time a coming and going of various drifting morons.[9] At the end of it all one sank back, convinced that America and Russia must be very alike, after all [...] the same sort of inconsequential madness, pursuit of the ego, etc., that you associate with Russian novels.

About three weeks ago, one would have left all this behind quite shortly, with a mild sigh of relief. Now, we've heard that we are likely to be able to get hold of some money to go to Chicago, St Louis, Minneapolis and places, and look around. It's not quite certain yet, but Hitchcock seems to think that it is, and is making arrangements for us to see Frank Lloyd Wright* in Wisconsin, Mies Van der Rohe* in Chicago, and so on. The thought of the glitter, heat, etc., is appalling, and one hardly expects to return from such places alive (Indians, bears, etc.), but the tour, presumably, is vaguely educational, and although it would be much pleasanter to be in Rome or somewhere, one has to suffer for experience.

About three weeks ago, one was making arrangements to come back in July or early August, but now it seems to be a good idea to come back in January or early February [...] see the year around and see places, etc. Without seeing them would really make coming to America rather absurd. So in the last 10 days or so our ideas have rather enlarged [...] Bill Jordy, whom I went to Newport with just before I last wrote, has just heard that he is coming over to Europe and wants to sell his car, which is a nice little Jeepster shooting brake.[10] We've priced them in used-car dealers at $1,100, and Bill will let us have his for $600. There is really no snag, since it's always been carefully used and is in very good condition, and Bill is supposed to be responsible for me and what not. So our ideas have now rather expanded. To buy Bill's car, to drive over to San Francisco, to work there for six months, with the money saved (one would get $60 to $70 and can live on $30), to return via Los Angeles; the Colorado Desert; Texas; New Orleans; Charleston; Nashville, Tennessee; Washington; etc.; to New York. After that, one would feel quite justified in feeling blasé about the American continent. It would have been seen and it would be quite unnecessary to see it again. And one would sell the car!

Now please don't be distressed about this, which I feel sure is your first reaction about everything I do. It would be ridiculous and fatal to go back to Liverpool—I've spent three years there and know all about how things are done in the School of Architecture.[11] It would be equally stupid to stay over here (had I wanted to, I could have had a job at $3,800 a year teaching architecture at Smith College, but I wouldn't want to stay over here for a year longer, and it would be silly to be stuck in Northampton, Mass., where one would be wasting time just as much as by going back to Liverpool). The American continent is always worthwhile having seen, particularly Chicago, the Frank Lloyd Wright buildings, and the Californian coast, and also for other reasons, we gather that it's going to be a good thing to delay return for some months. By early next year there are going to be a good many American architectural offices opened up on the Continent. One hears rumours of them going to be formed in Paris, in Rome, in Florence, in Munich. This rather stands to sense [...] since all the buildings that the Americans will require for the occupation of Europe will be fed out to American architects, and there will be a lot of hospitals, welfare buildings, residential buildings etc. that will go up in France and Germany and Italy and also in North Africa. Working in such an office one will be paid in dollars, at American rates, say $70 a week, one will be living in countries where $20–25 a week are quite enough, one will have the advantages of Europe plus those of the dollar too [...] and also no English income tax. This idea is so delightful as to establish itself as an irresistible aim, but to achieve it, I rather think that it would be a good thing to be around New York in six or seven month's time. A man called Lloyd Flod, who teaches here at Yale, is going out to Paris or Rome to open up an office for Edward Stone, for whom he works part-time. Eero Saarinen, who is a friend of Hitchcock's, is over in Munich and Paris with the same idea. Another man here at Yale is off to work in Florence. It seems to be a decided trend, but one gets into it in New York. Anyway that's the general aim, which work in San Francisco would rather help towards.

In view of all this, I've just turned down a charming invitation to give one of a series of lectures at Cambridge (England) in late August. The Society (or something or other) for Italian Studies, wrote and said they'd love a lecture on Inigo Jones* and Italian influences in English Seventeenth Century Architecture [...] other speakers in the series to be the Italian Ambassador, Dorothy Sayers, Donald Gordon, and Ellis Waterhouse, who is Director of the National Gallery of Scotland.[12] Sounds wildly distinguished, don't you think, and if one were on the Continent and working there it would be quite worthwhile doing... even though there is no money in it. But all told, I think that it's rather better to be here, intriguing so as to get a nice little American job, which will permit one to live in Europe in a reasonable semi-affluence, after which one could consider such tempting little diversions.

Anyway, you see the general aim. We hope to be able to get about $400 each for travel. We propose, in travelling, to sleep in the back of the shooting brake, so that daily expenses will be quite minimal. We have spaced people out nicely along the route, so that we hope to receive entertainment, hospitality, etc. I am taking a job for the next three weeks or so, helping a man here to build a house [...] I mean really to build it [...] social struggle, foundations, walls, and all. I ought to be able to clear about $120 on that, which will all add up, but there won't be quite enough to cover insurance and that sort of thing, and also the possibility of breakdown.

We need about another $150 each. Brian got in first with Hitchcock, who agreed to provide it here, in return for a cheque making the equivalent amount payable to him in England. Hitchcock doesn't want to take any more, but I found a girl here who is coming over to England and could use £50 or so. From the point of view of changing the money, that makes things quite alright, only the thing is that I shan't have £50 until Nikolaus publishes my article in some month's time.[13] Then it will be alright. The question is, could you finance the £50 business of this incredible Odyssey until then, when I'll let you have a cheque to cover it again? (It would have been alright if only the Ministry of Pensions would pay my pension directly into the bank [...] but I can't get them to do this [...] I have to claim it all, instead, when I get back).[14]

I am enclosing a cheque for £50 dated 1st January 1953, payable by the Midland Bank, Rodney Street, Liverpool. Could you pay £50 in to my account there and then I shall be able to make arrangements to have this girl paid cash by someone like Bob Maxwell* in London. If you can do this it will make everything quite clear, San Francisco and Europe will be a possibility, and I shall become an expert on the American scene.

Love,

Colin

P.S. Have bought a camera with a tripod, so as to be able to record all that is to be seen. Brian has also bought a light-meter, so as to be able to achieve effects of even greater accuracy [...] we expect to graduate as expert photographers and experts on all the more recent buildings on our route. We are also going to be lent a tape recorder, so as to be able to record variations of accent etc., in all the districts we pass through. Also, so that Frank Lloyd Wright can say a few words into it.

Please write and say <u>what</u> is happening at B.O.D.[15]

Colin

Please don't think this is a bad thing—David will tell you it's not.

Colin

1 William Osmun. See Rowe's letter dated 5 February 1952 (p 44 in this volume).
2 Balmoral Castle, Aberdeenshire, Scotland. Private property of the monarch (and not part of the Crown Estate) designed by William Smith (1817–1891) and constructed from 1853 to 1855.
3 Blunt, Maclagan, and Sitwell had been guests at the royal household.
4 Martin Charteris (1913–1999) was appointed private secretary to Princess Elizabeth in 1951.
5 Thomas "Sam" Stevens (c 1921–1992).
6 Vincent Michael Milone, architecture student, Yale University class of 1952.
7 George Howe* (1886–1955), architect in residence at the American Academy in Rome from 1947 to 1949, chairman of the Department of Architecture at Yale University from 1950 to 1954.
8 King-lui Wu (1918–2002) taught at Yale University from 1945 until his retirement in 1988.
9 Charles Chen was a classmate of Rowe at Liverpool. See Rowe's letter to Dorothy Rowe* dated 19 January 1989 (p 322 in this volume).
10 Jordy had received a Guggenheim Fellowship to travel in Europe. "Shooting brake" is a British term for station wagon.
11 Prior to coming to the United States, Rowe had been teaching in the School of Architecture at the University of Liverpool.
12 Inigo Jones* was the subject of Rowe's Master's thesis of 1947 at the Warburg Institute.
13 Nikolaus Pevsner* at London's The Architectural Review.
14 A disability pension Rowe received as a consequence of the spinal injury he had incurred in July 1943. See Rowe's letter to Ursula Mercer* 20 August 1943 (p 29 in this volume).
15 "B.O.D.": Bolton-on-Dearne.

To Robert & Margaret Maxwell, St George's Terrace, Primrose Hill, London   *June, 1952*   **010**

The School of Architecture, Yale University, New Haven, Connecticut

MY DEAR BOB AND MARGARET,

This is a business note.

I want 150 dollars quick (towards an automobile).[1]

It has to be got from England.

There is a desperate girl here, going over, who will let me have 150 dollars if I let her have £50 in London.

I would rather not write a cheque to her direct... conceivably it could be queried. But if she came over there furnished with a cheque from me payable to either one or the other of you, could you cash it and let her have the money. (This cheque won't bounce).

Would you be about in late June to do this sort of thing? Would you do it?

Can you write and let me know immediately. Time is short.

Also, if you can, where she should contact you. Suggest no more than a lunch meeting... I've met her about twice and she's hell.

If you can't who could?

Have told Hitchcock* to look you up?

Love,

> *Colin*

---

1   Rowe needed American currency to purchase William Jordy's Willys Jeep station wagon in which he and Brian Richards* planned to tour North America. A "desperate girl" had offered to give Rowe $150 in US currency in Connecticut in exchange for Maxwell* giving her £50 on her arrival in London in late June 1952.

011   *To Mr & Mrs Frederick Rowe,*
37 Highgate Lane, Bolton-upon-Dearne, Yorkshire, England   *15 September 1952*

Wright, Metcalf & Parsons, Architects, 2000 26th Street, Bakersfield, California.

Dear Parents,

At last, after three months, have achieved a settled address to which it is possible to write, and from which it is probable to receive a reply. Arrived here two days ago, and shall work here until Christmas, that is if the architects here can stand us or we can stand them for quite so long. However, if one does stay until Christmas it will be reasonable enough. There's nothing to spend money on here except trips to San Francisco, Los Angeles and the Yosemite and one is paid 450 dollars a month, which will allow one to return through the Southern States in comfort and ease. However I'll tell you all about Bakersfield in another letter. I think that I'd better send letters in a series of instalments describing the trip.

First day was New Haven to Rome, New York. We took with us the obese Lees Brown who lives at Rome where his people own a soap factory.[1] Drove up the Connecticut River to Northampton, where called on Hitchcock.* Northampton is rather a charming town. Western Massachusetts... one of the few picturesque landscapes and mature settlements in America. From Northampton to Williamstown and to Amherst, Massachusetts, to see houses by Frank Lloyd Wright* and Marcel Breuer.[2] Both of these are college towns and, before that, residential towns of extraordinary opulence. Late eighteenth century houses, immaculate lawns, huge elms and, quite soon, outside the settlements, rough mountains and jungle. From there, across the Berkshires to the Hudson Valley and crossed the river north of Albany at Troy. Troy was a boomtown of the 1840s and '50s, a river port when steam navigation opened up upper New York State. It was the metropolis and the sin city of the neighbourhood. Now it's a crude, abandoned, decaying little place. Neglected, with fine buildings if one cared to look for them, but not a place in which anyone lives. At Troy you definitely feel that you're out of New England. You come down quite steep slopes from the Berkshires, you cross the bridge and you drive out into a rolling, bigger country which rapidly becomes flatter and flatter. You feel here, for the first time, that you've struck the great west, (continually you feel this, all the way across the continent) and you feel, too, in this plain, that the ties with Europe have been quite decisively severed. A mild feeling of alarm and a growing distaste throughout all this country. We got to Rome quite late, only to discover that we were not to dine with the Browns at home but at the country club instead. (All American towns have country clubs and everybody seems to go there.) Lees is full of distaste for Rome, his family, his relations, the country club, etc. However, we are fed enormous steaks at great expense, taken on by papa and step-mamma to a night club where none of us wanted to go, etc. Step-mamma rather the OK style of thing, Papa disposed to talk of Republican politics. The next day we see Rome in the daylight. The wide, long, crude, rough main street, huge warehouse buildings of the 1840's, a vigour about things which reminds one a little of Rome, Italy. The Catholic Irish Monsignor walking down the street with buckles on his shoes, and talking to Lees in a mildly reproving tone as one of the impenitent members of the church. The gaol with windows overlooking the street and a prisoner in a tee-shirt sitting in each window, exchanging casual words with the passers-by. Rome, like Troy, was a port for barge traffic, but is a dead flat site in an apparently dead flat plain. Again, just behind the main street, the usual opulent, elm lined suburban streets. Lunch at another club, again on Papa's account. Interior of the place with splendidly lugubrious Victorian fittings, outside with the usual portico. In the evening Mrs Brown rises to a barbeque, again steak, after which Lees shows us the town.

Next day, on to Buffalo, through towns with names like Syracuse, Ravenna, Verona, Ilion etc. All these towns are early nineteenth century settlements. Those that haven't grown have a certain charm, the country is not quite as flat as first appears. It rolls about but there are no hills. In Buffalo, see three Frank Lloyd Wright houses, and a wonderful office block of Louis Sullivan's dating from the '90's.[3] But Buffalo, such a horror of filth, traffic, hoardings, neon, that we flee through the industrial squalor to Niagara, where cross into Canada and decide to go on quickly to Toronto. Arrive about ten-thirty, ring up Syd Key,* but they all have Mumps, and go to stay with a pleasant French woman called Marthe de Rakine, who paints.[4] Next day, Syd lets one know that Mrs Matthews (I think I told you about her) was really awfully anxious for one to go up to Lake Simcoe, so we ring her up. She enthuses and invites one up. So we drive eighty miles north through a countryside entirely devoid of charm and infested with mosquitoes. Mrs M. has a summer place by the Lake at a place called Roches Point which has belonged to her husband's (dead) people since the eighteen fifties, when it was a trading post where Indians came with furs and things. It is quite clear when we ask the way to the house that she is the local 'grande dame', peasants show respect and so on. A drive about half a mile long, cottages, stables and all the rest, indicate that nineteenth century England or Ireland are not dead yet. Drive up in front of the house, waves from dining room window, wash, are served drinks by a maid, and shown to the dining room where twelve people are sitting down to lunch. All this is a little grander than one had expected, especially when Mrs M. (Consy to the more gallant members of her generation) apologises for the age of her house party, had terribly wanted us to come, would have got up a younger one if only she'd had a month's notice, etc. Roches Point was very agreeable. I suppose there can be very few houses like it in Canada. Everyone wildly Anglophile, the Lake, a boathouse, with canoes, rowing boats, a sailing dinghy, a motor launch, an island in the lake which still had Indians. Mrs M. very grand manner pouring one drinks before dinner and then deciding to go out to inspect the village. Ourselves and an aged military type carrying drinks, and drinking them from time to time, Mrs M. conversing with the natives [...] one hadn't quite expected so feudal a setup in Canada.

We stayed for two days and then everything breaks up. Consy insists on providing an escort half way to Toronto. So we follow her car, which includes a dog, two maids, a parrot cage, and a lot of baskets of strawberries. After that we fork right and drive through northern Ontario, Guelph and places to Sarnia where we cross into Michigan. Northern Ontario is thin and cold looking, a clear strong light but very little colouring. A rolling country with no very decided hills.

Northern Michigan is just hell. Leggy, weedy trees. Messy settlements and lots of traffic down into Detroit. Are so depressed that almost decide to return. However go on to Detroit and look in at the Cranbrook Academy, where impose upon a mild and sensitive architectural student and spend the night.[5] Next day is very hot, and see houses by Wright, by Saarinen, the new General Motors building and other things. Drive on with increasing disgust to Toledo, Ohio, where the Willy's Jeepster place is, in the hope that they can fit the car with new piston rings. However, they won't, and next day leave for Kalamazoo. Country in Southern Michigan becomes unexpectedly charming. A sustained pastoral landscape with elegant towns and finished buildings. Albion and Marshall are towns of this kind. Kalamazoo not so nice. Guests of Norman Carver, a Yalie architect.[6] Arrive early and immediately whisked away to the country club where become immersed in the pool. Also in the pool are three dreadful Frenchmen whom we ignore (they have rubber flippers on their feet) and also the girl from Kalamazoo to whom we were introduced. Next day leave Kalamazoo, see one or two furniture factories, a couple of Wright houses, and arrive in Chicago in the late afternoon. Alarming volumes of traffic flowing through an outer industrial zone, suddenly one emerges on the fabulous Lake Shore Drive which runs along the Lake front. Terrifying road with eight or ten lanes of traffic, a beach and blue water to one side, yachts, etc, gardens on the other side with big apartment blocks, offices and so on.

We ring up some people called Boyden whose daughter Katrina had arranged for us to stay with, since they had a charming apartment in their basement which used to be Katrina's before she infuriated them by insisting on going off to Europe. We went round in a couple of hours or so. The Boyden house a stone terrace affair of the 1880's in the best part of town [...] the whole ground floor made over into one big living room. We arrived as a cocktail party was in progress, and just at the moment when old man Boyden, Chicago's leading divorce lawyer, had passed out on the stairs and people were trying to put him into bed. This was a source of confusion and embarrassment that was quite unexpected. However after half an hour or so Mrs Boyden rallied and was more or less able to cope.

Also staying in the house was a bad script writer and novelist called Harlan Ware, plus his family. Harlan, I think, had at an earlier age been rather addicted to Mrs B. but now seemed to spend most of his time reading his novels to anyone who would listen. The worst sort of American funny books [...] you know the sort of thing, only the most fantastic contortions of the muscles round about the mouth can make one seem to be amused. Harlan would say 'Now boys listen to this, this is funny' [...] His daughters would sit in corners and moan and say 'Oh no Daddy, not that' etc.[7]

Chicago was appallingly hot and terribly humid. Saw a great many Wright houses, office buildings and things. Have never seen streets so appallingly paved or slums so atrocious. About a third of the population seems to be Negro. Went round the stock yards and saw the mechanisation of animal killing, as a result succeeded in putting whole dinner parties off meat. Went outside to see the fabulous Farnsworth house by Mies van der Rohe,* which has just been completed at a cost of 95,000 dollars. It consists of one room and no more... so you can imagine how fantastic the finishes are.

Dr Edith Farnsworth for whom the house was built is about 45, unmarried, a former student of the violin in Siena, and a very successful G.P. with a taste for the arts. She inherited a certain amount of money and presumably has made more. She was in love with Mies and commissioned the house. It was the foyer of what she hoped was going to be their liaison. The original contract was for 35,000 dollars. Mies, the perfectionist, continually played upon her feelings, the details of the house became more and more immaculate, the expense increased accordingly. At 60,000 she wasn't having any more, she paid him his fee, he spent it on the house, he sued her for non-payment of fees, she is suing him for deceit. The case is proceeding and Edith sits in the house, in a marble volume as perfect as the Parthenon, surrounded by King Charles' spaniels, while the case drags itself out in the local courthouse. She is a friend of Hitchcock's and was charming. Kept us for a whole evening, gave us a lot to drink but fed us exclusively on anchovies because the refrigerator isn't big enough. The whole thing is a most suave comedy in the Somerset Maugham manner. She is torn between her delight in the house which she obviously can't afford, her chagrin about Mies, and her fury because she feels she's been tricked. Everything is acted out on the highest level, politeness and feeling for quality on both sides is quite extreme.[8]

Also in Chicago, learned from a man who teaches at Harvard that Mrs Holford had gone quite off her rocker. Just before they were due to leave Boston she caught viral pneumonia, which went to her brain and nothing could be done except to put the poor dear woman in a mental home. It's a very good thing that one didn't, as Holford proposed, go up to see them.

From Chicago went to stay with Paul Schweikher, who is a very good architect who it is supposed will be the next Professor of Architecture at Yale.[9] A timber house in a prairie. Wonderful detail.[10] He is appearing as a witness for Mies against Edith Farnsworth.

From Schweikher, as the guest of a pleasant Yalie called David Hilles who works in his office.[11] David lives in Lake Forest where, by an incredible fluke, he has an apartment at the top of a house which is almost always empty. In the garden, a swimming pool. Lake Forest, the really opulent Chicago suburb with enormous palaces jostled side by side. David gave an opulent party for us. Many penniless Englishmen haunt Lake Forest looking for heiresses.

From Lake Forest to Madison, Wisconsin, through another charming pastoral landscape.

Here I shall stop and tell you some more in another letter. I got all your letters in San Francisco a few days ago. But why did you keep on sending them to 333 George Street? I did give the Yale School of Architecture as an address.

Give my love to Auntie Mary, to the Lambert Laughtons, and so on. I feel that it is unfortunate that what has happened to Grandmamma didn't happen a year earlier.

Love,

   Colin

1 Lees Brown was a first year studio instructor at Yale University.

2 Wright's★ Theodore Baird House, Amherst, Massachusetts, 1940; Marcel Breuer's Robinson House, Williamstown, Massachusetts, 1946–1948.

3 Wright★ built four houses in Buffalo between 1903 and 1908: the George Barton House; the Darwin Martin Complex; the William Heath House; and the Walter Davidson House. The Sullivan office building is the Guarantee Building, 1895–1896. Both the Guarantee Building and the Martin House complex are cited in Rowe's "Chicago Frame" of 1956.

4 Marthe Rakine (1906–1982), a Russian-born French painter who migrated to Canada in 1948.

5 The Cranbrook Academy of Art in Bloomfield Hills, Michigan, 25 miles northwest of Detroit, was founded in 1932 and first headed by Eliel Saarinen (1873–1950). In the 1950s, Eliel's son, Eero (1910–1961), maintained an architectural office immediately adjacent to the academy.

6 Norman F Carver Jr (b 1928), architect and photographer, a native of Kalamazoo, Michigan.

7 William Harlan Ware (1902–1967) wrote a novel, *Come, Fill the Cup*, New York: Random House, 1952, as well as plays, screenplays, and scripts for radio programs.

8 Edith Farnsworth (1903–1978), a prominent Chicago physician who commissioned Mies van der Rohe★ (1886–1969) to design a weekend house for her in Plano, Illinois, 56 miles southwest of Chicago. Completed in 1951, the single-cell house is steel-framed with glass walls, an icon of Modern architecture. Details in this letter regarding the cost of the house are inaccurate.

9 Robert Paul Schweikher (1903–1997) was a visiting critic at Yale University in 1950–1951, and chairman of the Yale School of Architecture from 1953 to 1958.

10 Schweikher house and studio, Roselle, Illinois, 1937–1938.

11 David Ellsworth Hilles (1926–1997), graduated in architecture from Yale in 1951.

012   *To **Henry-Russell Hitchcock,** Smith College Museum of Art, Northampton, Mass.*   *September, 1952*

Wright, Metcalf & Parsons, Architects, Bakersfield, California

Dear Russell,

Thank you for your letter. I'm glad England was so enjoyable. We enclose a small cutting from an *Architects Journal* which you may or may not have seen but which in any case should be gratifying and amusing.[1]

I forget whether I told you what we are doing here. The principals of this firm are the world's worst architects who have on their hands a seven million dollar campus job.[2] They can't cope and a bad landscape architect from Los Angeles has provided them with a workable but intrinsically stupid *parti*.[3] We can't deviate from this very much, but all our effort goes into trying to make it appear reasonably plausible. So far the business is only one of plans... when elevations are reached I presume that the balloon will really go up... but meanwhile the project is becoming punctuated by our series of victories.

How much worth while this sort of thing is I never really know and one begins to wonder whether one's own experience must always be the experience of other people's stupidity.

We are anxious to get inside the Millard House and possibly the Ennis House.[4] We gather that both of these are difficult and we have been wondering if Masolink could be got to write to the owners, who presumably could scarcely refuse a request from that source.[5] If you could ask him about this we should be very grateful.

One is impressed in California by the provincialism of most things that are done... that is with the exception of Neutra... also it seems rather curious that he has never really succeeded in founding a school about himself.[6] The Bay Region, one has to face it, is rather *triste*[7] and Wurster just a little too much a clever operator disguised as a wooly bear intellectual.[8] Do you know anything about a man, Ernest Born?[9] Everyone in San Francisco speaks of him with awe. We called at his office but he has no work and no assistants, and was consumed by self-depreciation and an apparent sense of failure. He has built a charming and very European group of workers apartment houses.[10]

But California is so far away from the centres of authority. Nearly everyone here who is anybody can do a successful and highly personable small house. Beyond that they really cannot go and the great lay out is quite beyond them. I.I.T. and General Motors seem to have almost no reverberations over here.[11] In this expressionist wilderness you do see what legislative achievements these are.

One is also interested by the American hesitancy in handling any purely plastic thing. This stands out quite sharp and clear all the way across the country, so that the dis-relationship between structural and plastic disciplines seems to be one of the constituent factors of American architecture. Only Richardson and Wright* seem to have got over this. Sullivan* is particularly the outstanding victim of it. Does he ever succeed in fusing the two except in the Guaranty Building?[12] In general the forcefulness of structural statement is terrific and this seems to endow the plastic elements with a particularly endearing maladroit quality. They never quite achieve a rational context, a basic dislocation invests them with a curious punch, they are even slightly open (although God forbid) to a vaguely Mannerist interpretation.

And all this isn't only relevant to Chicago of the 80's but you can see it in the suburbs of Boston, in Mies'* McCormick House, and very pronouncedly in Eero Saarinen's office building at General Motors.[13] Only look at how that entrance has absolutely no relationship to the grid. One can't be quite sure whether this is a good or bad thing.

Did I tell you how Gothic we found America to be? The limitless, rather than the finite space of Europe, gives one very little sense of place. It prolongs a dream-like mood, and particularly in southern Michigan and in Wisconsin, going from one place without pronounced character, to another equally undefined, one quite often gets the idea that one is enmeshed in the web of an elaborate fifteenth century tapestry... because there is so little really memorable topography and very little to particularise the space one happens to be in. We found that this situation had great charm. When is Bill Jordy* coming west? Will you tell him that I'll write but tell him that we should like to involve him in our visit to the Millard and Tremaine House.[14]

With best wishes,

    Colin

P.S. Brian wonders whether you got to Kilmacolm?[15] Also asks me to enquire if the Kaufmann House which Neutra did is at all related to Edgar Kaufmann and if so whether you could provide us with his address.[16]

---

1 The enclosure is lost. "We" refers to Rowe and Brian Richards,* his traveling companion.
2 The "campus job": Bakersfield Community College, located on a 153-acre plot in Northeast Bakersfield. It opened in 1956.
3 *parti,* French: decision, course, choice; in architecture *parti* denotes the salient aspects of a scheme, primarily its plan.
4 Both are "textile block" houses designed by Frank Lloyd Wright:* Millard House (*La Miniatura*), Pasadena, California, 1923–1924; Ennis House, Los Angeles, California, 1924.

5 Eugene Masselink (1910–1962) was secretary and business manager to Frank Lloyd Wright★ since the mid-1930s.
6 Richard Neutra (1892–1970), Austrian-American architect in Los Angeles whose remarkable residential work, most notably his Lovell House of 1927–1929, established him as a pioneer in the early Modern Movement. His work was included in the International Style MoMA exhibition on Modern architecture curated by Hitchcock★ and Philip Johnson★ in 1932.
7 *triste,* French: sad.
8 William Wilson Wurster (1895–1973), an exponent of the Bay Region style, dean of the MIT School of Architecture and Planning from 1945 to 1950; dean of Architecture at the University of California, Berkeley, from 1950 to 1963.
9 Ernest Born (1898–1992), San Francisco architect, artist, and teacher.
10 North Beach Place, 1942–1950, San Francisco: a low-income housing complex designed by Born in collaboration with Henry Gutterson.
11 "IIT": Illinois Institute of Technology, Chicago, Mies van der Rohe;★ General Motors Technical Center, Detroit, Eliel and Eero Saarinen, 1949–1955. See Rowe's letter dated 15 September 1952 to his parents (p 54 in this volume). At this time the famed 'Case Study Houses'—many of them subscribing to Miesian aesthetics—were being built in Southern California.
12 HH Richardson (1838–1886), Frank Lloyd Wright★ (1867–1959), Louis Sullivan (1846–1924) and his Guaranty Building, Buffalo, New York, 1894. Hitchcock★ had published monographs on the work of Richardson and Wright: *The Architecture of H.H. Richardson and His Times*, New York: Museum of Modern Art, 1936 and *In the Nature of Materials: 1887–1941, The Buildings of Frank Lloyd Wright*, Cambridge, MA: Da Capo Press, 1942.
13 Robert McCormick House, Elmhurst, Illinois, designed in 1951–1952 by Mies van der Rohe★ as a possible model for manufactured housing.
14 Warren D Tremaine House, Santa Barbara, California, 1948, by Richard Neutra.
15 Brian Richards★ had studied at Trinity College, Glasgow, near Kilmacolm, a village in the west central lowlands of Scotland.
16 The Kaufmann House, Palm Springs, California, 1946, designed by Richard Neutra as a vacation house for Edgar J Kaufmann Sr, who in 1935–1938 had built Fallingwater, designed by Frank Lloyd Wright,★ in Western Pennsylvania.

013 *To Mr & Mrs Frederick Rowe,*
Highgate Lane, Bolton-upon-Dearne, Yorkshire, England   *1 October 1952*

Wright, Metcalf & Parsons, Architects, 2000 26th Street, Bakersfield, California.

Dear Parents,

This is really a continuation of the letter that began rather more than a fortnight ago when I'd taken you up to Madison Wisconsin. I don't think that I'd taken you any further than that.

Madison is a very elegant, completely residential city, situated between three excessively blue lakes. The dome of the State Capitol dominates all, and everyone appears to live in a condition of idleness and affluence. The University of Wisconsin which is situated there by one of the lakes is particularly fabulous and disgustingly rich. At Madison we saw a lot of houses and also went out to Taliesin to see Frank Lloyd Wright.★

At Taliesin Wright owns all the land which you can see from the terrace of the house and it's all a curiously English landscape. The Taliesin setup is surely the most feudal thing to be found on the North American continent, and Wright is the most complete autocrat in the middle of it all. The students pay 1,500 dollars a year for the privilege of working for Wright and he keeps a lot of them just working in the fields.

Approaching the house you rather get the feeling of approaching Chatsworth or something of that kind.[1] You sense the autocracy in the middle of it all. You pass farms and stables and all the outlying dependencies of a great establishment. Wright has never stopped building the house or altering the landscape in the last sixty years and the result is that it's so enormous that some parts are entirely forgotten, roofless and falling into ruin, while others are still in the process of erection. Mr Wright emerges some mornings and has a wall pulled down, or can't wait another day until a particular window is made [...] the result is that there is no plan, and no rhyme or consequence about the play [...] it's just an extraordinary un-American fantasy, which suggests something like Warwick Castle, or the Palace of the Dalai Lama, or the chateau of the Popes at Avignon. Internally the furnishings are of incredible richness. Wright spent about half a million dollars on Chinese carpets in 1916 and presumably at that time one still did get something for an expense of this kind.

We met Wright but he is really quite senile, and Taliesin would have been something of a desolation if it hadn't been for Edgar Kaufmann who was staying in the house (being treated like dirt and very bored).[2] Kaufmann is writing a book on Wright, is the son of a Pittsburgh millionaire and had persuaded his father about ten years back to build one of the most famous of Wright houses.[3] He showed us lots of plans, was witty, sympathetic, and disloyal to his host.

It's not until leaving Wisconsin behind that you really enter the prairie. Michigan and Wisconsin are rather a delightful pastoral interlude as regards scenery. Taliesin is situated in the first hills of any size after leaving New York State behind. From Madison we went in one day through Iowa to Des Moines. Here you definitely begin to hit prairie. You cross the Mississippi at Dubuque, a dirty town with a crazy bridge. The bridge is 100 feet above the river but made of iron slats, so that you see through it as you drive across. Dubuque to Cedar Rapids is high rolling country because the river is very deeply cut into the land. After Cedar Rapids we really hit prairie in the most exciting circumstances with an unreal sunset. The great heat of the day cooling off, the glitter of the chromium a little subdued, a note of nocturnal anxiety suggested by the neon of the motels, and nothing but corn fireflies and the headlights of cars. All this seemed basic prairie [...] only of course to be modified next day by even more extreme and more basic prairie. Next day we crossed the Missouri at Omaha to drive to Lincoln, Nebraska. Omaha, the start of the principal trails West a hundred years ago, has a certain sepulchral charm, a lugubrious splendour and seems quite incapable of shaking off the recollections of a glorious Victorian past. Lincoln, Nebraska, is quite different, brassy, neon lit and baked in an Italianate heat. The next day when we left at five in the morning for Denver, Colorado is completely memorable. I can't tell you how delightful it is to drive for an entire day through five hundred miles of the most interminable, unvaried, excessive monotony. You've only got to believe that it's terrific. The sensation of land extending on every side is overwhelming, you begin to believe that you are involved in a deliberate landscape in which all purely decorative incident has been thrown out in order to insist on the natural eloquence of the one single horizontal theme. All day you drive imperceptibly uphill. There's almost no traffic [...] this for 500 miles! [...] and about four o'clock you suddenly find yourself at the edge of an enormous trough with the Rockies at the other side and awful Denver in the hollow in between.

The Rockies are an awful bore, green, Alpine and banal, but once across them into Colorado proper you are in a wonderful country. Oasis valleys surrounded by blue mountains alternate with fantastically jagged deserts, in which without any warning at all the road suddenly plunges into quite terrifying canyons. There are stretches of 100 miles or so with no towns at all, and only very occasionally, strange peasant shacks from which incredible hoboes emerge [...] what they live on is rather a mystery. But one can understand why this country has generated a whole mythology of western films, and also one can understand people never wanting to leave it. It's the only part of America about which I can feel like this.

Salt Lake which we entered in pitch blackness through the most prolonged and winding canyons proved to be the most hospitable and entertaining of cities. It's got a population of 160,000. There's nowhere of equal size until Calgary 1,000 miles to the North, Mexico City 1,800 miles to the South, Denver 500 miles to the East, and Sacramento 700 miles to the West. These figures and the desert that you come through to approach the town make you aware of how great the Mormon achievement was in founding so elegant a city here 100 years ago.

The shadow of Brigham Young still lies heavily over the place, his name crops up in conversation at least twice every evening, his activities are the epic which makes Salt Lake quite different from other American Cities.

A charming man from Yale, Robbie Wicks, had invited us to stay with them. We descended on the Wicks' at breakfast time, to a most elegant meal in a little circular dining room. Everything was commotion and too much couldn't be done. In the next few days all doors in Salt Lake were opened. This was quite charming. Mrs Wicks' grandfather had come from Newcastle in the 1850's and founded the city's first bank, the Walker Bank, which is still in the family. Brigham Young had threatened his life and for twenty years he'd never been able to leave the house... (it was the same house we were in) without an armed guard of four men. There were continual stories about Brigham Young which I wish I could remember... but it was American finance as typified by people like Mr Walker that he particularly wished to exclude from the Mormon paradise.

But everyone in Salt Lake is fantastic, eccentric, and un-American. Mrs Wicks surprisingly turned out to be a cousin of Nancy Astor's;[4] but she quite paled into insignificance by the side of the fabulous Dorothy Allen.[5] We went with Robbie to stay in a summer cottage at a place called Brighton 9,000 feet up at the top of a canyon, and there complete with horse one day arrived our nearest neighbour, a Jewess who looked like a Toulouse-Lautrec circus artist. In her mid-fifties, she was a native of Salt Lake, had married into the American diplomatic corps, had spent years in Lima, had danced with the Prince of Wales, etc. etc. etc. represented the 1920's in their most complete form. She had a house that looked like something out of the film *Sunset Boulevard*, a wonderful, huge, elliptical swimming pool which she didn't use because she was frightened of water, and a positive menagerie of people who frequented her house. A charming elderly military type called Colonel Sweeney had been there for the last 6 years. He was writing a book on tactics, had been in the American Air Force, the French Foreign Legion, the Italian Army, and had lived in Paris until 1940. He had organised the Eagle Squadron in England in both wars, and had a very fine collection of Matisse drawings which he was delighted to show.[6] That was merely a sample of the human menagerie. Hemingway had been there the week before, and there were also tame deer, horses and quantities of dogs. The whole establishment conducted with a sort of gusto, naiveté, and tastelessness which approached a Somerset Maugham fantasy.

You get the idea of Salt Lake. Eccentric individuals who have no idea of their eccentricity. Following every whim. Isolated by 500 miles of desert which exaggerates all their attitudes to the point of caricature. All this conducted against a background where the memories of the polygamous rigours of the Mormons are still very close.

You become aware of how great a man Brigham Young was. A sort of mixture of Moses and Garibaldi. Ingenious, calculating and enthusiastic, quite ruthless. You realise how heroic was the trek through 2,000 miles of desert to found a city in the wilderness. Quite one of the major epics of the American nineteenth century. They thought of it as the trek from Egypt. The Mississippi was the Red Sea. The inland valley of Utah was the valley of the Jordan, the Salt Lake in which you can't sink was the Dead Sea. It's all quite extraordinary.

From Salt Lake we went north rapidly, through Idaho, Yellowstone, Montana, into Alberta. The Canadians of Alberta are very unpleasant, and Calgary is one of the most disgusting towns on the North American continent... and that's saying a lot.

Banff and the Canadian Rockies, the Chateau Lake Louise, and all the rest of it are dismal to a degree... it's all like being inside a Scottish Hydro... and nearly everyone you meet is dour and Scottish.

Canada really belongs to another letter which I will write in a day or so.

Love to everybody,

    Colin

P.S. I'm sure you are <u>still</u> writing to New Haven. Why?

---

1 Chatsworth House in North Derbyshire, England, rebuilt 1687–1707. Taliesin had been built by Wright* in 1911–1914 and was severely damaged by fire in 1914 and again in 1925. It was rebuilt, modified and extended several times during Wright's life.
2 Edgar Kaufmann Jr (1910–1989) studied and apprenticed at Wright's* Taliesin. His father commissioned Wright to design the famed Fallingwater in 1935 and later commissioned Richard Neutra to design the Kaufmann Desert House in Palm Springs, California. After the Second World War, Kaufmann was head of MoMA's Industrial Design department and from 1963 to 1986 he served as adjunct professor of Architecture and Art History at Columbia University.
3 Fallingwater, 1938.
4 Nancy Witcher Astor (1879–1964).
5 Dorothy Allen (1896–1970), an American movie actress active in the 1920s.
6 Mercenary Colonel Charles Francis Sweeney (1910–1993).

*To **Mr. & Mrs Frederick Rowe,***
Highgate Lane, Bolton-upon-Dearne, Yorkshire, England   *4 November 1952*   **014**

Wright, Metcalf & Parsons, Architects, Bakersfield, California

Dear Parents,

    I shall give up any attempt to carry this letter on as a description of Canada etc. etc. Vancouver was amusing in a way. The situation of the city is superb but is steadily being ruined by appalling buildings and as a town in its shops and things it is about as primitive as Barnsley.[1] You notice the change again every time you step over into America, particularly when you leave British Columbia for the Pacific North West. The Pacific North West is rather like England and all the settlements have a certain air of old established opulence which makes places like Vancouver and New Westminster appear extraordinarily tawdry.[2] Victoria is ridiculous.[3]

The Pacific coast in Oregon is damp and miserable.

Internally Oregon is more splendid.

We spent a night in a place called Eugene and then two nights in Reno, Nevada. This is one of the most awful places of all time. Gambling is completely mechanised. There is none of the colour or distinction of a European casino but just a lot of slot machines into which people put money and hope to get something out. The most fantastic thing seen was a circular bar. The gamblers sat round, each with a drink and a slot machine let into the bar. There was utterly no excitement and no animation. The slot machines occur everywhere. In blocks in the streets, in supermarkets and drug stores, and the entire population from the age of twelve or so upwards is continually using them. You get queues in a lot of places to put money into them.

From Reno to San Francisco via two very distinguished Nevada cities [...] Virginia City and Carson City.

San Francisco is the most finished of American cities. This is quite without a doubt. All white buildings looking mostly like large scale confectionary, a good deal of refinement of detail throughout the town, an extremely feminine atmosphere [...] this is very noticeable after Chicago and the Mid-West [...] but in San Francisco [...] dowagers parade the streets. The most shocking thing about the town though is the fog. It comes in between five and six every night, white and clammy. You see it creeping over the place in great white waves [...] rather like the spirit of the Lord visiting Elijah [...] and immediately it becomes uncomfortably cold. You can be crossing the Golden Gate Bridge and see neither the water, nor the pylons of the bridge, nor the other side. This seems to be the great drawback to San Francisco. It's a nightly occurrence and it makes it impossible to go out in the evening in any degree of comfort.

The other thing about San Francisco was that it was quite impossible to get a job there because there was absolutely no work. One had the most excellent introductions, the *entrée* to the most delightful societies but all to no use. However perhaps it was as well, as one would conceivably never have got away. Bill Crocker for instance I'd met in Italy. He was at Yale some time back and is now at Stanford.[4] The Crocker's are banking in California. It's the name that opens all doors. Bill took us to Sunday lunch at the parental palace in Burlingame. Quite the grandest sort of place so far. A private drive three miles long. A dining room about thirty feet high, and a butler and two footmen to serve lunch, which since we arrived by surprise was their normal Sunday corned beef hash and fried egg. Mr Crocker couldn't have been more charming, begged us to make use of the swimming pool and the squash court, to come often, etc. etc. But all this opulence did require some money from somewhere and quite plainly this was not to be had in San Francisco. So the only thing to do was to go on to Los Angeles.

The difference between the two places is quite extreme, and Los Angeles is awful, so the next logical step was to leave the coast for the San Joaquin Valley.

That's what brought us to Bakersfield which, since it was earthquaked this summer, is booming.[5] We are designing a whole State College which is to cost 9 million dollars and also getting a reasonably free hand.[6] However Bakersfield is quite devoid of society, so that although one can have money here one can meet absolutely no congenial people here. The sensitive in San Francisco shrink in horror at the name, and the fashionable like the Crockers flatly don't believe that anyone lives here. So what is one to do?

Bakersfield was founded in the 1860's by an Englishman, Colonel Baker, who fought for the Confederates in the Civil War. It is absolutely dead flat and is situated in the most disgustingly fertile plain in America. There isn't the vestige of a hill for ten miles if you travel East, or for 25 if you choose to go West. There are merely fields of cotton, orange, alfalfa, etc. etc. [...] all this interspersed with oil wells and also with Negroes, Mexicans and Okies who work in the fields. This is an amazingly peasant spectacle, particularly the Okies. They are the lowest of the low. There are Okies and Arkies. They are the people who migrated from Oklahoma and Arkansas in the 1930's. They are much the same and are quite shiftless. All Californians loathe and deplore all Okies, and the Okies spend their year doing casual labour up and down the valley all the summer and then committing a minor crime so that they can spend their winters in the State Prisons. This is completely Steinbeck country.[7] The ignorance in the small towns is unbelievable. For instance at Arvin, 20 miles from here, the mountain has produced an enormous chasm since the earthquake. It was widely believed that last Tuesday was to be the end of the world and that primeval monsters were going to come up out of the earth and going to make an end of all. There were ceremonies of prayer and everything else to keep off the evil day, and since it didn't happen they are now all doubly confirmed in their faith and have apparently been rolling and rocking quite frenziedly ever since.

Now if this was to happen in Africa you might believe it. But isn't it fantastic less than eighty miles from Los Angeles? [...]

1   Barnsley, former South Yorkshire mining and glassmaking town on the River Dearne, 8.5 miles west of Bolton-on-Dearne.
2   New Westminster, 12 miles southeast of Vancouver on the north bank of the Fraser River.
3   Victoria, the capital of British Columbia, 60 miles from Vancouver on the southern tip of Vancouver Island.
4   William H Crocker, a graduate of Yale in 1950, was studying anthropology at Stanford at the time of this letter.
5   Earthquakes occurred on 21 July and 22 August 1952, the latter killing four people in Bakersfield and destroying many of the town's historic structures.
6   Bakersfield Community College.
7   John Steinbeck's novel *The Grapes of Wrath*, New York: Viking, 1939, tells the story of Oklahoma tenant farmers ("Okies") driven from their home by drought, migrating to California.

To Mr & Mrs Frederick Rowe,
37 Highgate Lane, Bolton-upon-Dearne, Yorkshire, England   *27 December 1952*   **015**

Wright, Metcalf & Parsons, Architects, 2000 26th Street, Bakersfield, California

Dear Parents,

When I got your letter the other day I realised that I hadn't written since the beginning of the month, just in fact before going up to San Francisco for a weekend.

Since then a great deal has happened which only if you were intimate with Bakersfield could you understand. To understand places like this you should read Sinclair Lewis' *Main Street* which is a very dreary novel but amazingly evocative of the American small town.[1] Then you'd understand how complicated the position is with regard to the College we are designing. First of all there are the Trustees. Then there is the building committee which is desperately anxious to keep in the good graces of the local Chamber of Commerce and so insisted on giving the job in the first case to local architects who are incapable of handling it. Then there are the partners who are as complacent and as anxious to please as the building committee.

They are incapable of saying no for fear of giving offence and the result of course is they continually offend because they promise the impossible. The three partners are bound together by an interest in the profits and a dislike of each other which is intensified by the attitudes of their wives. So you begin to get some idea of the complexities of the situation.

The other day for instance we were fired, that is because we told Metcalf that he was "ludicrous and inept". So we said O.K. However the building committee went up in smoke [...] said that it should never have happened [...] and the other two partners were only too willing to take us back, both to propitiate the committee and as a crushing sort of snub to Metcalf. However we snubbed the lot by insisting on $25 extra a week or we wouldn't dream of coming back. The result now is that we are not on speaking terms with Metcalf but Wright's* wife can't enthuse too much over what has happened.

So you see political excitements of this kind add a certain amusement and stimulus to life but perhaps hardly sufficient to compensate for a basically fatuous situation. Imagine the three partners in this firm. An $8,000,000 college to design and they are hardly interested in it. The fees on the completed work will be in the region of $600,000 and even split three ways to $200,000 is not to be sneezed at. And yet if it hadn't been for the work we've done they'd certainly have lost the job. The situation is tragically inept. If one were an American citizen and sufficiently unscrupulous one could get the job away from under them and also get an international reputation for the finished work. As it is one has to fight all the time to prevent them making the most awful botch. However the elimination of Metcalf has made this a good deal easier.

While we were fired we made a trip to Death Valley which is awful and forbidding, like driving on the moon. You can go for sixty miles or so without any signs of life and absolutely no birds. You pass white lakes entirely of borax which look as though the most primitive forms of life should be emerging from them.

There are half abandoned towns occasionally, little collections of mining shacks, enormous sand dunes, canyons, rocks with notices like "Jesus Saves" or "Prepare to Meet Thy God" painted on them, and nothing in fact but utter desolation on the most enormous scale. Fifty years from now all this will most probably be irrigated, a lot of people will have made a lot of money, and a number of very prosperous, hideous little shanty towns will have sprung up.

We also went on a trip to Santa Barbara which is where Aldous Huxley and Thomas Mann live, although God knows why.

Also to see some friends of Bill Osmun's called the Seymour Slives who live at Pomona on the way to San Diego where he teaches art history. They are charming. Seymour spent last year in Holland studying Rembrandt, and Zoya, who is his wife, was most of the time in London or Paris.[2] They are Russian although Seymour was brought up in Chicago. Zoya lived in Moscow until she was eight, just opposite the Kremlin. Then in Berlin and later in Brussels. They have very fine things. Zoya's mother, who lives with them, has Faberge enamels and a collection of rugs which she has been forming for the last 45 years. Wonderful Persian, Rumanian and Navajo things. Also French and Venetian furniture and a wonderful collection of Mexican objects. They are really extremely Russian, particularly the mother whose English is not good, and also the small daughter who looks as though she might grow up to be a female partisan.

However nothing can convince me that California is really up to much. The weather is wonderful, there's lots of money, but apart from work, when the principal natural beauties have been seen there is absolutely nothing to do.

One could stay here indefinitely, the college could keep one here for another eighteen months easily. But that would be pure martyrdom. Neither the partners nor the town would recognise it as architecture when finished, so we are planning to get the project as it stands published... which more or less commits them all to the solution as it at present stands... and then one can clear out with the satisfaction that at least one has succeeded in laying down rather more than the main lines of the thing.

Since by the middle of January we shall both have saved about $1000, which isn't bad for four month's work, we think it's reasonable to call in on Mexico City on the way back. Seymour is quite enthusiastic about this. Everything apparently is preposterously cheap. One can buy native rugs, pottery of wonderful forms etc., and everything is both more European and more Indian than the U.S. The new University at Mexico City is the most remarkable architectural project just completed on this continent, besides being the oldest educational institution [...] since it was founded by Charles V in 1551.[3] You can also buy Aztec bronzes of the fifteenth century still quite cheaply [...] in fact everything in Mexico seems to be worthwhile, and the whole country will be a wonderful relief before facing Texas, Louisiana and other traumatic places.

So the general idea is to leave Bakersfield in the middle of January, to call on the Frank Lloyd Wright* setup at Phoenix Arizona, to see the Grand Canyon, and the Bryce Canyon and the Navajo Indian country. If possible to get some Navajo rugs cheap and then to go down to El Paso and through Chihuahua to Mexico City. Mercifully most things in Mexico are quite close to Mexico City. Puebla, Taxco, Cholula, Cuernavaca; everyone says should be seen. It would be pleasant to go on to Yucatan (possibly) before coming back.

The joy of all this is that one will completely miss the winter. Here apart from a few occasional fogs it's still like an English September, in Mexico City it should be like a North Italian August. There also will be something to write about... which is rather more than can be said for Southern California.

Really I don't know what you can do in B.O.D.[4] Can't Grandma be sent back to a nursing home again? I really see no reason why not. Other old women are. But in the Californian phrase, bungalows in Bridlington are 'for the birds'.[5]

Californian American is rather different, by the way, from other kinds. Everything in California is a 'deal'. There are raw deals, slick deals, rugged deals, tough deals, swell deals, lousy deals, big deals, Patio deals, two storied deals. When it isn't a deal it's a 'situation'. In that case you can apply all the same adjectives all over again. There is also 'darn tootin'. "I said to him 'darn tootin' you're right." "Darn tootin I will". This means "you can be sure I will", or "I completely agree with you". You can also, to signify approval, keep on nodding your head and saying "Slick, slick, slick, slick, oh slick". You can also, to emphasise things, say "man oh man" or "brother" (with emphasis on the last syllable). There's also, and I'd almost forgotten it, 'regular'. There are 'regular deals', 'regular guys', etc. etc. etc. Lots of these terms are quite old forms of speech one imagines [...] certainly one wouldn't hear them in the East. California I think imports its speech from the Mid-West. From Iowa, Nebraska, Arkansas (pronounced Arkansaw), and Oklahoma. That is because this part of the world is the paradise of the Mid-West. The Mid-Westerners when they can no longer stand their prairie or their climate come out here to retire. They build themselves little bungalows on Longbeach, or Pasadena and then they are perfectly happy. Los Angeles is all they ever dreamt of, or all they ever could have wanted.

Those are the reasonably well off ones. The others, the real Okies come to the valley and not to the coast. They too are well off, although you wouldn't imagine. They drive Cadillacs and eat steak every night so I am told. They live in shacks, but they keep their food stored in refrigerators and deep freezers. They are fundamentalist in religion, prolific and puritan, and they believe the *Bible* is entirely true. Jim Hicks, who works in the office, was telling me about a little Okie child the other day. He asked it its name. It said W.A. He said that couldn't be. The child persisted "Doubleyouay". He still didn't believe it. But its mother who had just come up said of course that's what it was. W.A. The letters stood for nothing but themselves. That's the peasantry of the San Joaquin Valley and of all the Mid-West. Isn't it quite fantastic.

You can go into any supermarket here and see them prosperous and buying, essentially transplanted peasants, from Hungary, Ireland, and Italy, Scotland, Sweden. They have a common style. American as opposed to that of the country they've originated from. But their behaviour is still that of a very prosperous peasant community. Basically they believe in food, fear God, and have no regard for art. It's very interesting.

The week before Christmas here all the local schools have a parade. Each school is preceded by the school band, by little girls swaying like a *corps de ballet* and dressed in the briefest little bits of luminous nylon.[6] There are floats with little Gothic churches on them and groups of girls in white nightgowns with wings. On these it might say "Daughters of Job (Bethel Lodge)" or something equally incredible. There were other floats with children from the local Indian reservation on them [...] these in luminous nylon too. Fat old men dressed up as hussars. The whole thing extravagant and indescribable. Something that you could never see in France or England. The peasant festival done without regard for New York or San Francisco. In a way, although very laughable, also rather amusing. The grotesqueness of the situation is that all the peasants have Cadillacs.

    Colin

---

1 Lewis, Sinclair, *Main Street: The Story of Carol Kennicott*, New York: Harcourt, Brace, and Howe,* 1920.

2 Seymour Slive (1920–2014), American art historian and director of the Harvard art museums from 1975 to 1991, and Zoya Gregorevna Slive, a social psychologist and connoisseur of the arts.

3 The Ciudad Universitaria, designed by Mario Pani, Enrique del Moral, and others, was built in the early 1950s and located in the southern part of Mexico City on an ancient solidified lava bed.

4 "B.O.D.": Bolton-on-Dearne.

5 Bridlington, where Rowe was taken on holiday as a child, is a minor fishing port and popular seaside resort near Yorkshire, England.

6 *corps de ballet*, French: in ballet, the group of dancers who are not soloists.

016   *To Mr & Mrs Frederick Rowe,*
Highgate Lane, Bolton-upon-Dearne, Yorkshire, England   *March, 1953*

Houston

Dear Parents,

    I thought that since I'd sent you one letter I might just as well send you two, particularly since you have had no real account of Mexico except for one letter which was probably illegible that I sent you from Palenque.

We crossed the border at El Paso, Texas on January 28th. This was quite a lot of trouble and after fixing things with the American authorities there were then the Mexicans to deal with. They were painfully slow, the customs house was filthy and one had to tip the customs officials to get them to do anything at all. Otherwise I suppose that we should have stayed there all night. The Mexican town used to be called El Paso del Norte but is now known as Ciudad Juarez which I think is a mistake. It is of no interest whatever and American tourists go over there in droves just to be able to say that they have been to Mexico.

We got out of Juarez at 5 p.m. to go the 200 miles which separates it from the next place, Chihuahua. Literally except for one or two customs posts, and two collections of mud-shacks there is nothing in between. The country is fairly flat though about 3600 feet above sea level and a frieze of mountains about twenty miles away accompanies the road all the way down. It is a mixture of scrubby grass, cacti, of all kinds, sand dunes. There was almost no traffic, there was nowhere to eat on the road, almost the only signs of life were the occasional fires with Mexicans sitting round them wrapped in *sarapes*. There can't be a more sudden change than this anywhere else in the world. Before getting to Chihuahua we ran out of gas, but were able to pour some in from an auxiliary tank which we'd got in Juarez. Finally the interminable drive was over, rounding a bend in the road were the lights of Chihuahua, the aerials of the radio station, a little neon, and then as you came up to it, a cemetery and a sports field. We couldn't face the town, so ate in a run-down little restaurant on the outskirts and spent the night in a ridiculous hotel, which has been built to catch tourists.

The next day Chihuahua revealed itself as a mountain village about the size that Wath must have been about forty years ago.[1] There was a bridge with women washing clothes in the river, there were shabby streets in which the shops had no glass. There was a large seventeenth century cathedral, an equally grand bishop's palace, an enormous lavish palace for [...] the Governor, and they completed the plaza. A few rather Frenchified houses for the upper bourgeoisie, and a collection of rough houses of mud-brick completed the place. There was literally nowhere to eat breakfast. The only thing to do was to buy chocolate and oranges and to go on.

South of Chihuahua the country becomes a little more charged with incident and occasionally you get the large village. Mexican villages in the plateau country are nearly all the same. The houses mud, built round courtyards, one story high, and with no glass in the windows. Also in the majority of cases no chimneys, since the smoke is intended to escape through a hole in the wall. The poorer villages have never been either plastered or painted and the effect is inconceivably depressing. When you drive through one of the richer villages, painted white and green and terracotta, it can be rather delightful.

From Chihuahua the next place of consequence is called Hidalgo del Parral but it is nothing to stay and look at. After that another two hundred miles, making about 450 in all to Durango which is the capital of the next state. Down along this road you begin to get more churches. You cross immense plains of about 30 miles or so extent, you drive for hours through cactus desert, you cross whole ranges of mountain. Indians sometimes wave from the sides of the road. The Tarahumare's are the local Indians up here and their principal pleasure is running barefoot. This you see them doing with cerise ribbons tied in their hair. They catch their horses by chasing them until the horses are exhausted, and they can run for days together and for hundreds of miles without showing any signs of fatigue.

As it was getting dark and before reaching Durango the countryside became really alarming. To have broken down in it would have been a nightmare. Dirty villages, deep ravines, bridges, narrow roads and gorges. Underneath most of the bridges fires were lit and Indians were sitting about there before settling down for the night. I'm sure they may have been charming but I should hate to have stopped.

After about an hour or more of this we came out on the great plain of which Durango is the centre. There were no villages here, and no light. Just from time to time, large shuttered eighteenth century *haciendas*. Finally Durango came as suddenly as Chihuahua had the night before.

It is rather a Sitwellian town of baroque facades, elaborate patios, and unlit side streets, and here it was quite a joy to sit in the gloomy elegance of the principal restaurant and eat what was to turn out to be the best cooked filet mignon that we were ever to get.[2] The restaurant had been made by roofing over the patio of one of the most splendid palaces in town, and although it was draughty and someone was tuning the piano, and we were literally the only people there, the whole meal had a certain atmosphere of achievement, which may be the cook felt as much as we did.

The next morning we had breakfast in a dubious little place surprisingly run by a Chinese and apparently extensively patronised by the police. Then again the same interminable road which by now was beginning to provoke a quite pleasant monotony. South of Durango the land gets higher and the Indians more gay. There were lots of them about and they always in this part of the country wave to anyone who goes by. Alongside the road from time to time you see the carcass of a dead donkey which the vultures are finishing off. Always there are peasants trotting along with donkeys. Just south of Fresnillo you cross the Tropic of Cancer, of which I'll send you a picture, and fairly soon about lunchtime you reach Zacatecas. This place is all of red brown stone, and is fitted out with aqueducts, entrance gates, cathedrals, churches and bridges, all of the most elaborate opulence. The Spanish thought a lot of Zacatecas, and from now on you are in Colonial Mexico, the part of the country which they really settled and subdued. From now on the churches all have domes, the distances are shorter and the towns increasingly grandiose, although the Indians seem just as poor.

I wish I could give you an idea of this extensive, continuous brown country and how extraordinary it is, but I suppose that it's quite useless to try. You go on and it goes, rather like a motion picture in which it's very difficult to isolate anything in particular. Aguascalientes and Leon are the next two towns. Leon in its position a little like Chihuahua, come upon round a bend of the road with a gentle slope leading down to the plain and the city. But villages along this stretch of road begin to develop quite *en hauteur*, with magnificent compositions of churches and bridges rising from the squalor. Leon is the first town which seemed to possess elegance and animation, with parades, statues, plazas, and walks. We drove through it and quite suddenly it became night and intensely black. Silao we went through in the dark and got on as far as Guanajuoto. This is a mountain city of incredible complication. Roads cross over roads, steps lead up and down, and the streets are completely crammed with a rabble who jump on to the back of the car and want to show you to an hotel. The only thing to do is to push them off, which we had to do.

The Guanajuoto hotel was totally depressing with damp sheets. This, and the atmosphere the following morning was sufficient to drive them out of the place. Walking round the town in the evening you couldn't help noticing the awful coldness of the air. You looked in through the doors of shops and inside you saw stacks of coffins, with little children sleeping in them. I can't tell you what a shock this was, but in the morning you realised that of course everyone up here just dies of pneumonia. The whole population the following morning was walking around with shawls and scarves over their noses and round their throats, and you did feel an awful piercing heavy atmosphere, which was quite an indication to get out.

This was the first town where we really ran into the standard rabble. Sitting on the side walks trying to sell dirty little cakes, cooking tortillas, and at midnight in every stage of dejection trying to catch buses around the doors of the hotel to places which I am sure were quite inconceivable.

We were able to feel a little more relaxed driving down to Queretaro because you did begin to feel that at last Mexico City was in reach.

Queretaro is really a very agreeable town. Just outside as you come in from the north is the hill where the emperor Maximilian was shot in 1867. You approach it up a little avenue of cypresses and at the top is a little chapel of red brick and I suppose Austrian Gothic architecture, which Franz Josef built to commemorate the spot where his brother lost his life. The chapel is so mean that one can only think that he didn't much care.

But you can't help wondering what romantic aberration induced Maximilian to give up being a Hapsburg prince, all the comforts of Milan, Trieste, and Vienna, to attempt so unlikely a career as that of being so-called Emperor of Mexico. Apparently he did a great deal of good, but the clericals didn't like him as being too liberal, too intelligent, too sympathetic, and advanced, and the Liberals didn't like him either since he had all their ideas but was theoretically on the wrong side. So Juarez, who was Indian and incorruptible, and apparently the only honest president that there's ever been in Mexico had him shot.[3]

This is Queretaro's principal interest [...] apart from its being quite a charming town. From here onwards you are really very high up, 8,000 feet or so and you go through some amazing irrigated valleys to Toluca. Toluca is just dull but is the last town before Mexico City 40 miles away. After this begins the real climb up to about 12,000 or 13,000 feet surprisingly through pine woods with wonderful cool air. By now the car was beginning to get a little exhausted and only just made it to the top [...] on a gradient that was almost nothing. It was very worrying and awful to think of being stuck there, but once on the top, all that was necessary was to glide down the last fifteen miles or so into the town, where there are no hills and consequently no difficulties.

Mexico City has a population now of about 3,000,000 people and appears to have no connection whatever with the rest of the country. It's rather too big a subject to comment on, but it has all the things you expect in a capital, including an imitation Champs Elysees. It has appalling slums and being very high above sea level people tend to get tired and go to bed early so that by 9 o'clock at night the streets are deserted. It's built on what used to be a lake and which is improperly drained, so that within the next ten years, according to competent engineers, the whole place is going to subside. No one appears to worry about this although buildings show alarming cracks and quite new ones are already eight or nine feet out of true.

It's not a particularly gay place and after getting the car looked after, and after paying our respects to the British Council, where we left a lot of luggage, we left for Cuernavaca and Taxco.

Cuernavaca is the Mexican equivalent of Richmond or Versailles or Tivoli. The semi-suburban town where people have villas. It's about eighty miles away and you approach it by two roads. One is quite good, a fairly normal Mexican road. The other is superb, a toll road with four lane highway that gets you there in no time at all. Specially built by the last president and his party to get them to Cuernavaca in the least possible time.

All over Mexico you come across things that the last president did. He was Miguel Aleman and had a passion for building.[4] Wherever you go you can't avoid his works.

He was apparently very popular, brought a lot of money into the country and even for a President of Mexico contrived to embezzle an extraordinary amount. During the six years of his presidency the British Embassy believes that he got together about £40,000,000. He is now a very rich man and lives in Rome.

In Cuernavaca we didn't stop, rather unwisely as afterwards we had to make a special trip to look at it and it wasn't worthwhile. It is the place where the more leisured section of the foreign colony live and indulge in literary attitudes, etc. They, and the majority of Americans rave about it, and no doubt it is a charming place to live, but the town itself is quite squalid.

From Cuernavaca to Taxco is about 80 miles and a drive through wonderful tropical scenery. You know the engravings in that old book of *Robinson Crusoe*.[5] I was amazed how true they are because everything looks just like that. Rocks, feathery trees, and little thatched cabins. All this is at a considerably lower altitude than Mexico City and has a delightful climate which never varies the whole year round from a steady 70 degrees. The little Indian houses down here are really no more than sunshades. The roofs are thatched with palm trees and the walls are just bamboo slatting which you can see straight through. The landscape is incredibly luxuriant with banana palms, blue flowering Jacarandas, and a lot of other quite unknown things.

Taxco was an old silver mining town in the eighteenth century which has now rather struck a tourist boom. It is another very complicated hill town, but you don't sense there the awful pneumonia atmosphere of Guanajuoto. We had been advised to stay at a place called "Casa Humboldt", formerly the Bishop's Palace and where the Baron von Humboldt stayed when he came to Taxco in about 1806.[6] It was very amusing but rather too long to describe. It belongs to a bogus architect, Alex von Wuthenau, who used to be a Counsellor of the German embassy in Washington, and his wife, who used to be married to an S.S. man (or at least so they say in Mexico City), runs it as a pension.[7] They are very German, very anti-American, and rather charming.[8] The house is a delight. An elaborate street front, a hall about 90 feet long, vaulted rooms, and a back which falls in a series of terraces into a ravine.[9] Little Indian maids who are paid almost nothing do all the work, and the von Wuthenau's are left with nothing except a rather tedious leisure during which Alex occasionally restores a church. For our benefit he wore a tartan shooting jacket which his father had got on a trip to Scotland in 1898.

From Taxco a trip to Acapulco two hundred miles away on the coast was an absolute necessity. It's the place where all good Americans go (by air) and which they rave about. Parts of the road quite close to Taxco lie through hostile Indian country and are not really very pleasant. But the whole road, Indians or not, is now being made into a superhighway although at the moment this seems to be more of an idea than a fact. For fifty miles before Acapulco there is really no road at all. You just drive through sand. These road works have been going on for years and sometimes you have to stop until they bulldoze a way through. Quite fantastic. All the time it keeps on getting hotter and hotter and the Indians get blacker and the total effect rather more tropical.

Acapulco used to be the place where the Manila galleons unloaded, and their stuff was brought across on pack horses to Mexico City and Vera Cruz for trans-shipment to Spain. This road then is hundreds of years old. It connects a modern metropolis with a sophisticated resort and yet the astonishing thing about it is that the country on either side has never been explored. Quite close by the land is called the *tierra desconocida* and if you go there you just don't come back.[10] That's the astonishing thing about Mexico, vast territories have never been explored and whole races of Indians live there who have never had contact with either the Aztecs, the Spaniards, or the modern Mexican government. Up quite close to the U.S. border just south of Arizona for instance, you get a tribe called the Yaqui's who in spite of all sorts of expeditions against them have never been subdued and still gaily practice cannibalism, although really one can't blame them because otherwise they get so little to eat.

Acapulco however is terrible. Just like Santa Barbara, or Malibu in California. There is a long marine drive, vulgar hotels, bad food, futile nightclubs, Mexican plutocrats and American slobs. After 18 hours of it we fled back to Taxco.

From here back again to Mexico City and on to Tlaxcala.

Tlaxcala is famous for *sarapes*, sort of woollen blankets and we bought some rather good ones here. A terrible hotel, and nothing to eat except scrambled eggs. Can you imagine it? This sort of thing happens all over the country. You never know what a meal is going to be, or whether you'll be able to get one.

On from Tlaxcala there is a place called Cholula which has 350 churches although quite a small village. It was interesting to look round one or two and also to climb the sacred pyramid, but one couldn't stay there long as the pangs of hunger literally drove you out. Except for the worst Mexican chocolate there was literally nothing to be had. Nothing. Not even a ham sandwich, and you find yourself living on these in Mexico. You see the natives don't eat bread, only the city sophisticates do that [...] the rest of them can't afford it. Cheese is unfit to eat. And the funny things they put on the little maize cakes [...] tortillas [...] are so formidable as to make one really run away.

So there was no other alternative but to go on to Puebla. Puebla is considered a fine town which is quite true, but also it is totally devoid of animation. Next day we went on to Vera Cruz. Beyond Puebla on this road you run into complete desert, places where there has been no rain for seven years. The poverty of the inhabitants is totally depressing and it is a known fact that they exist on grubs and bits of insects which they dig up. If they can get a lizard it is a great luxury [...] everyone accepts this state of affairs as a matter of course [...] and really no reason for surprise.

Suddenly in this desert you come to a ridge and below you lie the coastal valleys. They are a long way, thousands of feet below, but the character of the country and of the air immediately changes. As you descend everything becomes tropical, and humid and rank. The suddenness of changes like this in Mexico is quite amazing. Towering over it all you get Mt. Orizaba which is 18,300 feet high and has a permanent snow cap, behind you is desert and in front of you jungle.

The surprising thing about these tropics is how much one feels at home in them. Except for the occasional palm tree the effect is really very English, something like the New Forest or Hampshire [...] we were rather astonished by this but it was amusing that Jim Papworth who is British Consul in Vera Cruz thought so too. He was pleasant and hospitable, he was brought up in Madrid, and I believe I told you that his people used to live next door to Maria de Lara.

Vera Cruz is about the most animated town in Mexico and its plaza is just about the right size, taking the town into account to produce an agreeable atmosphere of congestion. It is just about the only place in Mexico where you can eat out sitting under the arcades round the plaza. Also being low down, at sea level, and very hot, it is late in going to bed. The life of the plaza here is indescribable. You would go there with Jim Papworth and take a table for dinner, but never anything went reasonably. Generally some awful fish stew would turn up. But the real thing were the beggars in every shape and form. First of all the people selling National Lottery tickets [...] in V.C. the National Lottery is a complete scourge, then small children selling Chiclets, a sort of chewing gum which was very popular with the Aztecs. They go around, pathetic little girls of about three shouting 'Chiclay, Chiclay', and clutching perhaps a single little piece of chewing gum. And then the shoe-shine boys who are always inexorable in their attentions. Also the inexplicable cripples, like the man with no legs, who'd drag himself round the tables with his hands at incredible speed in a manner which rather suggested a giant crab. And then the Marimba players, the marimba is a sort of xylophone, which it seems to take four men to play. They would establish themselves about 6 feet away, make any conversation quite impossible while they would presume that they were doing one an enormous pleasure. Then there was an Indian band which was completely ludicrous. All the time in the Square the town band would attempt to play the overture from "William Tell" or something of that kind and round and round the Square all the youth and beauty of the town would solemnly gyrate. This is no exaggeration and is not an attempt to describe this spectacle, but merely to give you a rough idea of Vera Cruz. Before going on to Yucatan we left the car in the garage of a man from Glasgow who is an automobile dealer and has been there for forty years. From here on for the next four days or so things were really rough. What you have heard so far was absolutely nothing.

You can go to the Yucatan by three ways:

By air which is terribly expensive.

In a boat called the *Emancipacion*. This is a very vague boat and no one knows its sailing dates. However it wasn't expected back in Vera Cruz for another ten days.

By the newly made railway which runs through the state of Tabasco to Campeche. Jim Papworth suggested we try this route.

From Vera Cruz a properly surfaced road runs as far as Alvarado, after that it is a dirt road to a place called Minatitlan. After that there is no road at all. But at Coatzalcoalcos across the river from Minatitlan the railway begins.

We were advised to leave the car at Vera Cruz since after that no one is really to be trusted until you get to Merida.

So we left by bus. The bus must have quite twenty years, without windows and without springs and bounced along to Alvarado where it crossed a river of enormous width on a completely antiquated ferry.

From here we plunged on through marsh and jungle until it began to get dark and we also began to get into hilly country. At San Andres Tuxtla it stopped. This is where we were to spend the night. It is a small town on a low hill with views all around into dense jungle. It has a little plaza, a place called the "Bar Bikini", an ice cream shop called "Alaska Eskimo", and the usual baroque bits.

The hotel was distinctly primitive. You approached your room down a long portico looking out over the square and the French door was the only means of ventilation, except for a window which opened into another bedroom. The room had three double beds which seems a little excessive, even though it obviously was the hotel's *Suite de Lux*. It is quite impossible to get information in Mexico, and anything might be possible but even so we were a little surprised to discover that the only bus the next day for Minatitlan and Vera Cruz left at 4 a.m. Anyway we were awakened to get it round the corner by the theatre. There was no bus for Minatitlan, however we were assured that there would be one at five o'clock from that same spot. So we went back again to the hotel only to discover they had let our room during the short time we were away. So we made a row and got it back again. The men who had moved into it were just getting undressed and hated us, but since it was our room we insisted. At quarter to five we went out again. Again we went down to the theatre. There was no bus and no sign of a bus, but after all it could quite possibly be late. We waited until quarter to seven which seemed long for a bus. After that we explored a bit and found another bus station in another part of town. Here the buses really did leave for Minatitlan and not only at 4 o'clock but at every two hours throughout the day.

So we went back to our hotel again. Again the room had been let. By now the whole thing was beginning to approach a bedroom farce. Wouldn't we take another room? We were offered one in which the beds were still warm with no proposal that the linen should be changed. No we would not. We had paid for that room and were going to have it. So the people in it were got up and again we entered in triumphant possession.

The bus on to Minatitlan was a complete nightmare. Heavy clouds hung over the jungle. The bus was unbearable with the windows closed and with the windows open the dust blowing in was suffocating. It was crammed tight with peasants. The occasional villages built round sugar refineries were the worst ever. Houses largely built of biscuit tins, pathetic little markets where there seems to be nothing to be sold, and pigs roaming in the streets [...] masses of them. Finally after five hours of it Minatitlan was reached. The problem now was how to get to Coatzelcoalcos across the river. Again another bus. A drive to a ferry. Everyone gets out. A little rowing boat comes across and people are taken over a dozen at a time. The boatmen just wade about in the mud. By the way, all the people around here have their eye teeth gold-plated which increases the general effect of a rather exotic barbarism. Finally we reach Coatzelcoalcos. Since no roads lead there, and there are no cars in the town, it's rather odd that Coatzelcoalcos should have wide concrete streets, double carriageways and all the effect of a new suburban development.

It seemed an unlikely place to have a British Consul but Jim Papworth had advised us to look up a Doctor Sparks there who had been consul since about 1908. This we did. He lived in a rather rundown wooden house overlooking the beach, with applied to the front all the usual consular insignia, the royal coat of arms and all the rest of it. The door was opened by his wife who had a rather timid manner with some antiquated mode of Kensingtonian refinement. When her husband was awake he came down. Fifty years ago Coatzelcoalcos was going to be a great port. The Panama Canal hadn't been built but a railway across the Isthmus of Tehuantepec was going to carry all the trade of the Pacific. None of this ever really materialised and the hopes of Coatzelcoalcos and of the Isthmian railroad were blasted by the opening of the Canal. Still in the few years in which there had been hope, he, a Newfoundlander and a physician had arrived as consul. He had never wanted to leave, and apart from a few years spent in Boston he never had left. He was completely adored and respected by the Indians and had a fine collection of pre-Columbian sculpture which would have distinguished any museum but which his wife wouldn't let him keep in the drawing room. They had a powerful radio with which they listened every day to the news direct from London. Isn't it a complete fantasy?

But into the middle of this suddenly breezed the daughter. W.V.S. type determined, vigorous, precisely the American idea of what every English woman is.[11] She said it was stuffy and promptly opened the windows. Married to a Frenchman with an estate in Burgundy, she lived in New York and was shortly leaving for Teheran!

The whole place had an English atmosphere, at once exotic, charming and totally depressing. How well and in how unlikely a place had they contrived to induce the atmosphere of a London suburb, how pathetic were they in the belief that Edwardian England, in which they still lived, would re-establish itself again [...] "when only times were better", how astonishing was the elaborate and poverty-stricken propriety of this establishment after the jungle which we had just come through.

Naturally we stayed to dinner, and naturally they gave their advice as to how to catch the train [...] which only leaves three times in the week and was due to go the following morning. The problem was when did the train leave and from where. Did it leave from Coatzelcoalcos or from Allende on the other side of the river (another river this time). Sparks had his ideas, Mrs Sparks had hers, the servants were of a whole variety of opinions. The railway station, telephoned, didn't really seem to know, nor were they quite sure at the hotel. It seemed to be the situation of the last night all over again.

However we got up at five o'clock and by now people did begin to think that the train left from the other side of the river. So that in the pitch blackness we went down to the quay and took a boat with about twenty other people for the other side. The scene was lurid. Oil jets flaring and just lighting up the tops of palm trees. The boat which had a little outboard motor wouldn't start and began, alarmingly to drift, out to sea. The peasants stood up and stamped and waved their arms and shouted *"freno"* and one really thought that the whole thing was going to capsize.[12] Mercifully another boat came up and towed us across [...] the river by the way, about three times wider than the Thames, with alligators and probably other monsters too. At the other side there was neither landing stage nor railway station, just a track and a train. You jumped off the boat into the sand. Indians in the darkness all around, Mexicans cursing, and the oil flares the only means of light. Don't you think this is all rather gay? The Indians, some of whom had been squatting for days waiting for the train to come.

We crawled into the First Class compartment. Again there was nothing to eat, and resigned ourselves to slow starvation for the rest of the trip. No one seemed to know how long it would last for. Finally after about two hours of waiting we were able to start. The train lumbered off, achieved a speed of about twenty miles an hour, which it never improved upon, and off we went, the whole thing lurching rather like a ship.

About the middle of the morning one summoned up enough vitality to explore the train. The Second and Third classes were indescribable [...] with the usual fantastic Indians cooking little things or attempting to sell each other little cakes. No Italian train could compare with it. That was on one side, but beyond our compartment somehow a dining car had been joined onto the train, and beyond that the alleged super luxury of a Pullman coach. A guard was stationed at the door so that only the right people got in.

The dining car was a wonderful discovery since no one had mentioned it. It was minute, antiquated, and we were the only people to use it. One had rather the feeling of a royal personage in a private train as this thing swayed down the single line track and windows were brushed by the banana palms [...] it's dense jungle on either side of the track, but we had an altogether excellent lunch which made the joy all the more complete. One can't go on boring you with all these details. At about two in the afternoon a charming German family got on the train and finally in conversation persuaded us to get off at Palenque to see the ruins there. We had no idea the line went by Palenque or that the ruins were in any way accessible, but they were travelling to see them.

Well I told you about Palenque. We were there for two days until the train came again to take us on to Campeche. It was still an overnight journey of 14 hours to get there, and once again the town was enough to put one to flight. The "Grand Hotel Cuaughtemoc" was just a slum, with dirty old men spitting around in the patio. The only thing was once more the peasant bus. This time to Merida.

Yucatan reveals itself as quite deadly and, except for its ruins completely uninteresting. It is a flat limestone country covered with scrubby vegetation, almost none of which succeeds in becoming trees. All the rivers flow underground and occasionally emerge in deep pools surrounded by cliffs called *'cenotes'*.[13]

There are only two towns, Merida and Campeche, and between these the life of a good Yucatecan revolves. They feel themselves completely independent of Mexico. They all spend the night in very large hammocks, some of them big enough to hold two or three people in complete comfort. The peasants keep tame snakes in the houses to keep away vermin and retire to their hammocks to loll about in the early afternoon. They are very clean and the Mayan women wear a sort of embroidered nightgown which they wash constantly. It is completely shapeless, and very long, and when the wind gets inside it they are apt to look like captive balloons.

Merida is an immensely proper town where everyone professes to be old Spanish. They live in charming houses and have neither water supply nor drainage. The infant mortality rate is very high. The theory is that the sewage just seeps away into the limestone as indeed it does, but the water comes out of the limestone too, which complicates matters, so that you have to drink only bottled water which gets a little tiring or beer which rather tends to send you to sleep. The Meridans accept all this as in the natural order of things, and of the Meridans quite one of the most outstanding turned out to be the British Consul.

Another consular household is probably a bit of a strain to hear about, but this one was far more incredible than the last.

    Colin

---

1 Wath-upon-Dearne, England, is a coal mining village two miles south of Bolton-on-Dearne. Both Colin and David Rowe★ were students at Wath Grammar School.
2 "Sitwellian", presumably a reference to Sitwell, Sacheverell, *Spanish Baroque Art, with Buildings in Portugal, Mexico, and Other Colonies*, London: Duckworth, 1931.
3 Maximilian I (1832–1867), proclaimed Emperor of Mexico in April 1864, was executed in Querétaro in 1867.
4 Miguel Alemán Valdés (1900–1983), president of Mexico from 1946 to 1952.
5 Defoe, Daniel, *Robinson Crusoe*, London: W Taylor, 1719.
6 Friedrich Wilhelm Heinrich Alexander von Humboldt (1769–1859), a geographer, naturalist, and explorer.
7 "S.S.": *Schutzstaffel*, a paramilitary organization under the German Nazi Party, 1929–1945.
8 Alexander von Wuthenau-Hohenthurm (1900–1994) and Beatrix Pietsch von Sidonienburg (b 1919). Von Wuthenau was professor of Art History in Mexico City from 1939 to 1965.
9 The Casa Humboldt became Taxco's Viceregal Museum.
10 *tierra desconocida*, Spanish: unknown land.
11 "WVS": Women's Voluntary Service was founded in 1938 as a women's organization to aid civilians.
12 *freno*, Spanish: stop.
13 *cenotes*, Spanish: natural wells.

To **Henry-Russell Hitchcock,** *The Museum of Art, Smith College, Northampton, Mass.* 6 May 1953 **017**
^c/o Howard Barnstone, Lovett Boulevard, Houston, Texas[1]

Dear Russell,

I have been intending to write to you for some months but have been a little uncertain as to your silence. I have been wondering whether you find this continuous jaunt around the North American continent irresponsible, or whether you were offended by a bad collage upon a Balmoral theme which we sent to you,[2] or whether you think that by now I should have published something about the compositional style.[3] Possibly I am wrong in all these guesses, and you are simply absorbed in all sorts of work. In any case I do feel that I should have written to you before now to let you know what I was doing.

We left Bakersfield towards the end of January. The place has now, in memory, become the dramatic symbol of the smaller American town. It was really, in spite of everything, an enjoyable heroic nightmare. To some extent we succeeded in imposing order upon the campus, beyond that I don't think that we should have ever been able to continue our success. We were used as a plan factory, and once we had gone it was naturally assumed that the elevations might take upon themselves, a more humane, less Miesian form.

We went by way of Phoenix, Arizona, where Mr. Wright* was very affable, and showed us designs for a palace on the Grand Canal that he's working on.[4] Taliesin West seemed to me more aloof than other Wright houses which I have seen—a very Edwardian quality, like that uncompromising *tenue* which women of the period so often possessed.[5] One had never expected to find it so acceptable a photographic background for *Vogue* models. Most impressive, I think, was the little auditorium, which has qualities of dryness and control that I haven't seen in any other Wright. It lacks that over-all softness which one so often finds in his things. That play of the Buddhist head in the roundel, the slots in the roof, and the Byzantine elegance of the seating arrangements is a complete joy.

From Phoenix there was the long drive to El Paso, and from there via Chihuahua, Durango, Zacatecas, Queretaro, etc., to Mexico City. You've never been to Latin America. One can't help thinking that some people are protected by their intuitions of horror, which make it unnecessary for them to explore such places. Colonial Mexico is really a great bore. All the towns possess the almost identical Baroque profile, which is very exciting as you approach them over the plain. Here, you always feel, is to be the revelation, but always it's a disappointment. As you approach the illusion dissipates itself, although if you drive through, something of it still remains, and you are still prepared to believe in some life-enhancing building you might have overlooked. If you stop, disgust begins to mount, and if you go into one of the buildings the impression finally crumbles. There is no substance, no reality behind it all, although perhaps this is really a restful state of affairs, since you come to realize that a Mexican tour can only be a *voyage pittoresque*, and that, unlike Italy, a personal exertion isn't really necessary.[6]

The University, as the third major layout on the North American continent, is what one principally went down to see. Again, this is not a necessary journey. In spite of Barragan's very brilliant landscape, he has not really been able to conceal the basically vapid layout. The stadium is not so fine as appears, since it is set in a hollow which conceals its real shape, and is being steadily defaced by Rivera's enormous bas-relief. Arai's playing fields, fronton courts, and swimming pool are very good, but the general impression which the campus makes is that of provincial and undigested Corbu.[7]* Internally, all the buildings are empty, since under the new regime funds are not yet available to continue the work.

There are some interesting things being done in Mexico City, principally by Juan Sordo Maddaleno.[8] He has just completed two elegant office blocks, one admittedly looking like a rather chic apartment house, the other a very distinguished small tower, a sort of miniature Mies* tower, with an ingenious overlay in the ground floor and mezzanine of Milanese elements. Maddaleno is always his own client, since he has apparently the means to realize any of the building which he chooses. He is rather despised by less fortunate professionals, is looked upon as the arch-dilettante, etc., but is much the most interesting architect practicing in Mexico City.

Juan O'Gorman, though, is someone who might amuse you. I think perhaps only in his own house. This, in the Pedregal, is still under construction, and is surely the most complete Guadian fantasy of modern times.[9] Partly dynamited out of the rock and partly imposed upon it, it is really a grotto, from within which an exterior is generated. All is to be either natural rock or mosaic covered concrete.

Tropical Mexico, experienced en route to Yucatan, is a complete trauma, but was worth it, in that we saw Palenque, Chichen, and Uxmal. These and other pre-Columbian sites, together with the natural magnificence of the landscape, are really the best things about Mexico, although it is really doubtful whether they make up for all the hardships of the hotels and lack of food.

We have now been back in the United States for some three weeks, relieved to find ourselves once more in an aseptic and rational atmosphere. We have fairly thoroughly 'done' Texas and Oklahoma, which are both, after the real west, rather depressing. I think that you were very right in not advising the South. For me it certainly lacks stimulus. Rank and small scale, without either delicacy or magnificence. Dallas, in spite of the Neiman-Marcus myth, failed to excite, but Tulsa, Oklahoma, is one of the most distinguished small cities. (The Lloyd Jones house is surprisingly impressive).[10]

It was the combination of Philip's De Menil House, the rumours of his church, Neuhaus' patio house, and Barthelme's West Columbia School, which brought us down here.[11] The combination suggested that something might be happening. I'm not sure whether it is, but meeting Howard Barnstone* down here has been a great pleasure. He is entirely delightful, ex-Yale, a Mies devotee, and carried out the final supervision on the De Menil House.

This house is very, very good, and something which I think you should see. I gather that at first Philip was opposed to the decoration, but has now come to approve of it.[12] One has never realized how admirable and how suave a background his architecture forms for an eclectic system of furnishing. The house is intricate, with a delightful feeling of privy passages and hidden rooms. Going round, and sitting in it, you do feel that every possible nuance has been explored. Everything has the appearance of calculated and subtle understatement. Barcelona chairs and stools are used casually, as though no particular significance were attached to them. The living room is very large, but so well scaled that its size is not apparent, and it becomes merely a saloon of modest magnificence. Sketches by Miro, Renoir, Picasso, are carefully concealed in a small drinks closet, only to reveal themselves to whoever is engaged in the intimate operations of mixing a martini. It is all a fabulous performance of opulent restraint. We hope to see Philip when he is down here in a few days time about his church.

Do you propose leaving soon for Europe? And are you to give a talk at the R.I.B.A.? One can only envy you those certainties. I feel now left with the satisfaction of having very thoroughly explored the North American continent. There is after this, a glow of conscientiousness, but a feeling of complete inability to take any more travel. I can't make up my mind at the moment as to whether to go back to England, whether to work down here for some time longer and return at a leisurely rate to New York, or whether to attach myself once again to some university. America, I think, has had a delightfully expanding effect. Before coming here I was beginning to feel like a gramophone record caught in a Corbu groove. Now, I've at least discovered that the groove is of no absolute significance.

I would very much like you hear from you,

With very best wishes,

   Colin

[handwritten]

P.S. Please give my regards to Bill Jordy if he has not already left on his travels.

1 Howard Barnstone* (1923–1987) was a Houston architect and a graduate of the Yale School of Architecture class of 1948.

2 On Hitchcock's* attempt to get into Balmoral Castle, see Rowe's letter to his parents dated 20 May 1952 (p 50 in this volume).

3 Hitchcock* had been encouraging Rowe to publish "Character and Composition".

4 Frank Lloyd Wright* lived part of the year at Taliesin West in Scottsdale, Arizona, near Phoenix. The "palace" design for the Fondazione Masieri was for a residence and library for architecture students to be located in Venice. It was never built.

5 *tenue*, French: holding.

6 *voyage pittoresque*, French: scenic journey.

7 Kichio Allen Arai (1901–1966), Asian American architect; "Corbu": Le Corbusier* (1887–1965), Swiss French architect.

8 Juan Sordo Madeleno (1916–1985), Mexican architect.

9 "Gaudian": like the work of Antoni Gaudí (1852–1926), Spanish architect of often curvaceous and colorfully tiled buildings.

10 The Richard Lloyd Jones House, Tulsa, Oklahoma, 1929, designed by Frank Lloyd Wright.*

11 Patio House, the Hugo V Neuhaus Residence, Houston, 1950; Donald Barthelme's West Columbia Elementary School, Houston, 1951; and the John and Dominique De Menil House, Houston, Texas, 1950, designed by Philip Johnson.*

12 The "decoration", vivid wall colors, and unique furniture were designed specifically for the house by Charles James, New York designer.

018   *To Henry-Russell Hitchcock, Smith College Museum of Art, Northampton, Mass.*   *17 May 1953*

Apartment 3, 3403, Roseland Street, Houston, Texas

Dear Russell,

Thank you very much indeed for your letter.[1] It was delightful to hear from you and to know that the East still exists. I was very sorry to hear about John Phillips, most pleased to know about Schweikher,* and shall look forward to the appearance of the Victorian studies.[2]

Down here it is depressing, with heat, humidity, chiggers, and the sensitiveness of the Texans. There is nothing here of Californian expansiveness. Instead the slightest lapse in pro-Texan enthusiasm is heresy, and this involves an attitude which it is a permanent strain to keep up. Ideas have been crystallizing very rapidly in an atmosphere where things are very trying and also not really worth while.

I would like your opinions on major problems.

The tour of the North American continent has now gone on long enough. To some extent in the first case it may have been an escape, but it has been very necessary and rewarding. One has learned a great deal, one's criteria have changed quite a lot, and the pleasure of travel and of buildings has often been extreme. The Mexican tour was altogether more blasé and less necessary. Further travel of this kind will I know be superfluous and irresponsible.

As I am sure you guess, the major problem revolves around America or England. On that I have no right to ask or expect your advice. I have at the moment a strong inclination to go back to England, to the known situation, and all the rest of it. Having seen America one could now justifiably return... which last summer was not the case. I am entirely uncertain as to the state of affairs in England, but assume that I could get along. Ultimately of course one has to go back, so as to know whether or not one wishes to stay over here.

The further problems revolve around whether one stays here longer, and on these I would really value your advice. If I stay it means that I have to look around for a degree of permanence and commodity... after a year of movement and of the west you find yourself wanting this desperately. I think that I ought to take a teaching job, and I assume that there are lots of these available and that most of them are in institutions without any academic standing.

Obviously my qualifications are good... obviously to borrow a term of yours I am now viable in this country. On the other hand, if I did stay on in the U.S., I should like it to be somewhere worthwhile, where the student has a certain intelligence and where there is a library.

For instance, one has got to know the Harwell Harrises rather well down here and I have an idea that there would be a job available at Austin.[3] If one were really modest, I suppose one would accept such a situation with delight... but I really wonder which would be more trying, the inconveniences of London or the amenities of so isolated a place. (Mrs. H. can't conceal her eagerness to get away... it becomes a mild hysteria... or is that usual?)[4]

Very reasonably I should like to find a place where society was less provincial and more stimulated, where one was not completely cut off from the facilities of research, and from where exhibitions and personalities were not too remote. I assume that I have no reason and probably no right to expect anything so agreeable. What do you think that I might expect? What opportunities are there in the East and how does one explore them? Certain institutions are so august as I suppose to be quite out of reach. Yale, Harvard and M.I.T. I conceive in this way; although I know that as a critic and instructor I should disgrace myself at none of them. The problem is... what other places are there, and how does one approach them?

I am so sorry to burden you with these questions at a time when your life must be an end-of-term and pre-vacation confusion; but, I wonder, if, in the middle of an architectural country, you have any suggestions to offer. If you have I should be very grateful for them.

At the moment I am in contact with Cunard about a sailing date early in July, I hope that I can be in New York before you leave, but if I do sail, I may in any case see you in Europe. I hope so.

With best wishes which Brian joins me in sending,[5]

Sincerely yours

    Colin

1   In his 11 May 1953 letter to Rowe, Hitchcock* wrote of both the death of John M Phillips (1905–1953), director of the Yale University Art Gallery, and of the appointment of Paul Schweikher (1903–1997) as dean of the School of Architecture at Yale.

2   Hitchcock, Henry-Russell, *Early Victorian Architecture in Britain*, 2 vols. New Haven: Yale University Press, 1954.

3   Harwell Hamilton Harris* (1903–1990) and Jean Murray Bangs Harris* (1894–1985). Harris was dean of the School of Architecture, University of Texas at Austin. In *Harwell Hamilton Harris*, Austin: University of Texas Press, 1991, pp 142–143, Lisa Germany* reports that according to Harris, Rowe and Brian Richards* had visited him at his Austin office in spring 1952 when "they had just come from Mexico". (As the two were in New Haven in 1952, the year would have been 1953.) Germany continues, "Later, when the Harrises were in Berkeley [...] they got a call from Rowe [...] Harris recalls the conversation, "'Can I get a job?' he asked [...] I didn't realize protocol called for all tenured faculty to select appointments. I just said 'Yes, come on.'"

4   See Rowe, Colin, "Texas and Mrs. Harris", *As I Was Saying: Recollections and Miscellaneous Essays*, Alexander Caragonne ed, 3 vols, Cambridge, MA: MIT Press, 1996, vol 1, p 28.

5   Brian Richards.*

019   *To Mr & Mrs Frederick Rowe,*
Highgate Lane, Bolton-on-Dearne, Yorkshire, England   *17 May 1953*

Apartment 3, 3403 Roseland Street, Houston, Texas

Dear Parents,

I'm so sorry that you appear to think that my letters haven't really been informative. Information is so complicated [...] or at least the kind that you want is [...] that it's very hard to give it in a letter.

First of all, in spite of many charming people Texas and Houston are totally depressing. There is nothing here of Californian expansiveness. The Texas myth and the Texas reality couldn't be further apart. Texas is rather small scale, cautious, conservative, small town and meagre. All qualities which are as disappointing as they are unexpected. The heat and the humidity of Houston are completely overwhelming. It's so hot that to emerge from an air conditioned building is really like penetrating a hot sewer. It's steamy, so much so that you have to have fans going all night if you are to get to sleep, and then finally the noise of the fan succeeds in keeping you awake. For the last week it has rained incessantly and very heavily so that all one's clothes are damp [...] and even when you take a tie to put it on it's like a limp rag.

All this sounds totally dismal and you will say how silly to stay. One has stayed so far quite against one's better judgement.

There seems to be two sorts of people in East Texas. The more established type of family is of old southern stock. From Virginia, North Carolina, and Baltimore. They were obliged to come here because of the circumstances after the Civil War. They have done very well for themselves, are very prosperous, very hospitable, but circumstances which led them here are ingrained somewhere in the sub-conscious, and they are unwilling to involve themselves in large scale operations. This type of agreeable society constitutes upper middle class Houston.

Out in the country there are far more small towns than one would ever expect, driving from here to Austin for instance they occur at intervals of every ten miles or so; which is really very frequent. They were mostly founded and built about eighty years ago, they have pronounced individuality, and they are falling into decay. The wretchedness of the lives that people live in these places I think must be quite extreme. They are all small-holders' villages and in none of them has the promise of prosperity been realized.

That's the other side of Texas. The remaining group which strikes one immediately are the Negroes. For the most part although they are not lacking in money, they live in appalling squalor, in unpainted houses which are gradually rotting and sagging. Of course all public lavatories, waiting rooms, etc. are duplicated for Black and White, and in Houston you can get quite a long term of imprisonment for sitting at a restaurant table with a negro.

Thirdly, Howard Barnstone* himself who really persuaded us to stay. Ex-Yale 1947, has been teaching at the University here. By reason of the Philip Johnson*-Yale connection is closely involved with the De Menils and in fact supervised the building of their house.[1] Howard has been the conspicuously successful outsider in Houston, does the best domestic architecture here, and being Jewish (although he doesn't look it) has succeeded in building up an all-Jewish practice and also a considerable amount of professional jealousy.

The attention shown by these three has caused us to receive quite a lot of attention elsewhere and also to inherit all the dislike that they have received, which of course hasn't been expressed to them. We have now discovered that in spite of trying to say nice things, in spite of showing genuine enthusiasm for landscapes and buildings (admittedly in other parts of the country) we don't really like Texas, in fact that we hate Texas, feel superior towards it, etc. This is of course the equivalent of being anti-American, because in the eyes of Texans, Texas really constitutes the major part of the United States.

People like the Harris's are very amused about all this but really it is rather sickening and makes an already not particularly delightful town, really rather awful.[2]

Brian Richards* is working in an office where the political situation has become rather tense. I was working for some time with a woman on the design of a hotel. The whole Texas issue welled up there the other day over quite a minor matter and I realised that the situation was quite untenable. Of course I knew before that it was, and that was one reason why I didn't write... general uncertainty, etc. Really one should have known that Texans are like this, since everyone else in the United States appears to know it.

However it will be a joy and a delight to get away. One has now seen the United States and the south seems to be too awful to face... (Russell Hitchcock* advised us never to go into the South). I am in contact with Cunard about a sailing date in mid-July, and the only thing that could impel me to stay is the possibility of a teaching job in New England which Hitchcock is investigating. This would be worthwhile, there are amenities there, and there are reasonable people. However even if this does come off I shall still I suppose be seeing you before the end of July.

Here, it really is awful. Rain and thunder and lightning have been incessant for the last four hours, there are rumours of an approaching tornado and it's as though the whole Gulf of Mexico had suddenly emptied on the town. It succeeds in being lugubriously funny.

Have just had a charming letter from Nikolaus Pevsner* with lots of proposals for writing about things which I have seen.

It's probably, I think certainly, not worth while writing to this address.

Love,

    Colin

1 See Rowe's letter to Henry-Russell Hitchcock* dated 6 May 1953 (p 77 in this volume).
2 Harwell Hamilton Harris* (1902–1990), chair of University of Texas at Austin School of Architecture, 1952–1955, and his wife, Jean Murray Bangs Harris* (1894–1985).

To **Henry-Russell Hitchcock,**
The Museum of Art, Smith College, Northampton, Mass.   *17 August 1953*   **020**

190 East End Avenue, New York, N.Y.

Dear Russell,

I rang Cunard the other day because I had the idea that you were arriving on August 15th. I couldn't get any information out of them so that I assume that you are probably travelling by some other line and are already back in this country. I do hope that this is so. One has heard all sorts of reports about your trip in Europe and it would be interesting to know what people are doing.

The summer here in New York has been totally frustrating, rather as one might imagine. It is so stupid not to plan ahead and then to be left with a space of ten weeks waiting for a boat, which at the same time is really entirely useless as regards taking a job in anyone's office. In all this I have changed my plans half-a-dozen times, have thought of going up to Canada, or looking for a more permanent job in New York, or going up to New Haven to work there. There always seem to have been some obstacles to these proposals, like joint ownership of a car or expiring visas and so on.

I am now back where I was at the beginning of June with Harwell Harris'* offer of a teaching job at Austin, Texas, which I have decided if possible to accept. I have thought this matter over rather carefully, and although I have no illusions about Austin, I like Harris, and I think that I would very much enjoy working with him for a time. I would also very much enjoy having America for some time to myself and not experiencing it entirely as a member of a team of two.[1] I am sure that you will appreciate this.

Harris has written asking me to supply two letters of reference for him to submit to the president of the University of Texas. I have written to George Howe* asking him if he could provide one of these, and I am wondering if you would be so good as to supply the other.[2] If you could I should be extremely grateful.

Assuming that I leave again for these remote places I should very much like to see you before going.

Sincerely yours,

Colin

Colin Rowe

P.S. Harris has asked that a letter be sent to him direct at the School of Architecture, Austin.

[handwritten]

I hope that this isn't an awful trouble—

Austin should leave me with some time for polishing up that thing about COMPOSITION which I am rather anxious to do.[3]

C.F.R.

---

1 For more than 20 months, Rowe had lived, traveled, and worked throughout the US with his friend and colleague, the Englishman Brian Richards,* with whom he had shared an apartment in New Haven.
2 George Howe,* chairman of the Department of Architecture at Yale University from 1950 to 1954.
3 "Character and Composition; or Some Vicissitudes of Architectural Vocabulary"; see Rowe's letter to Mr and Mrs Rowe dated 11 May 1952 (p 48 in this volume).

021   *To **Henry-Russell Hitchcock**, Smith College Museum of Art, Northampton, Mass.*   *24 August 1953*

190 East End Avenue, New York, N.Y.

Dear Russell,

Thank you so much for your letter.

What an immense number of houses you have contrived to see. You know that during the war I was stationed in a camp just below Hardwick for six weeks, during all this time it was a permanent apparition and a joy, but I never got in.[1] Did you meet the old woman at Easton Neston who is descended from the Comstock Lode and the Palace Hotel? Presumably she is the only reason for that house continuing to function.[2]

I'm glad that you approve of Austin.[3] Whiffen* will be there to teach architectural history as you say.[4] From Harris's inferences I assume that I shall be a design critic. This is one reason why I'm led to consider it a good thing since without lectures I shall be able to concentrate on the Inigo Jones* thesis and on the 'composition' piece... also on other things, and it will be rather a relief to get these things out of the way since one of them at least has been hanging about for rather a long time and one would never be able to face Margaret Whinney again unless it was disposed of.[5]

Rather belatedly *The Art Bulletin* has just sent me offprints of the Hamlin review and I must send one to you in this next day or so.[6] I was a little surprised at seeing it in print because on the whole it came out rather more lucidly than I thought it was going to. I must thank you for providing this opportunity for putting some thoughts in order.

I know nothing worse than writing letters of recommendation and do apologise for burdening you with this one. I hope the knowledge that I shall be design critic will help you in being suitably explicit.

Apropos of coming up to Northampton, I may be in New Haven later in this week and will try to get in touch with you then.

Sincerely,

Colin

1 For Rowe's recollection of Hardwick Hall, see Arnell, Peter, Ted Bickford and Colin Rowe, *James Stirling: Buildings and Projects*, New York: Rizzoli International, 1984, first ed, p 27.
2 Easton Neston, a country house near Towcester, Northamptonshire, England, designed by Nicholas Hawksmoor in 1702.
3 The University of Texas, Austin, where Rowe was to begin teaching in January 1954.
4 Marcus Whiffen.*
5 Rowe had written his master's thesis on the drawings of Inigo Jones* in 1947. In 1940 Margaret Dickens Whinney (1894–1974), a scholar of architecture and sculpture at the Courtauld Institute of Art, had written her doctorate dissertation at the University of London on Jones' work on Whitehall Palace and on the associated "Webb sketches".
6 Rowe, Colin, "Reply to Talbot Hamlyn's Recent Book," *The Art Bulletin 35*, no 2, June 1953, pp 169–174.

To Mr & Mrs Frederick Rowe,
Highgate Lane, Bolton-on-Dearne, Yorkshire, England   *17 September 1953*   **022**

190 East End Avenue, New York, N.Y.

Dear Parents

I shall be sailing from New York on September 9th, Wednesday, which means that by the time that you get this letter I shall be half way across the Atlantic. Hope to arrive Southampton on Monday and London on Monday night.

Will let you have a telegram when I arrive and have discovered what train to come down on.

There seem to be terrible frustrations and troubles about visas in this country and it is much easier to come back to England and settle things there.

Harris says that I can arrive in Austin whenever I want so that I shall apply for a visa when I get back.[1]

I do wish that all this sort of thing didn't worry you so much. I don't know what you would have one do. Stick around in Liverpool? Or live in London on about £600 a year like Bob Maxwell* and not have money left for anything. You know $120 is rather better than £12 as a weekly salary. I would never dream of staying in this country nor on this side of the Atlantic but one may as well make the best of it while one can. I shall see what the situation in London is like but I don't believe that it is particularly gay.

Love,

Colin

---

1 Harwell Hamilton Harris,* chair of the School of Architecture, University of Texas at Austin.

023   *To **Henry-Russell Hitchcock**,*
Smith College Museum of Art, Northampton, Mass.   *29 September 1953*

37 Highgate Lane, Bolton-upon-Dearne, Yorkshire, England[1]

My dear Russell,

I was so sorry not to be able to get into touch with you before rather unexpectedly I was obliged to flee New York so as to arrange Immigration Visas from over here. My last attempt to ring you was hopelessly frustrated by a long telephone call which you were having, after that you set out for the Museum, there the staff were expecting you in the next ten minutes but during that time the telephone service of the *Queen Mary* was disconnected so that it became quite clear that fate had interposed.

However one has now been back in England for about two weeks and a visa should be through in the course of the next three, so that then I hope that I shall be sailing back again and still able to see you before going down to Texas.

I was amazed and rather distressed about the aspect of England which really first reveals itself when one has got across Waterloo Bridge into the Strand. I had no conception that London is so slight, so intricate, so oriental, so over-detailed a city. The Strand has a general air of extemporized flimsy, but it was the whole town by daylight which seems even more amusing.

I had never before known how Edwardian a city London is. It is quite shockingly so. The buildings for the most part look like blowsy trollopes who have unloosed their stays, and bellied out over the public places... there is none of the admirable strictness of New York *Louis Seize*. But even more extraordinary, one discovered that streets which one had thought still to epitomize late Georgian urbanity etc., even they were caught in this same Edwardian predicament. I was amused, shocked and rather shaken, because seldom has one seen so much effort and so little result, English architecture is so reticent, so diffident, so unbelievably coy. Everything is qualified, elaborated, modified, gently inhibited. The total spectacle begins to promote hysteria almost like ones first visit to New York; but what layers of detailed indirectness the English do luxuriate in. I wonder if anywhere else in the world there are so many quoins, so many columns, such an excess of rustication.

One wonders if the neo-Corbu* is really a wise solution for the English.[2] It's so easy for them to distort it, even when they have the very best intentions, and really there seems to be surprisingly little difference between new-Corbu Paddington and the neo-Italian stucco city which it is replacing... and this isn't a tribute to any genius of any place.[3]

> *Colin*

[handwritten]

P.S. I have put you down on a form as a reference for immigration. I gather that there are no responsibilities attached. I hope this is alright.

> *Colin*

---

1   Rowe is writing from his parents' home in Yorkshire, England.
2   "neo-Corbu": neo-Le Corbusier.*
3   Reference is to the Hallfield Estate, a London housing project designed in the post-war period by the architectural firm, Tecton.

To **Mr & Mrs Frederick Rowe,** *Highgate Lane, Bolton-on-Dearne, Yorkshire*   *29 January 1954*   **024**

The School of Architecture, The University of Texas, Austin, Texas

Dear Parents,

I arrived down here just a week ago today after two nights and one and a half days on the train. All this makes it possible to understand the trans-Siberian Railway. All the first day I forced myself to look out of the windows of the train as southern Ohio, Indiana, and Illinois rolled by. Nine hours of continuous, implacably flat landscape with never a variation. Monotony on this level becomes something quite positive and inescapable, something quite definitely in its own right. After it the railway yards of St. Louis were an inconceivable relief.

The *Samaria* by the way wasn't quite as bad as all that: there were one or two amusing people on board. A Mrs. Fisher who was English and who after thirty years in Vancouver was going to live in Los Angeles and take out American citizenship so that she could work for Mr. Stevenson in the next election.[1] There was also rather a charming Anglo-American family called Moore who were most pressing that I went to spend Easter with them at Fort Lauderdale in Florida. This might be extremely agreeable.

This town is highly political.[2] All kinds and levels of politics from the state capitol downwards. The great object of every right thinking woman is an *entrée* to the governor, the great aim is to get him in your pocket. This is frustrating since as soon as the governor is changed then you have to start all over again.

The big feud of which I was made immediately aware is that between Mrs. Harwell Harris and Mrs. Marcus Whiffen.[3] I have dined with both and been told all. Whiffen* is over here from England as a Visiting Lecturer. The situation is one of Trollopian frenzy. Mrs H. says Mrs W. is plebeian. Mrs W. says Mrs. H. is psychopathic. Neither of them have got the truth. Mrs H. is uninhibitedly cranky, Mrs W. who is bouncy and a physiotherapist has all the opinions and prejudices of her type. Whiffen has a certain rather ineffective

Cambridge charm. Mrs Whiffen is one of nature's *memsahibs*.⁴ As a Canadian citizen Mrs H. is disposed to be an ardent American patriot; as an Englishwoman of correct education Mrs W. is disposed to look at it all as a colonial situation.

Mrs. W. is quite nice to look at.

I have given Mrs H. an azalea.

Other *dramatis personae* have presented themselves at the first faculty meeting.⁵ But no others has have so extravagantly identified themselves so far.

Everything here is transparent, everything known. I feel it is something to do with the strong light. I have been here a week and I have dined with the Assistant Attorney General to the State of Texas which gives me an unfair initial advantage. All is known. I feel the potentialities are infinitely amusing.

I may be made a member of the Governor's Committee for the Preservation of Texas. Only don't breathe a word: it would be sure to come back here. But the Preservation of Texas! Have you heard of it? Can you believe it? Can you imagine anything more Evelyn-Waugh-like and bizarre? I rolled over and over merely thinking of the possibilities of it. "From So-and-So to So-and-So, Mr Rowe served as member of the Governor's Committee for the Preservation of Texas." What a ludicrous fragment of biography.

This place, like a good deal of Texas, is Anglophile rather than Yankee by inclination. It's not as strong as it was but above a certain financial level a desire to establish background leads to identification with the Old South, which passes over as a form of social coercion into Anglophilia.

It is widely believed that by the next century Houston will be the biggest city in the world. Apparently Lloyds of London have said so. When Texans say this to you, you don't disagree, you don't express surprise, you merely show enthusiasm for their miraculous destiny.

I have a rather redwoodsey apartment which is hideously well equipped but a little discouraging since everything is built in and the whole impression just a little too earthy. However no doubt alternatives will reveal themselves.

What are you doing now about escape from B.O.D.?⁶

Love,

    Colin

1 Adlai Stevenson (1900–1965), the Democratic candidate for president of the United States in 1952 and 1956, was defeated in both elections.
2 Austin is the capital of the state of Texas.
3 Mrs. Harwell Harris★ (1894–1985), wife of Harwell Hamilton Harris,★ chair of the School of Architecture at the University of Texas at Austin from fall 1951 through spring 1955. Mrs Marcus Whiffen, wife of Marcus Whiffen★ who taught architectural history at the university.
4 *memsahib*, Indian: a married white or upper-class woman.
5 *dramatis personae*, Latin: persons or characters of drama.
6 "B.O.D.": Bolton-on-Dearne, the Rowe family home in Yorkshire, England.

025   *To **Henry-Russell Hitchcock,** Smith College Museum of Art, Northampton, Mass.*   *3 June 1954*

The School of Architecture, The University of Texas, Austin, Texas

My dear Russell,

I was delighted to have your letter and to hear that your leaving is to be delayed for a month or so. I should be up in New England before the end of the month. May I come and see you?

The bird life down here is so dense and tropical and noisy that it exhausts all patience. It begins so early that although at the moment it's only six in the morning, I am exhausted, but quite unable to sleep. I don't seem to remember that this sort of thing happens in New England?

The Whiffens* are leaving Saturday for New York, Boston and other places.[1] I imagine that you must have known how things were with them. All completely unsettled. The quarrel with the Tsarina was of so intense and sharp a nature that positively nothing could be done about it, and there is to be no reappointment for Marcus.[2] At the moment he seems to be quite uncertain what he is going to do, and I'm very sorry because they really liked it down here. The famous Whiffen-Bangs outrage you must have heard about from Marcus. If not, you will. It is at first difficult to believe, but I am now able to accept it in its entirety. Operations make Marcus' story only too plausible. However, all the same, they have been a little silly since by giving altogether too much cause for provocation.[3]

At the moment I am installed as Blue Eyed Boy but am entirely uncertain as to how long I shall enjoy the role. Quite frequently it is like waiting for the top of Krakatoa to blow off, and after any major *demarche* one literally expects the sunsets to be violet coloured for months.[4]

I was very glad to hear about your Latin American book and hope that you will be able to come down through here.[5] What order are you going to do it all in? Mexico first or last? If you were to do Mexico last perhaps one could see you there at Christmas. Are you to be allowed into Guatemala?

I look forward to seeing you.

    Colin

1 Mrs and Mr Marcus Whiffen.* Whiffen taught architectural history at the University of Texas at Austin during the 1953–1954 academic year.
2 "Tsarina", Rowe's nickname for Mrs Harris.*
3 For the "Whiffen-Bangs outrage", see Rowe's 1988 essay "Texas and Mrs. Harris", *As I Was Saying: Recollections and Miscellaneous Essays*, Alexander Caragonne ed, 3 vols, Cambridge, MA: MIT Press, 1996, vol 1, pp 25–40.
4 *démarche*, French: maneuver.
5 Hitchcock* was writing *Latin American Architecture Since 1945*, New York: Museum of Modern Art, 1955.

To **Henry-Russell Hitchcock**, *Smith College Museum of Art, Northampton, Mass.* *29 December 1954*   **026**

The School of Architecture, The University of Texas, Austin, Texas

Dear Russell,

I have just come back from giving a lecture at Berkeley and several people there,— Howard Moise,[1] Jim Ackerman,*[2] wondered whether you had yet got back from South America, and if so when and how. I have been wondering the same thing and am rather curious to hear whether you found the whole continent as deadly as you believed it to be a year ago when you told me that you could go nowhere where people called beer *cerveza*.

My experiences in Mexico do lead me to suspect that it is pretty bad, and I rather hope that you haven't been obliged to change your opinions.

I imagine that my last letter to you must have been rather late and suspect that by that time you had already left, but I had been trying to sell the idea of getting you to deliver a lecture here and by the time the Harris's could be got around to being able to receive the proposal, by then I think it was too late (you know you have always been unkind to Harwell... or so at frequent intervals I have been told).[3]

At the moment I am being tempted by the offer of a job at Berkeley.... It hasn't actually been offered as yet but it has been intimated that it will be and that is the reason why I was invited out there.

What do you think? Presumably the University of California is better than the University of Texas, only for me it happens to be in the wrong direction. Or do you suppose that routes East from Texas do lie through San Francisco?

Personally I find that the state of Texas has infinitely more style than that of California. I think that it is probably the equestrian motif, felt but not seen, that does it, but also I suspect that the intelligence of the students etc is rather more stimulating. California this time I found altogether too bland, too unemphatic; the climate, the topography, the architecture are all of a piece; everything is inconsiderately relaxed. And however beguiling San Francisco may have been one can't now eradicate the impression that it is all quite dead. Even the most convinced exponents of the Bay Region Style I suspect of being disquieted.... Where do we go from here, etc?

Am a little alarmed by these judgements since I would hate to find myself turning into a professional Texan and sometimes can't help feeling that it could easily happen. You know sometimes one feels ethnically implicated in Texas to an extraordinary degree. They are all so English and so lost that one doesn't know what to do about it... probably one ends by joining the Anglo-Texan Society of which Graham Greene is apparently the President, and eating a dinner over it all every San Jacinto day at the Savoy.[4]

This school is I may say a little tiresome. H.H.H. like Californian architecture is, as you know, bland and unemphatic, lost and distrait. Like all Wrightians he lacks the power of generalisation... in architecture they proceed from particular instance to particular instance with no desire to expose a general law... and so it is with education (one may suspect the same things at Berkeley). Unable to tolerate the Beaux Arts, which after all reposes upon generalisations, they end by mortgaging themselves as educators to the International Style, only to realise to their grief what they have done, and then to start kicking against it. This is the next stage of the little play at the U. of T. I pressed for an Albers drawing course, and now have it, I pressed that for a time at least all water colour presentation should be banned, and that was done.[5] The result has been a quite extraordinary change, which Harwell likes no more than he liked what was going on before.

I think that is all the information about this place. I'm sure you can fill in the details of it all. But I would like your advice on the Berkeley business... the younger faculty there by the way seem to want to swing away from all the Bay Region stuff.

Early Victorian Architecture I have enjoyed although at first I thought it was going to be rather forbidding.[6] I must read it again though so as to discover what a lot of things are all about. I am so glad that they got it up so very well and imagine that you must be immensely pleased and relieved to have it out of the way. I still think that you should republish *Modern Architecture: Romanticism and Re-integration*[7] with new illustrations and plans... because I find that everywhere now people are beginning to realise that it did contain some very penetrating observations... and if Sigfried Giedion can go on expanding *Space-Time* why shouldn't you bring it out again?[8]

Have come to the conclusion that you were much more judicious about Wright* at that time than you have been since. He is the GREAT CORRUPTER you know. It takes one a very long time to realise all this, but the new book *The Natural House* finally brings it all home.[9] The particular form of architectural consciousness which that man has promoted seems to have entirely destroyed that very splendid American capacity to arrive at architecture without having set out to look for it, and now all over the country in a thousand sexy little deals you see the effects of this. Perhaps of course it isn't as bad as all that since what he becomes in the end is a sort of purveyor of motifs for a peasant vernacular... but if the Guggenheim had been built every picture in it would have looked like a cheap print from the little gift shop around the corner.[10]

When I shall get East again I don't quite know.

Do you propose going to Europe again this summer or will you be around the North American continent? As yet I haven't decided what to do.

Do you know anything about summer schools in the East? Like the one Whiffen* taught at N.Y.U. for instance.[11] I can't help thinking that something like that would be a very agreeable solution for six weeks and would also help to finance a further six weeks trans-Atlantic excursion.

"Composition and Character" you may be interested to know has been completed for about six weeks or so. I am rather relieved since I hate to have the necessity of making abstruse deductions hanging over my head.[12]

At the moment I am interested in the rather obvious (but rarely emphasised) fact that Frank Lloyd Wright has never (to all intents and purposes) used the steel or concrete frame. And that coming from Chicago. When you think about this for some time it becomes really very extraordinary, I talked about all this at Berkeley.[13]

Best wishes for the Latin American book, and my regards to Martin Jones and other people.[14]

Yours,

   Colin

---

1 Howard Moïse (1887–1965).

2 James Ackerman.*

3 Harwell Hamilton Harris* and his wife, Jean Murray Bangs Harris.*

4 The Anglo-Texan Society, founded in London by Graham Greene in 1953, promoted conviviality between the British and Texans. The Society held a barbecue in London on 6 March 1954, Texas Independence Day.

5 Josef Albers (1888–1976), German-born American painter and educator, head of the Department of Design at Yale at the time.

6 Hitchcock, Henry-Russell, *Early Victorian Architecture in Britain*, New Haven: Yale University Press, 1954.

7 Hitchcock, Henry-Russell, *Modern Architecture: Romanticism and Reintegration*, New York: Payson & Clarke Ltd, 1929.

8 Giedion, Sigfried, *Space, Time, and Architecture: The Growth of a New Tradition*, Cambridge, MA: Harvard University Press, 1941.

9 Wright, Frank Lloyd, *The Natural House*, New York: Horizon Press, 1954.

10 Commissioned in 1943, the Guggenheim was completed in October 1959. See Rowe's letter to Alvin* and Elizabeth Boyarsky* dated 15 December 1958 (p 123 in this volume).

11 Marcus Whiffen,* had been assistant professor teaching architectural history at the University of Texas at Austin during the 1953–1954 academic year.

12 Although written by Rowe in 1953–1954, "Character and Composition" was first published in *Oppositions*, no 2, January 1974, pp 41–60.

13 Rowe's lecture at Berkeley was an early version of "Chicago Frame: Chicago's Place in the Modern Movement", *The Architectural Review* 120, November 1956, pp 285–289.

14 At the time, Hitchcock* was completing *Latin American Architecture Since 1945*, New York: Museum of Modern Art, 1955.

027 *To Mr & Mrs Frederick Rowe, Bolton-on-Dearne, Yorkshire, England*   *4 January 1955*

Austin, Texas

Dear Parents,

San Francisco was rather damp and cold which I didn't find very inspiring when I was there. I flew out. It took only about six hours from Fort Worth. Unfortunately it became dark before we were very far over the desert so one could only imagine what the scenery looks like. The lights of places like Las Vegas though were rather beautiful and the whole display of lights over San Francisco bay was quite fantastic. I imagine my lecture was successful.[1] People said how much they liked it, etc. But what does that mean. The dampness of the place after the extreme dryness of here was so dispiriting that one just wanted to curl up and die. It alternated clammy white fog and brilliant sunshine all the time, but although the light when the sun shone was overwhelmingly brilliant it was never warm.

I left after four days and flew down to Phoenix, Arizona, so as to be able to see the Grand Canyon from the air. Again not all that you might expect. But I imagine that one becomes blasé about landscape. Couldn't find any Navaho rugs in Phoenix which is what I was looking for. Everything there very pre-Christmassy. The hide-out for winter of the St Louis demi-monde, etc... or so one would imagine. Gramophonic carols with many bells relayed all over the town. *Adeste fideles. God rest ye merry gentlemen,* etc. A combination of spuriously modern and very olde-Englishe motifs, with no vegetation, a Rotherham, Yorkshire, England for miles around, except cacti.[2] All rather bizarre and bright like a sort of hygienic children's toy. You expected it to turn a handle and the whole town might do things.

Left Phoenix democratically by bus which got me into El Paso at midnight. All Mexican themes there. But a rather little dubious English crowd in a restaurant whom I imagine were *en route* to Acapulco from New York. Came on to here over night and arrived at about 3 o'clock in the afternoon.

A curious thing I realised is that you can't really take a train on this continent anywhere west of St Louis, or if by luck you manage it, it is only possible after extreme difficulty. You can get a train all right in New York, or even in St Louis and go to San Francisco, but it seems to be an altogether harder business to get a train in San Francisco and get to New York. The transcontinental terminals are about as big as the station at Rotherham and just about as primitive. This after all seems rather strange.

And now. Are you all <u>still</u> in a state of paralysis?

Have you <u>begun</u> to move yet?

If not, why not?

If I visit Europe this year I shall have to make up my mind within the next two months. I have no intention of <u>ever</u> visiting Highgate Lane again so that if you don't move out there is really no point in my coming.[3]

So I hope that you move.

   Colin

P.S. Please don't send a brief case although it would be very nice, because if you do I shall only have to pay inordinate duties on it. 30% or so which I don't want to have to do.

Please do move. After all there are <u>no</u> obstacles. And it <u>is</u> time.

---

1   At the School of Architecture, University of California, Berkeley. See Rowe's letter dated
    29 December 1954 to Hitchcock* (p 89 in this volume).
2   Rotherham, close to Bolton-on-Dearne.
3   "Highgate Lane": the Rowe family home in Bolton-on-Dearne.

To **Henry-Russell Hitchcock,** *Smith College Museum of Art, Northampton, Mass.   4 February 1955*   **028**

The School of Architecture, The University of Texas, Austin, Texas

Dear Russell,

   Very many thanks for your letter.

I wish that I could have been present at the S.A.H. Meeting but unfortunately New York is a long way and at the moment I simply could not afford to make the trip.[1] I would like to explode with pertinent things to say but I think that they must stay bottled up for quite a time.

Apropos of "Character and Compo", I like your S.A.H. idea, since the thing is perhaps hardly the *Review's* cup of tea.[2] I suspect though that it would take more room than the *S.A.H. Journal* usually provides—at about 25–28 typewritten sheets would it not engulf some ten pages? But I <u>do</u> think that that particular paper does require <u>some</u> material other than exceedingly obvious notices upon minor colonial monuments.

Would you like "Character and Compo" to be dedicated 'for H.-R.H.'? I would. Perhaps it would embarrass you. Would you like to read it again sometime in the next month or so and then you would know.[3]

The Wayne Andrews review I guess was to be expected since he and the Czarina are (so <u>she</u> says) the best of friends and from time to time eat out of each other's hands.[4]

I am so glad though to think that you and Marcus were a little concerned that I was placing too much emphasis upon her continued support.[5] The situation down here I think is now clear and I have incurred the same opprobrium as Marcus did before me. At least that is how I construe Madame's latest manoeuvres. In going to Berkeley I committed the odious crime of DISLOYALTY TO HARWELL or *LESE HARRIS*, and this as you may imagine is unsupportable.[6] One falls from grace easily and innocently. Reprisals have been taken and my whole scheme of programmes for the Second Semester has been torpedoed (a day before the opening) by the introduction at her initiative of a landscape scheme for a state park with chalets, Indian curio shops, California bungalows etc. This is to last six to seven weeks and is part of her programme of public relations for Harwell. In opposing it (which is very reasonable since the same class have already done this programme a year before) one is being doubly disloyal because the interests of Harwell and those of the students are not completely separated in her mind.

So you may imagine how I feel. Exhausted.

I have written to Jim Ackerman* asking how things are going on there, but about Kamphoefner a considerable embarrassment presents itself.[7] Hugo Leipziger down here has a private line up to Raleigh and he also has the implicit confidence of Madame... the only one of the faculty who has the School's interests at heart, a long range vision, etc.[8] Thus I can't help thinking that whatever representations are made in North Carolina will rapidly relay themselves to Austin.

So I don't know which way to proceed. Raleigh is geographically convenient, Berkeley I suspect culturally superior.

Let me hear from you please about "Character and Compo".

Sincerely,

Colin

---

1   "SAH": Society of Architectural Historians. On 31 January 1955 Hitchcock* wrote to Rowe, "It would have been nice if you could have gotten up to the SAH meeting last week in New York. I am sure you could have added something trenchant to the session on 'Architectural History and the Present Day Architect'. As it was, Vince Scully completely walked away with the show." Vincent Scully* (b 1920), architectural historian at Yale.
2   "Character and Compo": "Character and Composition", an essay Rowe had recently completed. See note 3 below.
3   "H.-R. H.": Henry-Russell Hitchcock.* Rowe had recently completed the essay, although it was published only in 1974. See Rowe's letter to Hitchcock dated 29 December 1954 (p 89 in this volume).
4   "Czarina" was Rowe's nickname for Jean Harris.* Wayne Andrews (1913–1987) had praised the work of Harwell Hamilton Harris* in his *Architecture, Ambition and Americans: A Social History of American*, New York: The Free Press, 1947, but was highly critical of Hitchcock's* *Early Victorian Architecture in Britain* in his review, "Victorian Buildings, from Soane to Pugin", *The Saturday Review*, 1 January 1955, p 67.
5   Marcus Whiffen,* with whom Rowe had taught in Austin from January to June, 1954.
6   *lèse*, French: injurious to, perhaps an allusion to *lèse-majesté*, an affront to the dignity of a ruler or state.
7   At the time, James Ackerman* was teaching at the University of California, Berkeley and Henry Kamphoefner (1907–1990) was dean of the School of Design at North Carolina State University, where Rowe was considering applying for a teaching position.
8   Hugo Leipziger-Pearce (1902–1988), a German-educated architect-planner who taught with Rowe in Austin.

029   *To **David Rowe,** London*   *28 February 1955*

The School of Architecture, Austin, Texas

My dear David,

I have been intending to write but was delighted to have your letter also to hear about the distilling people in St. James's Square. They occupy a Robert Adam on the west side don't they?[1] Which was designed for Sir Watkin Williams Wynn. I've always liked the name.

One may as well tackle the immediate problem.[2]

I entirely agree with buying a house.

Would it be leasehold or freehold?

Personally I don't much mind.

You say that you could keep up a mortgage of about 750 pounds. You want me to do the same.

Do you mean you want me to send you over 750 pounds or that you want me to send you over sufficient capital to make it possible to raise 750?

Would like to know this.

If you want 750 you could have it sometime like October. If you want capital to raise 750 you could have it I suppose by about the end of May. In other words by this time I could let you have $900.

This of course will mean that I shall have to postpone operations with Bob. However.

About freeholds and leaseholds, I think the former are very acceptable if there is the possibility of a conversion job in mind. [...] If not they convince me less.

I like Richmond and Barnes although I am not crazy about them.

There was a house going in St. George's Terrace, Camden Town, you know, overlooking Primrose Hill in November '53. It was leasehold of course, but struck me as being extraordinarily cheap. I forget how much it was, but I couldn't help thinking at the time that in such a situation the rents from a conversion would be extraordinarily high.

Anyway I don't mind much and would leave it entirely to your discretion, and I imagine that if a conversion were to be considered you could get it done by Bob.[3]

I suppose that the two possibilities are something like the Stevens House which Mother would prefer.[4] Or something like a big place which would be more immediately profitable as an investment. I doubt whether one has an enormous possibility of choice in these matters, so that I don't vote for either one or the other. The third possibility I suppose is a very small place, mewsy, on the edge of a good district, (there are such places in Richmond) which one makes elegant by Georgianising and including a first rate paint job.

What do they say?[5]

Anyhow I suppose that you could have my Regency from the Maxwell's,* and there is still a bit of it left in Liverpool too. Using that and adding one or two other things, and suppressing Mama's passion for dirty brown and gold, I think would make the final result very adequate indeed.

Am a little amused by all this though. Because do you remember how mother repudiated the idea of the Maxwell apartment (Rent 100 a year) simply because it would have meant spending about 400 on someone else's property.

I know that you can't tell me anything definite until you have something definite in mind, but will you let me know how much money and when. Then at least you will know when you can act.

Love,

    Colin

P.S. Please tell Alan C. and Alan C. that I will write soon.[6]

1 The Distillers Company Ltd, St. James' Square, London, with three bays designed by Robert Adam in 1771–1775.
2 The "immediate problem" is relocating their parents from Bolton-on-Dearne to London.
3 Robert Maxwell.*
4 The house of the parents of Rowe's friend, Sam Stevens.
5 "They" refers to Rowe's parents.
6 Alan Colquhoun* (1921–2012), British born architect, historian, critic, and teacher, and Alan Cordingley (1923–2009), an architect with whom Rowe studied at Liverpool and close friend of David Rowe.*

030   To *Henry-Russell Hitchcock,* Smith College Museum of Art, Northampton, Mass.   *5 June 1955*

The School of Architecture, The University of Texas, Austin, Texas

Dear Russell,

H.H.H. has resigned!!![1] That is the little piece of news which eclipses any other that I could send you. It happened last Monday, and I have merely been waiting to collect my impressions before writing.

On the whole it has been interesting. An experience that one wouldn't miss. After all it isn't given to everybody to be able to spend 18 months inside the framework of a novel by Dostoyevsky... and the relations between Harwell and the Madame are the nearest thing to Russian fiction which one has come across, or is indeed ever likely to.

He has been courting martyrdom and at last has achieved it. He couldn't have hoped for a better outcome. Together they have offended everyone and alienated every support and finally turn round to comment on the disloyalty and ingratitude of those they have raised from the dust. I do not think that I have ever met a more egocentric pair. Anyway as you can guess it's been a saga and I should like to tell you all about it before very long so that I am wondering what will be your whereabouts this summer. I plan to come up East early in September. I think that I must look around for somewhere else to go. Another year of this place will be quite enough. The people down here are all cannibals you know. They receive you with all the decorum of the savage tribe in the jungle, but the stew pot is always around the corner and they can't wait to put you in it. They would be pained if one told them so because they <u>do</u> have all the savage virtues, charm, lack of confidence, etc. One feels implicated with them, but one has to get away.

I think that I would like one more year here. Then one year somewhere in your part of the world. Then a return to England.[2]

However that is all by the way. They do have to choose a new director down here and I would think that it is going to take quite a time for them to do it. It would be an admirable place for someone who has the beginnings of a reputation and who would like to spend about five years here before going on to something else. There is here all the material to work upon. The students are very susceptible. I contrived to get the Albers drawing course started and the whole place would turn out results (in spite of Harwell and everyone else) in a matter of three years or so.[3] If someone with common sense, enterprise and a feeling for the proper publicity came here, they could leave it trailing clouds of glory. They would have some fight with certain members of the faculty, but with discretion and persistence (which the Harrises didn't possess) they should be able to steer their way through all that. What I was wondering is whether you could think of anybody. Do you think that Paul

Rudolph would be interested?[4] Is he not perhaps looking for just something of this kind? Could you let me know what you think about this and meanwhile I shall smell around and try to discover more exactly what is in the air.

Best wishes and hoping that the South America book is getting along well.

    Colin

1 "H.H.H": Harwell Hamilton Harris.*
2 Rowe had taught for three semesters under the direction of Harris and his wife, "The Madame", and would teach the 1955–1956 academic year at Austin after their departure. He taught the 1956–1957 academic year at Cooper Union followed by a year at Cornell before moving back to England in summer 1958 to teach at Cambridge for four years.
3 In spring 1954 Rowe suggested that the school appoint graduates from the Albers studio at Yale. See his 1988 essay "Texas and Mrs. Harris" in Rowe, *As I Was Saying: Recollections and Miscellaneous Essays*, Alexander Caragonne ed, 3 vols, Cambridge, MA: MIT Press, 1996, vol 1, p 22.
4 Paul Rudolph (1918–1997), architect and educator who became dean of the Yale School of Architecture in 1958.

To **Professor Henry-Russell Hitchcock,**
Smith College Museum of Art, Northampton, Mass.   *23 September 1955* **031**

The School of Architecture, The University of Texas, Austin, Texas

My dear Russell,

I was very glad to get your postcard and was delighted for you to hear that you are in London. I heard via Marcus in the first case and wonder whether you ever received the letter that I sent to you in Northampton in June.[1] I imagine that by then you were already in Europe.

Events here have been diverting in the extreme and, since the next year promises to be equally so, so long as one adopts an entirely detached position, I feel rather disposed to give you a full account of the circumstances leading to Harwell Harris's resignation (or dismissal).[2] One doesn't know which. I haven't seen you for so long, I shall not do so for another nine months at least. I would very much enjoy a conversation with you, so that I am going to write at inordinate length. You have lots of things to do. You may be amused by this letter. You may be bored by it, but please when you see its thickness don't feel inhibited by it.

To begin with I think one should present the Dramatis Personae for the succeeding action such as I found them when I arrived:-

The Czarina.[3] Since you know her there is nothing more to be said.

H.H.H. Again nothing more need be said except that you cannot possibly know the depths of his mind, his astonishing egoism, manic tendencies, etc. It takes a good six months to understand this, but all is not so innocuous as externally appears.

Buffler and McMath. Their principal opposition. Full Professors and both former directors of the school. The Czarina has rebuffed Mrs Buffler, insulted Mrs McMath, attempted to dismiss Buffler, but since they both have tenure nothing can be done. Constant sniping goes on on both sides. Buffler is a product of Pennsylvania, a contemporary and former acquaintance of Louis Kahn,* is mildly intelligent, embittered and vindictive. McMath is a product of North Dakota but some three generations back one suspects Belfast. Certainly the Ulster shows in a rather preposterous militancy and a more than necessary lack of subtlety.

Hugo Leipziger-Pierce. Full Professor. Of him the Czarina says that he is the only man apart from Harwell whom she can absolutely trust. Silesian, Jewish, ingratiating, suave, overtly liberal. Has built himself up a situation as a city planner, has the German passion for integrating all and sundry, and the primarily sociological limitations of his type. A former student of Bruno Taut.

Martin Kermacy. Associate Professor. Of Hungarian family. Competent, intelligent, but a little too obviously calculating to be agreeable at the first meeting. Possessed of a wife who is socially too energetic.

Leipziger and Kermacy are the two most influential supporters of Harris, but on their side are no more acceptable to each other than Buffler and McMath on the other.

Roessner. Associate Professor. From Cincinnati. A protégé of Pickering (!).[4] The 100% American boy of the 1930's. Sportif in dress, intellectually null, maintains a façade of neutrality, imitates Harris's work, but has no love for the Czarina, Leipziger or Kermacy. A Methodist. A good guy with the less discriminating students.

Bernhard Hoesli.* With whom I share an office. Swiss. Zurich. A former student of Corbu's.* Precise. Dogmatic. Cautious. Excessively attentive to details.

These are the main characters in the drama.

Subsidiaries might be added for the sake of local colour but their significance will not be intrinsic.

e.g. Leon White. A drinking companion of all the former governors of Texas from the late 1920's onwards. Is now pretty well corroded internally. A political appointee who draws a large salary, holds the rank of Full Professor and gives one or two lectures a week on structures.

Goldwin Goldsmith. Aged 86. A former director of the school. Columbia, Class of 1893. A goatee. Gives one lecture a week on specifications. Has the sentimental regard of McMath and a senile resistance to any innovation.[5]

Other characters it is not necessary to examine. There are here all the major ingredients for this first year's action. Only the stimuli, the irritants, the causes have to be added.

When I arrive it is apparent that I am unavoidably destined to enjoy an extraordinarily intense relationship with Mrs Harris. On three successive days she takes me on long automobile drives. Her conversation is continuous, and alternates protestations of the most extravagant regard for Harwell with remarks of considerable commonsense, frenzied expressions of hate for Buffler and a great deal of solicitude about myself. Another motif was ominously returned to now and then: the Whiffens.*

The Jean Whiffen-Jean Harris row had taken place a few weeks before. Marcus had seen the President about the Madam, and the Madam could become speechless with fury about Jean Whiffen. Going from one to the other had something of the charm of *opera bouffe*.[6] The *affaire Whiffen* had become a very celebrated cause, was known to the students, was discussed around the town, and had provided an opportunity for Buffler and McMath (who had resisted his appointment) to rush to Marcus's defence.

On the *affaire Whiffen* my attitude was one of neutrality, and it was apparent that on my arrival both Hoesli and myself were to be co-opted to the ranks of what Buffler called the Palace Guard.

In March '54 there opened a series of conferences at the Harris's. A *ukase* was sent out, and Leipziger, Kermacy, Hoesli, and myself were convened for several successive weekends at what I chose to call the Winter Palace.[7]

The weight of constructive suggestion was thrown to Hoesli and myself and after about three weeks I made my crucial suggestion.

To the great irritation of the Madam I brought along a copy of *Painting Towards Architecture* and also Vol. I of the *Œuvre Complète*.[8] She was extremely furious at the mere sight of these books. I was patient. I opened the first book at the Van Doesburg composition, the second at Corbu's skeleton of the Domino House and asked if one could not accept as a working hypothesis that the scope of modern architecture was delimited by these two drawings. I suggested that one need not be dogmatic about that, the situation was a factual one, that one could take either one or the other, or both, that there was a dialectic between them but that different minds might disregard it if they chose. Kermacy, Hoesli, and surprisingly Harris agreed. (Harwell I think saw them separately, with the concrete or steel skeleton in town, and Van Doesburg as the prototype of the suburban residence.) He accepted them as a common denominator whose implications it should be the purpose of a curriculum to explore. Seeing her husband's agreement Madam bowed to the inevitable but from this time onwards Leipziger, who did not understand the proposals, gradually withdrew from the meetings.

From that moment an apparent victory was won. A theoretical base was somehow provided. It became possible to proceed.

I pressed for an Albers course and as you know as a result H.H.H. made overtures to Yale. Hoesli made further suggestions and we got an ex-Cooper Union, ex-Harvard man at that time in Rome who would arrive in September.[9]

H.H.H. was delighted with his reforms. For the first time he had a programme, and when I wrote it down for him he read it to the faculty. I still think that it was an important document and someday I shall read it to you.[10] But what I had intended to be a manifesto of forceful, conservative, should one say Churchillian, compromise he read as though it were an invitation to come out to coffee.

This is the ending of the first act, with Hoesli and myself in full possession of the stage, and with the tableau completed by the Madam's gratitude and the director's deference. The enemy is apparently routed since Harris armed with my concordat has been able to persuade the President to order Buffler and McMath to comply.

The second act comprises the fall semester:-

During the summer Harris has been supervising the building of his deplorable exhibition house at Dallas, and the Madam has been operating in Dallas and Fort Worth society. Overcome by a quite new feeling of consequence she has bought an air-conditioned Buick.[11]

I return to Austin to be received with less warmth than I might have expected.

The situation is now further changed by the addition of three new faculty members.

Lee Hirsche.* A very long and agreeable Yankee type of South African background a generation or so back. A wife from Buffalo equipped with apparent means and aspiration to all things French. Oberlin, Yale, Albers boy.

Bob Slutsky.* Polish, Jewish, Cooper Union, Yale. Brooklyn, belligerent, a great devotee of Albers and a very critical enthusiast of Mondrian.

John Hejduk.* Hungarian by extraction. New York. Cooper Union, Harvard, the University of Rome. Immensely large, honest, intense, with an Italian wife.

Now with this material Hoesli and I are expected to make the wheels go round. But it is apparent at the beginning that something has happened—the Madam is not able to preside over this court. It is a little too extensive, too excitable for her to manage. It has its own private problems into which she cannot possibly penetrate. She makes attempts separately and *en bloc* and experiences failure.[12]

Meanwhile a little revolution is already taking place in the appearance of the students' work. It manifests itself first in the Albers course area. All the manifestations which one might expect, begin.

Other phenomena include the appearance of Miesian schemes in the junior years. Harwell is at something of a loss since the Van Doesburg-Corbu relationship is beginning to be accepted dialectically. Harwell can equate something of what is happening with Japanese prints, but I begin to suspect that he feels he has been tricked. The Madam too begins to act strangely.

First of all she goes on a diet consisting largely of peanut, secondly she asks one around, tells me that she is seeing too much of the younger faculty, and, when I do not go around again for several weeks, she rings me up with the loudest complaints.

Then there occurs the mad scene.

Hoesli is involved with a particular girl whom he has since married. The Madam asks me around to dinner in Harwell's absence and begins a cross examination. She has a pain in the back and alternately lies on the floor and stamps about the room. The upshot of it is that Hoesli, who has been acting with more than usual Swiss discretion, is endangering Harwell's position. Fantasy is piled on fantasy. This is pure disloyalty, ingratitude. He is to give her up, marry her, or to resign his position. And I am to tell him so. Within the next three days, the next three days, the next three days. If not we will both be guilty of DISLOYALTY TO HARWELL. I'm sure you can imagine the scene. The distraught woman, the frenzy superimposed upon the background of sparse japonaiserie.

What else <u>could</u> there be after this?

I tell Hoesli, as a matter of fact. Largely for my own curiosity as to how he will react. When she rings up I deny having told him. She raves and threatens and goes on and on. About ten days later she attempts apologies and a rapprochement. But it was the step from which there was to be no return, and although various conciliations are attempted success can be claimed for none. She retires in apathy and exhaustion.

Meanwhile the new programme continues to produce results, although they are results lacking perhaps in the 'human' interest which Harwell would like to see. I however experience great difficulty in getting money for slides and finally learn from Kermacy of Leipziger's policy to diminish the influence of Hoesli and myself.

He had paid two visits to Dallas in the summer. Had admitted to reservations about what was happening. Formalism. International Style. The Madam had listened, and the more she failed with our group the more she went on listening. Once having discovered this there were innumerable intimations that it was happening—one might pay a surprise visit and find them together, etc, etc.

However the new programme had now gathered momentum. It was irresistible and was not resisted, certainly not by Harwell anyway. He continued to express his usual reserved approval. Leipziger became progressively aware that we knew what was happening, and then on of course that we knew that he knew. There were the usual explanations. Madam was heard to speak of trades unionism.

At the end of the semester Kermacy left for Vienna. A year's leave.

The third act is inaugurated by a brief prologue:-

I have been since September in charge of Fourth Year design and before the Spring Semester begins a number of students come to me to ask about the scheme they will be doing. This they understand will be a design for the state park in west Texas. I tell them that I know nothing of it. They assure me that an announcement to that fact has already appeared in certain west Texas newspapers. I am baffled.

The semester opens.

A German expressionist called Waechter from Eugene, Oregon has been got to replace Kermacy.[13] He is the author of a book called *Schools for the Very Young*.[14]

At the faculty meeting nothing is said about The Park.

Privately I ask Harris about it, and he says oh yes of course, and Leipziger and Waechter are to assist me. I point out the impossibility of the programme, and Harris half agrees.

The following day Hoesli and myself make a joint *demarche* and Harris ends in full agreement.[15] The scheme will not be done.

The day after the Madam asks us to meet her. What is the trouble? What is wrong with the Park? It will be admirable public relations, besides H.H.H. has committed himself. But he has not committed himself to ten weeks of it, etc etc etc. This becomes excessively trying and as her hysteria mounts we inform her that Leipziger has merely constructed a noose, that we are aware of the manipulations that have been going on etc.

The following day there is another faculty meeting. Buffler, McMath and Roessner watch cynically while Harwell supported by Leipziger and Waechter insists that the Park scheme be done, and will simply not listen to the protests of the remaining faculty.

The Park scheme is done. For a place called Monahans, sand dune area which Leipziger has inadequately surveyed, and for which the students receive neither statistic nor programme. Revolutionary discontent breaks out among the students. Down with Leipziger is painted on the walls, Down with Waechter is written on the floor. I appear to attain an extraordinary moral ascendancy over the whole year. Relations all round deteriorate. A Mies*-Palladio* manner which would delight Philip becomes contagious in the lower school.[16]

From now on the action should take place on three distinct stages.

On the first should be Harwell, Leipziger, the Madam, and very occasionally Waechter (one learns that she finds him too stupid).

On the second should be Buffler, McMath, Roessner, who will from time to time communicate with spies entering through a secret door.

On the third should be Hoesli,* Hejduk,* Hirsche,[17]* Slutsky,* and myself.

The entrance to the first stage will remain blocked by Leipziger to all other actors except Waechter.

Waechter, who will only occasionally be admitted, will most of the time walk around the auditorium sublimely unconscious of what is going on, and will occasionally make remarks to the actors of a naivete so extreme as to throw some of them into paroxysms of embarrassment and others into ecstasies of delight.

The actors on the second stage will from time to time beckon to those on the third.

In spite of the way things are going Leipziger's position on as Grand Vizier remains guaranteed by the Madam. He is the Mayor of the Palace and the isolation of the Merovingian king becomes progressively more complete.

It is from April onwards that the catastrophe begins to take palpable shape. The Park fails, and with the students feeling desperate and frustrated, Leipziger abandons it before the scheduled time. I am allowed complete control once more—and it is complete control now since neither Leipziger nor Waechter chose to frequent the draughting room.

A confusion breaks out with the A.I.A. which could have been kept as a storm in a tea cup, but which Leipziger (so he can have the opportunity of calming it down afterwards) expands to alarming dimensions.

Harris has led Buffler and McMath to understand that they are going to teach summer school (or they expect it as they expect the revolution of the earth) and only in May do they accidentally learn that they are not recommended for it. The finesse of all this is too gratuitous to be comprehensible.

At the last faculty meeting Harris reads a letter from the President. He has been visited by Buffler and McMath. These gentlemen need to teach summer school, the money will certainly be provided for them to do so. Will Harris kindly find positions for them.

Harris leaves the situation. He invites discussion. He allows the faculty to become embroiled. He then states his resignation. A meeting exquisitely constructed by him—it collapses since during the final announcement, Hejduk, who has temporarily left the room, enters and falls over a chair.

———

The curtain opens once more to reveal Buffler and McMath comprising a somewhat debilitated triumph. Leipziger they are holding down under one of the stage traps, never they hope to rise again. Harris one knows to be sitting by the pay box writing letters of explanation to Douglas Haskell. Martial music sounds. Looks of repression cloud the faces of the two central figures. They compose them. Buffler with an ingratiating smile, McMath with the air of ferocity. Sounds of armament can be heard offstage. The lambs are to be sacrificed.

———

There, at the risk of boring you, you have the full story of this interesting debacle.

The dramatic critic will inevitably conclude that Hoesli and Rowe were deplorably lacking in insight. That they were immature, ingenuous. That they should have known that their best interests would only be served by insulating the Madam. But this they always knew. But to insulate the Madam was never easy. In the end they began to think it to be logically impossible, that it could only be achieved by acknowledging her every whim, deferring to her every suggestion, absorbing all her waking hours. Could only two *cavalieri serventi* have achieved this?[18] They thought in the end that it would require a regiment. On second thoughts the dramatic critic might think that they were right.

The situation too had the limitations of its possibilities, and short of endowing Harris with a mind, short of a divine intervention to provide him with the faculty of generalisation, the freedom they enjoyed was guaranteed only by their capacity to provide as stuffing ideas for the vacuum which he carries in his head. Their capacity to do this was determined by their capacity to control the Madam. When it was no longer possible to give her absolute and undivided attention, then they, then she, then Harris, and then Leipziger became destroyed.

If merely as material for his archives the dramatic critic might find this soap opera not unworthy of his attention. One of the actors at least asks him to consider the character who ostensibly is the central one—Harwell Hamilton Harris in the role of prince. He asks the dramatic critic to consider him as representative of the type, and asks whether he does not really consider the failure of the type to be perfectly well illustrated by the failure of its representative. Change the name of the actor, and the defects still show in the type. It is a type which deals only with particularities, with specific instances, which resists abstraction, which acknowledges no law, which dissolves knowledge and the possibilities of order, and which recognizes only personal sensibility. The redwoods of Oregon and those of California run together, contradicting the laws of geography they form an integral part with the pine forests of Germany. Lured by his expressionist tempters, like something out of Hansel and Gretel, the prince is led through these forests to his doom. The proponents of order attempt to drag him back to the plains of Illinois, but the horrible witch, at once wife, mother and symbol of sterility, bars the entrance to the forest. She urges him on to fight the dragon, but in the darkness of the forest the multi-headed beast is too much even for her.

———

But seriously though if you have been able to read so far I wonder what you do think. For me, as I say, it has been a most illuminating experience and I know that I could have only experienced it with such devastating charity in Texas. It has I think something to do with the light and something to do with geography. H.H.H. miscalculated Texas. He saw it as the new California. He did not understand how profoundly Texas wants to be Old South, not how really Southern it is. He did not understand that the Texans, because of geographical accident, will always prefer order to expression. That Texas is the predestined colony of Chicago and not that of the Bay Region.

Here on an enormous terrace provided by this state, with one's back to the Rio Grande, one feels it has been possible to survey both Europe and that Europe in America which lies East of here. To the West are the mountains and beyond that the mists of California—Japan. They are a fatal miasma which shrivels in the air of the plains.

Anyway one's prejudices are proved as far as I am concerned. Also one's experiment has been successful. The misfortune is that it was not given one year longer and that Harris did not have the discrimination to see what he was provided with. One cannot hope to stay here more than a year longer, and in any case, it would now be madness to attempt to do so. Already an underground railroad is constructed and refugee students are arriving in New Haven. At least only two so far, but I gather that they have been eagerly accepted and three others have been in to see me about it today.

In London does all this sound incredibly remote and banal, or can you possibly, like me, be amused by it?

———

Anyway, the forty days in the desert are now almost over, and one should make plans for returning, either to England or to the East. This is where I would very much appreciate your advice.

I assume five possibilities in the East:- Harvard, M.I.T., Yale, Philadelphia, and North Carolina.

In the Mid-West I presume that the Paul Rudolph regime at I.I.T. (which is rumoured to be imminent) offers another alternative.[19]

Harvard I think is still too much under the Gropius & Gideon regime to be tolerable.[20] About M.I.T. I don't know. Yale I would like although I gather that Schweikher is having trouble with Sawyer.[21] Philadelphia I understand to be sensible. With Catalano leaving North Carolina for M.I.T. I imagine that changes there are probable.[22] About England I don't know. My general plan is to get a job in the East for 1956–57 and also to visit England in the summer of '56 to have a look around and to attempt to arrive at a decision. Do you have any suggestions about the merits of the plans I have listed? Or about general strategy?

I would point out that we nearly did something quite big down here and do have rather impressive work to show—or at least I am told that Sert, Anderson,* and Louis Kahn* have all registered great surprise about the standard which was achieved in so short a time.[23] Really there is a whole machine here for sale. It only needs a discriminating buyer who would take in *en bloc*. As yet no possibilities really seem to present themselves of so dramatic a solution.

Can you let me have your ideas about all this?

Am glad that you visited Ronchamp.[24] But does it not vitiate all of Corbu's earlier conclusions? And however magnificent plastically does it not symbolise the despair of finding a public solution? Does it not pre-vision the impending crisis of rationalism? How would you compare it with Wright* and Mies churches?

Have you read *Scope of Total Architecture* and Walter Gropius.[25] These men, Gropius and Gideon, are frightened, desperate men. Why? Obviously because within the next five years the whole C.I.A.M. line up is going to collapse.[26] And here they are running around frenziedly trying to fill up, to conceal the central void which soon everybody is going to see, I am so annoyed by both books that I have begun to write a review of them. Whether or not it could be published I don't know. Who would publish it I can't think. But as soon as you start looking in the Gropius hypothesis it melts away.

It revolves around a number of extraordinary presumptions:-

i. that society is sick and that this is extraordinary and the fault of industrialism.

ii. that every healthy (?) individual is capable of creating form and that the artist who accepts the machine is the prototype of the whole man of the future.

iii. that modern architecture is whole i.e. not a manifestation of the sick society but a product of the 'elect' who have been exempted from the contagion. The more modern architecture that is built the more likely is this future civilisation of a rationalised technology is likely to come about.

iv. etc. etc. etc.

But the moment you examine it the whole thing collapses. Sickness of society is not unique, artist can never be prototype of whole man, has no right to consider himself 'elected' etc. It all becomes the patchwork of William Morris, fin-de-siecle aestheticism, vie-de-boheme, etc, etc.[27] Really this has struck me so violently in the last few days that I cannot help thinking that Gropius's days are numbered and that Hudnut must have been either extraordinarily self-controlled or extraordinarily stupid in not exposing him.[28] But I wonder if the time is ripe for a criticism of this whole position? Would it be too scandalous? Would all doors be closed afterwards? Or would some of them open with enthusiasm? Or would it be immediately so obvious that everyone would think, so what?

This all leads back into the Moholy-Nagy business, and I have just been reading Sybil's extraordinarily biography.[29] Moholy-Nagy was obviously the tame constructivist, the domesticated version of De Stijl whom Gropius was able to control. He was introduced so as to meet the challenge provided by Van Doesburg, but so that at the same time the party line could appear to be uncompromised with formalism.[30] All this is getting very interesting. But do you think that it is still too early and might have the effect of a damp squib?

I hope that London is exceptionally exciting, that Ennismore Gardens is not too lugubrious during the winter and I send you my best wishes and request you to convey my love to the Wittkowers.[31]*

    Colin

1   Marcus Whiffen.*
2   Harris* resigned as dean of the School of Architecture in June 1955.
3   "Czarina" was Rowe's nickname for Mrs Harwell Harris.*
4   Ernest Pickering (1893–1974), dean of the College of Applied Arts at the University of Cincinnati from 1946 to 1963.
5   The Harrises; Joseph Buffler; Hugh McMath (former Department chair); Hugo Leipziger-Pierce (1902–1998, taught at Austin from 1939–1974); Martin S Kermacy (1915–2007, at Austin from 1947–1983); Roland Gommel Roessner, Sr (1911–2001, began at Austin in 1948); Bernhard Hoesli;* Robert Leon White (1898–1964, at Austin from 1923–1964); Goldwin Goldsmith (1871–1962, at Austin from 1928–1955). See Caragonne, Alexander, *The Texas Rangers: Notes from the Underground*, Cambridge, MA: MIT Press, 1995.
6   *opéra bouffe*, French: comic opera.
7   *ukase*, French: a legally binding decree made by a Russian Czar or any absolute ruler.
8   Hitchcock, Henry-Russell, *Painting Towards Architecture*, New York: Duell Sloan Pearce, 1948 and Le Corbusier et Pierre Jeanneret, *Œuvre Complète, 1910–1929*, Willi Boesiger, ed, Zurich: Girsberger, 1937.
9   John Hejduk* was the ex-Cooper Union, ex-Harvard man. Josef Albers (1888–1976) was chair of the Department of Design at Yale at the time.
10 "Important document": "Comments of Harwell Hamilton Harris to the Faculty, May 25, 1954". See Rowe, Colin, *As I Was Saying: Recollections and Miscellaneous Essays*, Alexander Caragonne ed, 3 vols, Cambridge, MA: MIT Press, 1996, vol 1, pp 41–54.
11 This was the all-electric "Pace Setter House" on the grounds of the Dallas State Fair, commissioned by *House Beautiful* magazine and Dallas Power and Light. In 1957 the house was moved to a Dallas suburb. See Germany, Lisa, *Harwell Hamilton Harris*, Austin: University of Texas Press, 1991, pp 148–151. See Rowe's letter to Germany 14 July 1955 (p 435 in this volume) in which he remarks, "A pity you don't exhibit the plan of the Dallas Pace Setter House of 1955 because, surely, that is one of the very best plans by H.H.H. [...]"
12 *en bloc*, French: as a unit; all together.
13 Heinrich Hormuth Waechter (1907–1981), Berlin-born architect who studied under Bruno Taut (1880–1938), taught at The University of Texas at Austin from 1955 to 1956.
14 Waechter, HH and Elisabeth Waechter, *Schools for the Very Young*, New York: FW Dodge Corp, 1951.
15 *démarche*, French: move, maneuver.
16 Philip Johnson* (1906–2005).
17 Lee Hirsche* (1927–1998), studied painting under Josef Albers at Yale before teaching at Austin. After Austin, he taught primarily at Williams College in Massachusetts.
18 *cavalieri serventi*, Italian: gallant escorts.
19 Paul Rudolf would become dean of the Yale School of Architecture in 1958.
20 Walter Gropius (1883–1969), chairman of the Department of Architecture at Harvard from 1938 to 1952; Sigfried Giedion (1888–1968), Swiss architectural historian.
21 Paul Schweikher (1903–1997), dean of the Yale School of Architecture at the time and Charles Henry Sawyer (1906–2005), museum curator, art historian, and Yale's director of the Division of the Arts, overseeing the Colleges of Architecture, Art, and Drama; the Art Gallery; and the Department of History of Art.
22 Eduardo Catalano (1917–2010), Argentine-born architect who taught at the University of North Carolina from 1951 to 1956 and at MIT from 1956 to 1977.
23 Josep Lluis Sert (1902–1983), at the time dean of the Harvard Graduate School of Design; Stanford Anderson;* Louis I Kahn.*
24 Chapel of Notre Dame-du-Haut (1950–1955) by Le Corbusier* at Ronchamp, France: a radical departure from principles of the Modern movement architecture established before the Second World War.

25 Gropius, Walter, *Scope of Total Architecture*, New York: Harper & Brothers, 1955 and Giedion, Sigfried, *Walter Gropius: Work and Teamwork*, New York: Reinhold, 1954.
26 "CIAM": *Congrès internationaux d'architecture moderne* (International Congresses of Modern Architecture), an international organization for the dissemination of Modern movement principles in architecture, urbanism, landscape, industrial design, and other disciplines. Founded in 1928, it was disbanded in 1959.
27 William Morris (1834–1896), English writer, socialist and leading artist in the British Arts and Crafts Movement; *fin-de-siècle*, French: end of the century; *vie de bohême*, French: Bohemian life.
28 Joseph Hudnut (1886–1968), dean of the Graduate School of Design at Harvard from 1936 to 1953.
29 Moholy-Nagy, Sybil, *Moholy-Nagy, An Experiment in Totality*, New York: Harper & Brothers, 1950.
30 Theo van Doesburg (1883–1931) Dutch artist, founder and leader of De Stijl. In 1922 he moved to Weimar where Gropius directed the Bauhaus. According to Rowe above, László Moholy-Nagy, "the tame constructivist", was "introduced" as Bauhaus master "to meet the challenge provided by Van Doesburg".
31 Margaret and Rudolf Wittkower.*

032　　*To **David Rowe**, Gloucester Terrace, London*　　　　　　　　　*30 November 1955*

The School of Architecture, The University of Texas, Austin, Texas

My dear David,

Why not? Although you make it difficult for me to be enthusiastic by listing so many points altogether against it, it does seem to be a good and reasonable buy.[1] It would if necessary I presume be possible to turn it into two apartments by the simple process of inserting a bathroom downstairs, a kitchen up, and then proceeding to wall up the staircase. And two such apartments should I suppose bring in a minimum of Seven Pounds a week, don't you think?

Of course I am at a bit of a loss to know why they should want anything so big but I know that since they won't accept the sort of place that you got to live in after a conversion job, the size of this house is just about all that is left.

Is it Voysey-ish, i.e. has it got a certain external delicacy, quaintness, lightness, horizontality, etc., like the Stevens' house, or is it heavy, lugubrious, rather vertical, i.e. in the builder's tradition of 1880 onwards.[2] This I think is the crucial point. If it is the former I should have absolutely no doubt at all. If the latter I would have some reservations. I could then imagine crumbling brick, fog, the horrors of November desolation, etc.

But I think that particularly the duplication of kitchens is a good point since it does offer the possibility of a very convenient conversion. See over....

I think that to make it livable and agreeable one would probably need to lay down a new floor throughout the living rooms and kitchen and entrance hall. This is my own personal feeling since all English floors are so bad? Have you any idea of the cost of asphalt tile or plywood squares? All this would solve the carpeting problem I can't help thinking.

Looking at your plan, apart from keeping things as they are, I derive three possibilities.

Nos. 1 and 2 are variants on the idea of breaking the house up into two small apartments.

No. 3 is a move in the direction of making a rather grand and reasonable house. I.E. sitting room and dining room thrown together through some sort of proscenium arrangement, then dining room squared off as a 12'x12' room leading out into a rather narrow garden room, porch, flower room, conservatory etc. This I do think would make rather a fine space approximately 30' long and quite clearly divided into three separate functional areas.

I suppose that they would find it rather too grand, although lightly furnished and with a good floor and occasional oriental rugs I can't think that its upkeep would be too difficult.

Personally in spite of the expense I would favour No. 3, since it partly anticipates No. 1 and also makes the whole ground floor an excellent and a completely usable space.

I wonder if you will be able to sell the house to them.[3]

> *Colin*

---

1   Rowe is replying to a letter dated 25 November 1955 from his brother, David, in which David wrote that after several months of searching for a suburban London house for their parents, he had taken a 14-day option on a three-bedroom house at 8 Melville Road in Barnes, southwest London. The letter listed obvious problems with the house: "No room for a garage; the stairs are v. steep; no adequate electric power points" and David described the interior as "at present a series of awful browns and full of ghastly late Victoriana". He concluded, however, "This is positively the only house or flat I have found at a reasonable price which has shops and bus stops nearby, which is in a pleasant neighbourhood… and which appears to be well built and well proportioned." On the reverse of a page of his reply, Rowe sketched floor plans of the house showing three options for renovation described verbally in the letter.
2   "Voysey-ish" refers to Charles Voysey (1857–1941), an English Arts and Crafts architect. Sam Stevens, an architect with whom Rowe studied at Liverpool, was a close friend of both David and Colin Rowe, and was known by their parents.
3   On 23 March 1956 Rowe's father wrote, "David found a house at Barnes which he thought would suit us. Your mother went up to London to view the property and returned with a favourable impression. David made an offer for the house subject to a satisfactory survey. Messrs Tyler and Co. of Holborn Viaduct were instructed to make a detailed inspection but when the report came it was unfavourable. The house was not structurally sound and a considerable sum would have to be spent on it to put it into satisfactory condition." The letter concludes, "The surveyor thought that the price suggested, about £3500, was excessive so that scheme seems to have fallen through, but I do not think David has dropped it altogether." On 16 July 1956 Rowe's mother wrote him, "I was very disappointed that we did not get the Barnes house. I think you would have liked the situation, altho' it was not an architectural gem. That little effort cost more than twenty pounds. Surveyor's fees and my trip to London."

---

*To **Louis I. Kahn,** Architect, 1501 Walnut Street, Philadelphia, Pennsylvania*   *7 February 1956*   **033**

The School of Architecture, The University of Texas, Austin, Texas

Dear Louis,[1]

I am writing rather belatedly to thank you for the evening which you devoted to Bob and myself just over five weeks ago.[2] As a token of gratitude for the dinner and as a sort of memorial to the subsequent dialectics I am sending you a copy of Wittkower's⋆ *Architectural Principles in the Age of Humanism* which I do hope that you will accept.[3] You may have got it already and wondered where it came from; but if not, it should arrive within the next couple of weeks.

I chose the Wittkower book partly because of the influence it has had upon me, partly because I think that it may interest you, and partly because of matters arising out of our conversation. Did you see in the *Architectural Review* a deplorable article on 'the New Brutalism'—very chauvinistic and patronizing—suggesting first of all that you were a 'new brutalist', which as far as I know you would never claim to be, and then turning around and damning you because you didn't fulfill the N.B. canon.[4] Perhaps you did not. And if not then I suggest you don't look, as it would be merely an unnecessary exacerbation. But one little innuendo there was, condemning pseudo-Palladian formalism, which was meant for me. The implication was that between relapsed New Brutalists and pseudo-Palladian formalists (please forgive the terms) there might be all sorts of dubious and heretical and unorthodox rapports. This I think showed insight, because, although you are not an N.B. and I am not a pseudo-P., it was precisely a reason of this kind which had made me decide to send you the Wittkower book in which I think that you may discover attitudes with which you are profoundly in sympathy.

I remember that something of our conversation in Philadelphia revolved around principles which we designated as GROWTH and COMPOSITION. Principles which are opposed. And I took the side of COMPOSITION and then had great difficulty in explaining what I meant by it. You deplored COMPOSITION because it appeared to be no more than a manipulation of forms for the sake of effect. You wanted to GROW a building, and I, I think, suggested that I wanted to COMPOSE it. Or at least I was very emphatic about the *PARTI*.[5]

I still am; but I do wish that I had had the time to explain myself more completely, and had been able to indicate that the composition of which I was speaking was the result of a process of dialectic, and not of an irrelevant fantasy or purely arbitrary choice. For me, your cubes, your hexagonal cells, are objective data with a life of their own in which one can't intervene. They are independent, aggressively so, irreducible, intractable phenomena. This I like. At the same time, although they are independent, they are in fact the acts of your volition. Once born you can't violate their mode of being. But you are in a position (since they are independent) to argue with them.

It was no more than such argument that I meant by composition. I don't like the word. I prefer formal structure, or organisation, or perhaps better than anything ORDINANCE which implies to me the accepting of irreducible facts and the working out of their logical consequences. Basically to me your cubes are a very powerful system of ordinance which I would like nothing better to do than to attempt to bring into some sort of dialectical relationship with parti. Hence my feeling for them and the Rainaldi church, etc.[6]

This is really to ask you what are the possibilities of an appointment at the University of Pennsylvania? I don't want to sound like a sort of moral blackmailer, or to over-persuade, or to embarrass, or flatter; but I can think of nowhere I would rather be for the next two or three years.[7] And since I do sense the latency of some opposition between your cells and the idea of *parti* I would very much indeed like to experience it in myself and learn something from it, because now I feel that I can't really push my present attitude any further. It needs a disrupting stimulus.

I enclose with this letter a tracing of a Palladio* plan which I think might interest you. It is for an ideal building.[8] The transparency and the variety of reading of the forms is what engrosses me about it. It all holds together, and yet you can extract successively element after element and still it is always complete. Where cerebral appreciation ends and perceptual enjoyment begins in a matter of this kind I don't know. Maybe you would condemn my feeling for this plan, but I still feel that, being the curious, equivocal abstraction that it is, it would still possess a certain extreme visual tension. A modern version of this is what I mean by *Parti*.

I wish I could have expressed my feelings about all these things better than I have, but I do hope on some subsequent occasion to be able to try again.

Sincerely yours,

Colin

Colin Rowe

1 Louis Isadore Kahn* (1901–1974), distinguished American architect and teacher. At the time of this letter, Kahn taught architecture at Yale University.

2 Robert Slutzky* (1929–2005), American painter, writer, and teacher. Slutzky was teaching with Rowe at The University of Texas at Austin.

3 Wittkower, Rudolf, *Architectural Principles in the Age of Humanism*, London: Warburg Institute, 1949. Rowe had been Wittkower's* student at the Warburg Institute in London from 1946–1948.

4 Banham, Reyner, "The New Brutalism", *The Architectural Review* 125, December 1955, pp 354–361. See also Banham, Reyner, *The New Brutalism: Ethic or Aesthetic*, London: Architectural Press, 1966. Rowe reviewed this book together with Robert Venturi's *Complexity and Contradiction in Architecture*, New York: Museum of Modern Art, 1966, in "Waiting for Utopia", *The New York Times,* 10 September 1967, Sunday edition. The review is reprinted in Colin Rowe, *As I Was Saying: Recollections and Miscellaneous Essays*, Alexander Caragonne ed, 3 vols, Cambridge, MA: MIT Press, 1996, vol 2, pp 75–78.

5 *parti,* French: decision, course, choice; in architecture, the salient aspects of a scheme, primarily its plan.

6 The reference presumably is to Carlo Rainaldi's Church of Santa Maria in Campitelli, Rome (1662–1675). See "Two Italian Encounters" in Rowe *As I Was Saying: Recollections and Miscellaneous Essays*, vol 1, pp 6–10.

7 "I have been prompted by John Hejduk to write you", Robert Slutzky* wrote to Kahn* from the University of Texas on 25 October 1955 before describing his teaching activities at Texas. "By June of 1956 I will have had two years experience. After that I intend returning to the East, desirous of carrying on my own work in painting and teaching at the same time. Knowing of your contacts with the University of Pennsylvania, I am writing to inquire whether there might be an opening there next Fall [...]". On January 26, 1956, after he and Rowe had met with Kahn in Philadelphia, Slutzky wrote Kahn a second time saying that the two of them had toured the Universities of Princeton, Yale, Cooper Union, RISD, MIT and Penn earlier that month. "Only MIT and Penn seemed to know where they were", he stated, adding, "More than anything else I was, and still am, deeply impressed with your conviction and inner 'knowingness' and at all times I felt that I was conversing with a painter as well as an architect." In a "P.S.", not unlike Rowe's above, Slutzky wrote, "The new Architectural Review has an interesting (and to me, a most irritating!) article written by a R. Banham (?) about something or other called the New Brutalism…".

8 Plate LI in Palladio, Andrea, *Four Books of Architecture*, Venice, 1570, of the Vitruvian Villa of the Ancients. Beneath his colored traces, Rowe typed, "Sorry I didn't have any more coloured pencils because one could go on doing this sort of thing. Don't you really find it fantastic the way all the spaces here fluctuate, are alternately positive and negative, etc. Also the way in which you could almost turn the plan inside out because everything is entirely constructed?"

To Mr & Mrs Frederick Rowe,
Highgate Lane, Bolton-on-Dearne, Yorkshire, England   *4 & 7 July 1956*   **034**

43 Fifth Avenue, New York, N.Y.

Dear Parents,

This is such an auspicious day [...] when the Americans let off all sorts of fireworks, indulge in barbecues, read patriotic editorials, and think of democracy, all by way of celebrating their enthusiasm about their release from the accursed tyranny of George III that I suppose that I had finally better write a letter.[1] It happens to be raining rather hard outside, so that letting off of fireworks and the general celebration is a little dimmed. I am staying with Ian and Elma Mackenzie and they have gone off to the wilds of Connecticut somewhere to spend the evening with a terrifying woman from Aberdeen[2] (who gave me a graphic account of Laval's execution the other day) and because they have gone to Connecticut I am at least able to write a letter.[3] Trying to write letters here during the day is difficult because Elma never stops talking. Trying to write letters in the evening is impossible because then Ian never stops discussing the political situation in England, which harasses him.

So one takes one's opportunities.

This is a large and rather over furnished and rather over upholstered apartment which you might like. It reflects Elma's taste which I deplore. Although in everything else except visual matters she never seems to slip up. It is a rather dilapidated fifty years old apartment house down at the bottom of Fifth Avenue near Washington Square, which was designed by Stanford White and which was the setting for liaison with Evelyn Nesbit Thaw and which was also the home of Grover Cleveland after he had ceased to be president of the U.S.[4] So that it is an impressive building but has known better days and will no doubt shortly be pulled down.

I have been in New York for approximately three weeks or a little over and seem during this time to have acquired an intimate knowledge of Manhattan real estate. I have found myself an apartment between Madison and Park Avenue at East 90th Street. I shall move into it the day after tomorrow.

The address is 68 East 90th Street, New York, N.Y.

It is small but has all been painted white and I suppose is in an excellent part of town. Or perhaps it is just on the edge of an excellent part of town. After East 96th Street nobody lives. It is then first of all a Puerto Rican ghetto and then Harlem. Harlem is frightening. One doesn't go there. East 96th Street is the great divide. The descent from relative opulence to total squalor is precipitous. But East Ninetieth between Madison and Park exudes an air of Kensingtonian refinement which perhaps you might find appealing. It is one block from Central Park so that I suppose one may walk there if one chooses and it offers the alternative possibilities of reaching mid-town either by Fifth, Madison, Park, or Lexington Avenue, all of which (unlike so much of the rest of New York) contain relatively little to shock and a great deal to stimulate and please.

This I think is the first time I have ever been in New York without being in some way outraged by it. I don't find now that it afflicts me in any way. Climatically I am not oppressed. Visually I am not affronted. Socially I am not depressed. And in fact [...] though without enthusiasm [...] I rather enjoy it all. It has the flavour of a Glasgow or a Liverpool that has struck a boom and been able to buy all the relevant parts of Paris and then to have them done over with a good deal more discretion than the French nowadays could rise to.

I was intending to write from Texas for ages but first one obstacle to writing a letter and then another presented themselves. Texas being both so familiar and also so exotic, I mean as regards English experience, is a little difficult to write about. The relief of leaving it is I suppose extreme. Although I don't really know. But certainly it was worth going there. It is after all one of the American myths and having had first hand experience of it leaves one comfortably superior to the New Yorkers who although they affect to patronise Texas are really a little awed by it.

But Texas would require whole volumes of comment and I don't really feel up to providing it all.

At the moment I have one job to start in September teaching at the Cooper Union School of Architecture. I will look for another one soon [...] probably sometime next month when I have finished an article which I want to do, and by these means I suppose that I should have something like $6,000 a year or maybe with luck $7,000 which is perhaps not very much but which will be distinctly better than Texas and which I think will be quite agreeable. Also Louis Kahn★ who used to be at Yale and then at the University of Pennsylvania, and is a friend of mine is now going to be the director of the Yale School of Architecture and is interested, so that I think that I shall have lunch with him someday soon either here or in Philadelphia.[5]

That is where the Mackenzie's came back from Connecticut full of talk about the journey back and more tattle about this (to me) appalling woman Catherine Gavin who repeatedly tried to get herself elected as a Conservative member for various excessively left Scottish constituencies throughout the 1930's. The apartment in East 90th Street is still unfinished. The men haven't completely scraped the floor yet so that I still am waiting [...] with the slightly uncomfortable feeling by now of being in a big railway terminus with all one's luggage strapped up and absolutely no way of getting at the essential things because one has quite forgotten in which suitcase they might be.

That may explain my exasperation this morning with the *Sunday Times* for June 17th 1956 which suddenly arrived about three weeks late. I give you a sample:-

"Mr. Harry S. Truman arrives in London tomorrow as a 'man of the people', but during his brief visit to this country he will move in the suitably rarefied circles that should surround an ex-President of the U.S.A. At Oxford and at the Pilgrim's Dinner on Thursday night Lord Halifax will be his mentor and Mr. Truman is scheduled to see more academic gowns and white ties than cloth caps."[6]

Now is this innocuous? Am I all wrong to be exasperated by this sort of thing, and to find it far from innocent, and really symptomatic of all the trouble in England at the moment?

First of all there is an irrelevant phrase... Mr Truman is a "man of the people". This description might perhaps apply to the late of Mr Ernest Bevin, to a trades union leader, but obviously it is only completely applicable in a fairly stratified society where a certain amount of class hatred can be assumed to exist.[7] Am I wrong to assume that the phrase "man of the people" if it assumes appreciations of the figure who is so dignified, assumes a slightly contemptuous appreciation.

Second. Mr Truman "will move in the suitably rarefied circles that should surround an ex-President of the United States". And what is this to mean? That America does not provide such circles? Or that ex-Presidents of the United States can only be expected to be treated with the decorum which they deserve in Great Britain? Or that the United Kingdom is going to show the United States just how its ex-Presidents should be treated? It seems to me that all these assumptions are latent in these few words.

Third. "at the Pilgrim's Dinner on Thursday night Lord Halifax will be his mentor". Now what can this mean? Is one to understand that Lord Halifax will advise Mr Truman which knife and fork to use or assist him in a selection of the appropriate wines? What else can it mean?

Fourth. "Mr Truman is scheduled to see more academic gowns and white ties than cloth caps". Now this is really the ultimate absurdity. Since when has Mr Truman been habituated to the sight of cloth caps? Are they not the stigmata of the working classes in England and Russia exclusively?

Now do you see why at this moment I happen to be exasperated. This paragraph, ostensibly so urbane, is one tissue of naivete, patronage, and unwarrantable assumption. It is the product of abysmal ignorance, ungenerous instincts, and unimaginative pompousness. It is inflated and without percipience. It is calculated to make an American who might read it laugh himself silly (if he has a sense of humour) or alternatively it is calculated to make him very annoyed.

Now as far as I can see there can be no reason why Great Britain should not provide the United States with innocent amusement (galling though I might happen to find it). Nor I suppose should there be any reason why British newspapers should not chose to annoy individual Americans who might happen to read them since American newspapers so obviously reciprocate. That is obviously all right. But you don't have to look at a paragraph like this in isolation. At least I don't think so. It has a context. It is characteristic. It is a symptom of ever so much more.

Let us say that the paragraph is hideously provincial.

And then we will pick up a collection of old copies of *The Listener* which they have lying about here and we shall arrive very shortly at THE ENGLISHNESS OF ENGLISH ART.[8] And what <u>can</u> one say to that except Great God. The English being taught to be patriotic about English art by a German. How dreadful. One has thought that that peculiar brand of cultural chauvinism was a German speciality. How vulgar, how Germanically obtuse can people get to be able to tolerate such stuff? Since when have the English taken to care about being English? I thought that they just were. I didn't think that they need take pains to be so. I thought that they borrowed everything which they wanted with a splendid disregard for the consequences and that it sometimes (though very rarely) came off. But when you get around to the Englishness of English Art you begin to sense a rather nasty lack of self-confidence.

And then let us illustrate the problem a little more. While little Nikolaus is very shamelessly and very opportunistically flattering the national ego, Wittkower* (who has never played politics) is obliged to take a job in the United States. I had a long conversation with the Wittkowers at Christmas, who were very agitated and burnt up about things. Columbia University here in New York is offering him something between $12,000 and $14,000 to teach there. London offers him you can guess what. His particular seriousness, which presumably the Americans recognize and admire, apparently the English don't want. Apparently they prefer to be told by Pevsner* how English they are. So Wittkower is coming over to New York in September and I imagine that in about ten years time.... It will take ten years.... That this transaction will be bitterly regretted in England.

But what can you do about all this. These are merely journalistic and academic instances of the crass lack of perception which causes the loss of markets, the failure to develop Africa, and all the rest of it. It is so shocking. The ghastly parochialism of the whole situation becomes even more of a mockery when one is reminded that London still considers itself to be the centre of the earth and is blissfully and happily unaware of its horrible predicament.

The scandal is perfectly obvious to anyone who has been outside the country for more than two years and is perfectly illustrated by going through any representative collection of English magazines [...] which the Mackenzie's have in abundance. *Punch, The Listener, The Spectator, The Scottish Field, The Times Literary Supplement* etc. all show it. Perhaps that's not quite true. *The Spectator, The Times Lit. Supp.* and *The Economist* are all very well aware. But what else in God's name is?

Basically there is a terrifying small mindedness. Everything is picayune, snobbish, apologetic, and inhibited. You see this particularly in the advertisements. On this I could go on indefinitely but perhaps there is no point.

The corollary of this appalling condition of indecision is of course the assumption of airs of superiority. "Nowhere in the world does quality count so much as in Britain," and then, alongside, an advertisement that looks as though the commercial artist has seen nothing of the world since 1910. And then, when these people turn round to try to explain this situation (since they are dimly conscious that something is wrong), then how bland is the air of *savior faire*, and how particularly bland so far as the United States is concerned. The inference is of course we could do it too, but then we have chosen to pursue higher things, we, after all, are not ingenuous, if you really can't appreciate us then of course it's your misfortune."

This is of course almost as bad as the French and quite as unjustified at a time like this when Germany is leading all over again in quantity production while in design Italy and the United States are so far ahead that it's not funny.

After all this I have just been reading Edmund Burke and William Pitt and some of Disraeli's speeches which are like a breath of fresh air and which show an understanding and a breadth of mind which elsewhere you don't seem to find.[9]

Like Ian, at the moment I find the only small voice of sanity and perception issuing from *The Spectator* which as a Conservative and anti-government publication seems to be the only alive journalistic venture in the country. Is the Charles Curran who writes for it the Charles Curran from Goldthorpe?[10] I have, I suppose, presumably as a result of Texas, become a Conservative and an Imperialist. I must say that I never expected it. But then perhaps the scale of Texas does enlarge the mind.

But what shocks me in England is the incompetent gentlemanliness of most things. This associated with small mindedness and ludicrous assumptions of importance. And there is no reason why this should be so. The success of the United States is precisely because it was founded on English institutions. The English if they want, if they really want, can make of Australia and New Zealand another United States. It is patently in their traditions to do so. Why do they not want it?

Presumably the answer is in an incompetent educational system and also in an excessively class conscious society which is a form of society totally unequipped to deal effectively with mass production. The whole system has been running down, I can't help thinking, since approximately 1870 and what I am surprised about is how many people were aware of it fifty years ago and more, and who either were disregarded or were unable to do anything to stop it. Matthew Arnold for instance in 1882:-

"And therefore an English country gentleman regards himself as part of the system of nature.... If the price of wheat falls so low that his means of expenditure are greatly reduced, he tells you that if this lasts he cannot possibly go on as a country gentleman; and every well-bred person amongst us looks sympathizing and shocked. An American would say: Why should he?"[11]

Now obviously what Matthew Arnold was attacking was just the unwarrantable assumption of the gentleman regarding himself as part of the divine dispensation, taking so much for granted, and the whole thing just goes on. One discovers so little in the English press except exacerbated complaint, and so little indication that anything can possibly be done about it. This I assume to be the fault of the gentlemanly and I suppose the Anglican tradition.

The gentlemanly and Anglican tradition may undoubtedly be good in itself. But what does it lead to? Certainly it was not the tradition which founded Massachusetts. Maybe it was the tradition which founded Virginia. Certainly it was the tradition which made Anglo-Ireland. But it never had anything to do with Ulster. It was responsible though for present day Kenya. It has had very little to do with the foundation of either Australia or Canada. These simple statements obviously do not disparage the quality of the gentlemanly and Anglican tradition, but they do, one has to face it, constitute rather an indictment of its effectiveness. It has been eminently cultured, decorative, and agreeable but apparently has contributed remarkably little to the expansion of the English-speaking world. Therefore I think one might rightly guess that the gentlemanly and Anglican tradition is maybe not quite so important as the English believe it to be, and although there is no reason why it should not be encouraged to survive, it does seem demonstrably a little absurd that it should be regarded as pre-eminently the English tradition.

This does seem to me the root of the whole problem. The English, with that admirable romanticism which never deserts them, have put themselves rather in the role of the south before the Civil War. And the South was so magnificent in adversity, and so well mannered on the whole, and on the whole still is. But the South was impossibly obstinate, would not change, insisted on maintaining an obsolete social system (not slavery). And on the whole it was the preference for a manner rather than for prosperity or flexibility which ruined the South. And the South still is amazingly and enchantingly English [...] in terms of the gentlemanly tradition (One would be inclined in fact to say that it was more so).

You go through Virginia. The first English settlement there preceded anything in Massachusetts. Norfolk, Newport, Jamestown, all the towns on the shores of Chesapeake Bay surround the most splendid natural harbor on the east coast. But where is the great city which, given the great harbor, one has every right to expect. There is no Boston, and no Philadelphia, and no New York. The Virginians preferred to live like English country gentlemen. And for a time [...] but not for all time [...] this worked very well. But this Virginian preference (such an Anglican one) was scarcely favourable to the development of commerce or industry. And so you have Virginia today. A great tradition. An attitude. An admirable landscape. But ultimately an irrelevant place. And this is, after all, the first of English colonies and, I'm sure, quite the most endearing one as regards both climate and landscape.

But the whole thing is so obvious. The tradition of dissent, of Presbyterianism which founded Ulster, the Calvinist fanaticism which made Massachusetts, the Quakers in Philadelphia, all these were anti-Anglican elements, and all these places produced wealth and, like Manchester, they were all slightly disreputable in terms of the gentlemanly and Anglican tradition. Then sometime from about 1870 on all these dissenters became absorbed with the idea of trying to get in. They were no longer content to remain outside. They wanted peerages for themselves and education at Oxford for their sons. And so, sometime in the 1850's wasn't it, Oxford and Cambridge were opened to Dissenters and Methodists and Jews, and once absorbed they were all alike devitalised. Society became universally polite. Manchester took to becoming ashamed of itself, and an aura of Kensingtonian refinement was spread over everything. For some time of course it didn't show. What had happened seemed to be a blessing. There was the money to support it. One could believe that it had always been so, always would be. And so everything slowly ran down, became more introverted, backward-looking, precedent ridden, qualified. And there you have the present day [...] an eminently polite society with a supreme genius for vitiating any significant innovation.

The ultimate farce of course came when Mr Attlee accepted his earldom. This really was the supreme high water mark of the grotesque. One blushed. The Americans were vastly entertained by the vulgar spectacle. One had thought that Mr Attlee might have had better taste. Perhaps a little more integrity. Mr Gladstone,* after all, never accepted an earldom.[12] There was sufficient precedent to refuse it. And then assuming that it was irresistible, or that Mr A. felt that it was his duty to accept it, could he not have insisted on a life peerage only? Must he saddle the generations of his family to the most indefinite posterity with such a ridiculous burden. And assuming that his family do not have the money to keep up the title then the lack of money must ultimately be damaging to the peerage and of course to the House of Lords. Is this what he wanted to do? I doubt it. I'm sure he acted with the best of intentions and while he was quite prepared to question almost anything in the land, he was absolutely unwilling to question what by the mid-twentieth century is obviously a superfluous precedent.

But obviously this letter has gone on for long enough and is probably not very interesting or very informative either. There is almost nothing I can ask you, because obviously you are still in B.O.D. and I know all about that. There is at the moment almost nothing else that I can say except that I am immensely looking forward to moving into 68 East 90th Street, New York, N.Y. and hope to spend an interesting year there.

Then what. Must one return to England and be obliged to fight all the nonsense and the obscurantism that I have tried to draw your attention to. What a prospect. What fatigue. What bombs have to be dropped. I don't know at the moment whether I could face it. I know that in England I should feel emotionally obliged to fight. This might be a good thing but it WOULD be rather a strain.

Colin

1 4 July is Independence Day in the United States.
2 Ian MacKenzie, a native of Edinburgh and friend of Rowe's from Liverpool, moved to New York City in 1952 to serve as Managing Director and President of St. Martin's Press. Catherine Irvine Gavin (1907–1999), journalist and historical novelist, was Rowe's "terrifying woman from Aberdeen".
3 Pierre Laval (1883–1945), French politician, four times prime minister of France. He served twice in the Vichy regime, was found guilty of high treason, and was executed by firing squad.
4 Evelyn Nesbit (1884–1967), American chorus girl and model, one-time mistress of architect Stanford White.
5 Kahn* never became director of the Yale School of Architecture.
6 Harry S Truman (1884–1972), president of the United States from 1945 to 1952, traveled to Europe in 1956 where he received an honorary degree in Civic Law from Oxford University, met with Winston Churchill, and, on 21 June 1956, addressed a dinner of the Pilgrims of Great Britain in London. Lord Halifax (1881–1959) was the British Ambassador to Washington DC during the Second World War, staying until 1946.
7 Ernest Bevin (1881–1951), British trade union leader and Labour politician.
8 *The Listener*, a British weekly magazine that transcribed BBC talks. *The Englishness of English Art*, London: The Architectural Press, 1956 was written by the German-born Nikolaus Pevsner,* an expanded and illustrated version of the seven BBC radio talks he gave in 1955 as the "Reith Lectures". Pevsner was editor of the London-based *The Architectural Review* from 1943 to 1945.
9 Edmund Burke (1729–1797), Irish statesman, author, political theorist, and philosopher; William Pitt the Younger (1759–1806), a politician who became the youngest and the longest-serving British prime minister at the age of 24; Benjamin Disraeli* (1804–1881), Conservative statesman and literary figure, twice British prime minister.
10 Charles John Curran (1921–1980) was a broadcasting and television executive born in Dublin who grew up in Goldthorpe, a mining village adjacent to Bolton-on-Dearne, and was in the same class as Rowe at Wath Grammar School. An older Charles Curran (1903–1972) wrote for *The Spectator*, made regular TV appearances on *Free Speech*, and wrote frequent columns in the Sunday and evening press.
11 Arnold, Matthew, "Civilization in the United States", first published in *The Nineteenth Century*, no 23, April 1888, p 134.
12 Clement Richard Attlee (1883–1967), leader of the Labour Party from 1935 to 1955, prime minister from 1945 to 1951. Elevated to the peerage in 1955, Attlee oversaw legislation that transformed the United Kingdom into a welfare state. William Gladstone* (1809–1898), Liberal statesman who served as prime minister four times, declined an earldom and was not offered a peerage.

*To **Louis I. Kahn**, Architect, 1501 Walnut Street, Philadelphia, Pennsylvania*   *15 October 1956*   **035**

68 East Ninetieth Street, New York, N.Y.

Dear Louis,

I have been intending to write to you ever since I got a letter from you in March, but I suppose that I do have an infinite capacity for procrastination.[1] Short of writing I have been intending to phone but somehow that too has been continually postponed.

Anyway I was wondering if, between New Haven and Philadelphia, you are ever in New York, and if so whether some time we couldn't meet. I would very much enjoy doing so.

I have been around here for the last three months or so, generally relieved at having escaped from Texas, and working until a couple of weeks ago with John Hejduk* on that not very exciting competition for an old people's home.

I would like to hear from you—and I think John would too—sometime when you are in New York and have nothing else to do.

My phone number is TEMPLETON 1.3323.

Perhaps we could meet once again and have dinner together somewhere.

Sincerely,

Colin Rowe

---

1   On 22 March 1956, Kahn* wrote a seven-line letter to Rowe at the School of Architecture, University of Texas, Austin. "I have spoken to Dean Perkins", he said, "mentioning your knowledge and comprehension of history and modern design. I believe he needs a person like you. What he will do I don't know." He then noted, "Yale wants me back—the carpet is being rolled out. It's very tempting. I don't really know where I am."

036   *To **Morris Wells,** The School of Architecture, Cornell University, Ithaca, N.Y.*   *15 October 1956*

68 East 90th Street, New York, N.Y.

Dear Professor Wells,[1]*

   Peter Land tells me that he mentioned my name to you while he was up at Cornell recently and he pressed me to write to you when I saw him over the last week end.[2] He leads me to understand that you are not looking for any new addition to your faculty but would be interested in receiving an outline of my qualifications. He is himself so enthusiastic over both Cornell and Ithaca that he has communicated something of this to me and consequently I am only too happy to submit to you a brief biographical outline.

Perhaps though I had better expand it so as to cover the last few months when I have been working on finishing off a number of articles which I wish to publish shortly. I am at present teaching at the Cooper Union School of Architecture, and although I have not yet completed arrangements, plan to be working in New York until July 1957.

Should my qualifications prove of interest to you, as is suggested they might, perhaps we could arrange a meeting. I should anticipate it with great pleasure.

Sincerely yours

Colin Rowe

Colin Rowe

---

1   Morris Wells* (1902–1983) became head of Architectural Design at Cornell University in 1950 and the first chairman of the newly formed Department of Architecture in 1968.
2   Peter Land, a visiting critic brought to Cornell by Wells*, was a graduate of the Architectural Association, London, with a Master's degree in City Planning from Yale.

68 East 90th Street, New York, N.Y.

Dear Professor Wells,⋆

Thank you very much for your letter of October 18th.

I shall be delighted to meet you and Dean Mackesey at the time and at the place which you propose.[1] Since I have become involved in the Sydney Opera House Competition and since the designs are to be submitted on December 3rd I think that there is no danger of my forgetting the date![2]

May I say how much I do look forward to the meeting.

Sincerely yours,

Colin Rowe

1 Thomas W Mackesey (1908–1976), Dean of Cornell's College of Architecture, Art, and Planning from 1951 to 1960.
2 The international competition for Australia's National Opera House was launched on the 3 February 1956; closed on 3 December 1956; and the winner, the 38 year old Dane, Jørn Utzon, was announced on 19 January 1957.

68 East 90th Street, New York, N.Y.

Dear Professor Wells,[1]⋆

I hope that I have not delayed too long in replying to the proposal which you and Dean Mackesey made at our meeting on December 3rd; but thinking things over I have come to the following conclusions.[2]

1 It would be ungracious and irresponsible on my part to sever my connection with Cooper Union in the middle of the year.

2 It would be injudicious and extravagant on my part to come to Cornell in the middle of the year without some assurance that my appointment would extend beyond one semester.

3 It would be unwise on my part to come to Cornell with the rank of Instructor, however much I might be willing to do so, since having already been Assistant Professor for two years at the University of Texas, and having before that taught for three years as Design Critic at the University of Liverpool, I might well be putting both you and myself in a false position.

It is with considerable regret that I list these points. The first two are for me matters of crucial importance. The third is more a question of protocol to which I am advised that I should pay attention.

These are the circumstances and the difficulties which stand in my way of accepting an appointment for February. I suspect that they are almost insuperable ones. On the other hand I am most grateful for the offer which has been made and would be more than happy to accept a somewhat comparable one for which I could plan rather farther ahead. [...]

---

1   Morris Wells* (1902–1983), head of Architectural Design at Cornell University beginning in 1950; in 1968 he became the first chairman of the newly formed Department of Architecture.
2   Thomas W. Mackesey (1908–1976), dean of Cornell's College of Architecture, Art, and Planning from 1951 to 1960.

039   *To **Henry-Russell Hitchcock,** Smith College, Northampton, Mass.*   *15 October 1957*

68 East 90th Street, New York City

Dear Russell,

I supposed that I must have been too long in the South and become slightly torpid and equally fatigued because most of the way back from Northampton I found myself falling asleep and on getting back here I did go to bed at six o'clock and slept around until the following morning. This though is a tribute to your protracted stimulus over an elongated weekend which I did enjoy very much.

I was glad that after my being immured in Texas and your exposure to all the seductions of Latin America and Europe to discover that we did still agree on a good deal; and I have been wondering since, whether apart from the stimulus of travel, you really were immensely stimulated by any _new_ building which you have seen in the past two years or so. On the whole I am inclined to doubt whether you were.

I was sorry that I couldn't really interest you in the Transparency Gestalt line. I suspect that you were embarrassed by it, looked upon it rather as a passing obsession of the uncritical. Or maybe I am wrong.

On the way down from Northampton I got off the train in New Haven and walked around (without looking anyone up). You were of course quite right. Yale _is_ an anthology of Anglo-American architecture of the last 150 years or so. The only thing which it seems to lack are the equivalent of the ornamental villa and the Shavian house, but it could I think have been used to illustrate the composition business.[1]

Since you wanted to refer to it I'll send you a copy of that paper in the next day or so and I suppose that by the time your Pelican comes out one can have arranged to get it published.[2] My best wishes to Martin, to Wendell (whom I persist in wanting to call Barrett), my thanks to you for a charming and diversified weekend.

I do look forward to seeing you down here,

    Colin

---

1   "The composition business" refers to Rowe's essay "Character and Composition", written in 1953–1954, first published in *Oppositions,* no 2, January 1974, pp 41–60.
2   Hitchcock's* *Architecture, Nineteenth and Twentieth Centuries: The Pelican History of Art*, New Haven: Yale University Press, 1958 was published 16 years before Rowe's "Character and Composition".

122 Eddy Street, Ithaca, N.Y.

Dear Sandy,[1]

It would be so convenient if one kept letters. Then I should know exactly what I had said to you last time and also to be in some sort of position to find out exactly what you had said to me.

However, anyway, as you guess, I am writing because I am consumed with curiosity and various anxiety neuroses as to how my little cause is proceeding in your part of the world. I suppose that it is not now altogether premature to enquire and I feel tempted to do so because today is quite literally the first fine day which there has been here for a couple of months. There has been nothing but a miserable prostrating business of snow and melting snow and no day very cold. I don't know quite whether it has been as bad as an English winter. I feel tempted to believe that it is has not. But somehow after Texas and similar places one feels completely devastated devitalized.

Also this place breeds indifference. I think that I wrote and told Leslie that it was the liberal academy and all that that means.[2] I think that there is no need to dilate upon it. One lives the full horror of American relativism. Which is a little like being involved in one of those appalling arithmetical problems: if X is a leaky bucket which holds Y gallons of water escaping at the rate of Z pints per minute and A is a bath without a plug and the source of water is V meters away, how long will it take to get six inches of water into the bath and then maintain the level? Do I make myself clear? Somewhere Cyril Connolly does speak about the great American vacuum; and one must recognize it.[3] It demands to be filled. One is compelled to try to fill it. But then since it is equipped with an elaborate suction system unfortunately it never can be filled. It is like a man with a voracious appetite and an unappeasable dysentery. Really you ought to experience it.

In other words I feel exhausted rather than stimulated.

It was I think a painfully folksy little article that Peter Smithson wrote about his recent trip.[4] The tone was so *entre nous*, was it not?[5] And the things which he chose to get excited about—lavatories in Madison Avenue and all the rest of it. The thing is that if one were really to set out to explain the architecture of this country one ought to emphasize in the first case that Methodism dominates; and then, in the second, one should indicate that this, of all places, is where the eighteenth century survives. All else is virtually explained by these facts.

However I was amused to discover that apparently 'routine Palladianism' has been guaranteed a new lease of life by Louis Kahn.* 'Routine Palladianism', Miesian neo-classicism, Louis Kahn's neo-Beaux-Arts, Methodism, Thomas Jefferson, the Declaration of Independence and the doctrine of natural law—an explanation of American architecture today would have to concern itself with some obvious but difficult to analyze relationships in this area. I was interested for instance to hear that CLARIFICATION FOR CLARIFICATION'S SAKE had become an acceptable aim in Chicago, because frankly how can one set up any other? If the Zeitgeist fails one and one can no longer appeal to "the will of the epoch", if technology no longer arouses enthusiasm (and it never really did arouse much in the U.S.) what is left? And how can one justify what one is doing? By appeal to precedent—presumably of the 1920s? I take it this is one way out. But the Americans don't really like precedent so much as the English. And what then is left but some equivalent to Natural Law and—I suppose—Platonic forms? And if one is not convinced about either—then I suppose one has to be existentialist, in some way or other—about both.

Personally I see no other way of maintaining a reasonable level, and apropos of it I did come across rather a delightful little quotation in Pascal the other day—(one is obliged, you know, to read here).

"But what is nature? Why is custom not natural? I greatly fear that nature is itself only a first custom, as custom is a second nature."

"We need not feel the truth that law is but usurpation; it was introduced without reason, it has become reasonable; it is necessary to cause it to be regarded as authentic, eternal, and to conceal the beginning of it if we do not wish it to come soon to an end."[6]

Don't you think that this is rather cutting and also very apposite to a good many things at the present day? The Americans, when they are educated, are quite often motivated by this kind of disillusioned Whiggery. The English, I think, are not. And isn't this because they feel so safe? The angry young men and Peter Smithson and all the rest of it are surely just *The Yellow Book* turned inside out.[7] And how thoroughly they feel guaranteed in their traditionalism. Because in the end, although he doesn't know it and they certainly don't, behind them, like some vast combined father and mother image, eminently reassuring, there sits the Archbishop of Canterbury.

Please excuse this flappy little critical excursion. I leave it flabby because I believe you know perfectly just what I mean. These are the reasons why Lord Burlington and Dante Gabriel Rossetti are the patron saints of English art.[8]

However at the end of all this I do remain ridiculously eager to come and join you all.[9] One treads water here and one beats one's head against the sponge; so do please write and tell me how things are getting on. Or write and tell me if they are not. And please give my love to Muriel.[10]

Yours,

Colin

---

1 "Sandy": St John Wilson's* nickname.
2 Leslie Martin* (1908–2000), Director of the School of Architecture at Cambridge University.
3 Cyril Connolly (1903–1974), English intellectual, literary critic, and writer.
4 Smithson, Peter, "Letter to America", *Architectural Design*, March 1958. Smithson had visited the United States in fall 1957.
5 *entre nous,* French: between us; just between you and me.
6 Pascal, Blaise, *Pensées*, Paris: Flammarion, 1670. Translation unknown.
7 *The Yellow Book*, a quarterly illustrated literary periodical published in London and Boston from 1894 to 1897.
8 Richard Boyle, Third Earl of Burlington (1694–1753), English aristocrat and architect; Dante Gabriel Rossetti (1828–1882), English painter, poet, illustrator, and translator.
9 Rowe joined the faculty at the School of Architecture, Cambridge University, in fall 1958.
10 Muriel Lavender, St John Wilson's* wife.

041   *To Bernhard & Margaret Hoesli, Basel*   *April 28, 1958*

The Miller-Heller House,[1] 122 Eddy Street, Ithaca, New York

My dear Bernhard and Margaret,

I was delighted to get your postcard, but have been all this time replying to it because I simply did not have your address. I got it the other day from Werner Seligmann* in Austin.

As you see from the address I am at Cornell. I would have written before to tell you all about it if it weren't really too much. Also I didn't really want to write until I knew for sure what I would be doing next year. I am invited to stay here. Also I have had the expected invitation from Cambridge. On the whole it is easy to make up one's mind though I do have some misgivings. I cannot bear that moustachioed heartiness or that opinionated patronising refinement into which my compatriots constantly lapse. Still I do think that in Cambridge it is possible that some ideas might become articulated, whereas Cornell is altogether too much like banging one's head against a sponge. There is neither pleasure, pain nor profit attached to it.

So unless you plan shortly to return to the United States I do hope to see you soon. Maybe you will invite me to Basel. Maybe I can entertain you beneath the shadow of King's College Chapel.

Please do write and tell me how it has all been and what you plan to do. Have you been to Brou-en-Bresse for instance? Although I don't know why it is that I should be so eager about that place.[2]

It struck me the other day and I was going to write about it before I got your postcard, that a book on Corbusier as a city planner would be a very good idea. Nothing of this kind has been done. But what would you say about it? A moderately critical moderately enthusiastic survey. It's really an immense subject and with a reasonable text, a Zurich [publication might be expected] to have immense circulation. How would it be to collaborate? I think the material could be collected fairly easily and a summer—say the summer of next year—ought to establish the text.

Let me know what you think.

That's about all for the moment but please write soon.

My address I don't suppose will change to Cambridge until about the middle of August.

Hope to see you all soon,

Colin

---

1 In 1958 Rowe lived in one of the three visiting faculty apartments in Cornell's Miller-Heller House. See "Alvin Boyarsky: A Memory", Rowe, Colin, *As I Was Saying: Recollections and Miscellaneous Essays*, Alexander Caragonne ed, 3 vols, Cambridge, MA: MIT Press, 1996, vol 3, pp 331–340.
2 The Royal Monastery of Brou, built at the beginning of the sixteenth century by Margaret of Austria—its church in Flamboyant Gothic style—is located at Bourg-en-Bresse in central France.

3 Cambridge

1958–1961

Rowe taught at the University of Cambridge for four academic years, from the fall of 1958 through the spring of 1962, a time he later recalled as "the great folly of my life". From Cambridge, he regularly wrote to Alvin* and Elizabeth Boyarsky* in Ithaca, where Alvin studied regional planning at Cornell, warning them against moving to England and describing in detail his extreme dislike for the Cambridge School of Architecture and for the way of life that surrounded it.

Rowe's letters suggest that he had intended to stay in Cambridge only one year. He was still there in September 1959 when he wrote to Henry-Russell Hitchcock* in Massachusetts saying that he would have returned to Cornell already but current conditions were not favorable. "Certain complications have developed", he remarked, and "frankly the potential instability, the lack of guarantee, and all the ensuing politics, is something which after Texas I just can't bear."

Two years later, in fall 1961, he negotiated to return to Cornell as Visiting Critic in fall 1962. "Cambridge", he wrote in a December 1961 letter, "has raised no objections to my going [...]". When he arrived in Ithaca in September 1962, he accepted a three-year position at Cornell as Associate Professor and moved to Ithaca, NY.

[handwritten]

To **Alvin & Elizabeth Boyarsky**, Ithaca, N.Y.   *15 December 1958*   **042**

4a Castle Street, Cambridge, England

Dear Al and Elizabeth,

Thanks so much for your letter. I haven't changed my sentiments in the slightest. And I don't protest too much either. We all have to commit our follies. But for God's sake don't, don't, don't, don't come over here with the idea of staying a year or so.

My dear Elizabeth. It is a long time since you saw England in any other way than *en touriste*. You were visiting home [...] but in spite of that and although you didn't know—you were *en touriste*. Now the reality of the tourist is very different from that of the native—and maybe you have to come back here to learn it—as I have had to do.

If that is the case, there is no reason why I should attempt to dissuade you. But if it isn't please do accept the benefit of my experience. GO TO HONG KONG or VANCOUVER. Go to TOPEKA, KANSAS if you must—but don't seek a patriotic and sentimental martyrdom.

Saturday was the big day here for me. I was made M.A. (Cantab) in a ceremony which would surely have delighted any cultural anthropologist who might have been present. In the morning I was made a member of Queens.[1] They lunched, piled odd clothes on me and led me off like a living and acceptable sacrifice to the Senate

House. (Had there been tourists the tourist trade would surely have been stimulated by the sight. One felt like a quaint English custom.)

Once in the Senate House I began to feel slightly like Isaac being led up into the high mountain by his father and, since you never know what is likely to happen at these initiation ceremonies, I did begin to wonder if the roof of the building would be cleft in twain by an angel sent down in the nick of time to ward off the blow. However I was told that angels were only active in this way during full term and then I couldn't be told anymore since all was silent—the tribal magician had just come in. The tribal magician was all dressed in red and he sat himself down in a sort of Empire throne which looked as though it had been filched out of the Brighton Pavilion. On one side of him there was a formidable individual with a large silver club, on the other side two little men—one of whom did a sort of litany and the other made responses to it.

As things began to get worked up there was no doubt that the magic began to take effect—and finally an incantation began in which my own name appeared.

This was the sign. My sponsor gave me his right hand. I took it with my own right hand and we advanced up the building together—with the magician beginning to look more and more like the Grand Inquisitor as we approached.

Then some distance away the presentation began. There was more Latin—this time from my sponsor, and finally a slight kick upon the ankle, after which I prostrated myself (according to instruction) upon the floor. Then I raised myself, still kneeling; and putting my hands before me in an attitude of prayer I inserted them between the magicians knees. He pressed them slightly and a new incantation began—and then finally I caught a reference to the *spiritu sancto*, there was a squeeze of my hand, there was no doubt that the magic had worked.[2]

I rose, feeling slightly like a jelly. I stepped back, being careful not to get caught up in my gown. I bowed—I hope with all the decorum that the occasion demanded; and the exoteric part of the ritual was over. And apparently it was all over though I wasn't quite sure that there mightn't be something rather more arcane to follow.

So you see now I am part of a mystical body. I have been initiated, and I can enjoy the same sort of feelings as an American fraternity boy or a Trobriand islander. The sense of catharsis is quite extraordinary. Otherwise I would have written the day before yesterday.

Have I said enough? I think I have. I still think that the cold in this room is correlative with yesterday's ceremony, that the bad food, declining standards, almost Mexican incompetence are all connected with this obsessive passion for emphasising the sacramental bases of society. Because God knows although the bases of society are sacramental (and therefore in a sense these people are right), I would cheerfully declare that society was no more than a contract if only a little warmth would result. But even a powerful magician like Lord Adrian doesn't seem to be able to make warmth. He can make me a member of a mystical body—but then what's the point—if the non-mystical body is shivering around the knees?

So having experienced the laying on of the hands I still remain sceptical.

Obviously the magic hasn't quite taken.

Will try to find Nicholas a song book.

Give my love to people.

Have a nice Christmas.

    Colin

1 Queens' College, University of Cambridge.
2 *spiritu sancto*, Latin: by the holy spirit.

[handwritten]

To **Alvin & Elizabeth Boyarsky**, *Ithaca, N.Y.*   *9 January 1959*   **043**

4a Castle Street, Cambridge, England

Mes enfants,[1]

You know perfectly well how much my compatriots goad me into frenzy. Therefore you must (if the matter interested you) from time to time have meditated on why I wished to commit the unwarrantable folly of returning to live in their midst.[2] Then <u>why</u>, <u>why</u>, <u>why</u> didn't you tell me so? Why didn't you warn me that I should be subjecting myself daily to so interminable a sequence of minor trauma?

And of course this is just what I am doing? And the list is so many that I think I shall die of ulcers. Certainly I can't even begin to recite the half of it. But Michael knows it all—all of this world populated with variegated editions of Peter Self—some of them the *de luxe* kind with the majority, to be perfectly frank, just rather inferior paperbacks.[3] And all this becomes aggravated and exaggerated by the cold—and OH MY GOD----------THE FOOD.

Today the term began. And what a crowd these students are. There is scarcely a one amongst the lot that isn't an Inglese. And they do have bones in funny places. And they do look like odd balls of wool. And they do look like elderly bank clerks. And it can't be due to malnutrition. Or at least one can scarcely imagine it could be in the economic strata from which they most of them derive. But they can't eat sufficient meat. I'm sure they can't. And they work so hard at being little gentlemen and hardly at all at being students.

But the lethargic superciliousness of the upper class natives apart, I don't see how I'm ever to get warm. If you could feel my legs at the moment you would understand. It can't be colder in Japan. And how does one ever do any shopping when the shops open chiefly at improbable hours and simply to assemble a meal one has to trot around from place, and then from place to place in the same shop. Just don't talk to me about it. It just kills me.

So you see you really do, without knowing it, inhabit an island of the blest; and I'm sure you should become aware of it. But it was Proust, was it not, who said that '*les vrais paradis sont les paradis perdus*'.[4] And how right he was. Please for God's sake continue my campaign, Michael, to persuade Elizabeth NOT, NEVER to drag her family over here. The elegance, the style is all ancient. The present reality is neither stylish nor competent.

Hitoshi. I should have written to thank you for the kimono. Or at least I should have written to say that it had arrived. Please forgive me for not having done either. I owe you something for it. Well—Al has to send me a check for $25 or something of the kind and could you deduct it from this.

Tony.[5] I am sorry not to have seen you before I left. But everything was frenzied and hurried. Maybe I'll see you here sometime. You'll always be welcome. But maybe I won't. Because maybe you won't come or maybe I shall have gone. So perhaps I shall see you in New York.

Michael.[6] Thank you for the parcel and its miscellaneous contents. But could you write and tell me if I am still being flooded with book society and record club things. I hope like Hell that I'm not. But it's a little like trying to get the gas or the telephone disconnected. Things do get so aired (?). Also I don't know whether I've overstepped the mark or something. But since asking Al to get me a refrigerator I haven't heard a thing. Was I being tactless and demanding? Or is Al just looking like mad? Or did I write so much to him that it just becomes a dreadful chore to reply? I never do know about these things. Please let me know anyway.

Well that's about all. Perhaps my mood is just bad; but I would give a lot for the sight of some good neon. And though King's College Chapel is alright I would give it cheerfully away to anybody who could provide me with decent sandwiches at reasonable hours.

Pray for me. But not too hard. And remember me to Stuart.[7] And just shake Nicky's paw please the next time he comes around.[8]

Best love to you all,

Colin

---

1 *Mes enfants*, French: My children.
2 Rowe recently had returned to England to teach at the University of Cambridge after seven years in the US, the last months of which he had spent in Ithaca living in Cornell's Heller House along with the Boyarskys.*
3 Michael McDougall (1930–2007) lived in Heller House with Rowe and Boyarsky* from 1957 to 1958. Peter Self (1919–1999), social scientist, planning policy advocate, author of *Cities in Flood: The Problems of Urban Growth*, London: Faber and Faber, 1957.
4 *Les vrais paradis sont les paradis qu'on a perdus*, French: "The true paradises are paradises one has lost." From Proust, Marcel, *A la recherche du temps perdu*, vol 7, *Le Temps retrouvé*, Paris: Bernard Grasset, 1927.
5 Hitoshi and Tony, unidentified friends of Rowe in Ithaca.
6 Michael McDougall.
7 Stuart, unidentified friend in Ithaca.
8 Nicholas (b 1958), Alvin* and Elizabeth Boyarsky's* son.

044   *To Alvin & Elizabeth Boyarsky, Ithaca, N.Y.*   *14 April 1959*

10 Castle Street, Cambridge, England

Dear Al and Elizabeth,

How are you? The thesis?[1] Cornell? Nicholas?[2] I am told in these parts that Nicholas is too fashionable a name at the moment. So to avoid this kind of being in fashion some people I know here have called the child "Tristram". Isn't this rather sad—I mean in all ways—for it?

Nothing has happened of late to modify my feelings about this place. It is just tiresome. Noise of traffic, fatuous shops, dirty restaurants, woolly people, lack of hot water, expense, general aimlessness, appalling accommodation—I don't see why I should continue the list. But I do begin to realise what it must have been like in the Nineteen Thirties to have been unemployed. A lethargy descends so that it is as much as I can do to write this letter. It really is. I just want to fall into a coma so that I can forget about it all. I wouldn't like the coma to be fatal but I would like it to last for quite some time. I conceal my sentiments; but in spite of that the friendliness, the gregariousness of Cambridge is not exactly exhilarating. The vacation continues and, do you know, that since Monday of last week when I was in London, except for shopkeepers, I haven't spoken to a living soul. I find it hard to believe. But I decided just not to pick up the telephone and instead to wait until it rang. So I'm still waiting! And as you can guess I am also wondering whether I really can be as boring as all that.

From all this, what does one discern? One's real merits? Or the nature of Cambridge? I don't know. However I would have thought that in a live situation, simply as an indication of its liveliness, within a space of eight days something would happen that hadn't been entirely prompted by oneself.

Have you heard anything yet from Stanford I suppose you haven't.[3]

When are you coming here? Why?

If you do, and if I am not to be going there, I shall ask you to bring me one or two simple things.

Lots of love,

> *Colin*

---

1 Alvin Boyarsky's* Cornell thesis on Camillo Sitte.
2 Nicholas Boyarsky, Alvin and Elizabeth's son.
3 Stanford University.

To **Henry-Russell Hitchcock,** *Smith College Art Museum, Northampton. Mass.*   *19 September 1959*   **045**

5 Causewayside, Fen Causeway, Cambridge, England

My dear Russell,

I was so sorry to miss you when you were down here the other day, but I was in London and was rather hoping to get up there again earlier this week. However I didn't, so that I missed seeing you in both places.

Anyway what were your reactions to the Magic Box?[1]

To the pulpit from Santa Maria in Cosmedin? To the blackboard which has been Stijled by the Stijl?

To the English rushes? To the problematic core which tried, I think, to be Louis Kahn* and then got compromised by certain memories of Harvard in the later Forties because what else is it but a kitchen and bathroom which have in some way miscarried?

It is not, of course, all that important; and in any case I shall ask Michael, whom I find pleasantly catty about most things, just what you thought.[2]

As you see from the address I have not gone to Cornell; and the reasons are various: First of all, dragging oneself away is like trying to pull up a mandrake root; Secondly I have been told so often that I can't know my own mind as yet that I do begin to doubt whether I have any mind to know; And Thirdly, at the Cornell end, certain complications have developed. The present dean suddenly decides to resign in 1960.[3] And who is to be appointed one doesn't know. And frankly the potential instability, the lack of guarantee, and all the ensuing politics, is something which after Texas I just can't bear.

So here I am—at least for some time—and I suppose I shall make the best of it with certain regrets. The winter is hell (far worse than you could believe), the summer is exquisite, and the Anglican atmosphere continues to be suffocating so that one feels rather like the victim of some kind of cultural asthma. Far too often breathing is altogether too difficult. The insufferable privacy, the inverted turning in of everything, the morbid treasuring of the anomalous, the excessive pseudo-Gothic detritus—only principles of some kind or other can open it up—and the English are far too skeptical ever to assent to principles.

However all this has been said before and there is really no point in going on saying it. I just greatly regret that I shan't be in the position to drive over from Ithaca to Northampton. But there it is. I don't suppose that this is a sentence of death, and I shall always be able to go up to London and amuse myself buying mechanical furniture and other minor *objets de luxe* which I should never be able to afford in New York.

I don't know whether this is sufficient consolation. I doubt it. But I do think that I have to give England at least another two years try. Perhaps then one will love it and never ever be able to detach oneself. Or perhaps lots of things will turn up. Meanwhile there are few things that I should enjoy more than to go to Yale as visiting critic sometime in the Fall Semester of 1960 and I wonder if you could intimate to them that if they were interested I could probably be available. It would be a way somehow of coping with the situation in which one finds oneself. One could summon up enthusiasm for it.

Obviously this last request is the most important part of this letter and the rest is probably merely wrapping paper for it. I could provide more wrapping paper—but I think you know just what it would be like. Frankly, I would have loved to have seen you before you went off because the whole business of deciding not to go to Cornell was absolute hell. However, I do hope to see you next year—either here or there.

Love and best wishes,

> Colin

I hope too that the private hell of Northampton is not without relief.

> Colin

Sometime shortly I will write without ulterior purpose. I need to swamp someone or other with generalisations from time to time, and one can't swamp people here. They interpret it as criticism.

> Colin

1   Reference is to Alex Hardy and Colin St John Wilson's* 1958–1959 extension of the School of Architecture building behind 1 Scroope Terrace, Cambridge, UK.
2   Michael Jaffé (1923–1997), art historian and connoisseur, noted scholar of Rubens, and a Fellow of King's College, Cambridge, UK, since 1952.
3   Thomas W Mackesey was dean of Cornell University's College of Architecture, Art, and Planning from 1951 to 1960. He was succeeded by Burnham Kelly.*

046   *To **Elizabeth Boyarsky**, Eugene, Oregon*   *13 January 1960*

5 Causewayside, Fen Causeway, Cambridge, England

My dear Elizabeth,

I know exactly how you feel and am not at all in a good position to advise. The reason: I have just been over to Paris and on to La Tourette. *The Architectural Review* apparently decided that bygones were bygones. We had a feast of love. They asked me to do a critique of the building. Also they offered to pay the expenses of the visit. So naturally I went, stayed, saw—and it has all done me so much good. I feel increased. The building is eminently therapeutic. I am exhilarated. And consequently any advice which I have to offer will be coloured by my present state of mind and body.

O.K. you have to leave Eugene. I agree. I know just what it is like—a hole in the corner sort of place with all the worst qualities of New England minus cerebration plus that awful lost world sort of feeling that you get in the Pacific North West. It is not to be tolerated.

O.K. you could go to Cornell. Do think of it seriously. I know its defects—insufferable Rotarian tone and all the rest of it. But on the other hand it is a fairly solid institution. Also it might be possible to have something of a practice there. Not large—but the sort of thing Al might like.[1] The winter is obviously awful—but there would be the sabbatical every half dozen years or so and when you came over here you would have money, would be able to take an apartment in Florence or some other place and would be ENVIED. There would be politics. There are politics everywhere. There would be *faux bonhomie.*[2] There is *faux bonhomie* everywhere.

But of course, if all the time you were at Cornell you were to feel, not that you were living, but that you were just merely existing, then quite clearly something else is called for. So let's consider London. It is expensive. Not as much so as Paris—but a good deal more so than most American cities and I am inclined to think rather more expensive than New York. With Two Thousand a year you could just begin to get by. You wouldn't go to theatres. You wouldn't have a large apartment. It seems to be desperately easy to pay Fifteen Pounds a week for very little. Also it doesn't seem to be very hard to pay Seven Thousand for a 99 year lease on two bedrooms and a twenty four foot living room. On the other hand—though you don't want the great world, since you are so constituted that for relaxation and stimulus you require the illusion that the great world is just around the corner to be sniffed at—there is a great deal to be said for London which can certainly provide that illusion.

As to jobs in London. I suspect the Barlett to be a closed shop—I don't think Llewellyn Davies has too much of an opportunity there as yet also he is by way of being a bit of a statistician and a technocrat.[3] On the other hand the A.A. seems to be opening up a bit. At the moment though they are choosing a new principal so that I expect things will be some time sorting themselves out.[4] (Parenthetically: several people asked me why I didn't apply and though I found this flattering I didn't think there was a chance so that I haven't)—in five years time it might be a different matter—presuming that I am still around.

The A.A. would pay Al Twelve Hundred Pounds a year—which is not much. There would presumably be other sources of income. But the problem of course would be *entrée*. Thus it would have been a help to have been at Harvard—even more of a help to have been a student of Louis Kahn's.* Also for the A.A. Al should have some button down shirts, some rather Yalie clothes and some sort of vaguely American hair cut. With all that—supposing he could get in—he might go over rather big.

Myself—supposing I stay in this country—I am rather interested in the A.A. and am going up next week to give a talk to the fourth year students about their city planning scheme. Curiously, by now, though I don't know the institution, I do seem to know almost the entire faculty and I'll let you have a letter sometime soon as to the lie of the land.

But the big question about England of course is: "How much money do you have to make an establishment?" I don't think that I need press this point.

As to Vienna or a year somewhere in Europe: this would be a way of getting into England. You would acquire an agreeable international coloration and so on. But I think it would be rather expensive and really only to be considered if you could do it subsidised by some institution.

As to me: I've got over the worst of my culture shock. I could quite easily stay here and if I did I should love it if you came. But I should like to go into practice some time, I should like to have someone to practice with, I feel a certain rapport with your directions... etc. I also realise the limitations of the U.S. The New York area and the Bay Region are the tolerable situation.... Obviously one would accept offers from Yale, Princeton, Columbia, Berkeley... but they would have to be good and permanent. Also, given the right colleagues, frankly I don't think that I should find Ithaca too hard to take.

So that is approximately my advice. I don't really think it helps much. But I did get a letter from John Hejduk★ the other day who seems to have been having a hell of a time in New York and who I suspect rather regrets having left Cornell.

Seriously I think that unless Eugene is absolutely intolerable or unless there is the offer of something firm from elsewhere I would give it one more year. That you know was your advice to me. O.K., you can't stay there and maybe you can't stay in the U.S.; but coming back to England you don't want just to have to slum along. A little more money so that you could buy a house without difficulty would be very agreeable. Also within a few months I think that things might change for myself. Apparently I am no longer a foreigner here.

> *Colin*

P.S. This is if you decide that Ithaca is also out of the question. But if you think you can take the place for a few years I should take steps to transfer there. Don't you think?

P.P.S. I'm afraid I am confused and not very helpful

> *Colin*

1   Elizabeth's husband, Alvin Boyarsky★ (1928–1990).
2   *fausse bonhomie*, French: false geniality.
3   Richard Llewelyn-Davies (1921–1981), professor of architecture at the Bartlett, University College London, from 1960 to 1969.
4   William A Allen (1914–1998), principal of the Architectural Association from 1961 to 1966.

047   *To Alvin & Elizabeth Boyarsky,*
School of Architecture & Allied Arts, University of Oregon, Eugene, Oregon   *25 September 1961*

5 Causewayside, Fen Causeway, Cambridge, England

Dear Elizabeth and Al,

Am just back three days ago from the summer. A long and agreeable voyage through Holland, Germany, Switzerland, Italy and France lasting exactly thirteen weeks. A result is that I couldn't really feel better than I do and having got back here I feel that for the moment I am just arrived in simply another station of the journey. How long this will last I don't know. The old Cambridge miasmas will be creeping up any time now so that while I have a tolerably objective view of things I want to take this opportunity of writing.

First of all I would like to know what you are thinking of doing at the end of this academic year. That will have made three years in Eugene, Oregon which I imagine might be enough for anybody. Ideally then I take it that you are going to leave. But where for? Toronto? Montreal? Ithaca, N.Y.? London?

I ask these questions because sometimes I do think that it would be nice if we all happened to gravitate to the same place and since one only apparently gravitates by planning I am curious to know what—if any—are your plans?

As for me I know now how pretty definitely that I shouldn't have stayed around here two years ago. Since then nothing substantially has changed for the better, I still earn a pittance. I am still not a fellow of a college. I am—probably—as an Americophile— never likely to be viable in these parts. Nor has the school much changed for the better. There is still no organisation, no leadership, no staff meetings. And the myth that the Cambridge School of Architecture is the great white hope of England will soon be getting around to looking a little threadbare.

That is the situation in which I find myself. I am—for the present not in the slightest bit emotional about it. I only know—but now absolutely certain—that in the next few months I am going to have to act—that unless something very exceptional happened, to stay here after the summer of 1962 would be an act of frivolous procrastination which even I couldn't justify to myself.

I look at the possibilities:

i.   The A.A. Possibly good as regards ones colleagues. Also one is placed in a metropolitan and therefore a prominent situation. All this could be useful. But—I am not exactly, I think, *persona grata*[1] in Bedford Square. The powers are still a little too empirical and a little too welfare state in their orientation to be willing to tolerate what they surely regard as a subversive formalist line. Other English situations. Frankly I think there are none.

ii.   The so-called Commonwealth. Has become a little restricted and after one has really looked at it, can be narrowed down to Toronto and McGill. Michael Hugo-Brunt who was here in June on the day that I left for Italy offered his services at Toronto but scarcely succeeded in making it sound very enticing.[2]

iii. The U.S. For practical purposes surely succeeds in reducing itself to the East Coast and San Francisco. I could canvas Berkeley but would it be worth while and would it be a first choice? And on the East Coast what does one have? Pratt and such places? To exchange Cambridge for institutions so slight would presumably be a major act of [...] Harvard? A closed shop. M.I.T.? Bush-Brown* visited me in the summer.[3] For what reason I don't know. Perhaps he was smelling. He is I take it an accomplished politician. He is probably a little frightened of me. Possibly I could fly a kite in that direction. Yale? I understand that Rudolph is not well disposed.[4] I imagine that Mince Soully would probably not want to have me around.[5] I have discovered that several [times]—and since there have been no overtures from New Haven I don't think that there are likely to be. Columbia? In spite of all the conditions? which Colbert has been distributing I would believe that a position with tenure at Columbia would be very worthwhile indeed.[6] Princeton? Again would surely be just about as good as things are likely to be. And Cornell? There one is told an overture could be made with probably very good results. And from which one learns that Henry Ziger is anxious to withdraw in the direction of Stanford.

One runs over the list:

The A.A. has to receive many question marks. Berkeley v. The East is a major choice. And then in the East the issue would seem to narrow itself to M.I.T., Columbia, Princeton, Cornell. My preference would run: i. M.I.T, Princeton. ii. Columbia, iii. Cornell. But my possibilities of *entrée* would run i. Cornell, ii. M.I.T. iii. Princeton, Columbia.

1 *persona grata*, Latin: an acceptable or welcome person.
2 Michael Hugo-Brunt (1924–1988).
3 Albert Bush-Brown* (1926–1994), a PhD in architecture from Princeton (1958), author of *Louis Sullivan*, New York: George Braziller, 1960, and coauthor with John Burchard of *The Architecture of America: A Social and Cultural History*, Boston: Little, Brown & Co, 1961. He was president of the Rhode Island School of Design from 1962 to 1968.
4 Paul Rudolph (1918–1997), dean of the Yale School of Architecture from 1958 to 1964.
5 "Mince Soully": Vincent Scully Jr* (b 1920), professor of Art and Architectural History at Yale.
6 Charles Ralph Colbert (1921–2007) became dean of Architecture at Columbia in 1960, reshaping the curriculum to emphasize city and social planning rather than design.

048 *To **Morris Wells**, School of Architecture, Cornell University, Ithaca, N.Y.*   *10 November '61*

5 Causewayside, Fen Causeway, Cambridge, England

Dear Murray,[1]

I am writing to you at the same time as I am writing to Dean Kelly* because I am not entirely certain to which of you I should be addressing myself.[2] Should it be to you whom I do know or to him whom I do not? I am unaware of the protocol. However it is not a complicated question which inspires the dilemma. Quite simply I am writing because I wish to enquire what possibilities there might be of my returning to teach at Cornell.

As I believe you know very well I was immensely stimulated by the year which I spent in Ithaca. I also think that you have some pretty good idea how, at least two years ago, I felt about Cambridge; and I think that all that I need now say is that my judgment continues unchanged.

All the same, when I stayed on here in 1959 I do think that my decision might very well have been the right one.[3] Certainly it was a decision which has distressed me more or less continuously since. But I was told by so many people that after a mere twelve months in this country I could not know my own mind or that I was making a wholly emotional choice that I am still compelled to recognize that a choice made under these circumstances might have been one which lacked stability.

However, after a lapse of two years one emphatically does know one's own mind; one continues to recognize the area of the world and the style of the establishment in which one's capacities can best be employed; and, since it would be frivolous to procrastinate any longer, one feels compelled to write.

I think that perhaps I have said enough. I have no need to try to sell myself to you. And since further padding to his letter is not required I shall only conclude by sending my best wishes to Ruth and by expressing a hope that my question is not too much of a surprise.

Sincerely,

Colin

COLIN ROWE

1 A misinterpretation of Morris Wells'* nickname, "Morrie".
2 Burnham Kelly* (1912–1999), dean of the Cornell College of Architecture, Art and Planning from 1960 to 1971.
3 After a year teaching at Cambridge, Rowe decided to remain there rather than return to teaching in the US.

5 Causewayside, Fen Causeway, Cambridge, England

Dear Bush,

Since seeing you in the early summer I have been most of the time a tourist. I left for Italy in late June and got back here rather more than a month ago completely packed with miscellaneous and topographical experience. However I don't intend to talk about all this. We are now halfway through our eight-week Michelmas Term; there is at present something of a hiatus so far as the school is concerned; and, since in mid-December I shall become a tourist again—this time a Sicilian expedition, I am using the temporary opportunity to catch up with correspondence. To be perfectly brief about the nature of this letter: I would like your advice.

Someone recently described a move from Oxford to Cambridge as being like leaving a neglected rose garden for a horticultural research station in the wilds of Siberia; and though this is perhaps a little too neat to be accurate I thought you might appreciate something of its cogency. After all when you were here for a mere two days you did make it quite apparent that you had intuited a good deal; and for these reasons I think it would be quite gratuitous for me to enlarge on local problems, the status of architecture in this university, the collegiate 'system', etc. It is simply enough here to state what you already know: that I can scarcely regard myself as being very active at Cambridge and that I am probably a little too much affected by some trans-Atlantic virus to be as viable as I might wish.

Under the circumstances what does one do?

To some extent I have already forestalled your reply. I have written to Burnham Kelly* at Cornell.[1] But since there has as yet been no time for an exchange of letters, let us say that supposing his answer to be in the negative what sort of institution should then be considered approachable and what should be the strategy of approach.

I am not by these questions trying to put you on the spot. Nor am I making devious overtures to M.I.T. Obviously I should be interested if M.I.T. were to show interest. However I am not primarily trying to elicit that sort of response. Instead, quite simply, as a possible marketable commodity, I am anxious to have some sort of report on the condition of the market and the techniques of sale.

Thus I presume that it would not be clever, however easy it might be, to exchange Cambridge for someplace out in the boondocks. I further presume that, for a variety of reasons, it is better to be asked than to have to ask. And accordingly I deduce the field is not really extensive and that any transaction to be successful requires either luck or some considerable exercise of our diplomatic skill.

Have I said enough? I have given you the substance on a problem and wonder if you could think about it a little for me; and since I hate, myself, being asked to do this sort of thing I can only conclude by adding apologies to my best wishes for you all.

Sincerely,

Colin

COLIN ROWE

P.S. I think that shortly you may be hearing from Peter Eisenman.* He is anxious to teach and most probably will be coming back to the States next year. I am of course prejudiced in his favor—I traveled in Italy with him during the summer and shall visit Sicily with him at Christmas; but even if he were not a personal friend of mine I should still feel obliged to recommend him to you very strongly. It is a general opinion here that he is a most gifted, patient and exacting teacher. He came here simply as a graduate student. When he leaves he will for two years virtually have been running the first year with more success than might have been thought possible. May I simply risk the slight officiousness of this postscript because, if he writes, he will presumably not be able to say what a considerable impact he has made.

---

1 See Rowe's letter to Kelly* dated 14 November 1961 (p 134 in this volume).

050 To **Burnham Kelly**, *College of Architecture, Cornell University, Ithaca, N.Y.*   *14 November 1961*

5 Causewayside, Fen Causeway, Cambridge, England

Dear Dean Kelly,*

There is some confusion in my mind as to whether I should be addressing myself to you whom I do not know or to Maury Wells* whom I do. I am therefore—since I am not certain of the correct procedure—writing separately to you both; and, while I trust that you will be able to excuse the lack of any introduction, I think that it might be best if I were to open this letter by stating quite simply its business. Briefly: I am writing to enquire what possibilities there might be of my returning to teach at Cornell.

From my point of view in the year 1957–58 which I spent in Ithaca was an extremely successful one. I found the juries stimulating, the students plastic, the school animated. I was able to appreciate a sufficiency of colleagues; I could feel the presence and the support of definite institutional rhythms; and, above all I was in a position to believe that I was making some form of worthwhile contribution.

These are among the positive reasons which impelled my enquiry and no doubt they will permit inferences to be drawn as to the nature of negative ones which are less easy to specify with discretion. What were my initial reactions to Cambridge might possibly have been communicated to you by Tom Mackasey.[1] Perhaps they were hasty; and, because they involved certain repercussions at Cornell, I have not wished to write further until I could be convinced that my impressions were something more than mere intuition. But over the past two years, while I have deferred taking up this matter my judgments as to this establishment have not been subjected to any very radical change; and therefore I think it might not be any breach of confidence if I were not to assert that the system here is one which tends to debilitate both teacher and student by leaving neither of them very fully used.

This said, I suspect that I have concluded almost all which, at the present, can usefully be advanced and I experience a certain hesitation in speaking about matters which may be out of place. Perhaps, since I appear to be some sort of composite of architect, critic and historian, it might not be presumptuous of me to propose that I would always prefer to be active simultaneously in two or three of these areas; but as to what I might contribute, I believe that either Maury Wells⋆ or John Hartell⋆ could indicate this without the difficulties and embarrassments which confront myself. There is, I hope, much which might be discussed in a subsequent correspondence; but, while I would greatly value an exchange of letters, I would prefer to await your reply rather than now seem to anticipate it by irrelevant or premature digression.

Sincerely yours,

Colin Rowe

Colin Rowe

---

1   Thomas W Mackesey was dean of Cornell's College of Architecture, Art, and Planning from 1951 to 1960. Burnham Kelly⋆ succeeded him as dean.

To **Morris Wells**, *College of Architecture, Cornell University, Ithaca, N.Y.*   *5 December 1961*   **051**

5 Causewayside, Fen Causeway, Cambridge, England

Dear Morrie:

Many thanks for your letter of November 22nd which reached me here on Tuesday of last week. My reactions to it were immediate. I was stimulated both by its content and its tone; I appreciated its promptness; and I have only delayed replying until I could have some opportunity of talking over its question with Leslie Martin⋆ here.

The first opportunity I had to do so that occurred today and I can now report that Martin was highly accommodating. In principle he felt that the idea of my coming over as Visiting Critic next Fall was a completely reasonable one; and he also considered that, in practice, there was a sufficient time available to arrange matters so that my absence from Cambridge need not raise administrative problems. In other words there were no difficulties presented; and, since I was provided with a verbal assurance that I might go ahead to accept your offer, I can now feel justified in saying that I do look forward with considerable enthusiasm to seeing you in Ithaca towards the end of August or early in September.

I hope that this is an adequate answer to your proposal. But it would not be an adequate reply to your letter if I were not to conclude by saying how very conscious I am of the efforts and the generous adjustments which you and the Dean have made on my behalf.[1] I really am extremely grateful for these; and, if I simply add that my ultimate sentiments about coming to Cornell remain as previously expressed, I hope that you will not misconstrue this remark. It means that I accept with very great pleasure what you have kindly made available; but that I still wish to keep advertised my initial intention. I think that it is probably not out of place for me to say this.

Sincerely and with many thanks,

Colin

COLIN ROWE

---

1   Thomas W Mackesey was dean of Cornell's College of Architecture, Art, and Planning from 1951 to 1960.

*To **Thomas Howarth**, School of Architecture, University of Toronto, Canada   5 December 1961*

5 Causewayside, Fen Causeway, Cambridge, England

Dear Tom,[1]

Many thanks for your letter of November 14th. I can't tell you what an agreeable surprise it was; and I have only delayed replying until I could give some kind of concrete answer.

At the moment I can report the following: I shall not, as far as I at present know, be returning to North America in the near future; but I have received an invitation to spend the Fall Semester as Visiting Critic at Cornell; and, since Cambridge has raised no objections to my going, I do now hope to be not too far from Lake Ontario for a few months at the end of '62.

The idea of a lecture or lectures which you propose seems to me to be a very good one and I should be delighted to take up your invitation. May I write you further about it when my possible movements become a little more articulate in my mind?

My recollections of your visit to Austin in 1956 are quite clear by the way. Like other people who went through that town you constituted an event. You were some kind of punctuation of existence. Therefore can I send my best wishes to your wife.

Sincerely,

Colin

COLIN ROWE

---

1   Thomas Howarth* (1914–2000) was director of the School of Architecture at the University of Toronto from 1958 to 1974.

4
Cornell at First

In December 1961 Rowe accepted a one-semester appointment as Visiting Critic at Cornell for Fall, 1962. He moved to Ithaca from Cambridge and in September 1962 signed a three-year contract with Cornell that made him associate professor. Shortly before his move from England, John★ and Pat Miller★ had visited him. From Ithaca, Rowe wrote them of his satisfaction with his new setting, noting that there he had "everything that might have conspired to make Cambridge entirely acceptable—had it been obtainable there."

In 1963 Rowe initiated an Urban Design Program for graduate students at Cornell. "I really have got a very hot shot urban design thing going", he wrote Alvin Boyarsky★ in March 1965. "It's entirely empirical, pragmatic and accommodating. It is totally devoid of theory." Enthusiastic about the program, he was ambivalent about Cornell's school of architecture in general. In early 1966, he interviewed for the position of principal of the Architectural Association in London but was not offered the job. In 1965–1966 Rowe led his Cornell students in a design for the waterfront of Buffalo, New York. In 1969, he and a group of new students exhibited that work in Buffalo while completing a competition entry for urban renewal in Harlem. In 1967, though the letters make no mention of it, he wrote a review for the *The New York Times* of Robert Venturi's *Complexity and Contradiction* and Reyner Banham's★ *The New Brutalism*, two books seminal to architectural theory, both published in 1966, the year after Le Corbusier's★ death. And during this time, he wrote numerous memorandums to Burnham Kelly,★ dean of Cornell's College of Architecture, Art and Planning, formalizing his convictions regarding the program and noting ways to improve it.

German architect OM Ungers★ was appointed chairman of Cornell's School of Architecture in 1969, an appointment supported by Rowe, who had been, by this time, a full professor for three years. The semester that Ungers arrived at Cornell, Rowe went to Rome as resident at the American Academy. In fall 1970, he returned to Rome from where he wrote Pat Miller★ that he was not "all that turned on by this place or indeed by this town, [Rome]", which, "at the moment, contrives to look just like a junk heap of old warehouses.... If you sit down to dinner in any piazza you might just as well be eating in a garage."

53 *To **John** & **Pat Miller**, Stirling Mansions, Canfield Gardens, London*   *12 November 1962*

107 Cayuga Heights Road, Ithaca, N.Y.

Carissimi:

Panofsky, you may be interested to learn, has just delivered to the American Philosophical Society a disquisition entitled: *THE IDEOLOGICAL ANTECEDENTS OF THE ROLLS ROYCE RADIATOR.*[1] He argues, I am told, that the radiator—designed in 1906—is in reality a temple front—symbol of stability, permanence, etc. Then apparently he directs attention to the little figure standing up top (added in 1911) which he finds to be at variance (phantasies of movement, etc) with the implications of its base—and then all this he goes on to generalise and illustrate as indicative of a deep and permanent lesion in the English psyche. You are naturally fascinated? I am sure that what I have said so far makes you as eager to read it as I am and, therefore, in case you can't wait, as soon as I can come across copies I'll let you have one. Meanwhile—

I recently became installed in what I think should be called one of the *dependences* of a small, I believe French, fake chateau, erected c. 1923. You would probably like it. The planning is elaborately *en suite*.[2] The spaces are positively corrugated with axes. And the whole thing, in an innocent like way, aspires to be about as Palladian as you can get. One suspects the hand of some recently graduated architectural student who was determined to remain corrupted. It has that didactic, dogmatic quality and as a result I have a marble floored bathroom, five French windows, a terrace, a T-shaped living room 28 by 20—in fact everything that might have conspired to make Cambridge entirely acceptable—had it been obtainable there.

From here to the school of architecture is about a three minute drive or a ten minute walk. The walk is to be preferred but should not be indulged in too often. A tree lined road. Arrival on the top of an escarpment. Miscellaneous views of cataracts. A bridge. The ascent of a ravine. Sundry waterfalls etc. All this and with the Palladian villa left behind is apt to elicit Wordsworthian states of mind and to leave one feeling a bit like a Chinese mandarin and a bit like a British Prime Minister.

But as you see such establishment requires support. I don't mean that it's expensive—but it seems to require parties and the question is For whom? And it also seems to require furniture and the question is What? This is just to remind you that a chesterfield is rather a pressing necessity in this particular setting and I would be delighted <u>some</u> day to hear about one.[3]

However I am glad that you didn't like Greece. And though I didn't think Athens was absolutely a slum—I couldn't at Easter summon up the enthusiasm to stick it out for even 24 hours.

That's all for the moment. I am exhausted but felt that I might write just this. Am glad about the Hampstead apartment. Would love to stay but at the moment, 9.30 p.m., am just about to stagger in to bed—overcome no doubt by all the beauties of nature and what not.

Love,

    Colin

---

1 Erwin Panofsky (1892–1968), professor emeritus of the history of art, Institute for Advanced Studies, Princeton University; see "The Ideological Antecedents of the Rolls Royce Radiator", *Evening Lecture*, 8 November 1962, *Proceedings of the American Philosophical Society 107*, no 4, August 1963, pp 273–288. Republished in Panofsky, Erwin, *Three Essays on Style*, Cambridge, MA: MIT Press, 1997.
2 *en suite*, French: in succession; in a series or set.
3 The Millers* had been storing Rowe's "chesterfield" since he left Cambridge.

To ***Alvin & Elizabeth Boyarsky***, London   *15 January 1963*   **054**
107 Cayuga Heights Road, Ithaca, N. Y.

Dear Elizabeth:

Dear Al:

I was delighted to have your Christmas card because I had been wondering what your address might be and had only just lately arrived at the conclusion that I might reasonably address myself to the Bartlett. But my mental processes, sometimes, really are turgid.

Anyway I have an admirable apartment. It is large, quasi-Palladian, quiet. It is everything that Cambridge was not. And usually I walk to the school which happens to be about ten minutes away.

The school is not excessively stimulating—but since one never expected it to be so—one isn't seriously disappointed by this condition. If one were to analyse it one would discriminate three particular groups. There are the Academics, Morris Wells* would be the archetypal representative of these. Then there are the Anti-Academics. These are determinists, pragmatists, City planners. Finally there are the Neo-Academics. These comprise ex-Texans, miscellaneous juveniles and other representatives of the disaffected.[1] These three groups may be said to be incipient rather than crystallized; and obviously each is a little complicated by the relations of its different members with members of the other two groups. The Dean is—could it be otherwise?—basically an Anti-academic.[2] But the Academics are entrenched and the neo-Academics enlist his respect, and though a politician he is a nice guy—the students' friend and all that—so you get the picture?

Maybe Burnham will ultimately have his way. Does it sound like Llewellyn Davies?[3] He will have his way by a progressive enlargement of the faculty which will soon be so large as to form a mob—there are nearly fifty already—and most of his appointments will be of his persuasion, people involved in communications theory, theory of games, various forms of statistical analysis, in other words involved with definable activities, the sort of activities which [... missing page].

This summer I am sorry that I got your letter to Vienna too late to be able to do anything about it. Otherwise I would have done. Vienna is a so-so place. Far less grand than you would be disposed to imagine. A bit of an impoverished Amsterdam that a long way back decided to assume the Imperial role. The Hofburg is not very big. Nor is Schonbrunn. The Ring is not Paris. All the same it's a moderately sympathetic place to find oneself <u>and</u> both there and in Germany with a very little effort I think that you <u>could</u> put together quite a significant library for very little money of important 1920-ish and earlier publications. However Wagner (Otto) will probably send you up the wall.[4]

Would love to come to the Tuscan hills next summer but am not quite sure whether I can be able. There is a charter flight—I suppose several of them— round trip for $240—which is cheap enough; and I am half inclined to put my name down. However would also like some money and if I teach summer school here I <u>shall</u> find myself in the possession of another $3,500 which would be gratifying.

That's about all I have to say. Let me hear soon. Give my love to Bob (Maxwell)* if he is prepared to accept it. Tell me when you are coming back. Let me know if you think of coming back here.

Love best wishes and so on,

   Colin

P.S. Many, many thanks for the telegram to the *FLANDRE* in August. It was terribly nice of you and I have been going to write ever since to say so.[5]

1   The ex-Texans were Lee Hodgden,* Werner Seligmann,* and John Shaw; the miscellaneous
    juveniles presumably included Alan Chimacoff, Tom Schumacher,* Roger Sherwood, and
    Fred Koetter.*
2   Burnham Kelly.*
3   Richard Llewelyn-Davies (1921–1981), professor of architecture at the Bartlett School,
    University College, London, from 1960 to 1969.
4   Otto Wagner (1841–1918), Viennese architect.
5   The SS Flandre was the trans-Atlantic liner on which Rowe returned to the US after a
    summer in Europe (1962).

To **Pat Miller,** Stirling Mansions, Canfield Gardens, London   12 August 1963   **055**

107 Cayuga Heights Road, Ithaca, New York

My dear Pat:

Was delighted to have your letter. I got it in a mood when I was feeling rather more like Stendhal at Civita Vecchia than Gibbon at Lausanne.[1] Naturally it dispersed the mood. Everyone here, of course, has been captivated and enthralled by the English scandals.[2] You could have a *success à feu* just by paying a visit and making in-group gossip—or appearing to do so.[3] But it is all mildly entertaining as it seems to be compelling some kind of a revision of the American image of England. Trollope is down and Hogarth-Smollett-*Gin Lane* is up with the perennial wickedness of London now proclaimed.[4] However, though they like quite a bit to be told that London is bad-bad, bad-bad in its mere ideological aspects doesn't gratify them greatly and so for instance over the Queen of Greece affair their reactions were painfully sniffy and depressing.[5] The trouble, one supposes, is the ingrained—absolutely ingrained—American respect for authority. Sometime back *The New York Times* commented that the English had a tremendous preference for the *de facto* over the *de jure*.[6] Which is no doubt sufficiently true. But the Americans—who always always prefer the *de jure*—still do have the dreary habit of looking at all the facts so long as they are sufficiently extra-territorial and Byzantine as in some way legally established. And therefore Madame Thingummy in Viet Nam and all the rest of it become somehow just as valid and viable as the Declaration of Independence.[7] All no doubt—possibly or possibly not—very interesting. But I am still sorry that I missed the picture of the Duchess of Argyll in full coronation regalia sitting on the head of a naked Duncan Sandys.[8]

Actually at the moment life is hell. The reasons for this are not very complicated. I was left a couple of Siamese kittens (couldn't refuse) about two weeks ago. They are charming animals. They are called Per Mit and Per Suade. But the result of it all is that I live in a state of siege. The larger part of this apartment is given over to them. I exist, exhausted by it all, behind closed doors. I am trying to get rid of them—desperately. I try to manoeuvre the sentimental. But all that seems to happen is that while I try to soften people up by getting them drunk the animals just get excited with the abundance of admirers. Which all makes one feel like a rather ineffective procurer.

What else happens? I haven't been down to New York since the end of May. I occasionally buy a piece of gruesome nineteenth century mechanical furniture. Bought a superb cast iron shaving stand the other day. Much *terribilità*.[9] It has rather Crimean overtones or it might be the sort of thing that Victor Emmanuel took with him for using at Magenta and Solferino.[10] It is a bit dilapidated but has lots of presence as is also one of those chairs which used to stand on the railway stations in India for the use of British officials only, which I found the other day. And then in addition to these diversions I receive a steady dribble of Cambridge students doing the grand tour for whom I lay on the standard trip of the local waterfalls!!![11]

I look forward to Neave and would like if possible to use him as a minor camel but I hesitate a bit partly because I don't know what he could bring because I don't know whether he intends to come by air or sea.[12] If he comes by air he couldn't bring anything except perhaps cheese of which there is no abundance in N.A. But how is he coming?

It is so long since I wrote that I forgot to say that back in the beginning of April I did see the Corbusier building at Harvard.[13] It's much the best building there and is so nice because it's not slick and bitsy. There is, as John probably knows, a tendency in Cambridge, Mass. to write if off as a piece of expensive trivia or a French joke at America's expense. However....

At this stage when I thought that I had exhausted all possible topics I just got a letter— the post here is always in the afternoon—with a Como postmark from P.D.E. to tell me that he has married Christopher Cornford's American niece.[14] Somehow I almost expected as much. Anna—reliable antenna, surely a whole meteorological station in herself—had sniffed an inference.[15] And it was all very quiet with only the Eardleys, the Wellses,* the Hodgkinsons, the Wrights,* the Redpaths and Christopher's brother and sister in law, which I must say does begin to sound like quite a party. I'm sure it's all a good thing and I shall write congratulations as soon as I have finished this. Meanwhile—the thought does strike me: I wonder what sort of mileage I could get out of the Siamese if I converted them into a wedding present? Are they not part of the basic equipment for any up and coming *jeune ménage*?[16]

To conclude: herewith find a CHECK (dollars) to pay Beazer. And thanks so much for the chair business. Will not shift any furniture over here as yet. (It's costing me SEVENTY FIVE POUNDS to move books from Cambridge to the pier in N.Y.C.)

Lots of love and all that sort of thing. Will see you next summer. Am badly in need of several evenings really bitchy conversation. Am suffering maybe just a bit because everybody is so nice.

Tell John to write sometime if he can face the strain.

Hope the Palazzo Pitti was fine.

ARRIVEDERCI,

    Colin

---

1 Stendhal (1783–1842) once served as consul at Civitavecchia, a town he despised. Gibbon wrote of his "first emotion of joy on recovery of my freedom" after completing the last volume of *The Decline and Fall of the Roman Empire*. See Rowe's letter to Roger Conover* dated 2 August 1994 (p 412 in this volume).

2 The Profumo Affair and the Duke and Duchess of Argyll's widely reported divorce case.

3 *succès à feu*, French: blazing success.

4 Anthony Trollope (1815–1882), Victorian novelist; William Hogarth (1697–1764), painter, printmaker, and cartoonist, whose *Gin Lane* print supported the Gin Act of 1751; and Tobias Smollett (1721–1771), Scottish poet and novelist.

5 Frederica of Hanover (1917–1981), Queen of Greece whose state visit to London in 1963 was met by massive rioting.

6 *de facto* over the *de jure*, Latin and English: "the factual" over "the legal".

7 Madame Thingummy" refers to Trân Lê Xuân (1924–2011), who assumed the *de facto* role of first lady of South Vietnam from 1955 to 1963.

8 The Duchess of Argyll had been photographed with a naked man who was presumed to be Duncan Sandys.

9 *terribilità*, Italian: awesomeness.

10 Victor Emmanuel II (1820–1878), king of Sardinia from 1849 to 1861 and first king of a united Italy; commanded Piedmontese troops in the Battles of Magenta and Solferino against Austria.

11 Ithaca is noted for its scenic gorges and abundance of waterfalls.

12 At Rowe's suggestion, Neave Brown (b 1929), who had studied at the Architectural Association in London with John Miller,* was invited to Cornell as visiting critic for the fall semester of 1963.

13 Le Corbusier's* Carpenter Center for the Visual Arts, 1961–1964. See Rowe's letter to Judith DiMaio* dated of 28 July 1988 reassessing this building (p 292 in this volume).

14 Peter Eisenman* married Elizabeth Henderson, daughter of Jungian psychoanalyst Dr Joseph Henderson of San Francisco and niece of Christopher Cornford, painter, illustrator, and writer. Cornford taught at Cambridge with Rowe and later became head of the Department of Humanities at the Royal College of Art, London. On Cornford, see Rowe's letter to Michael Spens* dated 9 December 1996 (p 508 in this volume).

15 Anna Hodgkinson, Patrick's wife.

16 *jeune ménage,* French: young couple (or household).

To **Frederick Rowe,**
Highgate Lane, Bolton-on-Dearne, Yorkshire, England   *2 November and 1 December 1963*   **056**

107 Cayuga Heights Road, Ithaca, N.Y.

Dear Daddy:

Am not quite sure whether I owe you a letter or you owe me one. I rather think that you owe me. However I don't suppose that it matters because there doesn't really happen to be very much to write about.

The summer was moderately stimulating but overcast all the time and therefore, I suppose, in the end lugubrious. On the other hand the last few weeks here—since half way through September—have been brilliant. No rain, no wind, the leaves gradually disappearing, unbelievably blue skies, midday temperatures of about 90 in the shade (which one never got in July or August), in other words a physical situation tremendously animating in which one can live from day to day. But all of this came to an end on Sunday. Sunday was hot, hot; and then finally the rain began, and then on Monday incredibly cold winds blew in—either from Canada or from somewhere [...] so all the premonitions of winter were provided. However it won't happen yet. Everybody has said that this autumn is quite remarkable. On the other hand I find it exactly like last year. And exactly at this time last year it snowed. But this was just the overture for the winter. And nothing happened. It got hot all over again and finally, with desperate suddenness it did begin to snow about the first of December. Personally I find it gratifying to be subjected to such predictable conditions. The snow <u>will</u> fall, it will be around for about four months and at the end of March it will all melt within a week. There will be no spring. Suddenly we shall be precipitated into sticky, sticky, and hot, hot, summer and all this will be without nuances or overtones of any kind—reliable, crude, excessively trans-Atlantic. I suppose that this regularity—added to the systematic regularities of English Puritanism—does a good deal to explain the American temperament—including the occasional tendency to go berserk.

December 1st, 1963

I began this letter just a month ago. I had to stop because I had to get my typewriter repaired. I got it back—after an interminable interval—last week; and now re-reading what I wrote I find myself rather horrified by its prophetic tone.

First of all the weather was exactly as I proposed it would be. It got a little colder but not much. On November 29th, as I suggested it might, it began to snow and it has been snowing intermittently ever since. These are the great almost cosmic regularities which give one the idea that nothing is happening. Of course this is probably wrong.

People arrive and disappear. They talk a bit. Their comings and goings are elaborately lubricated with gin or bourbon or Scotch. Again of course, the predictable nature of this arrival, reception, departure, the complete absence anywhere of improvisation, the ceremoniousness—casual ceremoniousness of everything—makes all this social activity also something monotonous, also like a meteorological manifestation. You are left feeling a little detached—rather like a spectator of the laws of nature in operation. And if this sounds boring it isn't really so. Because although no one is so bored, I presume, as the inhabitants of North America, North America, for all its tedium, does have the capacity to make everywhere else seem boring.

And of course the events of last week do support my contention.[1] I did mention the occasional tendency to go berserk—perhaps as a reaction against the meteorological regularities. However when I re-read that part of this letter I didn't expect to be brought up quite so short. It is a little alarming to have one's random intuitions justified in quite that way.

Honestly though I wasn't surprised. It's a pity the setting had to be Texas. It could, with more justification, have been Alabama, or Georgia, or Mississippi; but, setting apart, the action did hold together. There wasn't too much extraneous in the whole affair.

Frankly, I wasn't wild about Kennedy. He was a going concern but I think slightly cheap—and now for a whole generation nobody who isn't disaffected will be able to utter a word of criticism—except in certain very specialized circles. What I was impressed by was Jacqueline Kennedy's behavior. Unlike most people here I thought it stylized, developed within a convention, involving the idea was her really great achievement—with the fact that by this means she was able to support the decorum of the American Republic, see it through a rather bad weekend and so on. People here didn't like the idea that she was playing theatre so were not terribly willing to accept this interpretation. On the other hand I got a phone call this evening from people who had been having lunch with friends of her parents, who (the friends of the parents) had been horrified and pained by what they thought was her excessively theatrical behavior and pointed out the second visit to the grave, the eternal flame and what not, as something quite beyond the bounds of decent Anglo-American behavior.[2]

So you see.

Will see you in June or so of next year,

    Colin

---

1 Reference is to the assassination of President John F Kennedy in Dallas, Texas, 22 November 1963.
2 Jacqueline Kennedy modeled her husband's funeral procession on the ceremonies for Abraham Lincoln in 1865. The casket was carried on a caisson and trailed by a riderless horse. Mrs. Kennedy followed on foot behind the caisson. The "eternal flame" at the graveside of the slain president was her idea.

057   *To **John and Pat Miller**, Stirling Mansions, Canfield Gardens, London*   *23 December 1963*

107 Cayuga Heights Road, Ithaca, New York

Pat and John, my dears:

I am, of course, conscience-stricken about not having written you for so long. I enjoyed your letters. I read some of them around to select circles. And I suppose that I haven't replied because I imagine that I am going through one of my understimulated phases. However, having just spent Saturday and Sunday in bed—because I felt tired—I believe that I might have gathered up enough strength to write—though about nothing in particular.

I suspect that you don't want belated news—very much—about attitude to the Kennedy assassination.[1] But it is rather interesting how attitudes really have changed. A few weeks ago when one tried to suggest that Jackie was playing the Spanish Infanta-Princesse de Cleves role with considerable distinction, almost too well, this was a style of remark which was likely to be deplored. But now........ It was, Cape Canaveral that did it. And then it was those Irish Catholic children who, in excess of zeal, put out the Eternal Flame by sprinkling holy water on it.[2] And then, somehow the Great American Public just didn't have too very much patience any more. Whereas when I had said that Jackie was playing a role and I meant it as praise and they took it as the reverse, now nearly everybody is disposed to say: Wasn't she being rather over-theatrical? And of course meaning it as condemnation. The Eternal Flame, of course, was Her Mistake. It was the only thing in her performance that didn't fit her very remarkable neo-seventeenth century act—that and the fact that Cardinal Cushing just ain't no Bossuet and therefore couldn't provide any adequate support.[3] But Cape Canaveral. Was that her mistake? Maybe it was. But one just can't help thinking that Lyndon Johnson did know what the results might be, knew what he was doing, and knew that it might hopelessly sabotage the Kennedy image. Very clever. Perhaps very desirable. But nothing, as yet, that can be said.

So what else is happening or has happened?

Neave, I suspect, has had grand success.[4] The somewhat *empresse* manner has charmed (Sorry the accent slipped). But Neave is really very good at the junior subaltern line: the eager, *ingénue*, boy architect. He has made a very great deal out of his being an Anglo-American anthropological anomaly. Perhaps he overplays his credentials. For some people I think that he does. However this is always a temptation and I think that the majority, because they like it, don't notice it. Neave is continuing to be very, very *Inglese*. I think that, just a little, he reprobates me. All the same I suspect that, behind the scenes, he is quietly acquiring some sort of transformation kit and that with this—which he is too proud to exhibit here—he will, when he gets back to London, imply the mildly, mildy Americano. Not enough to suggest that, in any way, he has become *deracine*;[5] but just enough to imply the sniff, to suggest the flavour of some kind of trans-Atlantic thing.

Or am I being captious and bitchy? Honestly, really, I don't think that I am. Neave is just a little prone to suppose that the axis of the world runs through Bedford Square, that in that architectural Mount Sinai there was, at some time, a divine revelation proffered; and he has, jerst a bit, the tendency to insist that, as well as a democrat, at the same time he is the member of an elite.[6] Which I believe means that, though I have been delighted to have him here, that though I got him here when I am told that he thinks Jim was responsible for it all, that though we met with considerable excitement, that somehow the relationship hasn't really prospered, and that oneself is left feeling rather like a Jesuit viewed by a good guy or a creature of the demi-monde surveyed by a lady of impeccable integrity.[7]

Which is enough about this and I must trust you not to repeat it. But what else? I don't think there is much else. People come and go through this place. They are ceremoniously lubricated with martinis and decorously drenched with bourbon. But by and large they tend to say nothing or nothing that I, at least, find very interesting.

December 24th, 1963

That was as far as my resolve to write took me yesterday and of course in sketching Neave I recognize that I have summarised certain aspects of myself. But the trouble is that both Neave and I have been inoculated with the American niceness and as you both of you know what is really needed in this world is not so much love but compassionate malice.

So what else has happened?

I could expatiate—it's absolutely fascinating on the climatic conditions of upstate New York (where Mme de Stael spent more than one winter)[8] but except for the fact that it's snowing at the present and has been doing so for the last two weeks I don't think that this information would be really very gratifying. Personally the snow leaves me a bit bored. The conditions are those for which masses of people in London pay lots of money to experience in Garmisch or Cortina d'Amprezzo and perhaps one should avail oneself of the opportunity. But do you really think that one should? I have two students—both of them professional ski instructors—one of them from Graz, the other from Zurich—both of them wild with anxiety to take me to some place called Greek Peek about ten miles from here. Do you think that I should buy the equipment which I am sure would lead to breaking every bone in my body? I suppose it would be one way of spending the winter and no doubt would exude a happy extravert uncontrollable air if one really took it up. But what do you think?

Maybe one should. And fishing too—at least when the streams melt—because one of the troubles here is that there is nothing to buy. Nor do I see all that much to buy in New York City (the City, as they tend to call it). American taste—I think this is true—was rather better about ten years back than it is to today; and, except for old Thonet chairs and old brass bedsteads of great magnificence, in the furniture line, New York at the moment doesn't really seem to have too much to offer.

It's the old problem you know. The problem that in England people don't know of, won't face. The problem that it is definitely quite impossible to be *chic* in a democracy. Thus certain strata of fantasy are eliminated. Thus irony disappears. Thus everything becomes matter of fact and considerate. And if in England people think that they have escaped this problem—as you know—they just don't know how they have deceived themselves.

Anyway about things. I have, to my surprise, lately got over-involved in, of all things chinoiserie. One regrets it a bit but it was rather too good to neglect. At a certain level the remoter provinces of the north eastern U.S. seems to abound in persian rugs and chinese porcelain and I was offered a pair of those blue and white garden seats in the form of tubs with lots of holes in them, not best quality but decidedly adequate and much below the price of New York and I suspect London. I think that you would both like them. And though I never expected to become chinoisy on quite such a scale, and since though late 19 C they are not overtly antique (perhaps nothing oriental ever is) it now becomes a problem of how to cope with them.

Which leads up to the fact that they would be extremely good against a black morocco chesterfield. That I bought them with this idea in mind. That the effect might be a little more opulent than your (John's) taste would be disposed to tolerate. That anyway you wouldn't despise it if handled with sufficient astringency.

Which leads to the next thing: what are you (John) going to do about it? One was of course ill-advised to dispose of the Eames chair, etc. They don't make them that way any more. Those were the good old days. Nowadays, though the price is the same or more, the footstool doesn't revolve, the leather is inferior, and the French polish is less evocative of Holman Hunt's awakened Conscience than in years gone by. So you got a bargain. You really did, you know, also with the proviso that you find me a chesterfield equivalent to yours. Probably you can't. Then don't you think one should have two or three made. Maybe you need another. Maybe I require two, and certainly it would be nice to pick one up next summer some time.

Write about this. My movements depend on whether or not I will ship a certain amount of furniture next year or not. Shall come over to Europe—Yurrup— some time towards the end of June. Whether one lands in London, Amsterdam, Paris, Rome, I don't know. Want to sell my Volkswagen here and though I am told it's stupid would like to pick up some kind of Alfa Romeo somewhere, so as to be able to move around. Would then ship it back here—either from Le Havre or Southampton—am not quite sure which because it all depends on whether one sails or flies back. One flies if it is not a question of baggage. One sails if it is. So it would be nice to know—would help to make plans—whether one could pick up one or two chesterfields or not.

No doubt all this sounds vulgarly large. But what can you do?

My love. And to whom else should you give my love? Alan? Maybe he would like it. Perhaps I will write to him in the next few days. Ken Frampton? Why not. But to whom else? One is of course being melodramatic but will see ya'.

> Colin

P.S. having just typed the address I am left wondering what Canfield Gardens and Stirling Mansions really are like.[9] Golders Green, builders Edwardian, debased Norman Shaw is what I suspect. There is a lot of *Haute Juiverie* in the vicinity, is there not?[10] If low down one keeps the curtains, some curtains, drawn most of the time? If high up one accepts the view over the roofs? I think that I have the picture. When you write tell me if I am correct. Lots of love, etc.

> Colin

1 American president John F Kennedy was assassinated in Dallas, Texas, on 22 November 1963.
2 Jacqueline Kennedy, President Kennedy's widow and mother of their two children, Caroline and John Jr. The "eternal flame" marked Kennedy's grave in Washington DC. Cape Canaveral was the site of rocket launches in a space program encouraged by Kennedy, who had visited Canaveral six days before he was assassinated. Lyndon Johnson, who became president upon Kennedy's death, changed the name from Cape Canaveral to Cape Kennedy, a change many Florida citizens bitterly resented.
3 Richard Cushing (1895–1970), archbishop of Boston, gave a televised eulogy for President Kennedy the day before his funeral. The comparison is to Jacques-Bénigne Bossuet (1627–1704), French bishop and theologian, renowned for his public addresses.
4 Neave Brown (b 1929), John Miller's★ former classmate at the Architectural Association, London.
5 *déraciné*, French: uprooted.
6 Bedford Square is the location of the Architectural Association in London.
7 "Jim": James Stirling.★
8 Germaine de Staël (1766–1817), French-Swiss woman of letters.
9 The Millers★ had moved to Stirling Mansions recently.
10 *Haute Juiverie*, French: High Jewry.

*To **Henry-Russell Hitchcock**, Smith College, Northampton, Mass.*   *16 May 1964*   **058**

107 Cayuga Heights Road, Ithaca, N. Y.

Dear Russell:

I am writing to say how nice it was to see you last week and even though there was no possibility of either any extensive or intensive conversation. Also I am writing to say that even though (in my view) the symposium did take quite a time to get warmed up I find myself a week later discovering that I was awarded a number of perhaps quite significant *apercus*.[1] When you invited me I didn't wish to talk because I had no idea of the style of the pitch of the group which was to be gathered together, hadn't tasted them, had no clue how microscopic—or alternatively—grandly synoptic they might be going to be. But on another occasion, if there is another occasion, I shall have no reservations (that is if you ask me).

This is because I think that nearly everybody else is in the same hole as myself—which is not ungratifying and some time I would like to talk about it. Perhaps in Germany for where best wishes,

    Colin

P.S. I would have liked to have heard something from you about your Barock kick. The whole subject of Barock-Rokoko seems to me to be surrounded by a Germanic fog. One ought I think to be able to achieve some sort of formula which could cover the rectilinear Rokoko......[2] I mean there are certain pieces of highly rectilinear Chippendale where just manipulation of an edge—say the internal surface of a table leg on the diagonal—where just this will imply the Rokoko in its entirety. What does one do about this? It is an aspect of things which seems to be obscured. Also I have a difficulty that so much of that Sought German stuff is better as an idea than as a fact and that I still think far the best interior that I have seen is in Turin, in the Accademia Filarmonica.[3]

    Colin

---

1 Modern Architecture Symposium (MAS 1964): The Decade 1929–1939, held at Columbia University, New York, 8–10 May 1964, recorded in *Journal of the Society of Architectural Historians* 24, no 1, March 1965; *aperçus*, French: insights.
2 See Hitchcock, Henry-Russell, *Rococo Architecture in Southern Germany*, London: Phaidon, 1968.
3 Music Room of the Accademia Filarmonica in the Palazzo Isnardi di Caraglio, Turin, 1840–1841, by Giuseppe Maria Talucchi (1782–1863).

059   *To **John** & Pat Miller, Stirling Mansions, Canfield Gardens, London*   *23 October 1964*

107 Cayuga Heights Road, Ithaca, N.Y.

My dears:

As an old Russian woman said to me the other day: "But you poor thing, you must be feeling so *dérouté*—I do", she went on, "whenever I go to Europe—or whenever I get back here again—for that matter."[1]

Well I am feeling *dérouté*—which is a new word with me—and I am giving it to you in the hope that it will be a new word with you and that you will be able to put it to use. I am finding America rather crude and unsatisfactory which is not a new sensation to me but since I wasn't all that excited about Europe either I am just left to meditate in a rather desultory way on the general failure of the Almighty who ought to have done just a little better with the world and also on the general failure of civilisation which ought—by this time—to have done something about patching up the Almighty's mistakes.

This sort of consideration leaves me feeling torpid and in need of an infusion of energy and hence I have not been writing letters since I got back here. But apart from that nothing very exciting has happened to write about. Michael and Ella

Jepson visited here last weekend and were in raptures about it all.[2] They have taken to bird watching and spent a whole day sitting around in the woods and looking at wild life through an enormously powerful pair of binoculars so that their excitement by the time it became evening was almost too much to bear. The weekend before that there was a Cambridge student—unknown to me and his name forgotten, who had to be driven around to take colour pictures of the Fall vegetation which seemed to have the same effect on him as the birds did on the Jepsons. And so it goes on.

The other day I heard Adlai Stevenson speak and had no idea until then that he was so very witty.[3] It was at a dinner to inaugurate the Cornell centenary celebrations and though the homiletic part of the Stevenson speech was platitudinous there was an introductory flow of anecdote which was remarkable.

There are only two items which I remember but—taking into account the susceptibility of the Americans to shock, their frequent moral prudery and their overt respect for religion—these two items were rather engaging.

At the height of the presidential campaign of '52 Stevenson is in Chicago (which he pronounces Chicawger) and is on his way to a meeting in the ballroom of the Hotel Ambassador or somewhere or other.[4] In the foyer are a group of supporters; among them is a woman so pregnant that he says I was really alarmed, I expected that any minute the child might pop out. But the worst of it was that she was holding a banner almost so over-sized as herself and on it there was no more than the simple inscription: Stevenson Is The Man.

The Minister says to Mrs Jones: Mrs Jones I was thinking about you until a late hour last night. And Mrs Jones replies: Why Reverend you don't have to do that, you didn't have to go on thinking, all you had to do was to pick up the telephone and, you know Reverend, I'd have been right round.

Perhaps not enormously amusing by themselves but embedded in an indefinitely extended context of the same stuff, delivered with great energy, and definitely not the sort of performance one expects from presidential candidates it all had great charm as a performance which obliquely criticised the occasion he was asked to lend his name to.

And now to come down to Chesterfields, Chesterfields, Chesterfields.[4]

I understand from David that to make one or two of them would be—he and you seem to think—a wildly expensive undertaking.[5] All the same, having thought about it, I don't really see any other way. David said something about a replica of yours costing Two Hundred Pounds. Would two copies of it cost correspondingly less? I presume that they ought to—just a bit anyway. So could you proceed to have two copies made and I shall hope that perhaps they are going to cost me about Three Hundred and Fifty the pair because frankly... and to repeat... I don't see the alternative and compared with Barcelona chairs and any of that stuff the expense would really be rather slight. Also with two of the things and all my other stuff, I am inclined to think that by then my major purchases of furniture might be at end.

Please, dear John, try to do this fairly soon.

   Colin

---

1 *dérouté*, French: confused.
2 Michael Jepson, English architect.
3 Adlai Stevenson II (1900–1965), American politician, unsuccessful Democratic candidate for US president against Dwight Eisenhower in 1952 and 1956.
4 The "chesterfield", an elaborate sofa, was a persistent subject in letters to the Millers.*
5 David Rowe,* Colin's brother.

107 Cayuga Heights Road, Ithaca, N. Y.

Carissimo:

And what else?

On December 1st the snow fell. And on December 3rd Furneaux-Jordan (visiting critic at Syracuse) arrived to give lecture.[1]

Should not these be listed among the significant and therefore the communicable calmatives of the season?

The snow you all know about and therefore why should I bore you? But F-J is something, though no doubt known to you, unknown to me, and therefore I suppose an anthropological specimen about which words could be uttered. But it <u>was</u> funny. It was like Bill Allen although just a bit more literate and ever so much more verbally elegant.[2] He gave a talk called the USES OF HISTORY and therefore one presumed—in one's grotesque innocence—some contact with Popper* and Geyl and Isaiah Berlin* and what all.[3] One didn't expect the contact to be elaborate or rigorous. One simply imagined that it would be recognized that these points of view do exist. That they have indeed existed for a good many years. But no.

Though Bedford Square is not all that remote from L.S.E. or Oxford or even Utrecht it is apparently, surrounded by an iron curtain through which ideas do not penetrate.[4] And that is just about all. We got a little Hegel, a little William Morris, a little Marx, a lot of romantic positivism, we were assured of the virtues of collaborative endeavor, of the values and enlightenment of English Bureaucracy, and the fact that all significant social change during the last one hundred and fifty years or so had been initiated in the British Isles. Do I have to tell you that the students squirmed and grimaced, and were agonized, that up-state New York is not quite so unsophisticated as all that? I don't think that I have to tell you any such thing. Simply I can imagine your embarrassment had you been here. But what still continues to surprise me is the self confidence, the unquestioning self-assurance of these travelling left-wing English. Myself I do have my Kiplingesque moments, from time to time I do empathize.

Am intending this letter also as a Christmas card and also as apologies to Alvin for any undue pain that I might have caused him in Italy last summer. I hope, in the end, that I didn't cause pain—although am still agitated from time to time to think that I probably bullied, hectored, was peremptory and so on. Also, Al, please forgive this untoward entreaty or apologia but I have been floating several letters on several drinks and by now it is 2.30—which is not necessarily either the most veracious or the most lucid hour.

Therefore will stop. Will felicitate you on Christmas on the New Year and all the rest and just let's hear about either ITHACA or the Visiting Critic thing.

Love and ciao, ciao,

Colin

P.S. To promote the visiting critic things—which I think you ARE interested in doing—suggest two letters one to DETWEILER who is your aficionado and other to Kelly.[5]* The letters would each suggest that the other one had been written to—and Kelly would then ask me, etc, etc.

But perhaps everything is going like a dream and I am offering irrelevant entertainments.

Colin

1 Robert Furneaux-Jordan (1905–1978), architect, critic, and teacher of architectural history at the Architectural Association, London, 1934 to 1963.
2 William A Allen (1914–1998), Canadian-born architect, principal of the Architectural Association, London, 1961 to 1966.
3 Karl Popper* (1902–1994), Austrian-born, British philosopher of science; Pieter Geyl (1887–1966), Dutch historian of history; and Isaiah Berlin* (1909–1997), British philosopher, social and political theorist, and historian of ideas.
4 Furneaux-Jordan taught at the Architectural Association in Bedford Square, Popper* at the London School of Economics, Berlin* at Oxford, and Geyl in Utrecht.
5 Henry Detweiler, associate dean, and Burnham Kelly,* dean, Cornell University's College of Architecture, Art, and Planning.

To **Alvin Boyarsky**, *London*   *14 March 1965*   **061**

107 Cayuga Heights Road, Ithaca, N.Y.

Alvin:

What to say with reference to your last letter?

First of all one does suppose that the College of Architecture is greatly changed. Wells* will retire very soon; so will Hartell* (in each case within about two or three years); Stuart Barnett will be a little longer to dispose of—but after all his is merely a passive existence anyway. Detweiler will retire—and will be very happy to do so—in two years time also. Well that is the picture of major routine eliminations. But the other aspect of things is the withdrawal of Canfield who says he is not going to teach design anymore. And with this, of course, goes the isolation of Alex Kira who will have to be promoted into something.[1]

As for the 'pragmatic formalists' being in and the 'country club' being out. What do I say about that? There is a group here who have been called the Texas Rangers. I do not belong to it; and; though I am thought of as having something to do with Texas, I exist, around these parts, very much by my own right. The Texas Rangers, I take it, are Lee Hodgden,* Werner Seligmann,* and John Shaw;[2] while possibly annexed to their party is Charles Pearman—who would always express some kind of reserve—and is nothing to do with Texas anyway.[3] Well the Texas Rangers <u>have</u> acquired a certain centrality—which of course is none of Lee's doing. In fact it is probably John Shaw's doing who has always been sensible even if a little Southern and repetitious, combined with my own doing who have always spoken well of them—though with <u>some</u> reservations—so that I have been able, precisely through not being a member of their party, to be of some assistance to it.

O.K. what else is there here?

Martin Dominguez—a very elderly 67(?) spanish type. Twice a refugee: from Spain and from Cuba. A charming person, perhaps not all that useful, but obviously not all that permanent.

Peter Cohen—Dominguez's partner—Harvard of the TAC period—with the limitations and contracted intellectual horizons of the type. A nice guy with a nice wife—but, as things are at the moment, apparently not to be retained.

The structures gang: Ludlow Brown—who can't be around for ever; Frank Saul, a possible sheriff type for Selma, Alabama—who is unfortunately likely to be here for some considerable time; Ray di Pasquale—who has lots of sense and although he is perhaps a little too much of a regular guy—is very agreeable to work with.

On the city planning front: Reps is recessive; Parsons is dominant and much more liberal than the previous regime; Barclay Jones is a little computer oriented bastard; Allan Feldt is a quiet and probably not too intelligent sociologist; and then, arrived last September, there is Michael Hugo-Brunt.........[4]

Well that is the general picture and I don't suppose that you can necessarily decipher it. However what it seems at the present to mean is the possibility of some rapprochement between city planning and architecture (Parenns, the Texas Rangers). Also, as you must realise, there is a considerable lobby for you:- Parsons, Texas Rangers, Detweiler, self.[5]

O.K. should you come?

QUESTION: Kelly?[6]★ A weak, quasi-liberalistic, quasi-technologically oriented personality. In fact a typical M.I.T. boy. How about him? He is being educated; he is always capable of doing the wrong thing; he has considerable charm, is susceptible to charm; and would eat out of your hand.

QUESTION: Group practice? At the moment I seriously think remote. But also, I think, that something which you, personally, could very easily precipitate. I have told Burnham that the only hope for this place is to base in Ithaca a go-go-go urban design office. Also I think that in general he believes that I am right in this. Also, though, in this area, he would look (and quite understandably) for someone rather more 'practical' than myself. In this area you could very well be the catalyst of the situation.

QUESTION: Me? What am I going to do? This is harder to answer. Eisenman,★ of course, wants me to go to Princeton and, accordingly, Geddes who is going to run the school down there invites me as visiting critic for the Fall Semester (as incidentally Paul Rudolph still presses Yale).[7] O.K. I put these problems to Burnham the other day and he countered by offering me two fellowships of $2,000 a year plus tuition and fees in order to buy more and better graduate students for my urban design situation. One supposes that this sort of thing is known as creative blackmail—but still, I must say that I scarcely expected quite so strenuous a counter bid.

Anyway, what about Princeton? And don't, don't talk about this! I like quite a lot of things up here. In spite of everything there is a topographical grandeur. Also there is certain crude democracy which is not displeasing—certainly not after Cambridge. Also I think that Peter is trying to do things too quickly e.g. the $50,000 for research into a linear city between N.Y.C. and Philadelphia.[8] Also I think that Peter has really got his buddy down there—Michael Graves★—and though neither of them realise and both say they want me—I still suspect that they might quite soon resent my arrival. They are a bit too much trying to railroad things—and they can't be told that that way lies danger.

Anyways, whether I stay here or not probably depends a good deal on you. I really have got a very hot shot urban design thing going. It's a composite of Ducerceau,[9] Aalto, Corbu,[10]★ Mexican sites, Chantilly, the Hofburg, etc. It's entirely empirical, pragmatic and accommodating. It is totally devoid of theory. But it is waiting to be publicised and bought.

Now this sort of town—not quite mid-West not quite Eastern, not quite Ivy League not quite State University—with no immediate architectural hinterland, could sponsor a practice at the urban design level at a national and international scale. Kelly★-Daniel Burnham could offer some kind of filiation. The city planners here could provide some sort of apologetic or alibi for the undertaking.

This is one aspect.

Another is that I, personally, can (for a few years in each case at least) command the loyalty and enthusiasm and labour of students. I am perfectly aware of this and don't have to be told how little or how much, this may count. All that I am trying to suggest is that I could furnish out such an office with sufficient of a personnel, having sufficient of the temperament of early Christians, to really get it in motion; and of course, once it was in motion, then one would get a snowballing with—if one were very rigorous—an increase of standards.

Would you not be interested in this which you could help to bring about and which I would not—COULD NOT—share with the Texas Rangers?

So that's the general situation.

As an initial salary you should probably ask for about $11,000. After all you are a sophisticated N. American type with lots of experience. Houses here begin at about $14,000 to $20,000 with 20% of the purchase price down. And, I am just telling you, you could walk away with it!

 Colin

P.S. I really have been very happy since being back here. Also I think that you would be too. In all the above I have been trying to tell you how much you, personally, would be presentable and would appear as an incisive, no nonsense, etc. type. Nor—to qualify— am I trying to buy you as a public relations man for <u>my</u> urban design operation. Instead I am offering shares in an operation which <u>together</u>, I think we could make go.

As to coming for a short time (in order to smell things out) or not—that is something which has to be left to correspondence.

The thing on the academic front is that there are three situations to fill: one in landscape and two in architectural design. You would be ineligible for the landscape— so, it would be architectural design, and lecture courses—if you wanted—<u>could</u> be history—of what you wanted.

Of course, on the filling of these situations a great deal does depend. But, as to the landscape appointment, I really shall try to lay down the law—over my dead body there will be no japonaiserie—Hiedo Sasakery-Californian-do-it-yourself-cook-out-stuff. As far as I am concerned it's going to be Le Notre, the Alhambra, Italian villas, Blenheim, etc.

Which is another reason why one would like you here.

 Colin

P.P.S. My love to Elizabeth and tell her not to despair.[11] Also tell her that you could soon be in a $20,000 to $30,000 a year situation over here. Also tell her that you all need some furniture and some clothes.

Best wishes,

 Colin

[handwritten]

P.P.S. Sorry for a week's delay in posting.

 Colin

1 Morris Wells,* John Hartell,* Stuart Barnett, Henry Detweiler, Thomas Canfield, and Alex Kira were all faculty at Cornell University's College of Architecture, Art and Planning in 1965.
2 See Caragonne, Alexander *The Texas Rangers: Notes from the Underground*, Cambridge, MA: MIT Press, 1995.
3 Charles W Pearman (1927–2013), practiced in Ithaca and began teaching at Cornell in 1962.
4 John W Reps, Kermit C Parsons.
5 Henry Detweiler (1906–1970), associate dean of the College of Architecture, Art, and Planning at Cornell since 1956.
6 Burnham Kelly* (1912–1999), dean of the College of Architecture, Art, and Planning at Cornell University from 1960 to 1971.
7 Peter Eisenman* and Robert Geddes, dean of the School of Architecture, Princeton University, 1965 to 1982.
8 The Jersey Corridor Project was funded by the Prudential Insurance Company and executed at Princeton University by Peter Eisenman* and Michael Graves,* 1964 to 1966.
9 Jacques I Androuet du Cerceau (or Ducerceau) (1510–1584), French architect, furniture designer, and engraver.
10 Alvar Aalto; Le Corbusier.*
11 Elizabeth Boyarsky,* Alvin Boyarsky's* wife.

062   To **Peter Eisenman,** *School of Architecture, Princeton University, Princeton, N.J.*   15 May 1965

107 Cayuga Heights Road, Ithaca, N.Y.

Dear Peter:

"Men living in democratic ages do not readily comprehend the utility of forms: they feel an instinctive contempt for them, I have elsewhere shown for what reasons. Forms excite their contempt and often their hatred; as they commonly aspire to none but easy and present gratifications, they rush onwards to the object of their desires, and the slightest delay exasperates them. This same temper carried with them into political life, renders them hostile to forms, which perpetually retard or arrest them in some of their projects.

Yet this objection which the men of democracies make to forms is the very thing which renders forms useful to freedom; for their chief merit is to stand as a barrier between the strong and the weak, the ruler and the people, to retard the one and to give the other time to look about him. Forms become more necessary in proportion as the government becomes more active and more powerful, while private persons are becoming more indolent and more feeble. Thus democratic nations naturally stand in more need of forms than other nations, and they naturally respect them less. This deserves most serious attention.

Nothing is more pitiful than the arrogant disdain of most of our contemporaries for questions of form, for the smallest questions of form have acquired in our time an importance which they never had before; many of the greatest interests of mankind depend upon them. I think that if the statesmen of aristocratic ages could sometimes despise forms with impunity and frequently rise above them, the statesmen to whom the government of nations is now confided ought to treat the very least among them with respect and not neglect them without imperious necessity. In aristocracies the observance of forms was superstitious; among us they ought to be kept up with a deliberate rate and enlightened deference."

DE TOCQUEVILLE, *Democracy......*, Vol. II, Book IV, Chapter VII.[1]

This is the quote which I half remembered and thought you might like.

Colin

1 de Tocqueville, Alexis, *Democracy in America*, 2 vols, New York: Vintage Books, 1954, vol 2, p 344. Rowe employs parts of this quote in the penultimate paragraph of "Neo-'Classicism' and Modern Architecture", part 1, first published (with Eisenman's* assistance) in *Oppositions*, no 1, 1973. Republished in Rowe's *The Mathematics of the Ideal Villa and Other Essays*, 1976.

*To **Pat Miller**, London*   *20 May 1965*   **063**

107 Cayuga Heights Road, Ithaca, N.Y.

Most Pat:

Was delighted to have your letter and am replying immediately enclosing a cheque for $1008.00 which I hope is the right amount and which therefore ought to satisfy Cripps.[1]

And now then begins the problem: when the chesterfields are sent (I got a letter from Dorothy the other day and already believed them to be in mid-Atlantic) but when the chesterfields are sent—and particularly if they are going to cost so much, one would like to arrange for a few other items in the same package. My original idea was to have them sent with the so-called cockfighting chair, the green velvet chaise, etc so that also the whole lot could come in looking like antiques and would therefore be duty free—they also would be duty free as personal effects, etc.

Now I don't know how much this would cost and though I don't mind paying there is another problem.

This don't talk about—please. But conceivably I might be asked to teach at Princeton probably beginning in September of 1966. I am going down there in November– January as visiting critic to look it over and also, I suppose to be looked over. Now if I chose to go there and if they chose to ask me they would pay all the costs of a removal while Cornell will pay long. And therefore, as you will understand, I find myself psychotically divided between my epicurean impatience and my meanness. Do I pay for having stuff moved to Ithaca where just possibly I would get only about nine months use out of it. Or do I wait and see and then maybe get everything paid for?

I take it that Pitt and Scott is a bonded warehouse or something of that sort and that there is a problem about purchase tax.[2] Because if there is no such problem I do, at the moment, feel a bit like saying:- why don't you take them for a few months and enjoy all the happiness of a Bernard Buffet arrangement with three in the same room?[3]

On the other hand if this is not possible it would be rational to consider three alternatives (and it would probably be rational to consider them anyway):
i.   what is the cost of their warehouse storage?
ii. what would their cost of shipping the chesterfields to N.Y.C. be if the spaces were filled with things like cockfighting chair, chaise longue, the two little white circular tables down in Chelsea, etc be?
iii. what would be the cost for the lot i.e. the foregoing plus two chest of drawers, revolving bookcase, telescopic tables and so on?

Also are they able to give a New York City to Ithaca estimate? Sorry to involve all this. As some amusement I send you a most interesting specimen of the style of public relations practised by the U.K. See enclosed and I will now read your enclosed.

Lots of love,

   Colin

1 Rowe had asked John* and Pat Miller* to have two copies of their chesterfield made in England and then to send the copies to him in Ithaca. Cripps was the firm that had copied Miller's chesterfield.
2 Pitt & Scott Ltd, International Removals and Storage, London.
3 Bernard Buffet (1928–1999), popular French expressionist painter.

064 To **Stanford Anderson,** *Department of Architecture, MIT, Cambridge, Mass.*   *18 June 1965*

107 Cayuga Heights Road, Ithaca, N.Y.

Dear Stan:

Since you keep on telling me that you have never received a letter from me and since I am now creating a precedent I am visited by immediate inhibitions about what to say. But I will begin by saying that, the semester being over, I have at last discovered the time and energy to transfer attention to all the papers which you keep on sending to me.

It was at this stage that I got your phone call—a coincidence which should probably be communicated to the Society of Psychical Research and which seems, for the moment, to make the rest of this letter unnecessary.

However to go point by point:

i. I am immensely impressed by all the work which you have done and I do feel a little ashamed and guilty about not having said so before now. I agree with your foundation statement and can't think of anything which I would wish to change—except of course the name CASE.[1]

ii. I have no proposals to put in place of CASE. SEMINAR sounds just dreary and CECA—or whatever it is—doesn't sound any better. One surely wishes for a title without naively activist overtones.

iii. I enclose a curriculum vitae.

iv. I shall try to append a description of the study group: Psychology of the architect.

Meanwhile I am not very impressed by the editorial statement that was put out from Princeton. It doesn't know whether it wishes to be a continuous piece of writing or an old fashioned nineteen-twentyish manifesto. It also has a sentimental activist, vitalistic tone. It uses the word 'total'—'total environment', 'total architecture', etc—God knows how many times. What is meant by 'total arch.'? Also one just cannot say things like this:

"We intend that this magazine should attempt to stem the flood; to this task we, and our contributors will bring all the rigor that we can muster. We shall be critical, analytical, philosophical, dialectical, polemical and political. Arch-is essentially organization, the laying waste must stop and a total architecture must begin."

"Stem the flood"—a political meetings c. 1910; "all the rigor that we can muster"—but ungrammatical and boy-scouty and therefore tacitly dis-implying any possibility of rigor; etc. etc.

Or am I being too captious?

June 22nd, 1965

It seems that though there isn't as yet available a study group statement, and since I have again been delayed, I had better send this as is. The study group will follow in quite a short time. But, honestly, I think that already there is a note of too great sobriety and liberalistic tolerance about our group. Can something not be done about it? We should talk about it while you are around in these parts.

Colin

---

1 In his phone call, Anderson* had asked Rowe to become a member of an organization he was initiating called CASE (Consortium of Architects for the Study of the Environment), a short-lived organization of select faculty members from a number of East Coast schools of architecture.

To **John Miller,** London   *18 October 1965*   **065**

107 Cayuga Heights Road, Ithaca, New York 14850

My dear John:

The Pitt and Scott invoice has come my way via David and Dorothy.[1] Therefore, for you, I am enclosing with this letter a cheque for Two Hundred and Sixty Six Pounds Eleven Shillings payable by the Westminster Bank in Cambridge.[2]

Perhaps it is a good idea that the furniture has not yet left?

If you think that it should not yet be dispatched then there is a situation to be solved at your discretion. Obviously it would be really silly to have this stuff sent and then— and perhaps while it is in mid-Atlantic—receive an offer from the A.A.. On the other hand—if the A.A. strategy begins to seem dubious—then perhaps this stuff could be sent off.

Anyway, I say, the cashing of the cheque and paying off of Pitt and Scott is to your discretion and if you think that it would be really opportune or circumspect to delay, then, by all means, do delay.

David rang me up the other day to tell me that he had become a father, etc.[3] When I mentioned (perhaps I should not have done) your A.A. demarches, he expressed a little skepticism. When I mentioned the possibility of flying over he intimated that the trans-Atlantic flight could seem more plausible if the financial sponsorship for it came from London. Personally, I am a little skeptical about this possibility. It is certainly the way you would deal with an American institution. But is it the way you can expect an English institution to work?

I ask these questions because I do have a propensity to undersell myself. And if you present yourself as financially difficult to deal with I have often noticed that you can gain more respect for your ideas. In other words, the more money you have or earn, the more people (including your employers, actual or prospective) are inclined to listen.

I do not wish to rub this stuff in *ad nauseam* and I would accept your advice. But this is the point of making oneself not viable by making oneself too available. Or do you think that this simply doesn't apply?

Anyway, my love to Pat and to Alan,[4]

Also my love and appreciation of your politics,

Colin

P.S. Apparently Aldo Van Eyck isn't going to be able to come here for three weeks in January.[5] In his absence I have re-iterated your name. Are you interested even though at this time the weather is likely to be lousy?

Colin

---

1 Invoices related to costs for shipping furniture from London to Rowe in New York sent to Rowe by Dorothy* and David Rowe.*
2 Pitt & Scott Ltd, International Removals and Storage, London. Miller* paid to have furniture shipped to Rowe in the United States from England.
3 James Rowe,* David* and Dorothy Rowe's* first son, was born in October 1965.
4 Pat Miller* and Alan Colquhoun,* Miller's* partner in the architectural firm Colquhoun and Miller.
5 Aldo van Eyck (1918–1999), pre-eminent Dutch architect.

066 *To **John Miller**, Stirling Mansions, Canfield Gardens, London*   *7 November 1965*

107 Cayuga Heights Road, Ithaca, N.Y.

My dear John:

The line was so bad that I could hardly hear anything and I am not quite sure that you could either.

However: as follows,

It would be extremely hard to withdraw from an American, or any other university, in mid-year.

One could send in a resignation quite well in March, April, May, and depending on one's position, even into August.

This resignation could become operative in September—or, depending on circumstances, could equally be made operative round about Christmas, etc.

For instance: if the A.A. thing became really firm I could send in a resignation about April-May-June and Cornell would then probably be happy to keep me on on very good terms.[1] Obviously so. Such an arrangement would be to everybody's advantage. They could say that I was going to be So-and-so after Christmas (if after Christmas were to be the date) and then they could expect (but need not necessarily receive) a favoured situation.

But quite obviously a situation would be more problematic in October-November if the idea were withdrawal at Christmas.

This is because the American academic year only synchronizes with the European at Christmas. Here there are two SEMESTERS with a break in February. *Chez vous* there are three terms with breaks according to the principal feasts of the church.[2]

Have I made the point?

If I have not it is because since your phone call I have been to dinner with the Michaelis's* and been given too much cognac.[3] However I think that I probably have made the point.

About coming over:

At Christmas I am supposed to go down to Dallas, Texas to be somebody's godparent. I may not go. But that is the present plan.

If I were to go I would prefer not to stay too long.

The reason is quite simple. I would like to spend Christmas trying to make a book via a Dictaphone. Have just been giving a seminar and realize that with what I have written and what I could produce I might quite well run to about 50,000 all new. This would be all the stuff you know that was lying around in Cambridge and the only way to get rid of it is via a big push and a Dictaphone and secretaries and all that—otherwise it would hang around for ever.

Well that is the situation.

Tomorrow, late, I go down to Princeton on the first of my little visits. I am to be visiting critic for a few weeks—about five, I believe—and they will pay for visits of three days or so during this period approximately $3,700. Say nothing about it. But I am amazed. Nor am I enraptured. I frankly believe that Pietro (who did engineer so much of it all) is for all that going to be that much of a problem.[4]

However this is also to say that if you ring up during the next month I am quite likely not to be around. It is also to say that the next time you ring please do it with charges reversed on me.

Love and all that and I do know that it would be possible to have a terrific thing going.

    Colin

---

1 "The AA thing": Rowe, a professor at Cornell University at the time, had been invited to apply for the position of principal of the Architectural Association, London.
2 *Chez vous*, French: at your house.
3 Dominic and Nina Michaelis.*
4 "Pietro": Peter D. Eisenman* (b 1932), Rowe's former student at Cambridge, teaching at Princeton at this time.

To **John & Pat Miller,** *Stirling Mansions, Canfield Gardens, London*   *13 November 1965*   **067**

107 Cayuga Heights Road, Ithaca, N.Y.

John & Pat:

    Here in Ithaca Alan is known as Al Colquhoun.* 'Hey, Colin, have you seen Al?' etc, etc.[1]

Now all this gives food for thought and I have begun to come to the conclusion that the <u>Al</u> in this case is like the <u>Al</u> in Al Hambra, Al Cazar, and—maybe—even in Al Kaseltzer.[2] Have you never thought of this?

Anyway my suspicions became confirmed the other day when looking through *Baedeker's Egypt* I came across a village or small town called Al Kahoun or (alternatively) Al Quhoun.

Which is not to say that Alan is of Egyptian descent. One must <u>presume</u> that there are other small Arab settlements—perhaps in Morocco, perhaps in southern Spain— one must allow for these. But this is surely enough to indicate something Moorish in the pedigree.

Interesting isn't it?

As for me I speculate as follows: Way back there is something Sephardic-Moslem in the picture. In the Middle Ages one has to imagine a location of several centuries in the Emirate of Cordoba—a blissful period on which the arrival of Ferdinand and Isabella brings down the curtain. So the Quhouns are expelled. They flee. First they go to Genoa and then *en route* to Edinburgh and possibly points North they are to be found in Freiburg in Breisgau, Leiden, Amsterdam, etc.

In Scotland the prefix "Col" they add to the name, partly as a result of pro-Celtic sentimentality (Col du Tarn, etc); and also, partly—and one has to face it—for purposes of dissimulation. But of course the truth will always out and the atavistic thing cannot be suppressed. And so—once in every three generations or so the existence of an Al Quhoun persistently testifies to the activity of the original genes.

Best love,

Colin

1　Alan Colquhoun* (1921–2012), renowned British architect and writer, was John Miller's* partner in the London architectural firm Colquhoun and Miller.
2　Alka-Seltzer was a popular, commercially available pain reliever for indigestion.

068　*To **John Miller**, Stirling Mansions, Canfield Gardens, London*　　　　*30 January 1966*

107 Cayuga Heights Road, Ithaca, N.Y.

My dear John:

You expected me, as I know, to be remiss in writing. Also, as I know, you are aware that this is because I am that much distracted (?) by events and things.

Anyway your last letter to me coincided with a letter from Carter asking me to apply. I send you a copy of it.[1] Ken, reading it, had reactions comparable to mine.[2]

The letter was accompanied by a Roneod brochure badly typed on both sides of the paper (?).[3] The brochure—perhaps you have read it—seems to me to be one of the most irritating little documents it has ever been my privilege to be exposed to. Its inference, so far as I can make out, is quite simple: We are liberal and believe in change and we are in no doubt that we are an *avant garde* and consequently we know what changes should take place; but though we believe (so passionately) in change we still want everything to be the same.

So I am asking you what to do about this? What line to take in stating my objectives, etc?

Meanwhile I get trying, and I can't help thinking sometimes hysterical—though, I believe, well meaning—letters and phone calls from Alvin Boyarsky* all about this same matter. The Boyarsky argument—which I don't necessarily believe—is as follows: that you are overdoing the sales job and failing to carry with you an important section of student and quasi-student opinion, that you represent an older (!) generation, etc. and that I am absolutely, in this picture, an antediluvian.

Frankly, as you know, I do NOT feel like something dredged up out of the debris of the flood. But I am confused by the style of the Boyarsky advice and would value some sort of memorandum which outlined the general political [scene].

I have no wish to play politics at any low level. I am not disposed to dissimulate my objectives, very much. But since I do have to write something about what sort of policy I should initiate some general guidance would, I am sure, by very useful. For instance: At what level does one take up the platitudinous insistence on change? I.E. one knows that change occurs but if change is as fast as it is said to be then presumably no one can teach anybody anything at all because things are obsolete almost as soon as they are enunciated, let alone put into practice.

The article in the *A.A. Journal* for February '65 by Wm. Bartley III called "On what is the House of Science Built", comes closest to representing my point of view.[4] Read it and tell me what you think because I am rather disposed to use this general position as a base.

My problem is, in any case, to tell the truth as far as I believe that I can see it. But it is also not to upset people unduly in doing so. For instance, one does believe that in order for genuine changes to be made it is necessary to question most of the premises which modern architecture implies. One has, one supposes, ultimately to deny such propositions as: facts are necessarily measurable and quantifiable; the hypothesis derives from the facts; the solution derives from the programme; the future is predictable so that in acting in the present we must consider this predictable future. This, I am sure, is at one level what has to be done BUT the big question remains how much of this sort of stuff has to be said or should be said?

O.K. There then emerges another issue. I am not averse to paying for a flight across the Atlantic. But also I know that I should not be expected to do so. In this context it seems that one would lose face and bargaining power if one displayed over-eagerness. And a flight across the Atlantic on one's own means in an issue of this kind could be construed as over-eagerness. Now either the A.A. will pay. Or we shall have to work out some Saint Simonian compromise so that I just happen to be in London-Europe on other business and am therefore enabled to take the A.A. *en passant*.[5] Now, as I say, I think they should pay because this is surely merely normal protocol. However, if it does turn out that they are so goddam mean that they won't, then some strategy must be elaborated. For instance, the Ungers* invitation to Berlin would be a useful gambit.[6] But that means being able to concert goings on at the A.A. with an invitation from Ungers and probably both of these events with the Cornell Easter Recess. But maybe, if we start thinking about this it won't be impossible.

Then there are other things:

Money. How much is likely and how much is necessary.

Practice. Possibilities of. I want big things or some involvement with them. But does this sound grasping? (I imagine, in any case, that it would make for a more influential position.)

A small Americano *equipe* as a part of the faculty?[7] Would this be tactful? Or would it be simply expected.

Please write to me about these things,

Colin

P.S. About re-publishing an article. P.P.S. Considering the power vacuum on the East Coast of this country one has no doubt that the A.A. could go, go, go and that Harvard, Yale, the lot, would just have to follow.

PAT, LOTS OF LOVE. WILL SEE YA'.[8]

Colin

1 The letter from Edward Carter, director of the Architectural Association, dated January 18, 1966, reads in part:

Dear Mr. Rowe,

Your name, amongst others, has been suggested as someone who should be encouraged for the post of Principal of the Architectural Association School. I enclose a copy of the advertisement which has been published widely and which you may have seen. I also enclose a copy of Notes which we have prepared for the information of intending applicants.

I must make it clear that this is not an invitation for a short list. I am writing to you simply because certain members have indicated that they think you might be interested to apply, and we naturally hope that you will do so. The final date of applications is 28th February.

2 Kenneth Frampton (b 1930), architect and architectural historian, at the time a visiting professor at Princeton University in New Jersey.

3 The "Roneo" was a British duplicating machine similar to the mimeograph.

4 A photocopy of the article by American Popperian philosopher William Bartley III (1934–1990) is among Rowe's papers in the Rowe Archive at the Charles Moore Foundation, Austin: Bartley III, William, "On What is the House of Science Built", *AA Journal*, February 1965.

5 Refers to Claude-Henri de Saint-Simon compromise in Paris, January 1832.

6 OM Ungers* (1926–2007), German architect and educator.

7 *équipe*, French: team.

8 Pat Miller;* this line was handwritten.

---

069   *To **Philip Handler**, West Hartford, Connecticut*   *20 March 1966*

107 Cayuga Heights Road, Ithaca, N.Y.

Dearest Philip:

Am delighted that Paris has finally arrived and that you are now faced with the problem of mounting it.[1] This is a problem which myself has never solved so that when you discover how please do let me know.

Am writing because if I go down to New Haven sometime shortly as it seems that I may I would rather like to come via Hartford and be shown everything that's happening—though this would be likely to be sometime in May.

Meanwhile on Thursday of this week I go off on a brief visit to London. Rather unexpectedly I was invited to apply for the job of being Principal (?) of the A.A.; and, as a result, I go over for a confrontation with them on March 28.[2] Frankly I am less than ecstatic about the whole thing. The politics are, I believe, hideous; but one can scarcely refuse such invitations and one can't very well, I suppose, refuse free trans-Atlantic excursions. So pray for me—though I don't know at all what would be the desirable outcome!

Of course, this means something else. Just suppose that I do go to London on terms acceptable to me—then perhaps Roger's record player which I don't think would travel well might be transferable.[3] Or am I all mixed up?

Also, of course, all that marching around which is so absurd sounds really quite enjoyable and maybe a whole party might come down from here someday to enjoy the joke.[4]

Must go now and try to pay a few bills,

My love to Maddy and

Willseeya, Ciao, etc.[5]

Colin

1 Rowe had sent the Handlers a wallpaper map of Paris as a wedding gift.
2 "A.A.": Architectural Association, London.
3 Roger Sherwood.
4 Handler* played the piccolo and the flute in the Connecticut National Guard marching band.
5 Maddy Handler, Philip Handler's* wife.

To **Marcus Whiffen,**
College of Architecture, Arizona State University, Tempe, Arizona   *6 May 1966*   **070**

107 Cayuga Heights Road, Ithaca, N.Y.

Dear Marcus:

I was delighted to get a letter from you and to be obliged to think of you and Jean in all that hot Arizona sunshine while here we are just moving out into a belated spring. Have also been through all that funny business about the A.A.—the <u>denouncement</u> of which you probably already know. Frankly, of course, I do not think that it is very much to be regretted except in so far as it concerns what one is convinced is the shortly approaching (effective) demise of that unhappy institute. Really I have delayed replying since, after coming back from London, I have been alternating frenzied activity in small circles and bouts of total fatigue. But Marcus, what do I know about Adolf Loos?[2] I have seen the bar off the Karntner Strasse and a couple of houses. I believe that he was a superb decorator but couldn't plan. I know nothing about Vienna, except that I don't like it. Therefore I want to say: Don't ask me to do a review of Adolf Loos. I would love to do a review on somebody whom I thought was important. But those Vienna boys! And what is the story of Adolf Loos, on his way back from Paris, being arrested at the Austrian border for trying to introduce a collection of dirty photographs?

Am sorry to sound so uncooperative but I think that you will understand. I am, of course, flattered to be asked; but I would prefer to do it some other time with somebody I knew something about.

My best love to Jean,

Yours ever,

   Colin

1 Rowe had been considered a candidate for the Principal of the Architectural Association, London. See Rowe's letter to John Miller* dated 30 January 1966 (p 160 in this volume).
2 Marcus Whiffen,* editor of the *Journal of Architectural Education*, had asked Rowe to write a review of Ludwig Munz and Gustav Kunstler, *Adolf Loos: Pioneer of Modern Architecture*, New York: Praeger, 1966. The American Bar on Kartnerstrasse in Vienna was one of Loos' best-known works.

To **John & Pat Miller,** *Stirling Mansions, Canfield Gardens, London*   *11 February 1967*   **071**

107 Cayuga Heights Road, Ithaca, New York 14850

John-Pat:

Write some time. I am sure that you have lots to tell me—though I, without giving a Proustian day-to-day account of existence—don't have too much to say.

The M.O.M.A. exhibition went off so so.[1] Drexler spent lots of money on the installation and, one can't help thinking, behaved a little bit like an interior decorator over the whole business.[2] Set up an interior that was a little bit like Giancarlo de Carlo out of Wright.* Turgid colors but the inferred violence muted—and therefore the general montage was neither scientific and objective nor did it have the qualities of that little room with the gravel floor in the Triennale of 1950, or was it '51.[3]

Then on top of this he blew some things up that were supposed to be little until they were 14' by 11' and reduced other things that were supposed to be big and then suppressed other items in quite a whimsical way—all very difficult. Also at the opening David Rockefeller, who is the aboriginal capitalist and quite awful, was there at 11.45 to welcome Lindsay who didn't arrive until 1.45!!![4] Also Lindsay then said nice things about our project going on for about five minutes—but then his speech never did get into the *Times*. So it's all rather difficult and I am told that this sort of thing is known as post-creative depression.

Nothing much else—that, God help me, I received a phone call the other day asking me if I was interested in being considered Dean at the S. of A. at the U. of Houston!!![5] Please say nothing.

Tell me about the Hodgkinson business.[6]

What about the chaise longue?

What about Dorothy's miscarriage? I got such an appalling letter from her about it yesterday that I don't know whether to write or to ring up or what.

It's now about five hours later and immediately after I typed the above words I did decide to ring up. Results were strange and distant.

What else?

There is only one thing that occurs to me. Do you think that you could bear to have two more replicas of your chesterfield made?[7] It would be one copy for me to put in the room with the books and another for some people who would like to take one with them to Chicago in the summer.[8]

Lots of love and all that,

   Colin

1 The New City: Architecture and Urban Renewal, an exhibition of urban design interventions for Harlem, New York, by teams from Princeton, Columbia, MIT, and the Rowe-led team from Cornell.
2 Arthur Drexler (1925–1987), director of the MoMA's Department of Architecture and Design from 1956 to 1987.
3 Giancarlo de Carlo, "Spontaneous Architecture Display", Triennale, Milan, 1950.
4 David Rockefeller (b 1915), honorary chairman of the MoMA Board of Trustees. John V Lindsay (1921–2000), mayor of New York City from 1966 to 1973.
5 "S of A at the U of Houston": School of Architecture at the University of Houston.
6 Patrick and Anna Hodgkinson were divorcing.
7 Miller* had had two "chesterfields" made for Rowe in 1965.
8 Stuart Cohen and his wife.

072

To *Alvin Boyarsky,* Associate Dean,
College of Architecture and Art, University of Illinois at Chicago Circle, Chicago   *18 September 1967*

Cornell University, Department of Architecture, Ithaca, N.Y.

Alvin:

Your visit to Ithaca and the attendant absurdities.[1]

Some day or so before you had arrived my information service had filled me in as to your expected presence. And, on the Thursday of your arrival, I was—such is the speed of communication in primitive societies—provided very, very soon with the news. On the Friday I was also re-provided with the same information as to your presence. And, of course, I was finally provided—by your chauffeur—with the circumstances and time of your exit.

By all this, I must say that I was a little chagrined and a little amused. It was Stendhalian Parma all over again; and, shortly after I was able to surmise that you were back in Chicago, Illinois, I began trying to ring up—curiosity, slightly damaged *amour propre,*[2] possibly malice on my part—but I began to believe that you and Liz were on vacation.[3] So that I desisted.

But would have liked to have seen you and would also have been happy if you had been more readily abstracted from the coils of the boa-constrictor in which both you and Tony are apparently caught. Need I say that I allude to the Circean charms of X.Y.Z.[4]

However, and serious, there really ain't no ill feelings. Just a sense of this entirely grotesque.

But do please try to manage better—I mean call—next time.

Lots of love and whatever,

　　Colin

1　Boyarsky* had visited Cornell from Chicago for a single day without having met Rowe.
2　*amour propre,* French: self esteem.
3　"Liz": Elizabeth Boyarsky,* Alvin Boyarsky's* wife.
4　"Tony" and "XYZ" are unidentified. Possibly Tony Heywood* and Astra Zarina.*

To *Pat Miller, Canfield Gardens, London*　　　　　　　*18 September 1967*　

073

107 Cayuga Heights Road, Ithaca, New York

My dear Pat:

Forgive me for ringing up you and John in the middle of the night. Actually it was enormously therapeutic—for me at least. I was simultaneously trying to write a letter to Ungers* and to yourself and was terribly fed up with both.[1] The Ungers letter was agony because he wrote to me in April offering me a chair at the Free University of Berlin and I was so *bouleverse* by the nonsense of the business that I just couldn't reply.[2] But I was trying to reply because of this symposium invitation which has arrived to compound miscellaneous feelings of guilt and indifference.

Your letter, too, was hell—really absolute hell. Something written again and again and all that—and always sounding malicious, or mean, or wrong in some way.

O.K. The mere act of phoning, however hysterical or obsessive or exaggerated it might seem, meant somehow the lowering of some entirely unreasonable threshold of inhibitions. So let's go—

To deal with first things first:

As I said last night I find myself enormously impressed with Alan's article which is just about the best critical thing that I have read for a long time.[3] I have sent a copy of it to Ungers and I hope that as a result of this little *demarche*[4] Alan does get invited (alongside Sam and Ken Frampton and Banham?*) to Berlin.[5] Then since nothing happens in isolation I gather from Boyarsky* that Alan is supposed to be in Chicago in the Spring. I gather this because I am supposed—as today—to write a letter of recommendation in this area—which seems ludicrous.

Also—and another thing—and to be talked about—I believe that I wouldn't on any long haul touch Boyarsky with a barge pole.[6]

But this is a big subject and would require development. But possibly you agree?

Furniture: though one scarcely dares to introduce the subject. But I did introduce it last night. It's a question of three more copies of your Chesterfield. One would be for me. The other two would be for Stuart and Susan Cohen. Stu is a former student of mine who can well afford it—just bought an early *seicento* table in Arezzo for $900.00 and all that.... So could this be expedited without massive inconvenience?

So what else?

There was of course the matter of our fire.... Or did the Koetters* not tell you? I had almost forgotten about it but at the time I was going to send you the newspaper cuttings. It was—how to emphasise the was—ARSON! The house was torched in three places and female underclothes treated with chemicals were used for purposes of ignition. And finally it appeared that the Cornell fire of last April in which nice people were killed was also arson. And apparently there is, one is told, a pyromaniac student around who is trying to fulfill various prophecies from Ezekiel—all of them about fire.

Anyway it was all very interesting and a bit like Dostoyevsky or Faulkner and Jerry rang me up at about 5.15 one morning to come and see the conflagration; and we learned a little about the apocalyptic intent of it all from the fire chief who was present—so went back and read Ezekiel (very rewarding) until breakfast.[7]

However, although the police can't decide who did it, I suppose that everything may still really be for the best in the best of all possible worlds, because we will not really be any the poorer for the fire. It's really been rather a gratifying little blaze in fact; and the insurance company seems to be paying something in excess of $6,000 over the costs of putting things right.

Which makes me think of how happy my little Control Bata stock still makes me. Bought at 30 in 1962. Split. 75 in March this year and now in the 130's. I find it all hard to believe—and if I hadn't been naive about this sort of thing I should have sold it. Doesn't this make you want to kick me.......?

Other snippety little things would be like a trip to Bermuda which is a composite suburb of New York and London. A bit like Newport, R.I. when seen from the water. A bit like Carmel, Calif. when the newer parts are seen at close quarters. Pink, white, blue and pseudo Portofino, etc. But inland might suggest bits of eighteenth century Yorkshire or Somerset—though the cottages for the negroes which are likely to be really very elegant and Ledolcian are distinctly more sophisticated than the equivalent sort of thing would be likely to be in England. However it's all very British and subdued and expensive. Nor are traces of action very discernible, so that all you can do is to work up a tan. Adele, however, did sell the house for Thirty Eight Thousand Pounds which I suppose must be a source of some satisfaction.[8]

The long haul things have obviously been—since February—working on this lousy book and then the New York business.[9]

As to the New York business in which Peter Eisenman* is very involved, it's probably going to be a go-go thing. We have an office floor about 90' by 25' and seem to be about to get a charter from the Board of Regents in Albany. Co-sponsored by M.O.M.A. and Cornell with miscellaneous trustees and advisors and all that, it is going to mean that I shall have to spend about half my time in N.Y.C.; and will have to look for an apartment down there, furnish, and all the rest of it.

As to the book: Well. To be brief I can only say that I have been helped—quite a lot—by Tom; [...].[10]

However, apart from all that that, the book progresses, and Tom will no doubt talk to you and Alan about it all [...].[11] But I would like you to make a Tom-Alan introduction since I think they would get along. And I would, as I said last night, like you to arrange a rapid and brilliant stucco tour—since one does like London to show its greatest grandeur to the naïve foreigner—and all that.

The Patrick-Anna affair is very *triste*.[12] It also imposes an inhibition about writing. Also one is led to believe that letters to Porchester Terrace don't necessarily get through to Cambridge.

For Alan, there is an article, "Hypothesis and Imagination", in that new Medawar book called *The Art of the Soluble*.[13] David gave it to me in the bar of the Waldorf at lunchtime on Saturday—and since then, though I don't think the book is remarkable, it's been turning me on and partly accounts for this letter.[14]

But the possibility of writing at such length has really derived from that phone call last night. I find this very odd. But that's the way things are. And, though this isn't a good letter, though it is worse than earlier letters I have rejected, writing I seem to have re-acquired an energy in which I seem to have been lacking for several months.

Anyway, if I come to Berlin from December 10–17, then I suppose that I shall be in London slightly later and conversation might be possible. Last night the line—your way—was really bad.

The best of love and all that,

    Colin

P.S. I have got on to an oriental rug thing. It's probably got the better of me. Eleven this year. It begins to embarrass.

P.P.S. By the way: about taking over the design department here?[15]
What ideas?
Boyarsky would like it I am told?????
Alan?
    Colin

1 OM Ungers* (1926–2009), at the time professor of architecture and dean of the faculty at the Technical University of Berlin. He was chairman of the Cornell School of Architecture from 1969 to 1975.
2 *bouleversé*, French: shocked.
3 Colquhoun, Alan, "Typology and Design Method", *Arena* 83, June 1967; later republished in Colquhoun, Alan, *Essays in Architectural Criticism: Modern Architecture and Historical Change,* Opposition Books, Cambridge, MA: MIT Press, 1985.
4 *démarche*, French: a diplomatic maneuver.
5 Sam Stevens, Kenneth Frampton, and Reyner Banham.* Alan Colquhoun* did not go to Berlin.
6 Both Alvin Boyarsky* and Rowe were being considered for principal of the Architectural Association.
7 Jerry A Wells.*
8 Adele Wells, wife of Jerry A Wells.*
9 It is unknown to which "lousy book" Rowe refers. Regarding "the New York business", Rowe led a team of urban design students from Cornell in a competition involving interventions around Harlem, New York. See note 1 to Rowe's letter to John* and Pat Miller* dated 11 February 1967 (p 163 in this volume).
10 Tom Schumacher.*
11 Alan Colquhoun.*
12 Patrick and Anna Hodgkinson; *triste*, French: sad.
13 Medawar, Peter B, *The Art of the Soluble*, London: Methuen, 1967.
14 David Rowe.*
15 Rowe regularly urged Miller* to apply for the position of chair of the design department at Cornell.

074   *To **John Miller**, Stirling Mansions, Canfield Gardens, London*   *24 June 1968*

107 Cayuga Heights Road, Ithaca, N. Y.

My dear John:

It is almost tropically hot, about 9.00 p.m., and I am just about to leave to spend most of the summer in N.Y.C. Tomorrow. I would have left a little before this—but getting out of anywhere seems to be a more than necessarily painful process.

O.K. So enclosed with this little note there is an inventory of things which it would be nice if they could be sent with the Chesterfields. Most of them, as you will notice, are at Cheltenham Terrace—but David writes to me to say that he will be in New York sometime in July so that I suppose that I could give him a copy of the inventory then—which ought to mean less sweat than either you trying to do the thing or me attempting to do it by letter.[1]

Then there is something else: I am at the present trying to make a lobby for a student, Steve Potters, who wants to come to London.[2] What has happened is that a sales job was almost done on Leslie for Steve to go to Cambridge but this now seems to have fallen through.[3] I think both Stephen and wife would have been terribly O.K. in Cambridge. Her propensity is medieval history and translating bits of Latin assisted by miscellaneous Jesuits and Dominicans, which always seems surprising; and Steve's propensity while at Cornell was every(one) form of athletics so that, naturally, he did acquire the reputation of not having a brain in his head.

So this particular assigning of personality types irritated me, and Steve became something of a project of mine—which he presumably still is. He is, as a matter of fact, intelligent, has good intuitions, is entirely reliable, displays great modesty, diffidence, etc; and one wishes that the athletics and rugby thing didn't go on because, otherwise, aggression which is now expended in this area might be altogether more usefully deployed.

But, in any case, there is almost nobody whom I would recommend to you more and I think that both you and Pat, as well as Alan, would greatly enjoy.[4] The duo-thing: scholasticism plus athletics—I think that you would all find entertaining and also you might like it all as a bit of Jewish New York. But, in any case, I wonder whether you could do anything to help? You and Alan would of course be perfect as employers—be interested and involved and all that. But then I also feel sure that you don't have the work to be able to take on this sort of thing. But who would and also be suitable? Douglas? Lyons, Israel? Denys Lasdun?[5]

As to other things: when you come here as visiting critic in February it will be coincident with the arrival of Mathias Ungers* to take over the architecture department here and I am sure that this will be amusing to watch. Myself initially, as you know, thought that Ungers would be a good idea. But then various somewhat Wagnerian personality traits emerged which didn't inspire my confidence, and still less that of people like Jerry and Fred.[6] However it was too late and since I set the great machine in motion I am now in the position to sit back wrapped in ironic speculations........

During this summer will mostly be at:
17 East 82nd Street, Apt 2A, N.Y.C., N.Y.
Telephone: 988.4090

Please write to me there any ideas you have about the Potters thing; and, after I have seen David, will let you know about the furniture and all that.

My love to Pat and tell Alan either himself to write or I will.

    Colin

P.S. You might expect a visit from the Wells's* later this Summer. At present they are in Spalato or Dubrovnik or somewhere but could be expected to be hitting London in the next two to three weeks.

    Colin

---

1 David* and Dorothy Rowe* lived at Cheltenham Terrace in London.
2 Stephen Potters, a student in Rowe's Urban Design Studio at Cornell.
3 Leslie Martin,* chairman of the School of Architecture at the University of Cambridge.
4 Pat Miller* and Alan Colquhoun.*
5 The Douglas Stephen Partnership, Architects, London; Lyons, Israel, Ellis, Gray, Architects, London; Denys Lasdun & Partners, London.
6 Jerry A Wells* and Fred Koetter.*

MEMORANDUM   *16 October 1968*   **075**

To: Burnham Kelly[1]*
From: Colin Rowe

Re: A New Lecture Course in the Urban Design Area

The subject of this memorandum is directly related to my notes on policy preceding the budget proposals for '69–'70.

By force of circumstances the Urban Design program has developed in a highly *ad hoc* and empirical fashion. Very largely it has relied on random suggestions and intuitions; while, as for structured academic input, it has depended exclusively upon offerings of the Department of City and Regional Planning.

It would now seem to be high time that some steps be taken to correct this situation and for this reason it is proposed that a lecture course, directed particularly to the needs of Urban Design students, be instituted.

I can describe this lecture course at length rather better than I can specify its contents succinctly.

Its bias would be analytical and critical rather than historical.

While it would include a survey of the standard and classic urbanistic set pieces its main focus of concentration would be elsewhere.

There exist, scattered throughout the cities of the world (or alternatively throughout the pages of history) a quantity of highly idiosyncratic and interesting building complexes which, for want of any better word, we might today call megastructures. These buildings which represent the effects of either the accretions of time or the adjustment to circumstances are among prominent but largely uncriticized contributions to the urban scene. They are, if you like, though at macrocosmic scale, among the *objets trouves* of the built environment, and are represented by such buildings as the Quirinale, the Palais Royale, The Hofburg, etc.[2] A study of such buildings and of the way in which, acting as both texture and object, they are stimulated by and in turn stimulate the context in which they are located would form an important component of the proposed course.

A further component of the course would include a study of the city as a compilation of neutral textures and prominent objects. It would discriminate the building as object from the building as texture and would proceed to the survey of textures and the analysis of such as might be possible or plausible today.

In this connection it would give particular attention to the dichotomy which existed between the city of history—the solid from out of which voids are carved—and the city as articulated by the early twentieth century—the void in which solids are juxtaposed.

Thus it would involve a study not only of such long received types as the *Palazzo*, the *hôtel particulier*, the *Maison de Rapport*, and the Row House, but it would also require a protracted notice of the elements of the *Ville Radieuse* and of the typical Central European *Siedlungen* c.1930.[3]

By such means the proposed course would proceed to more speculative fields enquiring whether—and, if so, in what way—it might be possible to mediate between opposed conceptions of city texture, between the existing and the new, etc. Here it might involve discussion as to the value, the limitations and the proper use of utopian fantasies.

This is some brief outline of the nature of the proposed course; and it is obviously believed that such a course could be of considerable usefulness to the more highly structured U.D. outfit that I have outlined. However, it is also believed that the visual material to support such a course is not at the moment available in our slide collection and that the putting of all this material together would involve considerable time and some money.

However, this is a proposal for next year:-

Question 1. How to implement it?
Question 2. Who to give it?
Question 3. Titles?

P.S. The Curriculum Committee has, I understand, approved a suggestion from Roger Sherwood for a seminar course: "Urban Housing" to be initiated next year.

As I understand it such a course would be in no necessary conflict with what I have here outlined.

Such a course, as far as I can see, would impinge upon the issue of urban texture but would be approaching such an issue from a different point of view—from a focus upon the individual residential cell rather than upon the macro-environment.

But in any case some of the same issues of visual aides are as obviously subtended as much by this decision of the Curriculum Committee as they are by this present memorandum.

---

1 Burnham Kelly* (1912–1999), professor of planning and dean of the Cornell College of Architecture, Art and Planning from 1960 to 1971.
2 *objets trouvés*, French: found objects.
3 *hôtel particulier*, French: large townhouse; *Maison de Rapport,* French: apartment house; *Ville Radieuse*, French: *Radiant City*, which was the title of Le Corbusier's* 1933 book on urbanism; *Siedlungen,* German: settlements.

MEMORANDUM   *26 March 1969*   **076**

To: Burnham Kelly* & the Graduate Faculty
From: Colin Rowe

Re: A Proposed Minor in Urban Design

The idea has been expressed that graduate students, if properly qualified, should have the opportunity of minoring in Urban Design. The proposal seems to be in principle a good one; but, of course, in practice, it raises a multiplicity of issues—specific and general, some of which I have already referred to in my Memo to Stephen Jones of February 14.

To deal first with certain specific issues: The Urban Design Program as at present constituted is very largely a studio course which relies for further academic input principally on courses offered by City and Regional Planning.[1] In the future it is hoped that the Urban Design Program will be able to offer lecture and/or seminar courses specifically related to its general tendency. But the time for this is not yet; and thus, for the moment, it seems that a minor in Urban Design would logically take the form of a studio course.

In this connection I have proposed that one full semester of studio could reasonably be regarded as fulfilling requirements for a minor; but this proposal necessarily ignores questions of space and faculty.

To turn to certain general issues: It might not be altogether injudicious to propose that the idea of a minor in Urban Design is something which is sponsored by the inadequacy of our present graduate offerings. Certain graduate students wish to continue an involvement with Design; but this is a wish which can only, as things are, be accommodated by the Urban Design Program.

This seems not to be a good situation, since while the Urban Design Program could take a limited number of students wishing to minor, it could scarcely go beyond a very limited number without proceeding to adulterating its content.

Therefore the problem of the graduate student wishing a Design involvement should probably be considered in a wider context.

In the list of our present graduate offerings there are at least three omissions which might be considered odd. Of these, the absence of a program designated "Graduate Architecture" is probably the most outstanding. Also the absence of "Landscape Architecture" is a matter which we should still continue to question; and, further, the non-existence of a program "Industrial/Product Design"—something cancelled with the mini-environment—ought to be considered as a serious omission on our part.

Certainly if programs in these areas were to be established, I believe that we should arrive at a much more stimulating and interesting structure of graduate studies and at a much wider and, probably, more logical spectrum of choice for the student.

---

1 Rowe's first Urban Design Studio was offered in fall 1963, one year after his return to Cornell from Cambridge.

077   MEMORANDUM   *4 April 1969*

To: Burnham Kelly★ & K. C. Parsons
From: Colin Rowe

Re: Certain issues which emerge from my memo: "A Proposed Minor in Urban Design"[1]

My proposal that one semester of Urban Design Studio could be seen as fulfilling requirements for a minor in this area is no doubt well intentioned; but also, seen retrospectively, it seems to me to be distressingly *ad hoc* and empirical.

It is certainly a possibility, but I really think that we have to try to envisage something just a little better and more logical; and thus, I wish to propose the following:

1. A studio course called *Elements of Environmental Design*
2. Supporting Lecture and Seminar Courses

1. Would be an equivalent at macrocosmic scale to the type of freshman design course, Bauhaus-styled, with which we are familiar.

Such a course, though it seems to be an obvious and necessary one, does not seem, as yet, to have been instituted anywhere; and at Cornell one could very well imagine it being jointly sponsored by both East and West Sibley and, perhaps, largely offered to non-architects, i.e., Historians, City Planners, possibly potential Urban Designers, etc..[2]

2. These courses might also be of interest to undergraduate architects.

The package of 1 and 2: *Elements of Environmental Design* plus Supporting Lecture and Seminar Courses could begin right away to service these graduate programs concerned with the macroenvironment, i.e., City Planning and Urban Design; while it could also, hopefully, lay the groundwork for a future re-establishment of Landscape Architecture.

Some such proposal as this is in line with the general tendency of the Kelly★-Stein-Hurtt★-Koetter★-Rowe conversations of April, 1968.[3]

1   See Rowe's earlier memo to Kelly* (p 171 in this volume). Burnham Kelly was dean of the college; KC Parsons was chairman of City and Regional Planning.
2   The east wing of Cornell's Sibley Hall housed architecture students. West Sibley housed planning students.
3   Burnham Kelly,* Stuart Stein, Steven Hurtt,* and Fred Koetter.*

To **Mary Stirling**, *Belsize Avenue, London*   *25 September 1969*   **078**

American Academy, Via Angelo Masina 5, Rome

Dear Mary:[1]

I am beginning to feel just a little bit established. I occupy two rooms which are, both of them, rather higher than they are long or square. They are about 20' high as a matter of fact and have tile floors which are already threatening to be rather cold.

This time, though, I am not particularly turned on by the Italian scene. The automobiles, the noise and the expense are all of them a bit much to take and one begins to think that the common market which one supposes has produced the so-called 'economic miracle' is perhaps just something of a curse. I may change my mind and get turned on. I hope so. But for the moment I alternate sensations of *deja vu* with spasms of mild dismay.[2]

All the way the cathedral of Coutances has been one of the best things seen (Cours Mirabeau at Aix and Villa Collodi at Lucca provide comparable stimulus)[3] and this is just to thank for the night at Coutainville and also for the stay in Belsize Avenue.[4]

Hope that this is not too polite and please tell Jim that I look forward to his arrival in November.

Will see you and all that and I include a little addition for the kitchen photograph collection.[5]

    Colin

P.S. And also my love to Mrs Thing![6]

1   Mary Stirling, the stepdaughter of P Morton Shand, was married to James Stirling.*
2   *déjà-vu*, French: already seen.
3   Coutances Cathedral (1210–1274), French Gothic; Cours Mirabeau, Aix-en-Provence, France, a wide tree-lined thoroughfare started in the seventeenth century; Villa Garzoni (Collodi) near Lucca, Italy, is renowned for its gardens.
4   Agon-Coutainville is in the Normandie region of France.
5   Mary Stirling kept current photographs on a pinup board in her kitchen.
6   Reference to Mrs Bonfield, the Stirlings'* Irish cleaning lady.

Rowe visiting Wells Koetter's architectural office, Ithaca, New York, 1967.

5
Disillusion

1970–1974

Although Rowe had encouraged the appointment of OM Ungers* to chair of Cornell's School of Architecture, he was soon unhappy with Ungers' leadership. In August 1971 he wrote John Miller* that he was "rather miserable and depressed", noting that, "You liked Ithaca in '66 because I had made a scene here. But this scene, apparently, aroused jealousy, so every attempt has been made to smash it [...]".

Nevertheless, he continued to develop the Urban Design Program, and in fall 1972 he and Fred Koetter* wrote a series of articles for *The Architectural Review* about the work of the program and its students. In December 1972, however, Fred Koetter, Alan Chimacoff, and Roger Sherwood, former Urban Design students of Rowe's teaching at Cornell, were fired: "the work of the Ungers-Shaw-Pearman troika" Rowe wrote John Miller, "an entirely remorseless vendetta". Klaus Herdeg,* another Rowe disciple, resigned in protest.

Rowe understood this as Ungers' dismantling of the Urban Design Program. He turned his attention to personal development, focusing both on writing and on publishing his previously written essays and lectures as books. "The catastrophes which have fallen on this place have resulted in at least one good", he wrote to Robert Slutzky* in August 1973. "One can say 'forget it' and, forgetting the lack of education which the students are now about to receive, one can concentrate upon the, personally, more advantageous." The year before writing to Slutzky, he had written an introduction to *Five Architects: Eisenman, Graves, Gwathmey, Hejduk, Meier*, broaching the subject of a legitimate Modern architecture. Immediately after this letter, from August to December 1973, he and Fred Koetter wrote *Collage City*.

To **John Miller**, *Stirling Mansions, Canfield Gardens, London*   *5 January 1970*   **079**

107 Cayuga Heights Road, Ithaca, New York 14850

John:

Quite uneventful trip.[1] Cannes is surely to be recommended as a place for comings and goings—that is if you must go by sea. No sweat. No fuss. I have lunch in the open overlooking the harbor and then stagger across the quay to get into the tender which takes us out to the boat. The *Raffaello* (the Raff- sister ship: the Mike) is quite pretty inside but is quite as tedious *en voyage* as we both guessed that it might be. Insipid food, bingo, returning Americans of indescribable dullness, a feeble library, *Mafiosi, monsignori*, and the religious—in fact much like any other ship. Nice departure—with snow over the Alpes Maritimes, and a nice morning and lunch in Naples—with snow over Vesuvius. Then lots of calm warm weather until the last day when the New York scene really began to afflict us. Landing late, awful cold, snow and all the works—worst snow in Albany since 1818, worst snow in Ithaca ever recorded, etc.

Of course the New York customs were entirely characteristic—except, being just before Christmas, they turned out to be drunk! I go to get the car. I stand waiting, passive, obedient. The bureaucrat continues writing. Finally, he looks up. "Yeah, I got ya whaddya want?" I explain and he gestures and I go to where indicated. The same wait, then the look, then the rolling of the cigar in the mouth and then I explain again. Another look and then "Waall and whakind of an automobile are ya talkin abaht?" I repeat. I tell him a "Lotus". He asks again. A further reiteration and then another and then a snort, and then—"A LOTUS, a Lotus, fella, that's not an automobile that's a flower."

Which is no doubt all very amusing if it were not entirely gratuitous, typical of Manhattan and degrading for all concerned.

Anyway, sitting on my table on the boat there was a guy called Robert Heineman who was returning to his house in Vermont from his house in Cagnes and the second night at dinner he set out to explain Cagnes to me. I said that I had spent some time there and he said: "Where?" I said: "A house"; but that I couldn't think of the name of the people but that I thought that I could draw it and that, in any case, there were lots of postcards of it. He said: You don't mean *La Gouldette*. But we live exactly three (or however many) doors down [...]

---

1 Rowe spent fall 1969 at the American Academy in Rome. This letter describes his return to New York, a journey made by boat from Cannes to New York City. The concluding pages of the letter are lost.

080   To *Alvin Boyarsky*, London   *12 January 1970*

107 Cayuga Heights Road, Ithaca, New York 14850

Alvin:

This is to suppose that you are still in London.

I was talking to Jerry the other night about your summer school business and my Lugano proposal.[1] Jerry was a little bit pre-occupied with other things but he did suppose that Mrs. Fleming might be quite interested.[2]

Now, if you are interested in pursuing this angle, he is to be in Lugano at the end of the month and, therefore, I suppose you should contact him here beforehand—presumably during the next few days.

Here, when I arrived, was said to have been quiet during the Fall. But certainly it is not quiet now. Ungers,* of course, is irrational and a maniac; but it isn't that—although I think that it has been brought on by that.[3] It is quite different. What it amounts to is a concerted attempt on the part of the old guard faculty and certain elements in Day Hall to oust Burnham Kelly* which, apparently has been underway since November but which has burst out in the last ten days during Burnham's absence in Mexico.[4]

You can imagine the line up: Kira, not Canfield, Barnette, Symonds, Saul, Brown, Detweiler.[5] With the exception of Canfield, it is the group which—way back—I wrote to tell Ungers would be likely to be against his appointment; and, personally, I think that they are unconsciously taking a grievance against Ungers out on Kelly.

But it's an interesting situation. By next Fall Burnham will have completed ten years as Dean—which is much longer than both Mackesey and the previous incumbent and which is a length of tenure not now in line with Day Hall policy.[6] Therefore, whatever Burnham's merits or demerits may be (and I can see a great many of both) and though nothing may happen just at the moment, I am inclined to think that this is the beginning of an end.

Do you find this interesting?

Does Elizabeth?[7]

    Colin

---

1 Jerry A Wells.*
2 Mrs Mary Crist Fleming (1910–2009), who ran Fleming College, a two-year co-educational program founded in Lugano, Switzerland, in 1968.
3 OM Ungers,* chairman of Cornell's Department of Architecture.
4 Burnham Kelly* (1912–1999), dean of the College of Architecture, Art, and Planning at Cornell from 1960 to 1971.
5 Alex Kira, Thomas Canfield, Stuart Barnett, presumably David Simons (not "Symonds"), Francis Saul, Ludlow Brown, and Henry Detweiler.
6 Thomas W Mackesey (1908–1976), dean of Cornell's College of Architecture, Art, and Planning from 1951 to 1960.
7 Elizabeth Boyarsky,* Alvin Boyarsky's* wife.

MEMORANDUM   *22 September 1970*   **081**

TO: Dean Burnham Kelly* and Professors Mahoney,* Levin, Lynn, Parsons, Peaman
FROM: Colin Rowe

RE: My Statement Made to the Architecture Study Committee on Thursday, September 11, 1970

This is to recapitulate, amplify, and add to my remarks.

I opened with observations from personal experience and stated:

1. that I had taught for eight years at Cornell;
2. that previously l had taught in the universities of Liverpool, Texas, and Cambridge;
3. that, from time to time, I had had intimate knowledge of Yale, the Architectural Association, Princeton, and Cooper Union;
4. that, while many of these institutions are (or were) supposedly illustrious, I am disposed to be highly impressed by the superiority of the Cornell product.

I continued that the formal curriculum of the College of Architecture had always elicited certain reservations on my part; that I believed that the three lecture sequences offered were, certainly in respect to the process of problem solving in design, just not adequate; that many aspects of problem solving could be taught, but that these are only taken up in an *ad hoc* fashion over the boards; that, in terms of graphics the School seems to me never to have been distinguished. But I added that in spite of all this there persisted a quality, and that Cornell graduates are generally highly regarded wherever it might be that they go to look for a job.

I then abandoned the discussion of the specifics of Cornell and made an attempt to speak about the general predicament of architectural education which became more broken up than I would have wished by a series of questions with reference to change, the personality of the Chairman, ideology, originality, imitation, etc. Therefore, in this context, I wish to amplify my remarks.

An approach to the problems of architectural education, I believe, might quite well take a stand on such a question as this: *With reference to a work of architecture, what propositions can be proved to be false or true?*

And an honest answer to this question will, I suppose, have to be based upon the acceptance of the situation that only a very limited number of statements indeed can be considered as empirically verifiable.

Pre-eminently these will relate to the laws of statics and to certain characteristics of the behaviour of materials; to a less certain extent they will relate to the structure of the human eye and therefore to the reception of the building as a visual manifestation; and to a still less certain extent they will relate to matters of function in so far as these are fairly directly concerned with the structure of the human body.

But, outside these areas, which—as to their verifiability—have been arranged in descending order, I suspect that we shall have to accept any statements made about a work of architecture as being largely conjectural or speculative.

This could also be said somewhat differently—and I quote myself:

"that, though a work of architecture in its practical aspects is very largely an affair of assembling bricks, stones, mortar, steel, concrete, glass, timber, tubes and entrails according to the principles of certain known statistical laws,... the supposition which is generally received that architecture is the coordination of these very miscellaneous materials for the purposes of use and pleasure already intrudes most of the ultimate problems of metaphysics. For, if the laws of statics can be assumed safely to be established beyond dispute, the "laws" of use and pleasure, of convenience and delight, have certainly not as yet been subjected to any Newtonian revolution; and while it is not inconceivable that in the future they may be, until that time any ideas as to the useful and the beautiful will remain opinions; they will rest upon untested and unverifiable hypotheses. And this we might propose as architecture's central glaring problem—a problem which neither the brisk conclusions of common sense nor the refined intuitions of an enlightened sensibility can ever quite suppress.

"Like the exponent of theology, political theory, philosophy, or any other discipline which seeks to order random experience, which cannot passively await an ideal future solution of its problems, which is obliged to disentangle significant and workable structures from a continuous flux of evidence, the architect is obliged to work upon an essentially 'uncertain' substratum, and in the end his formulation of concepts of use, beauty, improvement, etc., will rest upon ideological foundations. And thus, behind any architectural system or approach,"—however unconsciously entertained or strenuously disavowed—"there will always be implicated a variety of assumptions as to the substance of reality, the nature of truth, the significance of novelty, the natural man, the good society, and all the other criteria which typically are intruded in order to arbitrate problems of value."[1]

This is a situation which, for the architect and architectural educator is, for the most part, hard to bear; and rather than attempt to recognise it, they are apt to jump the gun and to insist that their procedures, their strategies, are based upon no more than a recognition of "facts".

But, of course, the architect's and the architectural educator's general notion of what constitutes a "fact" is something which presents inordinate epistemological difficulties. Thus, there is a disposition to attribute factuality only to that which is measurable and quantifiable, to that which has length, breadth, texture, smell, etc., so that rainfall in Florida or the prevailing wind in Iowa, the porosity of a brick, etc., are thought of as being "real"; while equally real phenomena, e.g. *The Communist Manifesto*, *The Declaration of Independence*, the notions of revolution and tradition, are apt to be dismissed as irrelevant. Therefore, while a separation is made between the physical and the "cultural", to only one of these is "reality" attributed.

This somewhat casual handling of a major problem has been characteristic of modern architecture; and, because it has always been glossed with sentimental overtones (the architect in the explicit service of mankind, the imminent dawn of the better social order, etc.), it continues to be a predominant determination. That is, there is widespread reluctance to face the condition of what architecture is (its mode of being, etc.); and the more disinclined the architect or educator is to do so, then—and the more he gets away from the empirically verifiable—the more violently he is likely to insist that his speculations are the undeniable revelations of scientific method.

I do not wish to appear obsessive about this issue; and I only labor it because I believe that it is from a lack of reasoning in this area that most of the problems of architectural education flow. It should be possible to put together a building with some degree of scientific rigor; but so long as the intrinsically subjective nature of an architectural work goes unrecognized, then the possibilities of a genuine rigor will always be aborted.

F. S. Northrop, in his *The Logic of Science and the Humanities*, states the following:

> Inquiry starts only when there is something unsatisfactory, when the facts necessary to resolve one's uncertainties are not known.

> The most difficult part of any inquiry is its initiation. One may have the most rigorous of methods during the later stages of investigation, but if a false or superficial beginning has been made, rigor later on will never retrieve the situation...

> Inquiry begins not with a method known *a priori* but with a specific problem; it is the problem which determines the method. Furthermore, in different portions of their experience, men are confronted with different types of problems raising different kinds of questions. Since it is the kind of question being raised by a given problem which determines the type of method appropriate for the answering of the question, it follows that there will be as many different scientific methods as there are fundamentally different kinds of problems.

> This is clearly recognized in the exact sciences. Certain problems occur in mathematical physics or in pure mathematics which raise merely questions of logical consistency. For such questions no one supposes the empirical methods of observation and experiment to be either necessary or appropriate. The methods of formal logic are sufficient.

> Again, there are problems where the consistency of a given theory is not in question and one is confronted solely with the problem of its empirical truth. Clearly such a question is not to be answered by the methods of formal logic alone, although they may be required in part. One must obviously also resort to empirical methods.

> But besides problems of logical consistency and problems of the empirical truth of theory, i.e., problems of fact, there are also problems which, for the lack of a better name, may be called problems of value. In the social sciences and the humanities where ideological issues are everywhere present, especially in the contemporary world, these problems are paramount. The characteristic of a

problem of value, such as the issue between democracy and communism, is that, in part at least, it raises a question concerning what ought to be, rather than what is, the case. Clearly scientific method appropriate for answering a question concerning what ought to be the case must be different from the method which answers a question concerning what is the case.

It is popular today to deny this thesis, affirming that problems of fact and problems of value are quite identical, the content only differing, and hence to be solved by one and the same scientific method.[2]

It may, perhaps, be pretentious on my part to produce a string of quotations such as these at such length; and if this seems to be the case, I must explain that, though personally I always prefer words about things, if pressed, I do use arguments such as these with students and only produce them to this committee because I believe they may illuminate the problems with which it is involved.

Architecture is concerned with amelioration. Therefore, it is to a great degree concerned with problems, not of what is, but of what ought to be the case. That is, it cannot be detached from problems of value; and that, therefore, these must be something which, in any system of architectural education, it is essential should be recognised.

Also, it should be insisted that to recognise the role of value is, to some degree, to escape it, i.e., once the role of value is recognised, it becomes possible to disregard the content of individual value judgements and simply to require that any particular person's value judgements (or fantasies), at least in so far as they are concerned with problem solving, should be articulated to their point of maximum clarity; and, in speaking to the committee I did suggest that an emphasis on the virtues of logical consistency might, in this way, have the tendency, if not to expel, at least to circumscribe the undue influence of ideological considerations.

And this is the crux of what I have to say.

However, though the architect is faced with these three categories of problem, so long as there survives the apocalyptic-messianic feeling that the millennium is just around the corner and that these intellectual distinctions—like the state after the Marxist revolution—will then vanish away, it is useless to insist upon them. They are necessary distinctions; but their necessity will not be believed. Rather they will be regarded, as specious and, to return to the particular, it is here, I suspect, that we might locate one of the central problems of the College: the romance of technology which means a great deal to the public means even more to the Chairman; and just as the public, through the agency of technology, seems often to anticipate a millennial dispensation, so does he; and therefore, while these intellectual distinctions become conceived as irrelevant, even their assertion (as a stage prior to their disappearance?) becomes impossible.[3]

But—just to enlarge and footnote this scene—because millennialistic and other fantasies have been able to insinuate themselves into the picture, we have already become very far removed from the simple Positivistic description of "reality" which so many architects and educators would still prefer to receive.

To make one further comment, rather than moving forward in an area concerning the knowledge of architecture, problem solving, and design, I believe that we are in imminent danger of taking a step backwards. In other words, I do not believe that we are welcoming the new or being particularly responsive to change. Instead, I believe that it is being urged that we accept the now largely discredited arguments that were made for modern architecture in the 1920s and '30s as though these were new and had not so far received our due consideration and attention.

**In order to elaborate and to comment upon these observations, I have attached to this memorandum two papers, both of which are mildly celebrated. These are:

William W. Bartley, "On What Is the House of Science Built?"[4]
Alan Colquhoun,* "Typology and Design Method"[5]

1 Excerpted from Rowe's unpublished address to the Architectural Association Council as a candidate for school principal in spring 1966. Similar passages are found in the talk Rowe gave at a conference, "Architectural Education USA: Issues, Ideas, and People", held at the Museum of Modern Art, New York, fall 1971, later published in *Lotus International*, no 27, 1980 and reprinted in Rowe, Colin, *As I Was Saying: Recollections and Miscellaneous Essays*, Alexander Caragonne ed, 3 vols, Cambridge, MA: MIT Press, 1996, vol 2, pp 53–64.

2 Northrop, FSC, *The Logic of the Sciences and the Humanities*, New York: Macmillan, 1947, pp 17–20.

3 O.M. Ungers* was chairman of Cornell's School of Architecture from 1969 to 1975.

4 William W Bartley III, "How Is the House of Science Built?: The Growth of Scientific Knowledge". At the time of this memo, Bartley (1934–1990) was professor of philosophy at the University of Pittsburgh, having completed a PhD under the supervision of Karl Popper* at the London School of Economics in 1962. It is uncertain if the paper was published. A typescript exists in the Rowe archive, the Charles Moore Foundation.

5 Colquhoun, Alan, "Typology and Design Method", *Arena* 83, June 1967, reprinted in the late 1960s and 1970s, the article appears in Colquhoun, Alan, *Essays in Architectural Criticism: Modern Architecture and Historical Change*, Cambridge, MA: MIT Press, 1985, pp 43–50.

To **Pat Miller,** *Stirling Mansions, Canfield Gardens, London*   *24 September 1970*   **082**

The American Academy, Via Angelo Masina 5, Rome

My dear Pat:

I don't know that I am all that turned on by this place or indeed by this town. About this place one might say something later; but the town, at the moment, contrives to look just like a junk heap of old warehouses. It's very expensive. If you sit down to dinner in any piazza you might just as well be eating in a garage. Driving is a little impossible. Walking about is a hazard. And as for the noise—this is a continuous assault.

Which is all a cue for John to say something.[1] And probably quite right too. So I think that I will give you a brief outline of my little *voyage* as it has been so far.

Well, after leaving you, I found the Lotus people with some difficulty and finally got out of town at about 5.30.[2] Found the country north of Nice rather exciting and drove through it a little too quickly to end up at a place called Barreme where I spend the night.

The next day up to Briancon and over the Mont Genevre. But to say <u>over</u> is a bit of an actual exaggeration because the real mountains seems to precede the actual pass and one suddenly finds oneself in Italy after only a dozen or so turns up the easiest of all possible hills. Then decided to avoid Turin and, therefore, on through rather bland mountainous stuff to Pinerolo which seems to be where the plain begins. Poplars and willows and all that stuff looking really quite nice and so decide because of some unspeakable nostalgia (or something) to spend the night in Alba—and perhaps even to gorge on truffles. But about 5.30 there were melodramatic flashes of lightening and, just as I get the top up, all hell breaks loose. And now...... the famous repair job done on the window in Nice turns out to be no repair job at all. The window will just not go up—and so I drive on getting wet and getting lost.

So Alba was an object lesson in the failure of memory and the distortions produced by retrospection. I had one picture of it from 1949 going there with Alan and Paolo Candiani and his father in some kind of horse drawn vehicle; and then I had another from '64, this time going with Alvin Boyarsky* to look for a Vittone church.[3] And I had the whole thing nicely placed and labeled. It was remote, untouched, subtly related to the *ancien regime*; and it was, in fact, rather clever to have been there and to be going there again.[4]

So do I have to say that the let down was awful, the town a little nothing place, the restaurant not good, the bed in the hotel awful, and—just for the record—that there was again NO SOAP? (One wonders now if that is where the expression comes from!)

So the following morning I start in the rain which is really a deluge and go on to awful Alessandria and dreary Pavia and take Mantua *en passant* round about lunch time. And then I got to San Benedetto Po to see the Guilio Romano church—a place which used to be the purest Stendhalian Italy. You approached it across the river by a bridge of boats and the piazza was sand and gravel and all this conferred remoteness, etc., etc. But now the economic miracle has struck and the bridge (where I tore out the muffler of the M.G.) is gone and the Mantua-Modena highway has now got a nice big wide bridge to go across. While as for San Benedetto—it has rallied to the occasion by paving the piazza and obscuring the church with an almost English accumulation of municipal *bric a brac*—mostly lampposts.

One now seems to have arrived at the standard situation and when one gets to Vicenza and the pleasures of a Jolly Hotel, it is obviously to discover that Vicenza is cluttered with cars, that Palladio* looks unendurably bland, and that—of course—it continues to rain.

Sunday morning I leave for Venice and, after stopping to get some gas, I run into a situation which could have been not good. Suddenly four cops come screaming down the road and trying to force the car ahead of me off on to the verge. He abruptly brakes and I follow suit—miraculously without running into; and then—as the car behind me doesn't manage so well—there is an awful scraping sound and while he pulls up ahead of both of us, the road is suddenly full of enthusiastic cyclists, six abreast. Of course, its all over in seconds and I get out to look at the damage and the driver who scrapes me comes up and things are a bit operatic but mercifully the damage is slight and the very minimum paint abrasions are at the moment being taken out at a *carrozzeria* around the corner.[5]

But apparently going to Venice on Sunday is not a good idea; and, although overtaking everything on the autostrada is really quite O.K., when I do get to the Piazzale Roma, it is only to find myself in a two hour traffic jam and to discover that there is absolutely no parking. It's hot, the engine gets hot, huge tourist buses desperately attempt to manoeuvre, obviously more cars are pouring in all the time; and about midday I decide that it might be a good idea to try a little later. Shouldn't I perhaps make a little trip to Chioggia at the end of the lagoon? Here surely there will be that undisturbed emptiness, that nineteenth century Henry James*-Augustus Hare scene?

It seems like a good idea and I progressively extricate myself, return across the bridge, negotiate the various spaghetti patches, and off I go through the awful smog of Mestre. But Chioggia turns out to be a mistake—a depressed little town with one main street which now apparently serves as an appendage to an entirely gruesome and absolutely new side resort called Sottomarina. Six story apartment houses, a cheap amalgam of reminiscences of the Second Empire and the Promenade des

Anglais with equally lower middle anticipations and fantasies of the year 2000. So one chocks it up to experience and recognises that perhaps by now the situation in the Piazzale Roma might be just a bit relieved.

So turn around and off we go and on the way back I am struck by a bright idea. Why not park the car in a garage in Fusina, take the tramway to the mouth of the Brenta, get on to the ferry and enter Venice in the classic way, landing on the Riva degli Schiavoni? It's obviously sensible and convenient. One has done something like it before. And wouldn't it, in any case, be cheaper?

Intuitions work like mad. I follow a sign saying "Seconda Zona Industriale".[6] I avoid several oil refineries and, suddenly, there is familiar territory. The Villa Malcontenta is just ahead; and, even though the oil tanks do press it close, there is a feeling of at least some achievement; and, accordingly, one decides to do a little Brenta inspection before one begins to think about the ferry.

Of course one notices that the tramway has gone. But one doesn't pay any particular attention to this. One is still infatuated by the ingeniousness of one's idea and so one drives along the river with the industrial landscape getting increasingly sinister, the sea marsh more and more desolate, the road more and more vacant, and one's sensations more and more poignant. But this is still the entrance made by the Grand Tourist and it is just the emptiness of this last stretch, the brightness of the sky and the sadness of the water which must have always contributed maximum impact to an arrival in the Piazzetta. Undoubtedly therefore one was doing the right thing; and, though the tramway had disappeared, there just ahead was the little terminal station—obviously disused but rather reassuring.

But by now you must guess that this is all the reassurance that there was. The Ruskinian entrance was just not to be made. The lagoon was there, Venice was there, the landing stage was there. But the ferry? Well, that was just a no longer available choice.

So there was the smog of Mestre, the weeds in the water, the sense of being in some very ancient place, a little time out for sardonic reflection, and—again—on to the Piazzale Roma. But this time it was just unbelievable. Quarter of the way across the bridge traffic was just at a standstill and, this time, we were an hour simply getting across—only to turn around quite obviously on arrival.

Which is how I saw Venice and although one might have plugged in to Bassano or somewhere for the night and then tried next day I decided not. Bologna seemed a sensible place. So south again with Chioggia once more coming up on the left, the terrible Lido of Ferrara, Germans swarming around the Abbey of Pomposa, Sant Apollinare in Classe with the oil tanks of Ravenna showing up above the trees of the *pineta*, and then threading one way through the usual one way street labyrinth just as it begins to get dark.[7]

Which was all a great object lesson in something or other and so, with illusions destroyed, after four nights in Lucca, one in Siena and three in Viterbo, one came on here. No great excitements anywhere. A nice dinner in Bologna, a pleasant academic couple from Pennsylvania who dosed me on Scotch which I didn't want, an elderly California architect in Lucca also an Oxford type, an interior decorator from Seattle in Siena, and—in Viterbo—a brief *rencontre* with the King of Sweden all mixed up with a hysterical female from N.Y.C.[8]—*la fanciulla del West* or *la piazza del Central Park*.[9] Won't go on about the K. of S. except that he was a nice old thing and wasn't able to get any excavating done because it rained all the time which was also *la pazza's* problem too except that she wanted to see gardens—and all this little group of people cooped up in a small sixteenth century villa turned into a hotel did produce an effect rather like the opening of some Isak Dinesen story.

This more or less completes the story and suggests what my mood might be. I have been here for just over a week. It has rained most days. I have contracted a cold. And, although I am feeling slightly less jaundiced than I was, I can't say that I am exactly exuding stimulation. Personally I believe the enemy to be the common market. Am beginning to suspect that it's the cause of everything bad and am even beginning to find myself sympathetic to those sections of the Labour Party etc. which are all opposed to it. It is the neo-Capitalist thing which is really the pain and its just as if all these places were trying to make a doctrinaire demonstration of their belief in *laissez faire*, *Time-Life*, the American 'way', *et al* by systematically wrecking whatever amenities they might still possess. It all seems to be both rather cynical and rather naïve—only both in the wrong way; and, out of it all, one wonders what the so called workers do get. As far as I can see the illusions of opulence and high prices and not much else. In fact the whole common market thing is obviously no more than an international managerial alliance. It's the sort of thing that is expected by managerial society in the U.S. of A. and, consequently, it's obediently provided—just as, for that matter, it's obediently provided in England—either by design or default—by both political parties.

Am not saying any of this very well because, as yet, am not quite sure what it is that I am trying to say. Only it does tend to become a bit clear here that there is just some point to the Socialist thing—however blunted and battered that might be.

Will write again when I have anything to say—and this letter is also for John.

    Colin

---

1 John Miller.*
2 Rowe's automobile, a Lotus, needed attention in Nice where presumably he had met Pat Miller.*
3 Alan Colquhoun.*
4 *ancien régime*, French: old order; a system or mode no longer prevailing.
5 *carrozzeria*, Italian: body shop.
6 *Seconda Zona Industriale*, Italian: Second Industrial Zone.
7 *pineta*, Italian: pine wood.
8 *rencontre*, French: meeting.
9 *la fanciulla del West*, Italian: the maiden of the West (as in the opera of this name by Puccini).

083   To ***David & Dorothy Rowe,*** *Cheltenham Terrace, London*   *5 September 1970*

The American Academy, Via Angelo Masina 5, Rome

David-Dorothy:

There is either a lot or not much to write about.

I got here just over a week ago. It has rained quite a lot. I have had a cold and still do a bit. And, for the moment at least, I am just not terribly turned on.

So far this trip has been like so: Coutances, Coutainville (Jim), Ruffec (Angouleme), Millaud, Aix, Haut-de-Cagnes, Barreme, Alba, Vicenza, Bologna, Lucca, Siena, Viterbo, Rome; and I suppose the most bizarre episode has been the hotel outside Viterbo where, because it rained, one was cooped up for several days with the King of Sweden—who just couldn't get outside to excavate Etruscan things.[1]

But the dominant impression I am left with is some sort of combination of *déjà vu* and dismay. Obviously one has seen most of it before; but also, and allowing for the betrayals of recollection, one is sorry to say that nothing seems to have changed for the better. In other words, in every town the dominant fact has become automobiles and if one thought that Woodstock and places were bad—well they just don't compare with the situation here.

This town is now a labyrinth of one-way streets and, with every piazza and every cortile jammed, you thread your way between the bumpers just as best you can. If you sit down to eat in Alfredo's or somewhere you might just as well be dining in a parking garage and if you set out to look at something—no matter what—you are more than likely to discover that the view is blocked by a ten ton truck. Then if you add the noise and also realize that everything has become very expensive, so that you can scarcely eat for less that £5.00–6.00, I think that you will get the picture.

I believe that I attribute half the trouble to the 'economic miracle' and the Common Market. Which seems to have lead to a naïve canonisation of capitalist principles. Which all, suddenly, sound rather pretentious but I suspect that you know what I mean. I.E. common market patronized by *Time-Life* and the usual U.S. corporate structure is an alliance of managerial etc. types and is oriented towards production-consumption and an idea (if any) of society in these terms. Therefore a rather dogmatically entertained idea of *laissez faire* becomes the ruling principle, *Time-Life* expects it, and the managerial alliance hastens to supply. And the more *laissez faire* the better—since it proves that you are not Communist. And a process something like this, I am sure, is at the bottom of the scene. And so if we loot the landscape and destroy the cities we not only have made financial profit but we have proved a theoretical point. Am not saying any of this very well but it does tend to look rather like an extension—at the international level—of the ruling mood in the France of Louis Philippe; and, in spite of the profits, just because it is so obviously destitute of any further idea it is surely about to run into really massive trouble.[2] Or don't you think?

Anyway, since then I have been out to lunch and weather has improved and so long as you only move around at siesta time—when you can see no churches or galleries which is a bit restricting—you can escape the cars and enjoy a few illusions. Meanwhile I will write again when I think that I have anything very significant to say—and please write and say how the lying in bed scene is getting along. I hope terribly well.

Lots of love and all that,

Colin

P.S. David. Do you think that you could so something for me in the area of the *Lotus*?

It is as follows:

They have still not sent me the log book of the car.

Nor have they sent me a list of *Lotus* dealers.

They understood that I would be arriving at this address on September 10 and these things were supposed to be here at this time. By now I do think that they should have arrived.

I am finding it just a bit tiring to be dropping into British Consulates to ask them for the name of the local dealer whenever I come to a likely town—and personally I think that they might do something about it—AND they might also send a list of

Lotus dealers in the U.S. of A.—and <u>if they can't do this then just what kind of an outfit are they</u>?

Then I want some parts and I would like them to send them to me here because Fattori e Montana, the people here don't seem to be able to supply.

I need the covers to two lights:

i. left hand rear—because with John's luggage on the rack in Coutances I couldn't see behind too well and, in reversing, I crumbled the red cover.

ii. left hand rear over wheel—because in Vicenza I ran into a bicycle race which forced the car ahead of me to a stop and me too, and which caused the car behind— which couldn't stop, to graze—very slight paint abrasions, no bumps, [...]

---

1 Gustaf VI Adolf of Sweden (1882–1973), an amateur archaeologist interested in ancient Italian cultures, participating in a dig to uncover an Etruscan city in the region of Viterbo.
2 Louis Philippe, king of France from 1830 to 1848, avoided the pomp and lavish spending of his predecessors. His support came from the wealthy bourgeoisie.

084   *To **John Miller,** Canfield Gardens, London*   *11 August 1971*

107 Cayuga Heights Road, Ithaca, N. Y.

My dear John:

According to Fred you are about to come here as visiting critic almost with the speed of light. Personally I think that you are mad and that when you get here you will find things so *triste* and lugubrious that you will wish that you had never come. But, if you know this and are still coming, then one can only say *chacun*, etc....[1]

But, if things are not amiable here and if you won't find the charming student situations that you found before, one guesses that your visit could still be put to a certain use. I mean with reference to things. For instance: you owe me money, you have reminded me of it, and I have no idea whether it's a matter of $10 or $20; but on the strength of this, do you think that you could bring with you something like two dozen Chesterfield buttons. I don't need so many but they could still come in useful. And then, if you could bear it and one won't mind if you cannot, there are miscellaneous effects, glasses, etc. some of which Paul Curtis was going to bring over last summer and some of which he did, but put them in the hold of the plane so that they got smashed. I believe that there is a collection of this stuff at the Stevenses...... but don't feel obligated about this, though I would like some buttons.[2]

So there is nothing any more to say except that I am rather miserable and depressed. You liked Ithaca in '66 because I had made a scene here. But this scene, apparently, aroused jealousy, so every attempt has been made to smash it by that insufferable Kraut.[3]

I am not paranoid and send my love,

   Colin

---

1 *triste*, French: gloomy; *à chacun son goût*, French: to each his taste.
2 Thomas (Sam) and Mary Stevens, friends of both Rowe and Miller⋆ in London.
3 OM Ungers,⋆ chairman of Cornell's School of Architecture from 1969 to 1975.

19 Renwick Place, Ithaca, N.Y.[1]

My dear Alvin:

Just a few notes about your New York project which in the abstract seems such a good idea but which then impels the most massive reservations.[2]

One notices, first of all, that quite a few people last year, although they were in London, insisted that, not knowing the town, they could not produce a design for a London site. A preposterous point of view perhaps—but a very common one, I am sure, with the people whom you will have around. And how do you overcome it?

One notices, secondly, the issue of time; and frankly one can scarcely see how, even in the comparative sobriety of a regular studio, any project of this kind can be done in five weeks. So that, consequently, one is left wondering just how, in what amounts to the atmosphere of a convention, any real contribution can be made.

Thirdly, you talk about simply a report. But is this <u>really</u> what you want. Frankly, I don't think that it is and I think that you are oscillating between fantasies of hard nosed planning and fantasies of generalised images.

Now with references to hard nosed planning I don't see how Jack Robertson* or Steve Quick or Terry Williams, or anyone else can propound to a highly disparate group in London the empirical realities of N.Y.C. and then make them stick.[3] Simply they won't stick; and there will be a great many people—like Peter Blake, etc—lying around to comment on just this.[4] Therefore why protrude your neck in this direction when what you are really trying to do is a P.R. job for your summer scene and, incidentally, for Con Ed?

Fourthly and in this context what really do we—meaning Fred, Terry or myself, have to contribute?[5] And what, for that matter is there in this proposal for us? Surely this is a little unclear—except that one senses that there is a general idea that we would be working for the good of humanity. But would we? I speak for myself; but I do think that one cannot but be encouraged to believe that we would be more definitely working for the greater good for Archigram because it does seem apparent that this is the image— tube city, pseudo-populist input—to which you fundamentally incline;[6] and since we do not (again I speak for myself) and since we are *retardataires* (back in '67), then could our contribution be of any value or significance?[7] Either for you or for us?

Now almost certainly these observations [run contrary] to the widely received ecumenical proposition that you put a number of people of widely differing backgrounds together and that, somehow, constructive miscegenation will occur. But then one does know that, whatever the useful qualifications a committee may interject, important first proposals are not ever the result of consensus. One knows, dear Alvin that you can't mate giraffes and hippopotami. And, supposing you could, one wonders whether it would be worthwhile anyway—and isn't it ever so much better to allow them both to be themselves?

And, finally, supposing that all these problems did not obtrude themselves, there still remains the entirely undiscussed issue of money which is surely not without relevance or importance. Alvin, when dealing with your friends and well-wishers you do display a rather strange propensity to gloss over this quite prominent matter; and I think that this does begin to dismay your friends because they cannot but be aware that people less well disposed towards you scarcely receive the same treatment—which is a question of general strategy requiring the most serious attention.

So O.K. and to revert to myself:

1. I don't see how a project of this kind can be done in the circumstances of S.S. '72 and I don't see the point in pretending that a later project or report was the work of the summer.[8]

2. Judging by the exposure which Covent Garden received I don't see any great reclame which derived from a lot of sweat.

3. But I can conceive of parallel projects representing different points of view and emerging from some condition other than that of S.S. '72 and I would be prone to place great emphasis upon this possibility.

So with all this said:

I may be in London but it is genuinely not certain that the I.R.S. will let me out; and, if I am in London, I would quite like to participate in the form of a lecture or something. But I will let you know about this when my income tax scene begins to shape up.

Ciao and all that

    C

And best wishes to Elizabeth, Victoria, Nicholas.[9]

    Colin

---

1 This is the first letter in this collection to be written from 19 Renwick Place in Ithaca, a house Rowe would occupy for the next 20 years.
2 Boyarsky* had written Rowe on 20 May 1972 that he was considering a Manhattan site as part of the forthcoming five-week design project for the International Institute of Design Summer School at the Architectural Association, London: "It may be that in addition to all else there will be a future New York project on an important site in Manhattan, and I am going to be in New York for several days casing it beginning Wednesday, 24th May."
3 Jaquelin Robertson,* director of the Mayor's Office of Midtown Planning and Development; Stephen Quick, senior urban designer; and Terrance Williams, deputy director, of the Mayor's Office of Lower Manhattan Development.
4 Peter Blake (1920–2006), German-born American architect, author, and critic and, in 1972, editor-in-chief of *Architectural Forum*.
5 Fred Koetter;* Terrance Williams.
6 Formed in the early 1960s at the Architectural Association in London, Archigram was a small group of paper-architecture futurists who imagined a megastructure urbanism of high-tech, lightweight, plug-in, mobile components.
7 *retardataires,* French: latecomers.
8 "S.S. '72": Summer Session 1972.
9 Elizabeth,* Victoria, and Nicholas Boyarsky—Alvin's* wife, daughter, and son.

086   *To **John Miller**, London*   *2 January 1973*

19 Renwick Place, Ithaca, N.Y

My dear John:

    A letter from Anne Engel at your prompting. But will you please tell who she is? Is she the new Mrs Joseph Rykwert?[1] She writes to me as though she knows me. But then I have absolutely no recollection of knowing her. So please let me have some info about this since I am, obviously, anxious to reply.

Presumably you have received intimations about the recent horrors here. December 7 Chimacoff got the axe—no adequate reasons provided; December 20 Koetter* and Sherwood got the axe—again no adequate reasons provided; and the Herdeg* execution is almost certainly imminent.[2] It is, of course, the work of the Ungers*-Shaw-Pearman troika; and it is also completely beyond the highest powers of my imagination to begin to conceive why people would do this—unless their paranoia and self-righteousness were altogether too over-developed with reference to whatever consciences they might possess.[3] But, if you add to this the Jerry tenure situation of 1970, then all you get are the evidences of an entirely remorseless vendetta.[4]

So, naturally, there will be repercussions; and, if I am relatively tranquil the *furore* of Seligmann*-Greenberg is to be imagined.[5]

Byby and love to Susan,

   Colin

---

1 Anne Engel-Rykwert, wife of distinguished architectural historian Joseph Rykwert (b 1926).
2 Alan Chimacoff, Fred Koetter,* Roger Sherwood, and Klaus Herdeg.*
3 OM Ungers,* John Shaw, Charles Pearman.
4 Jerry A Wells.* OM Ungers* had opposed his promotion to associate professor with tenure in 1970.
5 Werner Seligmann* (1930–1998) and Donald Greenberg, professor of Computer Graphics. See Rowe, Colin, *As I Was Saying: Recollections and Miscellaneous Essays*, Alexander Caragonne ed, 3 vols, Cambridge, MA: MIT Press, 1996, vol 2, pp 4–6.

To **Robert Slutzky**, *New York City*   *21 August 1973*   **087**

19 Renwick Place, Ithaca, N.Y.

My dear Robert:*

I have just read "Transparency II" and found some of the analysis overwhelmingly brilliant. But it is, of course, lost in that huge *Perspecta*.[1] But the Michelangelo-Mondrian piece—well there ain't nowhere nothing like it, though it has been suggested to me that, as of now, it could be opened up to make a comparison with the Free University of Berlin—showing just how 'literal' a grid exploitation this is in comparison.[2] And I think that you will probably agree.

Anyway, at the moment, I am still up here and able to walk now without a stick. Also, the A.R. piece is forming up very quickly and, at the moment, it is to be called: "Collage City: Towards a Pre-Millennial Urbanism", consisting of the following: "Introduction"; "Utopia: Decline and Fall"; "After the Millennium"; "Crisis of the Object: Predicament of Texture"; "Collision City and the Politics of Bricollage"; "Collage City and the Reconquest of Time"—and the first four are now complete.[3] Which is to say that the catastrophes which have fallen on this place have resulted in at least one good: one can say "forget it" and, forgetting the lack of education which the students are now about to receive, one can concentrate upon the, personally, more advantageous.[4] But there is, of course, irony—the substance of these papers would have formed part of the Cooper lectures which John was unwilling even to discuss in terms of money![5]

O.K., so today, this letter is also to incorporate two requests. I am working today upon the illustrations of the MIT essay book, to be called *The Mathematics of the Ideal Villa and Other Essays*, and I will, again provide you with a brief breakdown:[6]

1. The Mathematics of the Ideal Villa.
2. Mannerism and Modern Architecture.
3. Character and Composition. (unpub. Eisenman* wants for Oppositions but will probably be too late)[7]
4. Chicago-Frame.
5. Neo-Classicism and Modern Architecture. (unpub. Eisenman has for Oppositions)
6. Ditto.
7. Transparency I.
8. La Tourette.
9. The Architecture of Utopia.

Now it is obviously about "Transparency I" that my requests are concerned.

In strict chronological sequence it should be No. 5; but, in rational thematic sequence, as No. 7, it makes sense. I.E., if Nos. 5 and 6 are thematic outcroppings of No. 4, "La Tourette" is a derivative of "Transparency I"—"Transparency I" used for purposes of practical criticism—and so I would like to present it. In other words, in the intro, while Wittkower* is mentioned re "Mathematics"—, "La Tourette" gets a comparable treatment. O.K.?

So, the requests:

1. Does a copy of "Transparency I" survive from before the time that Jonathan Barnette so lavishly bestowed his editorial intelligence upon it?[8] Obviously, if so, I would like to publish this version and would like a copy; while, if there is no copy, I would like to attempt reconstitution. So, could I either have a copy of the original, or, if not, could I have your formal permission to reconstitute, subject to your editorial check?

2. Could I have a letter from you—this is strictly pro-forma—to lodge with the MIT Press who already have copies of such letters from *The Architectural Review* and *Granta*?

I hope all this doesn't sound too absurd; but I suppose that protocol <u>does</u> have its exigencies.

So please react and best wishes and all that,

    C

P.S. I also assume that the remarks made in the Introduction re "Transparency I" would be subjected to your general O.K.

P.P.S. An inference of this letter: I am in rather a go-go mood—for the first time in years—and I would like to get going on "Transparency III" just as soon as all this stuff is out of my hair. From now on I intend to keep my commitments to Cornell to a minimum—no sweat, no involvement, the place can go down the tubes in its own sweet way; and, therefore, I am working towards the following:

1. *The Mathematics of the Ideal Villa and Other Essays* (completed mid-September) by Colin Rowe 1974.
2. "Collage City: Towards a Pre-Millennium Urbanism" (published by A.R. December or January and republished as book by ?) by Colin Rowe and Alfred Koetter* 1974.
3. *Transparency* .... (published by MOMA?) by Colin Rowe and Robert Slutzky* 1974?
4. *The Architecture of Good Intentions: Towards a Critical Retrospect* (so much of this exists) by Colin Rowe 1975?[9]

As for 4: the hold up, you know, has been the inhibition about doing a demo-job on modern architecture; but, by now, the poor thing has been so demolished that a further attrition may be the only hope for salvation; and, probably, this book would include an excursus to be called "The Present Predicament of Architectural Education!"[10]

And, after all this, there could very well appear (1975-6?): *The Theoretical Drawings of Inigo Jones and John Webb!* The goddam thing exists in all its Wittkowerian horror and it only needs the employment of one of those intelligent females to check up a few things in Worcester College, Oxford (I have neither the time nor the inclination) to be on its way.......[11]

You say: How funny, and I do too. It's called going public and I have always had inhibitions about its vulgarity. But, if nasty, I suppose it may be necessary; and the joke of it is that, were I to stay at Cornell—or if I don't succeed in getting out, they would / will pay me far more for a neglect of my academic duties than for any strict attention to them.

My love and my love to Gabrielle,[12]

     C

1 Rowe, Colin and Robert Slutzky, "Transparency: Literal and Phenomenal, Part II", *Perspecta*, no 13 / 14, 1971, pp 287–301. See bibliography and Rowe, Colin, *As I Was Saying: Recollections and Miscellaneous Essays*, Alexander Caragonne ed, 3 vols, Cambridge, MA: MIT Press, 1996, vol 1, pp 73–106.
2 In their 1980 article, "The Crisis of the Object: The Predicament of Texture", *Perspecta*, no 16, pp 109–140, Rowe and Koetter* show a plan of the Free University of Berlin together with images of Mondrian's *Victory Boogie-Woogie* and Theo van Doesburg's *Steps of the Russian Dance.*
3 Rowe, Colin and Fred Koetter, "Collage City", *The Architectural Review*, vol 58, no 942, August 1975, pp 64–91.
4 The "catastrophe" is the recent firing of Alan Chimacoff, Fred Koetter,* and Roger Sherwood by OM Ungers* at Cornell; and Klaus Herdeg's* resignation in protest. See Rowe's letter to John Miller* dated 2 January 1973 (p 188 in this volume).
5 John Hejduk,* chairman of the Cooper Union School of Architecture in 1973.
6 Rowe, Colin, *The Mathematics of the Ideal Villa and Other Essays*, Cambridge, MA: MIT Press, 1976.
7 "Character and Composition" was published first in *Oppositions*, no 2, 1974. See Rowe's letters to Mr & Mrs Rowe dated 11 May 1952 (p 48 this volume) and to Henry-Russell Hitchcock* dated 15 October 1957 (p 118 this volume).
8 Jonathan Barnette was the graduate student co-editor with Michael Dobbins of Yale's *Perspecta*, no 8 (1963) which featured "Transparency I". See bibliography.
9 *The Mathematics of the Ideal Villa and Other Essays* and *Collage City* were published as books in 1976 and 1978 respectively. *The Architecture of Good Intentions* was published in 1994. See bibliography.
10 See Rowe, Colin, "Architectural Education in the USA" (a paper delivered at a 1974 Museum of Modern Art conference in NYC), *Lotus International*, no 27, 1980, pp 42–46; reprinted in Rowe, *As I Was Saying*, vol 2, pp 53–64.
11 In November 1947, Rowe had submitted a thesis supervised by Rudolf Wittkower* titled "Theoretical Drawings of Inigo Jones: Their Sources and Scope", to the University of London for the degree of MA in the History of Art.
12 Gabrielle, Robert Slutzky's* wife.

*To **John Miller**, London*   *18 June 1974*   **088**

19 Renwick Place, Ithaca, N.Y.

My dear John:

    They tell me you have become Mr Royal College of Art.[1] Do I congratulate? Or do I commiserate? I think that I should do the first—because it simply is a reasonably showy base (in spite of that dreadful pseudo club upstairs) and, if Bedford Square is the only competition, then surely there isn't any.[2] So happy, happy....

Here things are as you guess. They become more dismal everyday. Fred has accepted to go to Kentucky and leaves in mid-August; but is also going to do a visiting critic thing at Yale which might be a little exhausting though I am sure profitable. And Werner, I believe has accepted to go to Harvard in '75.[3] However, as for me (poor, poor thing!) apparently nothing has happened, as yet. Meaning that the expected overtures from Yale—expected by Jim—have not taken place—which I suspect to be the Scully* road block.[4] However Eisenman* alleges that he is setting up a series of 10, possibly 20 lectures for me in N.Y.C. at $600 a throw which <u>should</u> be useful and which will certainly keep the wolf from the door.[5]

But I seem to be so mobile nowadays. I went to Los Angeles the other day and was all overwhelmed again by what elegant domestic architecture there is in that town; and also there seems to me to have been a big Viennese influence. The Barnsdall House for instance and quite a few other Wright* [...] jobs are Wagnerian as much as anything else.[6] Also I am leaving in about two weeks time to get involved with Michael Dennis's* little summer school in Venice where I shall be between July 8 and August 3.

Would, on this occasion, like to come to London but don't quite see how because I have to get back to get involved with the MIT Press about lay out and things for the essay book;[7] and, if they accept it, which Stan Anderson* says they will, then to get further involved with them about COLLAGE CITY.[8] So will probably not see you all—unless you come to Venice.

However, to continue about here. The faculty voted Panos Koulermos chairman but I understand that he has been given such a bad offer as to nullify the vote; and, meanwhile, who is to be acting chairman but little Chas Pearman...........

Which is almost all—except for the real purpose of the letter. Some months ago Fred sat on one of the chesterfields with something of an excess of energy and the result is a broken front castor. It just snapped. Therefore and please, please do you think that you might get the people to send me a new one?

Lots of love to Susan, Alan, Jim and who ever may require it.[9]

    Colin

Also love to Sarah and Harriet, and pat the monstrous dog......[10]

[handwritten]

VENEZIA ISOLA DEGLI STUDI
FONDAZIONE QUERINI STAMPALIA
CASTELLO 4778 VENICE[11]

---

1 John Miller* was appointed head of the Department of Environmental Design at the Royal College of Art.
2 The Architectural Association School, 34–36 Bedford Square, London.
3 Werner Seligmann* taught at Harvard's Graduate School of Design from 1974 until his appointment as dean at Syracuse in 1976.
4 Vincent Scully,* professor of the History of Art and Architecture at Yale.
5 There is no record of such lectures.
6 Hollyhock House, 1919–1921, designed by Frank Lloyd Wright;* Otto Wagner (1841–1918), Viennese architect.
7 Rowe, Colin, *The Mathematics of the Ideal Villa and Other Essays*, Cambridge, MA: MIT Press, 1976.
8 *Collage City*, co-authored by Fred Koetter*, was published by MIT Press in 1978.
9 Su Rogers,* Alan Colquhoun,* and James Stirling.*
10 Sarah and Harriet Miller, John Miller's* daughters.
11 The address is that of the Michael Dennis* Summer School in Venice, printed in pencil.

Rowe with Peter Cook at the Rhode Island School of Design, 1975.

6
Publishing

In 1973 Rowe's former student and friend Peter Eisenman* began *Oppositions*, a journal dedicated to critical writing on architecture. When Rowe's "Robert Venturi and the Yale Mathematics Building" was rejected for publication by the editors of the catalog for which it was written, Eisenman agreed to publish it in *Oppositions*. Rowe wrote to him in 1975, describing in detail changes to be made.

The following year, Rowe published his first book, *The Mathematics of the Ideal Villa and Other Essays*, a compilation of remarkable essays written between 1947 and 1961. Although the book would prove a great success, when Rowe sent a copy to Henry-Russell Hitchcock,* he described it as a "graphically depressing little anthology", promising that his next work, *Collage City*, would "entertain far more".

Collage City was written by Rowe and Fred Koetter* between August and December 1973; however, it was not published until 1978. Intended as a journal article, when it proved too long for publication in *The Architectural Review*, Rowe's friend, Michael Spens,* contracted to have his publishing house produce it as a book. Only after several years of delays was the contract transferred to MIT Press. The awkward transition, along with Rowe and Koetter's concern for the size, length, and graphic presentation, are detailed in several letters in this collection—some written to Rowe's sister-in-law, Dorothy, who Rowe described as "so extraordinarily energetic on behalf of *Collage City*".

Shortly after the publication of *Collage City*, in 1979, Rowe wrote to Roger Conover,* its MIT editor, about the possibility of a Spanish edition of the book, but also about his plans for "two projects: *The Architecture of Good Intentions* and *The Disraeli Book*". *The Architecture of Good Intentions* would be Rowe's third book but was not published until 1994. *The Disraeli Book* was to be an "anthology of Disraeli pieces [...] concerning houses, people, politics. It involves this Jewish outsider (Disraeli-Proust) who finally comes on as prince". It was never written.

In addition to correspondence regarding publications, in spring 1978 Rowe wrote a remarkable suite of 37 letters to Judith DiMaio,* a former student who had become his close companion and intimate correspondent. Written over a period of 60 days, the letters present a daily diary of thoughts regarding the everyday occurrences in Rowe's life: "But you will see, when you get the letters that I do write to you almost every day: and my dear, my dear, my dear, I do have to tell you that I rely upon this writing—almost completely." Two of the 37 letters are featured in this collection.

089   *To **Peter Eisenman,** Institute for Architecture and Urban Studies*   *16 February 1975*
19 Renwick Place, Ithaca N.Y.

Peter:

Attached is the revised version of the Venturi piece.[1]

Revisions pay attention to most of your observations; but the thing must also not be too revised....

So, for matters left to your discretion:

p.7 end of first paragraph. I suggest an asterisk and then something like the following:

"*Is the assumption of a situation conceived to be public and standard necessarily and always a 'good' undertaking? Perhaps not always; but nevertheless the normative and the typical do possess their roles and it may be doubted whether themes deriving from nineteenth century suburbia can ever be promoted as usefully comprehensive generalizations. The role of these themes is essentially private; and perhaps one should never ask for the public parade of private virtues."

p.8 end of first paragraph. Suggest an asterisk and:

"*Surely for the most part true; but the name of Kurt Schwitters and, pre-eminently that of Marcel Duchamp should equally belong in this area."

p.9 'to the life of the art historian...........'

Personally I like, and do not wish to surrender, either "the art historian" or "the Mafioso hick"; but how about:

"may be seen as appealing to 'life' itself, to 'ordinary' life—the life of the art historian, the Mafioso hick, or the owners of the ranchburger around the corner, all being assumed to be equally 'real' and representable."

I suppose that this does soften the snobbery implied by "the petty bourgeoisie from Iowa"; and then I think that the further insert ("people as found without Utopian idealization") reasonably proceeds to help the meaning.

Have just read Scully's* effusion and questions:[2]

It's all about houses?

There, apparently, is an American *genius loci*—to be found hyper-distilled in Massachusetts; and, apparently, one neglects this distillation at one's peril?[3]

Apropo of this *genius loci*, the issues of determinism versus free will?

Internationally diffused ideas can never be nationalized; and the national spirit can only reflect itself imperfectly through the medium of these ideas? Therefore the imperfections of Neo-Classicism, Beaux Arts, 'International Style', etc? Therefore the pueblo and the tepee?

But is the constitution of the U.S. of A. so entirely indigenous a document, a product of Indian and Know Nothing ruminations, and does not S. admit English and French ingredients as components of the Shingle Style?

Anyway, these are little questions which erupt; and I think that, in writing a review of this essay, a way to fly might be like this:

English and European visitors to the U.S. of A. What they want to see and what they look at. Marvels of science and marvels of populism—the first to be regarded with awe, the second with slightly patronizing derision.

Small town America of the imagination: Laurel, Miss., Selma, Ala., Trumansburg, N.Y., etc. the fragility, poignancy, etc. of these places. The American Romantic suburb of 1910–1930: River Oaks, Grosse Pointe Farms, even Cayuga Hts.[4] Its adequacy in its time. The appearance of 'modern architecture' in both these places. So we look back at the U.S. domestic trade; and how often in France, Italy and even England we have felt its absence. It is this—so little estimated, so little regarded, so unprotected—that Furriners should be looking at—etc, etc, etc.

So all this before the <u>nevertheless</u>. And don't you think that this sort of tear jerky thing (<u>not</u> dependent on coastal Mass.) is really the way to begin.

  C

[handwritten]

*PLUS <u>x</u>: ONE OF THE GLORIES OF THE SHINGLE STYLE HOUSE WAS THE ECLECTIC INTERIOR (C.E. VICTOR NEWCOMB HO., ELBERON, N.J.). AND <u>WHERE</u> IN THIS NEO-SHINGLE STYLE <u>DO</u> WE FIND THIS LITTLE DISPLAY? WITH C.R. AND J. STIRLING PERHAPS?[5] BUT WITH BOB STERN OR ALDO GIURGOLA?

---

1   Rowe, Colin, "Robert Venturi and the Yale Mathematics Building", *Oppositions*, no 6, fall 1976, pp 1–23. Written at the invitation of Yale's dean of Architecture, Charles Moore, for a publication on the 1970 competition for a new mathematics building to be built on the Yale campus: Moore, Charles and Nicolas Pyle ed, *Yale Mathematics Building Competition: Architecture for a Time of Questioning*, New Haven: Yale University Press, 1974. When it was excluded from that publication without explanation, Peter Eisenman* featured it in *Oppositions*, a journal for critical writings on architecture and urban design that he started in September 1973.
2   Probably Vincent Scully's* most recent publication, *The Shingle Style Today: or, The Historian's Revenge*, Scranton, PA: George Braziller, 1974.
3   *genius loci,* Latin: the distinctive atmosphere or spirit of a place.
4   River Oaks, a national model for community planning in Houston, the wealthiest community in Texas; Grosse Pointe Farms, a small, fashionable suburb of Detroit on Lake St. Clair; The Village of Cayuga Heights, established in 1915, north of the Cornell campus.
5   Colin Rowe and James Stirling.*

090   *To **Henry-Russell Hitchcock***   *8 December 1976*

19 Renwick Place, Ithaca, N.Y.

Dear Russell:

  I thought that this graphically depressing little anthology might induce a couple of hours of nostalgic entertainment.[1]

Collage City, in both its English and German forms should be out shortly; and I am sure that it will entertain far more.

Affectionately and all that,

  Colin

---

1   Enclosed with this note was a copy of Rowe's recently published *The Mathematics of the Ideal Villa and Other Essays*, Cambridge, MA: MIT Press, 1976. *Collage City*, co-authored by Fred Koetter,* was published in English in 1978 and in German in 1984.

Cornell University Department of Architecture, East Sibley Hall, Ithaca, N.Y.

Dear Mr. Haywood:[1]

Many thanks for your letter of January 26 and its response to what may have been undue alarm on the part of Fred Koetter* and myself; but let me first of all clarify for you what were our reactions on the afternoon of Sunday, January 23.

As you probably know I had arranged with Roger Davies to have the rest of the visuals processed here in Ithaca (this in order to expedite matters); and the whole operation is now underway.[2] So in this connection Fred and I spent three days locating sources and all the rest of it; and, also, in working up (this as a help to Roger) our idea of an approximate layout. In London, Roger provided me with his general idea of the book which he intends should be highly visual; he also provided me with his general thoughts about layout (margins, integration of text, and illustrations, double page spreads, etc.); and I could only concur with what (to me are his highly acceptable proposals). However and quite simply, after attempting a layout which Roger will receive and of which I feel sure that he will generally approve, after quite careful measurements and checks, we found ourselves with a book approximately 130 pages long—and this after assiduous attention to location of text and illustration.

So judge our consternation (I have a book recently out from MIT of the same length but running to 200 pages);[3] and it was then that the issue of the point size of the typeface forced itself on our attention. Simply we began to look at other books (Siegfried Giedion, *Mechanization*; Sybil Moholy, *Matrix of Man*)[4] only to discover that, where their maximum pages run at about 490–550 words, ours tend to run at slightly over 600—creating quite considerable difference in volume and bulk which, we assume, can only affect price and sales.

And it is this which is the substance of our question. In other words, comparisons with *Oppositions* (which to my mind is very ugly) do not concern us, and we are absolutely convinced as to this visual distinction of what Warehouse will produce: simply we are concerned with size, volume, bulk, price, and sales.[5]

Are we wrong to assume that these may be correlated categories—that fatness, thickness, cost and circulation are not to be separated? Perhaps we may be; but, if most architecture books present a miniature text (some 8,000–10,000 words) inflated to large size, you will understand our dismay when our own, rather elaborate verbal sequence becomes correspondingly reduced, deflated and minimized.

To repeat: we may be wrong; but, concerned as we are, we are also to be persuaded. We are, for instance, sad that the book, with its present typeface, can only assume the format of an elegant and rarefied magazine; and we are aware that such a magazine as *Lotus* finds buyers and sells as a luxury product; but we are also dismayed at what here seems to be an imbalance: are we cheap or are we expensive?[6] Typeface infers one thing: visuals infer another.

So, fundamentally, this is our problem. We may be wrong: but, still, mild consternation reigns and we continue to be anxious for speed.[7]

Sincerely

Colin Rowe

Colin Rowe

1   Lyndon N Haywood, graphic designer for Warehouse Publishing, to whom *Collage City* was initially committed.
2   Roger Davies, graphic designer for MIT Press.
3   Rowe, Colin, *The Mathematics of the Ideal Villa and Other Essays*, Cambridge, MA: MIT Press, 1976.
4   Giedion, Sigfried, *Mechanisation Takes Command: A Contribution to Anonymous History*, New York: Oxford University Press, 1948 and Moholy-Nagy, Sybil, *Matrix of Man: An Illustrated History of Urban Environment*, New York: Praeger, 1968.
5   *Oppositions: A Journal for Ideas and Criticism in Architecture, 1973–1984.*
6   *Lotus International, Quarterly Architectural Review,* Milan: Electa, New York: Rizzoli.
7   In its final form, the MIT Press edition of *Collage City* ran to 186 pages, a 45 per cent increase in size over that initially planned for the Warehouse edition.

092   To **Dorothy Rowe**, *Cheltenham Terrace, London*   *16 February 1977*

19 Renwick Place, Ithaca, N.Y.

My dear Dorothy:

The mail appears to have become inconceivably slow. Meaning that your letter of February 3 arrived here today just after I had sent a letter away to you which included a copy of my own letter to Lyndon Haywood.[1]

So, and supposing this letter arrives first, to deal with your questions:

Sue's pictures <u>may</u> be the best obtainable and I have no doubt that they are.[2] However one does <u>not</u> have to write to the Bibliotheque Nationale for pictures from a book which was published in 1804. The B.N. would do no more than, after a typically French delay, reproduce from exactly <u>that</u> book which is clearly also available in London, Ithaca, Los Angeles and elsewhere; and the idea of such a process is a result of faulty instructions to Sue. So the Gemeentemuseum in Amsterdam cannot supply Van Doesburg—the pieces are destroyed; but the destroyed pieces are massively available and they are completely easy to reproduce without <u>any</u> loss of quality.

All of the missing items are now assembled (give or take about six) and should soon be processed (this is a little later than I had anticipated) when I will send them over with exhaustive notes of sources and all the rest.

The photos which I took away I brought back with me because they are mostly marginal and inadequate (Fred made the original Xeroxes and, probably, trusted too much to discretion); but everything will return—exactly and abundantly.

As a cover we are more or less decided on a Jaipur figure-ground and we do not have any anxiety to advertise either Richard Rogers or the horrors of Plateau Beaubourg.[3]

When I rang you the other day Fred and I <u>had</u> spent about 36 hours simply working on visuals and lay out; and, in this connection and with this type of face (and whatever Lyndon Haywood might say), it <u>is</u> going to be very hard to expand the book beyond 130–140 pages. Frankly, the typeface <u>is</u> ridiculous; and unlike us, <u>you</u> saw this immediately.... However, and since <u>we</u> are concerned with appalling delay, we are not <u>enormously</u> concerned to press the issue of what we <u>still do</u> regard as a gross mistake.

So do let me have the proofs and don't concentrate on the pics. These will all be in your hands—numbered and referenced—just as soon as is humanly possible.

Love, love, and *de la vitesse*.[4]

    Colin

P.S. The weather here is not quite so lousy as you may have heard that it is. There is here a frozen lake and the coldest January on record; but I am relatively untraumatized by these Siberian conditions. There is remarkably little snow and almost no ice on the roads, so, even though it has been almost continuously 20 below, life proceeds—

And then my two Rosa da Tivoli's arrived yesterday; and I like them.[5] They are big— each 54" x 39"; and, out of their Victorian frames, they are excellent country house pieces. Both show an amalgam of large scale erudition and naiveté. Beady-eyed sheep and goats, cows and horses, dogs and shepherds, Mons Soracte, ruins and funny hill towns, suggestions of Jacopo da Bassano, Caravaggio and Grandma Moses trying to be George Stubbs—this is, mostly, what they exhibit. They need working on; they are a bit blistered in parts; but I do like them; they belong to our museum—perhaps as part of the ante-library—; and I am thinking of asking Mr Rachs at Sotheby Parke-Bernet to find me a third.[6] In any case, they would cause David to become infatuated and they do come out of an area which, at present, is excessively low priced.

So a quote from Aldous Huxley, *Those Barren Leaves*: "An ancient shepherd, strayed from one of Piranesi's ruins, watched from a rock above the road, leaning on his staff. A flock of goats, kneeling ruminatively in the shade of an oak tree, their black bearded faces, their twisted horns sharply outlined against the bright blue sky, grouped themselves professionally—good beasts, they had studied the art of pictorial composition under the best masters—in momentary expectation of Rosa da Tivoli's arrival. And the same Italianizing Dutchman was surely responsible for that flock of dusty sheep, those dogs, those lads with staves and that burly master shepherd, dressed like a *capripede* in goatskin breeches and mounted on a little donkey, whose smallness contributed by contrast to the portly dignity of its rider."[7]

Anyway, so much for Rosa da Tivoli who obviously contributes to my happiness and self-esteem. At the moment I have Aldo Ross inviting himself to dinner on Monday night[8]—he's awfully *dernier cri* but I am at a loss to know why; and, while I don't quite know what to do with him, I shall try to lay on a performance.[9]

My best love to Simon on his birthday which, though I failed to recognize, I did not forget.[10]

C

P.P.S. David will be delighted to know that I have, at last, found a cleaning woman. It's a joy and soon I shall find a gardener and it helps the morale like nobody's business. Again best love,

C

1   Lyndon N Haywood was the graphic designer for Warehouse Publishing, who intended to publish *Collage City*. Dorothy Rowe* was preparing the book for publication in London.
2   Susan Lermon, who helped collect illustrations for *Collage City*.
3   Plateau Beaubourg refers to the Centre Pompidou, Paris, designed by Richard Rogers and Renzo Piano. Fred Koetter* later designed the definitive cover for *Collage City*, which was not of Jaipur but a figure-ground plan of Wiesbaden.
4   *de la vitesse*, French: let's move (literally, of some haste).
5   Philipp Peter Roos, later Rosa di Tivoli (1655–1706), a German Baroque painter who settled in Rome in 1677, painting Italianate landscapes populated with animals.
6   Parke-Bernet, one time the largest auctioneer of fine art in the US, was absorbed by Sotheby's in 1964.
7   Huxley, Aldous, *Those Barren Leaves*, New York: George H Doran Co, 1925; *capripède*, French: Satyr.
8   Aldo Rossi (1931–1997), Milanese architect, designer, and author of *L'architettura della città* (*The Architecture of the City*). 1966 and *Autobiografia scientifica* (*A Scientific Autobiography*), 1981. Rowe spelled "Rossi" as "Ross".
9   *dernier cri*, French: the latest fashion.
10 Simon Rowe* was born on 14 February 1970.

093

*To **John Miller**, London*   *27 April 1977*

19 Renwick Place, Ithaca, N.Y.

John:

    Enclosed is an X-large Wiesbaden T-shirt—a good idea I think but I imagine that you will agree with me that, at this size, the image is too small. At small size it is very good—we are thinking of using it for the dust cover of *Collage City*—and, though I am disappointed, I was going to let you have one anyway.[1]

Lots of love to Susan and so on,[2]

See ya' soon,

    C

P.S. I seem to have lost my info as to Patrick's new address so I am sending a letter to him via you. Could you, please, arrange for it to be transmitted.[3]

P.P.S. I made a little lec in Cincinnati the other day with John Meunier as Mr Big.[4] I was terribly amused and not by Cincinnati. He has 500 artichokes, I am sure that the salary must be Forty, and he is leaning over backwards to make gratuitously pro-American remarks.[5] I.E. what a beautiful, dynamic vital city is Cincinnati—dontyer think—and, when one can't quite stretch the imagination quite so far, then one feels the presence of the intervening chasms. But you get the picture.

    C x x x

---

1 The T-shirt sent to Miller* by Rowe is now lost. Miller recalls that the white shirt featured a 10-inch square figure-ground plan of Wiesbaden, Germany, in black. This Wiesbaden plan was adopted the following year for the dust cover of *Collage City*, Cambridge, MA: MIT Press, 1978.
2 Su Rogers.*
3 Patrick Hodgkinson (b 1930), London architect and former colleague of John Miller.*
4 John Meunier (b 1936), head of the Department of Architecture at the University of Cincinnati, where Rowe lectured.
5 "Artichoke" was Rowe's word for "architect".

094

*To **Dorothy Rowe**, London*   *23 May 1977*

19 Renwick Place, Ithaca, N.Y.

My dear Dorothy:

    The illustrations of *Collage City* are finally complete and you will receive both them and the proofs during the course of the next few days. So it has been longer than I anticipated in January and Hadley Smith, the photographer has been ill and slow. But he is a funny old man and has confessed that sometimes he was so interested that he took time off to read the books; and I think that you will agree that he has done a very good job.

With the illustrations you will find a schedule of illustrations noting what you already have, what we are sending, what is going to be supplied by Michael Spens,* etc.; and the illustrations themselves are included in what is a suggested dummy for lay out.[1] It is the size of the book; we have carefully measured the text; and, as a result, we have been able to dispense with captions since the verbals and visuals can so easily be made to collaborate.

You will also find a suggested dust cover. It is the photograph of a T-shirt pinned to a wall and with a plan of Wiesbaden printed on it; and presumably the values of the wall can be darkened as necessary. We think it has overtones of Bracquemond, Jim Dine, the *cuirasse heroique*—and Saint Sebastian; also that it is seriously enigmatic and provocative..........[2]

Now the proofs are something else. And they are something quite shocking. In the first case they are often almost illegible. In the second, quotations do <u>not</u> stand out from the text. Thirdly, words are inexcusably run together so as almost to defy interpretation. Fourthly, hyphens are <u>not</u> distinguished from dashes—so that again, meaning is frequently destroyed. Fifthly, <u>why</u>, if the typeface for the book is so small, make the typeface for the quotations <u>still</u> smaller? Most of which <u>you</u> had already noticed in January.

But it does look as if the proofs were the most appallingly rushed job; and it is <u>very</u> difficult to understand just <u>how</u> a typescript equipped with so few errors could have produced so messy a result. In which context, one more notice: we say DISNEYWORLD and DISNEYWORLD it <u>is</u>; but, in all cases, (whether from oversight or an assumption of superior knowledge who knows?), the compositor has come up with DISNEY WORLD, and DISNEY WORLD it is <u>not</u> !!!!

That is about all and I do hope that you will approve of the dust cover.

Love to everybody and repeated thanks for all your trouble.[3]

    Colin

P.S. I wonder if James⋆ has yet received the Sherlock Holmes books which I thought might be an appropriate present and which I sent to him a few weeks ago. Also I am sending Simon⋆ a copy of the Wiesbaden T-shirt which is a very elegant item and which I hope will not be too small.[4]

    C.

P.P.S. Am going to keep the proofs for just a few days longer. This is because there are about a dozen or so footnotes outstanding. But I am going to include with the dummy and the pix proofs and typescript for our terminal excursus. Proofs <u>and</u> typescript because it's a little stick together of terminal pieces which had never been arranged. This should be a help for Roger because when he sees our final collection of stimulants he might just be a little surprised.[5] But the piece is brief....

    C xxxx

---

1 Michael Spens⋆ (1939–2014) was initially contracted to publish *Collage City*.
2 Félix Bracquemond (1833–1914), French painter and engraver; Jim Dine (b 1935), American pop artist; *cuirasse héroïque*, French: heroic armor; Saint Sebastian (died c 288) was a martyr put to death by being tied to a tree and shot with arrows.
3 In *Collage City*, Rowe and Koetter⋆ write: "To Dorothy Rowe our obligation is not to be estimated."
4 James Rowe;⋆ Simon Rowe.⋆
5 Roger Davies, graphic designer for MIT Press.

095

*To **Dorothy Rowe**, Cheltenham Terrace, London*   *8 June 1977*

19 Renwick Place, Ithaca N.Y.

My dear Dorothy:

You have been entirely heroic about the proofs.[1] You caught certain things which Fred and I did <u>not</u>; and I return yours to you with my emendations—and also with a copy of our previous proofs and corrections, almost all of which are identical. Meaning with yours.

<u>Some</u> of your observations—like Albert Speer, Durand, Habermas—are <u>not</u> justified—for, after all, one is addressing a particular culture which is familiar (perhaps?) with these names. <u>Others</u> I have taken to heart—like not just Garches, but the Villa Stein at Garches.

You will also notice a couple of rather large deletions where, when we read it over, we decided that we were a <u>little</u> too opaque; and I think that you will agree that these are for the best.

However, I am glad that you were excited, stimulated, or whatever. Because so, on the whole, I continue to be. On the whole, the text still seems (despite certain *longueurs*) to move with reasonable alacrity; and some Americanisms—like 'implicated' and 'gotten' are deliberately introduced—either for emphasis or Anglo-Saxon value.[2] Which means that the set pieces are often a little eighteenth century and might, sometimes, need traces of 'with it' animation in order to place them as logical-rhetorical ornament.

In any case, I hope that you enjoy the pics which <u>did</u> take rather longer to deliver than I had ever expected. And we also, as you have observed, did sweat out a distribution.

In general, Fred's letter to Lyndon Haywood* of which I got a copy today; and which you will probably receive a copy before this little letter arrives, is also a summary of everything which I have to say. But, apparently, Fred will be over with you in the next week or so; and, no doubt, everything can then be settled.

Love and all that,

    Colin

P.S. I hope that Simon's T-shirt <u>really</u> does fit; and I am sure that you won't think it as exquisite as we do as a dust cover. However—and believe me—it really is not all that unapropos. Looking like Saint Sebastian and also Pop Art it grabs a lot of scenes—*cuirasse heroique*,[3] etc; and the little old photographer here absolutely caught the point![4] In any case it is a collage of implications; and much better than a simply architectural collage.[5]

    C

P.P.S. About me: the Harvard thing did not come through.[6] At the end of all their filtering of the situation I was the only person left; but then they decided <u>not</u> to make an appointment! There were three foci of opposition: Eduard Sekler (Austrian) who said that he would resign if I came there (probably a good idea); Tom Stifter who has a two year terminal appointment; and Mike McKinnell who is a Limey and whose position is not exactly solid.[7] So Sekler is a bad and timid historian and the other two are nuts and bolts types who suspect what they conceive to be undue cerebrality; and that is the approximate story. However—lots of shock and lots of comment on the marshmallow attitude of Jerry McCue who is the chairman, and

High Episcopalian, and rather Quakerish, and looking for a sense of the meeting.[8] And so the protestations (renewed) of fervor and all the rest from McCue: Will I, at least come there as visiting critic, etc., etc.?

So I have settled for this—at $12,000 for two days a week for the Fall Semester. Most people said that I should and Harvard students wanted me; but Steve Peterson* thought that, in so doing, I was demeaning myself. However, in doing so, I force my income for the next academic year up to $40,000 or so which, I suppose, is not to be despised—and this is whatever Harvard finally decides, because we speak *de puissance à puissance,* and if, in a year's time, they still want, then myself may not..........[9] However, it would be better than here; and, in default of money, there would be *réclame.*[10] But another however, and this for David, I begin to be appallingly sought after—and even on the East Coast! But no doubt, too much, too little and too late—and I feel like a Neapolitan monarch in 1860.

As for *autres choses*: Judy will be in London I believe very soon on her way to Paris where she is going to teach a little summer school before leaving for The American Academy in Rome; and I shall be confined here until late July, when I will go to Paris *en route* for Rome (there will be financial advantages attached—though very few); and that is as far as I know.[11]

About London I am frightened: there is always the Spens* peril which I cannot—for the moment—indulge; and, meanwhile, what are you people doing?[12] Meaning: that I just don't want to come to London but would love to see you somewhere else. As David said: James and Simon would just love it here and, of course, they would.... But let me know about all this kind of thing quick.

    Colin

MORE P.S.'s

Fred [...] is disposed to come on like a Montana cowboy; but he was brought up Catholic, and, ultimately his hero is Aquinas.[13] So Montana-Aquinas can also mean like carrying the weight and wait of the world!

Please let me know about where you are going to be

    C

[handwritten]

THE PROOFS ARE A SEPARATE ENCLOSURE

1   The reference is to Dorothy Rowe's* editorial work on the proofs for Rowe and Koetter's* *Collage City.*
2   *longueurs,* French: protracted passages.
3   *cuirasse héroïque,* French: heroic, or muscular armor. See Rowe's letter to Dorothy Rowe* dated 23 May 1977 (p 200 in this volume).
4   C Hadley Smith, photographer. See 23 May 1977 letter to Dorothy Rowe* (note 3).
5   Rowe had T-shirts made with what at the time was to be the *Collage City* emblem. One was given to Simon Rowe* but is now lost.
6   The GSD was seeking a new chairman for the Department of Architecture at this time.
7   Eduard F Sekler (b 1920), Harvard architectural historian; Charles Thomas Stifter; Michael McKinnell (b 1935).
8   Gerald McCue (b 1928).
9   *de puissance à puissance,* French: from power to power.
10 *réclame,* French: publicity.

11 *autres choses*, French: other things.
12 Rowe's close friend, Michael Spens,* was to publish *Collage City*. Ultimately, MIT published the book in 1978.
13 Thomas Aquinas (1225–1274), Dominican friar, influential philosopher, and theologian.

096   *To **Dorothy Rowe**, Cheltenham Terrace, London*   *1 July 1977*

19 Renwick Place, Ithaca N.Y.

My dear Dorothy:

A reply to your letter of June 6 and a sequel to my phone call of a couple of nights ago.

I am glad that everything is apparently going smoothly and that the cooperation of Fred-Roger has apparently, been successful and felicitous.[1] Am also glad that you like the pix; and I will let you have the outstanding, Napoleonic, quote in the course of next week.[2]

I am delighted that some furniture, at least, has begun to arrive and I am pleased that you find it agreeable and even useful. In a rather countrified way the chairs I find to be modest and pleasantly showy; but the red morocco on the library table!!! Anyway, I believe that the whole lot cost only Seventy Pounds which, by the standards of today, seems to be rather more than a bargain.[3]

But do you think that some day David and James could go over to a good shop—like Frederick's in the Fulham Road—and make arrangement to have the interior of the drawer restored? Because this surely needs doing and would surely be good for James. Also, should there be a fourth chair? And, if they are going to stick around in your house for some time, just what should they be covered in? Too early for horsehair, too rustic for silk damask. Velvet—or a cut velvet? A reversed suede? On the whole I am prone to think velvet would be too heavy (also you have too much of it) and that a very pale blue silk would be elegant but not quite serviceable. So what about a reversed suede which could be grey (unless dark and dull not enough body?), apricot (rather too fashionable?), or even purple (?)? But let me know what you think because I don't want to have these around in your house looking like a slum....

I will write to Stirling* next week about the couch *chez* Krier;[4]* it's his business and his job to put on pressure about repairs; and, if the worst came to the worst and you couldn't house it, I suppose—as Judy says—it could always be put on loan at the V. and A.[5]

I have just written Nina a letter and sent her a cheque.[6] Foolish perhaps because she doesn't need it and she has gotten a lot of mileage—ten years worth—out of those pieces; but no doubt, in the end, a good idea.

Love,

C

---

1 Fred Koetter* and Roger Davies, the graphic designer for *Collage City* at MIT Press.
2 See Rowe, Colin and Fred Koetter, "Collage City and the Reconquest of Time", *Collage City*, Cambridge, MA: MIT Press, 1978, no 7, 183.
3 Presumably, Rowe had sent furniture to Cheltenham Terrace, some of which was in need of minor repair.
4 James Stirling* and Léon Krier.*
5 "V. and A.": Victoria and Albert Museum, London.
6 "Nina" is unknown.

19 Renwick Place, Ithaca, New York

My dear Michael:

I am hopelessly and regrettably trapped; and I rang up Cheltenham T. the other night to ask them to see that this information (via West Central Street) could be made to reach you. In other words, I am not able to clear two, three, possibly four work sessions that lie ahead.[1]

1. To begin with there is Fred (and I gather that he and Roger Davies have enjoyed a happy relationship) who has arranged with *Perspecta* that we make something for them for September—and, as of now, I have no idea as to his movements.[2]

2. Then there is the whole business of the *Roma Interotta* exhibition (extrapolations from the Nolli plan) which has to be ready for the end of August; and, with Steve Peterson* still in London (?) and Judy certainly in Paris, I am beginning to get just a little frantic about this......

3. Then there is my commitment to appear in Paris in early August which I must do; and then, and if 1 and 2, get confused, there is the terrible prospect of a charrette in Rome in late August.

Just simply, when you rang me the other morning, I had not anticipated all these difficulties. But I have built myself into a mouse trap and I must apologise for what is here called 'standing you up.' But what to do?

At the moment it is terribly dull here and I would, just as soon, be anywhere else; but where are Fred and Steven and how long do I wait?

Now next year I am planning to make a little summer school in London. This is an idea which struck me about two weeks ago; and it will include Jorge Silvetti* from Harvard, Fred* from Yale, Steven Peterson* from Columbia, Michael Graves* from Princeton, etc. Its subject is to be English (or British) housing developments and lay outs mid-eighteenth to mid-nineteenth centuries; and obviously it is going to include Edinburgh, Glasgow, Cheltenham, Leamington, Scarborough, Bristol, Clifton, Bath, Brighton, etc.—all these apart from London plus certain more picturesque and fragmented organisations—Eastbourne (?), Sidmouth (?). And I think that it could be the first of two summer schools because the other would be the industrial revolution one.

So, my dear Michael, can you bear this procrastination? And could we make N.B. next year?[3] And, when I have said this, it is entirely likely that I shall be spending the next two weeks or so just waiting.

Best wishes and lots of regrets,

C

P.S. It is appallingly hot and humid here. There is, absolutely, no movement of air; and, though the trees are beautiful, I wish that I was anywhere else.

---

1 Rowe had accepted a telephone invitation to visit Michael Spens* in Scotland, but now finds himself obliged to decline. "Cheltenham T", London, was the residence of David* and Dorothy Rowe;* "West Central Street", London, was the address of *Studio International,* the publishing house where Spens was managing editor.

2   On Koetter⋆ and Davies, see Rowe's 23 May 1977 letter to Dorothy Rowe⋆ (p 200 in this volume).
3   "N.B.": North Britain.

098   *To **Dorothy Rowe**, Cheltenham Terrace, London*   *11 December 1977*

19 Renwick Place, Ithaca, N.Y.

My dear Dorothy:

I have been terribly remiss in acknowledging the profusion of your letters and you have been so extraordinarily energetic on behalf of *Collage City* that this is, first of all, just to say thank you and then, secondly, to say that I thought it better and less complicating if Fred were to take charge of the correspondence at our end.

But all the same, all the shuttling backwards and forwards to Harvard hasn't left much time for too many letters, though—on the whole—I have been very lucky with my airplanes.[1] Mostly everything has been approximately on time; but, of course, one worries that it won't be, and then, what with taxis, hotel rooms, meals, people not to be neglected and so on, one does begin to get a bit *distrait*.[2] However, taken altogether, it has been quite a pleasant episode; and the students at Harvard have been supportive, enthusiastic, and all the rest.

Last week I had Jim, Fred and Steve to my preliminary jury on Friday which made something of a grand occasion;[3] and this coming week (meaning this week) I shall go down once more before leaving for Italy the week after. I am still not quite sure about the date of my leaving for Italy (there are now cheap flights to Rome); but, obviously, on the return, I shall be stopping off in London for a few days and will let you know when well ahead of time. Then I shall return to Harvard for about a week and arrive back here for a more or less immobile period on January 21.

But I don't really want the visit to London to be very known. Jim knows that I shall be coming. But I don't want Spens⋆ to get wind of it.[4] (By the way, Jim tells me his latest fantasy is Westminster and as a Scottish nationalist M.P.!). So you get the picture. And my best love to you all. And my many, many thanks for all of your tremendous efforts.

    x x x x C.

1   In fall 1977 Rowe was teaching an Urban Design Studio on Thursday, Friday, and Saturday mornings at Harvard's Graduate School of Design.
2   *distrait*, French: distracted.
3   James Stirling,⋆ Fred Koetter,⋆ and Steven Peterson.⋆
4   Michael Spens.⋆

099   *To **Judith DiMaio**, American Academy, Rome*   *4 & 6 February 1978*

19 Renwick Place, Ithaca, N. Y.

Dear, dear Judy:

I think that in all this snow I am beginning to lose count of time. I find it stupefying, mind destroying, and wholly eventless. So much so that, while I am sure that it is less than a week since I wrote you, it seems like a century at least. For, simply, monotony produces inertia and inertia produces monotony; and then, whatever happenings do find themselves distributed throughout this time, become wholly inconsequential and minor.

4.00 p.m.

So, having told you so much and acquiring a certain animation from doing so, I thought that I would take a little time off and go and buy some things to eat because the driveway is approximately ploughed out and I got the battery for the car fixed yesterday. So I knew it wasn't going to be easy getting out and I knew that I probably wouldn't be able to get back in at all. But, Judy, I wasn't prepared to get stuck on the down slope in the way in which I now am! There was, first of all, some difficulty in making the reverse on packed snow. But I almost managed that with a scattering of ashes. Almost but not quite, because then I had to get out and give an extra push—a very little one: and then, before I could get the door fully closed, the wretched machine began to run away with itself and it is now firmly lodged with its front in a bank of snow—absolutely intractable to any efforts on my part.

"And, apart from that, Mrs. Lincoln, just how did you enjoy the play?"[1] Well, apart from that, I made two nice lectures this week; got visited by Jo Aronson again (a little exhausting);[2] and have been tending for obvious reasons, to go to bed about 7.00 p.m. if not earlier.

Sunday 5.00 pm: finally Michael D. came around yesterday with some students who pushed and lifted me into place and I got to the bottom of the driveway (the first time it has been traversed since December 15); but, since it was then about 6 o'clock, decided not to go out and I came back in, read a bit, ate a bit; and, deciding things were not quite tolerable, I went to bed to read and read at about 8.[3] Today: some work, some thoughts about Genazzano, a trip to the supermarket and, as I return to leave the car at the bottom of the drive, it begins all over to snow again.[4]

Hope all this doesn't sound mad or manic depressive or something; but I am trying to give you a blow by blow story. I have already written to you two letters ago to tell you how much you would, briefly, enjoy all this (James and Simon, of course, would love it); but, also how, after the brief spasm of excitement and amusement, it would all make you horribly angry, preparatory to making you (like me) just flat bored. And, anyway, your phone call this morning was a very enormous pleasure; and, if I could have gotten through the day without it, it has still provided a source of strength.

Dear Judy, I am not so depressed as I was when I began to write to you on Saturday; and, simply, because I now envisage about six weeks more of this horror and am, correspondingly, prepared to cope. But getting back was really very bad and overwhelming. But you will see, when you get the letters that I do write to you almost every day: and my dear, my dear, my dear, I do have to tell you that I rely upon this writing—almost completely. Judy, do I have to say that you and things that I find myself wanting to say to you are almost the serious total of everything that I have to think about.........?[5]

Don't really know much what more to say—because I don't and I can't really wish you here—in Sverdlovsk or Novosibirsk; because, instead, I prefer to imagine you in your nice studio—with John the Baptist and God and the little *strada dei palazzi*[6]— and with, outside, that view which, and I am going to sound silly, is an immense privilege offering all kinds of different presentations throughout the day.[7] And, also, I don't wish you here because I prefer to think of us in a place less evil than this one.

My dear, I cannot help thinking that this winter has to be the final one for me here. Confronted with Gerhard Kallmann and the snow, he said to me at Harvard: "But don't you find it invigorating?"[8] Well, all I could do was to shrug and to gesture because it's not my style of outdoors; and, therefore, I am seriously imagining myself as ready to be bought (at high price) by Maryland, then going to live in D.C. (at which stage a call from Jorge: the Boston airport is closed and he can't get here tomorrow).[9] But would you be interested in Maryland-D.C.? where they seem to have lots of money and to be enormously open to suggestion. But I asked you this in my previous letter—and would you?

Monday, Feb. 6.

Dearest Judy:

That was the condition of this letter when you rang this morning and I was so extremely happy to hear your voice because, being alone here with you in Rome, is very, very different from being alone here with you in Kentucky—and it didn't seem so very lonely until I got back because, somehow, until now it didn't really seem that you were so extremely far away—which leaves me wondering if memories of summer make time seem shorter and memories of winter operate to elongate time.[10] But, you see, I am very preoccupied with time; and, while I enjoyed myself enormously all the time I was with you, I am very depressed very often because June does seem to be so very remote.

Am writing so much having just gotten back from school and it's only about 4.30. Had to go to school via Route 13 and Triphammer because Fall Creek, all over again, is unmanageable (Ithaca High School is surrounded by frozen floods) and that particular approach is closed. So I made a little lec.—obviously this time about the architecture of Poussin and Claude; and then, and after seeing a few people and because the snow still continues, I decided it might be best to come back here—which, believe me, I accomplished with lots of difficulty. Came down here via University Avenue (Gun Shop Hill was closed because of Fall Creek) and stuff going both up and down was skidding all over the place.[11] Was once almost hit when someone skidded at me; and I twice mounted the sidewalk; and it seems that the way I came is now the only way to approach this house. It is just all more than a little bit bizarre; but, had I come the other way, I wouldn't have been able to get off Route 13 here—a matter of more frozen floods which they don't seem to be able to do anything about.

So that much is my outward life as of today; and later I shall try to ring up Steven and Jorge about the proposed jury tomorrow—because they surely won't be able to get here and I was looking forward so much to their arrival.[12] But, dear Judy, I have never known the like of this and also I began to discover that I have no recollection of recent winters here. Because, you see, last year there was almost no winter and the year before I was in Texas; and then the year before that you were still around which did make things completely different. But, as it is, I am, for the moment, just terribly glad to have gotten back here and simply to be sitting writing to you.

Judy, I miss you greatly, greatly, greatly; and I shall continue to write you approximately day by day scenes simply because I want you to know what I am doing,

Love, love,

C

P.S. And would love to come before June... but when and how?

Colin

1 Familiar quote attributed to Tom Lehrer.
2 Joe H Aronson, upstate New York architect who often showed Rowe the aerial views of Italian cities and building complexes that he was drawing.
3 "Michael D.": Michael Dennis.*
4 Rowe and DiMaio* had traveled to Genazzano in December 1977, visiting the ruins of Bramante's nymphaeum.
5 This letter and the 6 March 1978 letter in this collection are two of a 37 letter "daily diary" sequence—effectively a continuous 60-day letter written by Rowe to DiMaio* at the American Academy in Rome, where she was the Rome prize winner in architecture. DiMaio intends to publish this sequence as a separate collection, *The Roman Suite, 1977–1978*.
6 The reference is to the collection of engravings by Giovanni Battista Franco (1500–1561) and Giovanni Battista Falda (1643–1678)—some of them belonging to Rowe—with which DiMaio* had decorated a wall of her Academy Building studio.
7 The American Academy in Rome, located on the Gianicolo, has stupendous panoramas of the city.
8 Gerhard Kallmann (1915–2012), a Berlin-born Boston architect best known for his Boston City Hall, designed with Michael McKinnell and completed in 1968.
9 Jorge Silvetti.*
10 Before moving to Rome, DiMaio* taught at the University of Kentucky in Lexington.
11 "Gun Shop Hill" refers to the Fall Creek neighborhood of Ithaca.
12 Steven Peterson* and Jorge Silvetti.*

To **Judith DiMaio,** *American Academy, Via Angelo Masina, Rome*   *6 March 1978*   **100**

19 Renwick Place, Ithaca, N.Y.

Monday

My dear Judy:

Getting back today I found your letter of February 28 and am both pleased and distressed by it. Distressed because you have been so ill, and distressed because you think that my letters so far have been so terribly self-indulgent.[1] But, all the same, pleased to hear about so much else and also to know that, before you receive this little communication, you will also have gotten quite a number of letters from me which display a far more exhilarated mental condition.

Get it? I mean, Judy, that all I have wished to do was to keep you equipped with a diary of how I have felt, Lord knows, until, very recently, there has been very little, externally, to talk about. But, before you receive this letter, I am sure that, you will recognise that I have become fairly exuberant all over again. But, sweetest, and at the risk of distressing and boring you, I just could not pretend to a psychological condition other than that which I experienced and, absolutely, had I been as self indulgent; as you imply, I simply would not have written at all. Simply I would just have privately wallowed in misery.

And now: so what happens this week? Well, to begin with, Franz and Monika Oswald* arrived here from Zurich/Bern today and Monika has completed the German translation of *Collage City* which the ETH is immediately ready to go along with. All the same, [...] you know the Swiss-German fantasies and propensities of this place. The Gods, they promise, visit us from the Helvetic Confederation; they are stalking, lovely, head-up, through the cities; the Prince of the Deliverance can only emerge from Zurich; and so, therefore, there is Franz being extremely political and over charming—[...] (big parade of *gemutlichkeit, schwärmerei* and *kaffee mit schlagobers*),[2]

[...] sitting around with Greenberg and the residue of the Texas Rangers who are just eating his words.[3] My dear, it is just so despicably *sich*.[4] Meaning that Oswald wants to eat my words (I don't need it); and they want to devour just his.

Anyway, tomorrow, Franz will make his lecture and the following evening I shall have them both to dinner.

Wednesday

It's now 11.30 and I send you a further report. The lecture was utterly depressing and the dinner relatively charming.

But, first of all, the lecture. It was well constructed, well delivered; but the content, the content, the content! [...] It was all about the city of Bern; and it was all so 'urban history', conscientious and *folkloristico* and, while I did appreciate the effort and the delivery, like most other persons in the audience, I found the *longeurs* intolerable [...][5] What was spread out over about an hour and twenty minutes could have been compacted into ten. Of speculative dimension there was remarkably little; and what there was disclosed itself to be of the period c. 1962. Remarkable! Because there is Switzerland, located, conveniently for Paris, Milan, Munich, Vienna, Berlin, London, but receiving practically no reverberations of any kind. Insulated, clean, guileless; and, therefore, utterly appealing to the provincial, and the likewise, insulated. Of Levi-Strauss, Popper,* Piaget, and all the others belonging to the giants of the modern mind series, there were no traces whatsoever; and, instead, we received Aldo Van Eyck, traces of Kevin Lynch, cautious aspects of Team X—and all this kind of stuff introduced as belonging to the greatest (and most democratic) of revelations. Judy, it made me sigh. Because there is an ambitious person and a, reasonably, charming personality equipped with great *ad hoc* talent, who discharges in a manner which could only be exciting to K.C. Parsons—who was clearly hyper impressed.[6] [...]

On the other hand, the dinner was quite different. [...] There were only the three of us—Franz, Monika, myself; but it was all quite effortless and painless. Perhaps just a little too sugar coated all around; [...] That is: in their eyes it was a 'European' evening; and, accordingly, they switched sides and, also, switched gesture and posture. But, apparently, the big word in Germania is *Collage City*. Or, at least, so they said; and so, part of the dinner was concerned with production.

So, Judy, you do see that I am, at least trying; and indeed, in Swiss terms (though I can hardly believe it) my general way of acting approaches the dynamic. !!!!!!!!!!!!!!!!!!

Thursday

Gave up this communication last night shortly after 12.30 and I now resume after a completely clear, eventless day. So it's lack of event and recuperation; and I am, now, thinking about lots of things—just like an excited little clock.

So: TOPIC 1
The Dialectical Imagination. Some architects just 'compose' and others envisage building as a sort of visible argument. Bernini 'composes', Borromini argues. On the one side is Vignola—argumentative; and, on the other, mostly, Palladio* who prefers poetry to most else. Francois Mansart is dialectical. Inigo Jones* is not. Most *maniera* stuff is dialectical.[7] Most eighteenth century stuff is not. Michelangelo is and Wren doesn't approach. Soane is dialectical, not Nash. Richardson is dialectical, not Norman Shaw. Corbu,* not Gropius*/Mies.* Terragni-Cattaneo are dialectical but, scarcely, Rossi.

TOPIC 2

Quick and Slow. This is the discrimination of extraverts-introverts and their rates of response. Probably I am quick intro and you are quick extra. Slow extra are Rubens, Reynolds, etc; and quick extra are Whistler and Sargent (Is Degas quick intro or is he quick extra?). William Morris is quick intro. Vermeer is slow intro. Giulio is quick extra. Jerry Wells★ is slow extra. Mike Dennis★ quick extra. John Miller★ is quick extra. Alan Colquhoun★ is quick intro. Jorge and Rodolfo are, probably, quick extra.[8] Peter Eisenman★ is slow extra wishing to be quick intro; and, just possibly, the same might be the case with my brother. Is Stirling★ slow extra or quick intro? (this I can't even begin to envisage). Ungers★ is quick extra.[9] And on we go and on we go and on we go.

TOPIC 3

Ideas v. Talent. Begins in Torino. One architect with conspicuously good ideas but indifferent talent. Another architect with conspicuous talent but indifferent ideas. Guarini-Juvara, which can also become Hawksmoor-Gibbs, Kahn★-Saarinen, Borromini-Bernini; and, in the course of minutes, I might assemble some more. Like God knows whom.

Sweetest Judy:

Now it is Friday and it has been St. Patrick's Day here and nothing very much, as a consequence, has happened. So, today, I have spent about four hours making a little lec for Monday which will be mostly about St. Paul's and what a strange building that one really is—a bad building by an extremely intelligent individual who was more influential than one suspects but who, perhaps, was scarcely an architect.[10] But it would be a bore to go on with the details of all this.

Today has been a terribly nice day, as was yesterday, and the snow, at last, is beginning to melt—though I think that it will still be the end of the month before I shall be able to negotiate the driveway.

Sunday, March 12

I went to bed about 8.15 last night and was almost immediately asleep. Woke about one in the morning and read Freedberg for a couple of hours and then to, sleep again.[11] Went to breakfast/lunch today at Fairview Heights with Miriam Gusevitch★ and her mathematician boy friend, Richard Rand. There were present also Richard Becherer★ and David Roncayolo from Venezuela who is intermittently around these parts. Got back here at about 3.30 and for the first time since mid December was able to get up this driveway!!! What a joy, what a joy, what a joy. So since then, have been paying bills, sorting papers and what not; but I am about to be interrupted by Gil Rosenthal who seems to be in town and seems to be determined to see me.[12] Mercifully, there is nothing whatever to drink in the house; and then, in any case, he won't be able to stay too long because of my lecture tomorrow. But I think that I shall seal this letter before he arrives and then go on to send a letter, with check, to your mother.[13] Next week I have dinner with both the Ungers on Wednesday,[14] and on Thursday I go to Judith Holliday's★ celebration of her Fortieth birthday.[15]

Judy, lots of love and I am no longer at all depressed. Existence is rather dull but, at least, I am not depressed

Love and write to me about all that I have been asking you,

    C

1 DiMaio* had been hospitalized in Rome for influenza.
2 *gemutlichkeit, schwärmerei,* and *kaffee mit schlagobers,* German and English: friendliness, enthusiasm, and coffee with whipped cream.
3 Don Greenberg, Lee Hodgden,* and John Shaw: Rowe's faculty colleagues at Cornell.
4 *sich,* German: them.
5 *longueurs,* French: lengths.
6 KC Parsons, professor of architecture at Cornell.
7 *maniera,* Italian: manner; style.
8 Jorge Silvetti* and Rodolfo Machado.*
9 OM Ungers.*
10 St Paul's Cathedral, London (1668–1708), designed by Christopher Wren.
11 Sydney J Freedberg (1914–1997), historian of Italian Renaissance art.
12 Gilbert A Rosenthal (1953–2011) had been an undergraduate student of Rowe's in the 1970s.
13 DiMaio* notes that the check for Mrs DiMaio was "undoubtedly in exchange for some antique or *objet*" purchased by Mrs DiMaio on Rowe's behalf.
14 Mathias Ungers* and his wife, Liselotte (1926–2010).
15 Judith Holliday* (1938–2008), head librarian, Cornell's College of Architecture, Art, and Planning.

101   *To **Richard Meier**, Richard Meier & Associated Architects, New York, N.Y.*   *30 June 1978*

Cornell Department of Architecture, East Sibley Hall, Ithaca, N.Y.

My dear Richard:[1]

This is simply to remind you of an item in our conversation when Barbara and I were around in your place just before I left for Rome.[2]

This topic was Michael Manfredi* who wants very much to work for you; and the topic continues to be Michael Manfredi who proposes to visit you some time during the next few weeks.[3]

Michael's background is Trieste, Rome, Washington, Notre Dame, Cornell, and he has just completed his urban design thesis here which I am sure you will like.[4] He is sensitive, talented, conscientious, tough; he does not throw temperaments; he speaks voluble Italian and good French; over the last couple of years I have found him to be a rock of reliability; and, if you are able to use him, I am sure that your judgments will concur with mine.

Best regards,

   Colin

   Colin Rowe

   CR/la[5]

1 This is one of three 30 June 1978 letters of reference written by Rowe on behalf of Michael Manfredi.* The others were to Robert Stern and Charles Gwathmey.
2 Barbara Littenberg* (BArch Cornell, 1971), who earlier had worked in Meier's* office.
3 A recent graduate of Cornell's MArch program, Manfredi* had studied in Rowe's Urban Design Studio and in 1989 would become a founding partner in Weiss/Manfredi Architects.
4 For Manfredi's* thesis of 1978, "Upper Manhattan Development Strategy", see Rowe, Colin *As I Was Saying: Recollections and Miscellaneous Essays,* Alexander Caragonne, 3 vols, Cambridge, MA: MIT Press, 1996, vol 3, pp 37–40.
5 "la" indicates the initials of the Cornell secretary who would have transcribed this letter for Rowe.

Rowe in Caprarola, Italy, 1981

7
Renown

1980–1985

With the publication of *The Mathematics of the Ideal Villa and Other Essays* in 1976 and *Collage City* in 1978, Rowe's fame spread. Although he remained at Cornell, increasingly he taught as a visiting professor at other institutions. In 1980 to 1981 he taught in Rome for Notre Dame. In spring 1984 he taught as the Thomas Jefferson Professor at the University of Virginia. And throughout the mid-1980s, he lectured and was repeatedly guest critic for the Internationale Bausstellung IBA in Berlin.

During this time, Rowe wrote frequently to his brother, sister-in-law, and nephews in England, and began to write to former and current students. Obvious in these letters is his deep interest in personalities and provenance, in landscapes and architecture, and in the travels that unite them. His thoughts and advice are valued both in the United States and in Europe; and his unique writing style becomes more extravagant, knitting many topics into the cohesive whole of a single letter.

Rowe was 65 years old in 1985 when he became the Andrew Dixon White Professor of Architecture. In October of that year he underwent hip surgery in Boston. The year before, Bernhard Hoesli,* his contemporary and friend of many years, died unexpectedly. All of this led to a greater regard for legacy: an attentiveness to his library, publications, and personal wealth, and his concern for the upbringing and education of his nephews. His collections of prints, paintings, and furniture became recurring subjects in letters from this time.

---

102 *To Charles P. Graves Sr.,*
Chairman, Internal Review Committee, University of Kentucky[1]   *13 February 1980*
Cornell University Department of Architecture, East Sibley Hall, Ithaca, N.Y.

Dear Charles:[2]

Though your address seems suddenly to have become supremely elaborate and, I suspect, computerized, it is still an enormous pleasure to write to you and to be asked to write on behalf of the University of Kentucky's College of Architecture.

So what to say about it from a perspective and an experience such as mine, which is inevitably East Coast—though with occasional sorties elsewhere, most recently to Houston, Cincinnati, and Chicago/Notre Dame?

So, I believe that a fairly standard Eastern view might be expressed something like this. There is a group of institutions—Yale, Harvard, Princeton, Columbia, Cornell, Cooper Union, rarely MIT, and scarcely Penn, which appear to take in each other's students with, on the whole, satisfaction, mild skepticism and happiness; and then, around these institutions (and, obviously, in terms of their criteria) there is something of a twilight zone about which information is likely to be shady. For instance: I.I.T.? It was once felt to be a source of illumination, but now? Cincinnati?

Do they—indeed, can they—draw? Rice? Reliable, but not likely to set Buffalo Bayou on fire? U. of Va.? A provincial Princeton? Washington U.? Still a subsidiary of M.I.T.? Atlanta? Largely invisible and unknown. Maryland? Promising, but has difficulties as a commuting campus? Michigan, Illinois (Urbana and Chicago Circle), Minnesota? No discernible product? And then, way and beyond all this, there is a mysterious California, generally believed to be elaborate, but inherently supposed to be wacky and unstable.

But, if this is the way that an East Coast view reads, then it must be added that, out of this somewhat foggy condition of intuition and information, the University of Kentucky, nowadays, leaps into prominence. It possesses a respected product which, so far as I can perceive from recent experiences in London, Zurich, and Barcelona, is shortly about to be received as something more widely known; its student body appears to be reasonably informed, interested, and animated; its faculty appears to be tolerably happy and not to be unduly rent by feuds and politics; and, in short and compared with most places, Architecture at the University of Kentucky appears to be in a generally prosperous and enlightened condition.

So what problems can one perceive?

A wholly inadequate library; and one realizes that the building up of a library can only be a matter of much expense and many years.

A wholly inadequate slide library in which expansion and reclassification is imperative.

An absence of graduate programs. For, if these exist, I seem not to be aware of them. But, I do emphasize a graduate program(s) as a great potential source of vitality in a school in terms of a relatively free and easy impact upon younger students.

A difficulty in retaining younger faculty whom, it is my experience, are easily attracted to Lexington, who are apt to talk of Kentucky Architecture with great warmth and regard, but who are apt to be seduced by the bright lights of bigger (or more sophisticated?) places.

Now, I assume that most of these problems are interrelated. One couldn't conduct research in your library and, hence, the graduate absence and, hence, the attrition of younger faculty. And I assume that all of these issues are related to finances and endowments and, therefore, remediable.

However, all this being said, during the period in which I have known it, your college has struck me as being largely a model institution greatly distinguished by the sanity, the tolerance, and the modesty of its administration. And this is absolutely the reverse of faint praise. For, of where else is it easy to say so much which is so quietly positive? And where else does one not perceive the tedious filibusters of the academically disgruntled and the quasi-paranoia of the eternally inept.

But, could it be that I see Lexington in only golden light and, accordingly, paint it as a Bluegrass mini-Utopia? But, I don't think that this is the case; and, believing my letter to have been relatively objective, (and having stated four reservations) I can only congratulate your college on what seems to me to be its felicity.

Sincerely,

Colin

Colin Rowe

tb[3]

1 The complete address includes: ᶜ/o Vice President for Academic Affairs, 111 Administration Building, University of Kentucky, Lexington, KY.
2 Charles P Graves Sr★ (1927–2001), professor and a former dean at the University of Kentucky, as chairman of a 1980 Internal Review had asked Rowe's opinion of Kentucky's School of Architecture. This letter is Rowe's reply.
3 "tb" indicates the initials of the Cornell secretary who transcribed this letter for Rowe.

103   *To Judith DiMaio, Via del Teatro Valle, Rome*   *20 May 1981*

Cornell University Department of Architecture, East Sibley Hall, Ithaca, N.Y.

Dearest Judy:

It is a delight to be no longer in the Via dei Coronari, which doesn't mean that it's any great pleasure to be here—though it is agreeable to be surrounded by objects, books and all the rest.[1]

So received your postcard of "Il Papa" just before leaving for Minneapolis and, though you didn't envisage his present condition, I do think that you are right. And, with all his elaborately simulated humility, doesn't he just <u>continue</u> to be on a fake high?[2]

In any case, and as any one might guess, Minneapolis was flat, empty, abrasive, goody-goody and nothing-nothing. Also the convention was much the same. Also the medal is silver, apparently prestigious, and v. ugly.[3] All the same it's as well to have been there and even better to have left.

I got back here yesterday, I have spent most of the day in bed, I am still feeling a bit sleepy and I am wondering what else I can tell you.

There was an ex-Bennington girl at Minneapolis who is working for the AIA. After Bennington she did architecture at Carnegie-Mellon. Name: Beverly Sanchez; but I don't think that you know her. Anyway she wants to put together an AIA number on Women In Architecture for the *AIA Journal* for November or December of this year; and she, Jerry and Jason want to hold a little panel discussion in Ithaca at the Wells's★ in early Fall.[4] In other words (and don't scream or faint) there's some sort of an idea about Judy Wolin, Barbara Littenberg,★ Susie Kim,★ Judith DiMaio,★ (J. DiM!) and Grace Kobayashi (whom I scarcely know but who just won an enormous prize)all getting together in Ithaca talking, and then being published <u>with their works</u>.[5] Repeat: at the moment only a fantasy; but I think about your nymphaeum and other things and the Sanchez is apparently coming up here in a few weeks' time to look things over.[6] But will let you know more about this as it develops—and <u>if</u> you can bear it.

But Judy I am now in a very recessive mood. I have gotten the car activated but don't want to go out. I will go to New York sometime soon but don't know that I really want to. I mean that I just feel suspended, like up in the air, without contacts and no knowledge of the landing. Would have loved to come to *Sicilia* and want to hear all about it. But I really won't know where I am for several days.

Meanwhile, I gave your phone number to Jason Seely who will be arriving in Rome within the next day or so.[7] Probably I did wrong—but he did ask for it...........

Lots of love and would be wildly excited to discover that I related to <u>somewhere</u>

   C. xxxxxx

P.S More about the *medaglione*.[8] They didn't hang it around my neck and kiss me, which is the way I thought that sort of thing was always done. Instead they filled my arms with a large framed citation and just gave me the medal in a box. And it really is a bit crude. A perfectly ferocious-looking American eagle is standing on a rock and seems to be attempting, with its beak and its claws to devour what I suspect is a very feeble little olive tree. A strange iconography, or don't you think so?

Love, love,

    C

---

1 Rowe had just returned to Ithaca from Rome where he was a visiting professor in the Notre Dame Rome program.
2 Reference is to Pope John Paul II who was shot four times on 13 May 1981 in an attempted assassination.
3 Reference is the AIA National Convention in Minneapolis, 17–21 May 1981.
4 Professors Jerry A Wells,* chairman of the School of Architecture, and Jason Seley (1917–1983), dean of the College of Architecture, Art, and Planning at Cornell.
5 Grace R Kobayashi (M.Arch. Cornell,1982) received a $10,000.00 SOM Fellowship.
6 DiMaio's* "nymphaeum project," a waterwall for a garden in Rome, was executed while she was at the American Academy in 1978.
7 Jason Seley.
8 *medaglione*, Italian: medallion.

[handwritten]

To *Judith DiMaio*, *Park Avenue South, New York, N.Y.*   *8 August 1982*   **104**

1040 Dorsoduro, Venice, Italy

My Dear Judy:

Quite a big house (3,000 square feet) with quite a big garden. It's to the right of the Accademia, is six windows wide and confronts a small campo which opens off the Rio Terra Della Carita.[1]

Furniture—a lot of repro Empire which is adequate but not good and a rather nice set of very Viennese Bieder-mayer chairs in one of which I am at present sitting.

So it rained in the night and now is quite a nice sunny Sunday morning and Dorothy has just come back from San Marco. So as I look around, I am left thinking how nice it would be to redo this house—like you could make a Palazzo Spada false perspective out in the garden on the axis of the front door.

So Jim's building in Stuttgart is v. v. big and v. impressive—episodes dense and convincing, though I do think it could have a bit more of facade.[2]

Come soon and look forward.

    Colin x x x x x

---

1 Rowe is describing a house in Venice that David* and Dorothy Rowe* had rented in August, 1982.
2 Neue Staatsgalerie in Stuttgart, Germany, 1984, by James Stirling,* Michael Wilford, and Associates.

*To **Roger Conover**, Architecture and Designs editor, MIT Press, Cambridge, Mass.* November 1982

19 Renwick Place, Ithaca, N. Y.

Dear Roger:

I have long been looking forward to the appearance of this book and my first reaction to it is of some disappointment.[1] I know quite well what Klaus Herdeg* is trying to do; and I very strongly support both his intention and his idea.[2] All the same it seems to me that his intentions are not facilitated when they are expressed in what I would call a "Time-Life language." Since, surely, it is the very ethos of *Time-Life*, in so far as it concerns building, which Klaus is attempting to bring into question. So, on the whole, I find the language sometimes a little too cute and the emotional dimensions, sometimes a little too much without compassion.

But don't get me wrong. I am in complete agreement with Klaus about the ineptness of Gropius as both educator and architect; and I am also in complete agreement about the ineptness and the vulgarity of those individuals who emerged as prominent and 'successful' specimens of the Gropius/Harvard *equipe*.[3] Only I would have liked the mystique of Walter Gropius to have been properly laid out before the demo came on: and I am sure that this would have given more irony and punch to the text. But Klaus, I think, goes for the jugular before properly rehearsing anything of the pathos of the myth which inspires his polemic.

So I may be wrong about this and don't quote me about it to Klaus, because it's clearly irremediable......

However I do think that you must make just a little correction. On p. 6, Klaus speaks of the Errazuris House and places it in a "context" of middle class Chile of the thirties. Now Eugenia Errazuris whose great nephew I used to know, was born in Santiago in 1860, where you have to think of her frequenting a fairly opulent English, American, Latino and Greek society.[4] So, sometime before 1890, she transferred to Paris; and in Paris she remained—without any return to Chile—until, I believe, 1950. So her standards were scarcely middle class Chile—as Klaus may seem to allege. Instead she was the friend (and, in some cases, the relative) of the Lopez-Wilshaws, Emilio Terry, Carlos de Beistegui, Etienne de Beaumont, Marie-Laure de Noailles, Cocteau, Picasso, and you name it.[5] So the Corbu* project, a House for Mme. Errazuris, is to be placed within this scene.[6] It is related to the belated nostalgia for Chile expressed via some sort of SynFothetic Cubist, and rustic, fantasy. So, presumably, after some fifty years in Europe, Errazuris got a hankering for Chile (was it ancestral voices prophesizing war?); and, hence, the Corbu project. However, she couldn't tear herself away and didn't return to Chile until 1950 (after seventy two years absence!) when she, finally, met her death in an automobile accident in 1953.

So do send these Errazuris remarks to Klaus (he could check them out in Cecil Beaton, *The Glass of Fashion*)[7] and do tell that Eugenia Errazuris (whom I just could have met) was a rather grander version of Hélène de Mandrot and not,[8] exactly, the simple *bourgeoisie* from Chile which, it could seem, he imagines her to have been.

Then there is another imperative correction. For page 8, figure 7, Klaus has the caption "Errazuris House, View from Mezzanine"; but this image which is to be found in Le Corbusier *Œuvre Complète*, Vol II, p.51, is not of the Errazuris House which, obviously, was never built. Indeed it is captioned, by Le C. *"Pas la peine de se gêner"*;[9] and (see Le C., p. 52) it is part of the documentation of a house in Japan by Antonin Raymond which was published in *Architectural Record* in July 1934 and which

Corb considered to be a rip-off from his Errazuris project. So this must absolutely be corrected. For, if it is not, some picayune reviewer will pick it up; and, by doing so, will throw into question the whole of Klaus' brilliant analysis of the Errazuris project and Marcel Breuer's MOMA house of 1949—which Corbu chose to ignore as, presumably, beneath notice.

SO BOTH THESE CORRECTIONS ARE VERY NECESSARY FOR KLAUS.

Klaus is best, I think, with a one to one, morphological analysis as with Corbu-Breuer, and as with Schinkel and Philip Johnson;* but, then, I am of the opinion that he tends to vitiate these analyses by making them the lead pieces for an awful lot of schlock buildings and, possibly, this is inherent in the topic. But, all the same and if possible, I would still like a break to be introduced between the lead pieces and the schlock. For the reader could then be forewarned about the possibility of a primary and secondary reading. And such a warning: on p. so and so—primary, on p. so and so—secondary, which, I think, shouldn't be too hard to introduce, would, probably, immensely facilitate legibility.

Meanwhile, how about this for an endorsement?

"The persistence of the mystique of Walter Gropius is very hard to understand. For, as both architect and educator, Gropius was surely inept. With the Bauhaus almost a symbol of the Weimar Republic, he came to the United States as the widely advertised emancipator. Not only here but also in Europe it was supposed that Gropius was a supreme Moses-figure, preparing and illuminating the way; but, then, when the way turned out to be no more than relentless kitsch catastrophe, the mystique still survived and it continues to plague architectural education to this day.

"The confusions of so called Post Modernism are not only a reaction to Gropius but also an explicit product of that failure to recognize the complex nature of architectural discourse, which Klaus Herdeg, here, alleges was the ultimate result of the Harvard establishment sponsored by Gropius.

"This book abounds in comparative formal analyses, the most brilliant being the confrontation of Le Corbusier's Errazuris project of 1930 and Marcel Breuer's MOMA house of 1949. The inadequacies and the *non-sequiturs* of Breuer's exhibition house were visible long ago, as was his dependence upon Corbu's precedent; but not until Herdeg has this been made abundantly glaring. With this comparison alone Herdeg explains much of what has gone wrong with American architecture since 1937........."

Too long OF COURSE; but chop it around and use it as you like; and, meanwhile, since I have been very good and gotten this off to you before leaving I have a little request.

It is like this. Apparently in my tax returns of '79 and '80 there is a confusion about royalties and my accountant tells me that I will be investigated by the IRS. So no great problem; but, all the same, I would like from MIT Xeroxes of my royalty statements for these years. So could you transmit this request to the appropriate department?

Sincerely

    Colin Rowe

    Colin Rowe

[handwritten]

It's my own typing. Sorry. C.R.

1 Conover* had sent Rowe a copy of the uncorrected page proofs of Herdeg, Klaus, *The Decorated Diagram: Harvard Architecture and the Failure of the Bauhaus Legacy*, Cambridge, MA: MIT Press, 1983, hoping that Rowe might provide a comment for the cover.

2 Klaus Herdeg* (1937–2009).

3 *équipe*, French: team.

4 Eugenia Errázuriz, (1860–1951).

5 Artists and art collectors in Paris in the 1930s and 1940s.

6 For Le Corbusier's* design, see "MAISON DE M. ERRAZURIS, AU CHILI, 1930" in Boesiger, W and H Girsberger ed, Le Corbusier and Pierre Jeanneret, *Œuvre Complète, vol. 2, 1929–1934*, Zurich: Les Editions d'Architecture, 1964, pp 48–52.

7 Beaton, Cecil, *The Glass of Fashion: Fifty Years of Dress and Decor*, London: Weidenfeld and Nicholson, 1954.

8 Hélène de Mandrot (1861–1948), wealthy Swiss artist and patron of the arts and architecture for whom Le Corbusier* built a vacation house in Le Pradet, France, in 1931 to 1932.

9 *Pas la peine de se gêner*, French: not woth troubling or inconveniencing oneself.

106   To **Blake Middleton**, *Florence*   *11 January 1983*

19 Renwick Place, Ithaca, N.Y.

Blake:

Just got back here and am writing to say how much I enjoyed meeting you and your father at the Harvard Club yesterday and how sorry that I am that I had to leave you so quickly in 51ˢᵗ street.[1]

So I was thinking that, when you are driving your father down to Firenze, it would really be very nice to stop for a time (I think a night) at Parma which is a rich little town (shades of the Farnese and the Bourbons) (also Toscanini) where nobody goes very much.[2]

Last time I was there in '69 I stayed four days at the Albergo Torino (nice and modest but no parking); but, since you will be driving and papa, I suppose, paying, then I would recommend the rather more expensive Jolly Hotel Stendhal (!) where I stayed with Susan Potters in '72.[3]

But Parma would be terrific for an overnight stay. You could leave the *autostrada* at Piacenza which is strictly a thirty minute town; but it does have the two Farnese equestrian statues (Alessandro, Duke of Parma and Spanish general in the Netherlands and somebody else★★★) and these stand in front of the absolutely superb mediaeval *municipio*★★★, and then there is an unfinished Vignola Palazzo Farnese which looks rather more like a barracks (3 minutes).[4] So then, between Piacenza and Parma, you could stop at Pontellata where there is a little red brick *rocca* with in it a very small room frescoed by Parmigianino with the story of Diana and Actaeon. Think that it's terribly worth seeing—that is if the building is open.

So, in Parma, there's the Duomo (with Correggio frescoes), the Baptistery, the Madonna della Steccata (Parmigianino and elegant-sublime ★★★★★★), and—inside the Palazzo della Pilotta—the Teatro Farnese, early 17C ★★★ and the Pinacoteca.[5] Then also, if you had time to kill, you could look in at the small Museo Glauco-Lombardo which is dedicated to the memory of Napoleon's Maria Luisa, Grand Duchess of Parma from 1814/5 to 1846.

But I suggest all this in Parma because it would be a Farnese aperitif, a sort of overture to Caprarola; and also because of what seems to be your father's Farnese-Spain-Netherlandish interests. But I also suggest Parma because of the eating.

Blake, the eating is fantastic—and even Michelin gives stars. So, as far as I know, there are three good restaurants—L'Aurora, La Filoma, and a newish one by the Duomo which I find a bit pretentious (like it was designed by a half witted architecture student who equipped the bar with about 12 Eames chairs); but Michelin seems to prefer. In any case, the rooms at the La Filoma are rather small; and so little old me is quite content with L'Aurora.

But I am going on like a tour guide (which I imagine might be one of my lost *metiers*)[6] and, with all this, I don't really know whether or not you've been there already, or whether or not, like me, you swoon in La Steccata—which I find the most intimately spectacular church in the whole of Italy.[7]

So the tour guide continues. Because you see, if you left Parma early in the morning, you could enjoy a little adventure. I mean that, if the weather were good, you could forget the *autostrada* and drive directly down south over the mountains. It's not tough. I drove it in '72 with Susan. You can come out somewhere between Bagni di Lucca and Pescia (in any case, we did, and without a map) and it's all *molto suggestive* and *molto caracteristico*.[8] So, think it would be far better than the autostrada and, as I imagine this little trip, I only wish that I were going to be with you.

Which will cause me to continue just a little bit more with another little excursion per *il suo padre*.[9] So have you been to Artimino? So to get to Artimino, you turn left (coming from Firenze) at Poggio a Caiano and then you go on up and up the hill. And then, at Carbognano on the way, there is a beautiful church with elegant Buontalenti style trim (with Pontormo's Visitation inside).[10] And then, at Artimino, there is Buontalenti's La Ferdinanda—a hunting lodge built for the ex-Cardinal, Grand Duke Ferdinando in the 1590's. So it's worth looking at but you can't get inside and, in any case, much more important is the restaurant, La Delfina I think it's called, where, in January 1980, Judy and I had a completely sublime meal.[11] So we drove up on a wet misty day and I was in one of my moods—Let's just bug out this place is ridiculous. But J. said no; and it was a negative for which I remain—and will remain—forever grateful. There was a huge fire with all sorts of public cooking being carried on; and the triumph of the meal was an extremely rich and rustic *salsiccia*, the like of which I never expect to meet again.[12] It was terrific and, while we were sitting by this huge fire and eating it, the mists dissipated themselves; and, then, a landscape with Buontalenti became the prospect. So, dear Blake, it was sublime; and, therefore, you must excuse my carrying on so much.

Then you must also excuse what, as I reread it, seems to me to be the slightly patronizing tone of this letter. I agree that it sounds a little as though Italy were an exotic private possession—of mine. But this is just because we haven't met for ever so long; and, in New York, just to reach first base, we needed about three hours *tête-à-tête*.[13]

Ciao and lots of best regards,

    C

P.S. And again the tour guide—the *reisen fuhrer*.[14] But I like later sixteenth century Firenze—I like the G.D.'s Cosimo and Francesco Ferdinando personally I think it was a bit of a meat ball[15]—and, therefore, I wonder if you have been to the Castello?[16] If not do—and just to see the grotto which is the best Tuscan late *maniera*.[17] Again went there with Judy—as a matter of fact—three years ago today; and, again, it's a case of the fastidious, sophisticated elegant—sublime.

But then, there are so many things to talk about; and I am quite sure that you want to tell me as much as I do you.

So, as they say, *un abbraccio,*

  C

P.P.S. I have a dog temperament. I mean that I don't go out for walks unless somebody takes me on a lead.

  C

---

1 Rowe had met Blake Middleton* and his father, David Middleton, a physicist, at the Harvard Club in New York City for lunch.
2 David Middleton was arriving from Zurich in Milan, where Blake would escort him by car to Florence, visiting architectural sites on the way.
3 Susan Potters, the wife of Steven Potters, a former student of Rowe's and graduate of Rowe's Cornell Urban Design Program in the 1960s.
4 Rowe employs the '*' symbol to indicate a star rating for the various sites.
5 See note 4.
6 *métiers,* French: trades.
7 The Sanctuary of Santa Maria della Steccata in central Parma, 1521–1539. The dome of this Greek-cross design Renaissance church is attributed to Antonio da Sangallo the Younger (1484–1586).
8 *molto suggestivo* and *molto caratteristico,* Italian and English: very suggestive and very characteristic.
9 *il suo padre,* Italian: your father.
10 "Buontalenti style" refers to the architect Bernardo Buontalenti (1531–1608). The small church is called the Pieve di San Michele and is in Carmignano, a town west of Florence. Pontormo's *The Visitation,* 1528, adorns the altar of a side chapel.
11 Judith DiMaio.*
12 *salsiccia,* Italian: sausage.
13 *tête-à-tête,* French: a private conversation between two people; literally, head-to-head.
14 *reisen führer,* German: trip leader.
15 "G.D.'s Cosimo and Francesco Ferdinando": the Grand Dukes Cosimo I de' Medici (1519–1574) and Francesco I de' Medici (1541–1587).
16 Villa di Castello, the country residence of Cosimo I de' Medici, restored and enlarged by Giorgio Vasari, located in the hills northwest of Florence near the small town of Sesto Fiorentino.
17 The grotto of the animals (aka the grotto of the flood).

107 *To Daniel Shannon & Matthew Bell,*
University of Notre Dame, South Bend, Indiana   *15 April 1983*

19 Renwick Place, Ithaca, N.Y.

Wa-wa-wa-wa-wa; ra-ra-ra-ra-ra; wuff-wuff, wuff, wuff, wuff; dear Dan and Matt,[1] this is my new means of communication; and I suppose that it signifies, mostly, inhibited emotion.[2] You see I was so very happy to come to N.D. and to find so many alliances/liaisons in repair. Believe you me I didn't really expect it; and that's why, writing, I am presently so ridiculously, *emotionne.*[3]

Of course, it is absurd that, since we all left Rome, this was my first visit to N.D. Because, during the intervening time, it should have been at least my fourth visit.

So now let me tell you something. They were talking the other night about the N.D. budget for the Arch. Lib.—recently escalated from $900.00 a year to $5,000.00 a year.[4] So I checked out the same business here; and the budget for the Cornell Arch. Lib. (excluding periodicals) just happens to be $85,000.00. But what a difference; and this is not to talk about money so much as it is to establish the distance between concern and neglect—and I have written to Steve to this effect.[5]

Meanwhile my best love to Tom, Tom, Kevin, Fred, Janeanne.[6]

And also tell J.H. that I would like very much to receive a Xerox of her Armenian Embassy.[7]

Best of the best and thanks for din-din,

    Colin

1   Shannon and Bell* were students of Rowe's in the 1980 to 1981 Notre Dame junior year Rome Studies Program.
2   Rowe introduced studio reviews: "So let's get it up on the wall then, wa-wa-wa, ra-ra-ra, boom-boom, boom-boom-boom!"
3   *émotionné*, French: very moved.
4   "Arch. Lib.": Architecture Library.
5   Steven Hurtt,* a Cornell graduate (1976), taught architecture at Notre Dame from 1973 to 1990.
6   Thomas Rajkovich, Thomas Hofman, Kevin Hinders, Frederick Fredrickson, and Janeanne Hudson: Notre Dame students in Rome with Rowe, 1980–1981.
7   "J.H.": Janeanne Hudson.

To **Rodolfo Machado & Jorge Silvetti**, *Boston*   *17 May 1983*   **108**

19 Renwick Place, Ithaca, N.Y.

Jorge / Rudolfo:

I enjoyed the weekend—much, much; and I also enjoyed the review—jury—though not quite so much. Also, as I always do, I enjoyed *casa sua*—even though I do want to rearrange the drawing room and the library.[1] Then I also enjoyed all the fashionable publications which lie around and which are not exactly the same as those which I possess.

In any case you are always a great stimulus to me and a reassurance that life does exist and that's why I want to see you here during the course of the summer. So please do take a little time off and pay the briefest of visits.

I remained in your house this morning until about 2.00 p.m. and then, after locking myself out, I found taxis the greatest difficulty. However, as must be obvious, I finally found one.

So my great lesson was mirrors (which Nancy Mitford thought should always be called looking glasses,) with which designation I do not agree.[2] So, apart from the mirrors on either side of the fireplace in the drawing room (which I don't care for), I took time out to count something like fifteen mirrors in your house which, all of them, I thought, were provocatively distributed. Which means that, on a lesser scale, I am going to imitate; and which also means that, knowing all about mirrors, until now I must have inherited the mod. arch. inhibitions about.

Then, apart from this thank you performance, I have two requests.

i. I was foraging and reading this morning and I found a reference to a brilliant series of remarks which you had made about post-Modernism as an inversion of *modernita*[3] but obviously still preoccupied with the same *avant garde* fantasies.[4] So I suspect that it was all said so well that I want to read it and use it. So please equip me and, then, I will incorporate it towards the end of my new book—*The Architecture of Good Intentions* or whatever it is going to be called. Then,

ii. This morning I decided that the wing chair which, <u>Rudolfo</u>, you and I saw <u>is</u> worth buying. So, <u>of course</u>, it <u>requires</u> to be <u>fixed</u>, strengthened and all that; and, <u>of course</u>, the price is about $100.00 too high. But, <u>still</u>, it's a good chair—comfortable, big, authoritative. So I think that I <u>want</u> it—even at <u>her</u> price. I would have it fixed and then slip-covered in a white, pink, and green glazed chintz, which wouldn't be beyond the resources of Ithaca and which, incidentally, would be *molto inglese*[5] and (though nursery) *presque snob*.[6] So do please <u>get</u> it for me and have it <u>sent up here</u>; and, then, please recognise that I will, also, require its approximate partner. (Hope <u>not too</u> much to ask.)

In any case *un gran' abbraccio per lei* and my <u>very</u> great regrets that I was compelled to descend to a minor appropriation of wardrobe.

    Colin

---

1   *casa sua*, Italian: your house.
2   Nancy Mitford (1904–1973), novelist, biographer, and journalist.
3   *modernità*, Italian: modernity.
4   The quote to which Rowe refers is not known.
5   *molto inglese*, Italian: very English.
6   *presque snob*, French: almost snob.

---

109   To **Thomas Schumacher,**
University of Maryland Department of Architecture, College Park, Maryland   *27 May 1983*

19 Renwick Place, Ithaca, N.Y.

My dear Tom:

Thank you for your Vittoriano postcard; and I <u>am</u> sorry that you found my letter 'wonderful if somewhat embarrassing'. But, <u>believe me</u> it was written with <u>love</u>. I was only thinking about the two previous: [...] Emilia, who looked like a Bronzino and didn't understand the Bronzino role, and [...] Beth, who looked like a Dante Gabriel Rossetti and didn't understand the pre-Raphaelite predicament either. So it was <u>really</u> a letter of congratulations upon what, <u>I think</u>, is going to be a highly successful scene. So try to forgive me if I was unduly crude....[1]

Shall go to London in about ten days time. Shall then go, with DiMaio,* to Bavaria. May then drop down to Vicenza-Firenza. After all this should be here shortly after mid-July; and will hope to see you.

Best, best,

    C

---

1   Rowe's earlier letter to Schumacher,* a congratulatory note on his recent marriage to Pat Sachs, mentioned Emilia and Beth, Schumacher's first two wives.

---

110   To **William Pedersen**, *Kohn, Pedersen, Fox, Madison Avenue, New York, N.Y.*   *Summer, 1983*
19 Renwick Place, Ithaca, N.Y.

Dear Bill:[1]

I am writing to say thank you for lunch the other day and also to say how much I enjoyed meeting you and how much I appreciated your regard for the Cornell Product.

Back in January when Judy showed me your verbal presentation of the Houston building by the park, I was immensely impressed by your argument about Platonic Ideas and the contextual necessity for their distortion.[2] And <u>you</u> a corporate architect! Meaning someone who I would have expected to be utterly remote from <u>that</u> kind of reasoning!

Anyway, I was entirely convinced by the arguments about both of the Houston buildings; and let me say how much I appreciate both <u>them</u> and the <u>arguments</u>. Indeed, having read <u>over</u>, I would love to have Xeroxes of <u>both</u> these presentations—

Then to be truthful, I was <u>less</u> convinced by the Cincinnati job.[3] And I find it hard to say why. Is it because the site is more diffuse and, necessarily, the building is more of an aggregation? I think my reaction derives from such a situation, which is made evident in the problem of the garden, and, as far as I remember, this garden is indeterminate and doesn't really begin to accommodate the lateral and diagonal pressures which are implicit in the built solids. But I only say this because of what seems to be your scrupulousness.

I would like to have been able to show you some of our Berlin stuff. And before I leave for Venice, I will try to do something about this—though it's very complicated.[4]

Will also send you, in the early fall, when it appears, a copy of the second Cornell Mag, which is all related to what I have been doing for longer than I care to remember.[5] Then too, if we have anything worth while produced during the next few months, I should just love to persuade you to come up here as part of a jury.

Best, Best, Wishes,

[no signature]

1   William Pedersen* (b 1938), principal and partner of Kohn Pedersen Fox Associates, New York City.
2   Houston 265, a project that was not built.
3   Proctor and Gamble.
4   The "Berlin Stuff" is described in Rowe, Colin, *As I Was Saying: Recollections and Miscellaneous Essays*, Alexander Caragonne ed, 3 vols, Cambridge, MA: MIT Press, 1996, vol 3, pp 221–260: "Comments on the IBA Proposals"; "The Vanished City"; and "A Student Project: Berlin, 1983–84".
5   *The Cornell Journal of Architecture 2: Urban Design*, fall 1983: foreword by Léon Krier* and essays by Wayne Copper,* "The Figure/Grounds"; Steven Hurtt,* "Conjectures on Urban Form: The Cornell Urban Design Studio, 1963–1982"; and Colin Rowe, "Program vs. Paradigm: Otherwise Casual Notes on The Pragmatic, The Typical, and the Possible". See also Rowe, *As I Was Saying*, vol 2, pp 7–41.

To **John Miller,** *Regent's Park Road, London*   *14 July 1983*   **111**

19 Renwick Place, Ithaca, N.Y.

My dear John:

You know, <u>even on this inauspicious date</u>, the memory of the Germanic lands can <u>really</u> be quite charming.[1] Of course, *Struwwelpeter, Hansel and Gretel,* Bishop Hatto with his Rheinturm and his rats, the Pied Piper, belong to the Biedermeier picture and they scarcely represent the *horreurs*—though maybe, since such funny things happen in German children's stories, they are probably <u>some</u> sort of index.[2]

Anyway Berlin was much as usual—talk and acrimony;[3] and it was better to get down to Stuttgart where Jim's wild museum (which is now on the way) is well worth a special visit.[4] So, on the whole, the food was lamentable but the forests charming and they allow one to understand that nineteenth century taste for summers in Baden-Baden, Marienbad, Gastein, etc. At Wurzburg the staircase is very superb; but we tended to find the longueurs of Franconia rather over protracted.[5] For V. and A. reasons we went to Coburg and were compelled to think that Those People really struck it lucky when they reached England (the Coburg palaces look extremely minor when you think about Longleat and Hatfield, but in the *marktplatz* there is very large statue to Prince Albert (with an encampment of hippies around its base).[6] Bayreuth bored; then Regensburg was the dregs; but, with Salzburg and Munich things began to look up; and, of course, we did the *schlosser*[7] of the unfortunate Ludwig II whom I don't think was mad at all—just an extreme case of the family mania, their *bauwurm*,[8] occurring at far too late a date.[9] But the interiors of Neuschwanstein are, to say the least, highly indifferent and one feels how much better off Ludwig might have been if he could have made the acquaintance of Lord Bute and maybe engaged the services of Burges—a good idea, but, by English standards, execution is incredibly brittle and *retardataire*.[10] You see Neuschwanstein requires a bit of Pre-Raphaelite input rather than the deadly frescoes which are all over the place and even Wm. Morris would improve it.

On the whole though an engaging little trip with, for the most part, no crowds and you and Susan should try it—exquisite landscapes and beautiful air.[11]

So here it's rather hot. It's been about 95 for several days and, quietly, I am beginning to wilt. So I shall look forward to Germania again in August and perhaps we should all plan to meet in Munich.

Un abbraccio affettuoso for Susan and lots of love,

Also *bastia Francia*[12]

C

Suddenly violent thunder and lightening so, any minute, it's going to rain.

P.S. I picked up a copy of *The Observer* in the Zurich airport and so I learned the dismaying news about dearest Lionel.[13] <u>What</u> a vulgar, languorous, 1960's picture and <u>what</u> a martyrdom for the sweet 'Doctor' March. Also a copy of *Le Figaro* simultaneously informed me that there was to be <u>no</u> Paris expo in 1989 (strangely *The N.Y. Times* has still not reported this) and that, most probably, the Opera de La Bastille and the Parc de la Villette would be flushed down the tubes. So <u>what</u> a catastrophe for Alvin's *pauvre*[14] Tschumi![15] *Miau, miau.*

C

---

1 Bastille Day.
2 Reference is to German children's books, most from the nineteenth century. "Biedermeier" refers to the period between 1815–1848.
3 Rowe was in West Berlin to advise on the work and proposals of the *Internationale Bausstellung* or *IBA* for the architectural reconstitution of the city.
4 James Stirling,* Michael Wilford & Associates, Staatsgalerie, Stuttgart, 1977–1983.
5 Balthasar Neumann's main staircase in the Rezidenz, Wurzburg, 1719–1744.
6 *marktplatz*, German: market place.
7 *schlosser*, German: castles.
8 *bauwurm*: "building worm", a Germanlike word fabricated by Rowe.
9 Ludwig II (1845–1886), king of Bavaria from 1864 until his death, commissioned the construction of two palaces and the Neuschwanstein Castle, spending all the royal revenues on these projects and borrowing to complete them. This was used to declare him insane.

10 John Stuart, Earl of Bute (1713–1792), had Luton Hoo designed and built by Robert Adam. William Burges (1827–1881), Victorian, Gothic Revival architect, with overtones of Pre-Raphaelite; *retardataire*, French: outdated.

11 Su Rogers.*

12 *bastia Francia*, Italian: enough France. Rowe prefered Italy to France and disapproved of Miller's* love of France. In 11 June 2015, email to the editor Miller describes this phrase as a "playful dig at me".

13 See Davey, Michael, "A Right Royal Battle of Art", *The Observer*, Sunday 3 July 1983, p 14; Lionel March (b 1934), a Cambridge-educated mathematician, digital artist, and architect who became a professor in the Graduate School of Architecture and Planning at UCLA in 1985 and was appointed chairman in the following year.

14 *pauvre*, French: poor.

15 The Opera de la Bastille and the Parc de la Villette in Paris were public works projects of the Mitterrand administration, the latter designed by Bernard Tschumi, at the time a Unit Master in Alvin Boyarsky's* Architectural Association School, London.

To **John Miller**, *Regent's Park Road, London*   *15 November 1983*   **112**

19 Renwick Place, Ithaca, New York 14850

My dear John:

I think that my memory must be deserting me. Or <u>did</u> I send you a copy of that new edition of whatever the Cornell mag is called? A little odd I think it is and slightly like a highly premature obituary. However that's not the point. The point is that there I shot my third lec. for R.C.A.[1] So "Paradigm and Program" is *finito* and will shortly be incorporated in a publication to be called *The Eschatology of Modern Architecture and Related Essays*.[2] Which means that, for <u>you</u>, I have to think up something else.

Meanwhile, since seeing you and driving around Germania in June–July, yet again I went to Berlin in late August and, yet again, last week. So it's all <u>utterly</u> dreary and <u>cheap</u> jet-setty; and it's completely without rational *denouement*.[3] And last week was particularly horrid. It was the jury on the infill between Mies* and Scharoun; and you can imagine the *longeurs* of all that![4] What with the belated Expressionists and the Neo-Classicists <u>and</u> the Berlin temperament, death might be <u>much</u> better.......

Anyway, that's most of my history since I saw you. I shall go to Berlin again in February and, probably, in late January I shall be in London. However don't count on me <u>then</u> for any lectures; and, instead would like to be paid for my two little lecs in June.......????

Which is almost all except for a limerick which I thought that you might like:

> It's well known that the men of Westphalia
> Have unusually large genitalia
> Seeking the right size of wives
> They spend much of their lives
> A procedure which ends often in failure.

So I quoted this in Berlin the other day and, as you may imagine without <u>resounding</u> success. However, as related to some sort of Aubrey Beardsley extravaganza, I thought that it might amuse.

Anyway <u>do</u> send me a cheque; and <u>do</u> expect my presence in late January. I shall go from London to Berlin, then I hope to make a little Italian trip with Franz and Monika Oswald,* then for two or three weeks I shall go to Venezuela, and then for a couple of months to Jack Robertson* and the University of Virginia. Then, after that <u>and if I can stand it</u>, I should go to Madrid and Rafael Moneo. But <u>after all that</u>, I don't think that I can really cope with the Madrid piece....

Which is so much for my immediate future *istoria*.[5] Perhaps I plan a *retour d'Angleterre*;[6] but, maybe, this won't get further east than Boston where Fred and Susie seem to be determined to absorb me.[7] All the same I am proposing to come to London in Spring '85 and Spring '86; and, today, I have written a variety of letters to foundations which ought to make this not a financial dead loss.

Ciao amico and *un gran' abbraccio* for Susan.[8]

    C

---

1 "R.C.A.": Royal College of Art, London.
2 "Program versus Paradigm: Otherwise Casual Notes on the Pragmatic, the Typical, and the Possible", in *The Cornell Journal of Architecture* 3 (fall 1983): 8–19; also in Rowe, Colin, *As I Was Saying: Recollections and Miscellaneous Essays*, Alexander Caragonne ed, 3 vols, Cambridge, MA: MIT Press, 1996, vol 2. *The Eschatology of Modern Architecture and Related Essays* was never published.
3 *dénouement,* French: unfolding (of a plot) or outcome.
4 *longueurs,* French: lengths.
5 *istoria,* Italian: story; history.
6 *retour en Angleterre,* French: return to England.
7 Fred Koetter* and Susie Kim.*
8 *Ciao amico* and *un gran' abbraccio*, Italian and English: goodbye friend and a big hug; Susan: Su Rogers.*

113   *To **Robert Maxwell**, School of Architecture, Princeton University, Princeton, N.J.*   *6 March 1984*

Cornell University Department of Architecture, East Sibley Hall, Ithaca, N.Y.

Dear Robert:

No doubt it is incredibly *chic* that Princeton does not advertise its phone number on its note paper; but, all the same, it <u>is</u> a <u>trifle</u> inconvenient. You see <u>so</u> much can be done by the electric telephone (now <u>quite</u> established).

So while I look forward to the day when Princeton will abandon its Old South *langueur,* <u>you</u> look forward to a title which <u>I</u> can't provide.[1] So I don't want to be stupid or recalcitrant; but that is <u>just how it is</u>. I'll talk but I can't title.[2]

Meanwhile an *obiter dicta* of His Late Majesty King George the Fifth: "Abroad is <u>horrible</u>, I've been there and <u>I know</u>".[3] But I am also thinking so after my recent exposure to London and to Berlin.

My love to Celia and *un abbraccio affettuosissimo per lei.*[4]

Sincerely,

    C

    Colin Rowe
    Professor of Architecture

    dgb[5]

I'll perform OK but don't bug me about the dets.[6]

1 *langueur,* French: languor.
2 Robert Maxwell,* dean of Princeton's School of Architecture, had invited Rowe to lecture there.
3 *obiter dicta,* Latin: mentioned in passing.
4 Celia Scott, Robert Maxwell's* wife; *un abbraccio affettuosissimo per lei,* Italian: an affectionate hug for her.
5 "dgb" indicates the initials of the Cornell secretary who would have transcribed this letter for Rowe.
6 "dets": details.

To **John Miller**, *Regent's Park Road, London*   *15 March 1984*   **114**

19 Renwick Place, Ithaca, N.Y.

My dear John:

Happily I have avoided both the terrible Fourth and the even more terrible Fourteenth of July.[1] I avoided the Fourteenth (yesterday) because, somehow, I managed to sleep all day and I avoided the Fourth because I was on a plane from New York to London.

So I was in London for six days and I am miserable about it because I didn't call you and Susan who were always in my thoughts.[2] Anyway, let me tell you why. In the first case, because David just bought a house in North Oxford[3]—1888 and sort of garish Flemish and—in the second case, because I came for Chinese purposes—to meet my friend Charles Chen whom I haven't seen for years and years and years and who, during the cultural revolution, spent three years in solitary confinement.[4] So, to begin with, there was a dinner for Charles and then we went down to Oxfordshire; and then, coming back, there wasn't much time left and there were more entertainments for Charles which I had to go to. And, therefore, you see it all went by in a flash; and I came back here to chain myself to a typewriter. Which all means that I shall see you in September, coming or going from Berlin, and I shall look forward to the event.

Meanwhile I understand but don't understand Oxford. It's a big house, about 6,000 square feet but, then Oxford is so flat and nowadays, is so less than charming. However, it might [...] give me freedom of movement. So, at Oxford I shall probably build a small *orangerie* or hermitage at the bottom of the garden. I think that this might be for occupation around Christmas and during August. You see, what I am working for at the moment is to spend only September to Mid-December here and then to spend the rest of the time with Syracuse in Firenze. In other words, I am thinking about a protected base (Oxford, though I would prefer Bath) and diversity of small apartments which, in my absence, could be rented.

I am sorry that I was obliged to be so dreadfully remiss,

Love,

    Colin

1 American Independence Day and French Bastille Day, respectively.
2 Su Rogers.*
3 The house is at St Margaret's Road, Oxford.
4 Charles Chen was Rowe's fellow student and friend from Liverpool in the early 1940s and from Yale during 1951 to 1952. See Rowe's letter to his parents dated 20 May 1952 (p 50 in this volume) and his letter to Dorothy Rowe* dated 19 January 1989 (p 322 in this volume).

115   *To **Dorothy Rowe**, St. Margaret's Road, Oxford, England*   *20 March 1984*

Charlottesville, Virginia[1]

My dear Dorothy:

I haven't had time to scribble a word since I left you not quite three weeks ago. My two days in Berlin were nine o'clock in the morning until nine o'clock at night (not worth it); and then I left for Ithaca on the Saturday. So it was a nice crossing with easy connection and I arrived very smoothly at 4.00 p.m. Followed two days dealing with the expected accumulation and I left for Kentucky late on Monday.

So Kentucky was as you imagine—scarcely equipped with interest or with happenings; but, since the hospitality was extensive, life could only be embarrassingly cheap.[2]

In Lexington I did the round of the antique shops which were also predictable. You see the people who own the horse farms display an entirely standardized taste. They want instant heritage and, for those purposes, nothing but rustic Chippendale will do and, you gotta believe it, it crowds the shops. No Sheraton, no Hepplewhite, no Regency, no French, no Italian; but English, English, monotonously English—of a certain period.

Anyway, one result of this is that early to mid nineteenth century stuff goes for a song; and, as a result, I bought a very nice mirror which in N.Y.C., would be at least three times the price. It was $400.00. It is 59" long and 26" high, circa 1840, probably Philadelphia, with robust structure, delicate late Greek Revival decorations, and extremely well preserved gold leaf. The usual overmantel piece, I think that you and David will like it as much as I do, because it really does have a lot of presence.

Apart from all that, before leaving for Lexington I executed a codicil to my will making the trustees David and Judy; and, as soon as I get them here, I will send you Xeroxes of both these documents.

Have only been here for two days and so I don't have much to report; and I am, evidently struggling with an unfamiliar typewriter which is discouraging.

Best, best love and lots of thanks for the X-rays. When it came to taking them I could find neither string nor sticky tape.

Un abbraccio

   Colin

---

1 Written from the School of Architecture at the University of Virginia where Rowe was Thomas Jefferson Visiting Professor, spring 1984.
2 Rowe had returned recently from the University of Kentucky at Lexington where his host was Anthony Eardley, dean of the School of Architecture.

116   *To **David & Dorothy Rowe**, St. Margaret's Road, Oxford*   *15 April 1984*

Charlottesville, Virginia

Dorothy-David:

Contrary to what I had imagined I have been charmed during the last few days here which revolved around Thomas Jefferson's birthday (April 13) and the Aga

Khan.[1] So three lunches with the A.K. I agree are probably too many. So two of the lunches were quite small and I was placed at the A.K's table; and I think that he's a funny little man, with quite horrible suits (sort of Dacron and polyester) who, if you didn't know, you might quite well take for a rather bland used car salesman.

So this is the Imam of some twelve million Faithful who, presumably, all contribute to his well being; and, correspondingly, one is compelled to wonder whether (or how much) he believes. He is the son of Thingummybob Yarde-Buller (involving Guinnesses, Moynes and the Duke of Bedford) and he doesn't look in the least bit Indian. Then the Begum is apparently English, but with so much *tenu* that you would think—probably—Italian (in any case that's the model).[2] Then there is Yasmin, sister and daughter of Ali and Rita Hayworth,[3] whom Jack and I shared for the last of the three lunches.[4] And then there was Hassan who must be some sort of cousin, who was acting as an *aide,* who is indisputably Indian and who turned out to have been at the A.A. in the late '60's.

Therefore, altogether a very strange genealogical-marital mish-mash for an Islamic Prince and quasi-Pope; and one really is compelled to wonder just how he can believe.

A house in Paris, another outside Geneva, a racing stud ("I don't buy, I only sell") and, one imagines, the odd palace or so in Bombay and Karachi. If he were only slightly better looking the *ensemble* of all this would be positively Disraelian. But, with all this, he is diffident and completely without any traces of Oriental style and glamour.

In other words, I can only read him as a good and very well meaning man and as a victim. For, of charisma, there is nothing. Fundamentally, I think that he is the type of Louis Seize. But the predicament of an Enlightenment Prince, in a world which includes the Oil Rich and the Ayatollah, is surely very strange. So, though basically a boring sweetie, he invites sympathy; and, when I talked to him about his grandfather, as a Great Prince, he was prone to purr like the nicest of pussy cats.

But the money, and the secretariat, and the guilt, must all be equally enormous; and, as you know, he was chosen by his grandfather for the succession when he was aged twenty and an undergraduate at Harvard in 1957. So the old man whom, as an adolescent Qu. V. found highly interesting, overruled the succession of his sons Ali and Sadruddin; and I suppose that, ever since then, funny little Karim has felt doubly guilty and, hence, the massive distributions—hospitals in Dar-es-Salaam and elsewhere, an Islamic Institute at Harvard, and then the Architecture Awards which amount to $500,000 every two years! Frankly I hadn't appreciated the oddness of all this before meeting it in person; and, of course, I asked him his opinion of The Pyramid in the Cour Napoleon; and, of course, for reasons of state, His Highness could only wink.[5] So repeat: lots of *gemütlichkeit* and a minimum of charisma![6] But, all the same, with safe investments in Zurich, all this must continue to be an illustrious source of rational philanthropy.

Then, in all this, I was surprised, surprised, by how accommodating the Jeffersonian building of the U. of Va. turned out to be. Lunch at Jacque Robertson's* was exceptionally well done and it did serve to illustrate how much architecture (with a few pots of azaleas) is able to help. There were drinks before in one of the little gardens with the wavy walls. There was solicitous black service and then a retreat through the house to four tables in the loggia on the other side; and it all served to illustrate how grand a quite simple loggia can be. And, equally, lunch and a later dinner in the Rotunda were far more splendid than I had ever expected they might be. Simply food didn't matter and merely space imposed a modest decorum.

All the same I wouldn't like to live here!

    Colin

P.S. A little story from last night in the Rotunda which came from a guy who had been present on the occasion. It was an American Embassy luncheon in London where Churchill was present, and where, for a time, the conversation was about Duncan Sandys. So the conversation switched and they began to talk about great men; and, finally, they said: 'And Sir Winston who is the greatest man whom you have ever known?' To which Churchill replied: 'But, indisputably, Mussolini.' So the table is thrown into shock and consternation; and, when asked the reason for his judgement, Churchill replied something like this: 'Because Mussolini at least had the great courage to have his son-in-law shot.'[7]

Which could remind me of a story which I had the other day from a judge of the Supreme Court of Kentucky and which concerns Sir Thomas Beecham.[8]

So T.B. was conducting a rehearsal and was highly displeased by the performance of the leading cellist—who was a female. So he ceases waving his arms, he turns around, and he confronts her with his baton. So there is general suspense and then he utters the following:

"Madame, between your legs you possess an instrument of extraordinary delicacy capable of giving incomparable pleasure to untold thousands; and Madame, what do you do with it? Madame, you just sit there and scratch it."

But, for this, you surely need the full, and absurd, Edwardian intonation.

     C

---

1 His Highness Prince Aga Khan IV (b 1936).
2 The Begum Salimah Aga Khan, the Aga Khan's first wife, formerly British model Sarah ("Sally") Frances Croker-Poole.
3 Princess Yasmin Aga Khan (b 1949), the second child of Rita Hayworth and the third child of Prince Aga Khan.
4 Jaquelin Robertson.*
5 Reference is to the IM Pei-designed glass pyramid in the Cour Napoléon of the Louvre in Paris, a project presented in 1984 and completed in 1989.
6 *gemütlichkeit,* German: friendliness.
7 Churchill had two sons-in-law: Duncan Edwin Sandys (1908–1987), a British politician who married his elder daughter, Diana, in 1936; and Vic Oliver (1898–1964), an Austrian-born refugee, music hall and radio comedian, who married his younger daughter, Sarah, also in 1936. Concerning Scandys, see note 8, p 142 in this volume.
8 Thomas Beecham (1879–1961), English conductor.

117   *To **David Rowe**, St. Margaret's Road, Oxford, England 30 April 1984*

Charlottesville, Virginia

My dear David:

    Your letter of April 26 induces all kinds of fantasies; but I simply don't see what I can do to make them real. This last weekend I should have been in Berlin; but I didn't go for two reasons. The first is that all that racketing around can become a bit too much; and the second is that they are still being far too remiss about payments... even for expenses. And, also, there is probably a third: that the jury for the Prinz Albrecht Palais site was, on the whole, a little too provincial to be possible. You see, for reasons like my second reason, there were quite a lot of people who didn't show; and I was left as the only foreigner to contend with the populist lobby.

So I preferred to stay here and look at the trees, which, at the moment, are looking like a setting for Adam and Eve—or as visitors from Darmstadt said: 'But it's just a Paradise garden!'

Anyway, what a pity that Jim can't postpone his birthday party because attendance I cannot manage.[1] But do tell me all about it later, since I assume that a party given by Geoffrey at Carlton Gardens, on this occasion will have to include the German ambassador and representatives of Baden-Wurttemberg. But, in its Harvard U.S. components, will it also include the American ambassador too? Also will Mrs T. deign to show?[2] In any case do check out the Harvard people and, if Sydney Freedberg happens to be there, do not fail to give him my best regards.

Then, about Chen Chi Zien, if you meet him or if you have him to dinner at Cheltenham T. do give all that you know about my continuing love because there is no way in which I can come over. I shall leave here for Ithaca very, very shortly; and then I have to do certain things *chez moi*. And then I have to go to Knoxville, Tennessee to make an effortless, expensive lecture on May 22. And then, about ten days after that, I go for two weeks to Venezuela, which I think will be both flashy and *gemutlich*.[3]

So, you see, it is only sometime after that when it's possible for me to arrive in London; and, meanwhile, in all the interstitial *poche*, I have to try to indulge in a little slavery.[4]

Topographically, Charlottesville is an enigma. It is surrounded by elegant mountains; but there is so much local and 'bosky' incident that one can rarely see them—except from the air. Then, when you go out into the local version of the *campagna*, it is equally frustrating.[5] There are too many large roads and too little intimate detail. It's a red earth country which is, obviously, good for horses and cattle but not much else; and you can drive for twenty miles out into it without approaching any, highly visible, signs of settlement. In other words and so far as I can see, Charlottesville has no supporting communities. There seems to be a belt of the horse farms and the rich, occasionally interspersed with the 'dwellings' of the poor; but that seems to be about it. And, as Edith Wharton announced about ninety years ago, the foreground is invariably deficient.[6] You see, the local details do not anticipate the general panorama. There is no connection between them; and outside town, outside the opulent suburbs, the local dets are scruffy, ineffective second growth.[7] So, at Monticello T.J. really made the best choice; but, though it's grand, it isn't focused, and it ain't what you see from Frascati or Caprarola.[8]

Best, best to Dorothy, James, Simone.

    Colin

P.S. I still anticipate your reactions to my codicil.[9]

---

1 James Stirling,* born 22 April 1926. (Rowe believed Stirling was born in 1924.)
2 "Mrs T.": Margaret Thatcher, prime minister of Great Britain.
3 *gemütlich,* German: cozy.
4 *poche,* French: pocket, pouch.
5 *campagna,* Italian: countryside.
6 "The American landscape has no foreground and the American mind no background."
    Edith Wharton in a letter from the early 1920s.
7 "dets": details.
8 "T.J.": Thomas Jefferson.
9 See Rowe's letter to David* and Dorothy Rowe* dated 15 April 1984 (p 230 in this volume).

19 Renwick Place, Ithaca, N.Y.

Dorothy-David:

I came back here yesterday after a rather odd, protracted Virginia weekend. On the Friday, which was the day of my jury, Leon Krier* turned up; and Jack became determined to expose us to the world of the FFV.[1] So we went to two Jefferson houses—Bremo and Edgemont. So Bremo has an infinitely long driveway (I would think about two miles). It's about 1830, has been in the family ever since; and it is, simultaneously, miniature, grand and a bit beat up—like a house one might imagine in Ireland. But the thing about Jefferson houses is that, though they come on Neo-Classical, internally their style is <u>much</u> older. Internally, they come on like 1690–1740 (for instance, miniature Bremo has bedrooms twenty feet high); and, so though the external format is Neo, as you walk inside it becomes almost like Ham House—and this is <u>very</u> strange.[2] In other words, in Jefferson houses, there is the minimum of *aperture all' ambiente*.[3] They are very well ventilated, gales could blow through them; but there are no conservatories, few French windows, and very little related to Neo-Classical glitter. So, in Jefferson houses, the interiors are provincial William Kent.[4]

So, intuitively, at Bremo this was understood; and they had the nicest, understated things to make the point (no concern with style; but—this is the bedroom where Robert E. Lee often stayed; and, if <u>you</u> come again, this is the room which <u>you</u> will occupy.....).

However, all this is merely a prelude to a situation in which later we sat down fifty to dinner and, unfortunately, I was placed next to my hostess of Edgemont—and again the dreary French. But it wasn't <u>one</u> French. It was <u>two</u>. I had <u>two</u> impossible *Francaises*,[5] one on either side (no possibilities of conversation since the music was so loud) but all this in a kind of crazy *schloss*—Gothic, Art Nouveau and about two thousand feet above the view.[6]

Then on Sunday we went to lunch in Richmond with the Robertson* mamma in a very elaborate Queen Anneish sort of replica built about 1935 and really very good. Seven bays wide, a three bay pediment, and a beautifully paved forecourt in which four cars could be standing without even being noticed. So it's a small English manor, with all Am. Cons,[7] and apparently it's the masterpiece of a guy called Bottomley who was the leading eclectic architect of Richmond between the wars.[8] But, if the forecourt should be enough to stop the traffic (it is approached by gates, an *allee*, and then gateposts again, the garden side is something else; and here the house acquires two pavilions (based on the pavilions at Bremo) which are connected to it by two five bay loggias.[9] And all this is very high above the James River, with woods falling down the escarpment and the view to the river framed by a couple of huge Prussian eagles, bought cheap because they were intended for a German Embassy in Madrid but were never installed.

Anyway, these strike a quite appropriate Frascati note; and, of course, in the garden which you see, there are <u>no</u> flowers. It's one of <u>those</u>; and, if you want to find flowers, you either have to go down into the woods or into a couple of little walled secret gardens. But after all this, which is <u>rather</u> overwhelming, inside it's all a bit too predictable.

Five b.r's, each with its own b., a library of about 18' by 36' with drawing room and dining room not quite so ambitious, large entrance hall and very fine staircase.[10] So I begin to sound like an advertisement in *Country Life*; and now I shall cease to do so because the furniture is equally predictable. Almost all good quality, highly conservative repro with too much French polish gloss, all the chintz and the damask in unimpaired condition, there is scarcely an amusing piece in the whole house. Apart from a pair of very good Charles II chairs (the kind with high backs, arms and tapestried upholstery which appear to be a must in Virginia), most of the rest of the place looked like a very well furnished club; and I've noticed this as being characteristic of this kind of American taste—opulent, immensely safe and terribly boring.

So a few mementoes of Pekin and Jacquelin's mamma (who is almost a memento of Pekin herself), aged 84, is in the middle of all this supported by an almost equally antique butler ("Davies has been with us ever since the house was built"), a highly decrepit parlour maid and, somewhere backstage, a reasonably enterprising cook and a moderately juvenile chauffeur. But what Jack does with this house when it becomes his God knows. I don't think that it would sell for what it's worth since, in spite of the grandeur of its lay out and its view, its approaches are now locked in a suburban development. It's an expensive suburb, with houses all like smaller versions of Millburne; but its distribution is no way as good as Cayuga Heights.[11] So, all in all, a funny white elephant and Mrs R. wants me to go down to stay, where I think that I would be involved in readings aloud from Trollope and Jane Austen. So I think not....

C

P.S. Richmond has a very fine cemetery dating from the 1850's. Lots of temples, obelisks, broken columns, urns, etc. So it all looks like a version of the *Hypnerotomachia* which is made more so by a Confederate cenotaph in the form of a large version of the Pyramid of Caius Cestius around which there are buried the appalling quantity of 18,000 Confederate war dead![12] It sure makes ya think.......

C

1 Jaquelin Robertson;* "F.F.V.": First Families of Virginia.
2 Ham House, built in 1610, overlooking the Thames south of Richmond by Thomas Vavasour.
3 *aperture all' ambiente,* Italian: openings to the surroundings.
4 William Kent (c 1685–1748), English architect, landscape architect, and furniture designer.
5 *Françaises*, French: French women.
6 *schloss*, German: château.
7 "Am. Cons": American conveniences.
8 William L Bottomley (1873–1951), American architect and preeminent Colonial Revival designer.
9 *allée*, French: a tree-lined axis, typically paved as a driveway or pathway.
10 "Five b.r's, each with its own b.": Five bedrooms each with its own bathroom.
11 "Millburne": presumably the small English village of Milburn, Cumbria. Cayuga Heights: a small residential village north of the Cornell campus in Ithaca, New York.
12 *Hypnerotomachia Poliphili*, Venice, 1499: an allegory in which Poliphilo pursues his love, Polia, through a dreamlike landscape.

*To **Dorothy & David Rowe**, St Margaret's Road, Oxford*   *25 May 1984*   **119**

19 Renwick Place, Ithaca, N.Y.

Dorothy-David:

I found my new little trip down South, to Knoxville, so interesting that I stayed another day. Of course, apart from being appallingly folksy (all that country music) east Tennessee is quite lyrically pretty. The mountains are exquisite, the rivers are charming, the houses are unassuming, and, all in all, if you drive through it quickly, it is one of the most engaging little Utopias that you might ever wish to see. There seems to be nothing at all in Tennessee like the grandeurs of Virginia.

But I knew all this years ago. I knew that the landscapes between Knoxville and Bristol, Va, were completely ravishing (I have driven them several times); but, all the same, I went down to Tennessee in order to check out.

So it's a country of small sharecroppers (little people and Scots-Irish without the money for slaves); and, one hundred and fifty years later, even today it still so presents itself. Because, you see, they are little, little people. They are just themselves. They are completely uninfringed; and I received all this when I was invited to dinner at <u>five</u> o'clock. But <u>can</u> you believe it? The lecture was at eight; and, <u>as a preliminary</u>, I was to be exhausted by a hospitality which, utterly, I didn't want. Or, as Astra Zarina★ has just said to me over the phone: "But isn't it positively archaic?" (you see Tony comes from there....).[1]

Anyway, equally instructive was a very miniature tour of one or two adjacent TVA works—I have already forgotten which.[2] You see I have always been depressed by the New Dealiness of TVA; but, of course, I have been wrong. You see it was, and is, an utterly enormous undertaking, such as I had never imagined. From its source to its entering the Mississippi (or is it the Ohio?) The Tennessee River is 640 miles long; and all this, the length of England and Scotland, or the Italian peninsula, or Paris to Marseilles, has been dammed and turned into a chain of lakes and hydro-electrical etceteras since 1933. So, though Ronald Reagan <u>does</u> and Mrs Thatcher <u>would</u> object to all this, I don't really see the reasons because, when all opposition has been entertained, these works must surely be the greatest of the twentieth century, comparable in grandeur to the chain of Vauban's fortresses and to De Lessep cutting of the Suez Canal. In other words, I am <u>almost</u> converted to F.D.R. because the whole thing (and, now, I would like to see it <u>all</u>) is understated, pragmatic and without pretence.

So the initiation of <u>anything</u> like this is <u>inconceivable</u> at the present day. It would disturb the ecological balance (<u>if</u> we do <u>this</u> in Tennessee then <u>what</u> will happen to the pompano in the Gulf of Mexico?). And so the liberals have come full circle. Fifty, forty, thirty years to be obstruction; and, on the opposite side, the attitude simply seems to be <u>Nothingness</u>. On the one side, we <u>can't</u> build a road because this <u>may</u> endanger the existence of a few fish in the Hudson River; on the other side, interventions of government are impossible because these can only be violations of the impeccable doctrines of Adam Smith.[3]

So <u>what</u> a bore to be <u>this</u> trapped; and, needless to say, all these reservoirs—lakes have abundantly altered the micro-climate. It <u>must</u> be more humid, it <u>must</u> be more overcast than was previously the case. However I take refuge from all this because I still have a <u>horror</u> about the Confederate dead who all seem like they might have been my students.

So I told you about the 18,000 at Richmond; but, at Chattanooga, it's <u>very</u> much more shocking.[4] And it <u>must</u> be at Chattanooga that the <u>descent</u> into the modern age begins. In the words of the song 'three hundred thousand Yankees lie dead in Southern dust'; but, in <u>one</u> of the battles of Chattanooga, out of 120,000 engaged, there were 30,000 casualties![5]

However I shouldn't bore you with all this which reflects: one, the influence of Jack Robertson★ and Virginia; and, two, that book which I read in your house called *The Face of Battle* (incidentally written by an Oxford friend of Jack's).[6] But, since slavery would surely have disappeared anyway, I am simply left more and more wondering what <u>was</u> the point of this entirely disabling confrontation.

My best love to James and Simon,

    Colin

P.S. Some time in the course of July you <u>may</u> receive a phone call from a student of mine called Elliot Barnes who will be travelling around with his younger brother. Elliott is expensively educated, *café au lait* black; and I have entertained his parents. Papa is some sort of important medical type in Beverly Hills and Elliott, who is generally ironic, sardonic and anti-liberal, for some reason is prone to sit at my feet. So I told him to call; and he had reservations about being pushy, so perhaps he won't. But, <u>should</u> he do so, I think that you would enjoy. Modest, intelligent and polite, what <u>they</u> used to call 'an American of the better sort', he would be a specimen to add to your menagerie; and Papa seems to have the fantasy of the younger brother being sent to Eton for a year or so. In other words, <u>if</u> he calls, I send him to you as possibly worthwhile acquisition.

    Colin

---

1 Tony Heywood,* Astra Zarina's* husband.
2 "TVA": Tennessee Valley Authority, a federally owned corporation created under Franklin D Roosevelt's (F.D.R.'s) administration in 1933 to control flooding and generate electricity in the Tennessee Valley, resulting in a series of immense dams.
3 Smith, Adam, *An Inquiry into the Nature and Causes of the Wealth of Nations*, first ed, London: W Strahan, 1776.
4 See Rowe's letter to Dorothy* and David Rowe* dated 9 May 1984 (p 234 in this volume).
5 Possibly from "I'm a Good Old Rebel" by James Innes Randolph, 1866.
6 Keegan, John, *The Face of Battle: A Study of Agincourt, Waterloo and the Somme*, London: Jonathan Cape, 1967.

*To **Judith DiMaio,** Park Avenue South, New York*   *21 July 1984*   **120**

19 Renwick Place, Ithaca, N.Y.

Dearest Judy:

    I hope you will like this book which I bought in London the other day.[1] So Russell Page is apparently Famous; but I had never heard of him until David directed my attention. So I thought that you might like it and went out to buy. And this is because I have, finally, decided that gardens <u>must</u> be your thing. But see what I have underlined on p. 144.

Anyway, this guy seems to have known most of the great gardeners of the century; and I am thinking about what sort of garden D. and D. are to make at Oxford where, while the house was built in 1888, there is virtually no planting.[2] So I am thinking about it. To the left of the hallway (too narrow) there are two rooms which, combined, will comprise a space about 15'–16' wide and about 43' long. Unfortunately, it is principally lit from the ends (like the affliction of my living room); but there is also <u>some</u> side light which might be manipulated. In other words, a potential grand room which might be the first reception room and a library (David sees it as the library, as do I, but I think that Dorothy sees it as the drawing room).

Then, from this 43' library/drawing room, one can extend an axis for about another 150'. But, unfortunately, the greater part of the garden is to the north of the house; and it is there that the terrace <u>has</u> to be made. It will receive sun in the morning and the evening; but, otherwise, it will be shadowed. So I am thinking about a very umbrageous space (the kitchen will be a pavilion to this spa with lots of *treillage* and green density.[3] So, from there (a paved space of about 15' by 30') one would then, via a false perspective *allée*,[4] penetrate a miniature *bosco* to arrive at the principal garden scene—and about this, my dearest, I just don't know.[5]

In any case, the axis of about 170' <u>could</u> be spectacular; and, also, it <u>would</u> be like nothing known—to Oxford where, as you know, there is no visual sense whatsoever. So, at the end of the axis, there would be my <u>own</u> pavilion, *orangerie* or *ermitage*.[6] And that is the story.

Both D. and D. are quite exceptionally sensitive about plant <u>material</u>. In fact, in this area, they are extraordinary, as witness their backyard at Cheltenham, T. which I don't think that, in the summer you have ever seen. But, Judy, it is an incredible oasis; and the trees breathe around you and it is of astonishing quality.

In other words there is no prob about knowledge of trees. <u>They</u> know it all. But there is a prob about the grand (miniature) design. And I want to involve <u>your</u> interest in this. Through the *boschetto*[7] the *trompe-l'oeil* perspective is going to lead to the *eremitage*; but then, there is going to be about 60' before we get there and <u>what</u> is to be done about all this?[8]

Dorothy says there <u>has</u> to be water and I agree. So I assume the possibility of a small Mozarabic canal (twelve inches wide) leading down the false perspective. But, then, what to do with it?

You see all this, for absence of better, is occupying my mind and I also want <u>you</u> interested.

Cara mia I will send a copy of this letter to Dorothy.

Best, best love,

Colin *x x x x x*

P.S. The house <u>plus</u> the garden could be <u>very</u> good; but I always seem to imagine it as a garden party. As I imagine it, champagne and fruit punch are, eternally, being served; beyond the *boschetto* there is croquet; little nibblies abound; and, involved in all this, there is to be a little cheap shit collection of nasty impoverished snarling academics who will all go home and make rude remarks.

So you imagine all those nasty people as well as do I; and, as for me, on the whole I would prefer the WOPS.

C   *x x x x x*
             x x x x x

---

1 Page, Russell, *The Education of a Gardener*, London: Collins, 1962.
2 "D. and D.": David and Dorothy, who had recently moved to St Margaret's Road in Oxford.
3 *treillage,* French: latticework.
4 *allée,* French: an axial path or driveway bordered by trees.
5 *bosco,* Italian: woods.
6 *orangerie* or *ermitage,* French: orangery or hermitage.
7 *boschetto,* Italian: little woods.
8 *trompe-l'œil,* French: optical illusion.

19 Renwick Place, Ithaca, N.Y.

Dearest Dorothy:

I don't think that I told you about the horrors which occurred in this house while I was away in Boston. But, when I got back, everything was very strange.

In the kitchen an *epergne*, standing in the window was smashed and lying on the floor, while lots of other things from the top of the refrigerator were overturned and scattered in a complete disarray.[1] So, briefly, I wondered about burglary; but this didn't seem to make any sense unless the burglars were totally irrational—which I suppose does happen. So then I looked around, in the living room and upstairs; and all the craziness—things thrown to the floor—was related to the back wall of this house. So then I said obviously there must have been a small earthquake—though it is not an Ithaca possibility.

So I had some nice Miami Cubans to dinner and they were infinitely amused by my concern. No small earthquake had occurred, they said; and they seemed to think that the whole story was a fiction invented for their entertainment. But the next day, when I came back here, there were further disarrangements. For instance, a picture had been thrown through 45°; but, as I began to think about a poltergeist visitation (though I thought that these were associated with young girls approaching puberty), the source of all this misery suddenly became visible. In fact it came down the chimney and disclosed itself to be a frenzied and dangerously rabid squirrel. But where in the world but in Amerika......?

So it ran away upstairs; and I thought: O My God! But the occasion seemed to be one for bravery and action. So I close the doors to the library, because if it had gotten behind the books, then devastation would have been complete—it would have sat there, every minute getting more furious and mad, and chewing and eating. Then I opened the doors to outside and, to make a corridor, I closed the bottom of the staircase with large pieces of cardboard. So, then, I went upstairs; and, my dear, it was hideous and ferocious; but, looking under the beds, I said "Boo". And so, with incalculable heroism, I drove it out of the house. But, all the same, it really was a terror. It was a monster and it was like a large rat....

However, that isn't all which I have to report about my little friend. There then came three charming guys, ex Notre Dame to spend Saturday and Sunday. These are part of the Roman residue, in the best sense 'Christian gentlemen', and 'Americans of the better sort' as they used to say. So, to continue a parenthesis in which I am now involved, I am delighted by these visits from the N.D. product. They come to me, as they come to Judy, with the greatest appreciation; and then, having arrived, all they seem to want to do is to look at picture books. And I am embarrassed because I think they, like, want, to do more. But picture books seem to be the story; and, about this, I am immensely impressed by the Americans. They will sit around and talk about places like Civita Castellana and persons like Vignola. Even coming from Indiana, they know these places and people. But they know them without affection; and I am prone to compare this with a possible display of picture books to James and his Charterhouse, Westminster and Eton friends.[2] For, simply, I think that in that case, the reactions would be supercilious, bored, class ridden and, completely, without appropriate *disinvoltura*.[3]

Therefore to return to the monster. It was the N.D. guys who finally discovered all its depredations. In desperation, the poor brute had eaten its way through three glazing bars—or almost completely through. So that the basement window is now, literally, stuck together with Scotch tape and is going to have to be replaced.

And, meanwhile, I learn that squirrels are not Acts of God!

Best, best,

   Colin

P.S. Finally, Judy has approximately resolved her scene. It is to be Rome all over again and she is going there at the end of the month. So she told me not to tell anybody; but she must have told enough people herself because the N.D. guys had already heard about it in D.C. So, since they are quite devoted to her, they seemed to think it was an extremely good idea; and I think that, after more than two years of riding the rush hour subways of N.Y.C., it really <u>must</u> be a good idea. All the same she is still vacillating and thinking that, perhaps after three years or so, she will come back.

Like a Henry James* predicament isn't it?

   C

---

1 *épergne,* French: an ornamental centerpiece for a dining table.
2 James Rowe,* Colin's nephew.
3 *disinvoltura,* Italian: ease, casualness.

122 *To **Dorothy Rowe**, St. Margaret's Road, Oxford*   *4 August 1984*

19 Renwick Place, Ithaca, N.Y.

Dearest Dorothy:

   On this dreadful day which I suppose is, more or less, the seventieth anniversary of Great Britain's ultimatum to the Second Reich about the invasion of Belgium, on the whole I have been rather hot and damp; but, all the same, quite a lot of work has been done and, also, quite a lot has been learned.

For instance, I am told that the dreadful Peter Eisenman* has left his wife of twenty one years for a little girl aged 22, whom (I presume) is Jewish and whom (I presume) he picked up at Harvard. This was related to me by a mischievous little guy, ex-Cornell, called Warren James, who is something to do with William and Henry (though I don't see how), and who is now sort of *intime*[1] with Barbara Jakobsen.[2] So I checked it out with Peterson*; and all true. So, being evil, I rang up Fred who was delighted and said then <u>that</u> will bring <u>that</u> bastard, finally, down the tubes.

So I don't know; but I am more concerned with poor Elizabeth who will not know how lucky she is; and I say this because it was I who made the introduction of Eisenman to the Wedgwood-Darwin-Cornford descent.[3] And, about all this, I feel calamitously sad.

You see Eisenman has kept Elizabeth obscured, in a quasi-Islamic purdah; and the whole history has been, more or less, like a Gothick novel. For instance, at Bennington, Judy's best friend was a girl called Pamela Skewes-Cox; and Pam's parents lived next door to Elizabeth's in Marin County. So this is Judy's relationship to Elizabeth. But, <u>then</u>, the development of anything like this was excluded by Peter, who has been <u>macho</u>-patronising to Judy—for rather obvious reasons, for Elizabeth was to be kept in a condition of isolation, in subservience and without friends of her own; and, when Judy wanted to go to luncheon in Riverside Drive, this was forbidden to Elizabeth. Really wild, but really true; and I have had phone calls from Elizabeth when she was sobbing and distraught about her own predicament. But, all the same, she was quite unaware of its origins and reasons. She was still unable to perceive that she had been absorbed by a terribly insecure, terribly ambitious, slightly mad, somewhat oriental, version of Heathcliffe.

So Peter got his WASP; and, for Jewish reasons, he needed his WASP. I was his first; Bill Ellis, from Shreveport, Louisiana, was his second; and Jacquelin Roberston is his third. However, we have all had the sense to perceive—at least something; and, meanwhile, the worst is for poor, abused, Elizabeth. Of course, she has always been slightly scatty; but that is neither any excuse nor any explanation. Eisenman wanted her for Lithuanian-Jewish reasons and he craved the 'important' Bloomsbury connections.

But all this was visible to Peter Bicknell two years ago. He had come from Cambridge to look at the Wordsworth collections here (they are alleged to be important); and, sitting across the table, he said: Of course, you know that Elizabeth is at present in a psychiatric institution in Connecticut? So, when I said that I did know and could well understand, then Bicknell said: but I am not surprised. It isn't Elizabeth's psychology. It is primarily the fate of anybody associated with that man!

Therefore, Moses, Mephistopheles, Faust and Don Giovanni, with these names, I dismiss Eisenman (rather melodramatically I must say) and hope for a call from la sposa.[4]

So I have just been Emily Bronte. I have just rewritten Wuthering Heights, with a location in New York; but, dearest Dorothy, how ever Gothick it may seem, everything that I have said I believe. This has been the situation; and this is the denouement.

But now to move to another topic.

In my letter of the other day I was desperately crude and absurdly populist in my remarks about James and his Westminster-Eton friends. But, was I, altogether, wrong? Of course, I jump to antique conclusions which, maybe, have no relationship to the present day; but, all the same, I remain convinced that, for something like a hundred years there has been something appallingly wrong with English education. And this is what I want James to escape.

So he is interested in physics, which must be good; and he is not interested in history, which must be bad. So I see no hope of J.A.R. becoming interested in the events of political history or in genealogies. Absolutely these are not his schtick. But, on the other hand, there is dear James who is extremely interested in things and visuals and I think that he has a good eye for these. So things and visuals will, inevitably, lead to ideas; and it is in this area that I want to 'catch' James. Via the furniture and the pics which are a part of his background, he is going to be obliged to know, at least, the history of ideas.

But what I want to know is quite simple. Is there anybody in Oxford who gives the intellectual and cultural history of Europe since the Enlightenment? Here it is given by Dominic La Carpa who was a student of Levi-Strauss; but is there anything like this at Oxford? I assume that there must be; but all the same, one scarcely hears about it. And, because James is interested in physics, I assume that he must become interested in the history of general critical theory.

Meanwhile a little phone call from Bill and Jane Ellis in New York who are exceptionally fond of Elizabeth. They utterly agree with what I have just written to you. I read it to them and they said that my description (observed from a distance) is entirely without exaggeration. They are appalled by Eisenman and they tell me that E. is now with her parents at Sausalito or wherever; but, though papa is a Jungian analyst, I don't quite imagine how that is going to help.

Best love to you all; and I do hope that Scotland isn't going to be too wet and cold with everybody feeling like damp sheep.

    Colin

P.S. I know there is no point in advising; but there is a book by Peter Medawar which I think that James might like. It is called *Art of The Soluble* (a definition of science which must be related to Edmund Burke's definition of politics as *The Art of the Possible*) and it was given to me years ago by David in New York.[5] So it is a series of essays in Popperian bias which are related to scientific method and I still find it wildly stimulating.

But, you see, if I had been taught science, as the history of science—the history of discarded hypotheses—I think that I would possess <u>some</u> comprehension. We would have begun as Babylonians looking at stars and framing explanations; and we would have gone on and on, confronting phenomena and framing theories, <u>all</u> making discoveries but <u>all</u> of them to be faulted. So, from all this, one would have [understood], quite early in life, the value of the false hypothesis as an heuristic agent; and, in this context, Medawar's two most brilliant essays contrasting John Stuart Mill and William Whewell (mid-nineteenth century Master of Trinity) as philosophers of scientific method, I think that James might like very much. But I am assuming that, as a physicist in this day and age, James has first to learn the critique of Inductivism and, then, whatever critique is to be made of the Hypothetic-Deductive method; and, inevitably, this is going to be embroiled with the history of ideas.

But, also, tell James that there is a very interesting book, *Science Since 1500* which was put out by The Museum of Science in South Kensington.[6] It is an absolutely charming book, much above my head, but immensely regarded by my friend La Carpa; and it has headings like this:

Strevinus, hydrostatics; Galileo, dynamics. Two fold importance of <u>glass</u>: telescopes and the end of Ptolemy, and barometers, defining the concept of a gas and of the physical. Thence, choice of mass as fundamental. Conservation principles in science. Gravitation, action at a distance. Light. Minimum principles in science. Waves and projectiles. 18th Century instruments. The idea of compensation: achromatic lenses and compensated chronometer.

So, mostly about the seventeenth century and it could <u>almost</u> be the history of art. But I doubt whether this kind of stuff was taught at Westminster; and, at the same time, I am presumptuous enough to assume that this is the kind of thing which might excite J.A.R.

No doubts about James. If he wants to be called JIM, I'm only going to do it if he calls me FRITZ. But I look forward to his arrival

    C

And I <u>don't</u> look forward to his calling me Fritz!!!

---

1 *intime*, French: intimate, close.
2 Warren Antonio James (BArch, Cornell University, Ithaca; MArch, Columbia University, New York), architect; Barbara Jakobson (b 1933), New York City art collector, patron of modern art and architecture.
3 Elizabeth Eisenman (née Henderson), daughter of Jungian psychoanalyst Dr Joseph Henderson of San Francisco and niece of Christopher Cornford, painter, illustrator, writer, and Rowe's teaching colleague at Cambridge University, married Peter Eisenman* in summer 1963. See Rowe's letter to Pat Miller* dated 12 August 1963 (p 141 in this volume).

4   *la sposa*, Italian: the bride.
5   Medawar, Peter B, *The Art of the Soluble*, London: Methuen, 1967.
6   Pledge, Humphrey Thomas, *Science Since 1500: A Short History of Mathematics, Physics, Chemistry and Biology*, London: His Majesty's Stationery Office, 1939.

To **Simon Rowe,** St. Margaret's Road, Oxford, England   *30 August 1984*   **123**

19 Renwick Place, Ithaca, N.Y.

Dearest Simon:

I received your postcard of Dunrobin for which many thanks;[1] but the substance of your message appears to be a putting green and then you seem to think that the appearance of such an item will shatter what you, a little cynically, imply are my baroque fantasies.[2] But, dearest feller, in <u>no way</u>. It simply causes them to become dilated. Because, you see, after the terrace and the *trompe l'oeil* perspective and before you reach the pavilion, I <u>never</u> knew what to put in.[3] And, therefore, why <u>not</u> a putting green—as the space is too small for a tennis court anyway? But do tell me how big a putting green should be, whether it might also be used for croquet (I rather think not), and how much the presence of water might disturb the activity of placing a small ball into a small hole?

You see *la sua mama* wants water in the garden and I am sure that she is right.[4] But, then, <u>where</u> do you put the water and the, presumably, goldfish? It's got to start somewhere and to end somewhere; and, ideally, it should be initiated in front of the pavilion and it should be terminated close to the terrace. But perhaps this is no problem and there must be all sorts of solutions for it. So baroque sculptures <u>and</u> a putting green! And <u>what's</u> the sweat?

Meanwhile, today, the mere <u>thought</u> of water is a bit more than I can bear. It has been a day of quite excruciating humidity, with everybody looking and feeling like alligators or wet sea weed. Seriously it has been like Alabama, Vera Cruz, or the former *Congo Belge*.[5] It has been unimaginable and it is only the exhaustion which I have derived from it which has inspired me to make such an immediate reply to your P.C.

I have an invitation to Berlin for the middle of the month; but I have declined it. The thought of the night trip, the Frankfurt airport early in the morning, then the crowded Pan Am flight to Tegel, exceeds any reserves of patience which I may possess. I am going to Berlin in December anyway and, therefore, <u>why</u> should I go <u>now</u>.

In Berlin they sign letters *Ganz herzlich* which, I assume, means love of heart greetings, so lots of love...

      Colin xxxxx

P.S. I have a present for you which I hope that I can persuade James to bring back with him. It is a repro of the *Nolli Map of Rome* and I hope that you will like it. About 1740 I think (but I always forget this date). Anyway it is something which <u>every</u> O.K. guy <u>must</u> possess. It's stupendous cartography; and it is to be hung either in an entrance hall or a library.

      C

Ganz herzlich = very heartfully yours

1. Dunrobin Castle in the Scottish Highlands.
2. Simon Rowe⋆ had proposed the inclusion of a putting green for a garden renovation Rowe was designing for the newly acquired residence at St Margaret's Road, Oxford.
3. *trompe-l'œil*, French: trick the eye.
4. *la sua mamma*, Italian: your mama.
5. *Congo Belge*, French: Belgian Congo.

124   *To **Dorothy Rowe**, St. Margaret's Road, Oxford, England   31 August & 3, 5, 15 September 1984*

19 Renwick Place, Ithaca, N.Y.

Dearest Dorothy:

Yesterday I went at 5.00 p.m. to a little convocation of the faculty here. So it was an obligation. I had been absent; I hadn't been to a faculty meeting since December; and, therefore, judge my shock. I had forgotten, or I hadn't observed, the total lack of distinction of my colleagues—physical, sartorial, verbal, intellectual. They looked awful, what they wore was awful, they mumbled their words and, even with the mumbling, they had <u>nothing</u> to say. And all this with very few exceptions. So we were all <u>good guys</u>; things needed to be done but, all the same, everything was O.K.; and the general idea was aspiration and open debate. Really I had never expected to live to hear such trash. If everybody is sincere, above board and openly democratic, the College of Architecture will, *ipso facto,* become a better place. My dearest, it was positively Unitarian, like the worst convention of slushy liberals, without wit and without style; and the only charming thing that happened to me was a meeting with J.O. Mahoney⋆ who must be about 77.[1] So J.O. said something like this: "Well at least I have acquired one IMMENSE gratification. Burnham Kelly⋆ is SO much younger than I am and I found myself highly delighted to observe that he is looking SO much more DILAPIDATED." All this said, quite loudly, was about the only moment of truth in whole afternoon.

September 3rd, 1984

I was writing on Friday to fill in time—before my weekend guests arrived; and, obviously, I stopped when they did arrive. So I will now continue with a few more details about that Symphony of Sincerity to which I was subjected.

You see, it's a curious thing that while, privately, the Americans are so sardonic, publicly they are apt to be so banal (could anything be <u>more</u> appalling than the choice of Mondale or Reagan?)[2] So you have people who, privately, will be highly engaging and witty and then you have the <u>devastating</u> platitudes of 'the corporate man'. And, of course, all this is something to do with 'democracy' which, one supposes, is a political institution likely to inflate rhetoric (and <u>lack</u> of truth) and prone to discourage accurate (and, <u>maybe</u>, savage) observation. So, in the U.S. of A., <u>wit</u> appears to belong, <u>absolutely</u>, to the private sector (where it is <u>abundant</u>); but, then and as you approach the *res publica*, the prevailing tone becomes <u>painfully</u> sanctimonious.[3] Houses becomes 'homes', God is more often invoked than should be desirable; the 'Nation' becomes a geographical entity; 'we are the most religious nation on earth' (Mondale); and the escalation of low class, baroque pronouncements proceeds.

So I don't know why I have set all these remarks down, because everybody knows about those two American personalities, about private integrity and public squalor. Anyway, it has helped me to write all this; and this is because on August 30, apart from the shock of my colleagues, I received another one. Meaning that the activities of the college were paraded; but what was ignored was any reference to the activities of the U.D. Studio and Berlin. A sin of omission rather than commission, I am sure; but, all the same highly displeasing. You see, we have <u>two</u> exhibitions in Berlin in mid-September; but, such is the absence of mind, that never a word about all this.

Which is to say that this has completed my disaffection. Deprived of society, exposed to banality, I am <u>not</u> depressed. Simply, I am made furious.

Meanwhile, over the weekend, I had Erich and Katia Dluhosch.[4] At my suggestion Erich once translated a book from the Russian about St. Petersburg for me; and it's published with a sort of dedication to me.[5] Anyway, though they live in Boston, they are Canadian citizens; and, by origin, he is Czech and she is Hungarian—with all the hyper-vivacity which belongs to those people.

So, from Katia, whose hysteria is a little bit like that of Astra Zarina* (ages ago Judy and I invented a composite personality called <u>Kastra</u>) I received endless lectures. I <u>must</u> sell this house, there are too many stairs (I agree) and it is <u>very</u> bad for me (I don't quite understand); but then the lectures continued that we must all go to Montecatini next year. So <u>all</u> means them and <u>you</u> and <u>Judy</u> and <u>me</u>; and, by about this time, I was almost deprived of speech. So I put in words which were supposed to be questions. I said: Salsomaggiore, Chianciano, Abano? But, with the speed of light, all these were turned down. Montecatini it was to be.

But <u>how</u> to sell this house and to go to Montecatini in the same summer is something which eludes my capacity to imagine.

Lots of love,

    Colin

Meanwhile a phone call from Mahoney: "I don't want to go to India. It's a dirty place, with repellent sculpture showing people doing what they ought not to do. Just how could it have been that, you British were so absurdly interested?"

September 5

P.S. My dear Dorothy, I received a phone call from Zurich at 9.00 this morning; and, after that, I have received calls from Zurich, and elsewhere, all day long to tell me just the same thing: that my friend from Texas, Bernhard Hoesli* suffered a heart attack in the Bangkok airport and, promptly, croaked—there and then. So, being reasonably callous, sardonic and cynical, for several hours I received <u>no</u> immediate impact; but, after all the calls, I have, quite suddenly, found myself completely shattered and I am now behaving like a Victorian lady in the most violent extremities of grief. And, really, I <u>don't</u> know <u>why</u> since Bernhard and I were <u>never</u> all that close.

So I was thrown into this condition about midday, when there were a number of students in my office and I received a phone call from John Hejduk* and, then, I was irrationally thrown into an absurd consternation of tears. My dear, it was too ridiculous but all the students were *molto simpatico* because, quite suddenly, I disclosed, quite unexpected, sensibility.[6]

But, dearest Dorothy, though I have been in tears for several hours (Bernhard had just completed the German translation of *Collage City*), I can only conclude <u>that</u> <u>grief is self-indulgence</u>. Qu.V. could grieve for Albert because it was for the bed which she was missing; and, without such intimacy, I suppose that one grieves for people because they are no longer available for dinner, because one had planned little dinners for them and little drives around places in Toscana. In other words, I suppose that death dislocates the dinner table and compromises the conversation; and, as I write this it, somewhat, relieves a misery.

> Colin

Dearest Dorothy, *September 15th*

So I have kept on forgetting to get new envelopes; but I did get some today and, as a result, I continue—though nothing much to say.

Last weekend I had Judy and Bill, and Elizabeth Pedersen;* and Bill, who is Judy's boss, gave me a very pretty Neo-Classical urn which looks like Paris but isn't. Then Judy left for Rome on Wednesday and she rang me up from her old apartment last night—Did I do the right thing, etc? Also, her apartment opposite the Teatro Valle has apparently been used as a major setting in a new novel by that Texas/Roman guy, Michael Mewshaw whom we both know and she was diverted by all that.[7] (It was the small Mewshaw child who, when I was excited, once said to me: 'Hey, coolya jets, will ya'.)

Then I picked up James (but you already know this) from the bus station at about midnight; and, for dinner or whatever it might be called, he had soup, a sandwich of salami and cheese with Major Grey's chutney and a slice of chocolate cake.

Then it has been wet and dirty today. So we have done a little shopping and (at the moment—7.00 p.m) he is nibbling on little bits of Jalapeno cheese and smoked oysters.

Also we are awaiting an infliction—a Japanese type who had obviously invited himself to dinner. Tonight it will be chicken and tomorrow it will be *boeuf bourguignon*. And tomorrow for breakfast we shall have bagels and lox.

> Colin

1 James O Mahoney* (1907–1987), painter, Cornell University faculty member since 1939. See 21 October 1987 and 14 August 1990 letters to Dorothy Rowe* (pp 286 and 348 in this volume).
2 The United States presidential race of 1984 featured Walter Mondale as the Democratic candidate and Ronald Reagan as the Republican candidate.
3 *res publica,* Latin: public affairs.
4 Erich Dluhosch, historian of architecture, professor at MIT, and authority on El Lissitzky and Russian architecture.
5 El Lissitzky, *Russia: An Architecture of World Revolution*, Cambridge, MA: MIT Press, 1970.
6 *molto simpatico,* Italian: very nice, friendly.
7 Michael Mewshaw (b 1943), American fiction writer.

125 *To **Judith DiMaio** Via del Teatro Valle, Rome* *23 & 24 September 1984*

19 Renwick Place, Ithaca, N. Y.

Dearest Judy:

It's now six p.m. and James left at 12.55 today. So I can now sit down and attempt Wordsworth's definition of poetry—a recollection of emotion in tranquility.

So, my dear, it was all much easier than I expected and, very, much more expensive than I imagined. But, really, he was extremely quiet, very considerate, not at all obstreperous and extremely well behaved. So I don't know whether this is age or absence of family; and I suspect that it may be a bit of both.

But anyway there it was. We drove around the lake (a terrible bore) and went to Voorhees who was delighted to see me (Colin bring me more customers like that);[1] and we went to Homer to buy shirts (for J.);[2] and we went to Groton to see what was on display there (and Mrs. WhatNot was v. excited about you).[3]

So Jas. was mostly only excessive when there were guests in the house when he was holding my Leica (which I don't know how to use and to which he is very attached). So the guests all told him that the Leica was worth $2,000.00 and I repeated that I haven't the slightest intention of giving it to him; but, with very occasional apologies to me, Jas. went on about light meters and how did it work. In other words there was a certain ennui; my own conversation was pre-empted by a technological *disinvoltura*....[4] But then, about all these episodes, I later received apologies; and, therefore, what now do I say?

Obviously a highly intelligent boy and quite wildly unintellectual. My dear, Brian Kelly★ took him to a lecture given by Dominic La Capra on Jeremy Bentham and the English Utilitarians and, quite seriously, all this was news—to James. Music, mathematics and physics are his *schtick*; but literary, visual, historical stuff—my dearest, forget it.[5]

And not that you are so good on that literary stuff either; but, at least, you compensate in other areas; and in this scene, it is ALWAYS, ONLY, GOLF.[6]

Dear Judy, of course he is very young; and, of course, I have read to him all sorts or things about scientific method—but not to any effect. However I think that he can still be rescued by *comedie des moeurs*.[7] For instance, he was crazed for Max Beerbohm''s *Zuleika Dobson* (an extravagant version of Edwardian Oxford) which, with the greatest histrionics, he insisted on reading all the way through until three o'clock in the morning; but, otherwise, to look at even a picture book seems to be almost an insuperable effort.[8]

September 24 '84

So James came on Friday, after you and the Pedersens★ had left on Sunday; and therefore, except for four days of the intervening time, James is my history. On the Saturday Shin Onishi dropped in and stayed for a quite interminable time, on Tuesday Paulo Berdini★ and Brian Kelly★ came to dinner, on Wednesday Douglas Fredricks [...] called to report on his trip to Berlin and said that our display was looking very nice, and on Saturday there was a visit from Richard Becherer.★[9] Then the studio is still very slack and that's about all.

Then I can guess what you are up to. The weather is beautiful and blue. You are taking students little walks around Rome to show them things which you have seen time and time again before [...] you have been to lunch with the Einaudi's and you are about to go for a weekend to Porto San Stefano. You have been twice up to the Academy. [...] You have the occasional little dinner with Jeffrey,[10] the occasional little dinner all by yourself, Plinio Nardecchio is overjoyed by your arrival,[11] and Ellen is not in town.[12] In any case that's the story which I guess. But, oh yes, while I have bought nothing, you have been to Porto Portese and bought???[13] And then you have also bought an irresistible pair of shoes and, at least, a little skirt or sump'n. And, while you are looking like a little pocket Venus, you are also lamenting the tediousness of existence.

Which is to tell you about me and which is to guess about you; and now what else is there to tell you?

Richard Becherer* who is here for the year at The Society for the Humanities provides the information that one of the persons who was against Tom at the U. of Va. was Mario Valmarana![14] So it may not be true; but, all the same, I am finding it relatively easy to believe. But can you believe it? Myself can see that Mario might find Tom a threat—his Italian is so good and his Venetian knowledge so extensive—and I can also see *la Contessa* observing Tom (Bronx) through the optical instruments of Philadelphia (Main Line); but, all the same, I find it a little bit shattering.[15] However, when you see Mario, as surely you will see him, in Venice next month, I would suggest steering clear of the subject, as it might just be conjecture....

Today is a horrid wet day here and as you imagine the leaves are just beginning to turn. In other words, another little bereavement which makes me wish that I were somewhere else. But, *speriamo*, and I will write again to try to induce exhilaration.[16]

Un abbraccio fortissimo and all that,

    Colin

    XXXXX

---

1 Mrs Voorhees, owner of an antique store in Interlaken, New York.
2 Homer Men and Boys, a clothing shop in Homer, New York. See Rowe's letter to Matthew Bell* and Brian Kelly* dated 6 September 1989 (p 334 in this volume).
3 Rowe employed "Whatnot" in instances of forgetfulness.
4 *disinvoltura*, Italian: ease, casualness.
5 *schtick*, Yiddish: a person's signature behavior.
6 James Rowe* was an enthusiastic golfer.
7 *comédie des mœurs*, French: comedy of manners.
8 Beerbohm, Max, *Zuleika Dobson: Or, An Oxford Love Story*, London: William Heineman, 1911; a satire of undergraduate life at Oxford University where James was studying physics.
9 Onishi, Berdini,* Kelly,* Fredericks, and Becherer* were students of Rowe at Cornell.
10 Jeffrey Blanchard, architectural historian residing in Rome, winner of the Rome Prize Fellowship, the American Academy (1978–1979).
11 Plinio Nardecchio was a print and engraving dealer in Rome on the Piazza Navona frequented by Rowe and DiMaio.*
12 Ellen Shapiro, architectural historian and former student of Vincent Scully* at Yale, winner of the Rome Prize Fellowship, the American Academy (1984–1985).
13 Porta Portese: Rome's flea market staged every Sunday in Trastevere.
14 "Tom": Tom Schumacher;* Mario di Valmarana (1929–2010), professor of architecture at the University of Virginia from 1973 to 2000; began UVA's study-abroad programs in Venice and in Vicenza, where his family owned Palladio's* renowned Villa Capra-La Rotonda of 1560.
15 *la Contessa*: Valmarana's wife, Betty Baker Supplee of Philadelphia.
16 *speriamo*, Italian: we hope.

---

126   *To **David Rowe**, Cheltenham Terrace, Chelsea, London*   *26 September 1984*

19 Renwick Place, Ithaca, N.Y.

Dearest David:

I think that James enjoyed this house because, though very small for its size, it is incredibly elaborate. It's not English, it's not American, it's not Italian, certainly it ain't French; but, whatever it may be, it does possess a degree of presence—which, as I remember James already recognised in '79.

Meanwhile I am both quietly exhilarated and moderately depressed. Happy with my own house, such as it is, happy with Cheltenham Terrace soon to be dismantled, happy with Belsize Ave. and Regents Park Rd.[1] I am made horribly miserable to set foot in the houses of my colleagues not only here but also in Princeton, Boston and New York. For you must know that these are all dreadfully unamusing, all—as a matter of principle (?) *existenzminimum*.[2] All the usual Mies*-Corbu*-Breuer (none of it cheap) and, in the worst cases all the abominable Scandinavian teak. But, all of them, dreary beyond relief and nowhere is there anything to approach my own mini-*grandezza*.[3] And, though I say it myself, of course there is not.

So, obviously, this is to resume our conversation of a couple of nights ago; but, first of all to make a couple of interjections. On Tuesday it was stifling. The humidity was excessive. The temperature at midday was about 90° BUT TONIGHT IT'S GOING TO BE BELOW FREEZING POINT. But WHAT a dreadfully shocking transition which James (who thinks the skiing here might be fun) will find it hard to believe. But, of course, this is a mild version of Russia and no doubt about it.

Then, before I wrote the preceding paragraph, I had just come back from a little affair which my students had mounted for the opening of a brief exhibition which they had arranged; and, in the middle of all this, a little girl (second year I would think) came up to me and said that she had just come back from London a couple of weeks ago and her godmother, Elizabeth Wade, had asked to be remembered to me. So naturally, I was overthrown. I said: Elizabeth Wade, Elizabeth Wade, Elizabeth Wade? And the nice little girl said: She works at the British Museum, you know; and she has lots of books though I don't think as many as you. So I was still *bouleverse*; and I continued to say Elizabeth Wade.[4] And then it all came back to me, Pamela and Betty Wade with whom I used to play when you were a baby (in some way they are remote cousins of ours). So, rather tactlessly, I then said: but she ain't very bright is she? And, after that, I lost the god-daughter of Elizabeth Wade. She was a charming girl; and I was such an ignorant and futile brute that, now, I don't think that she will ever approach me again.

But, genuinely, I had never thought of Pam and Betty Wade as being particularly bright and the last time I had met either was [...] when Pamela was about to marry someone from New Zealand (I think); and, responding to a description of a mirror, Betty said: But what's elliptical?

Which explains my reactions; but, now what to do about them?

Or should we do anything?

The Wades, as you know, are some sort of cousins of ours; and, at the time of our last meeting, their papa had bought an apartment house in Buckingham Gate—one of those Eighteen–Eightyish bay-windowed jobs. So it is demolished now but it must have sold quite well because I am still marveling at the situation of Betty Wade at the B.M.; and at what must be the transformation of an ignorant (with money) provincial girl.

So is she nothing at the B.M.? or is she quietly distinguished? And I must confess that I long to know. Because I am still curious how somebody aged 21–2, as she must then have been, would find the word elliptical a difficulty and how she would then proceed to the B.M. In other words, would a few discreet enquiries be possible?

Or is this too absurd, since I think that the Wades were my playmates rather than yours? But I am sure that you must remember. They are the granddaughters of Leger Hawksworth, great uncle of Michael and next door neighbor at Wath Road. And, then Marie Beaumont who died of influenza in 1918 was also married to one of the Hawksworth boys and so operates as a long defunct aunt-in-law of Pamela and Elizabeth. And, then, I think that grandmamma Beaumont was a cousin of their grandmamma Wade; and, then, I believe that there is some further connection through the Halletts......

In any case, this letter has gone on for quite long enough. It began as remarks up St. Margaret's Road and it has turned itself into *une recherché des temps perdus.*[5] All the same am wildly interested and would love to know.

Meanwhile a frenzied *abbraccio* from Wuthering Heights, a plausible birthday and very best love.[6]

    Colin

P.S. Will continue—and how very inexorable that is apt to sound.

    Colin

---

1 Cheltenham Terrace, Belsize Avenue, and Regent's Park Road: the residences (by road names) of David★ and Dorothy Rowe;★ James and Mary Stirling;★ and John Miller★ and Su Rogers,★ respectively.
2 *existenzminimum,* German: subsistence level, a term synonymous with public housing in architectural circles.
3 mini-*grandezza.* Italian: mini-magnitude / greatness.
4 *bouleversé,* French: shattered, overthrown.
5 *une recherche des temps perdus,* French: search for times lost, an allusion. to Marcel Proust's seven-volume epic, *À la recherche du temps perdu.*
6 David Rowe's★ birthday is in early October.

127   *To **Judith DiMaio,** Via Teatro Valle, Rome*   *10 October 1984*

19 Renwick Place, Ithaca, N.Y.

Dearest Judy:

I was just thinking about what happened here since I last wrote and it ain't much. I have been scribbling a little piece for *The Harvard Architectural Review*—to their topic: "Precedent and Invention"; I had Bill McMinn,★ the new Dean, to dinner on Saturday night—interesting; I received an overture from the New York Chapter of the A.I.A.—and they, unanimously, wish to propose me for the *A.I.A-A.C.S.A. Distinguished Teacher Award*; and that's just about all.[1]

So McMinn seems to be determined to have a Cornell Program in Rome. You see, he discovered Rome in 81–82 via Mid Career Fellowship at the Academy. Apparently there is no place like it; and, therefore, I told him that you would be the most eligible person to run the outfit. In other words, expect a phone call within a few weeks. He's off next month to Istanbul and will stop in Rome on his return and I've given him your number and all that.

But are you not greatly amused by the Q. of E. in Ky. trying to find stallions to breed with. You know, the fees for a good stud in the Bluegrass are up to $800,000.00—with no guarantee; but the most amusing piece was in *The New York Times* yesterday. It was a horse farmer reported as saying that all the stallions were booked up for the next year; but, if the Queen of England really wanted one, then he was sure that everybody would be willing to make arrangements.[2] So shades of the Czarina Catherine.......![3]

Best, best love and do write

Un abbraccio affettuoso e fortissimo

C

x x x x x

October 11

P.S. The enclosed was in today's *Times* and I still do like immensely the two Ledoux towers.[4]

    C.

---

1 Rowe, Colin, "Precedent and Invention", letter to the editor, *The Harvard Architecture Review*, no 5, January 15, 1986; reprinted in Rowe, Colin, *As I Was Saying: Recollections and Miscellaneous Essays*, Alexander Caragonne ed, 3 vols, Cambridge, MA: MIT Press, 1996, vol 2, pp 367–370.

2 Crist, Steven, "Queen playing matchmaker for Her mares during Her visit", *The New York Times*, October 9, 1984.

3 Catherine the Great, Empress of Russia (1729–1796), died at the age of 67, fabled to have been crushed while attempting intercourse with a stallion and the harness supporting the horse above her broke.

4 The enclosure is lost.

*To **Dorothy Rowe**, St. Margaret's Road, Oxford, England*   *12 October 1984*   **128**

19 Renwick Place, Ithaca, N.Y.

Dearest Dorothy:

H.B.M. lookin' around for stallions in Ky., is just about the most extraordinary thing; and, news from Ky., among the horse fan people, a civil war has broken out between those invited and those not.[1]

But the most amusing piece (quite innocent) was in *The New York Times* the other day; and it was a horse farmer who said something like this: Well, all the stallions were booked up for next year; but, if the Queen of England really wanted one, then he was sure that everybody would be willing to open a slot and to make accommodations.[2]

But, dear Dorothy, is she completely off her rocker? And just why is she rompin' around in those circles? And can you imagine Q.V., Q.A., or Q.M. ever being so astonishingly involved?[3]

Personally, I think it all very odd (effects of Freud upon the British Monarchy? Or resurgence of madness in the House of Braunschweig?); and, by the way, the fees for a good stud in the Blue grass are up to $800,000.00—with no guarantee.

Much amusement and best love.

    Colin

P.S. So a crude letter but it refers to a crude interest.

    C x x x x x

---

1 "H.B.M.": Her British Majesty; "Ky": Kentucky.

2 Apple Jr, RW, "Alure of Thoroughbreds Shapes Elizabeth's Itinerary in U.S.", *The New York Times*, 5 October 1984. See also Crist, Steven, "Queen Playing Matchmaker for Her Mares During Her Visit", *The New York Times*, 9 October 1984.

3 "Q.A. and Q.M.": Queen Alexandra (1844–1925) and Queen Mary (1867–1953).

Cornell Department of Architecture, East Sibley Hall, Ithaca, N. Y.

TO WHOM IT MAY CONCERN:

I have great difficulty in assessing the capacity and the potential of any individual in terms of numerical points; and I hope that my reluctance to do so will neither prejudice this application nor cause you grave inconvenience.

I have known Mark Hinchman* since the academic year '80–'81 when I was attached to the Notre Dame Architecture Program in Rome when he was a third year student and, as I judged him, one of the better members of his class.[1]

Unlike so many Notre Dame students who would probably rather be in South Bend, Mark Hinchman reacted very rapidly and positively to an Italian environment; and, therefore, it was a great pleasure to watch his development. Then, since the Fall of '83, he has been enrolled in the Graduate School at Cornell; and so I have had had further opportunity for observation.

In the first case, he is something of a linguist and fairly adventurous as a traveler. In other words, he is quite self-reliant and will always be likely to make a good impression in foreign parts. He is serious, assiduous, reasonably knowledgeable, modest; and, in his approach to architectural (and stylistic) issues, I believe that he displays excellent intuitions and considerable powers of generalization.

Also, I find his topic to be intelligently set out and one which obviously requires his presence in Berlin, where Schinkel scholarship can only be a matter of intense concentration. Moreover, I think that it is clever that he proposes to direct primary attention not to Schinkel's architecture but rather to his very important scenographic production which is, comparatively, less explored. And this is a line of research which ought to open a highly profitable field.

Indeed, one can imagine leading backwards to such renaissance architect-scenographers as Peruzzi and Serlio, through such figures as Buontalenti and Inigo Jones,* and on through the great reputations of Juvara, the Bibbienas and Piranesi. But Schinkel's historical location, at the interface of the Classical tradition (Nicolas Poussin?) and the attitudes of *Sturm und Drang* (Caspar David Friedrich?), is what I think really renders the investigation of his scenographic activity particularly interesting at the present day.

I have enlarged upon the potential of this project because this candidate has a tendency to be laconic and, sometimes, not completely to advertise all that he is thinking about. But, all in all, I judge him as an excellent prospect whom (though I don't like comparisons between students) I would place several notches higher than Tom Davis—at present in Florence on a Fulbright Award.

Colin Rowe

COLIN ROWE

CR/rp

---

1 In October 1984 Mark Hinchman,* a former student of Rowe's, applied for a Deutscher Akademischer Austausch Dienst with the intent to study Schinkel's theater designs in Berlin. This letter of reference was in support of that successful application.

19 Renwick Place, Ithaca, N.Y.

Dearest Judy:

Being determined to remember both your birthday and Picasso's and to send a telegram, I promptly forgot—for a very simple reason.[1] You see I was down in Washington for a little symposium on Classicism organized by Hank Millon at the National Gallery.[2] So it was a very *recherché* little affair (no audience, no tapes); but all the same, in the general sweat of it all, I got carried away. In other words, my memory lapsed until I got back here yesterday, when it immediately turned on again just as though someone had put a dime in a slot. So I am abject because I know that you are saying: 'Well just what I expected'.

Since writing this I have been out to pick up the mail and have just opened the Palazzo del Te book.[3] But it has a lot of nice pictures, like those of the Sala degli Stucchi and the Appartamento della Grotta, which I haven't seen before. And now I have just had a phone call from Bill Pedersen* and, when I mentioned the P. del T., Bill said he had a very funny story about you and said that he wasn't quite sure that you hadn't taken up residence there—because you were opening the door to people after hours........

It is still very, very warm here—like about 75 at midday; but I am told that the weather in Rome is not quite so benign. I discovered this from a postcard sent to me by Steve Fong whom I had forgotten is living in the Via Garibaldi this year. So Steve is Canadian-Chinese Cornell U.D., ex a couple of years with Werner at Syracuse (with one year in Firenze), and now with the University of Toronto/Ontario (?) in their Rome program. So you will probably meet and, then, I am sure that you will enjoy—quiet, sardonic and lots of facility.

And now another phone call: This time from Werner who has just told me that the business about me and Firenze is, more or less, completely settled, that, more or less, it only requires signatures and stamps.[4] So guess how relieved I am; but don't, don't breathe a word about it to <u>anybody</u> until the whole thing is in black and white.[5]

However, dearest Judy, I am proposing you for the Cornell program in Rome; and mightn't this be nice? Because we might have a little house somewhere in between and be able to go on little trips and all that....

Am writing all this while waiting to go off to dinner with Josef-Paul Kleihues* which is an event that I do <u>not</u> expect to enjoy. J-P.K. is Berlin and IBA and here to give three lecs, Wednesday, Thursday, Friday.[6] So, I introduce him Wednesday and, since I <u>cannot</u> sit thru three lecs, on Thursday I am goin' to be 'absent'—maybe in Toronto. But it isn't J-P.K to whom I object. It's to Jerry's choice of restaurant.[7] Dear Judy, it's bizarre. It's noisy, folklorist and *macho*. [...] and its absolutely the worst place—redneck and *troppo caracteristico*—for a fastidious and slightly neurasthenic Berliner like Kleihues.[8] So it's my dearest Jerry, the seventeen year old, high school football hero who <u>never</u> grew up.

My dearest, it's all going to be *macho* Peter Pan.

Un abbraccio per la piu bella e la piu intelligente[9]

    Colin

1 Pablo Picasso was born on 25 October 1881.
2 Precedent, Paradigm and Norm; The Value of Ancient, Renaissance and Later Classical Architecture, Urban Design and Landscape for an Architect of the Late Twentieth Century was held on 26 October 1984; Henry Millon (b 1927), American architect and historian of Renaissance and Baroque architecture, was the dean of the National Gallery's Center for Advanced Study of the Visual Arts in Washington DC.
3 Erbesato, Gian Maria, *Palazzo Te di Mantova*, Novara: Istituto geografico de Agostini, 1981.
4 Werner Seligmann.*
5 Seligmann,* chair of the Syracuse School of Architecture, had arranged for Rowe to direct the Syracuse Program in Florence.
6 "I.B.A.": Internationale Bauausstellung.
7 Jerry Wells,* chair of Cornell's Department of Architecture.
8 *troppo caratteristico,* Italian: so characteristic.
9 *Un abbraccio per la più bella e la più intelligente,* Italian: A hug for the most beautiful and the most intelligent.

131

*To **Paul Zygas,***
College of Architecture, Arizona State University, Tempe, Arizona   *10 December 1984*

Cornell University Department of Architecture, East Sibley Hall, Ithaca, N.Y.

Paulo:[1]

Your letter from 'Tempe and the Vales of Arkady' reached me in Ithaca, N.Y. yesterday which is just as I am about to leave for Berlin (and this will be the eleventh visit in an apparently unending sequence—meaning that I am getting tired of the Frankfurt airport at eight in the morning).[2]

So it's delightful to hear from you in your irrigated oasis where the beautiful yellows and browns of the desert have been made to yield (I am sure) to a meretricious simulation of Killarney or whatever. And doesn't that passion for green, green, emerald grass and permanent sprinklers just produce extra humidity and make life extra hell? But, all the same, I think that I would prefer Phoenix / Scottsdale / Tempe to an eternity of L.A.[3]

Anyway, as to the Big Question, my answer is going to be NO.[4] You are aware that I genuinely, but quietly, loathe the architecture of Frank Lloyd Wright,* who occupies that Kantian category, the genius with no taste; and, therefore, you can't imagine me really coming to Scottsdale to put my head in the lion's mouth—Wesley Peters and all that.[5] No, dearest Paul, in no way—since what would be the point of talking, in that location, about the ineptness and general lousiness of F.L.W.'s furniture, the horrors of the Robie House, etc. Or should I come as the dissenting voice?

My very best love to Nijole,[6] my best love to the Whiffens* and, *per lei, un abbraccio fortissimo.*[7]

   Colin

   CR/sb

P.S. Marcus may be distressed to hear (shades of Texas and the Tsarina Harris) about the death of Bernhard Hoesli.[8]* It occurred in the Bangkok airport in October; and about it, I sobbed and sobbed and sobbed. But, of course, all grief is self indulgence. But isn't this true? And isn't it true that one is more irritated than sad—irritated because until The Second Coming (and then we'll have forgotten what we we're going to say)—there is no possibility of another word?

P.P.S. Tell me about Globe, Arizona.[9] Is it quite so entirely antediluvian and promisingly archaic as I remember it from years ago?

1 At Cornell, Rowe had supervised Paul Zygas'* dissertation of 1978, "Form Follows Form, Source Imagery of Constructivist Architecture, 1917–1925".
2 Allusion to John Keats' "Ode On a Grecian Urn", 1820.
3 Before moving to Tempe, Zygas* taught at the University of Southern California in Los Angeles.
4 Zygas* had invited Rowe to speak at a national conference on Frank Lloyd Wright* to be held in Scottsdale, Arizona, the location of Wright's Taliesin West.
5 Wesley Peters was then head of the Taliesin Fellowship, the architectural office and school established by Wright* in 1932.
6 Nijole, Paul Zygas'* wife.
7 Marcus Whiffen* and his wife, Jean. Whiffen taught architectural history at Arizona State University at the time of this letter.
8 Bernhard Hoesli* had taught with Whiffen* and Rowe in Austin in the mid-1950s.
9 Globe, Arizona, a former copper-mining town in central Arizona founded in 1875.

To **James Rowe**, *Oxford, England*   *3 February 1985*   **132**

19 Renwick Place, Ithaca, N.Y.

Dearest James:

I do hope that, in the dreary upper Thames valley, and after Sestriere, you are still not repining for snow; because, here, you could now have it in abundances.[1] Not by any choice of mine I got back to this place rather too early, or so it seems; and, for rather more than a week, everything was clear. However, four days ago IT came and, since Wednesday, I haven't left this house. Nor have I been able to do so, since they only came to plough the driveway about an hour ago.

But GOD WORKS IN A MYSTERIOUS WAY and I am sure that you would love it. All the same, I'd wish that, after ALL THESE YEARS, the ALMIGHTY could be just a bit more inventive and make some attempt to diversify HIS effects. And you've got to think about it, because if we were to install Mozart up there, the Acts of G. might become a wee bit more interesting.

Anyway, I miss you; and, in Rome the other night, I was talking to Karen Einaudi about where you might go to in Italy.[2] So Karen said: Never Perugia, a waste of time, the wrong politics and the wrong place. So then she said: What about Urbino—very little and very pure? And then, when I said mathematics and physics, Karen said: 'Well Pisa, of course—Galileo, old university, nice people, proximating to sea and swimming'. So, about Siena/Montalcino, she expressed surprise: 'Of course, the best Italian is alleged to be spoken there. But does it really matter (not like England)?'

In other words, I would check out Montalcino with Tom Madge, son of James and Jennie in Ifield Road; and, then, I would prevail upon your Mamma to send a copy of *Robert Adam and His Circle* to Karen Einaudi at: Vicolo delle Grotte 52, Campo dei Fiore, Roma, because, if you choose Pisa, the Einaudi's have a house not too far away at Orbetello.[3]

Apart from all that, I am going down to NYC next week to buy some clothes and, since Brooks Bros. have a charming cotton sweater which will look v. *chic* in Italy (see enclosed), I shall have one sent to you as an alternative to the much cheaper stuff at Homer Men and Boys.[4] I think that it is devastatingly good style and I think that you will like it.

Best, best love,

    Colin

P.S. Am going to order it <u>large</u> since Brooks Bros. style is generally too tight.

    Colin

---

1 Sestriere, an Alpine village where James skied.
2 Karen Einaudi, wife of Roberto Einaudi,* director of Cornell's Rome Program. Rowe was encouraging James to study in Italy.
3 Fleming, John, *Robert Adam and His Circle in Edinburgh and Rome*, Cambridge, MA: Harvard University Press, 1962.
4 Homer Men & Boys Store, Inc, in Homer, NY, where previously James and Colin had shopped for clothing for James.

133   *To **Rodolfo Machado**, Boston*   *19 February 1985*

Cornell Department of Architecture, Ithaca, N.Y.

Dear Rudolfo:

    Many thanks for the copy of *Ultra*.

So, minutes ago, I rang up Houston and *il mio amico* to congratulate him on his house.[1] But <u>is</u> he off his rocker, or <u>is</u> he a leprechaun?

Anyway, he was <u>unimaginably</u> soft voiced and fey; and you are <u>entirely</u> correct. He was glad when I liked the house; and then, when I mentioned you, it was: 'Oh yes, just a year ago he was my gardener. He did very good work for me; but then he left.......!'

So I was worried. Was this just <u>defensive</u>, protective, *chic*? Or was it <u>offensive</u> something else? In any case, the voice was that of a <u>small</u> child just having been woken up (but, since this is characteristic of H.B.) this didn't severely, demolish my powers of address; and, simply, I said: 'But was he a good gardener—the topiary, the palm trees, the leaves around the pool?'

And <u>then</u>, of course, he lamented your disappearance: 'Yes Rudolfo did all those things for me; and I am so sorry that he has gone.'

But <u>is</u> this simply the *enfant gate* of Houston (no client with less than a Hundred), or is it a prospect, quite appalling, for me?[2]

Best love and will see ya' in Vancouver, Minneapolis,

    Colin

    Colin Rowe

P.S. Drugs and dementia? Or is it simply living with <u>the rich</u>?[3]

1   Howard Barnstone;* *il mio amico*, Italian: my friend.
2   *enfant gâté*, French: spoiled child.
3   Barnstone* suffered from manic-depressive psychosis.

To **Dorothy Rowe**, *St. Margaret's Road, Oxford, England*   *3 March 1985*   **134**

19 Renwick Place, Ithaca, N.Y.

Dearest Dorothy:

I send you some pages out of today's *New York Times*; and this is not because I approve of them.[1]

Instead, it is because I want <u>us</u> to be rational.

The last I heard, in January, was that David was threatening to throw away the big Chesterfield from Cheltenham T.; and I remonstrate about this—because it's the silliest idea that I ever heard about.

I mean that <u>my</u> two Chesterfields (black) will go in the lib; but, as an anchor piece in the drawing room, you are going to need <u>something</u> else; and the Chesterfield there has to be what they call here "English country house". In other words, it should be a rather elaborate loose cover affair.

But, <u>as such</u>, it would <u>establish</u> the drawing room and make it quite distinct from the library.

So, <u>please</u>, don't allow David to disdain this argument.

Best of love,

> *Colin xxxxx, March 5*

P.S. There's been five inches of snow this morning. I am marooned. It is desperately boring and it is rather more than I can stand.

> *C.*

1   Simons, Mary, "Taormina's Stop for Sybarites" in the Home and Garden section of *The New York Times*, Sunday, 3 March 1985.

To **James Rowe,** *Christ Church, St. Aldates, Oxford, England*   *4 March 1985*   **135**

19 Renwick Place, Ithaca, N.Y.

Dearest James:

For the love of God (or as Oliver Cromwell would have said: 'I beseech you in the bowels of Christ') just why should <u>myself</u> be expected to know the arcane details of every Oxford address?[1] I <u>did</u> think that Christ Church College <u>was</u> wrong: but then I did <u>not</u> want my letter (as I thought that it might) to be delivered to that funny chapel/cathedral which you have somewhere in the back there.

However, I am <u>now</u> instructed; indeed I am almost rendered *declasse* by my apparent ignorance; and, correspondingly, I find myself thinking about George III and George Washington.[2] For must the limeys always be so sticky and uppity with colonial and foreign *disinvoltura*?[3]

Anyway, enough for that and now to go on to more important topics. The other day in N.Y.C. I couldn't get you that rather dazzling jersey from B.B.[4] It was out of stock. So, instead, I bought you a quite ravishing dressing gown. It is velvety and voluminous; it has a hood; and it is an affair of green and navy blue stripes. Also, it's an affair of 'one size fits all'. In any case, it is certainly jealousy-promoting—which, I think, must always be an object; but I should add that it is <u>not</u> entirely comfortable since the sleeves are a little too big and a little too short. But, as all the world <u>ought</u> to know, by now, <u>great</u> style inevitably involves <u>some</u> suffering....

So where shall I send it? To Choochoo, to Chel.T., or to S.M.R.?[5]

I will await your instructions; and, meanwhile *un abbraccio fortissimo per le*

    Colin

P.S. D. and D. seem to be unreachable and I simply don't know where they are.[6]

    C. x xx x x

---

1 "I beseech you, in the bowels of Christ, think it possible you may be mistaken", from Oliver Cromwell's letter dated 5 August 1650 to the General Assembly of the Church of Scotland.
2 *déclassé,* French: of inferior status.
3 *disinvoltura,* Italian: ease, casualness.
4 "B.B.": Brooks Brothers.
5 The three are various addresses for James: "Choochoo", unknown but seemingly related to James' Christ Church College address; "Chel.T." for Cheltenham Terrace, London; and "S.M.R." for St. Margaret's Road, Oxford.
6 "D. and D.": David* and Dorothy Rowe,* James' parents.

136   *To **David & Dorothy Rowe,** St. Margaret's Road, Oxford, England*   *28 March 1985*

19 Renwick Place, Ithaca, New York

Dorothy-David:

    Getting to Vancouver and back was incredibly exhausting.[1] It is really far easier to cross the Atlantic than to arrive in British Columbia; and each way, it took a bizarre ten hours. All this plus the canonisation, when Jerry (I was mildly surprised) made a highly distinguished speech on my behalf.[2]

Anyway, it was all very effusive; apparent good will abounded; and I was compelled to recognize what an awful lot of people I do seem to know in North America. So I am beginning to feel a bit like a public monument (*o statua gentilissima del gran commendatore*); and I returned to learn that I shall shortly be approached by the Aspen Foundation (it's an American outfit located in Wannsee or somewhere) to become something associated with it which I don't quite understand.[3] And then there was a further information. Apparently there is a lobby in Zurich which is exerting itself to persuade the ETH (Eidgenössische Technische Hochschule) to award me an honorary degree. And then there was a letter signed by the entire

Harvard faculty saying: 'Dearest Colin, we are all your students.' So it seems (does it not?) that epiphany threatens......

You will guess that Vancouver is a bore; and, of course, it is. It was warm; it was overcast; it was humid. There were snow-capped mountains, semi-fjords, and the site is sublime (Jerry thought it superior to San Francisco); but the town itself is quite vile. Thirty years ago it was just shabby; but, now, it's like any other corporate headquarters and just as well might be Phoenix, Arizona or anywhere else. However, there must be a lotta money and the suburbs are amusing. They must have lots of Chinese gardeners; and, since you can grow anything there, there is an abundance of pine and spruce, a fabulous presentation of rhododendrons and azaleas; and, most curiously, a wild addiction to topiary. But, in the opulent suburbs, it's like an England that never was. The hedges are maintained in the most strict and linear precision; and always, as in England, the enclosure of the property is complete. I imagine that New Zealand must be rather like this. It's the same Pacific situation—only upside down; and, in the end, it must be just as remote from the constrictions of S.M.R. as it is from the openness of the American suburb.

So what else do I discover? First, that I have to go to San Francisco in June to receive this award (or something else?) all over again—which means that I have to think of something else to say; and, second, that everything seems to be goin' well both in Firenze and Roma. In Rome it seems that the Villa Svezia (built for Louise Mountbatten, Queen Louise of Sweden, the wife of my King of 1969) will probably be taken over by Cornell; and it doesn't seem to be all that bad.[4] Next door to the German Embassy to the Holy See, it's about four or five doors away from the Villa Taverna (American ambassador). So, though not in the *centro storico* and perhaps a bit Hampstead, it can't be completely appalling; and I have seen the plans. It's Stockholm quasi-modern of about 1925 and it was presumably built to accommodate Gustaf on his little Etruscan digs. Really a Scandinavian interpretation of a large farm house, grounds are very small, it's built around three sides of a courtyard, and it has something like thirty five rooms, including a small apt. which I could use should I elect to alternate Syracuse in Florence with Cornell in Rome. But, where it is, you take taxis into town [...].

My best, best love and my most extravagant love for the *nipote*, dearest Dorothy, basically this letter is for you.[5]

    Colin

P.S. I send you a copy of my acceptance speech at Vancouver, in which I quoted both Igor Stravinsky and Edith Wharton. And, surprisingly, this was well received, though I am sure that I don't know why. But, maybe, the delivery might have been more vivacious than the text.[6]

    C.

P.P.S. I seem to have misdated this letter because it's still only March 27; but I hope you understood that, when I had your call at 5:00 p.m., there were people in the house which inhibited my response. Anyway, I am terribly shocked about the expenses of S.M.R. But have you seen the Charles and Maggie Jencks* affair in Lansdowne Whatever It Is;[7] and it must be very nice to be a large part of Jardine Matheson.[8] Indeed it must convey great calm. So they have spent One and a Quarter Million on the conversion; and as Geo. Baird* said to me on the plane back from Vancouver: 'And they haven't gotten a single Goddam room out of it'.

    C.

1 Rowe went to Vancouver to receive the ACSA-AIA Topaz Medallion for Excellence in Architectural Education.
2 Jerry A Wells.*
3 *O statua gentilissima del gran commendatore,* Italian: "Oh, most noble statue of the great Commendatore", from Mozart's opera buffa, *Don Giovanni,* 1787.
4 See 5 September 1970 letter to David* and Dorothy Rowe* and 3 March 1985 letter to Judith DiMaio* (pp 184 and 257 in this volume).
5 *nipote,* Italian: nephew, or grandson (depending on context).
6 "Address to the 1985 ACSA Annual Meeting in Vancouver" (ACSA/AIA Award for Excellence in Architectural Education), *Journal of Architectural Education,* fall 1985, pp 2–6.
7 Charles Jencks* and Terry Farrell, 19 Lansdowne Walk, Holland Park, London, 1979–1984: redesign and extension of an 1840s terrace house.
8 Maggie Keswick Jencks, Charles Jencks'* wife, was "a large part of" Jardine Matheson Holding, an international conglomerate with extensive business interests in Asia.

137 *To **Judith DiMaio**, Via del Teatro Valle, Rome*   *20 April 1985*

19 Renwick Place, Ithaca, N.Y.

Dearest Judy:

I got your letter on April 3 when I got back here from Minneapolis the other day. And you might well ask what I was doing in Minneapolis!? Well it was all Mickey Friedman all over again.[1] She was having a conference on skyways (otherwise *passerelles* over streets); and she wanted me to open it and Jacquelin Robertson* to conclude it. So there it was. There was really no way to say no; and, though the Friedmans still like the architecture of Ed Barnes,[2] they are really very charming and sympathetic and, probably, I shall go to Minnesota again in late June—but this time to some Benedictine monks (!) Marcel Breuer, et al., in Collegeville (as a consultant at $60.00 an hour!)[3]

So your news about Frank and Alan and Friedrich was all which I would have expected; but, perversely, I still like Frank, whom I tend to regard as a museum specimen, a specimen which requires to be preserved for inspection.[4] But you see, for all my intellectual super-structure, below that I am apt to be deplorably pragmatic and my infrastructure (like Frank's) is apt to be pretty nuts-and-boltsy. In other words, with Frank I am passive (why argue with a pre-Columbian ceramic?). Instead, forbear the argument, concede a bit, and then get it all your own way anyway. But, all the same, I would still find the denial of typology v. hard to bear. But, my dear, that is just the way in which a *retardataire,* uncomprehending convert to 'modernism' behaves.[5] Absolutely no surprise. It is just like Morrie Wells,* chairman here before Ungers.* And, by the way, Morrie is still the best chairman whom I have known here. But, my very dearest, you must know that antiques exist to be polished....

Then, about the story of *Francia*; and I skip Torino.[6] But La Tourette remains one of the greatest revelations of my life;[7] and it has never left me, ever since been my datum for any talk about MikeAngel[8] and the Chapel of the Propaganda Fide.[9] But, about Belaud and Favre, I know nothing;[10] and, so far as I can see, Pere Couturier was able to exert no real influence on the De Menils-Schlumberger's in Houston.[11]

All the same I am, I am shocked by the Gothic cathedrals, and no Chantilly and no Vaux-le-Vicomte; but I am very poor and I don't know (saving money) if I can go so far as India.[12]

Meanwhile, I shall come in July and we shall discover that town north of Ascoli-Piceno. Meanwhile I shall have Matt Bell,* Dan Shannon, Kevin Hinders, Robert Goodill* here in the Fall, so your presence will be required and inevitable.[13]

So what more do I say?

Have just rung up David, and Dorothy was asleep; but I grabbed James and Simon—James voluble, Simon shy. But maybe you should pay a visit to Oxford *en route* to N.Y.C. But, if you go, don't be rude.

Lots of *abbraccio*

    Colin.   *X X X   X   X   X   X X X*

P.S. I also send you this funny house in Hartford which I visited rather more than thirty years ago. So why doesn't the *N.Y.T.* spell it out for real? Vincenzo Scamozzi, Villa Ferretti, Dolo?[14]

When I visited this house I sat in a Piedmontese Room and was impressed; but now I am no longer so.

    Colin

---

1 Mildred "Mickey" Friedman, wife of Martin Friedman, director of the Walker Art Center, Minneapolis.
2 Edward Larrabee Barnes designed Minneapolis' Walker Art Center, which opened in 1971.
3 Saint John's University and Benedictine Abbey, near Collegeville, Minnesota, by Marcel Breuer, completed in 1961.
4 Frank Montana, Alan Colquhoun,★ and Friedrich St Florian, an Austrian-born American architect and professor at Rhode Island School of Design.
5 *retardataire*, French: latecomer.
6 *Francia,* Italian: France.
7 See Rowe, Colin, "Dominican Monastery of LaTourette, Eveux-sur-Arbresle, Lyons", *The Architectural Review* 129, June 1961, pp 401–410; revised and reprinted in Rowe, Colin, *The Mathematics of the Ideal Villa and Other Essays*, Cambridge, MA: MIT Press,1976, pp 185–203.
8 Michelangelo Buonarroti.
9 Borromini's facade to the Jesuit Collegio di Propaganda Fide, Rome, 1662.
10 Eric Belaud, ballet choreographer. Emmanuelle Favre, set designer.
11 Father Marie-Alain Couturier (1897–1954), co-editor of *L'Art Sacré,* promoted the work of modern artists—most notably Le Corbusier★—in contemporary church building.
12 Reference is to a tour led by Frank Montana with visits to La Tourette and many Gothic cathedrals but no gardens and no Chantilly or Vaux. After the tour, Rowe was asked if he wanted to visit Le Corbusier's★ capitol complex at Chandigarh, Punjab.
13 Bell,★ Shannon, Hinders, and Goodill★ had studied with both DiMaio★ and Rowe earlier in Rome, in the Notre Dame Rome Program.
14 Rowe sent a clipping: Brooke, James, "A Rare Glimpse Inside an Italian Villa in Hartford", Home and Garden section of *The New York Times*, 18 April 1985. The article describes the Hartford, Connecticut, "Chick" Austin house, 1929–1930, as a copy of Scamozzi's Villa Ferretti Angeli,1596–1606. See Rowe's letter to Eugene Gaddis★ dated 13 September 1985 (p 273 in this volume).

To **Judith DiMaio**, *Via del Teatro Valle, Rome*[1]   *23 April 1985*   **138**

19 Renwick Place, Ithaca, N. Y.

Dearest Judy:

    Three quotes from *Italian Hours* by Henry James★ which are guaranteed to send you up the wall:

'Straight across, before my windows, rose the great pink (!) mass of San Giorgio Maggiore which has for an ugly Palladian church a success beyond reason.'

'I walked down by back streets to the steps mounting to the Capitol—that long inclined plane, rather broken at every two paces which is the unfailing disappointment, I believe, of tourists primed for retrospective raptures. The hill is so low, the ascent so narrow, Michael (!) Angelo's architecture in the quadrangle (!) of buildings at the top so meagre, the whole place so much more of a mole-hill than a mountain, that for the first ten minutes of your standing there Roman history seems suddenly to have sunk through a trap door. It emerges however on the other side, in the Forum... The dwarfish look of the Capitol is intensified, I think, by the neighbourhood of this huge blank staircase (of the Aracoeli).... Above, in the piazzetta before the stuccoed palace which rises so jauntily on a basement of thrice its magnitude... You recover in some degree your stifled hope of sublimity as you pass beyond the palace... to descend into the Forum. Then you see that the little stuccoed edifice (!, couldn't he observe travertine?) is but a modern excrescence...'.

'You don't care to remind a grizzled veteran of his defeats, and why should we linger in Siena to talk about Beccafumi? I by no means go so far as to say, with an amateur with whom I have been discussing the matter, that "Sodoma is a precious poor painter and Beccafumi no painter at all"; but, opportunity being limited I am willing to let the remark about Beccafumi pass for true.'[2]

So there, dearest: Judy, you have them; and they confirm a suspicion that H.J. was not only a supercilious bastard; but, above all else a visual illiterate. Because, Ruskinian aesthetic apart, just how could he publish such stuff? But it's bland and insipid and idiotic; and I have just had to set it all down to get it out of my system. But it's fearful isn't it???

Lots of love,

Colin

P.S. You and the Sphinx is a beautiful pic and you at Schonbrunn is even better; but you standing in the little door at Salona is an absolute joy and delight. It's just gotta be your house.[3]

C X X X X X

BUT IT FITS DOESN'T IT?

Suddenly it is quite appallingly hot here. By midday it was 85 degrees and only a week ago it was snowing.

---

1 Judith DiMaio* was director of the Notre Dame Program in Rome during the 1984–1985 academic year.
2 James, Henry, *Italian Hours*, London: Heinemann, 1909, a collection of essays written over the preceding 40 years; Giovanni Antonio Bazzi (1477–1549), Il Sodoma, a High Renaissance painter; Domenico di Pace Beccafumi (1486–1551), Mannerist painter.
3 DiMaio* had sent Rowe pictures of herself at Schonbrunn and at the Upper Belvedere in Vienna with a Sphinx sculpture. A third picture shows DiMaio in the doorway of a small 'house' in Salona, an ancient city on the Dalmatian coast.

19 Renwick Place, Ithaca, N. Y.

Dearest David:

Something which, after all these years, I could never have imagined is the hysteria which is being worked up in this country about the President going to Bitburg. It exceeds commonsense, it defeats belief; and it seems to be impossible to propitiate.[1]

So, forty years after Waterloo, Qu.V. found herself capable of laying a wreath on the tomb of Napoleon;[2] and, though, if the D. of W. had been living, he might have found this slightly distasteful, one has never heard of any contemporary *furore* in London about this activity.[3] And this makes the implacability of U.S. opinion all the more devastatingly bizarre.

Of course, from Jewish New York one would expect it; and the reasons would be good, though not overwhelmingly so; but, that the reactions of New York should be echoed and reechoed from coast to coast, I do find mildly frightening.

In other words, and for the first time, I <u>do</u> feel sorry for Ronald Reagan—ill advised though he <u>may</u> be and without historical sense though he <u>must</u> be. Initially to veto Auschwitz or Dachau was a crazy, pro-German sentimentality, a thoughtless idea of reconciliation; but a German cemetery and, forty years later, just what's the sweat—even though two and a half per cent of the occupants are ex-S.S.

Of course, the model was Valery Giscard d'Estaing and Francois Mitterand who, both of them, did this kind of thing with distinction.[4] So I am baffled; I don't understand; I already hear, by telephone, the German reactions; and I am completely horrified by the naivete of the whole situation.

So, just tell me, <u>are</u> there <u>any</u> reactions in London <u>whatsoever</u>?

Love,

   Colin

P.S. And <u>don't</u> be inhibited. Because, <u>very</u> briefly, I just want to know.

P.P.S. And now I have just had the full blast from New York, from John Hejduk.* If this were <u>only</u> a parliamentary government Reagan would be out <u>right</u> now; but, <u>as it is</u>, the Senate and the House are, alike, alienated and almost ready to impeach. Etc, etc, etc. All this, of course, plus all the world knows (and all this very nicely) I am a Fascist hyena pig and my influence has been <u>completely</u> destructive of American architecture.

   Colin

P.P.P.S. But that wasn't the <u>worst</u>. I have just had a call from Arthur Drexler (MOMA and Jewish) who is totally opposed to all that endless Holocaust talk; and Arthur says that Reagan is a genius beyond belief because, quite inadvertently, he has restored <u>Isolationism</u>. <u>Why</u> all the troops in Germany? Why not let the Russians take it <u>all</u> the way to the Rhine? And, <u>as</u> for the French, then <u>why</u> shouldn't the Russians take France too. From which situation England and Italy are <u>then</u> to be absolved.

But, dearest David, this is the most dangerous situation which has occurred since 1945; and <u>my</u> Bishop in Berlin, preoccupied with anti-Prussian sentiments, Hamburg and Schleswig-Holstein, will <u>never</u> understand.[5]

    Colin

And I am <u>very</u> serious and <u>very</u> terrified. A good speech by Reagan would calm and pacify; but, his being so plastic, I don't see the possibility. He is neither Washington, Jefferson, Lincoln, Baldwin or Churchill; and therefore, excessively, he is out of his depth.

    Colin

---

1 In April 1985 the White House announced that President Reagan would lay a wreath in the German military cemetery at Bitburg to fulfill a request made by West German Chancellor Helmut Kohl (b 1930; chancellor 1982–1990). The event was to mark the fortieth anniversary of the Allied victory in the Second World War. A large number of American Jews, veterans, and members of Congress were opposed to a visit.
2 Queen Victoria visited the Invalides on 24 August 1855.
3 "D. of W.": Duke of Wellington.
4 Valéry Giscard d'Estaing (b 1926), president of the French Republic from 1974 to 1981, staged a summit in Rambouillet that brought together former Allied and Axis powers. François Mitterrand (1916–1996), France's president from 1981 to 1995, met with Chancellor Kohl at the Douaumont cemetery in Verdun, in recognition of the seventieth anniversary of the outbreak of the First World War.
5 The Right Reverend O'Kelley Whitaker (b 1926), Bishop of the Episcopal Diocese of central New York from 1983 to 1992.

140   *To **Dorothy Rowe**, St. Margaret's Road, Oxford*   *9 May 1985*

19 Renwick Place, Ithaca, N. Y.

Dearest Dorothy:

Very strange things are happening <u>here</u> at the present moment; and I don't know whether they signify an *envoi* or a blandishment.[1] But, in a confused way, I rather think that they represent both.

You see I am <u>now</u> to become Andrew Dickson White Professor of Architecture, which I believe is the oldest chair in this university. But <u>what</u> is the <u>purpose</u> or the <u>use</u> of this distinction when I <u>only</u> propose to spend a further <u>three</u> semesters?

It is all very ironical as I perceive this gesture, since the Andrew White Chair has been in abeyance since 1968—and this largely for political reasons.

So the last occupant of this chair was Frederick Morris Wells,* chairman of the Architecture Department for about twenty two years; but, when Mathias Ungers* came, it was decided that the chairmanship and the A.D. White Chair should no longer be combined—and this was because, seventeen years ago, there were people who said that, if Ungers were going to be chairman, then the A.D. White Chair should come to me.

But dearest Mathias would have <u>nothing</u> to do with my receiving it. The mere idea consumed him in a <u>slightly</u> hysterical sequence of negatives; and then, during the period when K.C. Parsons was Dean ('71–'81), it became apparent that <u>he</u> wanted the chair, for himself after he ceased being Dean. And, while I always suspected this, I have recently learned that my suspicions were correct: Jerry Wells* tells me that Jason Sealy, later Dean, was approached by Parsons about this and refused to confer the Chair.

In other words, this has been odious, grotesque and crude politics for quite a long time; and it now reverts to me when I can have no possible use for the title. But it also seems that there is no way in which, gracefully, I can refuse. Like a lunch with the president the other day: "But we can't lose you"...!!???.

But, of course, this binds me to nothing. The mysterious they have been told that I am the bees knees and all that stuff: and, maybe, it may help a very little bit.

For instance, if it only produces $10,000.00 a year extra, then it is hard to see it being all that bad. But, all the same, this is a serpentine form of address: 'Dear, dearest Colin, please do stay and please don't go to Syracuse in Firenze'; and I am quite repulsed by it.

This is not like Jowett, becoming Master of Balliol after twenty years in outer darkness.[2] However, I imagine that it is still fate; though now, I can do nothing with the title, I am going to purr like a Cheshire cat and offend nobody about it.

But, Dearest Dorothy, this particular situation could have been useful.

Best, best love to you all.

    Colin

P.S. I send you some clippings from today's *New York Times* about "treillage"; and I am sure that erecting "treillage" is an alternative to golf.[3]

P.P.S. All very Trollope and *Chronicles of Barchester*![4] Or don't you think so?

    Colin

P.P.P.S. To all this stuff there is now added the potential of an apartment in Louis Mountbatten's Villa Svezia—that is if Cornell buys it.

However I suppose that it must be me who has made this transformation—although this is by distant influence. But, only a very few years ago, Cornell was incapable of imagining such things as Stirling's* Performing Arts Center and the Queen of Sweden's villa in Rome, Parioli.[5]

So, no doubt, that myself—remote control—has brought all this about.

    Colin

---

1   *envoi,* French: send-off.
2   Benjamin Jowett (1817–1893), theologian and master of Balliol at Oxford University from 1870 to 1893.
3   Yang, Linda, "Gardening, Trelliswork: A Country Idea in City Gardens", Home and Garden section of the *The New York Times*, 9 May 1985.
4   Anthony Trollope (1815–1882), English novelist who wrote *Barchester Towers*, London: Longman et al, 1857.
5   References are to Cornell's Schwartz Center for the Performing Arts by James Stirling* and Michael Wilford, and to the Villa di Svezia in Parioli, which, ultimately, Cornell did not buy.

141   *To **Judith DiMaio**, Via del Teatro Valle, Rome*   *22 May 1985*

19 Renwick Place, Ithaca, N.Y.

Dearest Judy:

I have just received your letter and I agree with every word that you say. But, my dear, you must understand that, in the course of '84, I saw orthopaedists in New York, London and Boston. These were Doherty from The Hospital of Special Surgery, Churchill-Davidson in Harley Street, and a guy, in Boston, whose name I forget; and they all disadvised an operation—which now I have been entirely willing to have for about three years.

So that is the story on that; and I have no developed plans for the summer because what I really want is exactly that op. So, remember the previous op; and two weeks afterwards in Princeton plus another two weeks on Riverside Drive. Well, it is that subsequent four weeks on the flat which encourages me to think about Boston where I could spend this time with Fred and Susie in their large Beacon Street apt.

Meanwhile, I think that your two Empire seats are incredibly beautiful (they were a very good buy); and that my Guido-Raphael display in your dining room is entirely superb.

Love, love, love,

    Colin X X X X X

P.S. My brother tells me that now Simon wishes to become an' artichoke (! ! !).[1] He tells me too that, apart from the house in Oxford, they still have an apt, somewhere in Cheltenham T. (???). Then he also tells me that I should have the op, quite immediately.[2]

    C

---

1 Simon Rowe.* Rowe used the word "artichoke" to mean "architect".
2 Cheltenham Terrace, London. The "op" to which Rowe refers here and in the first paragraph of this letter is a surgical operation on his hip. See Rowe's letter to James Stirling* dated 16 August 1985 (p 268 in this volume).

142   *To **Dorothy Rowe**, St. Margaret's Road, Oxford*   *2 August 1985*

19 Renwick Place, Ithaca, N. Y.

Dearest Dorothy:

A little recipe which you might use. It is very cheap and goes a long way. Two boneless breasts of chicken hammered v. flat; lemon juice; flour; dip in eggs and breadcrumbs; then lightly fry in butter. Is completely foolproof; will serve six; garnish with slices of lemon and anchovy. But D., S. and J. would love it—chicken subjected to *wiener schnitzel* treatment.

Anyway, last night we had: jellied consommé, shrimps, this chicken, strawberries with kirsch, mascarpone, and sorbet with triple sec. All this washed down with Fontana Candida and Perrier; and, dearest Dorothy, the sequence is completely effortless and absolutely to be recommended.

Of course, not that I did <u>anything</u> except conduct operations from afar. But it was all quite charming; and <u>we</u> were: Paolo Berdini* from Rome; his 'friend' Mary Kaplan from New York who <u>always</u> says Petersburg and <u>never</u> Leningrad; and a woman whom they brought along and whose name I failed to catch.

So Mary is Russophile, of an earlier dispensation; and, therefore you first have to go through Lermontov, Gogol and Turgenev before you get anywhere.¹ And, meanwhile, Paolo wants to talk about Mies Van der Rohe,* Grabriele D'Annunzio, Eleanora Duse, Giulio Romano, Cardinal Pole and the Council of Trent. So, to cool Paolo down, Mary who is fundamentally Hungarian begins to imitate her father imitating Fidel Castro; and it was all v. amusing. Papa was in sugar in N.Y.C.; therefore had considerable interests in Cuba; abominated the Trujillo regime; and was, originally pro-Fidel, whom he dared to advise about relations with the State Department in D.C. But, needless to say, no use. Papa made an exposition of about half an hour and Castro took about three hours to reply; and, as Mary said: "My Father's attention span was always <u>very</u> limited."

However, this only served to produce the bombshell of the evening. The <u>incognita</u> had been sitting quiet. But it now turned out that she had been married to a New York Warburg, and so the most bizarre information was divulged: "But <u>whom</u> do <u>you</u> think <u>paid</u> for that special <u>sealed</u> train which took Lenin from Zurich, through Germany, to the Finland Station in St. Petersburg? <u>You</u> think that it was the German government. But <u>no, no,</u> it was Felix Warburg on behalf of Warburg's, N.Y."

So <u>do</u> you believe it? And, <u>should this be true,</u> the world contracts <u>still</u> more. But, <u>if this is the case,</u> then playboy, yachtsman, Felix Warburg, made a <u>far</u> greater intervention in history than ever Aby did <u>in spite</u> of <u>all</u> his library in Marburg.²

So <u>what</u> a bore and <u>what</u> a sweat. I send you pictures of Aby and Felix.

Best love,

    Colin

P.S. Felix eludes discovery; but I send you Aby, 1895–'96, as Jewish, cowboy anthropologist in New Mexico.³ And this was, apparently, the turning point of his life. All you had to do was to add Pueblo serpent ritual to the study of Botticelli and, *ipso facto*, revelation would ensue—or, alternatively, mental breakdown. But find a picture of Wall Street Felix and compare.

---

1 Mikhail Yuryevich Lermontov (1814–1841), Nikolai Vasilievich Gogol (1809–1852), and Ivan Sergeyevich Turgenev (1818–1883) were important Russian writers.
2 Aby Warburg (1866–1929), German art historian and cultural theorist who founded the *Kulturwissenschaftliche Bibliothek Warburg,* a private library for cultural studies in Hamburg, which was moved to London in 1934. In 1944 the library was incorporated into the University of London, where Rowe studied at the Courtauld Institute from 1946 to 1948.
3 Rowe's photocopy is of plate 231 from Saxl, Fritz and Hugh Honour, eds, *Lectures,* London: Warburg Institute, University of London, 1957. The caption reads: "Warburg and a Pueblo Indian". Aby Warburg suffered a mental breakdown and was hospitalized from 1919–1923. He gave a lecture in the psychiatric clinic in Kreuzlinger in which he recalled his trip to New Mexico. His explanation of the Hopi Indians' serpent ritual proved to his doctors he was fit to be released.

143 *To **Michael Handler**, West Hartford, Connecticut*   *5 August 1985*

Cornell University, School of Architecture, Sibley Hall, Ithaca, N.Y.

Dear Michael:

Many, many thanks for your entirely charming letter which is one of the nicest that I have ever received; and, since all tribulations go away in the end (by some means or other) I am delighted to hear that even the poison ivy has gone away.[1]

But who was it who made the distinction between trials and tribulations? Between trials which are capable of ethical resolution and tribulations which can only be endured, can only be resolved in terms of esthetics? I think that it was Auden.⋆ But, in any case, no matter since, in spite of tribulations, personally I enjoyed having you all stay so much.

And, now, a little bombshell which I think that your Papa might enjoy. It was dinner the other evening; and because of its constituents, the conversation was a little Russian. So the woman who had been quiet, the incognita who turned out to have been married to a New York Warburg, suddenly produced the question: "But who do you think paid for that special sealed train which took Lenin through Germany to the Finland Station in St. Petersburg? You think that it was the German government. But, oh no, it was Felix Warburg on behalf of Warburg's, N.Y.!"[2]

But, if so, what an intervention! From playboy Felix it was much more than the equivalent of his brother's library in Hamburg!

Anyway, I think that Philip will enjoy this story; but, also, do give my thanks to both of them for the juice machine which is called Rowoco.[3]

Best, best love,

    Colin

    Colin Rowe

    CR/rp

---

1 Michael Handler (b 1968) was suffering from poison ivy when he and his parents, Cornell graduates Philip and Maddy Handler,⋆ visited Rowe in his Ithaca home in June 1985.
2 See Rowe's letter to Dorothy Rowe⋆ dated 2 August 1985 (p 266 in this volume).
3 The Handlers had given Rowe a Rowoco manual juicer.

144 *To **James Stirling**, London*   *16 August 1985*

19 Renwick Place, Ithaca, N.Y.

Dear James:

Many thanks for the *Wissenschaffzentrum* catalogue;[1] and about the Cornell building, I particularly like the *"Aussicht auf den Campus und den Cayuga-See"*.[2] But the info for which I asked, about what President Rhodes is up to, you didn't send me;[3] and I wish that you would, because there are quite a lot of people here who are concerned about the rumors that he (heavy handshake) doesn't like stripes.[4]

So I shall be in Boston on October 17–18; but I doubt very much whether you will see me at your opening.[5] And the answer is very simple. I am going to have a little op on my little hip. It's called HIP HIP HOORAY; and, as a result, almost certainly I shall be in a hospital bed. So what a sweat; but then you will all be able to come and [tell] me all about it.

Best regards to everybody who you think might welcome them.

  Colin

P.S. But Wolfgang von Eckhardt! And was he not appalling.

---

1 The *Wissenschaffzentrum Berlin für Sozialforschung* (Social Science Research Center Berlin), designed by James Stirling* and completed in 1988, featured alternating pink and blue stripes.
2 *Aussicht auf den Campus und den Cayuga-See*, German: "Section through the Campus and Lake Cayuga".
3 Frank HT Rhodes (b 1926), president of Cornell University from 1977 to 1995.
4. Stirling*—who "striped" the Fogg Art Museum addition at Harvard, the Staatsgalerie in Stuttgart, and the *Wissenschaffzentrum* in Berlin—designed the Schwartz Center for the Performing Arts at Cornell, completed in 1989.
5 The opening of the Stirling*-designed addition to Harvard's Fogg Museum.

To **Dorothy Rowe** St. Margaret's Road, Oxford   *18 August 1985*   **145**

19 Renwick Place, Ithaca, N.Y.

Dearest Dorothy:[1]

I am reminded of a little rhyme of Edith Wharton's of about 1905. It goes like this:

Climbing cliffs and fording torrents
Here we are at last in Florence
Or rather perched upon the piano
Nobile at Settignano.
Seeing picture galleries, no sir.
Driving out to Vallombrosa,
Bellosguardo, *tutti quante*[2]
High above the dome of Dante.[3]

And the occasion was a drive down from Paris to visit Berenson.[4]

So did not D.H. Lawrence and Frieda live at Scandicci in the 1920's: but I get the idea that, since the building of the autostrada which is very convenient, the whole area has become very built up. However, since I've never been there, I may be wrong.

Anyway, not too far away, you find the villas Careggi, Petraia and Castello—all worth while and all Medicean. So Careggi is early and castellated; and the other two are located in the same park, with the better gardens at Petraia and a completely elegant Buontalenti grotto at Castello (where the location of the house is a little depressing). Then, very close to all this, at Doccia you could find the porcelain outfit of Richard-Ginori which, since it's the third in Europe (after Meissen and Vienna) might be interesting.

Then, if that doesn't sound like too long a morning, you might round it off in the afternoon by a visit to La Pietra since, after all, Harold Acton did go to Christ Church and, therefore, on James' application, the place might be shown (But you know this place was offered to Oxford and turned down; and it was only afterwards that it was offered to and accepted by N.Y.U.[5]—But this is, perhaps, appropriate since I believe that Hortensia Acton's money was Chicago and Marshall Field (?).

After which maybe another day, you could do a little inner suburban tour. You could go up to Fiesole where there is a lot to see, though I doubt that the Villa Medici would be shown. So it was an English house, almost continuously from the mid-eighteenth century down to W.W.II and here it was that lived the famous Lady Sybil Cuffe-Cutting-Scott-Lubbock (mother of Iris Origo) from about 1907 or so onwards. But, also, there might be the Villa Palmieri (Walpole, later Crawford and Balcarres) where Queen Victoria stayed in the early '90's. Then, afterwards you could go over to Vincigliata, which is another English house. This is a Gothic restoration, very authentic of the mid-nineteenth century Temple-Leader; and T.-L., I believe, was a Liberal M.P., large villa in Clapham or somewhere, who gave it all up for his Tuscan fantasy; and, after that, you could come down to Settignano, take a brisk look at I Tatti (shades of Berenson and presence of Harvard); and then, after Ponte a Mensola and if you have the strength, you could go on to the south of the river.[6] But, before this, you should certainly attempt the Villa Gamberaia.

So forget south of the river, because the Villa Gamberaia and its gardens are enough, enough, to complete this little excursion. Occupied during the earlier years of this century by two famous Lesbians, the Roumanian Princess Ghyka and her American friend, Miss Blood, these two restored it and, after being wrecked in W.W.II, it is impeccable all over again. In other words give it *****.

And, now, south of the river belongs to another story.

You would have to start early; and you could start with a drive around Bellosguardo, where the Villa L'Ombrellino might amuse. You see it was at L'Ombrellino that Galileo was under house arrest for about fourteen years (1617–31) and it was after that that Alice Keppel (ex-Edward VII) spent another thirty years.[7]

O.K. after all that (these Anglo-American-Russian scenes of the Bel Epoque), you then have to go to the Certosa del Galluzzo (15 minutes, with faded Pontormo frescoes and traces of Le C.), you then have to go to Poggio a Caiano (Giuliano da Sangallo, Medici villa, more Pontormo frescoes); and then you have to go up the hill to Artimino and you will do this by turning left.[8] But, on the way, there is a charming village with a rustic *maniera* church (10 minutes **); and then you move up to enormous heights to La Ferdinanda, a Buontalenti hunting lodge of the 1590's.[9]

But at Artimino I have been three times, with Susan Potters, with Judy, and with Werner Seligmann;* and the food is terrific. You are on top of the world. They have a wonderful open spit and wonderful *paesano* sausages. So GO. It's a famous restaurant and is now about a quarter of a mile from La Ferdinanda.[10]

Well, that might be enough for another day. But then, what about Lucca? And, on the way, you could drop in to the Villa Garzoni at Collodi—midway between Lucca and Pescia. And the Villa Garzoni, which is v. grand is the Pinocchio place and is a super must. And then Lucca is supremely good—*maniera* palaces, Romanesque churches and antique shops of quality—for at least an extremely concentrated date. But Lucca has an excellent self service restaurant which you will find easily—stand in front of San Michele, look away from the façade, the street will enlarge into a little *piazza* and there you will find it. But, in 1980, it was incredibly good.

So, needless to say, this is just minimal advice and nothing about the town (Firenze) where I suspect that there will be far too many Tourists. But, with all this motion and all these places, personally I see no, <u>no</u> possibility for gold!

Finally, the Ciano stuff reads like this:

September 18, 1940.... As for England, von Ribbentrop says that the weather has been very bad and that the clouds even more than the RAF have prevented final success.[11] However the invasion will take place as soon as there are a few days of fine weather.[12]

So, darling Dorothy, the final descent into Heathrow: and <u>all</u> is understood.[13]

Lots of Love

    Colin

P.S. Also do go and see the Medici Treasure at the Palazzo Pitti. It is approached by its own entrance in the front left corner of the courtyard. There will be nobody there; and you will think that they bought a new toy every day for over three hundred years.

    C.

---

1   This letter is a reply to Dorothy Rowe's* request for advice regarding a tour of Florence and the surrounding areas.
2   *tutti quanti*, Italian: all of them.
3   Postcards of I Tatti sent 17 October 1911 by Edith Wharton (1862–1937) from Florence to Henry James* (1843–1916) at the Reform Club in London.
4   Bernard Berenson (1865–1959), renowned art historian, lived at I Tatti, Settignano.
5   James Rowe,* Dorothy's son, studied physics at Christ Church, Oxford.
6   Villa I Tatti in Fiesole, Italy, the home of Mary and Bernard Berenson for nearly 60 years, was willed to Berenson's alma mater, Harvard University, in 1959.
7   Alice Keppel (1868–1947), British socialite and mistress of King Edward VII, lived at L'Ombrellino through both World Wars.
8   Le Corbusier* (1887–1965) cited the Certosa del Galluzzo, the Carthusian monastery of Ema near Florence, as a model for collective urban dwelling. See, for instance, his *Precisions: On the Present State of Architecture and City Planning*, Paris: Vincent, Freal & Cie, 1929, p 91. Panofsky refers to one of Ema's "faded Pontormos" in "What is the Baroque?", 1934.
9   Medici Villa, *La Ferdinanda*, Bernardo Buontalenti (c 1596).
10 Ristorante Da Delfina, Artimino.
11 From the 1936–1944 diary of Gian Galeazzo Ciano (1903–1944), Italian Minister of Foreign Affairs.
12 "RAF": Royal Air Force.
13 Heathrow: London's largest international airport.

To **Dorothy Rowe**, *St. Margaret's Road, Oxford*   *7 September 1985*   **146**

19 Renwick Place, Ithaca, N.Y.

Dearest Dorothy:

    What a <u>very</u> grand affair Jim is going to be put through for the opening of the Harvard museum for which I received one of those highly ambiguous American invitations only yesterday.[1] For $1,000.00 you can be a patron of the Dedication Ball and for $500.00 you can be a sponsor. Or, alternatively, you might just buy a couple of tickets at $125.00 each; and, if you <u>can't</u> accept, you are still given <u>no</u> option but to enclose a <u>gift</u>—that is <u>if</u> you select to RSVP.

So the enclosed will tell you all about it; and, as of the end of July, what with patrons and sponsors they seem to have picked up a minimum of $123,000.00 out of this little affair. So I suppose not bad; but, all the same, I am not able to hope for the best from a Ball which is going to be held in three separate places. And, my dearest, just what is Mary going to wear?[2]

Anyway, while all this is taking place I shall be reclining in The New England Baptist Hospital just a few miles away and the sound of 'revelry by night' will scarcely reach me; and the telephone will be: 1.617.738.5800. Then the Koetter*-Kim* telephone is: Home 617.262.5027 and Office 617.536.5027.[3]

But, as they are supposed to have said after the assassination: "But, apart from that Mrs. Lincoln, just how was the play?";[4] and, of course the question encourages me to ask: but, apart from the golf clubs, just how was Florence?[5]

I do hope that the days were beautiful and that the skies were superlatively blue. I also hope that you went to lunch at Artimino and went to Lucca and the Villa Garzoni at Collodi.

Judy is, finally, returning from Rome and is proposing to come up here [...] but over the last few days the weather has been atrocious and, as of now, the humidity leaves me feeling like an alligator.

Best lurv to y'all,

 Colin

P.S. I went to Buffalo the other day to be examined as to my potential as a U.S. citizen and the examiner was called Ralph Palermo. And it was all very entertaining—as he felt too.

Apart from driving to Buffalo, which is about equivalent to driving from London to York (with nothing to see on the way), everything was an affair of great discretion and, contrary to what I had expected, I didn't have to wait and was treated *en grand personage*.[6] With apologies I was asked the names of the President and the Vice President and then the names of the Senators from New York; and, then, I was asked about *The Bill of Rights*, 1791. So I recited the first ten amendments to the *Constitution*; and, feeling pushy I announced that I could also do the following sixteen. So I did it; and, after that, Mr. Palermo said: 'Evidently you know everything about it.' So I am mildly shocked by all this (even with a guy called Palermo the English preference is gross); but, anyway, there it is; and all that remains is to abjure allegiance "to all foreign, princes, potentates and powers" which is the eighteenth century part of the declaration.

So problem: I cannot do this in Ithaca in November (I shall be in Boston) which means that I shall have to come back here in May to raise my hand and all that stuff. But, at least, doing all this must put me outside the theatre of British estate duties; and I assume that this will relieve the mind of David.

 C

This is a very curious commentary upon the Blunt affair.[7]

In 1945, when A.B. assumed directorship of the Courtauld Institute his credentials were scarcely elaborate.[8] He had written one book, on Italian art and theory during the fifteenth and sixteenth centuries, which would—nowadays—seem like a not very good Ph.D. dissertation, whereas Waterhouse had a major publication behind him: *Roman Baroque Painting*, 1937.[9]

But Waterhouse always wore the most <u>dreadful</u> shirts; and then I am sure that you can grab the rest. In spite of Marlborough and New College it was an outside-inside career.

Then I thought that the further enclosed—from American *H. and G.*—might possibly entertain.[10]

1 James Stirling,* The Fogg Museum New Building, Harvard University, 1979–1985.
2 Mary Stirling, James Stirling's* wife.
3 Rowe was to have hip surgery in Boston at this time and intended to convalesce in the Boston home of Fred Koetter* and Susie Kim.* The quote "There was a sound of revelry by night" is from Byron's *Childe Harold's Pilgrimage* (1812–1818).
4 Attributed to Fletcher Knebel (1911–1993).
5 See Rowe's letter to Dorothy Rowe* who had recently returned from a visit to Florence dated 18 August 1985 (p 269 in this volume).
6 *un grand personnage,* French: a great person.
7 This "curious commentary" regarding Blunt and Waterhouse was one of two enclosures now lost.
8 "AB": Anthony Blunt (1907–1983), director of the Courtauld Institute from 1947 to 1974, was exposed as a Soviet spy in 1979. The book to which Rowe refers is *Artistic Theory in Italy, 1450–1600,* Oxford: Clarendon Press, 1940.
9 Sir Ellis Kirkham Waterhouse (1905–1985), author of *Baroque Painting in Rome: The Seventeenth Century*, London: Macmillan, 1937, was educated at Oxford where he became a lifelong friend of Blunt. He died in Oxford on 7 September 1985, the date of this letter.
10 This second enclosure, from *House and Garden*, is lost.

To **Eugene Gaddis**, *Wadsworth Atheneum, Hartford, Connecticut*   *13 September 1985*   **147**

CORNELL ARCHITECTURE

Dear Eugene Gaddis:[1]*

The other day, as I told you, I was completely delighted by your phone call about the Austin House where I was taken to luncheon sometime in 1952.[2]

So, since I was taken by Russell Hitchcock,* I could not be unaware that, apart from its visual merits, the house was also to be interpreted as a theater of historical confrontations and then to be equipped with a whole stage of characters. For, apart from Russell Hitchcock and Philip Johnson,* here were also received Alfred Barr, James Johnson Sweeney, James Thrall Soby,* Lillie P. Bliss (didn't Berenson call her Perfect Bliss?), Lincoln Kirstein, Pavel Tchelitchew, Salvador Dali, Gertrude Stein, presumably Le Corbusier,* and <u>you</u> name it. In other words, the house is an important *mise-en-scene* for the policies of art in the 1930s, and, as such—with its own slightly Surrealist bias—is to be intimately linked with MOMA.[3] Meaning, all of this that—in terms of associations—it is quite as much one of the important monuments of Hartford as is the house of Mark Twain.[4]

But now to come to the building itself. When I first saw it I immediately said: "Well, it's Scamozzi's Villa Ferreti south of the Brenta at Dolo and, of course, it's date is 1596"; and I was wildly excited by the acuity that this choice of model presented. Because, even today, the incredibly important—and astringent—Vincenzo Scamozzi (interviewed by Inigo Jones,* concerned with the *Dom* at Salzburg, the author of *L'Idea Universale dell' Architettura*) is a person far too little known;[5] and, for Scamozzi to be a choice of model in the early 1930s is to indicate the extreme precocity of Austin's* taste—simultaneously modern, *maniera* and historicist.[6]

Then there was that room, which I remember well, either from Turin or somewhere in Piedmont; and recollection of this room causes me to believe that the Austin House should be regarded as a carefully constructed and integral ensemble, at least the equivalent of a place like Caramoor.[7]

However, in terms of style, intellectual daring and associations, it far exceeds Caramoor; and as the visual document of an important artistic personality, I can only think that it is to be placed, not alongside the house of Sir John Soane in London, but—at least—alongside the house of Giorgio Vasari at Arezzo and the studio of Eugene Delacroix in Paris.[8] And, if preserved intact, then I am sure that it will come so to be seen.

Then, finally and obviously, I can only think that for the Wadsworth Atheneum to maintain and to preserve this house would be a major service to Hartford, to New England and the nation.

Sincerely,

Colin Rowe

Colin Rowe

Andrew Dickson White Professor of Architecture

CR/mc

cc: Philip Handler*

P. S., The house should be regarded as a private, and important, version of what was done in the museum.

---

1   Eugene Gaddis,* curator of the Wadsworth Atheneum's Austin House, wrote *Magic Façade: The Austin House*, Hartford, CT: The Wadsworth Atheneum, 2007 and *Magician of the Modern: Chick Austin and the Transformation of the Arts in America*, New York: Alfred A Knopf, 2000.
2   A Everett ("Chick") Austin house, Hartford, Connecticut, 1930. Rowe had telephoned Gaddis* in 1985 after having read an article in *The New York Times* on the Austin house. When Gaddis became curator of the house, he asked Rowe to write this letter.
3   "MOMA": Museum of Modern Art, New York City, where, in 1952, Hitchcock* and Johnson* were curators.
4   Mark Twain house, Hartford, 1874. Twain lived there from 1874 to 1891.
5   Vincenzo Scamozzi (1548–1616), Venetian architect and architectural theorist.
6   On the Chick Austin house, see Rowe, Colin, "Henry-Russell Hitchcock" (1988), *As I Was Saying: Recollections and Miscellaneous Essays*, Alexander Caragonne ed, 3 vols, Cambridge, MA: MIT Press, 1996, vol 1, p 18; and Rowe, Colin, "The Avant-Garde Revisited", RE Somol ed, *Autonomy and Ideology: Positioning an Avant-Garde in America*, New York: The Monacelli Press, 1997, pp 60–64.
7   Caramoor, 50 miles north of New York City, is an 81 acre estate featuring the Renaissance Revival Rosen House, 1929–1939.
8   Soane House, London, 1792–1812; Casa di Giorgio Vasari, Arezzo, 1547; Eugène Delacroix's apartment and studio, Paris, 1857–1963.

19 Renwick Place, Ithaca, N. Y.

Dorothy-David:

I am so sorry that you went to Artimino in the dark—for dinner and not for luncheon; because I intended lunch at Artimino to be a substantial little break on a minor sight-seeing tour and Buontalenti's La Ferdinanda, which was completely invisible to you, is very, very grand.[1]

Anyway, I send you a few Xeroxes from a book called *Architettura Rurale in Toscana* just to discover the kind of *casa colonica* which you might like.[2] Me, I adore the group shown in Fig 4 which, I guess, no longer exists. Also, I am very fond of Figs 15 and 78, with their suggestions of an enclosed entrance courtyard. But, then, there is the *ex-castello* type like Fig 17.[3] However, though J. and S. would certainly like running up the towers I think that, probably, in the end it just might be a bit of a nuisance. After which there is the type of regular block with small tower for pigeons, like Figs. 35, 37, 59–60; and, of these, there are quantities; but, in general, myself prefers the picturesque, like a possible combo of Figs 85 and 131. However I add a few more for your inspection.

The book was given to me a couple of months ago by Paolo Berdini,* whose family I learned recently (but not from Paolo) have been Lawyers to the Holy See since about the mid-nineteenth century; and Paolo, whom I shall miss, has just left Cornell U. to do a Ph.D. in Art History at Columbia. He wanted to go to Princeton; but, because of the internal politics of that institution his admission was vetoed by my former student, Tony [...] Vidler, whom I placed at Princeton. And, if Maxwell* and Colquhoun* deny that this is the case, this is to illustrate not my paranoia but their naiveté.

All the same, one must not pile on the parentheses; and, though I may be furious with Princeton and the supine attitudes of certain people who are unable to recognize Othello's Iago when they see him, all that I really want to say is that: Paolo, being Anglophile, or Londraphile, had to buy a copy of *The Observer* once a week, which he invariably handed to me.[4]

So do look at *The Observer's* real estate ads; and notice that, apparently, there are lots of outfits in London concerned with Tuscan properties—at inflated prices I am sure.

Then notice that little German girl, Ulla, who works for Jim; and she has a boyfriend, Irish, who lives on the Fiesole slope.[5] Therefore, why not contact her too.

And then there is this Phyllis Burden from Philadelphia who has lived in Florence for twenty-five years and who seems to wheel and deal in rentables at places like Bellosguardo and Ponte a Mensola; and, immediately that I know more about her, I will let you know.[6]

For my visit from mid-June to beginning of May I shall, of course, hire a car (and, needless to say I shall require it); but I shall hire it from here, when it will also be much cheaper and also tax deductible.

Best love,

   Colin xxxxxx

P.S. I believe that my house sitters are impeccable and that all of you would approve of them. They are what you might expect—from me. They are ex-Notre Dame, mid-

Western, Catholic (not too much so), Christian gentlemen, ex-Judy and me in Rome; and, with great solemnity, I have explained that they are to be the Great Danes and to allow <u>nothing</u> (except the garbage) to leave the house.[7] So I think that it is all O.K.; and, as a result, I shall leave the house with a complete consciousness of their regard and their responsibility.

Should you ever wish to call the house <u>they</u> are Kevin Hinders and Matt Bell.★

    C.

P.P.S. If <u>you</u> are really serious about Toscana then <u>I</u> am delighted. An English house, where the fires are not frugal and lights are not dim, an English house equipped with American conveniences in a Tuscan landscape, all this plus a swimming pool, all this must <u>surely</u> be a *beau ideal*.[8]

    C.

P.P.P.S. Have just looked through yet another catalogue; and, from this, I discover that (including the previous books which I have told you about) just TEN of my books come to NINE THOU!!!!! However <u>and obviously</u>, it cannot <u>all</u> be <u>quite</u> so pricey.

    C.

<u>Hardly</u> a POSTSCRIPT but <u>probably</u> an EXCURSUS

I am wondering what the Koetter★-Kim★ baby is going to come out looking like. It is going to be a boy and I presume that the black hair will prevail over the blond—as it usually does. So I assume a rather presentable version of that somewhat Roman style of oriental physique which is a variant all the way from Japan down to Maori New Zealand.

However, the baby—as you will imagine—is going to be a little bit of a nuisance for me. For, big though the apartment on Beacon Street may be, and calm though Susie usually is, I think that following this so called 'happy event', it's not going to be possible for me to recuperate there.[9]

But Michael Dennis★ offers the first alternative: I can stay with him; and then, for after that, Philip and Madeline Handler★ in Hartford, Connecticut offer me the second: I can stay with them. And so it goes on. Paul Curtis, whom I remember you do <u>not</u> like, offers to accommodate me and tells me that his father is a director of New England Baptist;[10] Blake Middleton★ whom you met in Jim's house in '78 (attenuated Yankee person) tells me much the same;[11] and, as for Rudolfo Machado★ (Argentinian), Rudolfo is *senza dubbio*.[12]

So, you see, I am promised a reasonably entertaining recuperation; and, meanwhile, I am sitting here—10 p.m.—waiting for the arrival of Hugh Aldersey-Williams. Just wish he'd come <u>soon</u>.[13]

September 22

Which, at that moment, he did and, then, stayed for two nights.

So, on the whole and in spite of the voice over the telephone, I was <u>not</u> disagreeably surprised. He read chemistry at Cambridge (John's) and so we were able to talk Cantabrigia—though I <u>must</u> say it <u>was</u> hard work and bridging the gaps was, sometimes, a bit desperate. You see, though he has acquired an architectural interest, it's more about *fabbricazione*[14] than *spazialita*;[15] but, anyway, I had some students to dinner on the Saturday and, therefore, the whole occasion was slightly less fatiguing than I had anticipated. But, all the same, I would say remarkably little visual interest (J. and S. naturally have very much more and, utterly, no curiosity about objects or books in the house). Indeed, for all little Hugh saw (and I wonder what he did see) this house and all its toys might have been any old banal place in Upstate, with shag rugs, Grand Rapids teak pseudo-Scandinavian, and 1950's chenille bedcovers. In other words, so much for me; and I am left wondering what he writes to tell his parents about my totally benighted taste.

E.G.W. used the Trieste / Nizza service but it evoked no notice.

Best love,

    Colin

---

1 Dorothy⋆ and David Rowe⋆ had recently toured Italy. In his 18 August 1985 letter to Dorothy, Rowe had recommended lunch at Artimino and a visit to Buontalenti's La Ferdinana (see p 269 in this volume).

2 David and Dorothy were considering buying a vacation house in Tuscany. Enclosed with this letter were photocopies of pictures of farmhouses (*casa colonica*) from Lorenzo Gori-Montanelli, *Architettura Rurale in Toscana*, Florence: Edam Editrice, 1964, p 35 (fig 4), p 42 (fig 15), p 85 (fig 78), p 44 (fig 17), p 57 (figs 35, 37), p 73 (figs 59, 60), p 89 (fig 85), and p 125 (fig 131).

3 *ex-castello*, Italian: former castle; Captioned *"Incisa Val d'Arno. Antico castello trasformato in case coloniche"*, fig 17 shows a farmhouse with a six-storey tower.

4 *The Observer* is a weekly British newspaper published on Sundays.

5 Ulrike (Ulla) Wilke (b 1955), at the time an assistant architect with James Stirling⋆ and Michael Wilford.

6 Bellosguardo and Ponte a Mensola, on the outskirts of Florence.

7 Rowe intended to visit England for ten and a half months from mid–June 1986 to May 1987. The "Great Dane" reference is to "Bounce to Fop: An Heroic Epistle from a Dog at Twickenham to a Dog at Court", Alexander Pope's satirical poem of 1736 about his dog and loyal protector, a Great Dane named "Bounce".

8 *bel idéal*, French: the perfect type.

9 Ultimately, Rowe convalesced "for the better part of a week" at the home of Fred Koetter⋆ and Susie Kim⋆ on Beacon Street in Boston and then with the Handlers in West Hartford, Connecticut.

10 Paul Alden Curtis, Boston architect.

11 "Jim" is James Stirling.⋆

12 *senza dubbio*, Italian: without a doubt.

13 Hugh Aldersey-Williams, Cambridge-educated natural scientist, author, and journalist from the United Kingdom.

14 *fabbricazione*, Italian: making, building, manufacturing.

15 *spazialita*, Italian: the condition or concept of space.

8
Withdrawal

In July 1986 Rowe wrote to his friends John Miller* and Su Rogers* that he was "feeling dull and uninspired and making plans for the eventual (and not too remote) withdrawal to Rome I think".

Both Syracuse and Notre Dame Universities—as well as Cornell—competed for Rowe's involvement in their Italian ventures. From January to June, in both 1986 and 1987, Rowe taught for Syracuse University in their Florence program. From January to June in 1988 and 1989, he taught for Cornell in Rome, a city he preferred greatly to Florence. He left Rome for Houston in fall 1989, where he taught as a visiting professor at Rice University.

The following February, in 1990, while still in Houston, Rowe badly injured his back. To convalesce, he moved to the residence of Steven Peterson* and Barbara Littenberg* in New York City. A few months later, he turned down an invitation to deliver the Charles Eliot Norton Lectures at Harvard in 1992–1993, citing as reasons the fragility of his back and a reluctance to divert his attentions. Sufficiently recovered in 1991, he proposed to the University of Miami that he teach two lecture courses there beginning in fall 1992, courses he described as "all ready to go: 'The Architecture of Good Intentions: Towards a Possible Retrospect' and 'Italian Architecture: Bramante to Scamozzi'." In January 1992 he taught for the last time—in Rome, for Cornell.

Rowe corresponded with many different people at this time. Most frequently and most regularly—and with a directness and familiarity that one seldom finds in other Rowe letters—he wrote to his sister-in-law, Dorothy.* He wrote to her of his impressions of Rome and of Houston, of his concerns for his nephews' intellectual and financial wellbeing, of his own health, of his travels through Italy and of his daily activities in Ithaca. Most touchingly, in 1987, he wrote her of his thoughts on the sudden death in 1987 of his Cornell friend, JO Mahoney,* and on the events that followed in Ithaca where "the setting was sublime—it only needed the Temple of Vesta from Tivoli on the cliff across the gorge; but the details become slightly sordid".

---

*To **John Miller & Susan Rogers**, Regent's Park Road, London*   *9 July 1986*   **149**

19 Renwick Place, Ithaca, N.Y.

Dearest John and Dearest Susan, my dears:

It was wonderful—or, at least, most agreeable—to be in your house again the other night; and, therefore, to begin with this is a thank you letter. "Mr. and Mrs. Miller it was just great to [be] with ya"; and, needless to say, to escape the prison of Oxford—however briefly—was also a further joy. So, <u>Sir and Maam</u>, lots of slightly ironical thanks....

But, by now, I think I have had almost enough of this particular *stazione di villeggiatur*.[1] I stayed with Fred and Susie for the best part of a week in Boston, and I got coerced into doing things in the office, which was nice; and now I have been back here for just about two weeks. But, pristine to begin with, it has now become putrid. There have been three or four days of the most shocking and inexcusable humidity, during which everything which one has touched has been slimy. But, really, in all this tropical absurdity—while one keeps alive by absorbing a combo of orange juice and champagne—one, absolutely, <u>does</u> expect to find alligators crawling and snapping around the door. Ghana, may be not; but Louisiana almost certainly.

In other words, I am feeling dull and uninspired and making plans for the eventual (and not too remote) withdrawal to Rome I think; and this brings up the whole topic of *objects*—what to sell, what to give, what to take, etc.

Which means, dearest John, that—as a beginning—I have two requests to make of you; and the first is the simplest.

I. Back in November '73—while we were writing *Collage City*—Fred, in a moment of animation and excitement, broke one of the castors of one of those chesterfields, which <u>still</u> waits repair.[2] Therefore <u>could</u> you supply………???????

And now the second and much more painful for you.

II. This is the question of that mechanical chaise longue which I bought on your advice and which you have had ever since. Now I happen to think (just happen) that this will look particularly good in Palazzo Massimo, where you all will come and stay.[3] The P.M.'s furn—such as it is—is either rough/tough/peasanty Baroque or extremely modest Biedermeier—related to the Massimo connection to the House of Saxony? But in any case, and even supposing that one acquires <u>anything</u> of it, it needs a little bit of sprucin' up and a little bit of *inglese* ra ra (you know, we might be about to convert at any minute (possibly May); but, if not English, we are still <u>at least</u> American), so *caro mio*, you grab the pic?[4] And, with this noticed, <u>we</u> will go on to visit the wildest, the most remote and the most bizarre places, all Romanesque and all in the former *Regno delle Due Sicilie*.[5]

Then, and if you can scarcely bear this, myself has lots of beautiful American wire which would look <u>very</u> well in Regent's Park Road but <u>not</u> in Palazzo Massimo.[6]

Meanwhile lotsa lurv,

 Colin

---

1 *stazione di villeggiatura,* Italian: holiday resort.
2 Fred Koetter.*
3 Palazzo Massimo housed the Cornell Rome Program.
4 *inglese,* Italian: English.
5 *Regno delle Due Sicilie*, Italian: Kingdom of the Two Sicilies.
6 "American wire", garden furniture; "American wire stuff—four chairs and a *jardiniere*" as described in Rowe's letter to Dorothy Rowe* dated 10 October 1986 (p 281 in this volume). "Regent's Park Road" refers to the residence of John Miller* and Su Rogers.*

150 *To **Mary Stirling**, Belsize Avenue, London*   *8 July 1986*

19 Renwick Place, Ithaca, N.Y.

Dear Mary:

  I am vividly aware that I still owe you for the ticket from Venice to London the other day. Also I have received a notice from Gloucester Place telling me how much.

And, slob, I have lost this notice. Therefore I am wondering whether you get them to send it to me all over again. And, of course, I am immensely sorry to be such a nuisance.

The climate here is putrid—quite literally. It's like being in a tropical rain forest—without the rain—and almost everything which you touch is slimy with humidity. So, while I am half expecting alligators to walk in, my typing deteriorates; but, all the same I press on.

You see the other night I had a fantasy about St. Margaret's Rd.[1] I thought that it might be nice to have a couple of big obelisks somewhere to the rear of that over large drawing room—where they might help to frame the vista of the garden (if it ever comes about). So I think they would have to be about seven feet high (approximately the top of doors and architraves), of the cheapest carpentry and mount-on concealed castors (so that one would move them around). And then, needless to say, they would have to receive a simulated marble paint job (what everybody in this country suddenly calls *faux marbre*).

Now I have the dimmest idea about what they would be like in detail—whether they would have pedestals or mouldings or not, but I rather think they would not— the more abstract perhaps the better; but I am sending you a notice of this fantasy because I would like to secure your advice and collaboration.[2]

I can't imagine that building the obelisks should cost all that very much; and it's my experience that this is the kind of thing that workmen like to do. But the simulated marble job, I guess, is likely to be something else; and I wonder if you could, quite casually, give me an idea—assuming say a *giallo de Siena* or a *verde antico*.[3]

You see I plan these [as] a little Christmas present for the house.

Best, best love,

    Colin

---

1 St Margaret's Road, Oxford, refers to the home of David* and Dorothy Rowe.*
2 Mary Stirling offered her ideas to Rowe, but the project was never executed.
3 *giallo di Siena*, Italian: yellow marble from Siena; *verde antico*, Italian: antique green marble (from Egypt).

*To **Dorothy Rowe**, St. Margaret's Road, Oxford*   *10 October 1986*   **151**
19 Renwick Place, Ithaca, N.Y.

Dearest Dorothy:

    Dallas was something else. It's a town that I seem to visit at ten year intervals— and always with something like dismay. My dear, IT IS NOTHING, absolutely nothing. NO *genius loci* and nearly everything trash.[1] However I was received as a Texan come back home; and this was flattering and diverting—with a combo of politeness, ineptness, and quite a lot of *simpatico* decorum. But it is so very strange because they do regard me as one of them; and, as a result, although the auditorium had seven hundred and fifty seats, there was scarcely standing room in the aisles. You see, by myth-representation, I now seem to belong to the history of Texas; and, therefore, protracted ovation with lots of handshakes and kisses to follow.

So, while I was repulsed by the physical setting, I was *etonne* by the extravagance of the reception—and, incidentally, though hopelessly naïve, they do have better manners down there than in N.Y.C.[2] I believe deplorable violence in the air hostess category (also I wouldn't trust the Southern Baptists); but, above that scene, when it becomes Episcopalian, there is that great anxiety to play at ante-Bellum South.

All the same, this is not a letter about Dallas—that diffident city which attempts to play ra-ra. Instead it is a reaction to your communication about conservatories/pavilions which I received just before I went down there.[3] All very much more interesting than Big D.

1. The bird table I like. It's like something which you might expect to find in a sacristy for the use of a cardinal.

2. The Gothic garden seat is also quite nice; but it would be a bit too small for the end of the axis. Only 4'6" wide.

3. The hexagonal pavilion at 7'2" is surely slightly cramped and, from the pic, it really looks as though it could only comfortably be occupied by one person.

4. The octagonal pavilion seems to me to be quite the best. But do you get it without the seats?

Question: what are the roofs made of? I suspect that they might be aluminum trying to look like something else and I wonder whether they might not look just a little cheap.

5. I was not wildly impressed by the prices and I still think that the Rousham garden seat would look best. Being Kent, its membering is much more robust.[4] Also it is the right size; it is directional; and, seen from the drawing room, it would be legible.

The conservatories which they produce I find quite charming; and I wish I had seen them before. You see I had intended to give you my American wire stuff—four chairs and a *jardiniere*[5]—and these have lately become quite expensive (Voorhees saw two chairs sold at a country auction the other day for $1,500.00).[6] But you can't put these outside (rust); and you don't have anywhere under cover where they could go. So, problem, what to do?[7] So I didn't pay more than $75.00 apiece for any of my wire (and Peterson* thought that I was being extravagant); but, had not already built the terrace, I would have been disposed to think of a conservatory on the axis of the drawing room.[8] However that, I believe, is now too late; and the kitchen does not provide enough height to attach a conservatory to it.

Best, best love,

    Colin

P.S. To what address shall I have the Eames chair sent? I think that Cheltenham T. would be best since, presumably, the work on it will have to be done in London.[9]

P.P.S. I still owe the Stirlings* for my flight from Venice to London.[10] I lost the letter from Jim's office telling me how much this was; and, though I wrote to Mary about it, she hasn't replied as yet. So I wonder if you could pay them and then I could pay you.

Brilliant autumnal day here; but it's no longer hot. The weather changed while I was in Dallas; and I was shocked by the chill—after three days—when I returned.

Am told that the Eames chair is now priced here at over $2,000.00. Can this be so? If so, a v. good present for dear James. But, since Simon is so visual and so art historical, I am thinking of sending him a pile of books—and, probably, he should have the candelabra and that sort of stuff too.

Ask David whether or not I should send my Regency dining chairs to Sotheby's. Like a lot of things in this house, they are a bit in the way—too small for too much stuff.

    Colin

MATT BELL⋆ WHO IS MY ASSISTANT, LIKES (WAS IN ROME—NOTRE DAME—WITH JUDY) THINKS THE GOTHIC SEAT O.K. THINKS THAT IT MIGHT MAKE THE GARDEN LOOK BIGGER. I DISAGREE. BUT HE HAS GOOD JUDGEMENT AND, OF COURSE, IT SORT OF CONCURS WITH YOURS.

    C.

1 *genius loci*, Latin: distinctive atmosphere or pervading spirit of the place.
2 *étonné*, French: astonished.
3 Presumably Dorothy had written Rowe of her intentions to buy a prefabricated conservatory, garden furniture, and two garden pavilions for the newly purchased house in Oxford on St Margaret's Road.
4 "Being Kent" refers to William Kent (1685–1748), designer of the Rousham garden in Oxfordshire.
5 *jardinière*, French: in this context, a receptacle for holding potted plants.
6 Voorhees operated a small antique shop in Groton, New York, where Rowe purchased his wire furniture.
7 Rowe eventually gave this cast iron ensemble to Dorothy.
8 Steven Peterson.⋆
9 David⋆ and Dorothy Rowe⋆ owned a house in Cheltenham Terrace, London. The Eames chair was a gift from Rowe to his nephew, James.
10 James and Mary Stirling.⋆

---

*To **David & Dorothy Rowe**, St. Margaret's Road, Oxford*   *14 October 1986*   **152**

19 Renwick Place, Ithaca, N.Y.

Dorothy-David:

Franco Purini who came here with his assistant on Monday was the usual Italian Hegelian Marxist.[1] Or maybe not quite. And I say not quite because the moment he walked into the room he began to notice everything. "But this room is a tribute to Rome; but these are Rosa da Tivoli; and don't you know how much one of these sold for at Sothebys / Christies, Rome, the other day. I proposed it for a bank and they bought it for $20,000.00."

So I knew the Rosa da T's were going to escalate. I bought them for Three; but, I suppose, for the pair—in Rome at least—you could now expect Forty. But wild, or don't you think?[2]

The reports are that Peter Eisenman⋆ has sold his library to the Getty Foundation for One Million Dollars!!!. It is mostly magazines which he began to collect in '61 at my instigation; and Geoffrey Steele, antiquarian bookseller, who was here the other night was in a state of horror. Apparently the market has been totally transformed by the transaction; and very elderly Geoffrey was in a condition of dismay. But Kurt Forster⋆ (Getty Foundation) will be here later this week and will be *chez moi* to dinner on Friday.[3]

So shall I surrender my library too?

By my standards it is far better than Peter's.

    Colin

1 Franco Purini (b 1941), Italian architect.
2 See Rowe's letter to Dorothy dated 16 February 1977 for a description of the two Rosa di Tivoli paintings (p 198 in this volume).
3 On 28 October 1986, Rowe wrote Dorothy: "Kurt Forster [...] now tells me that it is completely untrue about Eisenman's* library, tells me that it is a rumor created by Peter himself in order to inspire curiosity and raise prices".

153   *To Matthew Bell*   *23 July 1987*

19 Renwick Place, Ithaca, N.Y.

Dear Matt:

Robert, Cheryl and I gave a little dinner for Richard last night; and Cheryl gave me your address and so I am writing—probably not so briefly.[1]

So she tells me that she has told you about the circumstances of my coming back here, with the electricity and telephone disconnected [...]; and all this stuff [...] has taken me the best part of two weeks. Because, every time you think you are thru, then there is just more to follow. For instance: parking tickets incurred by my car; failure to pay Vicky (she walked out in February); and, finally, a letter which I only discovered yesterday which was mailed on March 27.[2] It is from the Univ. of Cincinnati; and it proposed that I go there as Distinguished Professor of U.D. and, apparently, bring a team which would address itself to the problems of Ohio's older cities. Matt, this might have been the solution to so many problems; but alas........?

Then, thirteen days in England was, more or less, what I expected thirteen days in England to be like. Jim's dinner party was Jim and Mary,[3] John and Susan Miller,* Leon and Rita Krier,* Anne Rykwert (Jo was in hospital and Anne was [...] talking about the Frescobaldi and her other connections in Firenze);[4] and, also, Tom Muirhead.* Then Dorothy had a champagne and orange juice garden party in Oxford for the sake of <u>my</u> garden (which I have no wish to recognize as <u>mine</u>). About forty people; and—again—Tom Muirhead (who seems to think that Annabelle and I are <u>fatally</u> close—the message which both Mary Stirling and Dorothy had, unaccountably, received).[5] Then there was a further little trip, with James and his *inamorata* to Wilton, to Stourhead and to Bath—about which I will comment later.[6]

Then I have also talked to Lee about a summer school which, he thinks, might start in Italy and end in England.[7] So as you must see from all this, we haven't been able to get very far on the slide business, and though we are looking forward to your arrival, we are not exactly excited by the exhibitions of *terrlbilita* which are likely to ensue.[8]

However, this is only a prelude for what is to follow. I have been sitting today with one of those financial management guys who (after going thru all the bonds and that kind of stuff) has disclosed to me that I am worth rather more than I believed. I had thought that I had about $170,000 in loose cash; but it now seems to be more like $220,000 which, given, my income (it will, from this and that, be rather more than $100,000 next year), and given tax-free municipal bonds at 10 to 14 p.c., and given my cheap habits, mean that between now and 1990 (when I propose to withdraw from Ithaca), the total estate (house, lib., furn., etc) can be built up to something round about *Un Millione*. Not very good; but not terribly bad for someone, like me, who has never, seriously, thought about mon.

So this now prepares the argument for the next piece.

It is evident that James has no literary or visual interests whatsoever, though, in a lazy way, he is happy to go and look at what he has been told is important; and it is no longer clear, to me, that Simon's visual interests prevail. And, therefore, what to do with the lib.?[9] Sell it? Give it to Cornell? Give it to the American Academy? As I think you know I am reluctant to indulge in any of these performances. But, then, <u>what</u> to do? And this question brings me out in a will-dangling mood which, as I now see, was already my state of mind when I gave you the Leoni *Alberti* in December, with the subsequent presents to Robert and Paolo (and, by the way, I have given Cheryl a very elegant seventeenth century engraving of the Duke of Berwick—illegitimate son, by Arabella Churchill, of James II of England and ancestor of the Dukes of Alba).[10] But, then, it seems that I frequently make casual, expensive presents—like giving Fred a set of Letarouilly.[11] However <u>this</u> is different; and now to resume the will-dangling state of mind.

If Simon is <u>not</u> interested (and, now, I don't anticipate his interest) do I leave the lib. to Judy or to <u>you</u>? David and Dorothy, of course, would love to have it—as a cultural trophy—of this I am sure but, not liking that sort of possession, I want it—after I croak—to be the property of someone who finds it rewarding; and, as a consequence, this is the reason why I <u>now</u> think of <u>you</u>. Dear Matt, potentially this is an appalling bequest; and I don't expect you to accept with enthusiasm. Unless you enlarge it very much (meaning the lib.), it may be a horrible item to be cursed with. It would be extremely, irrefutably <u>me</u>, like having a ghost around all the time; and I don't know that is the best of situations.

Nevertheless, in default of Simon, I am compelled to think of <u>you</u> as the destination: and it is to that scene, <u>if</u> you can bear it, that we <u>now</u> have to address ourselves.

Since the estate (though it will still be minute) now promises to be much more than I had ever anticipated, I am now encouraged to diversify my will. One Hundred Thousand each to James and Simon is surely enough (those boys are going to be quite rich anyway); and Judy <u>is</u> considered in my <u>present</u> scene (though she is going to be quite rich anyway). And, then, what to think about the rest?

So I am assuming that the lib. requires a support situation. Like, apart from the value of the lib., about $200,000, which would secure an income of, at least, $25,000. But I get confused by all that math and at the moment, I am assuming that you are principal beneficiary. Don't think this is, in any way an unreasonable idea; and, Dear Matt, I am addressing you in this way—remote—because I think that it is far better than a confrontation *de face en face*.[12] What I am trying to say is without emotion and it illustrates what is becoming my intention.

Best, best,

   Colin

P.S. I have shown this letter to Cheryl and she agrees that it is not as extravagant as it may seem. You see, even if I were to croak tomorrow, the estate (ready cash) would still be worth rather over $500,000.00 (this is secured by insurance—Estate of Colin Rowe). So, if even I were to croak *domani* (don't expect), the estate would still be rather more than a meagre $1,000,000,00.[13]

Matt, when you arrive do not address me on this topic. I want you to think about its possibility. Instead, bring it up two to three days after you arrive. There are situations of great disputation here; but, unless the very idea is improbable/impossible, they may rest for a few days—though I think that they will have to be settled (one way or the other) by the end of September.

   Colin

1 Robert Goodill,* Cheryl O'Neil,* and Richard Role,* Cornell graduate students.
2 Rowe's housekeeper at 19 Renwick Place, Ithaca.
3 James and Mary Stirling.*
4 "Jo" is Joseph Rykwert (b 1926), architectural historian and educator.
5 Annabelle Selldorf, Rowe's student at Syracuse in Florence.
6 *innamorata*, Italian: loved one or sweetheart.
7 Lee Hodgden,* Cornell professor.
8 *terribilità*, Italian: emotional intensity.
9 "lib.": library; that is, Rowe's personal library.
10 Robert Goodill* and Paulo Berdini.*
11 In a letter to David Rowe* dated 11 August 1987, Rowe wrote: "To Fred Koetter, I have
   already given Letarouilly, *Édifices de Rome Moderne*". Letarouilly, Paul Marie, *Édifices de
   Rome moderne*, Paris: Didot frères, 1840.
12 *face-à-face*, French: face to face.
13 *domani*, Italian: tomorrow.

154   *To **Dorothy Rowe**, St. Margaret's Road, Oxford*   *21 October 1987*

19 Renwick Place, Ithaca, N. Y.

Dearest Dorothy:

The events of the last five days have been interesting and shocking.

After my lecture last Friday J.O. Mahoney,* who has assiduously attended, came up to me and said; "But what about the Carlton House conservatory.[1] You are going to have to show that and where do I find pictures of it?" So I said: "Why not try that Regency publication, Pyne's *Royal Residences*?" So he found it; and, late on Saturday, he rang me up to thank me and say how much he was enjoying it.

Then, on Sunday morning at 5.00 a.m., apparently there was great pain; and he was taken away in an ambulance to the hospital. It was an inoperable aneurism; and he died in the hospital at 7.00 a.m. Monday.

But that is the bare outlines and now I must fill in the details. I didn't know about the Sunday morning calamity (I was out in the afternoon) until eight o'clock in the evening when I was called by a totally distraught Judy Holliday:* "He will not survive the night," etc. So this is the first time that I have known someone was going to die and was obliged to think about it; and, needless to say, I told Judy that I would do anything to assist, sit in the hospital with her, etc. But I didn't seem to be wanted. So I rang different people; and, in a specially chartered plane, his friend, Henry Jova, independently rich and, apart from that, a highly successful architect in Atlanta, Georgia, came up here quickly and was in time to be in at the death.[2] He was in intensive care (quantities of morphine); and they were not admitted until six, when one of the things (Henry told me this) was: "Do please thank Colin for the Carlton House conservatory."

So much for the outline and, needless to say, I cried a bit, and I made an acknowledgement in my lecture today. But, dearest Dorothy, the nerve racking scene this morning was the scattering of the ashes—highly private, about twenty persons altogether—the ashes to be scattered from the south terrace, over the parapet, into the gorge.

So, initially, I thought a good idea. The stormy autumnal sky, the drifting leaves, the big lake, the gorge, the two waterfalls surely made the perfect setting for some arcane Neo-Classical celebration of death. It promised to be Hubert Robert and Piranesi all in the same package;[3] but it was nothing like the disposal of Shelley at Lerici.[4] They did things better in those days.

It began with a mild grandeur—salmon mousse in a fish mould, pate, brie, choice of Asti Spumante or Veuve Clicquot no less! But, during the course of this little *ricevimento,* about 10.30, I found myself talking to Henry Jova about the disposition of the estate (we were the only persons who could so communicate); and, at this point, I began to sense the degringolade to follow.[5] Henry gets the pictures, Judy Holliday gets the mynah bird (as a compensation for her cat which has just died?), I might get something (Henry thought the blue and white Cantonese china of which there is a great deal—but I very much doubt it), while the house and the property, which is large and choice, are left to the Unitarian Church of Ithaca![6] And what do you think that institution will proceed to do with it? Sell the outer parts for building sites I am sure. Well, as you will now guess, things went quickly from bad to worse.

Shortly we were shepherded out into the east courtyard, where has recently been completed a sort of baroque grotto (shades of William Kent and quite good) which I hadn't previously seen; and, here, we were encouraged to dispose of ourselves in a circle; and, then, there ensued interminable mumblings mostly about 'spirituality'. But it was a little chilly and a little damp. I didn't have my overcoat with me, I had left it in the car; and I was highly relieved when Alex Kira suddenly said: "Don't you think that we ought to get on with the business. Otherwise there might be more deaths—of double pneumonia this time."[7]

Well this didn't quite bring this little conclave to an end; but it acted to do so; and most people were highly relieved to get back into the house again—so much so that half of the crowd remained in the house and chose to witness the next act from behind the big dining room window—with the mynah bird screaming, in Russian (!), from inside its enormous cage.

So, in end, it was quite a small group on the south terrace, where little old me had expected some kind of plinth or pedestal with a nice looking urn on top of it. But NO!, NO!, NO!!! The Unitarian minister came sanctimoniously on to centre stage WITH A TRANSPARENT PLASTIC BAG (a little blue ribbon around the top of it); and, in THIS, was enclosed the debris of the deceased!

The bathos, the failure to understand the Neo-Classical idea, I think would probably have amused Mahoney; and I saw that Henry Jova thought so too. Then the minister scooped some of the stuff out of the bag and invited others to do so, following his lead as he threw some little white pebbles over the edge. Naturally myself did not imitate; but Judith Holliday and Gillian Pederson-Krag ran around like frenzied Greek maidens (maenads perhaps, anyway quasi-Isadora Duncans) in a positive orgy of pebble throwing until supplies were completely exhausted; and I swear that I'll never look at a little plastic bag again without this spectacle coming to mind.[8]

Repeat: the setting was sublime—it only needed the Temple of Vesta from Tivoli on the cliff across the gorge; but the details become slightly sordid. Then, when only Alex Kira and myself were left on the terrace with the plastic bag, he tried to set fire to the bag—curiously the Unitarian minister had left it behind; but the wretched little thing wouldn't ignite. And it was on this spot that, underneath a large blue and white umbrella, I had lunch in July.

Sounds like a fragment from a cynical novel by some minor follower of Evelyn Waugh.[9] Don't you think? And what a way to spend the hours between 9.45 and 11.15, when I left to recover for my lecture at 12.30.

Best love to all,

Colin

It continues to be a week fraught with events and, today just before 2.30 along with about fifty others, most of them of oriental origin, I really did become a U.S. citizen.

The ceremony was highly folksy. A man came in and rang a bell; "Ye, ye, ye" (can you believe the mediaeval English) "the court is in session. All stand". So enter the judge, who turned out to be a charmboat. Called Frederick Bryant, I realized that I had met him sometime, quite a time ago; and, outside the law, his hobby is being a magician. He begins his allocution by saying: "My name is Frederick Bryant and, as you may guess from that, I'm a wasp. That is a White Anglo-Saxon Protestant; and let me tell you folks that, apart from the American Indian, we were here first." But all jokey rather than arrogant/supercilious, all underplayed; and, as I noticed, particularly appreciated by the orientals.

Then, after the allocution, communally, we all sweared to 'abjure allegiance to all foreign princes, potentates and powers'. All very eighteenth century; but what a relief from the turgid, Unitarian unctuousness of yesterday. It was Bryant's last day on the bench; he was given a protracted round of applause; he was visibly moved, was unable to speak, bowed, withdrew. After which all the rest of us were given our Certificate of Naturalisation. I was the third to be called; and, though I haven't examined details yet, I took a brief look and found that the folder—among other bits and pieces—also included a small silk American flag. Then, at the door, there were members of the D.A.R. (Daughters of the American Revolution) who gave all the new citizens three red roses—very well intentioned I am sure but I find the symbolism to be mildly elusive.

But there it is. It was painless. It's been done. And I am immensely relieved—although I know that, in Rome, the Polish Pretender would <u>not</u> have appreciated the opening reference to the WASP origins of this country.[10]

But, dearest Dorothy, I am sure that you would have enjoyed being present and would have appreciated the casual decorum. Also, I hope that, with this action today, I have defeated the doctrine of *animus revertendi*[11]—which I am sure will give David at least <u>some</u> pleasure.[12]

All the same, <u>what</u> a week. However, tragedy, trauma, anti-climax, and climax have left me highly resilient; but what <u>else</u> can the week have in store? But is 6.45 and I must now prepare my little lec *per domani*.[13]

> *Colin*

---

1 James O Mahoney* (1907–1987), Cornell art professor, renowned muralist and painter, was born in Texas and educated at Yale University.

2 Henry Jova (1920–2014), Atlanta architect, received his BArch degree from Cornell University in 1949.

3 Hubert Robert (1733–1808), French painter of landscapes and picturesque ruins; Giovanni Battista Piranesi (1720–1778), renowned Italian engraver.

4 Percy Shelley (1792–1822), English Romantic poet, died at sea at the age of 29 when sailing back from Livorno to Lerici. His body was cremated on the beach where it was found; his ashes interred in the Protestant Cemetery, Rome.

5 *ricevimento*, Italian: reception.

6 "In spite of disclaimers", Rowe wrote, "J.O. Mahoney was fundamentally a Texan; but, like so many Texans, a Texan Italianized [...] the years J.O. spent as a fellow of the American Academy in Rome were the decisive years of his life. [His] ultimate references were mostly Italian; and the house remains a witness to considered impressions gathered from Frascati, Tivoli, [...]". Rowe described Mahoney's* Ithaca house as "an Italianate villa done on a budget, [... his] major achievement and his major act of self disclosure." See Colby, V, et al, "J.O. Mahoney", on Fingerlakes Artists, http://jsuttongallery.com/artists-pages/j-o-mahoney (accessed 29 March 1914).

7   Alexander Kira (1928–2005), Cornell architecture professor, author of *The Bathroom*, New
    York: Viking Press, 1976.
8   Gillian Pederson-Krag, painter and professor of fine arts at Cornell University.
9   Evelyn Waugh (1903–1966), English writer of novels, biography, and travel books.
10 "The Polish Pretender": Karol Józef Wojtyła, Pope John Paul II (1920–2005).
11 *animus revertendi*, Latin: with intention to return.
12 David Rowe* had encouraged his brother to take United States citizenship for legal purposes.
13 *per domani,* Italian: for tomorrow.

To Chairman Wells and Architecture Faculty   *27 October 1987*   **155**

Cornell University, School of Architecture, Sibley Hall, Ithaca, N.Y.

MEMORANDUM
RE: The Rome Program   *C.R.*

    A major problem with the Rome program is that we have not enough students
and not enough faculty.

The Architecture Department of the University of Syracuse in Florence has some
fifty-five students with four full-time and two part-time faculty. The Architecture
Program of the University of Notre Dame in Rome has some sixty students (it is
capable of accommodating seventy) with an administrative director, three full-time
and two part-time faculty. Also both students and faculty are either in Florence or
Rome for a <u>full</u> year or longer; and it should further be noticed that, with this critical
mass of students and this student-faculty ration, both of these programs show a
financial profit—indeed it would be hard to imagine either Syracuse or Notre Dame
undertaking a foreign venture that was not profit making.

With this information in mind, whatever the relevance of the Syracuse/Notre
Dame know how/experience, I suggest that, at this stage, we should not act with
uncharacteristic precipitancy by casually committing faculty for the next three years.
Rather, we should attempt to define what our objectives in Rome may be.

Needless to say, I do not require to be told that the establishment of the Rome program
was scarcely received with universal enthusiasm: but I believe that initial doubt is partly
mitigated and, in any case, the program is now a *fait accompli*.[1] Located at an illustrious
address, with space that could serve a much more expanded activity, now it is surely up
to us to use this space in a way which could stimulate and animate the college in general.

When I was with Syracuse in Florence during the spring of this year, I tried to get
down to Palazzo Massimo to give a lecture every couple of weeks; but, though I
wasn't completely successful in achieving this schedule of visitations, nevertheless, I
received impressions as to how the program was getting along.

With the students to whom I spoke, obviously, it was an inordinate success and they
communicated their feelings with vivacity; but, all the same, I found myself wondering
if sending an isolated faculty member from Ithaca to Rome for a mere four months
(may not know the city, may not speak the language), to live in an apartment where
you are obliged to dine in the bedroom and the only saving grace is a Pompei Batoni
portrait of an eighteenth century Massimo, is an entirely good idea.[2] Instead, I began
to wonder whether this might not be designated as '<u>cruel and unusual punishment</u>'.
For instance, I several times went out to dinner with Astra Zarina* (University of
Washington) and, several times, we found Charles P. glumly eating a solitary little meal

in some restaurant close to the Campo dei Fiori.[3] It was a depressing spectacle; and I want to compare it with animated collegiality which prevails at Syracuse and Notre Dame—also with Washington at Palazzo Pio. The Einaudi's, Roberto and Karen, are sympathetic, charming, and hospitable; but even though Roberto did happen to be born in a taxi in New York City and, subsequently, brought up in Ithaca, they must have their own social life and can scarcely be expected to attend to the isolated depressions of the solitary faculty member whom we chose to send over. Alone, the isolated faculty member, there for four months, will be lost in a highly gregarious city.

So, dear Jerry, this is my primary response to your memo, addressed to Rome Program Faculty, of October 21. Decisions are not to be rendered in quite so perfunctory a manner. We will not be able to solve the problems of Palazzo Massimo on an entirely routine basis. It is too much of an undismissable challenge; and we have to face it with more consideration.

For instance, is Palazzo Massimo an albatross (a huge bird suspended around the neck of Coleridge's mythical sailor)?[4] Is it a monstrous ornithological curse or is it, quite merely, a lame duck which requires help and generosity? Myself thinks that the lame duck story is that which applies; and it is, hence that I write at such length.

In other words, let's have a bit of 'thought'; and with 'thought', I am sure that, among lamentable proposals, brilliant results will ensue.

So what do I talk about now? The specifics of Palazzo Massimo or the generalities of foreign programs? And, which first? I think Palazzo Massimo.

At present it is being under-used. Too many rooms of 'parade' which are not good enough to excite any sentiment more than weariness. There is the first room, the entrance gallery over the loggia or the cortile—empty (could be used as reception-secretary-telephone). There is the second room (used for casual lectures; but there is the alternative space downstairs). There is the third room (big; but only housing a secretary and a few bookshelves—Roberto's triangular office relates to this room). And, then, there is the fourth room, the *ante capella*, which enjoys no purpose whatsoever. And what to do about the *ante capella* which looks like Munich and Bavaria c., 1740–50 strange, crude rococo, interesting, no doubt, for *la famiglia Massimo*; but I don't think for others. And then there is the faculty apartment, two difficult rooms which might become the first a library and slide room and, the second a badly needed faculty office.

I calculate that these under-used rooms, with the rest of the premises which we lease could hold twice the present number of architecture students, however, these were to be distributed.

But, now, to consider foreign programs in general.

Neither Syracuse nor Notre Dame appear to consider their Italian programs as disruptive of their own campus teaching back here in the U.S. of A.; and, at both institutions, the year in Italy seems to be regarded, not as an exotic excursion, but as an integral part of the curriculum, informing and transforming the domestic endeavor. Indeed, at Notre Dame, the Rome experience is mandatory; and, as I happen to know, this proviso has frequently served as a magnet to attract students to South Bend. But Syracuse offers something more—a graduate program of one year's length in Florence (not ideal in terms of either length or place); and, again, this serves as a magnet for applicants. For instance, there are ten graduate students at Syracuse in Florence this semester and none of them did their undergraduate work at Syracuse— notably, one is from Cornell, and some others are from outside this country.

The upshot of this argument is my suspicion that we don't fully recognize the asset which we have acquired—an asset which can be put to profit, both intellectual and financial. We remain hermetic; and we are half disposed to interpret an asset as though it were an affliction. Indeed, I am not sure that our attitude to the development of Palazzo Massimo is not equivalent to that of Day Hall to the development of the Cornell campus: let us not think about it; let *ad hoc* day to day decisions prevail; let us pursue a policy of 'benign neglect' and *dolce fa niente*: there is absolutely no plausible reason for any comprehensive plan.[5]

So, while we despise and lament the negative activities of the bureaucrats of Day Hall, in a certain way might it not be that we are serving as their mirror?

Therefore, can't we begin to think BIG? For isn't Daniel Burnham's *'make no small plans'* a dictum which illuminates our consciousness?[6] And, rather than tinker with the details (which often may be appropriate politics?), in the case of Palazzo Massimo don't you think we should begin to project some major revisions in our undergraduate curriculum?

This extended memo should not be construed as a *rappel a l'ordre*; but as the ruminations of an approximately logical capitalist.[7] And this doesn't mean money. It means the capital of ideas, memories, emotions, and experience.

So, at Cornell, we <u>have</u> this composite capital well in excess of <u>any</u> other school; and it's a capital which may well be lost unless we invest it in the assets which we have available. There used to be that *graffito* in the New York subway: *Jesus saves; but Moses invests*. So, are we to emulate Jesus (in terms of Wall Street a holding operation) or are we to emulate Moses and place, reasonably conspicuous, venture capital in Rome? The dividends are reliable, sometimes brilliant and, never, have they been less than good. In any case, far, far better than committing any capital to Washington, D.C.[8]

P.S.
I have cited the examples of Syracuse and Notre Dame because I happen to know both these outfits reasonably well; but, also, there should be cited three other Roman situations: Rhode Island School of Design at Palazzo Cenci, University of Washington and University of Illinois—both at Palazzo Pio. It would be reasonably easy to discover the precise statistics from each of these three institutions: but, over the weekend, I haven't been able to do so. However, apart from lavish studio space, University of Washington (which also sends classicists) includes six, recently converted, two room, faculty apartments; and this might offer some clue.

P.P.S.
I have a suspicion that the size of a profitable venture relates to the size of a bus (field trips, etc.); and the average bus holds approximately fifty. Thus, field trips for as few as sixteen become immensely expensive; and this probably means that some thirty to forty undergraduates and some ten graduates is the ideal to aim at. Note also that such a disposition would permit graduate students to serve as T.A.'s to undergraduates; and this is the case with Syracuse.

CR/rp

---

1 *fait accompli*, French: accomplished fact.
2 Pompeo Girolamo Batoni (1708–1787), Italian painter.
3 Charles Pearman (1927–2013), Cornell architecture professor.
4 Reference is to Coleridge, Samuel Taylor, *The Rime of the Ancient Mariner*, 1798.
5 *dolce far niente*, Italian: sweet do-nothing.
6 Daniel Burnham (1846–1912), Chicago architect and city planner: "Make no little plans. They have no magic to stir men's blood and probably will not themselves be realized."
7 *rappel à l'ordre*, French: call to order.
8 Cornell had a small program in Washington, DC. A faction of the faculty preferred to strengthen that program rather than commit money to Rome.

19 Renwick Place, Ithaca, N.Y.

Dearest Dorothy:

My little trip with Susie was very amusing and a great disappointment for Susie.[1] Poppi, *presso* Bibbiena turned out to be <u>impossible</u>, as far from Pontassieve as Pontassieve is from Firenze, over tough mountain roads and at least three hours from the Pisa Airport.[2] And, though Poppi is a surprisingly charming town (a little bit Venetic) the house which she had in mind turned out to be the usual pig sty with a view—the view being of the Levi d'Anconas property down the hill (shades of Lisa Benaim and all that).

So Poppi was flushed out and then went to Siena where Susie was convinced that she had the most charming little modest Swiss real estate man. But, alas, it didn't turn out to be like that. M. Quendet, at Grove about 15 km from Siena, turned out to be one of the most ruthless Swiss entrepreneurs (Zurich banks and, for propriety, on the board of directors the Barone Ricasoli and H.H. the Duca Amedeo d' Aoasta). So you get the pic/Quendet is the great man for organizing the renting of Tuscan places.

So, then we went to Volterra (Susie was devastated by the landscape) and spent a night at Montepulciano. It was a good and very cheap hotel. Judy tells me that I like driving Susie because she is so rich whereas Judy doesn't have a penny; but, *quant a moi*, I <u>haven't</u> noticed the difference.[3] But, anyway, the country south of Montepulciano met with approbation and, then, we returned to Rome.

All in all an interesting little trip because it gave one ideas and made Susie realize that, if she wanted to find something, she would have to settle somewhere for a month or so and start looking in depth.

Susie has the fantasy that she would like to move to London, like to open an office in London (they seem to be getting work in London); and, so, she was interested in proximity to Pisa, which is one of the reasons why Volterra aroused interest; but to Lucca, of course, we didn't go.

Meanwhile, I have said NO about the *palazzo* in Bagnoregio,[4] though the enfilade (four rooms making a perspective of about 70 feet on the *piano nobile*) is, or could be, spectacular and, also, at $70,000.00 it's cheap.[5] But, without a *cortile*, without a garden, without a terrace, without a view, without a garage you can guess how cooped up one would feel; and the observation of all comings and goings I am sure would produce neurosis.[6] Lots could be done with it at a price—take off parts of the roof (it would have to be redone anyway) and you could get a whole promenade of internal terraces, winter gardens, etc; but it would be money down the tubes. You could sink the best part of $300,000.00 into it; but the basic deficiencies would never be remedied. Why drive so far into the country without the prospects which one drives out to look at?

Dear Dorothy, there are times (David may be right) when I turn to think about Bath.

On the other hand, the Notre Dame/Via del Teatro Valle fantasy <u>is</u> moving ahead— with more than the speed of a glacier. As I was told that they would be, they are intrigued and only seem to want further details (like how many days a week would I need a secretary, how much would she cost, etc? exactly the details which I <u>don't</u> think about) in order to become really active. So I'm working on it.

Then, as you would expect, the Notre Dame interest has produced a little flurry in this neck of the woods. Werner Seligmann* came to dinner yesterday with all sorts of proposals for Florence; and things, <u>even</u>, move <u>here</u>. Of Roberto Einaudi* it seems that my own evaluation is quite the mildest and the gentlest. Tactless Roberto amuses me; and, because he amuses me, I like him—a little bit. But my own tranquility about Roberto is <u>absolutely</u> mine alone. Everybody who has worked with Roberto is hostile (in so far as their extremely docile and cow-like characters allow them to be); and Ithaca John Miller,[7]* who goes to Palazzo Massimo in September, already, has refused to work with Roberto.[8] Instead he takes with him John Coyne, one of Judy's little *proteges* from Notre Dame of '84–85, a highly talented and *simpatico* guy from Tennessee (Judy caused him to transfer to Cornell), as <u>his</u> equivalent of Matt Bell.[9]* So you get the pic? I applaud John Miller's choice; and, at the same time, it is little me, who remains the only, slightly insipid, partisan of Roberto. But dearest Roberto, with all that *fa figura*, if he <u>only</u> knew.[10]

So Ithaca remains as you might imagine it to be: hot, humid, repulsively green; and I have bought a postcard of a waterfall in order to send it to Pierina, *portiere* at Palazzo M.[11] And I shall tell her that it's just at the bottom of my garden (I gave Pierina a book called *Viva Il Re*[12]—because she is so devoted to the *Casa di Savoia*[13]—though very choosy; but, in a nineteenth century way, Pierina will be <u>very</u> impressed by the waterfall—with a *cascata*[14] like that it will assure her that everything here is *molto signorile*.[15]

At Civita, of all places, I found a book called *The Year of the French*—about a French, 1797, invasion of County Mayo; and, as a result, I have become absurdly interested in Dublin / Belfast politics of the French revolutionary period: Lord Edward Fitzgerald, Wolfe Tone, and all the rest.[16] Edward Fitzgerald, fought in the wars of the American Revolution, was a bit of a military hero, marched through forests, and became, correspondingly, infatuated by Rousseau. You get it—all that North American stuff with a bit of French rhetoric added. So do find some books on The Society of United Irishmen for David because I think that they would absorb his attention.

And now I have a little book list for James which <u>you</u> will have to buy at Blackwell's because dearest Giacomino is <u>never</u> going to do it himself.[17] These are:

Trevelyan, <u>the three volumes on Garibaldi</u>.[18] I was brought up on the hirsute Garibaldi myth; and I think that the same is true of you and David. But I have discovered that James knows nothing at all about the heroics of the Risorgimento; and, in this condition, I want him to be first introduced to the English, Edwardian, liberal version.

Denis Mack Smith, <u>a whole number of books</u>.[19] Used to be at Cambridge is now at Oxford, an antidote to Trevelyan's sentimentality.

Harold Acton, *The Bourbons of Naples, The Last Bourbons of Naples*.[20] This is, obviously, a pro Neapolitan production (absolutely contra Trevelyan).

Try to get these things for James,—he is willing, highly, to learn but is desperately without info.

Love,

    Colin   *x x x x x*

July 29

But everything here is desperately meager and, is the word, *mesquin*.[21] Horrid small scale with the ceilings too low and everything impossibly bitsy; and <u>this</u> James will understand perfectly. I realize that never before have I found Rome so elevating and so grand; and I am supposing that this must be the result, strangely enough, of

Palazzo Massimo. And James will, also understand this because, in his own way, he found Palazzo M. much more impressive than I thought that I did.

So it's the usual story about Rome. It's horrible; it's crude; it's a collection of mountain villages pretending to be a city; it's a lot of old warehouses grotesquely described as palaces; but, though it's impossible, there seems to be no escape from it. The Upper East Side? Pony Street? Cadogan Whatever It May Be Called? The Rue de Varennes? None of these add up to the squalid, and hideously paved presence of that little *centro storico*.[22] There is no polish in Rome. Repeat: it's just crude; and this causes me to think of Russell Hitchcock,* years ago, in New Haven. The last granddaughter of <u>the</u> Vanderbilt had died; and Russell looked at the pic (she was nothing to talk about, Mrs. Twombly)[23] and snorted: "Just imagine, so much *tenu* and no looks".[24]

So I think that Mrs. Twombly must have been a bit like Rome; and the only explanation for Rome must be in terms of *tenu*, absolutely not in terms of looks.

Extremely interesting all this; but I still, desperately, want James (who is so good) to become conversant with the history of Italy.

Un abbraccio

Colin

Out of all this, by the way, I have acquired a constituency. James' friends Nadine Hippolyte and Helen Kim will come to dinner tomorrow night; and Neale O'Shea and John Maniscalcko threaten to come later. *Ridicolo*, or don't you think?[25] But should I invite James here? You see I am picking up his friends.

Colin

---

1 Rowe accompanied Susie Kim* on her search to purchase a vacation house in Tuscany.
2 Poppi is small town in Tuscany, just north of Bibbiena; *presso*, Italian: at.
3 *quant à moi*, French: as for me.
4 Rowe was considering purchasing property in Bagnoregio for himself.
5 *piano nobile*, Italian: the main story / floor of a plazzo containing principal rooms.
6 *cortile*, Italian: courtyard; enclosed area, typically roofless and arcaded, within or attached to a building.
7 John Clair Miller,* professor of architecture at Cornell University from 1977 to 2003.
8 Palazzo Massimo alle Colonne housed the Cornell Architecture in Rome Program.
9 *protégés*, French: disciples.
10 *fa figura*, Italian: fine appearance or impression.
11 *portiere*, Italian: doorman at Palazzo Massimo, location of Cornell Architecture in Rome.
12 Quartara, Giorgio, *Viva il papa? o Viva il Re!*, Milan: Fratelli Bocca Editori,1949.
13 "Casa di Savoia": The House of Savoy. Formed in the early eleventh century, it ruled the Kingdom of Italy from 1861 to 1945.
14 *cascata*, Italian: waterfall.
15 *molto signorile*, Italian: very elegant.
16 Flanagan, Thomas, *The Year of the French*, New York: Holt Rinehart & Winston, 1979.
17 "Giacomino": Rowe's Italianized name for his nephew, James Rowe;* "Blackwell's" is a bookseller on Broad Street in Oxford.
18 Trevelyan, George Macaulay, *The Garibaldi Trilogy*, London: Longmans, Green, 1911–1919.
19 Denis Mack Smith (b 1920), British historian specializing in Italian history, best known for his studies on Garibaldi, Cavour, and Mussolini.
20 Acton, Harold, *The Bourbons of Naples, 1734–1825*, London: Methuen, 1956; *The Last Bourbons of Naples*, New York: St Martin's Press, 1961.
21 *mesquin*, French: mean or shabby. Rowe is describing his Ithaca house.
22 *centro storico*, Italian: historic center.
23 Mrs Hamilton McKown Twombly (1854–1952), the last surviving granddaughter of Commodore Cornelius Vanderbilt from whom she inherited $100 million in 1877.
24 *tenue*, French: bearing or poise.
25 *ridicolo*, Italian: ridiculous, laughable.

19 Renwick Place, Ithaca, N.Y.

I came back to this house late on Tuesday to find it in completely shocking condition.

A first notice of this was at the garage with a collection of smelly garbage so distributed that, apart from the stench, it was impossible to drive a car into it; and, then, the spectacle of the basement confirmed this initial impression—a carpet rolled up so as to obstruct entrance and God knows how many bags with old bottles of wine and beer. Then, the basement stairs were further cluttered with old cases of beer.

So I began to receive the idea that the house had been recently abandoned by an army of occupation which had behaved in characteristic style only to leave the returning owner to contemplate the debris; and, upstairs, this impression could only be expanded. In the entrance hall there were crooked pictures and the lights had failed; in the kitchen there was a quaintly inextricable confusion of pots, pans and imperfectly washed plates; and in the living room a pile of newspapers four feet high.

But WHY? Don't normal people, normally, take out newspapers at least once a week?

But, also, in the living room there was a very prominent clue to this behavior pattern. It was, I am sure, intended to be read as an 'amusing' manifesto. In the mantelpiece, in place of two plaster caryatids had been submitted two empty cans of Piels beer. An attempt to *epater les bourgeois*?[2] But it was so like the behavior of silly children that it might have been endearing if it were not symptomatic of so much else—a slovenly and destructive carelessness.

For, of course, in the living room, there was further illustrations to be found of the attitude which I have identified. There were rugs upside down, one walked on grime encrusted floors, and everything one touched was grimy and sleazy. It was like the residence of less than white trash in somewhere ever so much worse than Alabama. And, then, there was the wrecked condition of the chaise longue; and how does one get that fixed in Ithaca?

However, now to go upstairs into the bathroom, where one light had failed, another was about to expire, the Corian lining of the bathtub was peeling off the wall, and the drain encrusted with, presumably, pubic hairs.

But the condition of the little bedroom was even more mysterious and was, obviously, connected with the condition of the front bedroom. From the little bedroom all the books had been removed and put on the floor of the front bedroom; and, apparently, this was to allow Y. to put his clothes in the bookshelves. But WHY? Except for the drawer in the front bedroom, there were eight drawers which had been emptied for a general accommodation. So WHY go to all this bizarre trouble and inconvenience? But, also, in the front bedroom the window shades had been removed and one was left wondering what abrupt decision had sponsored this little gesture—an irrational gesture because the room faces south and, in addition to this, outside there is a street light which, for most people, makes the shades absolutely indispensable at night.

And, THEN, on the Wednesday morning, with the phone ringing, I go to the front bedroom, I pick it up, there is complete silence, and WHAT do I discover. I DISCOVER THAT THE CORD HAS BEEN RIPPED OUT ITS SOCKET!!! ???

So I spent the last three days—and today—attempting to restore a little order and a degree of cleanliness. I took the huge 4' pile of newspapers downstairs; I took seventeen (17) sheets and God knows how many towels to the laundry; I laid out X.'s clothes and other belongings (WHAT are they doing here anyway?); I put the books back into the small bedroom (no small job); and, today, I involved myself with the kitchen and the refrigerator.

First of all, pots, pans, plates and everything to be washed; and, then, the refrigerator washed and cleared of decaying food. And then, there was the problem of the ants. The cupboard second left from the sink was swarming with them and had to be completely emptied and washed.

So, last night, I took down eight bags of garbage; and, as a result my general irritation has become increased. Just WHY are you guys so PIG-LIKE, so PEASANT (but good peasants would never behave like this so ABOMINABLE? Or is it, SIMPLY, that you are REGRETTABLY childish and naïve?)

I shall have to take down at least another twelve bags of garbage next Friday night; and this leaves me wondering JUST why do I have to clean up after YOU—having received, as yet, not a trace of a small and generous rent?

I am rather more sad than mad about all this.

---

1 This memorandum was addressed to two Cornell graduate students who rented Rowe's house at 19 Renwick Place in 1988. Rowe taught in Rome from January to June 1988. See Rowe's letter to "X." dated 24 August 1988 (p 298 in this volume).
2 *épater le bourgeois*, French: to shock the middle classes (a rallying cry of the late nineteenth-century French Decadent poets).

158 *To **Dorothy Rowe**, St. Margaret's Road, Oxford*   *1988 August 12*

19 Renwick Place, Ithaca, New York

Dearest Dorothy:

Finally I have come to understand why, in the nineteenth century, one went to spend the summer (if one could afford it) at a German spa, surrounded by good German forests. Of course, I had already had intimations of this taste in '79 when, after spending four broiling days by myself in Parma, I changed trains in Milano and, en route to staying with Franz and Monika Oswald* in Bern, I spent a night in Brigue where the air was exquisite. But, if Rome wasn't exactly cool before I left, then, ever since I got back here twenty-five days ago, the heat and the humidity have been completely intolerable. There's been occasional rain; but it hasn't really helped; and I—who like heat—have become so prostrated by it all that I think that I shall either fly to Alaska (to do what?) or buy an air conditioner which I suppose, will be the cheaper and more intelligent alternative.

As it is, at the moment, I am apt to take refuge in an air conditioned car and just drive around to cool off. So what am I doing with an air conditioned car? Well, one afternoon rather more than three weeks ago, I lent my own V.W. to Matt who got sideswiped by an idiot who wasn't looking where he was going.[1] So it was totally the fault of the idiot and his insurance is going to pay for all repairs. Meanwhile, I drive around in a grotesque rental car, a Ford with automatic shift (which I hate and despise); and, as a result, I don't know which is worse, enduring the heat or enduring the automatic shift.

It's a terrible car, with bells that ring and seat belts which envelop you automatically. So it's not only the absence of gears; but I believe that I'll get my own car back before you receive this letter.

At this stage I broke off and went out to drive around a bit so as to cool down; but, when I returned with a copy of *The New York Times*, the air was just as baleful; and this house, although it's an oven is still cooler than the great outdoors.

Well, all this is to tell you that, having contemplated the immediate future scenario as envisaged by *The Times*, I am as of right now, become an ecological partisan. Up in Civita di Bagnoregio five weeks ago, I thought that Astra was being hysterical when she was talking about the greenhouse warming effect; but I can imagine her hysteria if she had been here over the last twenty-five days. In all the meteorological records of this town, going back 150 years, apparently there hasn't been a summer like it; and I realize that myself hasn't been cool since I came back from Civita and had lunch at a little *ristorante* overlooking the Lago di Vico. It was called "La Bella Venere" and it was backed up by all those beautiful forests.[2]

But, you see, it must be a matter of forests, and forests, and forests. Acid rain, coming from the U.S. is destroying forests in Canada. Acid rain, coming from France and England is destroying forests in Germany. The forests of Tennessee, Alabama, the Carolinas, etc. are said to be wilting. And, as one reads, the worst offender must be Brazil; and, for instance, do you know that, over the last five years in the Amazonian jungle, an area the size of New York State has been stripped of trees by felling and burning and that the fumes from all this (like the fumes from the explosion of Krakatoa—only more so) have radically affected climate in places so far away as the South Pole and Chicago?

So, maybe, I am becoming messianic, which I don't think is my temperament; but, all the same, I am convinced that some great climatological catastrophe is about to impend. The absurd Wojtila, the Polish pretender, condemns contraception; and the population, therefore increases just as catastrophe threatens.[3] But, as the polar ice caps melt, there are worse things to be anticipated. The levels of the ocean will rise and you know all the rest of that story.

But there is more to this apocalyptic of *The New York Times* than simply the flooding in New York, New Orleans, Amsterdam, Hamburg, London, there is also the story of A New Ice Age which can happen very quick—and this is likely to destroy everything in which, during my life, I have taken pleasure and delight.

Apparently, the last Ice Age, which was an imponderable horror, descended within twenty years following a general heating up; and The New Ice Age is to be expected about the year 2000. Apparently, it's going to descend on northern Europe and northern America, with huge glaciers and all those dreadful things; and everything is going to be obliterated. I don't know; but, being a survivor, I am thrown into a condition of consternation and concern.

But I can believe this happening, with the inept floods of refugees coming down to Italy from Sweden and Germany and England. And what are we to do with them?

Get a good house, protect it with guns, and just hope to continue is what I think; but I don't think that the collection of *trulli* in Puglia (I have a dazzling collection outside of Martina Franca) might be the most perfect solution.[4] All the same, as they did before, I think that the Alps will block the glaciers.

Perhaps I am thinking in terms of too great a calamity; and, in any case, we will mostly be dead. But, for your entertainment I enclose a few clippings from today's *New York Times*.[5]

"Pollution, Waste, Toxins" and "It's a Jungle Out There" correspond to my present state of mind; "Harbingers of Gloom" might amuse James, because it describes exactly the role which he wishes to avoid and the affair of the McMillan shares might interest David.

You know that it's exactly thirty-five years ago that Macmillans, London sold McMillans, New York. This was to pay for Harold's political career.[6] But I think that they sold it cheap with no conception that it could become so valuable—like, nowadays, someone offering $1.1 billion for just a part of the company!

So it was Ian Mckenzie who went to work in N.Y. for the new version of McM's which they called St. Martin's Press. But just think about this: the Macmillan folly and Ian and Elma Mckenzie from Edinburgh whom I haven't seen for years.

Lots of best, best love,

> *Colin*

But you must know that something like this terrible weather is predicted to continue through to the end of September and that, therefore, I must get two air conditioners—one for upstairs and one for downstairs. I don't see any other way.

P.S. My sluggish air conditioned automatic has been wished upon me by the other guy's insurance company who are paying for this combination of torture and relief.

I enclose another clipping for you. It displays Barbra Jakobsen's latest adventure.[7] Isn't it quite a bit awful?

> *C.*

---

1 "V.W.": Volkswagen automobile.
2 *La Bella Venere,* Italian: The Fair Venus.
3 Karol Józef Wojtyła (1920–2005), Pope John Paul II.
4 *trulli*: dwellings of boulders with conical or domed roofs, indigenous to southern Puglia.
5 The four clippings from *The New York Times*, 13 August 1988: Reuters, "Ipanema is Lovely No More"; "It's a Jungle Out There"; Russell Baker, "Observer; Harbingers of Gloom"; and Geraldine Fabrikant, "Maxwell Adds a Twist to Offer for Macmillan".
6 Maurice Harold Macmillan (1894–1986), British Prime Minister from 1957 to October 1963, the son and grandson of the founders of MacMillan Publishers of the United Kingdom and, in 1952, of St Martin's, New York City.
7 Vogle, Carol, "Design: Period Pieces", *The New York Times*, 14 August 1988.

159 *To X.*   *24 August 1988*

19 Renwick Place, Ithaca, N.Y.

Dear X.:

I received your letter of 8/12/88 with amazement and amusement. I am particularly surprised that you should intimate your supposition (?) that my reactions represent my guilt at not returning for your review.

No, far from it. My reactions are to the conditions of the house when I arrived; and I append a list of 'things' discovered when I arrived.[1]

These are, altogether, some twenty-five 'acts of omission'. My awareness of them was successive; and, as I hope that you will be able to notice, my increasing awareness of negligence is associated with increasing irritation.

The rent which I proposed was exceptionally generous. In fact, it was less than I pay for the mortgage of this place. So heating expenses were high; but it was still far less than you and Y. would have been obliged to pay for a deplorable place in Collegetown.

No, in these matters, details of money do not concern me; and I am much more concerned that 'my' graduate students should live in 'suggestive' places with appropriate circumspection.

However, all my hopes you and Y. violated. Obviously you abominated/patronized the house. It was a *retardataire* joke; and, so far as I can see, in this way you treated it.[2] I offered you, I gave you, an instructive womb; but all I gave merely provoked hostility. And that is the general story, interpretation, of what I found.

I have just paid:

$126.00 for cleaning (the place was filthy)

$30.00 for garbage clearance; and I am about to pay $156.00 for window cleaning.

But why should I have to suffer all this nonsense? And why should I pick up all the tabs?

Simply, all this I don't see, although you may.

Anyway, I just append a list of the horrors which I found in the house. (see over)

Best of best wishes,

    C.R.

    Colin Rowe

A list of 'things' discovered:

*A pile of newspapers four feet high. But why? Is it not obvious that someone has to get these down into the basement: and why did I have to do this?
*Two cans of Piel's beer inserted as ornaments of the fireplace. But did you not apprehend that these would piss me off?
*Ashtrays with an accumulation of cigarette ends?
*A green Thai silk cushion recklessly, (?) destroyed.
*An 'important' chaise longue, part of its frame smashed and its green velvet mattress bursting at the seams.
*Plants evidently not watered.
*A collection of Y.'s papers littering the library.
*Smoky discoloration of mantelpiece and no attempt to do a repaint job.
*A dirty refrigerator equipped with rotting food.
*An oven filthy inside.
*Greasy dishes in the drainer. Why not clean dishes put away?
*Ants in the cupboards. They all had to be emptied and sprayed.
*One of the fluorescent tubes in the kitchen not working.
*None of the lights in the entrance passageway working.

And this is so much for the living room floor; but, now,

*Some filthy goo on the staircase; and I cannot imagine what it is.
*In the bathroom the fluorescent tube flickering, the other light not working,

simulated (Corian) marble peeling off the wall, general decay of plaster.

*In the bedroom which Y. selected to use: his sheets on an unmade bed, his clothes strewn all over the floor and distributed throughout the bookshelves, and the shades—removed from the window—awaiting rediscovery.

*In the front bedroom the telephone disconnected from its jack. But why did I have to pay for its reinstallation?

*Further in the front bedroom: a pile up of books from Y.'s room which has taken an immensely long time to sort out and to restore their positions.

*In the back bedroom: not much, except that condition of the shaving mirror in there belied any stories of attempted cleaning. It had about a sixteenth of an inch of dust upon it. And, now, to go outside:

*It was apparent that X. and Y. had recently mowed the grass and, probably, weeded the terrace; but there didn't seem to be much more evidence of concern and conservation:

*for instance, the rear terrace littered with cigarette butts;

*the trees along the driveway not clipped back;

*and the condition of the steps and outside lights. So the steps were never good; but, now, they are downright dangerous and what to do about the outside light at the bottom of the steps, as yet, I don't quite know.

*Then, in the basement, the accumulation of garbage was something frightful; and, even after Y. removed things, I still had to pay $30.00 to get the garbage men to take it away.

But was it, really, necessary that I should have had to face any of these problems. The rent was generous; and I had assumed—foolishly trustingly, it seems—that you two guys would be responsible.

    C.R.

---

1 Rowe had rented his house to "X." and another Cornell graduate student, "Y.", earlier in 1988, and was unhappy with the condition in which it was left. See his memo of August 1988 (p 295 in this volume). The initials, "X." and "Y.", are fabricated for the purpose of this publication and not those of the actual tenants.
2 *retardataire*, French: latecomer.

160 *To **Dorothy Rowe**, St. Margaret's Road, Oxford*   *7 September 1988*

19 Renwick Place, Ithaca, N.Y.

Dearest Dorothy:

    I now believe that the Notre Dame proposition is getting along very well. Genuinely they are interested and inclining to my program. So the *appartamento* in Via Teatro Valle is, perhaps, not all that remote.

Problem is: whether it's January next year or September; and, about this, I await info.

Of course, I would prefer January. [...]

Meanwhile, in the story of Firenze, there is a house which Joel Bostick wishes me to consider.[1] It is in Bellosguardo with a panoramic view of the city. It is very small and has no more land attached to it than its terrace. On two floors, there are two rooms five meters square, plus kitchen and bath; but below this is the *cantina*.[2] It includes the garage and extends underneath the terrace; but Joel is of the opinion that it might be excavated/manipulated to produce a little *cortile* and a library.[3] Repeat: the whole scene is very small—not much more than a cottage with very tall rooms and a terrace; but I think that it might be a spectacular acquisition; and, in any case, I imagine that it could always be rented at profit.

The owner is Swiss, from Lausanne; and, returning to Lausanne, she only wishes to dispose of it (according to Joel) to some 'appropriate' person who would just love the house.

So I am thinking of going over in a few weeks time to check all this stuff out. You see, after the apartment in Via Teatro Valle, this might be a logical and charming, retreat. Also, it has the merit of offering only one guest bedroom. Other guests would just have to stay at the Pensione Annalena down the hill.[4]

You see I have just acquired a new typewriter ribbon—and about time too! This is to assist me in typing up that little lec which I gave in Rome in April and at Harvard in December; and you see, in a crazy way, Lotus International in Milano is just frantic to publish it.[5] BUT EVIDENTLY SOMETHING HAS GONE WRONG WITH THE NEW RIBBON!

      LOVE, LOVE,   *Colin!*

P.S. The typewriter seems to have recovered; but the only thing else that I want to tell you is that I have a new student who comes from Nicosia, Cyprus. He's a nice guy and his name is Socrates![6] Rather alarming; or don't you think? But even more intimidating when I learn that his grandfather was called Aristotle and that he has an Uncle Plato. Pity that they have the chronology reversed; but he must get rather bored when people constantly say to him something like this: "Hey Socrates, try a little hemlock. It's extra *strong* today!"

   Colin

---

1 Joel Bostick (1947–2004), former student of Rowe's (MArch, Cornell University, 1974), who was teaching at Syracuse University in Florence at the time.
2 *cantina*, Italian: basement.
3 *cortile*, Italian: courtyard.
4 On the Pensione Annalena, see Rowe, Colin, "Two Italian Encounters", *As I Was Saying: Recollections and Miscellaneous Essays*, Alexander Caragonne ed, 3 vols, Cambridge, MA: MIT Press, 1996, vol 1, pp 3–10.
5 "Ideas, Talent, Poetics: A Problem of Manifesto", given as the annual Walter Gropius Lecture at Harvard University in December 1987; published in *Lotus international* 62, 1989; and reprinted with a 1994 postscript in Rowe, Colin, *As I Was Saying: Recollections and Miscellaneous Essays*, Alexander Caragonne ed, 3 vols, Cambridge, MA: MIT Press, 1996, vol 3, pp 277–354.
6 Socrates Stratis.

To **Cornell Curriculum Committee**   *3 October 1988*   **161**

Cornell University, School of Architecture, Sibley Hall, Ithaca, N.Y.

MEMORANDUM
TO: The Curriculum Committee
FROM: Colin Rowe

As meetings often do, the meeting of the Curriculum Committee the other week left me stricken with concern; and I allude to the topic of 'History, Theory and Criticism'.

Simply, I find this painfully pretentious. It is about on a level with the proposition that Cornell should go into business to train potential teachers of architecture how to teach—a fantasy, I think of Jerry's based upon further fantasy, <u>his</u> evaluation of the Urban Design Studio over the last so many years.[1]

But, surely, there are <u>certain</u> topics which can, in <u>no</u> way, be institutionalized.

So anti-intellectual and philistine, no doubt, my position will appear; but I shall proceed to enlarge upon it.

The existing curriculum, drawn up before I came to Cornell, is something of a tribute to the cultural ingenuousness of its author, Tom Canfield; and I have always deplored and lamented its deficiencies.[2] I believe that it articulated three areas of concern: structure, technology, and history (but correct me if I am wrong); and I further believe that, with the student subjected to a bombardment of lectures in these three areas, it was supposed that 'good' design would, necessarily ensue.

But <u>such</u> a <u>regime</u> I can only believe to be <u>intolerably</u> cruel to the student—and, also, to the historian.

In the bombardment of messages, so far as I have been able to see, it appears to have been anticipated that structure and technology would provide the basic equipment of 'facts', and that 'history' would provide the necessary cultural 'catch-all'.

But <u>nothing</u> could have been more wrong and demeaning to the historian and the student. There was no 'how to do it' scene in which the student was to be equipped. Supposedly, all of this was to be taken up over the board and in the studio. Simply there was to be a <u>congestion</u> of detail; and, out of this, there was to follow an <u>inflammation</u> of capacity.

That, out of such a structure of lectures, <u>anything</u> good might have ensued, says much for the intelligence and the vivacity of the Cornell architectural community— both faculty and students, who, without addressing the <u>highly</u> obvious questions to this <u>regime</u>, have tolerated its intrinsic absurdities and suffered its, entirely, monstrous distortions of common sense.

So, today, when I hear about <u>additions</u> to the curriculum—'History, Theory and Criticism'—I find myself reduced to a trembling jelly. <u>No</u> thought about revising the curriculum <u>itself</u>; but <u>every</u> thought about adding appendages to this <u>hopelessly</u> deficient central body.

Really, <u>do</u> we have to be <u>quite</u> so myopic? And, if we face it, are we not sufficiently intelligent to know better?

When I talk about Julien Guadet, *Elements et Theorie de la Architecture*,[3] I am talking, so I think, about something which only Lee understands; and I am talking about Guadet from a position of, original, hostility.[4] It is the cream of Beaux Arts doctrine; and years ago, at Liverpool, I can remember how violently Bob Maxwell,* Jim Stirling,* and myself objected to the Guadet message we were obliged to receive. These lectures, in the style of Guadet, were intolerable. They assumed 'eternal' principles; and they were a violation of historical sense.

We found them abominable.

So <u>what</u> was Guadet, super pontifical, all about?

As far as I remember, he told you all about beginnings, middles, and ends; about *portes cocheres*,[5] vestibules, incorporated vestibules, circulations, types of staircases, where to place them, the gradients of stairs, how to arrange an *enfilade*, and all the rest of the stuff which is now forgotten because it seemed assumed that, with the arrival of modern architecture (unlimited freedom?) all such issues would vanish away.[6]

However, this did not turn out to be the case; issues unrecognized simply become problems unsolved; and the results are only too evident in pretty nearly all recent buildings; absence of appropriate vestibules (think about the Johnson Museum!);[7] stairs scarcely to be negotiated; labyrinthine circulations (sometimes you are apt to feel that, somewhere, there must always be a minotaur); bathrooms not to be discovered (at the Hotel Schweizerhof in Berlin, the men's johns are down two flights of stairs from the entrance and, in order to find them, you have to ask); and, in short, there has occurred more or less a complete collapse of the capacity to produce a coherent plan.

Now, such might be the greatest indictment of the style of architectural education which has prevailed since the fifties; but it ought to be comparatively easy to remedy. F.L.W.,* Corbu,* Mies,* all derived from a background in which something like the 'doctrine' of Guadet was implicit; and they, then, proceeded to subtract from this doctrine.[8] But to subtract from a 'position' which permeates the exclusive values of Synthetic Cubism, Constructivism, De Stijl, a 'position' without furnishing further ideas as to the distribution of space and function...? Well, however self-conscious this 'position' may be (and, usually, it is not), probably this is to invite catastrophe.

So, no doubt, I have become over-excited (I often do); but, fundamentally, what I am appealing for is the establishment of a lecture course comparable to Guadet's which would be of equal status and prolongation to the courses in structure, technology and history. I do not suppose that Guadet is really 'theory'; but I do think that, if 'theory' is, really, to be considered that, first of all it should make a humble and pragmatic entrance and not be conceived as an exotic sauce for the entertainment of graduate students. I believe that, only after we have contracted to essentials, should we be willing to conceive the luxury of additions.

Of course, myself should be all in favor of 'theory' (which exists in opposition to 'history'); and, in a little lecture the other day, I quoted Erwin Panofsky on just this problem. Circa 1940 Panofsky wrote:

> The relation between the art historian and the art theorist may be compared to that of two neighbours who have the right of shooting over the same district while one of them owns the gun and the other all the ammunition. Both parties would be well advised if they recognized this condition of partnership. It has rightly been said that theory, if not received at the door of an empirical discipline, comes in through the chimney like a ghost and upsets the furniture. But it is no less true that history, if not received at the door of a theoretical discipline dealing with the same set of phenomena, creeps into the cellar like a horde of mice and undermines the groundwork.[9]

This quote is to me the best text (or pretext) upon which a course (or outfit) involved with the theory of architecture might rest itself; but it is, also, a council of perfection. The possibility of any elegant theory depends upon the ability to define; and, at this stage, one should be thinking about that throw-away remark of Nietzche's: "only that which is without history is capable of definition"[10]—a little *obiter dicta* which places 'theory' in an extremely precarious predicament.[11]

For one sees only too well what 'theory' would become. It would become a history of theories; and, right now, I can imagine it.

From antiquity there would be Aristotle's *Poetics,* Longinus *On the Sublime,* and Vitruvius. Then there would ensue a big gap (?). After which, there would follow: Alberti, Palladio,*

Perrault, Laugier, Lodoli, Milizia, Quatremere de Quincy, Cesar Daly, Viollet-le-Duc, Pugin, Ruskin, perhaps Paul Valery's *Eupalinos,* Semper, Von Hildebrand, Geoffrey Scott, and a bit more of late nineteenth century Vienna. Then, as we approach the present, there would follow observations rather more abstract; and, I suspect that, very suddenly, upon the scene there would be paraded: Wittgenstein, Levi-Strauss, Jurgen Habermas, Jacques Derrida, Peter Eisenman;* and, God knows, even me. (You see that, though I shouldn't say it, myself is the subject of a couple lectures at the University of Hamburg (?) and two more, this is *per annum,* at the Architectural Association).

Now I want to suggest that all this is pretentious, absurd, and detrimental to undergraduates, who have no idea of how to put a building together.

And this is my primary objection to history, theory and criticism.

If theory, real theory, is a precarious undertaking, then criticism has, lately, become absurdly intellectualized (*Vide* Peter Eisenman).[12]

And, almost certainly, this is my fault; and it is painful for me to say this. But, since I am a believer in rigorous analysis (of both architecture and academia), finally, the blame belongs to me. It was me who began all that nonsense; and why did I do it? Perhaps because of an infatuation with St. Thomas Aquinas (known from Jacques Maritain).[13] Perhaps because of Rudolf Wittkower* (for whom St. Thomas wouldn't have meant all that much). Perhaps, perhaps…?

But, anyway, there it is, and; after all this, what to say about 'criticism'?

Myself would say that there is casual, empirical criticism (which I have practised); and, then, there is great criticism (from which I have always been remote). So, I think that casual criticism has no particular standards; but great criticism, inevitably, has to involve something else. Great criticism, which can only very rarely be employed, must be related to notions of nature, history, scientific method, the legitimacy of government, etc.

But how are we, limited and ignorant as we are, to presume to teach all this? Or do we suppose criticism to be merely journalism and Paul Goldberger?[14]

I ask these questions because I am concerned with what, to me, appears to me to be over-ambition.

If we are to attempt to teach criticism (and I believe this to be impossible), I know that we have to spread our constituency very large in this university.

But, after all that, I don't know what we will have succeeded in doing? Or, rather, perhaps I do. We will have produced a tribe of horrid, snotty guys who, with no visual sense (and no understanding) will pronounce arcane 'judgment'.

But what a terrible denouement. Or don't you think?

P.S. I wrote this a week ago and I have been reluctant to send it on, but now, advice of Vincent, I do.[15]

Copy: Dean McMinn*

---

1 Jerry A Wells.*

2 Thomas H Canfield (1916–1993), professor of architecture, Cornell University from 1946 to 1976.

3 French architect and theorist Julien Guadet's (1834–1908). Guadet, Julien, *Eléments et théorie de l'architecture,* Paris: Librairie de la Construction moderne, 1910, became the standard history-theory text for architecture students in the years following his death.

4 Lee F Hodgden* (1925–2004), who taught architecture at Cornell University from 1961 to 1995.

5 *portes cochères*, French: a porch or portico-like structure at the entrance to a building through which a horse and carriage can pass.
6 *enfilade*, French: a suite of rooms formally aligned with one another.
7 Cornell University's Herbert F Johnson Museum of Art, Ithaca, New York, 1973, designed by IM Pei.
8 Frank Lloyd Wright* (1867–1959), Le Corbusier* (1887–1965), and Mies van der Rohe* (1886–1969): all renowned twentieth-century architects.
9 Erwin Panofsky (1892–1968), quote from "The History of Art as a Humanistic Discipline" (1939); republished in *Meaning in the Visual Arts: Papers in and on Art History*, New York: Anchor Books, 1955, pp 1–25 (quote on pp 21–22).
10 "Only something which has no history is capable of being defined", Nietzsche, Friedrich, *The Genealogy of Morals*, New York: Boni and Liveright, 1887, essay 2, sec 13.
11 *obiter dicta*, Latin: said in passing.
12 *Vide*, Latin: See, consult.
13 Jacques Maritain (1882–1973), French Catholic philosopher, author of more than 60 books.
14 Paul Goldberger (b 1950), architecture critic at *The New York Times*.
15 Vincent Mulcahy, associate professor of Architecture, Cornell University.

To **Thomas Muirhead**, *Upper Montagu Street, London*   *7 October 1988*   **162**

19 Renwick Place, Ithaca, NY

Dearest Tom:

Many thanks for your letter of September 17 which, I am horrified to say I only opened yesterday.

This is because I have been so busy—a retrospective memoir on Texas way back; trying to cope with *Lotus International* who want to publish my Harvard lecture of December 9 last year, but don't seem to understand that this must take time and will require illustrations; making lectures; paying bills; and God knows what all.[1]

But it was nice to have your, highly cathartic, letter; and, having opened it, I am stimulated to reply.

So my advice on Americano universities requires to be expanded.[2] You see, in a provincial way, I gave you simply East Coast advice. But, if we are to think about *Mittell Amerika*, then I also think that we should have our eyes on Notre Dame.

This is not a provincial institution, as Matt Bell* would tell you. It has had its scene in Via Monterone for something like fifteen years and it requires its students to do two years of theology, which renders them intellectually agile, casuistical and eclectic—as, for instance, Matt.

So, think about Notre Dame and address yourself there to Steven Hurtt,* who is an ex-student of mine and devoted to whatever it might be that we, jointly, might represent.[3]

Werner thinks highly of Notre Dame;[4] and, by the way, he is not the *Tedesco* monster of what seems to be your interpretation.[5] Not at all. Werner knows perfectly well how hostile am I to the traditional, Giedeonesque, Framptonesque, versions of mod. arch.;[6] and, therefore how hostile are my former students. But, nevertheless, he continues to buy my former students, I suppose not because he shares their convictions but, presumably, because he appreciates their vivacity.

So Werner is not the traditional Germanic horror of legend. Not really. And myself finds it rewarding to recognise that, while only one of my former students has been hired by Cornell during all the time since 1965 (this is Matt Bell, after a great deal of effort and pressure on my part) the situation at Syracuse is completely different; and, for a supply of teachers, Werner has been largely dependent upon my product.

True, Art and Joel were at Syracuse before Werner arrived there; but, as of now, among my most recent graduates, there are: Cheryll O'Neil,★ Pamela Butz, Richard Role, Robert Goodill;★ and, recently left, are Shin Onishi and Esteban Sennyey★ (he, for better or worse has been dragged by Annamaria to San Juan, P.R.); and, then, in receding but scarcely distant perspective: Ken Schwarz, Bruce Lonnman, the outstanding Blake Middleton,★ Jeff Nishi, and quite a few more whose names do not, immediately, come to mind.[7]

In other words, though it may not be 'liberal', Werner's judgment is, at least, 'catholic'; and, in all this, the loss to Cornell has been the gain to Syracuse. And, as things are, I think that even Matt, for all his ability, conscientiousness, and presence, is not appreciated here, accepted as my slightly *outré* and bizarre *protégé* (I hate all those French words, but they will keep croppin' up).[8] But, somehow, except in 1965 (Fred Koetter★ and Roger Sherwood who were both fired in '73) my own nominees have never been acceptable at Cornell; and, as for Matt, we will soon see how long, after I withdraw from this place, he will survive.

Now, dear Tom, as of now I, genuinely, don't know what I am going to be doing in the first part of next year; and I don't want to appear paranoid about this. There was an original 'agreement' with Bill McMinn,★ the Dean, that I was to spend future Spring Semesters at Palazzo Massimo; but this seems to have evaporated, or dissolved.[9] Less an act of bad faith, I think, than a failure of communication. So the Architecture Department here, for at least the next three years or so, seems to be resolved (through inertia?) to perpetuate its present, absurd, policy: faculty members, ignorant though they may be of Rome, will continue to go there for one semester; and, as you can see, they will scarcely be recovered from their 'culture shock' before the time comes for them to pack up and return to Ithaca, N.Y. So it—Palazzo Massimo—seems destined to be a case of the ignorant leading the blind. All very sad.

But, *vis a vis* Notre Dame, nothing has, as yet, occurred. And, of course, this is my preferred solution, the solution which keeps me in Rome. But, you know, apart from all my many friends (and we all love each other to extravagance), in that cold, outer world, I believe that there is great hostility to me; and, hence, I don't know whether I am not going to be compelled to accept Werner's Syracuse/Firenze offer.

This would take me to Firenze, I am led to suppose, at my present salary—say $68,000.00 and I really don't know what else. But, perhaps, add another Forty in terms of stray investments, etc. And this is, surely, good—if not very good. But, then, I don't, I don't, want to go to that *citta miserabile*.[10] I don't want to be condemned to drive around those horrible *viale* day after day.[11] The proximity of Via del Teatro Valle and Via Monterone is entirely perfect for me.[12] A walk of two hundred yards at the most—but this is perfect.

So, dear Tom, what am I going to do? Because, though I hope, I don't think that my spectrum of choice can exist for very much longer.

I can, certainly, come to Firenze as tolerably rich; and I can, perhaps, go to Rome as tolerably poor.

Meanwhile, little old you (by the way you are still too paranoid and thorny), should be thinking about Notre Dame—which, though it has become obscured, is the primary topic of this letter. Meaning that I rank Notre Dame very high.

Best, best regards,

    Colin

1 The "memoir on Texas way back" was published as "Texas and Mrs Harris" in Rowe, Colin, *As I Was Saying: Recollections and Miscellaneous Essays*, Alexander Caragonne ed, 3 vols, Cambridge, MA: MIT Press, 1996, vol 1, pp 25–40. In December 1987 Rowe gave the annual Walter Gropius Lecture at Harvard University, Ideas, Talent, Poetics: A Problem of Manifesto, which was subsequently published in *Lotus International* 62, 1989 and reprinted in Rowe, *As I Was Saying*, vol 2, pp 277–354.
2 Muirhead* knew Rowe from the Syracuse architecture program in Florence where he taught until he moved to London to work for James Stirling* in mid-1986. Rowe had previously advised him on teaching in the US.
3 Steven Hurtt* taught at Notre Dame from 1973 to 1990.
4 Werner Seligmann* (1930–1998) was, at the time, dean and professor of architecture at Syracuse.
5 *Tedesco*, Italian: German.
6 Sigfried Giedion (1888–1968) and Kenneth Frampton (b 1930), historians of Modern architecture.
7 Arthur McDonald* and Joel Bostick, professors of architecture at Syracuse.
8 *outré* and bizarre *protégé*, French and English: outraged and bizarre disciple.
9 Palazzo Massimo housed the Cornell Rome Architecture Program.
10 *città miserabile*, Italian: miserable city. Rowe is referring to Florence.
11 *viali*, Italian: avenues.
12 Where Rowe lived while teaching for Cornell in Rome.

To **Dorothy Rowe**, *St. Margaret's Road, Oxford*   *14 October 1988*   **163**

19 Renwick Place, Ithaca, N.Y.

Dearest Dorothy:

This is a very belated reply to your letter of September 13; but I have had so much to do—like a memo on Texas way back and a version of my Harvard lecture of last December for *Lotus International* who, prompted by Purini, seem to be very eager to publish but not quite willing to recognize how much work is involved.[1]

Now, about Simon, I don't know what to say beyond the obvious. I know that he's a charmboat and an angel; but, if he wants nothing any more to do with Eng. Lit. and history, and, as you say, "completely went off" architecture, then I think that you should <u>not</u> persuade him to take up history of art.

I know that you and David have frequently seen in Simon the latent connoisseur; and this is a fantasy which I appreciate. But connoisseurship, which is an aspect of the history of art, also requires great knowledge of political and intellectual history; and, if Simon is simply not interested in history, then—*ipso facto*—his pursuit of the history of art IS LIKELY TO BE IN VAIN.[2]

I say this with regret because I tend to imagine that Simon has a good eye. He derives that from David and myself who, probably, derive it from our completely un-instructed grandmother Beaumont. But I, also, suspect that his linguistic ability is considerable; and, as does James, he derives that from you. But, if Eng Lit. is to be a closed topic, then <u>how</u> is he to proceed?

Really, I am beginning to think that English education must, lately, have become terribly bad, unimaginative, neglectful. Because I cannot conceive how a boy as visually susceptible/excitable as Simon (and I have always been delighted by his visual acuity) could fail to be interested in the temporal <u>provenance</u> of the objects which he finds stimulating. Gibbon speaks of the absence, in the Oxford of his day, of "skillful and vigilant professors"; and I am dreadfully afraid that, at Canterbury, Simon can have found <u>very</u> few of these.[3]

Also, what about German? And this is the Freiburg-im-Breisgau motif yet again. How myself ever crept into the Warburg Institute I will never know. Perhaps because my German accent is said to be so good—this on so many of my recent visits to Berlin—they just <u>assumed</u> a knowledge. But the knowledge is nil; and I have always found this lack to be deplorable. Because, without German, in art historical terms, I am a provincial.

So, Dorothy, while I know that you prefer that members of our family should remain attached to the New York-London-Paris-Rome cultural axis I think that this is slightly myopic; and, hence, my repetition of Freiburg-im-Breisgau (but it could be Munich/Vienna, and Salzburg would be supremely O.K.).

But what is all this going to do for Simon, <u>if he proposes to study history of art; but, at the same time, professes to have no interest in history, political and intellectual?</u>

And I confess that I am at a loss to know.

If Simon were to get a good degree at one of those new, and minor, English universities, the mere existence of which (without adequate libraries) slightly frightens me, then I guess that, for graduate work, he could go on to the Courtauld, which is perhaps less of a high *bourgeois* finishing school than it was in my day.[4] But these would be the basic credentials; and no doubt, then, if you were to know the appropriate people in the Bond Street establishment, there would be an equally appropriate position available.

But, personally, I am entirely convinced that histrionic Simon is, also, intellectually brilliant; and, as a consequence, I scream and yell. But it is just possible that language courses in Paris, Firenze, and (as I would hope) in Salzburg will, as they say, <u>shape him up</u>.

Otherwise, <u>whaddya goin' to do?</u>

Send him to Australia, Canada, New Zealand, Texas—the invariable late nineteenth century solutions? "Take up the white man's burden, Send out the best you breed, Go send your sons to exile, To feed your captive's need." This was Rudyard Kipling in Vermont to Teddy Roosevelt in New York.[5] But it isn't any longer, an available exit. Is it now? And, therefore, what to do for dearest Simon?

I <u>would</u> say: <u>don't pressure him</u>; and, by all means, send him to language schools in France, Italy <u>and</u> the Germanic lands. And, after that wide, wise, and generous exposure, it is just possible that he may discover that, after all, he is much more interested in history than he, at present, supposes.

Of course, he may <u>not</u>. Ten months in Rome don't seem to have sponsored much knowledge of Italian history in James; but, then Simon is a different product—more susceptible, I suspect, to *genius loci*.[6]

But don't push and scream; because, that way, won't work.

Maybe Simon <u>does</u> want to become an art historian; but your letter gives me no indication of any inclination or propensity. And, as a consequence, I am left wondering what he really <u>should</u> be doing.

Of course, I immensely love him as he is, just now—but development can scarcely be arrested to secure a perpetual adolescence. And, therefore, I <u>am</u> concerned.

Should it be law school which I think, perhaps, it should? Or should it be art history—and a grand auctioneer at Sotheby's (and this Simon would do superbly well—but, this, after a <u>lotta work</u>).

As I see it an antique shop would be far too 'low' for Simon; and, being curator of an important museum might be far too 'high'.

Anyway, these are my reactions to your letter.

Best of Love,

Colin

P.S. From all this you must see that, very shortly, I am going to have to make a quite different will. You see I have become terribly disappointed. My library is a tolerably important instrument; and James, in '84, spent ten days in this house without ever opening a book—not even a picture book—of which, here, there are so many. So I had to read to him every night the sort of things which I thought that he would enjoy; and, now that Simon has, allegedly, no interest in architecture, history and Eng Lit., the whole purpose of my intended bequest becomes baffled and obstructed.

In other words, as I now know, for the library (which is very valuable) and for its location and appurtenances, I am going to have to find another destination. And this is going to reduce legacies to J. and S., though, God knows, they will be sufficient enough. But I am obliged, as I see it, to encourage and to protect the life of the lib; and, no longer can I see this as being an affair of *la famiglia*.[7] But, if Judy told me all this long ago, I am now extremely aware that the library and related *objets*, have to have their independence and their endowments.

Dearest Dorothy, I derive this new policy, on my part, from you. In Rome you told me that it was very wrong of me to propose such large distributions to J. and S. You intimated that this was likely to produce irresponsibility; and you said that you would never do anything of that kind. Instead you said that you would be leaving all of your money to your Edinburgh niece; and, at the same time, you suggested that I should be thinking in some comparable way.

Well, reluctant though I may have been to accept this argument, I have begun to perceive that you were, probably, right; and, as a consequence I must begin to discover other destinations for bequests.[8]

For instance, an endowment to Cornell for a scholarship, fellowship, lecture series? To be called The Colin Rowe So and So? Possible; but I doubt Cornell's judgment in interpreting an endowment of this kind. Something for the American Academy in Rome, the proceeds to be spent exclusively on books about architecture? Liverpool? I scarcely think so. Cambridge? Never. The Warburg Institute? Don't be silly. The Graham Foundation in Chicago? Interesting; but too rich already. And, then, over the last few years The Paralyzed Veterans of America has, for obvious reasons, been my preferred charity. But I suppose them to be a horrible group—populist and hostile (see the enclosure). However, all the same, they have had a terrible raw deal; and, in terms of simple mercy, they do require support.

None of this, of course, solves the problem of the destination of the library, which I know that it would be wrong to disperse; which is too small to be an institutional gift; and which is, still, too elaborate not to be considered as a problem. So, about this, I must now begin to think.[9]

Lots of Love,

Colin

---

1 See 7 October 1988 letter to Thomas Muirhead,* (p 305 in this volume); Franco Purini (b 1941), Italian architect.

2   This sentence was handwritten by Rowe in capital letters.
3   The King's School, Canterbury, an independent, co-educational secondary school.
4   Courtauld Institute of Art, London.
5   From Kipling, Rudyard, "The White Man's Burden", *The Times*, London 1899, written in response to the American occupation of the Philippines after the Spanish-American War.
6   *genius loci*, Latin: distinctive atmosphere or pervading spirit of the place.
7   *la famiglia*, Italian: the family.
8   On 13 August 1987, Rowe wrote to his brother David: "The present [will] is 'family' oriented—J. and S.; but it now seems to be that I shall be able to make ample accommodations for J. and S. [...] and, after that to proceed to completely fascinating fantasies of my own invention [...] This is the first time that I have ever felt that I have any money whatsoever. But you get the pic? There will be no indiscretion; but, from now onwards, there may be the idea of a mini foundation".
9   The complete Rowe Library is housed currently at The Charles Moore Foundation in Austin, Texas.

164   *To **John Miller** & **Su Rogers**, Regent's Park Road, London*   *8 November 1988*

19 Renwick Place, Ithaca, N.Y.

Dearest John and Susan:

It seems that I shall be <u>finally</u> leaving this place at the end of this year; and, on the whole, I am immensely relieved, because there hasn't been all that much extremely gratifying here since Fred Koetter⋆ was fired by Ungers⋆ and since Mike Dennis⋆ left for Harvard in '80.[1]

On the other hand, since Mike left, I haven't spent all that much time here. '80–'81 I was in Rome, Spring '84 I was in Virginia, Spring '86 I was in Firenze, also Spring '87; and, this year, I was in Rome again from the beginning of January until the end of July. But, still and <u>all the same</u>, in spite of other little trips I <u>really</u> have spent <u>far</u> too much time—with a faculty which is now <u>incomparably</u> dreary.

So now I am planning, in just a few weeks time, to remove myself to Wopland, either Firenze or Roma I am not quite sure which. Notre Dame would like me to go to Rome as 'scholar in residence'; and Syracuse would like me to go to Firenze in an equivalent role. So, while these options are not exactly an *embarras de richesses*, they are still, both of them, pleasing.[2] I don't like Florence; but I suppose that my aversion to that *citta miserabile* might be conquered;[3] and Florence, apart from the horrors of driving around those wretched *viale*, though it would produce more money, would mean more work.[4] Also, where to live, I wouldn't know, though I imagine this problem might be soluble. But I hate that dreadful Piazza, I hate the Ponte Vecchio, I hate those long, sleazy, tedious, gridded streets. Seen from Fiesole, or Bellosguardo, or the Piazzale it's all sublime; but, nowadays, from any of these places, you can't get into the *centro*—with a *macchina*.[5] So what to do?

My accountant tells me that, what with this and that and the offer from Syracuse, I could go to Firenze with an income of rather more than $100,000.00; and, in Rome, I don't believe that my income could be more than $80,000.00. On the other hand, I know that I would find Rome both more stimulating and more relaxed. Firenze is now an automobile city; and Rome is, still, a charming, walkabout, collection of villages. Anyway, I have until Friday this week, three days, to make up my mind about this.

Dearest John and Susan, as you must perceive, this letter is an incredible self indulgence; and, partly, I have been writing to clarify my own intentions.

You will say: why not Provence? Why not London/Bath? But in Provence, after Italy, I always feel that I am a leftover member of a crude football team. And London/Bath? My income there would be more diminished. In London/Bath I would have very little more than $65,000.00; and, so far as I can see, a pauper in S.W.3, S.W.7, Cadoganland, and all those other dreadful places now subject to American and Iranian takeover.[6] (But isn't Pont Street, just now, a little Teheran in exile? The Iranian females arrive here—their parents in Cadogan Gardens—and they are like wonderful greyhounds; but whaddya do with them? They are immensely over-bred and *racees*).[7]

So, indisputably, illustrious *chiquitas* of the Iranian type which I know, are going to be taken for a ride in the U.S. of A.[8] Much better for them: London, Paris, even Rome; but this letter is getting to be too long; and it must now converge upon two separate messages:

Once I am established in Italia I want you to come pay a visit. But why not? If I accept Rome it could be quick; if I accept Florence it will be longer. But this is the general invitation for something which would give me immense pleasure.

That mechanical *chaise longue* which you have had for years and years I would like it to be sent to the Rowe outfit in Oxford to be later shipped with other things.[9] So try to send it to Oxford, after which it can be sent to Roma/Firenze with the rest.

I hope that you enjoy the idea of coming to me in Italia. There are, still, the most ravishing drives and the most ravishing places to see; and everything we'll go look at will be exceptional.

Best of love,

    Colin

P.S. November 9. The plot thickens; and playing roulette with academic institutions becomes increasingly amusing. Suddenly, Cornell cannot bear to be outdone by Syracuse and Notre Dame. It would be too scandalous; and so, today, I am offered the same terms by Cornell, in Rome (with much less work—only one lecture a week), as I am offered by Syracuse in Florence.

But, though this is grotesque, it's not entirely baffling. No offer until you give notice that you are about to quit; and, then, this sudden abundance. In a mild way it leaves me feeling like a highly sought after professional football player; and, at this very late stage, it is the first time in my life that I have ever felt particularly wanted. Bizarre, is it not?

All the same I am not exuberant about any of this. With $105,000.00 or so in Rome I don't see myself very much above the level of penury; but this may depend upon the apartment. Meanwhile, today, I gave an entirely brilliant lecture (possibly my last lec in this awful place?). It meant a lot of work; but it was delivered *ad hoc*/ impromptu, casual, serious/frivolous. In other words it was a throw-away, self-consciously English amateur. But I like talking to audiences this way—in which any trace of effort is concealed. Also, in the end, I received student applause which has equipped me with a continuing glow of satisfaction.

Dearest John and Susan, fundamentally I am a disgusting, horrid, theatrical monster; and, if you won't come to Italy to see me, I shall well understand.

    Colin

1 OM Ungers* (1926–2007), German architect and theorist; chair of the Cornell School of Architecture from 1969 to 1975.
2 *embarras de richesses,* French: embarrassing surplus of riches.
3 *citta miserabile,* Italian: miserable city.

4   *viale,* Italian: avenues.
5   *centro,* Italian: center of city; *macchina,* Italian: automobile.
6   The Cadogan Gardens neighborhood of London.
7   *racée,* French: distinguished, classy.
8   *chiquitas,* Spanish: young women.
9   "The Rowe outfit in Oxford": David* and Dorothy Rowe's* house, St Margaret's Road, Oxford.

165   *To **Dorothy & David Rowe**, St. Margaret's Road, Oxford*   *11 November 1988*

19 Renwick Place, Ithaca, N.Y.

Dearest Dorothy-David:

It appears that Cornell cannot <u>bear</u> to be upstaged by either Syracuse or Notre Dame; and so what I <u>never</u> expected to happen <u>did</u> happen yesterday. I was offered a four to five year contract as 'scholar in residence' at the program in Rome, one lecture a week to give, the rest of the time to be devoted to 'literary' production.

So I rang up Werner Seligmann* about it; and I was surprised to discover that Werner had known about all this a day before I did. The reason being that Werner had divulged the Syracuse offer to me to Cornell; and had told them that they should act quickly if they wanted to grab me. Werner said, to me, that he knew that I preferred Rome and he knew that I would be happier there; and that, although the Firenze/Syracuse offer still stood, he was aware that I would, now, probably turn it down.

In other words, Werner's intervention was crucial to Cornell's action; and, as I see it now, this is why the Cornell offer is so closely based on that of Syracuse. It's not financially superior; but it means infinitely less extraneous work.

Now what Cornell offers, as <u>does</u> Syracuse, as <u>will</u> Notre Dame (?) is a basic $40,000.00 for part time 'work' between now and 1993; and <u>what</u> am I to do about this?

Taken <u>in the abstract</u>, it's penury; but, taken with a concern for detail it might be a modest opulence.

For instance, retiring from Cornell, I understand that there are 'fringe benefits' which, in no way, can be alienated; and, without success, for the last three weeks I have been trying to find out <u>what</u> these are.

So, with repeated efforts, I haven't been able to get too far with a turgid and recalcitrant bureaucracy, both here and in New York. They tell me that they'll reply and they don't; I ring up and they apologise; and so it goes on.

November 14

All this means that, apart from the basic <u>Forty</u>, I don't know very much—for certain; and I can only suspect. The 'fringe benefits' from Cornell, which I learn <u>absolutely</u> belong to me, derive from a capital of $283,000.00; and, in no way, I believe, can I get at the capital. What a bore! Because, during the course of twenty-six years, I think that even myself could have done better than this which, at ten per cent (perhaps more), promises, approximately, another <u>Thirty</u>; and this is shockingly little.

But, then, apart from this, there is probably about another <u>Twenty</u> to <u>Twenty-Five</u> (this is tax free income from municipal bonds at ten per cent; and I must consult my accountant about this); and then there are Royalties.

Therefore, all this seems to mean that, in Rome or Firenze, I should have an income, for a few years, of rather more than One Hundred; and I am excluding from this calculation what I might get from the sale of this house. But the house next door sold for One Hundred and Eighty last year. Not much; but, dear David, as you were able to see the other day, the Ithaca market is suddenly escalating.

So, what about an income of $100,000.00 in Rome or, maybe, Firenze? Enough for abstemious, miserly, me to be able, at least, to get along. On the whole, I think so; because, in spite of my apparent extravagance I have always bought wisely; and everything which I have bought (I wish I had bought much more) has appreciated immensely. For instance, the two Rosa da Tivoli,[1] bought from Cornell at $6,000, in twelve years time (information from James deriving from information from Christie's) have escalated at least to $60,000.00 and, would sell for much more in Rome. *Per fabbricare una dimora signorile questi quadric sono indispensabile, a*nd so it goes.[2]

Therefore, I think that I shall be able to survive in the very simple style to which I am accustomed: but will One Hundred (allowing for rent, servant, and all that—to which I allow—for the servant—$10,000), enable me to make the further accumulations which are my habit? And I don't know.

But, if I can make the further accumulations from the projected *train de vie*, then I think about J. and S. whom I love, particularly S., to extravagance; and, meanwhile, I think of what I said to you, the other day, about the library.[3]

I shall be immensely happy to drive with Simon, and perhaps with Alessandra, in April or May, through the Marche; and we shall be able to look at places which Italians and 'mere' tourists never visit. So we shall be in the possession of enormously *recherché* information; and all this might make Simon a monstrous little shit for life.[4] However, since I perceive Simon as being resilient, I don't think so.

But this doesn't get me off the hook; and, as a result, I return to the library and what I perceive to be related to it.

In terms of the lib, I don't perceive James (I watched him in '84) as having the slightest interest in it. But, then, why should he? And, apropos of Simon I don't know. But the library, in a minor way, is Warburgian.[5] Apart from literature, it involves history of politics, history of ideas, history of objects; and, with the best will in the world, as yet, I don't see Simon as being so preoccupied.

November 20

Finally, I receive not very satisfactory info from the flaccid bureaucracy: my pension from Cornell will be rather more than $31,000.00 p.a.; but, then, we can escalate from this. For instance, in '88, retiring in the summer, I can count on an income of $55,000.00. This is from Cornell; but, then, there are the etceteras, which should produce $95—100—perhaps more.

So, since I assume accumulations, 1990 might be better; and, with accumulations, might produce as much as $120,000; and 1991 should be better still. Income for 1991 I would estimate at $140,000.00; and income for 1992 at something like $160,000.00.

However 1993 is the cut off date. In '93 the basic Forty Thousand will vanish; and myself will be returned to fundamentals. Of course, returned to fundamentals, I shall be able to acquire $6,000.00 p.a. from U.S. Social Security, into which I have paid since 1951. But, apart from this grotesque and odious little accruement, I suppose that I shall be, still, able to imagine an income of about $120,000.00.

With reasonable accumulations such as I <u>will</u> make between <u>now</u> and '93, my accountant tells me that this <u>can</u> be done. But, then, <u>why</u> attempt to do it?

Reason is that I am utterly obsessed/hysterical about J. and S. <u>and</u> the lib, which <u>cannot</u> be put together. No <u>these</u> are opposed agenda. In June, in Civita with Astra and Tony,[6] I realized how foolish I had been not to have bought the Vescovado—for $70,000.00.[7] I wouldn't, as Astra and Tony said, have noticed the money, and this little *palazzo*, with a chapel frescoed in the early 1520's, might have provided the O.K. setting for the little foundation which I imagine. It would be in collaboration with efforts of Astra and Tony; and, also, it would have produced an extravagant theater for great profit—profit both intellectual and financial.

So James, very well, saw all this. He very well saw what I had missed; and, as a result, in Civita a few months ago, I was left in my usual condition of wondering what to do. To buy a house next door to Astra and Tony for J. and S.? It's a very little house; but quite ravishing. And it's a disappointed woman from Oregon who, maybe, wants to sell it. But all this brings back the library <u>once again</u>; and, about this, I am no longer convinced by <u>anything</u>.

For, if the lib and other items, are to become a small foundation, with Judy, Steve Peterson,* Matt Bell,* perhaps Simon, among the trustees; then I don't see how I will <u>ever</u> acquire the money to bring this about.

So I am schizoid. There's J. and S. and <u>then</u> there is the lib; and I want to make appropriate gestures in both areas. But, for me, this is going to be a mess.

My money is American money; and my collections are American collections. Also, upon <u>your</u> advice, I am <u>now</u>, myself American. Therefore the destination of the library and related collections <u>must</u> be Americano. In terms of what might be my ethical consciousness, I can see no other way.

So <u>should</u> it be the American Academy, should it be Cornell (in Rome), should it be the illusory foundations, should it be Judy, should it be Matt, or should it be Astra?

Personally, I am inclined to suppose that either Astra or Matt could cope with the library; but I am not entirely convinced and I await your reactions.

Best love,

   Colin

P.S. The story is not quite so desperate; and, perhaps, there is rather more money attached to this than I have alleged. To begin with there is rather more than $60,000.00 in bank accounts. Shearson/American Express (this for covering my Am Ex, expenses without the dreariness of having to write them lots of checks) and Tompkins County. Then, there is rather more than $200,000.00 in tax free, 10% municipal bonds—Franklin, Dean Witter, Nuveen, Lord Abbett, Shearson—and this, I am entertained to tell you, I have been able to put together within the last six years. Then, there is life insurance (I don't know why) from the Prudential for, I believe, $280,000.00 assigned to James and Simon. However, this is costing far too much money; and I begin to think that I could do better by withdrawing from and putting the money myself into municipal bonds—which is where the Prudential has it any way—and do I really need their expensive mediation.

So, after adding in the conjectural value of this house and its contents—perhaps $450,000.00, <u>as of a year ago</u> this seems to result in an estate of $990,000.00. Or, alternatively, but I am skeptical about this, if we count in that other $280,000.00

from the American University system, an estate of $1,270,000.00, which is an idea by which simple minded me is quite naively excited.

So, then, there are the accumulations which will accrue in Italy. In '89 I shall be subject to American taxation. In '90 to no taxation whatsoever. Beginning '91 to Italian taxation. GET THE PIC.

Now, I think that you will both agree that giving half a million dollars each to J. and S. would, really, be serving their best interests; and this is what my present will would do. My new will is intended to be an interim affair based upon the value of the estate as of the end of this year.

But, in any case, J. and S. will be carefully—even lavishly—provided for; and this is one of the reasons—there are others—why I am compelled against my inclinations to stay here through December and into January.

Best, best love,

    Colin

---

1 Rosa da Tivoli (Philip Peter Roos; 1657–1706), German Baroque painter.
2 *Per fabbricare una dimora signorile questi quadri sono indispensabili,* Italian: to build a nice, high class home is essential.
3 *train de vie,* French: lifestyle.
4 *recherché,* French: uncommon, rare.
5 Reference to the Kulturwissenschaftliche Bibliothek Warburg, the famed private Library for Cultural Studies founded by Aby Warburg (1866–1929). In 1933 the library was moved to London and transformed into a cultural institution—the Warburg Institute—where Rowe studied with Rudolf Wittkower* in 1946–1947.
6 Astra Zarina* and Tony Heywood.*
7 Vescovado: the bishop's house at Civita.

To **Dorothy Rowe**, *St. Margaret's Road, Oxford*   *27 November 1988*   **166**

19 Renwick Place, Ithaca, N.Y.

Dearest Dorothy:

In your letter of November 18, which I received yesterday, I think that you have totally failed to understand the new direction of my ideas which, in any case, was instigated by you at that disastrous dinner on June 11, when James (so much resembling you that it was entirely charming) said: "Mom, I can't stand this any more" (myself had no idea what this was), got up, left the restaurant, and proceeded to storm away down the Via del Monserrato.

Dorothy, though not a diarist, I do make notes of scenes like these, and I made further notes of your misery (deriving from various causes) and of your determination to leave all your money to your niece. You had already said something like this to me, by the way, after I had given dinner to you and James at *La Costanza* and then, while James diverted himself with my students at Palazzo Massimo; you and I waited for him for forty five minutes at *Tre Scalini* in Piazza Navona. This was on May 10; but only gradually, imperceptibly, did your argument begin to inseminate my mind.

So I am responding to your arguments of May and your more vociferous arguments of June, when you told me that too much money was very bad for people. So, now, do you really want J. and S. at age twenty-five (supposing that I am dead by then—

not likely) to have unrestricted access to something like half a million dollars each? If I had called your attention, that evening of June 11 when you were so unhappy, to this circumstance of my will, you would have said: "Absolutely no way can this be."

But my own particular excoriation has followed more recently. It now appears that James displayed a propensity to tell his friends in my studio that he would never seriously have to work; and the story which I have received from these people (I couldn't help receiving it) is that, from his father and his uncle, he was going to receive so much money that he was assured for life!

To know all, of course, may be to forgive all; but, while I am perfectly willing to assume naivete and *romanza della famiglia*, I still find it very hard to conquer my dismay.[1] Simply *l'oncle d'Amerique* did not expect any such 'romantic' disclosures of his financial affairs—to his students.[2]

Dear, charming, exuberant, gregarious, easy, urbane, glib, fascinating James! I hope that, in three years time, he will begin to observe the dreariness of the career to which he has consigned himself; and then, if he begins to think about graduate work at MIT (because, if not Cambridge, England, then isn't Cambridge, Mass. the obvious place—for physics?),[3] then I shall be most happy to attempt to provide such *entrée* as I might and such support as I can.[4]

All the same, I don't have all that much optimism about James and MIT. In his position in three years time, I would both seek and look forward to the opportunity; but, in a breezy (and rather tactless) way, James has repeatedly proclaimed to my students: that "American schools are no FUN, that they are dreadful, that you have to do FAR too much work in America, etc". And I have heard this myself; but, though I hope for a change of mind, if not, so be it.

Now Simon, I trust, is something else. But is it a case of "the heir and the spare"—to quote Consuelo Vanderbilt? And, sometimes, I think it may be. He won't take a good degree, the Courtauld is out of the question, perhaps he should exercise his social gifts by working in a bar.[5] All these statements, prophecies, and prescriptions I derive from your letter of November 18; and, to me, they seem to disclose a conviction of Simon's inherent inferiority which, in no way, can I assent to.

Exhibitionist, of course he is; and this has been visible, to me, since he was six years old. But he is exhibitionist in a charming way; and he's never brash. Adorable we both know him to be, as does David; but, for me, he is, potentially, *personaggio importante*.[6] That he is bored by the histories of the Stuart kings and the Romantic poets I fully understand (ME TOO; but why do English schools still lazily produce Wordsworth, Keats and Shelley— with Byron admitted as a kind of low level classmate?). But there are many other themes, as you well know, which can be compelled to elicit Simon's excitement and attention.

About his coming to Ithaca I don't know. There are lots of summer school courses, I believe, which would be suitable for him; and I must find out what these are. But, of course, I only hope to be here to sell this house; and I would prefer to see him in Salzburg learning German. However, more about this later. Meanwhile, I am completely convinced that Simon must go either to the Courtauld or to the Fogg at Harvard. It's just the case that, for art history, he has to have a graduate degree.

But now to take up the topic of the library.

Dorothy, in your letter to me you seem to suggest that I equip the books with a book plate; and, then, give them away to be dispersed in a large library. But this solution is equivalent to sending Jews to Auschwitz or Dachau. It is the final, the 'total' solution which obliterates everything. I have seen what happened to J.O. Mahoney's⋆ books which he gave to Cornell.[7] With his bookplate in them, I turned up an awful lot of his books in a store in Owego. So I was grieved and shocked; and I bought about $200.00 worth myself—as some sort of memento. But this is what, also, would happen to my books in <u>any</u> large library. It would sell everything which it already had; and, then because of ingrained bureaucratic behavior, it would disperse the rest through several departmental libraries—Eng. Lit., French Lit., history, philosophy, visual arts, theology, etc, so that any traces of <u>me</u> would be effectively lost. No, no, no. The library <u>cannot</u> be so disposed. Its parts are intrinsically connected. In its little way, it's a Warburgian whole; and as <u>such</u> it <u>must</u> be transmitted. About this you may accuse me of suffering from a John Soane or a Mario Praz syndrome. But, you see, you don't know the way in which the library is used as a teaching instrument.

It's like an improvised version of the Cambridge-Oxford tutorial, in which we look at visual images, produce a variety of texts which might, curiously, relate, and all the rest. And it is in order that this kind of conversation may be continued that I plan the "Fondazione Rowe".

This will comprise not only the library—by itself that would be banal—but it must include, as supporting apparatus, everything that there is in this house and everything that I may have in Rome—this to make the congenial *ambiente* for its 'conversations.'[8] Simon will enjoy the *serate* of the *Fondazione*,[9] a minor theater for Italian-American debate. But its goin' to mean lotsa work.

Dearest Dorothy, since that evening in Via del Monserrato these have, gradually, become my ambitions. I took your line; and, as a result now I feel much more exhilarated and clear. But I don't think that, if I were to croak right now, the equivalent of $450,000 each (and maybe more) would really be very good for James and Simon; and, under the terms of the present will, that is what they are getting each. Simply, when I made this will in January '84, I didn't anticipate such rapid escalation. So, effectively, it is now a different estate; but I very much doubt that, under a new dispensation, James and Simon will be receiving appreciably any less.

Un abbraccio and lots of love,

    Colin

P.P.S.   *December 5*

I continue to be very concerned that Simon should learn German; and, in a letter that I have just sent to him, I have told him how imperative this is. And I have also suggested that Salzburg would be a highly O.K. place for these purposes. For purposes of his Italian it is, of course, ridiculous that he should be thinking of spending only <u>one</u> month in Firenze; and James, I am sure, will tell him as much.

Now, if Simon is prepared to spend <u>two</u> months in Firenze, then I shall be only too happy to support him for a further two months in Salzburg, where I am convinced he would enjoy both profit and happiness.

    Colin

---

1 *romanza della famiglia*, Italian: family novel.
2 *l'oncle d'Amérique*, French: the American uncle.
3 James Rowe* had studied physics as an undergraduate at Oxford University and was considering graduate schools.
4 *entrée*, French: the privilege of entering; access.
5 Courtauld Institute of Art, London.
6 *personaggio importante*, Italian: an important person.

7   James O Mahoney,* professor of art at Cornell and a friend of Rowe. See Rowe's letter to
     Dorothy Rowe* dated 21 October 1987 (p 286 in this vol).
8   *ambiente*, Italian: ambiance.
9   *serate*, Italian: evenings.

167   *To **Simon Rowe**, St. Margaret's Road, Oxford*   *2 December 1988*

19 Renwick Place, Ithaca, N.Y.

Dearest Simon:

I am in complete agreement with you about Paris. I used to love it and find it liberating. One used to go over on the night boat Newhaven-Dieppe; and in the train Victoria-New Haven there was wonderful bar which was, positively, a museum piece. It must have dated from about 1905; and it was like nothing you would see nowadays outside of the remotest provinces of Russia. Its walls were lined in green silk damask and, sticking out from them, there was a little green velvet upholstered shelf, so that you could sit on it. But it was the ceiling of this piece of rolling stock which was its most fantastic component; and believe it or not this was painted with sky and clouds! About goddesses I don't remember; but I think they must have been there. Because this little bar compartment had, patently, been fitted up by some slightly mad devotee of Tiepolo—the sort of person whom in the eighteenth century might have fitted up the most sumptuous boat for navigating the waters of the Brenta.

This, then, was a sort of English overture to the promise of French emancipation; and, after Dieppe, in the first, very palest light of morning, there followed that rapture which French river scenery still provides me with. Those big, wide, placid rivers, like nothing in England, Italy, or Germany; but which you do find reproduced in Texas about a hundred miles inland from the Gulf Coast. And, afterwards, then was St. Lazare at about 6.30—with a ritual walk down to an almost empty Place de La Concorde.

But, dearest Simon, except for some of the rivers flowing into the Loire (and I forget their names) it's a long time since I felt anything like this; and, about Paris in particular, I begin to feel as George V felt about 'abroad'. He must have been a terribly irritating and irritable man, that little, splenetic king who is reputed to have said: "Abroad, ABROAD, can't stand the place, NEVER COULD!"; and, to me, I am sorry to say, *la grande nation,* with all its pretentiousness and machinations, has become the entirely tedious, presumptuous equivalent of Geo V's 'abroad'.[1] The land can be ravishing; but the people are apt to be UGH....

And all that silly *gloire*—The Rue de Rivoli, the Avenue de Sebastopol, the Font de Jena, the Avenue Foch; and all that further recitation of *les victoires*—Marengo, Austerlitz, Wagram, Pyramides, and all the related names *ad nauseam*, like Massena, and Soult, and you name them. It all reminds me of the much traveled taxi driver in New York who said to me about the French: "And, with all their fancy names for streets, by themselves when did they ever win a war? Feller," he said, "Waterloo Station, Waterloo Place, Trafalgar Square, that where it's real. You limeys, you never make in London a Blenheim Avenue. You got far too much sense for that; and Trafalgar Square! Well that's nutten to write home about, is it now?"

But enough for Paris and the fatuous French; and now to approach the issue which your mamma simply doesn't want to face. This is; that, if you are to be an art historian, absolutely you have to learn German.

Dear Simon, reluctant though your mother may be to understand this basic requisite, horrible though the memories of the Third Reich may be, everybody will tell you just what I am saying. You will never be able to occupy any position, either academic or curatorial, without at least, a reading knowledge. You just gotta have it.

But is the idea all that depressing? Way back in the nineteenth century one went to Dresden (but mostly for 'finishing' and music), one also went to lugubrious Berlin (but mostly for philosophy), and the British diplomatic service sent people like Harold Nicolson to Hannover.[2] Of these places, Dresden seems to have been the most entertaining; but I can scarcely believe that it would be nowadays; and I find Berlin a big yawn—likewise Hannover which has never recovered from its bombs. So one never went to Cologne, Frankfurt, Karlsruhe, Stuttgart and, nowadays, there's even less reason. Which seems to leave Salzburg (after all the *geburtsstadt* of Mozart) as one of the most promising of possibilities.[3] So music, Baroque architecture, landscape, cream cakes, mountains—with all this I think a couple of months in Salzburg could be completely idyllic, very *gemutlich* and not at all a pain.[4] And, if you've got to take a dreary pill, why not take it slightly glazed with the best sugar?

(which reminds me that, to reduce the size of my distended testicles, for the last week I have been taking four antibiotics a day and it seems to be working!)

They tell me that there is snow all over northern Italy, from Turin almost to Venice. 'They' also tell me that there has been two feet of snow in Zurich. Here, except for an aberrant little storm when David was here, so far there has been nothing, though I am convinced that it will begin about seven o'clock tomorrow morning; and that's why I am dreading the next few weeks. But, all the same, I don't see how I can get away from here before mid-Jan.[5]

So tell me when you are going to come to Firenze.

Con tanta affezione,[6]

Colin

P.S. Of course, I remain convinced that you should have given Paris until Christmas. For all I say about it, after all, it is inexhaustible. Did you, for instance, go to the Musee des Plans Reliefs, in the Invalides? You went to the Louvre and the Musee d'Orsay; but did you go to the Musee des Arts Decoratifs? Did you go to the Musee Cognacq-Jay, the Musee Marmottan, the Hotel Carnavalet? Did you go to the house of Delacroix in the Place de Furstenberg? Did you go to St. Cloud, St. Germain, Malmaison, Maisons-Laffitte? Did you go to Fontainebleau? How about Vaux-le-Vicomte? Did you walk around the Faubourg St. Germain—Rue de Varennes, Rue de Grenelle, Rue de Bellechasse, etc? Did you go the Val-de-Grace? How about the Bibliotheque Sainte-Genevieve?

Forgive the questionnaire but I long to know.

---

1 *la grande nation*, French: the great nation.
2 Harold Nicolson (1886–1968), English diplomat, author, politician, and husband of Vita Sackville-West.
3 *geburtsstadt,* German: birthplace, hometown.
4 *gemütlich,* German: friendly, nice, agreeable.
5 Rowe intended to teach spring semester 1989 for Cornell in Rome.
6 *Con tanta affezione,* Italian: with so much affection.

19 Renwick Place, Ithaca, New York

Dearest Dorothy:

About the new will, I had a meeting with my lawyer yesterday. He's called Henry Theissen (ex-Cornell law school); and he grabbed the significance and the danger of the present dispositions immediately. He said that himself had a boy aged twenty-two whom he was convinced would be quite unable to handle any such inheritance until he was, at least thirty to thirty-five. He also advised an investment in ten per cent tax-free municipal bonds.

Now this was so exactly like Judy's mother that I found it mildly amusing. It was Livia DiMaio who first insisted that such bonds were O.K. and that I should buy them. [...]

So, now, I want you to think about several sums of money, invested Di Maio style and compounding over a period of ten years.

To J. and S. each:

1.	$150,000	should produce	$388,000
2.	$100,000	" "	$258,000
3.	$80,000	" "	$228,000
4.	$50,000	" "	$129,000
5.	$30,000	" "	$77,000

Now, none of these alternatives are exactly 'disinheritance'; and the general strategy behind them is much less lamentable than the present 'blanket' disposition. So Alternatives 1 and 2 I suppose to be too extravagant; but Alternative 3 is, maybe, mildly 'interesting'. Though you can't live comfortably on $26,000 a year. I am lead to believe that there are a great many academics in England (and even some in the U.S.) who scrape along on about this or less; and, as of now, it's probably about this much that Judy is getting for her three days a week at Yale. But, in any case, it is not my object that either J. or S. should be able to live comfortably upon what I leave them. Instead, this is intended as a challenge and a stimulus; and, personally, I would prefer it not to be used as a casual extra income.

Anyway, myself did not achieve an income of even $30,000 until 1976 (and I picked up this much by going down to Texas on a sabbatical). Then, when I went to Notre Dame in 1980 and was paid $35,000, this was still the highest income which I had ever received (why it has shot up so quickly to $68,000 I don't know). Then, two years ago I didn't have even an accessible $100,000 to my name (that's when I began to get worried). But, with $100,000, if you're interested in moving, then you can move; and, if you are not interested, then you are simply fatuously extravagant and silly.

This is me in my new Calvinist mood—partly induced by you; but, now to transfer attention to the foundation or institute.

Rather more than a year ago, having dinner with Werner and Jean Seligmann,* suddenly they said to me: "Colin, why are you so immensely preoccupied with your nephews? Why are you skimping and saving your money for THEM—as you obviously are? We know that you have excessively high aspirations for your nephews; but, in the end, you know, too much money may be detrimental to the ambitions which you hope to inspire. And by now shouldn't you be spending it on yourself and don't you, finally, deserve this indulgence?"

Though they went on for quite a long time, that was their message. So, when I said that I wouldn't quite know how to spend it, that there was a limit to books, engravings and taxis, that I was not very interested in expensive automobiles, New York restaurants, grand hotels, or clothes, then they began on a new line. "Well, what about endowments which will carry your name? What about doing something extremely particular for the American Academy: we don't think you will; but why not...? Or what about the Colin Rowe lecture series at Cornell—all lectures to be published? Or what about a number of travelling scholarships?"

Very flattering when people advise and suggest in this way; but, also, very irritating I find it. Very American all this too; but, of course, it is this particular American state of mind which is one of the reasons why this country is so profuse—like so many, many endowments here (it's a form of secular religion) and so very few elsewhere—particularly in Italy where family is all.

I suppose, therefore, that it must have been the Seligmanns* who impregnated me with new and 'charitable' thoughts; but there was still the problem of the library and, as a simplification of a process of thinking, I shall now write down the following equation:

The Seligmanns + the library + Dorothy Rowe* = the foundation or institute.

It's going to be a sweat and a lot more saving; but, if I succeed with my negotiations, it will have been worth it. And, if I don't succeed, well there always remains Cornell; and there is always the possibility of special negotiations with the American Academy.

Love, love,

    Colin

To **John Miller** & **Susan Rogers**, *Regent's Park Road, London*   *28 December 1988*   **169**

19 Renwick Place, Ithaca, N.Y.

Dear John and Susan:

    I don't expect to get away from here for another three weeks and, meanwhile, I am quietly enjoying it—nothing to do with Ithaca but the thought of leaving it. And, of course, the thought of leaving this faculty—Corbuphilia, object fixation, and spasmodic high tech—is just absolute joy.[1]

In 1515 or thereabouts, on the briefest of visits Leo X Medici found Firenze *citta miserabile— insupportabile*;and I cannot think that things have improved over the last four hundred and fifty years.[2] So I hope that the Roman scene will work out (better than Bath I think); and I hope that I find somewhere of appropriate size and convenient location. Because, if not, then I'll have to take a second look at Firenze—for something in Fiesole or Bellosguardo.[3]

In Rome in the first few months of this year representatives of *la famiglia*, needless to say, were a continuous presence.[4] First of all there was James who seems to have scarcely learned anything at either Westminster or Christ Church; and he was there from September to June for the purposes of Italian. And then there were David and Dorothy and Simon in March; and, adding all these to James only produced a situation of confusion and irascibility. Then there was Dorothy who decided, not to James's pleasure, that she just must spend a couple of months at his Italian school. And then there was David again, for a week end, and Simon for a week. So the violence was something awful

(Dorothy thinks that, quite properly, Nelson Mandela should be in jail "because, after all he is a terrorist"; and James sees nothing too bizarre in <u>two</u> main courses and <u>two</u> desserts and taking it upon himself to order extra bottles of wine—all at <u>my</u> expense).[5]

So it was apt to be <u>very</u> trying; and this might provide <u>some</u> reason why I don't want to go to Oxford (don't like it anyway) for quite some time.[6] James, to say the very best of him, is a little 'exuberant', Dorothy, as ever, is completely *detraquée*, David is preoccupied—as well he might be, and Simon?[7] Well Simon seems to be the only equable, tractable temperament; but, only eighteen, while James postures as the 'heir' Simon is relegated to the role of the 'spare'.

However too much about all this and it should be enough just to say that, separately they <u>may</u> be adorable but the combo is something else....

More amusingly, I got back here after several days to find two hysterical squirrels in occupation. One of them hid behind the curtains in the library and I was able to get him out; but the other retreated behind a fuse box in a closet in the kitchen and just couldn't be shifted, refused all enticements—crackers, bits of cheese, etc. So I had to call some pest control people and, first, there arrived a nice boy called Patrick—"C'mon, buddy, c'mon"; and, with this failing, then Patrick had to call the *maestro*, a real Upstate redneck, rather like something out of *A Midsummer Night's Dream*, who came with a rather elaborate cage and seemed to have a complete understanding of squirrel psychology. So we all sat in silence round the table for about ten minutes or so; and, then, suddenly there was a snap. The little guy had incarcerated himself and, after I had paid $40.00 cash, I opened the back door and—minus a bit of his tail—we let him out on the terrace.

Amerika, oh *Amerika*, scarcely is there ever a dull moment!

Lots of lurv,

    Colin

Modeling themselves on S.C. the squirrels came in down the chimney![8]

---

1 A Rowe-fabricated word, "Corbuphilia" refers to an intense love of the architect Le Corbusier.★
2 *città miserabile—insopportabile*, Italian: miserable city—unbearable.
3 Rowe has been considering purchasing a residence, preferably in Rome but perhaps in Bath, England, or in Fiesole or Bellosguardo, in Florence.
4 *la famiglia*, Italian: the family; meaning David,★ Dorothy,★ James,★ and Simon Rowe.★
5 Nelson Mandela (1918–2013), South African antiapartheid revolutionary, politician, and philanthropist; president of South Africa from 1994 to 1999.
6 The Rowe family lived in Oxford.
7 *detraquée*, French: deranged.
8 "S.C.": Santa Claus.

170   *To **Dorothy Rowe**, St. Margaret's Road, Oxford, England*   *19 January 1989*

19 Renwick Place, Ithaca, N.Y.

Dearest Dorothy:

    The weather here continues to be exceptionally benign, with still no snow. But the light has been brilliant—almost like a Roman light in September-October;

and, on the whole, I have found it entertaining to have been in this house with the minimum of disturbance.

Also, I have achieved quite a lot. First of all I prepared my '87 income tax for my accountant (getting papers ready for accountants is almost like cleaning the house before the cleaning woman comes to do it); but the '87 papers which should have been sent in long ago were in terrible confusion—stuff sent to Rome too late and then coming back here much later. However the Internal Revenue Service has no reason to bitch since I now find that they owe me $4,500—so my apparent delinquency has only been defrauding myself. And then, on top of this I now feel completely clean since I have already prepared the income tax *materiel* for '88 and given it to the accountant, so that all that remains is to slot in the few pieces which will arrive in the next week or so; and, then, it will all be painless and finished.[1] But, simply, I couldn't have left without performing this completely horrible and protracted work.

And what else have I done? Well, I have almost completed the typing of two articles— one for the Cornell Mag and the other for *Casabella*.[2] But, with all this, and a minor operation, and the squirrels, I can now begin to feel relaxed.[3]

For the weekend I had Paolo Berdini* (he was at that dinner which I gave for all of you at La Costanza) and *La Favorita*—otherwise Mary Kaplan, New York-quasi Hungarian Jewish and, presumably, fairly 'comfortable'. Or, otherwise, what would no occupation, a house in the East Eighties and an apartment in the Rue de Grenelle seem to imply?[4] Anyway, Mary arrived with characteristic profusion—lashings of Beluga caviar and three bottles of *Moet et Chandon*. Meaning that the weight of the caviar had already destroyed the possibilities of dinner before we had even begun to think about it.

Then a few days before Craig Cowden, one of my Texas *aficionados* from Florence, dropped in with the most absurd and romantic proposition.[5] We should go down the Rio Grande, through that sublimely heroic canyon—we and some others equally bizarre—on a raft. "No," he said, "you are not too old for that sort of thing and we want to take you down the Rio Grande—on a raft." But imagine it; and Paolo thought it was terrific (I'll come too). But a combo of me and Paolo and Craig and his friends navigating the south of the Big Bend, although it might be a historic event, is—perhaps—a little more than I am prepared to concede. J. and S. might enjoy the Big Bend; but the Anglo-Texan-Wop descent, all the way from El Paso to the Gulf of Mexico...?

Paolo, of course, is a little *extravagante*. He is either a godson or was baptized by Pope Pacelli; and let's not forget that.[6] But Paolo has equal *liaisons* with the *Brigate Rosse*.[7] Big buddies of Paolo are Billi Bilancioni (papa ambassador in Prague) and Toni Negri now in jail, who taught Eng. Lit at the Univ of Padua.[8] So get the pic? Well heeled Wop, embarrassed about a previous leftish scene, devoted to me (if not the Big Bend we, together, might drive around the Marche), doing a Ph.D. at Columbia.

Meanwhile, today, I gave luncheon to Charles Chen*—Chen Chi Zien—; and it was exhausting. We had *prosciutto e melone*, scrambled eggs with shrimps snow peas and very small carrots (I made it all myself and I thought that it was a little bit *cinese*); and then we had *formaggio* and *petits fours*. On the whole, I think, an elegant and thoughtful lunch (we drank *acqua minerale*, the leftover bottle of Moet et Chandon, and Lapsang Souchong); but it was tough work.

Dear Charles is to be teaching here for the semester—to the planners; and he is far from completely suckered by the Commies and the Determinists—which he recognises the Cornell planners to be. All the same it was heartbreaking and difficult.

He said that the forty years which he had spent in China, since leaving London, had been absolute hell; and I knew about that but didn't want to press it. Charles, way back, used to display a lot of *folie de grandeur* which he has now lost.[9] He used to talk about parties at <u>Claridges</u> which, for some unknown reason, we would give together; and Hugh Casson once told me that, after the Revolution, he was still wearing the Savile Row suits which he had made in London.[10]

But, that way, lay tragedy; and, when I <u>dared</u> to mention it, he said to me: "That was the reason for my Waterloo." So I knew that he had spent three years in a concentration camp in Szechwan but I didn't press or probe. However it all came out <u>very</u> quick.

Originally, it appears that Charles had a traditional Peking courtyard house and he'd furnished it with elegant Ming, eighteenth century pieces. But it was charming. But, then, <u>they</u> took the house and the furn and all the <u>new</u> books—because these were glossy. But they didn't take away the <u>old</u> books because they didn't understand them. "So, dearest Colin, I was left with the copy of Leoni's Alberti which you <u>gave</u> to me"; and THEN I knew what was going to happen: "I spent three years translating Alberti into <u>Chinese."</u>

Dearest Dorothy, the elegant lunch was also shattering. More than ever I had imagined I was dealing with an impossibly wounded person. The background Shanghai Banking, the father a friend of Chiang Kai Shek, the <u>complete</u> destruction of anticipation: "Oh, dearest Colin, it's so charming to be in your house—all these books and things."

In other words, it's been an interesting day. For instance, I have learned that I am highly regarded in various universities in China! But <u>can</u> it be true?

I will leave for Rome on Sunday; the house is then to be occupied by Matt, who is totally reliable—almost excessively conscientious; and I shall be in that Notre Dame apartment in Via del Teatro Valle. Dearest Dorothy, if you wish to come, please do. But give me warning as I anticipate a sequence of visitors.

Did J. and S. receive my hopelessly inadequate Xmas presents?

Best of love,

Colin

P.S. I enclose a clipping from today's *New York Times* about English boxwood which has always been highly popular here.[11] You see, it has occurred to me that a discreet use of box hedging might tune up the front of St. M's R.— that and some flanking green stuff on low trellis.[12]

C.

P.P.S. If you are leaving a place for a long time and, maybe, for ever; and, if you want to leave everything in order, the exit is inevitably protracted—like mine has been. But it's an <u>overwhelming</u> relief to be leaving everything in a supreme condition of order.

C.

---

1   *matériel*, French: material.
2   Rowe, Colin, "Grid/Frame/Lattice/Web: Giulio Romano's Palazzo Maccarani and the Sixteenth Century", *Cornell Journal of Architecture*, 1991, vol 4, pp 6–21; *As I Was Saying: Recollections and Miscellaneous Essays*, Alexander Caragonne ed, 3 vols, Cambridge, MA: MIT Press, 1996, vol 2, pp 103–169. No article by Rowe was published in *Casabella* at this time.

3 Regarding squirrels, see Rowe's letter to John Miller* and Susan Rogers* dated 28 December 1988 (p 321 in this volume).

4 Regarding Mary Kaplan, see Rowe's letter to Dorothy Rowe* dated 2 August 1985 (p 266 in this volume).

5 *aficionados*, Spanish: fans.

6 Eugenio Pacelli (1876–1958), Pope Pius XII (1939–1958).

7 The Brigate Rosse (Red Brigade), an Italian Marxist paramilitary organization formed in 1970 to create a revolutionary state through armed struggle.

8 Guglielmo "Billi" Bilancioni, professor of architectural history, living in Rome at the time of this letter; Antonio "Toni" Negri (b 1933), Italian Marxist sociologist and political philosopher.

9 *folie des grandeurs*, French: delusions of grandeur.

10 Claridge's, a five-star hotel in the Mayfair district of London; Hugh Casson (1910–1999), British architect.

11 Yang, Linda, "Not Quite a Maze, Perhaps, but Amazing Nonetheless: A Garden Tied in Knots", *The New York Times*, 19 January 1989.

12 "St. M's R.": St. Margaret's Road, Oxford, David* and Dorothy Rowe's* residence.

To **Dorothy Rowe**, *St. Margaret's Road, Oxford*   *6 April 1989*   **171**

Rome

Dearest Dorothy:

I've got to set the stage for a little happening of last night at about six o'clock.

My next door neighbour is called Kenneth Featherstone and, obviously, he teaches at Notre Dame. English, tall, elegant, short white beard, invariably very well dressed, he operates as a professional Limey; but, being slightly under-educated, he doesn't completely succeed. Also, he comes from Matlock, Derbyshire; it is demonstrable in his voice; and the younger faculty at Notre Dame deplore him very much.

So the former Mrs. Featherstone came from Buenos Aires (they split over the Falkland/Maldives war); and, living with Kenneth, there is his daughter Annamaria— twenty-two (?), feckless, sexy, provocative and, I suppose, intelligent.

Anyway, Annamaria seems to make a point of leaving her keys behind and last night was no exception. Therefore the bell rang and it was Annamaria trying to get into their apartment from mine—papa being in Sicilia. Problems, problems. She proposed to get in from my courtyard balcony; but then we couldn't open the immediately adjacent window and, on my advice we took a hammer and smashed the pane so that we could get at the *chiusura*—with a big piece of card so that the glass wouldn't fall downstairs.[1] So it was a neat job; Annamaria clambers in and returns in triumph a minute later with the keys.

Out of politeness and some curiosity (Matt had a thing about her) I offered her a drink and the conversation began with Caravaggio and went on to Firenze, to Parma and, via the Bourbons de Parme, to the Empress Zita. And it was at this stage, that I said to her: "Annamaria, just what do you do?" "Well," she said, "I try to go to see my grandmother in England as little as possible—this because I find the whole country stifling." So I was intrigued but the next of this little *chiquita* from South Bend, Indiana, absolutely laid me back.[2] "You see what I am really doing is working hard to become a duchess!" Outrageous and bizarre, or don't you think? But it continued. "The Duca Salviati has a charming villa just outside Pisa. I want it and he's the man. But is it true that Carlo Massimo is really going to marry the daughter of Ibi Amin, rich, black and fat?"[3]

Well, needless to say, my mind reeled at this further dimension added to Henry James* subject matter. "Of course, I don't know Carlo Massimo but I understand that he's quite mad; and Ibi Amin is very evil is he not?" So I concur. "But all of my friends—so and so Ruspoli, Ludovisi, Aldobrandini, Borghese, Buoncompagni—all of them tell me that this is obliged to happen." However, my little mind still reeled. I thought it was a nice story; but I still couldn't (as Coleridge might have said) cause my disbelief to become suspended.[4] *SE NON E VERO E BEN TROVATO*[5]

Three hours later

I have just been at a party at Palazzo Massimo for Bill and Joan McMinn;[6]* and I thought that it might add a little dimension if I asked Roberto whether or not he knew anything about this.[7] So, in his pedantic way, Roberto, first of all, said: "Dear Colin, not Ibi, Idi Amin"; and then he said: "No, I haven't heard that one; but, on the whole, I wouldn't be at all surprised. Carlo, don't you know, has a very developed taste for black women—he's often to be seen around with them. But rather beautiful than fat...".

But an interesting rumour? Derived from a certain 'high' society which Annamaria, apparently, really does frequent. Matt told me last year that she was on to big stuff, had stayed with the Ruspoli at Vignanello and the Aldobrandini's at Frascati. So I am left wondering whether she is simply ingenuous or simply conniving, or—like Edith Wharton's Undine Spragg (also a mid-Westerner) maybe a bit of both?[8]

However, I must say that I do find this little story of the potential *duchessa* from Matlock, Buenos Aires and South Bend, to be entirely fascinating; and, when I make a party for my students, I think that I shall include her and some of her 'friends'.

But, from Matlock, Derbyshire, from this perspective, I can only think that Annamaria's 'exotic' *train de vie* must be highly disturbing and utterly incomprehensible.[9] However, I am sure that what I am on to is a dime novel or strip cartoon which will produce, later, interminable developments; and, so, I shall keep in close touch with my subject matter and I shall, also, keep you informed—as the action develops.

Best love,

 Colin

P.S. In the mildly dreary and highly sycophantic biography of Princess Alice, Countess of Athlone, which I gave David to give to you, I was intrigued by one detail.[10] At Claremont, Esher, on separate occasions, the Albany's entertained both John Ruskin and Edward Lear! And this titillates—or massages—my *culte de royaute*—the more minor the better. Because, among the sons of Q.V., who else than Leopold would have committed so outrageous an intellectual indiscretion? Among the daughters, obviously Louise and, just maybe, the Empress Frederick. But among the sons? Informed that Canon Somebody was an authority on Lamb (meaning Charles Lamb), as a gastronomic authority the P.O.W. laid down his knife and fork; and, non-plussed, looked down the table at this wretched little canon—to whom he could attribute no understanding of meat whatsoever; and the P.O.W. said: *Lamb?*

Among the more absurd remarks of the B.R. F; this must surely be like the Duke of York's: "another book Mr. Gibbon. Nothing but scribble, scribble, scribble, eh?"; like George III's: "What, what, what, shot, shot, shot" (this on hearing that his brother-in-law, the King of Denmark, has been assassinated); like Geo V's remark to Iris Origo's grandfather: "Oh, dear Lord Desart, I am so delighted to learn that you don't wear pajamas either. Can't stand them myself"; and, like the immortal remark of Geo VI to John Piper, about his watercolor of Windsor: "Oh, Mr. Piper, what a pity that you have had such trouble with the weather. But you just must come back when the light is better."

No, Leopold, Duke of Albany, haemophiliac, alone among the boys of that generation, was an 'intellectual'. Augustus Hare—and Henry James—would lead you to believe something like this about the Duke of Edinburgh (musical and naval); but myself doubts this. And, then, the Duke of Connaught? Well, it's highly respectable: banal, moustachioed and military. Or don't you think so?

But Leopold is something else. Strangely close to the pattern of Albert, had he lived longer he would have transmitted these patterns to an, otherwise, barbarous family—otherwise the descendants of George V. But no hope. However, it is from the little Leopold, I think, there is to be derived the elegance, the stamina and the, surprising 'modernity' of Alice Athlone.

She is <u>much</u> to be regarded.

    Colin

P.P.S. For Simon: QUEEN VICTORIA CONSTANTLY EATS COLD APPLE PIE Quirinale, Viminale, Capitolino, Esquilino, Celio, Aventino, Palatino.

    C.

[handwritten]

WHAT A LONG TIME IT HAS TAKEN ME TO SEND THIS LETTER OFF.

---

1 *chiusura,* Italian: lock.
2 *chiquita,* Spanish: girl.
3 Idi Amin Dada (c 1925–2005), president of Uganda, 1971–1979. Rowe consistently refers to "Idi Amin" as "Ibi Amin"; Carlo Massimo (b 1942), the son of Prince of Arsoli and the Princess of Savoy.
4 In 1817 Samuel Taylor Coleridge described fiction as "a willing suspension of disbelief".
5 *SE NON È VERO, È BEN TROVATO,* Italian saying: "Even if it's untrue, it's well conceived". This sentence was handwritten by Rowe in capital letters.
6 The Cornell Rome Program was housed in the Palazzo Massimo; Bill McMinn,* dean of Cornell's College of Architecture, Art, and Planning.
7 Roberto Einaudi,* director of Cornell's Rome Program.
8 In *The Custom of the Country* (1812), Edith Wharton tells the story of Undine Spragg, a Midwestern girl with a talent for finance who attempts to gain entry into New York high society.
9 *train de vie,* French: way of life.
10 Aronson, Theo, *Princess Alice, Countess of Athlone,* London: Cassells, 1981; "David" is David Rowe.*

*To **Judith DiMaio**, West 67th Street, New York, N.Y. Giornata della Liberazione[1]*   25 April 1989   **172**

Cornell University, College of Architecture, Art & Planning, Rome

Dearest Judy:

So you went to Egypt and returned without ever calling? But I know why. It's because of airports, like Kennedy, Heathrow, and Fiumicino.[2] They are so entirely horrible that we wish to have nothing to do with them. One doesn't want to add to their miseries and complications; and, so far as I can see, with all these places (Frankfurt included) it will only get worse.

Meanwhile, to add to the miseries, Plinio Nardecchio has abdicated in favor of his son [...][3] [While] my other little old man in the south east corner of Piazza Borghese [...] has croaked. But he was wonderful. He had a tape deck which always played Haydn and Mozart quartettes; and, whenever he saw me arriving, last year he always brought out the best *maniera* stuff.[4] But, now, no longer; and the next of these scenes to go away will be the *gesso* man opposite Palazzo Taverna.

No, all of the Rome of just a few years back is going, very quickly to disappear— including our framers in Via dei Greci. The jeans shops in the northern part of the Via del Corso are taking over; and, after 1992, it's going to be worse.[5]

Because of the *metropolitana*, dumping people in Piazza de Spagna, the deprived *borgate* types are coming in in the evenings.[6] Piazza Navona is now them and they flood over to Santa Maria della Pace, where the prices have become a bit mad.[7] In the *centro storico* they don't, as yet, invade the restaurants (these must be too expensive); but the result must be jeans, jeans, and more jeans.[8]

I look out of the window in Via del Teatro Valle and I see jeans and jeans; but, then, just how can I object to this?[9] Myself, when I go out, is likely to wear a jeans jacket from L.L. Bean. So what's the sweat?

April 27

Just picked up my mail in Palazzo M.[10] and have been reading a clipping which Matt sent me about the burial of the Empress Zita.[11] But what a terrifying life! One of the twenty-four children of the last Duke of Parma (shades of Paul III Farnese), ultra Catholic (after her husband's death in 1922 she always wore black) I receive the impression that she must have been a bit of a trial; and in Ottawa, in W.W.II, apparently they (the mysterious they) found her so. Queen Wilhelmina was completely with it; but not so Zita! This I was reading the other day in a rather sycophantic biography of Princess Alice, Countess of Athlone, Qu. V's last surviving grandchild, and like Zita, in her day a great beauty. But the book was more than I could bear, so that via David who was here the other day, I sent it on to Dorothy, being completely aware that she will adore it.

By the way, I have just learned a trick for remembering the Seven Hills of Rome. It's a nineteenth century English schoolboy bit; and it reads:

QUEEN VICTORIA CONSTANTLY EATS COLD APPLE PIE

(Quirinale, Viminale, Capitolino, Esquilino, Celio, Aventino, Palatino); and I thought that this item of highly unlikely information might amuse you. All the same I find it regrettable that the BRF (HBM or the Q. of E.) sent no representative to Zita's funeral. IT or SHE, I suppose, was just too shit scared to be able to cope with elementary decency.

At Palazzo M. (which is more lugubrious than ever) I have been repeating myself. Meaning: that we are just finishing off yet another Armenian Embassy for the Vicolo della Moretta site; and after all these years![12] But the results are going to be good and I shall send you Xeroxes.

Susie K. was here the other day [...]; and I later met Fred and Werner in Firenze (the Syracuse 'work' being so deplorable that W. became mildly frenzied);[13] but S. and F. are excessively preoccupied with where to live in London. North of the Park I said and avoid Belgravia like the plague—no services, prestige but no shops. Don't know that the

Marlborough Man is <u>all</u> that excited by *Londra.* It appears to be Susie's determination, though the M.M.,[14] as I hear, in that Americano invasion seems to be goin' down big.[15]

But, dearest Judy, would love to see you. For instance, you have never seen the *maniera Deposition* which I bought in Via Monserrato a year ago. It was from a genuine junk shop and it cost me six hundred dollars. So a very provincial little item—charming and poetic dets—which myself thought of as northern Lazio or southern Umbria of c. 1560. Not Rosso, not Pontormo, not <u>even</u> Vasari—it's *minore, minore.*[16] But Richard came for it the other night (this is for *ripristino*[17]—about five hundred); and, while he agreed with my dating, he doubted my locality.[18] "No," Richard said: "Ferrara or, possibly, Brescia"; but, quite simply, I <u>cannot</u> see how such a minor but distinguished picture (if from Ferrara or Brescia) could have migrated so far south.

Therefore, to see what happens to it. Not exactly a national treasure it is; but, when I've finished with it, this little piece is going to be a knockout; and, also, it will receive a knockout frame. So THEN it <u>will</u> become a national treasure; and how to get it out <u>will</u> present a problem.

Dearest Judy, come, call,

  Colin

---

1 *Giornata della Liberazione,* Italian: Liberation Day, the anniversary of the liberation of Italy in 1945.
2 International airports in New York, London, and Rome, respectively.
3 Plinio Nardecchio: print dealer in Piazza Navona in Rome frequented by Rowe and Judith DiMaio.*
4 *maniera,* Italian: Mannerist.
5 Rome celebrated a jubilee year in 1992.
6 *metropolitana,* Italian: subway.
7 *borgate,* Italian: lower class outskirts of the city, slums.
8 *centro storico,* Italian: historic center.
9 Rowe's apartment was in the Via del Teatro Valle.
10 "Palazzo M.": Palazzo Massimo alle Colonne, which housed Cornell's Rome Architecture Program.
11 Princess Zita of Bourbon-Parma (1892–1989), wife of Emperor Charles of Austria and the last Empress of Austria, Queen of Hungary and Croatia, and Queen of Bohemia.
12 Rowe had conducted the Armenian Embassy studio project several times before.
13 Fred Koetter* and Werner Seligmann.*
14 "Marlborough Man" ("M.M."): Rowe's nickname for Fred Koetter.*
15 Americano invasion: American architectural firms during the late-1980s building boom in London.
16 *minore,* Italian: minor (as in minor work or artist).
17 *ripristino,* Italian: restoration.
18 "Richard": Richard Piccolo (b 1943 in Hartford, Connecticut), a painter, muralist, collector of sixteenth-century engravings and works by Piranesi, who has lived in Italy since the early 1970s.

To **Dorothy Rowe,** *St Margaret's Road, Oxford*   *27 July 1989*   **173**

19 Renwick Place, Ithaca, N.Y.

Dearest Dorothy:

What a terrible day it was yesterday! At 9.30 James drove me to Fiumicino; and, after the usual horrors, we got away at 11.30.[1] So it was an eight and half hours flight to Boston (TWA) where we arrived shortly after 2.00 p.m.; and, then, all hell broke loose.

American Express in Rome had booked me on a Piedmont flight at 5.10 to Ithaca; but because some fatuous Cornell professor (I've met him but forget his name) gave his advice to Reagan on the deregulation of airlines (this in imitation of Thatcher) I found everything in a condition of complete confusion.

The Piedmont desk told me that the 5.10 flight to Ithaca no longer existed. It had been abolished on July 1; and they were surprised that this was not known by American Express in Rome. They said that they were sorry but, now, I could only reach Ithaca via Philadelphia. And then they had second thoughts which were not quite so *outré* as Philadelphia.[2] I could leave on a flight at 6.00 for Newark, N.J.; and from there, at 7.55, I could get a flight to Ithaca. So what else to do? And, at Newark, from one terminal to another I traversed the airport at absurd expenses only to wait for a plane that was two-and-a-half hours late.

Therefore it took me just as long to get from Fiumicino to Boston as it took me to get from Boston to Ithaca. Seventeen hours altogether. Believe it you must but I scarcely can.

Arrived here, I found Matt and his girl friend, Cheryl O'Neil* in the greatest alarm as to what had happened to me. Had I been kidnapped, etc. They had rung up James in Rome who was sure that I must have left. Then they had rung up Fred and Susie in Boston who became equally alarmed. To all intents and purposes I was *sparito*.[3] T.W.A. would not provide the information that I was on the Rome-Boston flight until they were required to do so by the Sheriff of Tompkins county (and all this is getting a little hysterical, but don't you think); but, after Boston, I remained untraceable, with the threatening question: What has happened to the notoriously incompetent C?[4]

But all this has been made worse by what Matt told me. He went to meet the flight on which American Express had booked me; and this flight did arrive in Ithaca—though about an hour late. Problem was that it is no longer a Piedmont flight. It was acquired (effective July 1) by T.W.A.; and the Piedmont desk clerks were unacquainted with this info. So much for pseudo-capitalism and deregulation; and, as a result, I went through three hours of extra hell. So much for the entirely gratuitous intrusions of academic neo-Conservatives.

However, getting back to Upstate, N.Y. I suspect must be a little like arriving in nineteenth century Russia. I have had this fantasy before but never quite so strongly as today. It is voluptuously warm rather than hot and it is, almost oppressively, green, that overwhelming intimacy with trees, that profusion of greenness which, after Rome, is so soft as to be almost incredible. I think of what I imagine Russia to have been like—all those big rivers, meadows, hedges of sunflowers and big stands of trees; and I sit inside with the light filtered by the leaves and I look around this house at all the Neo-Classical references and Italianate bits; and, somehow, in some funny way I feel that I have just crawled into a story by Gogol or Turgenieff.[5]

For instance, this evening I just went out to see an important settee. Vienna 1840's I would think. A good Biedermeier piece, *bois clair*, original upholstery.[6] It came from the Seward house up the lake; and the Sewards have lived in Auburn since 1823, the most prominent member of the family having been Abe Lincoln's Secretary of State. So a good provenance; and it had just arrived in Matt's apartment (where I had never been before) and I was to give my opinion. So he got it for just over $2,000 and what a steal and what presence! But, though I am jealous, I am immensely happy that it was Matt who bought it. Quite up to Jim's standards, it indicates what an awful lot he's learned from living in this house and looking at the furniture books in the library.[7]

Judy, when she sees it, will also be consumed with dismay; but Matt tells me that, apparently, there's an awful lot of Biedermeier around these parts—neglected by New York dealers, who cleaned up the quilts and the brass beds, and underpriced by the locals, who only appreciate what they call 'country' pieces. So, since he is leaving in about two weeks time for the U. of Maryland and has already found himself an apartment in Washington, D.C., he proposes, in the next few days, to introduce me to what's going; and maybe (who knows) I shall buy some. Not anything that I had <u>ever</u> thought of doing over here; but, if the prices in Rome are so high and the prices here so little, it <u>might</u> be a good idea.

Dearest Dorothy, lots of love,

    Colin

P.S. I constantly think of your predicament—all alone in that great big house; and I think of the irony of it all.[8]

James, for the few days that I saw him in Rome, was v. charming. Only trouble is that both he, and Simon, are v. hard to get started in the morning.[9] He (they) are impossible, so far as I can see, to get out of bed before ten-thirty; and then are apt to sit around for at least an hour deciding what they are going to do. So, before they get going, it's, already, almost too late. Now this is <u>very</u> David and, on occasion, its also <u>very</u> Me. But, way back, when I first came to Rome (July 15, 1947!) with that Canadian guy Sidney Key* who, though a potential director of National Gallery of Canada, later committed suicide (don't know why); but to cut an over-protracted sentence short: we always went out at six o'clock every morning and saw four churches before doing anything else. But <u>not</u> J. and S.[10]

But, of course, I hated Sid's churches; and ya' gotta' believe the quite enormous number of Early Xtian mosaics at which I was obliged to look at 7.00 a.m. But it has been an immense relief to have seen them all. Because it now means that one only sees what one wishes to. <u>And</u> I <u>never</u> prescribe Early Xtian jobs to J. and S.

I will return to Via del T, V. on August 22 and I hope that Judy will be there before that—perhaps until the end of the month. Do you think that Simon might/could/ should pay another little visit in September?[11]

    Colin

---

1 Fiumicino: the Rome airport.
2 *outré,* French: outrageous.
3 *sparito,* Italian: disappeared.
4 "T.W.A.": Trans World Airlines.
5 Nikolai Vasilievich Gogol (1809–1852) and Ivan Sergeyevich Turgenieff (1818–1883), Russian novelists, short story writers, and playwrights.
6 *bois clair,* French: light wood.
7 "Jim": James Stirling.*
8 Separated from David Rowe,* Dorothy Rowe* was living alone on St Margaret's Road, Oxford.
9 James* and Simon Rowe* had just visited Rowe in Rome.
10 Sidney Key.*
11 "Via del T, V.": Via del Teatro Valle 51, Rome, Rowe's apartment at the time.

*To **Dorothy Rowe**, St. Margaret's Road, Oxford*   *12 August 1989*   **174**

19 Renwick Place, Ithaca, N. Y.

Dearest Dorothy:

    I am sure that James enjoyed himself in Rome, where he was charming and amenable and I enjoyed his presence. Simon, on the second occasion that he came down, less so. I think that Simon and myself both share the same personality—slightly hysteric, slightly histrionic—previously demonstrated by Margaret I-L.[1] But Simon came down with his *amici di Firenze* who were, to say the very least, a bit of a drag.[2] Simon insisted on staying with them in an adjacent *pensione*; but, effectively, they occupied the apartment, sat around the table reading, didn't talk too much, but fatally inhibited conversation. On the whole I am quite unsure why the *amici* came down because they didn't seem to be interested in looking at anything whatsoever and, really, they seemed only to leave the house with the greatest reluctance. But J. has much more *savoir faire* than he displayed last year and I am sure that S. will soon learn. He spent a lot of time reading a book on Donatello.

Am just in the throes of having the outside of the house repainted: and it's now an immaculate and dazzling white. The boss of the team is called Philip Genova—with the accent on the <u>Gen</u> ("Hey, Colen, call me Phil"); and, of course, there is nothing Italian left in his makeup. He is a hefty Upstate redneck with a beard (since he was hired by Matt I guess this figures);[3] and, like some incredible contagion, all of his distinctly juvenile team, also have beards and it makes a kind of Germanic Gothic effect, like something that you might have expected to find in Tyrol many centuries ago.[4] They work quite hard; they are immensely polite; and they are as typical of these parts as they are a curiosity.

So, while they have been working I have just stripped the house of almost all *maniera* images in order to take them to Rome; and I have plugged the gaps—with great success—with German and Dutch/Flemish stuff.[5] And, therefore, all in all the house doesn't seem to be seriously depleted. But, all the same, I find it difficult (for the most part) for German and Netherlandish stuff to be in the same room with Italian. I have suddenly remembered Dominic Michaelis,* years ago, saying: "Alveen this morning. I had too much Boyarski last night" (he'd had a lecture in my house on his inherent frivolity); and I remain amused by the idea of Alvin as an intoxicating drink—some appalling Jewish potion, perhaps a minor version of Eisenman?[6]* So I enclose a Xerox of a letter which I have just sent to him; but that <u>this</u> might have <u>any</u> impression or effect I <u>very</u> much doubt.[7]

Lotsa Lurv',

    Colin

P.S. I suppose that I shall return here next year (*D.V.*)[8] in order to try to sell this house and perhaps Simon should join me for a couple of weeks in order to look at books, help in sorting/packing them and observe how *il zio* has existed over quite a period of time.[9]

    C.

P.P.S. I have just discovered a book here which I had completely forgotten about: Jane Kramer, *Europeans*, 1988. It is incredibly brilliant and do read.[10] American, apparently she lives in Paris, and these are articles from the *New Yorker*. But read her on Mitterrand, on Germany, on the Vatican, on the Bishop of Durham, and read her on London.

Though written as far back as '81 her analysis of English society and Mrs. T.[11] seems to me to be amazingly astute and accurate. No doubt because she tends to say everything which I have been saying for years and years. As the basis of the English 'problem' she postulates the equivalent of Disraeli's* 'two nations' who do not speak the same language; and, if this is Walter Scott and *Ivanhoe* all over again, then what to do?

She is correct, I imagine, in intimating that the 'problem' is 'social' rather than 'political'. Nobody coming to do a paint job in England would say: "Hey, Colen, call me Phil"; and, instead I am reminded of the social subservience of Cambridge: "Well, sir, if you are going to make a dinner party sir, I could come to do it. I've often cooked for officer's messes sir."

But isn't this the hopeless, the irremediable, 'problem' of the C. of E. (Disraeli defined it as *'the Tory party at prayer'*),[12] of the House of Lords (abolition was proposed in the Parliament Act of 1910), of the Honours List (surely a cheap, Frenchified and Napoleonic importation), of Oxford/Cambridge (where the fellows of colleges are still so many enlightened *abbés* of the *ancien regime*),[13] and of the public schools which, *faute de mieux*, scarcely should be made to go away.[14]

In Italy way back Queen Margarita spoke with a Piedmontese accent; but catch a Q. of E. sounding like she came from Lancashire! But the Queen of England and the Queen of Scots! And you see how Scotland anticipated the populist titles which came on after the French Rev. But, as we all know, this intense and absurd social stratification (also guaranteed by the Monarchy and the Brigade of Guards) isn't the least bit American, French, German, Scandinavian, or even Italian. It is the crucial *specialita d' Inghilterra*: it operates to cause industry and commerce to wither; and it seems not to be questioned by any political parties.[15]

To Dissenters from Birmingham/Staffordshire like Josiah Wedgwood, Joseph Priestley, Erasmus Darwin, Matthew Boulton, all this would have appeared incomprehensible; but perhaps not. For rather like a contemporary English football mob, in the 1790's the Birmingham mob yelled: "for King and Church and down with the Philosophers." And, hence, neither social nor political revolution in England.

So is it that we have to put up with English desuetude or over-rationalized French folly? Joseph Priestley was given a rousing reception in New York and went away— from Birmingham, to live in Cumberland, Pennsylvania where, not knowing it, he became the grandfather of the greatest American architect, H.H. Richardson.

But all this is very, very, very strange.

> *Colin*

---

1   "Margaret I-L": Margaret Thatcher (1925–2013), the "Iron Lady", prime minister of the United Kingdom, 1979–1990.
2   *amici di Firenze,* Italian: friends from Florence.
3   Matthew Bell.*
4   Tyrol, Austria.
5   *maniera,* Italian: mannerist.
6   Alvin Boyarsky* and Peter Eisenman.*
7   The enclosure is lost.
8   *"D.V.": Deo volente,* Latin: if God is willing.
9   *lo zio,* Italian: the uncle.
10 Kramer, Jane, *Europeans*, New York: Farrar, Straus & Giroux, 1988. Kramer's weekly "Letters from Europe", published in *The New Yorker* since 1981, formed the basis for this book.
11 Margaret Thatcher.
12 "C. of E.": Church of England.
13 *abbés* of the *ancien régime*, French and English: abbots of the old order.
14 *faute de mieux*, French: for lack of better.
15 *specialita dell'Inghilterra*, Italian: speciality of England.

175 To **Dorothy Rowe**, *St. Margaret's Road, Oxford*   *6 September 1989*

Rome

Dearest Dorothy:

"It all takes work for the working man to do." Well the workmen came here at ten o'clock this morning—to do various things here and next door. They are moving the water heater (quite correctly James thought it was dangerous); they are repainting the bathroom (perhaps about time); they have brought a microwave oven (I already hate it) and they are putting in smoke detectors all over the place (or at least that's the idea—it's the new regime at Notre Dame.[1] But, so far, only the microwave job has happened. They ceased work at one; God knows when and if they are going to come back; and, meanwhile; I am in a state of suspended animation.

I wrote you a long letter over the weekend. Did I mail it or did I lose it? But I think that I must have lost it.

Anyway, today, after deluges of rain over the last few days, at last it is *una bella giornata Romana*, warmish-coolish, with exquisite September light; and, coming back and without the furniture, I find this room to be almost august, the stuff on the walls (have brought more to be added) highly impressive.[2] J. and R. left the place in impeccable condition;[3] and Astra continues to rave about Giacomino, whom, apparently, I do not fully appreciate.[4]

But, then, just what am I to do? He's a charming guy; and I wish he were literate and possessed some historical knowledge. I tried to corrupt him with books about Lady Ottoline Morrell and Anthony Blunt; but, while he finds Lady O. to be outrageous, positively living in a cesspool, he seems to take the horrors of Blunt in his stride.[5] However, even though Garsington is just outside Oxford, all this is Cambridge.[6]

Was a little disappointed, this time, with Simone.[7] He seemed to lack his usual *brio* and brilliance.[8] However he's very young and we will see.

Love,

   Colin

---

1 James Rowe,★ who had been visiting Rowe in Rome.
2 *una bella giornata Romana*, Italian: a beautiful Roman day.
3 James Rowe★ and his future wife, Rosie.
4 "Giacomino": Rowe's Italianized nickname for his nephew, James.
5 Lady Ottoline Morrell (1873–1938), English aristocrat and society hostess who befriended intellectuals and artists of the day, renowned for her many extramarital love affairs; and Anthony Blunt (1907–1983), British art historian who was exposed as a Soviet spy late in his life.
6 Garsington was at one time the home of Lady Ottoline Morrell. James grew up in Oxford and was an undergraduate at Oxford University.
7 "Simone": Rowe's Italianized name for his nephew, Simon.
8 *brio*, Italian: vivaciousness.

176 To **Brian Kelly & Matthew Bell**, *School of Architecture, University of Maryland*   *6 September 1989*

Cornell University, College of Architecture, Art & Planning, Rome

Hey you guys:

It's silly and it's inconceivable but I'm missin' both of you a terrible lot. Never expected to feel like this but there it is. It's just perhaps that, for the first time, I feel completely bereft of the U.S. of A.

Got here a week ago. Three days steady rain. Positive *diluvio*.[1] Dinner with Astra Saturday. She lectured me on how I didn't properly appreciate James. Dinner with Derek Tynan and wife on Sunday.[2] They were on their way from Amalfi to Dublin-London. Drinks to Shaw and Hodgden★ Monday.[3] Shaw as negative as you could imagine him to be, Lee highly impressed by the things on the walls. So, simultaneously gruesome and stimulating.

However, I do <u>not</u> anticipate the year as going to be 'interesting'. Think that I shall stagger, with great success, in Houston in November and February (Brian, come for Christmas); but, about May if nothing else happens, I really think that I might croak; but forgive me being so morbid.

You see I need animation which I cannot, entirely, supply for myself; and I need a degree of red kneck presence which is scarcely available in this town.[4]

The U.S. is charming and hospitable. Or is it me that has made it so? But <u>this</u> town which I know so, excessively, well—I don't know that it doesn't bore me.

So Houston will set me up; but what I really need is a couple of trips—Pippo, Billi, Alessandra; otherwise expect me to croak in May.[5]

Losta lurv,

Colin

---

1 *diluvio*, Italian: flood.
2 Derek Tynan, Irish architect and former student of Rowe's Cornell Urban Design Studio.
3 John Shaw and Lee Hodgden,★ Rowe's faculty colleagues in Cornell's School of Architecture.
4 Regarding the "k" in Rowe's "red kneck", Brian Kelly★ wrote to the editor that he thought it "a deliberate affectation meant to encourage the reader to get into a kind of LL Bean/ Homer Men and Boys, backwoods, down home, style of speech".
5 Pippo Ciorra and Alessandra Capuano, architects in Rome; Guglielmo (Billi) Bilancioni, architectural historian from Rome. All were friends of both Rowe and Paulo Berdini.★ Regarding "croak": "Well, he was always about to 'croak'." Brian Kelly★ wrote the editor, "He would often talk about dying and he'd ask that we never refer to it as 'passing on', 'passing', 'expire', or some other sentimental language." Rather, he "asked that we (his friends) refer to his death as 'croaking'."

To **Judith DiMaio**, *West 67th Street, New York, N.Y.*   *25 November 1989*   **177**

Cornell University, College of Architecture, Art & Planning, Rome

Dearest Judy:

There was <u>no</u> way in which I was able to get to <u>that</u> corner of Yukon and Graustark to which <u>you</u> directed me.[1] Simply, although <u>they</u> would drive me by it, it was impossible to persuade them to stop. However, from what I have seen of it, I assume that it is an area in which there are <u>no</u> contextual problems. Close quarters you get the other De Menil jobs—University of St Thomas, Rothko Chapel, and Renzo Piano's *pinacoteca*[2]— and, forgetting Richard Rogers, the Piano item is far the best.[3] (A different thing from Jungle Jim at Stuttgart; galleries, lighting, display are infinitely superior).[4]

So don't worry. Make an early Christian church with an atrium; and make it stripy. Even though the presidents of Harvard and Cornell do <u>not</u> like stripes, because of Rice they are a big deal in Houston and, quite infallibly, <u>stripes</u>, with a bit of local idiosyncrasy, <u>are guaranteed to structure ANY vertical surface</u>.[5]

But don't get too agitated about local particularity. Because the particularities are apt to change, in Houston this is silly. I saw an Irving Phillips* job the other day and I remembered it from the drawings—a small library designed with assiduous concern for adjacent circumstance. But, <u>since</u> building, adjacent circumstance is all gone away; and, as a result, Irving's little building looks like a gesture <u>in vain</u>. No, far better to build a strong building and to hope that its <u>presence</u> will take care of itself. And I think that this <u>must</u> be true even in what threatens to become an ill organised De Menil enclave.

After Houston, where you are highly regarded, I went to Notre Dame, where there was snow and where Father Hesburg's buildings are, indeed, hideous and inexcusable.[6] Then, on Wednesday, Steve Hurtt* drove me from South Bend to O'Hare.[7]

So this was <u>very</u> kind; and after the outrage of Gary, Indiana, there was then the different shock of south Chicago, where I simply thought about multiplication.

I thought about sheets, knives and forks, cups and saucers, kitchen equipment being multiplied beyond belief; and, believe you me, this produces nightmares.

Un abbraccio stravagante

    Colin

P. S. I've already explained to you the [...] hysteria of Rajkovitch with whom Smith seems to be so desperately infatuated.[8]

    Colin X X X X X X X

P.P.S. To add insult to injury, yesterday, when Gorbachev went to Piazza Venezia to lay a wreath on the Altare della Patria, when he broke away from his security guards and all the wives of ambassadors the first person with whom he shook hands was—Rajkovitch![9]

<u>Believe</u> it! The Italian press was <u>very</u> pissed.

    Colin

---

1 Yukon and Graustark in Houston, Texas, the site for a Kohn Pedersen Fox project on which Judith DiMaio* was working.

2 *pinacoteca*, Italian: art gallery.

3 Philip Johnson* designed Strake Hall and Jones Hall at the University of St Thomas. Johnson, Howard Barnstone,* and Eugene Aubry designed the Rothko Chapel. Louis Kahn* had been commissioned to design the Menil Collection art museum, but John de Menil died in 1973 and Kahn himself died in 1974. Renzo Piano was commissioned to design the museum, which opened in 1987.

4 James Stirling's* Staatsgalerie in Stuttgart, Germany, which opened in 1984.

5 Stripes are a salient feature of James Stirling's* MD Anderson Hall at Rice, 1981, which houses the School of Architecture. On stripes at Stirling's Performing Arts Center at Cornell, see Rowe's letter to Stirling dated 16 August 1985 (p 268 this volume).

6 The Rev Theodore Martin Hesburgh, CSC, STD (b 1917) was president of the University of Notre Dame from 1952 to 1987, during which time the University grew rapidly.

7 Notre Dame is in South Bend, Indiana. "O'Hare" is Chicago's O'Hare International Airport. Gary, Indiana, and South Chicago lie between the two.

8 Thomas Norman Rajkovitch, architect, visiting associate professor of architecture at the University of Notre Dame, from 1989 to 1992; Thomas Gordon Smith, architect and chair of the School of Architecture, University of Notre Dame, from 1989 to 1998.

9 Mikhail Gorbachev (b 1931), leader of the USSR in 1989.

Cornell University, College of Architecture, Art & Planning, Rome

Dearest Dorothy:

I spent almost a week at Civita and nobody could have said that it was exactly warm.[1] But how those people do eat! The drive up from Rome is about an hour and three quarters; but it's unthinkable to attempt it unless you have a two hour lunch break on the way. And, likewise the return trip. So you have just had breakfast and are about to leave, and Astra says: "Now where will we stop for lunch?"—when I would have thought that lunch would have been the last thing that she would be thinking about. But, then, they also spend a tremendous amount of time cooking—or having Domenica, their Civita treasure, bake little things for them.

But the big *salone*, 9 metres by 6, even when you were close to the huge fireplace was excessively cold and dark; and, at Christmas, Astra feels compelled to produce traditional Latvian dishes—all of them with the same sauce or stuffing made of shredded prunes, walnuts and cognac, which (though it keeps you regular, as they say) for me is apt to become a little trying, particularly when you may also have to eat mashed potatoes.[2] However she is vivacious, good and kind; but, all the same, it's better when she is not attempting trad. Latvian in Italy. Simply, from how I grab it, the Latvians succeed in making turkey taste like pheasant, taste like chicken, taste like goose. Simply, the dressings obscure any evidence of the original bird.

Matt breezed in and out on his way to see the *innamorata* in Firenze;[3] and he left me a clipping from the *Pittsburgh Post-Gazette*.[4] So the Princess Ileana of Romania is a nun living in a mobile home just outside of Pittsburgh where, apparently, she receives regular greetings from 'Lilibet and Philip'.[5] Very, very strange; but stranger still to recollect that Qu. V. wanted the future Geo. V to marry his cousin Marie of Edinburgh and that she turned down London ('the best position in the world') for Ferdinand of Hohenzollern-Sigmaringen and Bucharest ('where I understand the tone of society is so bad').[6]

It all makes one think of those lines of Ogden Nash:

Have you heard of Mme Lupescu

> Who came to Romania's rescue?
> It's a wonderful thing
> To be under a king
> Is democracy better?
> I escu.[7]

I once met a nephew of Magda Lupescu's in N.Y.C. The Lupescu and King Carol, I seem to remember, both died in relative opulence in Rio de Janeiro; but he didn't seem to do too much for his sister did he? A mobile home in Pennsylvania, in the mountains, far, far away from Balmoral, Osborn and Windsor! Far, far away from the Hohenlohe-Langenburg and the other German cousins. One imagines Qu. V. nodding her head: 'I always predicted that only the worst could ensue'.

But I am also reminded of an occasion outside a supermarket in Austin, Texas. An old lady with a laurel wreath in her hair (!) came towards me and she said:

"Are you Shareman?" And I replied: "*Nein,* Engleesh."

So, "Oh," she said: "Do you know which church;" and when it turned out that she meant Whitchurch, Shropshire, I said that I did. "So do you know ze portal?" To begin with I thought it must be a monumental gateway; but it turned out to be a family. "Ze Portal never write to me. And I write to Queen Marie of Romania. I ask: what has happened to ze Portal? And, do you know I have had no reply."

Finis. Tableau.[8] And <u>very</u> odd. Particularly so as Marie of Romania had already been dead for quite a long time. But the U.S. of A. must still be absolutely stuffed with characters like this—combos of inept memories and poverty.

David comes on the twelfth (I hope <u>solo</u>). He thinks about the Hotel Raphael. But isn't it too expensive. I concur and I propose the Inghilterra, only to discover later that it's even more pricey. I give dinner to James Madge* and his new wife (didn't take <u>him</u> too long to get over the death of Jennie Drew) this evening; and I am <u>not</u> looking forward to it.[9] Matt will return, I suspect, while David is still around and is determined to assist me on my two books—footnotes, pics, layouts, indices, a lot of work.[10] But, since Rice allots Twenty Thousand for these purposes, I don't see that this should be any great financial sweat; and it should be something of a *coup* to have <u>two</u> books appearing at the <u>same</u> time.[11]

I leave for Houston about Jan 24 and will return shortly after the beginning of March.

My best of best love,

    Colin

P.S. My little pleasure (?) for tomorrow threatens to be a lunch given by my assistant, David Foley, for his landlady, Jean Louise Campbell; and, since I have the soul of a butler, it might turn out to be interesting, since Lady Jean is obviously very mixed up. She is the first wife of Norman Mailer, a convert, she divides her time between a convent in Connecticut and an apartment a hundred steps up in Piazza Margana which she sublets to miscellaneous English, Americans and Neapolitans, she advertises herself as a granddaughter of Lord Beaverbrook. Nothing about Clan Campbell and nothing about Inveraray.[12] So I pointed out to David that she must be a daughter of the Duke of Argyll and, possibly, of that celebrated Mrs. Charles Sweeney who, after becoming duchess, got herself mixed up in a shocking sex scandal at the same time as the Profumo affair. So I was correct and <u>that</u> is Lady Jean. *Ci vediamo.*[13]

    Colin

P.P.S.   *January 9, 1990*

This is threatening to become one of my interminable letters; but, since I've returned from Civita, *'ah've been thinkin'*—as <u>they</u> would say in Texas.

I <u>need</u> an automobile and this, automatically, excludes pedestrian cities like Rome, London, New York. I think that it even excludes Oxford. Too much walkin' is apt to be absolute hell. I need to be able to <u>drive</u> up to monuments, see what I want to see, and, then, bug out.

Rome in the winter is <u>not</u> agreeable. It's underheated and all these thick walls <u>sweat</u> with damp. Even Judy says this to me: "Colin, I <u>cannot</u> go to La Pollarola, La Costanza, Archimede, Pierluigi, <u>et al</u>. Simply I would catch rheumatism. Indeed, in your apartment I feel it <u>already</u>." And, if this is Judy, then think of <u>me</u>! About 1830, freezing to death in a Paris drawing room, Mme. Vigée Lebrun and her great friend, the Princess Dolgoruki, both said to each other: "in order to get warm we'll both have to go to Russia." And I agree. In order to keep warm you gotta' go to a cold country. See all those terrible monuments in the Protestant cemetery here. Think about all those tubercular girls from Berlin, London, St. Petersburg, Boston, who were brought, 'for their health', to 'enjoy' a winter in Rome. Almost they all croaked; and it's not very hard to understand why.

Suddenly and after all the food here, I find myself yearning, not for roast beef and Yorkshire pudding (they give that to me in Texas (where the y. p. is called 'popovers' and is very much better). No, what I desperately need is a roast leg of lamb with mint sauce, new potatoes and green peas. After all the elegant, and manipulated, stuff that I eat just this very simple truth to materials would be absolute heaven. But did you ever expect to hear this from me?

The *siesta* is an intolerable tyranny.

All reasons for not staying in Italy throughout the winter. Apart from financial criteria, all reasons why Texas, and the thought of Texas, has become such a conspicuous pleasure, I just don't think that I would have survived the winter here without maniacal depression—and I leave again for Texas in less than three weeks time.

Which is all preparatory to saying that I would like to leave Rome at the end of April to come to London/Oxford. Of course the 'embarrassments' remain but, by now, I think that I can cope with them and, you know, that I want to investigate the possibilities of a place in England. In early March Steve Peterson* will drive me to look at various places in New York State; but I don't have too much confidence in these possibilities and, hence, my English fantasies. And, hence London/Oxford and you/David.[14]

So, do I come to Oxford at the beginning of May?

Best, best love,

    Colin

P.P.S. To all this is added an appendix about what I am proposing to do over the next three years.

    C.

SCHEDULE OF POSSIBLE ACTIVITIES, 1989–1993

June 1989 — officially retire from Cornell and assume four-year contract as Scholar in Residence. This pays Forty Thousand a year; and it assumes that I make one lecture course a year either in Rome or Ithaca

Sept 1989 — come to Rome, lectures to Cornell and Notre Dame, also to Rice

---

II

Spring 1990 — Spring, complete the lectures to Cornell, Notre Dame and Rice. These are the basics of the sixteenth century book.[15]

June 1990 — Retire to Ithaca for a work session on all this; and this is because libraries, assistance and photography are all so much easier there.

August 1990 — Matt arrives for a concentrated four-week work session.

September — I remain in Ithaca until Christmas and give the <u>second</u> lecture series required by the contract. This is "The Architecture of Good Intentions"; and, since it's mostly a re-tread, it shouldn't involve too much sweat. Also, Matt will come up from time to time to assist.

_____

III

Spring 1991 — I will be in Rome and will work on the setting up of the two books with Matt.[16] So, by the end of the summer, I hope that this <u>should</u> be done; and, then, I propose to remain in Rome for a couple of months to give the <u>third</u> lecture sequence required, which will be the sixteenth century replay with qualifications, emendations.

Now it is after this that I want to <u>get out</u>; and I want to come, <u>finally</u>, to *Ingilterra* to make the *opera ultime*, Disraeli* and Inigo Jones.[17]*

So, should we assume that in the Spring of 1992 I will be in Oxford/London to work on Disraeli/Inigo Jones; and, whichever of these I choose, would then be given as the <u>fourth</u> lecture sequence in the Fall of that year, most probably in Ithaca in September-October-November, so that I get out before the snow?

Disraeli, of course would be better; and I impose all this austerity upon myself (which, incidentally, is a pleasure and is <u>all</u> that I understand) because, some time back, David told me that I should scribble a bit more. But then, after November '92, I should be able to romp around to all sorts of funny places.

Let us try to think about this.

    Colin

_____

1   Civita di Bagnoregio, Italy.

2   *salone*, Italian: living-room.

3   *innamorata*, Italian: sweetheart.

4   Rishell, Grace, "Romanian princess has prayers answered", *Pittsburgh Post-Gazette*, c December 1989.

5   The clipping features a photograph captioned "The Reverend Mother Alexander, 80, daughter of King Ferdinand and Queen Marie of Romania" and opens, "One of the most interested observers of the political upheaval in Romania is that country's former Princess Ileana, who has lived for the past 22 years in a monastery near Ellwood City." She is, it says, "now a nun, whose religious name is Mother Alexander", and she lives in a "double-width mobile home on the monastery grounds". She came to the US when Communists forced the royal family to leave Romania in 1948 after which she had six children, divorced, became a nun, and helped to found a Romanian Orthodox monastery near Pittsburgh. At the time of this article, Romania was attempting to free itself from the "24-year rule of Nicolae Ceausescu".

6   Marie of Edinburgh: Marie Alexandra Victoria (1875–1938), spouse to King Ferdinand and queen of Romania.

7   One of the several variations on this classic limerick about King Carol II's mistress, Elena (Magda) Lupescu (1895–1977), a divorcee who married him following his abdication.

8   *Fini*, French: The end; *Tableau*, French: stilled (as at the end of an act in the theater).

9   Jennifer Ann Shirley Alliston-Drew (1937–1986), James Madge's* first wife, daughter of the renowned English architect Jane Drew.

10 Rowe, Colin, *The Architecture of Good Intentions*, London: Academy Editions, 1994; Rowe, Colin and Leon Satkowski,* *Italian Architecture of the Sixteenth Century*, New York: Princeton Architectural Press, 2002.

11 *coup*, French: blow.

12 Inveraray Castle, Scotland, seat of the Duke of Argyll, Chief of Clan Campbell.

13 Margaret Campbell (1912–1993), British socialite and Duchess of Argyll who famously divorced her husband in 1963, initiating a sex scandal of epic proportions; *Ci vediamo*, Italian: I'll be seeing you.

14 Here Rowe is considering places to which he might retire.

15 Rowe, Colin and Leon Satkowski, *Italian Architecture of the Sixteenth Century*, New York: Princeton Architectural Press, 2002. Rowe would spend much of spring 1990 convalescing at the New York City residence of Steven Peterson* and Barbara Littenberg.*

16 The two books are *The Architecture of Good Intentions* and *Italian Architecture of the Sixteenth Century*.

17 *opere ultime*, Italian: last works. Rowe was planning to write a book on either Benjamin Disraeli* or Inigo Jones,* Inigo Jones having been the subject of his MA thesis written in 1947 under the supervision of Rudolf Wittkower.*

[handwritten]¹

To **Dorothy Rowe**, *St. Margaret's Road, Oxford*   *3 February 1990*   **179**

Houston, Texas, The Hilton Houston Plaza-Medical Center Hotel

Dearest Dorothy:

Funny town this but quite restful after Rome. I got into the hotel after twenty hours of traveling about 11.00 p.m. on Tuesday night—rather tired, rather overwrought; and, after all that movement, I found it rather impossible to get to sleep. K.L.M., which I flew all the way, was very good; and, of course, I should have bought myself a small bottle of whisky in the Amsterdam airport so as to stupefy myself.² But I always forget any such commonsense ideas.

Anyway *me voici* (or *me voila*).³ I am in an absurd suite in a Hilton hotel adjacent to this enormous Texas medical center. There are <u>three telephones</u>, two bathrooms, a bedroom with <u>two</u> double beds, no kitchen, but a 'wet' bar eight feet long! But <u>who</u> would <u>want</u> all this when the basic writing table is underlit and just a minor <u>escritoire</u>, about eighteen inches by thirty-six inches in size.

But ever since I arrived the weather has been <u>excessively</u> ominous/lugubrious, not a trace of sun, heavy low banks of black cloud, all the phenomena of the tropical rain forest. So I look out of the window and, from the twentieth floor, I try to see what I might see. However, it's never very much—just banks of dirty mist with a few towns looming through.

Sound cheerful? But I assure you that I do <u>not</u> repine. I go down to the restaurant (where the waiters are apt to look like Aztec frescoes) admire the stamina of the natives and, occasionally, have room service send a dinner up here.

Made my first lec. on Thursday night (I am told a success), make my final lec. on February 21, and then I am really to leave and <u>never</u> return.

But there are charming people here whom I love and who love me and the pathos of it all—the opulence and the squalor—is very strange.

Love

    Colin

P.S. Have you noticed that elevator doors are becoming increasingly impatient? They no longer move with their old Edwardian *tenue*.⁴ In Berlin they operate with the speed and snap of guillotines and, in this town, they are particularly quick on the draw—they hardly allow you time to get in. But observe the consequences of this: and, tonight, I almost witnessed a great calamity.

I have just been down to dinner in the sort of all-purpose palm court garden/lounge/restaurant/foyer which they have downstairs, where the Mexican *maitre a foyer* is always to be found bowing obsequiously; but tonight he was outdone.[5] As I sat there, there entered a group of about thirty Japanese lead by a capo who could bow even more abjectly than the Maitre D. So I first witnessed a tableau of rival bows; and I presume that the Japanese capo felt emboldened by this performance because, as he welcomed each member of his group to the elevators the inclination of his head and the upper part of his body became increasingly excessive. And then the predictable occurred.

When he had succeeded in getting his first elevator so crammed that it began to look like a can of sardines or the black hole of Calcutta, he made a particularly profuse bow and, snap-snap, the elevator doors closed around his neck! His head was inside, and the rest of him was outside! And though not exactly guillotined, he was certainly trapped in the mechanical jaws of the monster?

Therefore, to be expected, consternation. Bell boys rush up, retro-active buttons are pressed and the monster is compelled to retract its victim. But it all goes to show, doesn't it?

Anyway, it was a nice diversion during dinner; and I found myself almost regretting that the mechanism, apparently inexorable, had been thwarted. But Italian restaurants do not provide such thrills and Texas elevators now threaten to become almost as exciting as those high-tech, francofied, London public elevators which, infallibly, drown little old ladies.

Reactions were phlegmatic, even from the Spanish component which saw it all. But I found myself regretting the headlines which had been lost:

Japanese Visitor to Texas Medical Center Done to Death by Elevator in Hilton Hotel. Architect Observes Speed of Elevator Doors as Contemporary Hazard.

Can't help thinking that it would have looked well in *The New York Times*.

　　Colin

1　This letter was printed by hand with a felt-tip pen in all capital letters.
2　"K.L.M.": Royal Dutch Airlines.
3　*me voici* (or *me voilà*), French and English: Here I am (or there I am).
4　*tenue*, French: bearing comportment.
5　*maître du foyer*, French: master of the house.

180　　[handwritten][1]

*To **Alan Colquhoun**, School of Architecture, Princeton University*　　　*3 February 1990*

Houston, Texas, The Hilton Houston Plaza-Medical Center Hotel

Dearest Alan:

　　Have you observed how increasingly impatient elevator doors have lately become?

This is not true of Rome, scarcely true of N.Y.C., true of Berlin where they act like a horizontal guillotine, and abundantly true of this town where they are particularly quick on the draw.

So, observe the consequences of this. Tonight I was sitting downstairs, having dinner in the all-purpose lounge/restaurant, foyer of this hotel, when in there came a group of about thirty Japanese lead by a capo of highly polite and samurai style, compelled to bow, obsessively and frequently to all of his escort. Therefore, as you can imagine, the decorum of the procedure is endless: but, when the elevator is beginning to look like the black hole of Calcutta, as an *envoi* he takes a particularly protracted bow.[2] And the predictable occurs.

Inexorably and with great speed the elevator doors close upon his neck; and, with all his old style *politesse*, this capo is left with his head inside and the rest of him outside![3] A curious confrontation of two patterns of behaviour which I was able to witness from less than forty feet away. But Italian/Roman restaurants can offer you no such thrills.

But, to introduce Italy, I am remembering the occasion a very long time ago when, at the border, you were taken off the train and interrogated as to whether you were Archibald Colquhoun.[4]

So, ever since then, I have been wondering about this other Colquhoun who was/is a friend of Harold Acton,* lived in Naples in the late 1930s and, after W.W. II returned to Italy as a rabid Marxist. Did a translation of *La Chartreuse de Parme*,[5] did another translation of Manzoni's *I promessi sposi*,[6] was hauled in by the police in Venice and told that, if he went on [in] his present way, quite soon he'd be doing a translation of *Le mie prigioni*.[7] But just think about this: and this must be where you came in...!

However, if it amuses you, read about it in Harold Acton's slightly dreary book (mostly a big yawn) *More Memoirs of an Aesthete*.[8]

As you might guess, this town, for me, is a little bit like the last act of Proust— so many confirmations and so many surprises, so many people whom I love and so many people who reciprocate my affection. But this is difficult since, without exception, I find them all retarded. And, apart from that, this ambiguity is decidedly lugubrious. I have now been here for five days and, during all this time (me looking out from the eighteenth floor of this hotel) everything has been cataclysmically black, misty and obscure. All in all, a terrible view of a frustrated tropical rain forest.

So, I gather, from Judy, that you have had a bad scene with John; and I must admit that, for all sorts of reasons, I am not surprised.[9] But then, *che fai*?[10] And I presume Primrose Hill.[11] But, as for me, *che faccio*?[12]

Simply, I don't know but I am beginning to know. And I now do know that Rome is impossible for me, and, in spite of all my love, anywhere else in Italy is inadequate. One means that one knows this most superb landscape but one also knows that, in these scenes, the L.S.Q. (the *Literate Societe Quotidienne*) is completely lacking.[13]

So what to do?

It seems, for me, to be that the British government's *Animus Revertendi* doctrine is about to apply, that I will return.[14] To Newbury-Hungerford?[15] I wonder and I don't know.

    Colin

P.S. My best love to Roberto.[16] It's so long since I saw the two of you.

    Colin

---

1 This letter was printed by hand with a felt-tip pen in all capital letters. "It has nothing in it about architecture", Alan Colquhoun* wrote the editor on 6 August 2009, "But it shows Colin in a typically extravagant mode; his love of parody, and his often rather cruel wit, a bit reminiscent of Hilaire Belloc."

2 *envoi*, French: send off.

3 *politesse*, French: courtesy.

4 In an August 2009 letter to the editor, Alan Colquhoun* explained, "This event took place in 1949, en route, with Colin, for Italy (by train). Archibald Colquhoun was <u>no</u> relation of mine, but the frontier police mistook me for him…. He was in the Foreign Office during the War and was sent to Italy to work with the Resistance. Unfortunately, he was also a Communist spy, and in 1949 he was on the run. I knew of his work with the Resistance and thought I was being welcomed as a Resistance <u>Hero</u>. As it turned out, I narrowly avoided being arrested as a spy!"

5 Stendhal [Marie Henri Beyle], *The Charterhouse of Parma*, Paris, 1839.

6 Alessandro Manzoni, *I promessi sposi*, Florence: Massimo, 1827. Translated with intro by Archibald Colquhoun: Manzoni, Alessandro, *The Betrothed: A Tale of Seventeenth Century Milan*, Archibald Colquhoun trans, London: JM Dent and Sons, 1951.

7 Pellico, Silvio, *Le mie Prigioni: Memorie*, (My prison: memoirs), 1832.

8 Acton, Sir Harold, *More Memoirs of an Aesthete*, London: Methuen, 1970; for Archibald Colquhoun in Naples, see pp 50 and 293. Sir Harold Acton (1904–1994) is mentioned in several of Rowe's letters.

9 Alan Colquhoun* and John Miller* were partners in the architectural firm of Colquhoun and Miller from 1961 to 1989. The partnership was dissolved shortly before Rowe wrote this letter.

10 *Che fai?*, Italian: What's up? What are you doing?

11 Primrose Hill was Alan Colquhoun's* address in London.

12 *Che faccio,* Italian: What do I do?

13 *Literate Société Quotidienne*, French: Literate Society Daily; the everyday literate society.

14 *Animus revertendi*, Latin: with intention to return. The British government's *Animus revertendi* doctrine addresses the legal rights of an Englishman returning to England after cessation of his employment in a foreign country in which he owned land.

15 Newbury and Hungerford are small Berkshire towns 60 and 70 miles west of London.

16 "Roberto": Robert Maxwell.*

181   *To **Judith DiMaio**, West 67th Street, New York, N.Y.*   *25 July 1990*

19 Renwick Place, Ithaca, N.Y.

Dearest Judy:

Borbone di Parma e Borbone di Napoli[1]

For your instruction:

Presumably Parma became annexed to the states of the Church about 1530–40 and it was then promptly alienated by Paul III (Alessandro Farnese) when, in 1545, he created his illegitimate son, Pierluigi, Duke of Parma; and this is one of the reasons why Palazzo Farnese was scarcely ever occupied by the family. Though they never again lived in quite so grand a house, they became rather more splendid than mere Roman princes.

So Pierluigi was assassinated in 1547 (for good reasons); but, by now connected with the Habsburgs, the Farnese continued to thrive—as generals, viceroys, and all that stuff; and it was Elisabetta Farnese who became married to the first Bourbon king of Spain, Philip V, great grandson of Louis XIV: so, about the war of the Spanish Succession and the great victories of the first Duke of Marlborough—Blenheim, Oudenarde, Ramillies, and Malplaquet—read Winston Churchill's biography of the first duke.[2] It is really very good; and it involves Marlborough's nephew, illegitimate son of James II of England, Duke of Berwick, fighting on the Franco-Spanish side.

However, because of internal English politics, Philip still became king of Spain (for their pains the English merely got Gibraltar, which they seized in 1704); and when the Farnese, in the male line became extinct in 1731, it was Elisabetta, daughter of Ranuccio II Farnese (obit 1694) who by the terms of the Quadruple Alliance (London 1718) became the reason why the *Borbone di Spagna* came to inherit.

Well that's mostly the story.

But the second son of Elisabetta spent only three years in Parma; and, in 1734, left to become Charles III of Naples (hitherto a Spanish viceroyalty); and it was Carlo who shipped all that Farnese stuff, both from Rome and Parma, down to Naples and Capodimonte. But you gotta imagine the trip which those items took. From Parma the Correggio's, Tizianos, Parmigianinos, *et al*, obviously travelled flat (were they shipped via Venice?); but, from Rome, when you begin to think about the Farnese Hercules and the Farnese Bull, you have to imagine the packaging job, my dearest, it must have been a super Bolliger that was required.[3]

O.K. so that is part of the story about the *Borbone di Parma* and the *Borbone di Napoli* (*ou des Deux Siciles*).[4] Carlo III di Napoli, one thinks of as an enlightened but somewhat extravagant prince; and, in Naples before going on to become Charles III of Spain, he seems to have done everything—begun the works at Portici, Capodimonte, Caserta, and all the rest, and pity it is that all of these now seem to be as lost as if they were in a Mexican or African slum. But a town like Martina Franca makes one recognise that the B.D.N. could not have been so lousy bad as the nineteenth century English liberals imagined.

Both the B.D.N. and the B.D.P. invariably married Habsburg and Bourbon cousins. As ruling houses they were obliterated in Parma in 1859 and Naples in 1860; but a conservative like me still, as you know, wonders why. The B.D.P. married well. The Empress Zita of Austria, who croaked last year, was a B.D.P., daughter of the last Duke of Parma. But I rather suspect that the B.D.N. assisted their own disappearance. They <u>are</u> around but, they, mostly, <u>went away</u>.

Best love,

    Colin

P.S. But <u>why</u> didn't I give this to you when you were here the other day.

    C

P.P.S. A phone call from Peter Eisenman:* Alvin Boyarsky* died this morning—very shocking; but the message was transmitted to Peter before me and the date is now August 6.

    C

---

1 *Borbone di Parma e Borbone di Napoli*, Italian: Bourbons of Parma and Bourbons of Naples.
2 Churchill, Winston S, *Marlborough, His Life and Times,* 4 vols, London: Harrap, 1934–1938.
3 Bollinger Roma SpA, an international moving/shipping and storage company.
4 *ou des Deux Siciles,* French: or the Two Sicilies.

*To **John Shearman**,*
Harvard University, Department of Fine Arts, Cambridge, Mass.   *26 July 1990* **182**
Cornell Architecture, Ithaca, N.Y.

Dear John Shearman:*

    I have just returned from a trip to Oxford/London where, <u>again</u>, I found myself without access to a typewriter and secretarial assistance; and, hence, still no letter to

Michael Spence. But, perhaps, all this delay has been as well because, on good advice though contrary to my own inclinations, I am now writing to him in the negative; and I enclose a copy of my letter.[1]

You see, I found myself the subject of debate. There were those who said: "Of course, you have something to say, it is very illustrious, the money is excellent, and who but you?"; and, then, there were my brother and sister in law who said: "by no means, it will divert your attention, you have enough to do already, you don't need either the money or the prestige, and, should you get excited—who knows—there may be another—and worse—muscular spasms, and how embarrassing this will be for both Harvard and yourself."

So these were the arguments and, on the whole and with reluctance, I felt compelled to accept my brother's.

Repeat: I am very reluctant about this. My physical condition is now much better than it was when I saw you a few weeks ago; but I am made aware that, <u>with strain</u>, it could easily deteriorate. And I know that, for a couple of years, I MUST NOT impose strain.

Pity it is. But that's how it is. And, only the other night in London, I was thinking of what was to happen to modern architecture's apologetic now that the Marxist empire has gone away. In spite of Imperial Russia <u>does</u> the Marxist <u>ideology</u> survive? And, if so, just what are Kenneth Frampton, Manfredo Tafuri, Francesco dal Co going to say?

This, of course, could have been one of the great topics of The Charles Eliot Norton Lectures: how to preserve an ideologically Marxist critique when political Marxism has gone away; or, alternatively, how to preserve a principle of resistance in a world where consumer capitalism throbs, excites, disgusts.

Best love and many regrets,

> Colin Rowe

P.S. You know that a great topic is at St. Benedict and Subiaco, William Morris, the Bauhaus and Capitalism.[2]

---

1 John Shearman* (1931–2003), chair of Harvard's Department of Fine Arts from 1990 to 1993. The enclosure, a letter to Michael Spence declining Harvard's invitation to Rowe to deliver the prestigious Charles Eliot Norton Lectures, is lost.
2 Subiaco, Italy, site of the first convents, founded in the sixth century by Benedict of Norcia.

183   *To David Rowe*   *31 July 1990*

19 Renwick Place, Ithaca, N. Y.

Dearest David:

Emmanuel Héré de Gorny was born in Lunéville in 1705 and died in Nancy in 1763.[1] He was the father of sixteen children by <u>one</u> wife (poor thing) and at one stage set up a factory for making starch out of horse chestnuts which, obviously, failed.

He never travelled; it is not certain that he even visited Paris; and, apart from his job in Nancy, in that city, apparently, there are to be found: the Seminaire des Missions Royales des Jesuites, 1739, the church of Bonsecours, n.d., and, surviving from his city gates, the Porte Stanislas. Then, outside Nancy but still in Lorraine, there were works at Chanteux, Eiville, Malgrange, Commercy and Lunéville (which, of course, was the residence of Stanislas).

Within his lifetime he was the subject of two publications:

Recueil des plans, elevations et coupes tant geometrales qu'en perspective des chateaux, jardins et dependances que le Roy de Pologne occupe en Lorraine, 2 vols, n.d.; and

Plans et elevations de la Place Royale de Nancy et d'autres edifices batis qui l'environment batis par les ordres du Roi de Pologne, duc de Lorraine, 1753

See also:

Compte General des Edifices et Batiments que the le roy de Pologne, Duc de Lorraine et Bar a fait construire pour le embellissement de la ville despuis 1751 jusqu'en 1759, Lunéville 1761.[2]

So, even though he croaked quite young, he must have felt that his immortality was assured.

All of this I picked up from what Rudi Wittkower* thought was a deplorable source: Reginald Blomfield's *A History of French Architecture from 1661 to 1774*, London 1921.[3]

But why this sudden interest in Lorraine? And have you been to Charleville which has a quite exceptional early seventeenth century *place*, the twin to the Place des Vosges?[4]

About tennis balls, Susie said: "I don't want to hear. I know that it's some dreadful macho joke"; and Fred said: "Sure, it's something you get between your legs if you play too much tennis." However and ineffectively, we explained some of <u>your</u> problems with the E.E.C.[5] and she, gradually, came to understand. But, the other day, I found something called 'sneaker balls' (for putting in tennis shoes) and Judy, who was here, thought that I should send some to you. However, though a good idea, it's a nuisance and a sweat to follow up.

Judy came in like the inevitable <u>scirocco</u>, flung open all the windows and then complained about the monsters that got in. She had just come back from Napoli-Amalfi-Capri, where she went with Michael Graves.* "But Michael said: you know that I tire him and he asked whether I didn't exhaust you too. He said that he didn't like Roman ruins and, sooner or later, he likes to see a building with a roof on top of it. He only liked Bramante's nymphaeum at Genazzano; and it all sounded so much like you. But WHY do you and Michael have this prejudice?"

"Well my dear"... but there ensue interruptions, interruptions, interruptions, and, finally, I feel compelled to quote Tennyson:

Man for the field and woman for the hearth
Man for the sword and for the needle she
Man for the head and woman for the heart
Man to command and woman to obey
All else confusion[6]

So, though excruciating and Victorian at its most monstrous, it calmed her down and she would love to come to St. Tropez during the first week of September.[7] May she? We would arrive on that outfit which flies New York-Rome with an early morning stop at Nice/Nizza. It's a very O.K. flight full of rich New Yorkers going to see kids at school in Provence or, alternatively, taking kids at school in Provence on to places in Wopland.

So may she come?

    Colin

P.S. Please, please send the plans of that apt.

    C.

P.P.S. Capri seems to have been less than charming. Like me, Michael didn't like Axel Munthe's Villa San Michele; and, of course, Judy raves about it.[8] And then, at the 1930's house by Libera[9] (which neither of them liked) they ran into Charles and Maggie Jencks;*[★] and, over dinner, C.J. told Michael that he was a Fascist hyena pig. All this because there are swans on the roof of the new hotel that he's done for Disneyworld down in Florida.[10] Because apparently—but don't you see it—the swans evoke recollections of Lohengrin; and from Ludwig II to Third Reich is the merest of steps!

WOW!

    Colin

---

1 Emmanuel Héré de Corny (1705–1763), court architect in Nancy, France, to Stanislas Leszczynski (1677–1766), Duke of Lorraine, former king of Poland.
2 *General Account of Structures and Buildings that the King of Poland, Duke of Lorraine and Bar, Constructed for the Embellishment of the City from 1751 to 1759.*
3 Blomfield, Sir Reginald, *History of French Architecture: From the Reign of Charles VIII to the Death of Mazarin* and *From the Death of Mazarin till the Death of Louis XV, 1661–1774*, 2 vols, London: G Bell and Sons, Ltd, 1911, 1921.
4 *place*, French: urban open space.
5 "E.E.C.": European Economic Community.
6 Tennyson, Alfred Lord, *The Princess*, London: Edward Moxon, Dover Street,1847, pt V, ll, pp 427–431.
7 Presumably, David Rowe* had rented a house in Saint Tropez.
8 The Villa San Michele, above Capri in the village of Anacapri, Italy, was converted from a ruined chapel in the late 1870s by Swedish physician and collector of antiquities Axel Munthe (1857–1949).
9 Casa Malaparte on Punta Massullo, on the eastern side of the Isle of Capri, Italy, designed in 1937 by architect Adalberto Libera (1903–1963); redesigned and built by Curzio Malaparte (1898–1957), journalist, writer, and involved in both the Fascist and anti-Fascist movements.
10 The Swan Resort, Walt Disney World, Orlando, Florida, 1987.

---

184   *To **Dorothy Rowe**, St Margaret's Road, Oxford*   *14 August 1990*

19 Renwick Place, Ithaca, N.Y.

Dearest Dorothy:

You know that book *The Rose and The Ring*.[1] It has a Prince Giglio and a Prince Bulbo, a king of Crim Tartany, a Countess Gruffanoff, an Angelica, and a Betsinda. It is a Victorian children's classic (I had it as a kid) and it was written by Thackeray for Alice Storey, daughter of William Wetmore Storey, in the 1840's for that enormous apt. that the Storey's occupied in Palazzo Barberini.[2]

So the Storey story is quite <u>bad</u> enough and is a super Boston piece. Papa was a chief justice of the United States and, when he croaked the mysterious 'they' said to him: "but why don't you make your father's monument?" So Bill Storey is supposed to have said: "I can't do that until I go to Rome and learn to be a sculptor;" and, therefore, to Rome he went, occupied a forty-room apt. churned out academic pieces and, presumably, entertained—the statue of Buddy Boy Peabody outside the Royal Exchange is a Storey piece.[3]

So Bill Storey never left Rome; but that is no matter. We are concerned with *The Rose and The Ring*, I imagine a book now quite difficult to find. But I would like it to be your present to the Peterson's;* and, with this particular provenance it would be absolutely terrific.[4] Betsinda is, of course, a Cinderella character who turns out to be the Princess Rosalba and marries Giglio and the Countess Gruffanoff is finally disclosed to be the wife of the footman, Jenkins; but the weather is so black and sinister that, even in the middle of the afternoon, I can scarcely see to type.

Anyway, they have the manuscript—illustrated by Thackeray—at the Morgan Library in N.Y.C. and they publish a facsimile; but too expensive and not very useful and Mr. Thingy in Blacklands Terrace I am sure would provide at the drop of a hat.[5] But it is an adorable book which I had aged five or six.

Also, Mr. Thingy could equip you with a copy of Ruskin's *King of the Golden River* (this is a Tyrolean affair) which you could also send to the Petersons for the little Miriam.[6]

Have just, while typing this last sentence, received a phone call from Astra and Tony at Civita. The house next door to them is for sale and I had thought about it for J. and S. Dates from the thirteen hundreds and is quite large. But, with the apartment in Gloucester Avenue, I now am completely strapped.[7] So whaddya think?

Do you think that J. and S. should sell Ledwell and buy Civita?[8]

Personally, since I find Ledwell depressing, I think that it would be a clever move; but I also, think about it more cynically. Civita is superb and ravishing. Myself adores Astra and Tony; and they adore Giacomino; and, had they met him, they would adore Simone.

But this is a cheap *entrée* into an important property.[9]

Best love,

    Colin

P.S. While you were out at Scottish dancing I rang James and talked to him and Rosie. So wildly excited but reluctant to dispose of Ledwell. But to raise a mortgage on Ledwell and to buy Civita seems to be the idea; and this would be absolutely terrific. James, with his Italian, would rapidly become *primo personalita* in Civita; you would be able to stay there; maybe I could still make my *fondazione*; and Astra would be assured of the support which, I think that she needs. It's still very black and silly and thunderous.[10]

    Colin

P.S. Today, Sunday, cleaning out papers I came across the enclosed cheque/check from the Trustees of F. Beaumont Ded'd, which, apparently I had overlooked.[11] I think that it must have reached me in Rome just after I had left for Texas and I suppose that this must explain my neglect of it.

So will you please re-issue.

    C.

P.P.S. I send you a tear out from *The RIBA Journal* (about all that it is good for) but I thought that you might like the pics of Brodsworth Hall.[12] They are much better than those published by Mark Girouard.[13]*

    C.

Am told that I should put this house on the market at $225,000 and I will get further advice; but, anyway, I am quite pleased. Though it's not much, it is still rather more than I expected since the house next door (same date, same builder) sold three years ago for $180,000 which seems to suggest that property values in Ithaca have not slumped as they seem to have around New York City, Houston and elsewhere. But *speriamo*.[14] The house cost $30,000 in 1971 and the mortgage was completely paid off earlier this year.

Greenberg/Monteverdi paid so much for the Mahoney* house because of ten acres of land attached to it; and he proposes to demolish and develop.[15] A pity to demolish, though it does need a lot of work; and, completely empty, a lot of it doesn't look much more than a warehouse. However, the street is zoned for two acre properties. So Monteverdi can get five houses on the property and still retain the best location (secluded and with view) for himself.

But WHY did Mahoney leave all this (and more) to the UNITARIAN church? One perceives that by this transaction that grease-ball institution has received a bequest of at least $425,000; and the poor Mahoney didn't think that he had a penny to his name!

    Colin

---

1 Thackeray, William, *The Rose and the Ring; Or, The History of Prince Giglio and Prince Bulbo*, London: Smith, Elder, and Co, 1855, written under the pseudonym MA Titmarsh.
2 William Wetmore Story (1819–1895), American sculptor, poet, and art critic. Rowe consistently spelled "Story" with an "e".
3 Erected in 1869, a larger-than-life bronze of a seated George Peabody (1795–1869), American British entrepreneur, banker, and philanthropist.
4 Steven Peterson* and Barbara Littenberg,* whose daughter, Miriam, had just had her eighth birthday.
5 John Sandoe of John Sandoe (Books), Ltd, 10 Blacklands Terrace, Chelsea, London.
6 Ruskin, John, *The King of the Golden River; Or, The Black Brothers: A Legend of Stiria*, London: Smith, Elder, and Co, 1851.
7 Rowe was in the process of purchasing, through David Rowe,* an apartment in Gloucester Avenue in London.
8 Ledwell refers to a two-and-a-half bedroom cottage in Ledwell, a small village in Oxfordshire, which David Rowe* purchased in 1967 for use by the family on weekends and holidays.
9 *entrée*, French: entrance.
10 *primo personalita*, Italian: first person.
11 The enclosure is lost.
12 "Brodsworth Saved", *RIBA Journal* 97, no 6, June 1990, pp 64–66. Brodsworth Hall,1861–1863, lies six miles north-east of Bolton-on-Dearne, where Colin and David Rowe* grew up.
13 Girouard, Mark, *The Victorian Country House*, Oxford: Clarendon Press, 1971.
14 *speriamo*, Italian: let's hope.
15 "Monteverdi" is Rowe's italianized name for his neighbor, Don Greenburg, who bought the Mahoney* house for $350,000.

185   *To **David Rowe***   *17 September 1990*

19 Renwick Place, Ithaca, N.Y.

Dearest David:

    As you have always known this place is social desolation; and, though the students <u>may</u> have been brilliant, the faculty has <u>always</u> been banal.

All the same so many of the students, like Alex Caragonne,* Fred Koetter,* Peter Szilagyi, Matt Bell,* were so wonderful that one could forget the faculty and simply give brilliant parties. However, now as I cease to teach and the students go away, though the new ones try to grab me, I am left with a total absence and vacuity.

I am sure that the students who came to see me the other night (and it was very nice of them and they expected revelation) were awful good guys but, still, I can no longer see myself endlessly providing diversion for people not so much older than James.

And this means the quicker the exit the better because I entirely depend on week end visitors and, otherwise, the isolation is quite excessive.

So people come from Boston and Miami and New York and Los Angeles; but this isn't exactly like Voltaire at Ferney.[1] People ring up from Rome and Bilbao; but never, never have I received a phone call from any colleague here. Nor, do I think, will.

Tough? Or doncha think? But, of course, they are busily concerned in repairing the 'damages' which have been provoked by my presence.

So don't mind and you'll probably see me before you receive this letter.

Best love,

    Colin

P.S. My service *equipe* seems now to be entirely Hispanic—from Madrid, Caracas, Miami and Bilbao; and they are going to help me get the garbage out of the house tomorrow night.[2] Meanwhile I learn that Xavier Cenicaceleya, from Bilbao, is to be Dean at the University of Miami.[3] Never met him; but this is the product of my ex-Cornell, Miami team—Jose Gelabert, along with Jorge and Luis Trelles.[4] Xavier is pleased and also am I. But, for long distance politics, don't you think? And, actually, it's a great combination. Xavier seems to own the Bilbao magazine, *Arquitectonica,* which is very distinguished; and all the guys in Miami are just rearin' to go with, among them, Liz Plater-Zyberk* and Andres Duany* who are the particular pets of the P.O.W.[5]

So this is a little combination which myself has brought about and it must have its own internal politics. But, whenever the P.O.W. goes down to play polo at Palm Beach, it seems to be really this group that he wants to see.

Interesting? Maybe. Important? Perhaps not.

    Colin

---

1 Voltaire (1694–1778), French Enlightenment writer. Having been banned from Paris and Geneva, for the last 20 years of his life Voltaire resided in Ferney, a village on the French-Swiss border. As Ferney possessed no inn, Voltaire invited his visitors to stay overnight in his chateau.

2 *l'équipe*, French: team.

3 Javier Cenicacelaya.*

4 From Venezuela, Jose Gelabert-Navia (b 1954) earned his bachelor's degree in 1974 and master's degree in 1978 from Cornell University. He is professor of architecture and former dean of the School of Architecture at the University of Miami. The brothers Jorge (b 1958) and Luis Trelles (b 1956) were students of Rowe's Urban Design Studio at Cornell in the early 1980s.

5 Elizabeth Plater-Zyberk* (b 1950) and Andrés Duany* (b 1949), planners who helped develop Seaside, Florida, in the late 1970s. Regarding Seaside, see Rowe's letter to Cynthia Davidson* dated 31 July 1993 (p 399 in this volume).

Rome

Dearest Dorothy:

It seems that, for all of my scribblin', I haven't yet thanked you for the P.O.W's book which, I think, is better than you give it credit for.[1] It is naïve and populist; but of course. Also, it doesn't say any more than what *The Architectural Review* has been saying for about the last thirty years; and, if this has not elicited <u>any</u> controversy, then it says much for the prestige of the monarchical institution in the U.K. that, when the Heir Apparent simply reproduces old style arguments from *The Architectural Review*, the 'liberal' establishment should become so inflamed.

Honest to God you might believe, from this quarter's reactions, that mod. arch. was still a going and an heroic concern. When, in *Collage City*, Fred and I intimated that this was scarcely the case there was scarcely anybody who even flickered an eyelid; but, when H.R.H. says the same....[2] Well, Jesus Christ, the 'liberal' establishment begins to approach *lese majeste*.[3]

But <u>they</u> can't say, as <u>they</u> do, that the poor guy's water colours are fuddy-duddy and no good. Because the contrary is true; and everybody, *Italiano* or *Americano*, who has looked at the book, has been astonished by his discernment and capacity. Of course, I wish that he didn't always get pictures of himself painting wearing a double-breasted suit. Apart from being prissy and uncomfortable, it seems to be at variance with the populist image of himself which he is, otherwise, anxious to promote; and <u>what</u> is really wrong with shirtsleeves anyway?

In any case, apropos the water colours, it must be obvious that, since V. and A, only Princess Louise possessed anything like Carlo's capacity; and, when the 'liberal' establishment dumps on this capacity, then it only discloses its ignorance and desperation.[4]

Pity that he has <u>so</u> little knowledge; and, pity it is that Prince Albert would have handled all this with much greater *seriosita*.[5] But, ya' gotta take the rough with the smooth; and, after the barbarism of Ed. VII and Geo. V (think of Geo. V, with his awful swearing and his Royal Command Variety Performances—while Covent Garden languished under the auspices of Thomas Beecham and Lady Cunard) then, apart from Q.M. as a collector, this is the first one, out of <u>that</u> crowd, to have displayed the slightest traces of visual interest.

Also pity it is that the P.O.W. doesn't dare to dump on Thatcher, who is a primary source of his agitation.[6] But in general, though ingenuous, his prejudices are justified. But unfortunate that he didn't read *Collage City*.

Best love,

    Colin

P.S.

The members of the corps
All hate the thought of war
They'd rather kill em off by peaceful means.
But all we want the world to know
Is we support the status quo.

They love us everywhere we go,
And, when in doubt,
Send the Marines.[7]

Ref. is obviously to the U.S. 'affair' in Panama. By what argument is it thought that an American court can try a foreign head of state however criminal he may be? And why is it even possible to think about it. Because everybody tells me that the dirt on Bush will then 'get out'.[8]

    Colin

---

1 HRH Prince of Wales, Charles, *A Vision of Britain: A Personal View of Architecture*, London: Doubleday, 1989.
2 Colin Rowe and Fred Koetter,⋆ *Collage City*, Cambridge, MA: MIT Press, 1978.
3 *lèse-majesté*, French: defamation of the ruler or sovereign power.
4 "V. and A.": Queen Victoria (1819–1901) and Prince Albert (1819–1861); Princess Louise Caroline Alberta, Duchess of Argyll (1848–1939), was the artist daughter of Queen Victoria.
5 *seriosita*, Italian: seriousness.
6 Margaret Thatcher (1925–2013), British prime minister from 1979 to 1990.
7 A variation on Tom Lehrer's satirical song of 1965, "Send the Marines".
8 In December 1989, during George HW Bush's presidency, the US invaded Panama ("Operation Just Cause") and took its military governor, Manuel Noriega (b 1934), into captivity. He was awaiting trial in Miami at the time this letter was written.

To **Thomas Muirhead**, *Upper Montagu Street, London*   *15 December 1990*   **187**

19 Renwick Place, Ithaca, New York

Dear Tom:

When you invited me to Lugano you didn't appear to recognise under what extreme pressure I was a year ago.[1] Simply there was no way in which I could have done it. Damp and unheated buildings in Italy and then monstrously air conditioned buildings in Texas had done their worst; and, apparently, I had contracted arthritis.

Very shattering; but there it was, though I didn't know it.

So my second trip to Houston was worse than the first and, towards the end of February, leaning over to pick up a Palladio⋆ slide (!), I experienced a muscular spasm which kept me flat on my back for almost three months.[2] But I understand that this is quite common, almost endemic, in Houston and Los Angeles.

Therefore, grab the idea that this was a shattering event and that I have not, yet, completely recovered from it. But it's rough; and when Harvard, the University and not the G.S.D.,[3] asked me to make the Charles Eliot Norton Lectures for 1992–1993, on the advice of family and friends I had to refuse.[4]

$120,000.00 for six lecs! It was pretty hard to refuse; but I saw no way to do otherwise.

However, as you may know, I have now acquired an apt. just up the road from you in Gloucester Avenue, just where it joins Regent's Park Road, and I now hope to move in April.[5]

See ya,

    Colin

1 In fall 1989, while teaching a design studio for SCI-ARC in Lugano, Thomas Muirhead* had invited Rowe—who was teaching in Italy at the time—to lecture on the Lugano-born architect Francesco Borromini (1599–1667).
2 At the time, Rowe was visiting professor at Rice University. The injury forced him to leave Houston. He convalesced for several months at the New York residence of Steven Peterson* and Barbara Littenberg.*
3 "G.S.D.": Graduate School of Design.
4 The appointment was filled by Umberto Eco, who delivered *Six Walks in the Fictional Woods*, Cambridge, MA: Harvard University Press, 1994.
5 Muirhead's* apartment in Upper Montagu Street, London, was just to the southwest of Regent's Park; Rowe's apartment in Gloucester Avenue was just to the northeast. He resided there in July and August 1992 and from September 1993 to October 1994.

188   To **Robert Goodill**, *Syracuse University, Florence Italy*   *1 January 1991*

19 Renwick Place, Ithaca, N.Y.

Robert:

The best of wishes for this year!

Do you think that there is going to be a war?[1] And, if there is, is Syracuse going to get out of Florence. But, certainly, Cornell is going to get out of Rome because <u>why</u> allow American students to be sniped at and bombed by a combo of Lousy Arab sharpshooters? And, you <u>must</u> know, that <u>they</u> will do <u>this</u>.

But, almost, I hope that there is going to be a war because this will bring you back to Syracuse and, then, at least I shall have somebody to talk to.

Feller, it's been total desolation here; and, sometimes, I feel that, perhaps, I have croaked and <u>not</u> known it. There is the ruling junta, Val, Andrea, Mulcahy, Zissovici, obviously served by the obsequious John Shaw, and there is Lee, obviously out on a limb; but, for any of these people, do I have <u>any</u> existence?[2] *Per questi sono completamente finite.*[3] Gone and, happily, forgotten. Dear Robert, until now, I never knew that myself was such a lousy bastard!

However, I do not repine and, occasionally, I feel radiant; but, the other day, I had a phone call from Wilvan van Kampen who told me that you, too, were not exactly popular with the American community in Firenze, that you were widely regarded as a Fascist hyena pig. So, dear hyena/pig, I do hope not; but, if so, what matter? Just a bunch of excruciatin' liberals anyway.

Dear pig, tell me whom <u>do</u> you see. Xtiano Toraldo di Francia? Gianni Pettena, Joel's sailing companion? Marco Mattei?[4] Matt almost vomits over all these names; and he is coming up with Paolo the day after tomorrow.[5]

Best love,

   Colin

But Firenze as one always has known is <u>not</u> a cheerful city. Cold and lugubrious it certainly is.

1 Operation Desert Storm began 17 January 1991.
2 Val Warke, Andrea Simitch, Vince Mulcahy, John Zissovici, John Shaw and Lee Hodgden:* faculty in Cornell University's School of Architecture.

354   The Letters of Colin Rowe

3   *Per questi sono completamente finito*, Italian: for these people I am completely finished.
4   Joel Bostic, a sailing enthusiast who taught for Syracuse in Florence. Gianni Pettena, Marco Mattei, and Xtiano Toraldo di Francia were Italian guest critics in the Syracuse Florence program.
5   Matthew Bell* and Paolo Berdini.*

To **Dorothy Rowe**, *St. Margaret's Road, Oxford*   15 March 1991   **189**

19 Renwick Place, Ithaca, N.Y.

Dearest Dorothy:

I have just been reading an incomparably dreary biography called *Eleanor and Franklin*—obviously by a passionate devotee.[1] All the same it did have its moments. For instance, when F.D.R. was running for his second term, the Republicans had a little jingle which they ascribed to Eleanor:

> I'll kiss the negroes
> And you'll kiss the jews
> And we'll stay in the White House
> Just as long as we choose.

Awful, of course; but, in that ultra sardonic Americano way, quite true and very amusing.

Then I send you a little student piece, "Useful phrases to know when traveling in terrorist areas of the world", because it belongs to the same category.[2]

Then I add a clipping on the Einaudi's and don't you think that Cornell is being very effusive about them?[3] And this is particularly amus/ironical because the architecture faculty wants to get rid of both Roberto and the Palazzo M.[4] But, until reading this, I didn't recognise that Roberto's State Department brother is now the U.S. Ambassador to the Organization of American States. However, most understated of all is that Papa Mario "by spring expects to settle down on the farm where he was born in Dogliani, Italy". So folksy this is; and doesn't it make it sound all like Upstate? But the truth is that the Villa San Donato just happens to be an ex-monastic affair with an extremely lavish and pretty mediaeval cloister, and not at all 'simple'.

And about the rest?

Well, about the beginning of February, I received here John O'Brien* from Tennessee, suddenly separated from his wife of eleven years and in great distress.[5] So I scarcely knew him but, since he was a sort of friend of Matt's, I presumed that he had to stay here and he has turned out to be a, temporary (?) treasure. The Southern accent is so very thick that, sometimes, I don't understand him at all—*paa* and *waan,* but he is devoted to Piedmonte (*aace box paa and all that*)[6] and wants to make a dissertation on Vittone.[7] So he intends coming back to Cornell to make his Ph.D. and, meanwhile, he has a little job working out space standards for Bill McMinn;* but, best of all, he turns out to be quite a good cook and, also, quite obsessively tidy. So, in other words, what with Barbara (who is a sweetie) to do the general cleaning on Wednesdays and Saturdays and John to cope with the kitchen, life is very much relieved;[8] and with John helping me out on footnotes and pics, it's like having found one of those improbable English manservants, a Bunter or a Jeeves, in any case a staple of the detective story.[9]

But the tidiness is drivin' me crazy (and I think it must have driven his wife crazy) because it just can't be stopped; and books are put away almost before you can take a look at them. So you get the idea? A devout Catholic but never been to Rome, approves of the Benedictines and the Dominicans, doesn't approve of the Jesuits and the Franciscans, deplores (I don't know why) what he and Matt call the Polish Pretender.[10]

People come to look at this house; but the real estate market is not moving.[11] Perhaps, with the end of that war, in April or May it will.[12]

Speriamo,[13]

    Colin

P.S. Michael Dennis* has been coming up every Wednesday to teach the U.D. studio and staying every Wednesday night. Yet never has he called me? Fred thinks very odd and I do too. Fred and Susie have gone to San Juan, P.R. and, at the moment, it must be very agreeable down there. However, apart from little flurries, still no snow here.

    Colin

P.P.S. A little bit of extra horror. When Kaiser Wilhelm II's wife, Augusta Victoria, known as Dona, returned home late her favorite meal was cold pork and potato salad! Believe it? Qu. V. called her *eine kleine Deutsche prinzessin*, impoverished and pathetic; and you begin to grab the judgment.[14] Absolutely no possibility of cold pork and potato salad at Windsor! But the Schleswig-Holsteins were totally down to their last penny because of Bismarck's annexation; and it was probably for these reasons that P. Christian of S-H (who was Dona's uncle) married Lenchen, Pcesse. Helena of G.B. and I., and proceeded to shack up in a minor house in Windsor Park.[15] But it was still Bismarck who selected Dona as a suitable breeding mare of Willy; and, in this role—because of the cold pork and potato salad?—of course she performed extremely well.[16]

All the same poor Willy! And no wonder how much he hated his mother. Contrary to the Anglo-American version of the story, I am beginning to see Vicky as pretty much a bitch on wheels. For instance, in front of guests, she would tell Willy that he was little more than a cripple; and just try to imagine the effects of that upon a painfully malformed and self-conscious young man!

No, though it's difficult to take the cold pork and potato salad, I don't think that the *Englanderin* was a bit nice.[17] A tragic figure who could only be lead to regard Willy as an inadequate codicil of Prince Albert's will, like her father an intellectual? All the same, I can't imagine that this can excuse her and, consequently, I am now beginning to take the German position on the Empress Frederick—an excessively tactless, indiscreet and opinionated woman who, in herself, explains why Willy over-leapt his parents and reserved his regard for his grandfather in Berlin and his grandmother in London. But, on the whole there should be no wonder that Bismarck did everything he could to destroy her.

P.P.P.S. Strangely I had a Manfred Bismarck to dinner just before Christmas. Why? Because of Berlin? Because of Annabelle?[18] Because of Annya, Jacquelin Robertson's* East Prussian wife? But, somehow, he just drifted in (at this stage I knew nothing about the cold pork and potato salad) and so we had a little Chinese din and a little desultory conversation; and, since I didn't have enough clean sheets, I didn't feel disposed to ask him to stay the night. A retrospective brush with 'history'? But very, very different from what the Bismarck scene would have been one hundred years ago!

Best love,

    Colin

N.B.[19] Like Adele Wells used to think when she was still with Jerry, sometimes I think that, like Mozart, I shall be buried in a pauper's grave; and even <u>any</u> money seems to me to be a <u>great</u> illusion.[20] But this is in my worst moment; and, at my best, I begin to realise that I am tolerably rich though, by no means, opulent. Meaning that the estate, for J. and S., should come in at rather more than a million dollars and, perhaps, more like a million and a quarter.

So get the pic. But, all the same, this requires an attention which David doesn't seem able to attribute to it.

For instance, with reference to what Simon calls the King Lear syndrome, with suitable protections I would give them everything right now.[21]

I.E. we want to escape horrid estate duties but <u>what</u> can we do about this?

Colin

1   Lash, Joseph P, *Eleanor and Franklin: The Story of Their Relationship, Based on Eleanor Roosevelt's Private Papers*, New York: Norton, 1971.
2   The enclosure is lost but presumably was from a Cornell student newspaper.
3   The clipping, "International center named for Einaudi" and "Grant honors Einaudi's widow", is from the Cornell University newspaper (no date, c March 1991) announcing that Cornell's Center for International Studies was renamed the Mario Einaudi Center for International Studies and documenting Mario and Roberto Einaudi's* extensive involvement with international studies at Cornell. Roberto Einaudi was director of the Cornell Rome Program.
4   Palazzo Massimo, Rome, which housed the Cornell Rome Program.
5   John O'Brien,* a PhD student in the Cornell Art History program, lived in Rowe's Ithaca house from February 1991 through 1992.
6   *paa, waan, aace box paa*: Rowe's rendition of O'Brien's* pronunciation of pie, wine, ice box pie.
7   Bernardo Antonio Vittone (1704–1770), Baroque architect from the Piedmont region of Northern Italy.
8   Barbara Littenberg.*
9   Mervyn Bunter is the fictional butler and cook to Lord Peter Wimsey in the detective stories by Dorothy L Sayers (1893–1957). Bunter's character was in part based on the fictional Jeeves of PG Wodehouse (1881–1975).
10 Pope Saint John Paul II, Karol Józef Wojtyła (1920–2005).
11 Rowe's house at 19 Renwick Place, Ithaca, was for sale at this time.
12 The Gulf War, 2 April 1990–28 February 1991.
13 *Speriamo,* Italian: let's hope.
14 *eine kleine Deutsche prinzessin,* German: a little German princess.
15 Prince Christian of Schleswig-Holstein (1831–1917) married Princess Helena of Great Britain and Ireland (1846–1923).
16 Kaiser Wilhelm II (1859–1941), who, in 1881, married "Dona", with whom he had seven children. His mother was Victoria, Princess Royal, the eldest daughter of Britain's Queen Victoria.
17 *Englanderin,* German: English lady.
18 Annabelle Selldorf, a student of Rowe's at Syracuse in Florence, Italy.
19 "N.B.", *Nota Bene,* Italian: Note Well.
20 Adele Wells, wife of Jerry A Wells.*
21 In Shakespeare's *King Lear*, the aging Lear's troubles begin when he decides to abdicate the British throne and divide his kingdom evenly among his three daughters.

To **Dorothy Rowe**, *St. Margaret's Road, Oxford*   *25 April 1991*   **190**

19 Renwick Place, Ithaca, N.Y.

Dearest Dorothy:

I send you one of the minor editorials from today's *New York Times*.[1] It is written by Harold Brooks-Baker of *Burke's Peerage.*

So, obviously, this woman, Kitty Kelley, is a journalistic abomination; and the hatchet job which she has just done on Nancy Reagan, though a lot of it seems to be well justified, seems to be generally deplored.[2] But, then, <u>what</u> can she be going to do on Philip of Schleswig-Holstein-Sonderburg-Glucksburg, alias Philip Mountbatten?[3]

Is she going to tell us that his mother was born stone deaf but had become able to lip-read in four languages by the time she was eighteen? Is she going to tell us that the three daughters of Prince and Princess Andrew of Greece and Denmark, Philip's sisters, were all married into German princely families, that Philip's rather blowzy middle-aged niece is *hofdame* to Margaret von Hessen und bei Rhein (the former Margaret Geddes) who, because her father was British ambassador in Washington, speaks English with a slightly American accent and seems to have many friends in Albemarle County, Virginia?[4] Is she going to tell us that, though Margaret Geddes-von Hessen und bei Rhein is well received at Balmoral, the R.F. has always chosen to 'blank out' the quantity of Philip's Hannover and Hohenlohe-Langenburg relations? Is she going to tell us that, at Wolfsgarten, I.K.H. Prinzessin Margaret devotes her time mostly to spastic children?[5] But, I think, not <u>this</u>, since, quite evidently, the object is <u>so</u> worthy; and, therefore, to begin with, she will rip apart a few books and present this as the result of 'research'.

She will present the career of Prince Alexander of Hesse who went to Russia with his sister when she married the future Czar Alexander II, and who, with great brilliance, participated in the Russian conquest of the Caucasus (the Koran of Shamyl is at Broadlands and, by persons of the Russian descent, myself has been allowed to handle the sword of Shamyl in Houston, Texas). So what next? She will dilate upon the elopement of Pc. Alexander with the Polish chick who wasn't *ebenburtig*.[6] She will talk about morganatic marriages and she will present the Polish chick as, ultimately, becoming Princess of Battenberg.[7]

So what is so rough and tough about all this? I had thought that everybody knew it; and, then, whatever dirt is <u>she</u> going to acquire?

She will present Philip as a racist—remarks to English students in China 'if you stay here much longer you'll get little slitty eyes'; and she will dredge up certain sex scandals of 1963, related to the Profumo case and the Duchess of Argyll's divorce. So what's new and just <u>why</u> should *Burke's Peerage* begin, by its standards, to get worked up about all this?

Must say that I am consumed with curiosity.

Then I also send you a p.c. of Arenenberg, Thurgau, C.H., which I have just received from former students at present teaching in Zurich and Firenze.[8] Arenenberg is a very small house, scarcely as big as St. Margaret's Road; and it was in this rustic version of Malmaison that Hortense de Beauharnais spent her life of exile. And very convenient too, since, across the water, she had cousins, and sons and nieces happily established in the houses of Baden and Bavaria.

The ex-Q. Hortense spent the winters in Rome in an apartment in Palazzo Ruspoli, corner of Via dei Condotti and Via del Corso, and the summers here where the views are fabulous.[9]

One wonders, of course, how long in the 1820's it took her to make the annual move; but it's not about that I wish to digress.

Back in Trieste in '82 Judy and I had to go through the most extravagant arguments to persuade David to buy a couple of Sevres white and gold *epergnes* which, he thought, were not up to his standards; but the same *epergnes* are here at Arenenberg to the left of the door.[10]

So think about that now.

Best love,

>   *Colin*   x   x   x
>
>   COLIN ROWE

1   Brooks-Baker, Harold, "Kitty Kelley Could Rock the Royals", *The New York Times*, 25 April 1991.
2   Kelley, Kitty, *Nancy Reagan: The Unauthorized Biography*, New York: Simon and Schuster, 1991.
3   At the time, Kelley was writing *The Royals*, New York: Warner Books, 1997.
4   *hofdame,* German: maid of honor.
5   "I.K.H. Prinzessin": *Ihr Koniglichen Hoheit Prinzessin*, German: Her Royal Highness, Princess.
6   *ebenbürtig,* German: of equal birth.
7   Princess Julia of Battenberg, née Julie Therese Salomea Hauke (1825–1895).
8   A postcard of Schloss Arenenberg, an early sixteenth-century chateau on the shore of Lake Constance in Thurgau, Switzerland.
9   "ex-Q.": ex-Queen.
10 *épergnes,* French: an ornamental centerpiece for a dining table used for holding fruit or flowers.

To **Javier Cenicacelaya**, *Dean, University of Miami School of Architecture*   *7 June 1991*   **191**

19 Renwick Place, Ithaca, N.Y.

Dear Javier:

I was entirely delighted to learn from your call the other day that *Arquitectonica* is to publish my sixteenth century article so very soon.[1] Though it was written for the occasion of that *convego* way back in 1976, I am still highly impressed by it (though I say it myself); and of course, it is completely lost in the pages of *The Cornell Journal of Architecture*.[2]

Meanwhile, a number of things to say about the Cornell publication:

The pic of Villa Lante on the Gianicolo (figure 7 on page 8), as you said, is too small and should not be so casually thrown away. Also, as you recognize, the view must be frontal as, otherwise, it is without <u>any</u> value as information. But a frontal view exists in Frederick Hartt, *Giulio Romano* (New Haven, 1958), though, unfortunately, soft focus. However, I am sure that other frontal views are relatively easy to find.

With reference to the Loggia dei Banchi at Bologna (figure 15 on page 11), you might, just possibly like to include a further pic. This is an early seventeenth century drawing which, better than anything else, seems to me to illustrate the way in which protuberance erupts from flatness in this façade. I send you a Xerox of it; and it is from Anna Maria Orazi, *Jacopo Barozzi Vignola* (Rome: Bulzoni Editore, 1982), plate 487.

On page 16 I am at a loss to understand why the student editors chose to illustrate Michelangelo's Capitoline palaces with rather bad measured drawings rather than with very good photographs.

Caption 37 on page 17 should read: "Antonio da Sangallo, Palazzo Ducale (?), possibly for Castro"; and, on the same page, caption 44 should read: "Giuliano da Sangallo, Uffizi 2794, Palazzo dei Penitenzieri (?), Rome".

Then, at this stage in the argument, I am unable to comprehend why my editors chose to omit frontal <u>and</u> diagonal views of the Medici tombs at San Lorenzo. But this last omission is particularly damaging as it results in a failure to provide visual information about Capella Medici in its relationship to Sala di Costantino.

And, finally, on page 21 I say "research-in the archives-"; but, later on, when I obviously intended to say "the 'researcher in the archives'", my editors made it "the 'researcher and archives'".

So, if these are the remaining probs, I am confident that *Arquitectonica* will give attention to the most glaring ones and that the results will be a superb job.

Best regards,

Colin

COLIN ROWE

P.S. As to my coming to Miami. Of course, I would love to come and this for the obvious reasons: down there I would find not only yourself but lots of my friends—Gladys Margherita Diaz,★ Jorge and Luis Trelles, Jose Gelabert, Pablo Hernandez, Juan Calvo, all my former students and I know their extreme goodwill. And, to go on with the Cornell list, I know there would be the inevitable visits from San Juan—Esteban Sennyey,★ Hector Arce, Jorge Rigau; and, maybe we could even bring Juan Antonio Cortes (something of a Don Quixote) from Madrid! So all of this, with Andres and Liz[3] (though perhaps, not with Bernardo and Lorinda), myself would find immensely stimulating.[4]

In other words, tell me what is in your mind; and, while waiting to hear this, I will tell you how I am placed.

Obviously I am *d'un certain age* and can scarcely go racketing around indefinitely.[5]

To fulfill my obligations to Cornell I have proposed going to Rome in the Spring of '92; and, particularly since in Rome I shall be well taken care of in Palazzo Pio, I cannot back out on this assignment.

I cannot be lured down to Miami for an entirely new lecture course; and, apropos of this, I have already (perhaps foolishly) turned down the Charles Eliot Norton Lecture at Harvard—offered by the University and not by the G.S.D.[6] And the requirement for these lectures, the most prestigious which Harvard has to offer, is the delivery of six lectures, spread out over six months, at a fee of $115,000.00! (But I suspect that this also means lots of dinners with the Harvard establishment which I felt that I just didn't possess the energy to cope with).

I have two lecture courses all ready to go: "The Architecture of Good Intentions: Towards a Possible Retrospect" and "Italian Architecture: Bramante to Scamozzi"; and I would like to give them in that order. But there is here a problem. "The Architecture of Good Intentions" is promised to M.I.T. Press; and, unless they are very slow, I suspect that, as a lecture course, it might already be superseded by publication. That is: if we plan for "The Architecture of Good Intentions" in the Fall of '92. However, maybe we could put restraints on M.I.T. so that they published for Christmas (which I think that they prefer), in which case Fall '92 would surely be O.K.[7]

But, everything considered, I would prefer to give "The Architecture of Good Intentions" in the Fall of this year, '91, because, then, it would still be immediately fresh in my mind.

Javier:
Perhaps this is impossible; but let me know what you think; and then we could go on to talk about money and all those dreadful things.

In both courses it would be a matter of eight to ten lectures, delivered weekly (?) throughout the semester; but this is not intended to exclude some general exposure like seminars, juries and all that.[8]

Then, in terms of reimbursement, I have not the faintest idea what Miami is paying Vincent Scully;* but I merely assume that I should be at more or less the same rate as *caro Vincenzo*.[9]

So grab the general pic; and I know that you know that, in all this, I am <u>not</u> being monstrous and grasping.

Un abbraccio fervente,

   Colin

   COLIN ROWE

P.P.S. Please send me a copy of your mag to *il mio fratello*:[10]

David Rowe*
Buckingham Court 32
78 Buckingham Gate
London SW1 E6PD
England

1   Rowe, Colin, "Grid/Frame/Lattice/Web: Giulio Romano's Palazzo Maccarani and the Sixteenth Century", *Cornell Journal of Architecture*, no 4 1991. The article was republished in *Arquitectonica*, 10 March 1993. See also Rowe, Colin, *As I Was Saying: Recollections and Miscellaneous Essays*, Alexander Caragonne ed, 3 vols, Cambridge, MA: MIT Press, 1996, vol 2, pp 103–169, in which Rowe notes that the article was first presented as a lecture in the Palazzo Massimo, Rome, at the opening of the Cornell Rome Program on 14 March 1987.
2   *convegno*, Italian: conference.
3   Andrés Duany* and Elizabeth Plater-Zyberk.*
4   Bernardo Fort-Brescia and Laurinda Hope Spear, partners in the Miami architectural firm of Duany Plater-Zyberk and Company.
5   *d'un certain âge*, French: of a certain age.
6   "G.S.D.": Graduate School of Design. See Rowe's letter to Thomas Muirhead* dated 15 December 1990 (p 353 in this volume).
7   *The Architecture of Good Intentions* was first published in 1994 by Academy Editions in London.
8   Rowe did not teach this proposed course.
9   Vincent Scully* (b 1920); *caro Vincenzo*, Italian: dear Vincent.
10 *il mio fratello*, Italian: my brother.

To **Simon Rowe**, *Brevard, North Carolina*   *19 June 1991*   **192**

19 Renwick Place, Ithaca, N. Y.

Dearest Simon:

   I hope that you enjoyed being here quite as much as I enjoyed your presence here; and this is partly because, by my standards, you and I comprise the volubility/volatility of *la famiglia*.[1] So grab this and grab that I appreciate it.

But am I quite so *molto vecchioso* as I assume that you are prone to imagine?[2] The Duke of Wellington was born in 1769 and his adored and adoring friend, Angela Burdett-Coutts (of the bank) was born in 1819; and, at Strathfieldsaye, the D. had a special staircase put in to connect their bedrooms (though there was nothing of <u>that</u> sort between them—even though she <u>might</u> have wanted it).[3] However, when

Angela—she was Miss Angela—became a little too exhausting for him, the D. would quote what must have been a popular piece of early Victorian verse:

Speak gently to the aged one
And sooth his careworn heart
The sands of life are running low
And he is ready to depart.[4]

But I found you, as Bernard Berenson would have said, "life enhancing" rather than exhausting; and I can only hope that yourself didn't occasionally repine under the remorseless bombardment of my relentless conversation.[5] For it's all the same—architecture, furniture, historical anecdote, royalty—is it not? All the same, I can assure you will infallibly get to the same way. Heredity? Certainly I acquire my own garrulousness from Margaret Lambert-Laughton.

So, when you find time, tell me about North Carolina, where they found her vagina.[6] Are you in the middle of a forest? Is it deliciously cool? Or are you infested with mosquitoes? How are the brats? How is Asheville? And have you been to Biltmore which I am sure is an absolutely horrible house?[7] You see, never having been in that part of the world myself, I would just love to know.

Un abbraccio fervente

 Colin

P.S. Also you can't be very far away from Black Mountain College where Josef Albers and a lot of other *Bauhausler* used to teach.[8] So it was quite Famous in its day and I wonder what it could be like now. Pretty moribund I should expect.

 Colin

---

1 *la famiglia*, Italian: the family.
2 *molto vecchioso*, Italian: very old.
3 Arthur Wellesley, Duke of Wellington (1769–1852), British general who defeated Napoleon and was twice British prime minister; Angela Burdett-Coutts (1814–1906), Victorian philanthropist.
4 Paraphrases "Speak Gently" by David Bates (1809–1870). In *Alice in Wonderland*, Lewis Carroll parodies the poem with "Speak Roughly".
5 Bernard Berenson (1865–1959), American art historian specializing in Renaissance painting.
6 Simon Rowe* was a camp counselor in North Carolina during summer 1991.
7 Biltmore House, 1889–95, Asheville, North Carolina, designed by Richard Morris Hunt in the Chateauesque style for George Washington Vanderbilt II.
8 Black Mountain College, near Asheville, an experimental school founded in 1933, renowned for its faculty, which included Josef and Anni Albers, Merce Cunningham, John Cage, Franz Kline, Robert Motherwell, Buckminster Fuller, and others.

193 *To **Simon Rowe**, Brevard, North Carolina*   *27 June 1991*

19 Renwick Place, Ithaca, N. Y.

Dearest Simon:

So nice to have your letter and Dorothy and James told me all about the vicissitudes of N.C. which doesn't exactly seem to be like the Garden of Eden.

But, all the same, it's awful hot here—89 degrees at 10 o'clock this morning! And now, at 3.30, it must be about 100. So have you ever thought how people <u>did</u> get along in this country before air conditioning, the refrigerator and all that? Particularly in the deep South it must have been absolute hell and any attempt to cook, what with the big hot hearth and no screens on the windows, must have been complete torture. All that you could do really, I am sure, was to have a slave operating a big fan and to slump around drinking mint juleps. But, then, just <u>where</u> did you get the ice? Like the ice they used in order to cool drinks in Calcutta I assume that it must have been imported from Boston—or, in certain areas, down river from mid-West places up north.

June 29 '91

It isn't excruciatingly hot today and, as a result, I am thinking of what a really charming *stazione di villeggiatura* this place happens to be—appalling, mostly, in the winter but, as that old waiter in the Station Hotel in Perth used to say: "But you should see it in the summer, sir. Oh, sir, it's lovely in the summer".[1]

In other words, I am looking at the trees and at the *cortile*/patio/nymphaeum/terrace out back; and, just briefly, I am finding it entirely ravishing. Indeed, I bought the house, in the first case, <u>entirely</u> because of the trees; and a woman who came here the other day was equally overcome by them—"It's just like England"; and, when I said, "No way", she said, "Yes you're right. Actually I am thinking about Italy". Truly unfortunate that she doesn't have the money to buy the house because she, obviously, has a passion for it.

A little small it is; but, for six months of the year, as they used to say, it is possible to live here with *otium cum dignitate* (trans: ease and dignity).

All of which has lead me, via a process of lateral, flip-flop thinking: to make a decision and to envisage a possibility.

The <u>decision</u> is to enlarge this house by building a pavilion adjacent to the front door—this pavilion and its approach to comprise another bedroom, with *en suite* bath, and a guest cloakroom/powder room; and I am now beginning to think that I could get all this for a, more or less, moderate price.

Because of some funny old inhibition about money, for a long time I have been <u>blocked</u> in seriously considering this; but, now, it seems to me to be entirely reasonable.

Reasons why? Most people seem to be no longer able to conceive of existence without at least two bathrooms and they are also beginning to think of four bedrooms as a necessity. Also the pavilion <u>could</u> serve as rental unit likely, as things are at the moment, to produce at least $4,000.00 p.a. And, then, for all its charms this house is not up to the quality of its location—incredible seclusion, etc., etc.

So I have just been talking to David about this; and, since he believe in ideas, he expressed himself as completely in favour; a "good idea", that is what he said.

And then I went to present the possibility; and he was completely enthusiastic about it. Or, at least, so I thought.

So <u>what</u> is the <u>possibility</u>?[2]

Dearest Simone, it is simply that you <u>forget</u> the U. of Sussex and come <u>here</u> to Cornell U. Yes, yes, yes? No, no, no? But <u>why</u> not?

David said: But <u>what</u> would he study? And I said, "Law"; and David said, he <u>just</u> couldn't bear it. So David said, "hotel management", 'management' in general? And I said, not quite 'humanist' enough. And David said, Icelandic literature (the collection here is the very best). And I said, no money in it. And I said, "Art history"; and David seemed to shrug.

But the most amazing thing that your papa did say (because I had _not_, so far, thought about it) was: And when James is graduated from Cambridge next, then he might like to come to Ithaca for post graduate work!!!

Anyway, this is how my own thought is moving.

I _cannot_ unload this house in a low market—one should always buy _low_ and sell _high_:

This is a _positive_ asset rather than a liability;

Intrinsically this house belongs to you and James—or, at least, what I derive from selling it does;

David's argument has _always_ been that I should _not_ sell—though I think that the arguments against it have only just emerged. Dearest Simon, spend a few days in thinking about this. At the time of the Revolution families split—in Boston. Some stayed and some went up to Ontario; so they were covered, and the money was covered, in spite of _what_ might happen. And, presumably, I am advising something like this.

As a family, apart from being pro-Italian, almost without thinking about it, we are also pro-American; and this house would give both _you_ and _James_ an American presence and _personae_.[3]

Think so? In any case do think about the possibility.

Obviously I think my advice, like David's advice, must be the _very best_, you _must_ know that, to me, it would be a great happiness to think about you here even though I might prefer to see you in London.

Best, best love, _un abbraccio_ and all that,

    Colin

P.S. Sweetest fella', nothin' at all seriously coercive about any of this. Coercion, without torture, gets you nowhere; and even, plus torture, I don't see how it gets you very far. No. No. No. All this relates to unpleasant (?) paternal and avunculat concern about your 'best' interests—which can be rescinded at _any_ minute.

    Colin

---

1   _stazione di villeggiatura_, Italian: holiday resort.
2   In a letter dated 17 July 1991, Rowe sent Simon "a copy of a letter which I have sent to 2 Buckingham Gate and to St. Margaret's Road. Don't let it agitate you because the idea is probably more valid for James anyway." He then wrote, "[...] all the same, you do seem to like it here and, though your mamma doesn't seem quite to grab the pic, nowadays you really do have to have a graduate degree. However, if hotel admin seems too utterly odious, obviously not." See his letter to the Rowe family dated 14 July 1991 (p 364 in this volume).
3   _personae_, Latin: voice or character.

194   _To **David Rowe**, 78 Buckingham Gate, London_   _14 July 1991_[1]
       To **Dorothy, James & Rosie Rowe**, St. Margaret's Road, Oxford

       19 Renwick Place, Ithaca, N.Y.

Dear y'all:

On this day of all days, with memories of that deplorable event, with a lot of Frogs behavin' like lunatics and shootin' off their mouths, I am writing a letter to a collectivity: to David in London and to Dorothy, James and Rosie in Oxford.

Topic: my Cornell fantasies for J. and/or S.

Fantasy 1: James to do graduate work at C.U.[2] Pro: this may not be such a bad idea and it was David who first suggested to me. Nor need it cost very much. With a degree in physics from Oxford and a degree in engineering from Cambridge, James should be able to walk right in. I think that they would drool at the prospect; and, what is more, they would probably award him an assistantship, with free tuition and a stipend of perhaps $800 a month. And that with no rent to pay, would surely be a good, helluva good, deal.

Useful American connections which could be built upon in the future whether in London or wherever it might be?

On the other hand, it is quite possible to think otherwise. A too protracted academic exposure? Though I am not quite sure that this applies.

Fantasy 2: Simon should do undergraduate work at Cornell. David said: "to study what?" And then he said: "why hotel management." And I said: "But surely not. But God forbid."

However, on second thoughts I am not so sure.

You see, without a medical degree, I don't see what you do with psychology; and the C.U. School of Hotel Management, skeptical though I have always been about it, is by no means a little hole in the corner operation.

Its graduates, one is told, start with a basic salary of $50,000 p.a. which is quite a lot and much more than you could get with a degree in psychology from the U. of S.;[3] and they are apt, quite rapidly to ascend to much more than that. Then, for instance, the manager of the Villa Medici-Hassler in Rome is a C.U. graduate, as also, is the case at the Albergo d'Inghilterra; and, neither of these is exactly a low class establishment.

Demeaning: 'my son who is the manager of a hotel'? And we know that New York Jewish parents are apt to run along the beach screaming. 'Help, help, my son, the doctor, is drowning'; but, just as business management doesn't involve daily tour around any workshop, nor does hotel management mean sitting at the front desk or supervising the chambermaids or the waiters.

Not Humanist? Of course not! But then what is so very humanistic about being a stockbroker?

However, with this background, Simone could very well expect an income of $200,000 p.a. and not necessarily in N.Y.C./L.A.

All the same, let's forget about hotel management, because were he to come here, Simon could study (with his background) quite a lot of O.K. humanistic things.

More expensive in his case than that of James? Yes, it would be; but I do have to iterate that, in general, some sort of graduate work is absolutely vital and that, with the background of Oxford, Cambridge, Cornell, plus his pronounced linguistic ability, James could call the tune in England, the U.S., Italy, France. He would be just exceptionally to be sought after.

And, then, let us call attention to Ithaca as a place for short time residence—not long time. Skiing in the winter? Not for me; but it means that you don't have to make trips to Cortina, St. Moritz, Sestriere, or Kitzbuhel. A charming *stazione di villeggiatura* in the summer, with a lake and sail boats (again not me).[4] A *macchina* available for use, bought in 1984, with only a mileage to date of 18,000.[5] For just two or three years, the place is a little Utopia.

Siren songs? Siren songs? Am I Circe trying to seduce a couple of versions of Odysseus?

And then there is this house which, by the time I have finished with it <u>should</u> have four bedrooms and two and a half baths. Enough for parents and others to pay brief visits which need not entirely reduce them to extremities of boredom?

So <u>such</u> is my argument. I am suggesting a stint at C.U. for both J. and S. and David has, always, advised me <u>not</u> to sell this house; and <u>now</u> I have put the two scenes together.

I <u>want</u> to sell but, since it is absurd to sell in a low market, involving a loss of maybe $80,000, then <u>just why</u> should I do it? This house or its sale price belongs in equal terms to both J. and S.; and, by <u>them</u> being able to occupy, either together or successively, would not <u>everything</u> be gained? Educationally too?

Certainly, though I would have to take out a little home improvement loan (my credit is exceptional so nothing rough). In other words what I seem to be talking about is a *marriage de convenance* made in heaven.[6] In the end J. and S., my dearest friends, would be able to control the selling price.

A small sweat but a large benefit for such, mostly educational, gains.

Un abbraccio fervente per tutti,

   Colin

P.S. Dearest Rosie: in all of this <u>you</u> may think that <u>I</u> have excluded <u>any</u> consideration of <u>yourself</u>. However this is <u>not</u> the case.

Shitty though I may be, I think about <u>you</u> all the time. So, as I believe, an application to mod. lit. at C.U. could grab you the same advantages as James. But <u>not</u> so much money. And you know why? It is because the *scena mechanocratica* possesses pre-eminence.[7] But come (after conversations in London), next year *chez moi*, and I will immediately have evacuated this house for you and J.[8]

P.P.S. I am entirely Italian about *la famigilia*.[9]

See you in September and I'm keeping my fingers crossed.

   Colin

---

1 Bastille Day.
2 "C.U.": Cornell University.
3 "U. of S.": University of Sussex.
4 *stazione di villeggiatura,* Italian: holiday resort.
5 *macchina,* Italian: automobile.
6 *marriage de convenance,* French: marriage of convenience.
7 *scena mechanocratica,* Italian: machinary-ruled (bureaucratic) scene.
8 *chez moi,* French: at my house.
9 *la famiglia,* Italian: the family. On 17 July 1991 Rowe sent a copy of this letter to his nephew, Simon, in North Carolina with a note. See Rowe's letter to Simon Rowe* dated 27 June 1991 (p 362 in this volume).

195 *To **David Rowe**, Buckingham Gate, London*   *17 October 1991*

19 Renwick Place, Ithaca, N.Y.

David:

A quite perceptive observation just came my way—from a book by Bernard de Voto.[1] The original settlers in the West <u>were not poor</u>. For, just simply, if they had been among the employees of a factory in Lowell, Mass. or Providence, R.I. then <u>how</u> could they have afforded it?

The factory has shut down; they are out of work; but doesn't this mean that they don't have the wherewithal to move? You've got to imagine the covered wagon, the horses, the provisions and the endless attrition of capital involved in any such move! No such a move could only be undertaken by the fairly well heeled, anxious for a bit more money and, maybe, a bit bored and anxious for excitement.

If you think about it at all, which I never have until now, this seems to be entirely obvious and to be something which is also visible in the seventeenth century. Meaning that to forget the Roundheads and Cavaliers, Massachusetts and Virginia nonsense and to concentrate on the so called 'Pilgrims', who couldn't exactly have been Lincolnshire and East Anglican peasants! After all, before setting out, these persons were able to spend a couple of years in Holland; and, if they were entirely strapped, then how did they contrive to do it in that highly opulent little society?

Of course, from a very early time, there were always slaves and indentured servants and scarcely anyone, either north or south, was armigerous; but, as for a 'proletarian' immigration, I think that one may forget it. It only begins after 1850—with the Irish—and after 1860–1870—with the Neapolitans. Because, even the Germans who came after 1848, as liberals were also distinctly bourgeois specimens.

So, all of the crap about give me your poor, give me your downtrodden, is fundamentally the most distressing late nineteenth century pseudo-liberal nonsense, even though it has since become one of the basic Americano platitudes—presumably related to the cherished idea of dragging yourself up by your bootstraps.[2]

So, fantasies of cheap democracy and semi-Marxism apart, I send you a pic from today's *N.Y.T.*—Senator-Galahad-Joseph Biden, Jr, arranging his profile;[3] and it reminds me of Monsignor Gilbey of the gin outfit trying to convert me at Cambridge long ago.[4] But the insufferable vanity of this windbag doesn't even begin to allow him to perceive what derision this pic has incited in N.Y.C. today. The fucking bastard is looking out at the light and <u>yearning</u> for inspiration!

<u>This</u> is the guy who plagiarized Neil Kinnoch; and, now take time out to vomit.[5] But, all of it, is probably the result of Montesquieu and his *Esprit des Lois* of 1748.

Sorry to burden you with all this stuff but I conceive that you will understand. However, apart from 'vicious' New York, the population of this country is too supine and too drugged by the so-called 'media' to begin to understand anything <u>whatsoever</u>.

George W. and Thomas J. will be done in by the avid deconstructionists next year,[6] Abe Lincoln the following and, after that, *distruzione* and <u>what</u> to do.[7] Because, grab the story, the *denouement* of this affair is not going to be 'merely' cultural.[8] No way. Within a few weeks it also going to affect Wall Street.

Un abbraccio fervente and best love

    Colin

P.S. Next time when you ring me give me the address and the phone number at Darwin Court.[9] It would be a great help.

    C.

1 Bernard Augustine de Voto (1897–1955), author of *The Year of Decision, 1846*, Boston: Little, Brown & Co, 1943.
2 "Give me your poor, give me your downtrodden" paraphrases "The New Colossus" by Emma Lazarus (1849–1887), a sonnet of 1883 about the Statue of Liberty.
3 The *New York Times* article featured a photograph of Biden in profile, looking off into the distance.
4 Alfred Newman Gilbey (1901–1998), son of the wealthy gin and wine merchants, who became a Roman Catholic priest and chaplain at the University of Cambridge.
5 The lines of Senator Biden's speech of August 1987 in Iowa—"Why is it that Joe Biden is the first in his family ever to go to a university? [...] It's because they didn't have a platform on which to stand"—were nearly identical to those in a speech given three months earlier by British MP Neil Kinnock—"Why am I the first Kinnock in a thousand generations to be able to get to university? [...] It was because there was no platform upon which they could stand".
6 "George W. and Thomas J.": George Washington and Thomas Jefferson.
7 *distruzione*, Italian: devastation.
8 *dénouement*, French: final outcome.
9 Darwin Court, the London condominium on Gloucester Avenue that David Rowe* had secured for Colin.

196   *To **Daniel Naegele**, Philadelphia*   *9 November 1991*

19 Renwick Place, Ithaca, N. Y.

Dear Daniel Naegele:*

Many thanks for all your stuff about me which I received here yesterday.[1] Matt Bell* had conjectured its existence; but, in no way, had he been able to form any idea as to its extent and its quality.

All the same, and while you were writing all this, just why didn't you come up here or, at least, give me a call? You see, had you done so, I would have been able to put you right about so many things.

For instance, about the publishing history of *Collage City*.[2]

This piece was written in this house between August and December 1973; and it was like this. Fred Koetter* sat scribbling in the library and, while I sat scribbling at this dining table, Susie Kim* reclined on a chesterfield and made meals as they seemed to be necessary. And that is so much for beginnings.

So Fred and I took it over to London in late December and there followed various polite luncheons at the Reform, the Travellers, the Athenaeum etc., and the ultimate upshot: the *A.R.* simply cannot publish anything quite so long.[3] And, therefore, I spend several months contracting the piece for the purposes of *A.R.*

Then meanwhile, back at the ranch, there have been movements; and these concern Michael Spens* (Sir Patrick Spens is the skeeliest skipper that ever did sail the sea);[4] and Michael (gruesome chateau in Scotland, Eton and Trinity) is, in this scene, the really bad news. He sent me a telegram to Venice in '74. Although this was in complete contradiction of his anxiety to be a Scottish Nationalist M.P. for the Orkneys (or the Shetlands), Michael had just bought Studio International; and it was from thence that all trouble flowed.

You see, once M. had gotten hold of *C.C.* in '74, he sat on it and diverted funds towards his political aspirations. This until we threatened a lawsuit in '78 (Dorothy was involved with this);[5] and, from thence, a treaty ensued. MIT was going to publish the book; but, to avoid excessive litigation, we were obliged to accept the layout made by Studio International.

Which is the story of *Collage City* about the ikkustrations of which you have made so many ingenious surmises. Both Fred and myself objected to the pseudo chi-chi format which reduced our text to a coffee table book; but, after five years of frustration, just what can you do?

Hence do not attribute the pics in *C.C.* either to me or to Fred. They are the result of a *force majeure*.[6] As part of the American takeover of this book, MIT felt obligated to accept the work of the English compositor already appointed by Studio International.

Then about other things.

"Transparency" was written in Austin, Texas in late '55 and early '56 and was sent to the *A.R.* where it was conceived by Nikolaus Pevsner★ to be sacrilegious and, hence, it was rejected—not to see the light of day until years later in *Perspecta*.[7] And the two pieces, "N.C. and M.A.", were both written at a small apt. which I had in N.Y.C. on East 9th between Madison and Park.[8] It was in a brownstone, now demolished for a large new apt. building on Madison, at the center of what developers now like to call Carnegie Hill; but it wasn't called that in my time. And my time there was '56–'57. But where to publish?

Pevsner, and perhaps Banham★ too, had deprived me of the resource of the *A.R.* and these two pieces, slight though they may be, were *un po troppo intellettuale*[9] for the American architectural press of that period.[10] So, yet again, they languished in darkness, only to see the light of day after P.D.E. set up *Oppositions*.[11]

And now a quote from Alexander Pope:

> Oh let me flap this bug with gilded wings
>
> This painted thing of dirt that stinks and stings.[12]

So my bug during these years was, primarily, Peter Reyner Banham, that populist (I think card carrying) Marxist about whom I could say so much—not susceptible to publication. But just one thing: aesthetic "nerve" or aesthetic "verve"? But very different implications. And don't you just turn a letter upside down to make a point? But this is exactly what happened in the Mumford article of way back. My text, which said "nerve", was sent for my correction as "verve"; and I wrote a special letter back to insist on 'n' rather than 'v'. However, no matter, it still came out as 'v'.[13] And, in this as in much else, I feel entitled to perceive the manipulations of P.R.B. Because "verve" is a bit cissy isn't it? And "nerve" is strong. Oh Iago, oh Iago; but, Othello apart, doncha grab the pic?

It was a fantasy totally in Banham's mind. I was erudite, *sans gene*, presumably rich, and I wrote like someone escaped from a late Henry James★ novel.[14] So tough shit and ideal target. Ideal target for a pseudo-proletarian.

Now, *caro Daniele*, just why did you not speak to me before you wrote all this. For, on the whole, I am affable and easy, always willing to accept invasion from someone so obviously intelligent/perceptive as, patently, you seem to be. And, therefore, why leave the situation so late?

Do I finish this letter with the Italian *un abbraccio fervente per tu* or with the Anglo version, which is terribly tepid, "Sincerely"?

Anyway I sign myself,

> *Colin Rowe*
>
> COLIN ROWE

P.S. Of course you are entirely right about Hoesli,* who screwed up both *Transparency* and *Collage City*:[15] And let me say that Fred wouldn't even accept to read the German version of *Collage City*. Indeed we both screamed about it; but to no avail. Hoesli had croaked—heart attack in the Bangkok airport, was installed in the Pantheon of saints at the E.T.H. and it is impossible to speak evil about the dead.[16] No?

But, having gotten so far, I rang up Fred and Fred (pseudo cowboy from Montana) said to me: "But why are you being so protractedly nineteenth century, your sort of letters were gone away long ago. Just ring the bastard up." Not what Fred exactly said but what he intimated; and, therefore, my phone call.[17]

    C.R.

---

1 In October 1991 Daniel Naegele,* at the time a student in the PhD Program in Architecture at the University of Pennsylvania, sent Rowe his Yale thesis of 1990 titled "Rowe's Erection: A Private Proscenium and the Elliptic Illustrations of *Collage City*".

2 Rowe, Colin and Fred Koetter, *Collage City*, Cambridge, MA: MIT Press, 1978.

3 "A.R.": *The Architectural Review*.

4 "O, Sir Patrick Spens is the skeeliest skipper, that sailed upon the sea" is lyric from a traditional Scottish ballad that tells the tale of the ill-fated voyage of the seven-year-old Princess Margaret (1283–1290).

5 Naegele* had known Dorothy Rowe* since 1987 when she assisted him by writing a brief biography of Colin Rowe. Regarding Dorothy Rowe's involvement with the publication of *Collage City*, see letters to her in this volume: 16 February 1977 (p 198); 23 May 1977 (p 200); and 8 June 1977 (p 202); 1 July 1977 (p 204).

6 *force majeure*, French: superior force.

7 First published as Rowe, Colin and Robert Slutzky, "Transparency: Literal and Phenomenal, Part I", *Perspecta* 8, 1963, pp 45–54. Reprinted in book format in German, French, and English. See bibliography.

8 "N.C. and M.A.": Rowe, Colin, "Neo-Classicism and Modern Architecture, Parts 1 and 2", *Oppositions*, no 1, September 1973, pp 2–26.

9 *un po troppo intellettuale*, Italian: a bit too intellectual.

10 Nicolas Pevsner* and Reyner Banham,* editors of *The Architectural Review* in the late 1950s.

11 "P.D.E.": Peter David Eisenman.*

12 Pope, Alexander, *Epistle to Dr. Arbuthnot* (1735).

13 Rowe, Colin, "Roots of American Architecture: An Answer to Mumford's Analysis", *The Architectural Review* 116, August 1954, pp 75–78. Rowe repeats his nerve-to-verve complaint in Rowe, Colin, *As I Was Saying: Recollections and Miscellaneous Essays*, Alexander Caragonne ed, 3 vols, Cambridge, MA: MIT Press, 1996, vol 1, p 129, a re-publication of this article.

14 *sans gêne*, French: without embarrassment or constraint.

15 Naegele's* Yale thesis speculated that Bernhard Hoesli's* German translation of *Collage City*, Basel: Birkhäuser, 1984, unintentionally removed a positive ambiguity that he, Naegele, understood as essential to the text.

16 "E.T.H.": Eidgenössische Technische Hochschule Zürich (Swiss Federal Institute of Technology Zurich), Switzerland.

17 Rowe telephoned Naegele* at 3:00 am on 10 November to read him this letter before mailing it to him on 12 November.

---

197   To **David Rowe**, *Buckingham Gate, London*   *5 February 1990 & 24 November 1991*

19 Renwick Place, Ithaca, N. Y.

Dearest David:

    The moving men were here two days ago to pack and they are coming back tomorrow to take away; and, meanwhile, the house is occupied by quantities of cardboard boxes—and, really, I quite like the look of them.

So, while sifting, sortin' out and, quite often, destroying my own private papers, I came across a little letter which I began to write to you on February 5 1990, and I think I had better transcribe it for your entertainment.[1]

Houston, Texas   *February 5, 1990*

Sitting here on the eighteenth floor of this not very interesting hotel and looking out over a frustrated tropical rain forest is <u>not</u> my idea of ultimate bliss. And, then, take into account the immediate setting. I am in a so-called suite. There are two bathrooms; in the bedroom there are two double beds; there is no kitchen; but, of course, there are two t.v. sets and, in the *salone*, there is a 'wet' bar eight feet long, with endless supplies of ice.[2] So you grab the approximate pic.

However, I do <u>not</u> repine; and, rather, I begin to <u>think</u>. In spite of my horror of determinism, I begin to think about how very little free will one actually possesses.

A long time ago when our great uncle, Henry Hallett, died, our grandfather's sister, Annie, burst out into a spasm of spending and exuberance—the Grand Hotel in Scarborough, equivalent hotels in Harrogate, the Humber Snipe and, occasionally, the liveried chauffeur. In fact all of the appurtenances of the far from inconsolable widow which so promoted the derision of Elizabeth Beaumont. Because Annie's behavior reduced her to absolute shock.[3]

So, looking out at this tropical rain forest which, to the north west gradually turns into savanna and prairie, I have dredged up a recollection of a grand visit which Annie paid to Springwell Farm—complete with chauffeur in peaked cap and leggings. "Oh Lizzie," she said (and I thought quite correctly) "you know this house has such a poor approach; and, if you MUST know it, it has NO entrance of ANY kind!"

Now, as an attentive adolescent, I perfectly remember this (it must have been the impressive figure of the chauffeur): and, though I do not remember the details of Lizzie's outrage, I imagine that they were something like this: "Unwarrantable extravagance; and apart from that, she doesn't even have a stick of furniture in her house, or anything else in her house, that I would even look at twice."

But, at Linden Villa, Annie gave the most charming children's parties with our cousins Joyce Hallett and Pearl Hollins (musical chairs, "Oranges and Lemons say the bells of St Clemens, Here we come gathering nuts in May, who shall we have to pull her away? We'll have Colin Rowe pull her away"); and, because it was charming, little me was immensely impressed by what seemed to be an 'openness' and 'sophistication'.

But not so Lizzie; and, when grandpapa croaked, Lizzie by no means proceeded in Annie's way. She didn't have the *allegrissiama*.[4] So all she did was new bedroom furniture and a new, quite dreadful, fireplace in the drawing room. She could, of course, have done <u>much</u> more. The Hallet and the Beaumont estates were of the same size; but pleasures and hotels in Harrogate were not Lizzie's way. Rather than a happy bourgeois *apertura*,[5] I think that she really preferred <u>Wuthering Heights</u>.[6] "Let us, at all costs, endure"; and thus, she endured for another seventeen years, without <u>any</u> traces of amenity, without fun for herself or for anybody else. Harrogate and Scarborough were, emphatically, <u>not</u>; for all that she enjoyed, in a supremely un-intelligent way, was her silver and her mahogany. But the sociology of Emily Bronte still applies. For, if we were brought up in Wuthering Heights, then the Halletts to me always represented that other house down in the valley, that infinitely more genial house, Lynton Grange (?)[7]

David: I wrote all this way back; and I send it to you now for obvious reasons.

During my personal packing I have been much hampered by the well-intentioned efforts of Barberini who, like so many other fanatically tidy people have hidden things away and then forgotten where he put them.[8]

---

1 Presumably, the original letter was printed by Rowe probably with a felt-tip pen similar to the two letters—to Dorothy Rowe* and to Alan Colquhoun*—written from the Hilton Hotel in February 1990.

2 *salone,* Italian: salon.

3 In a letter dated 29 January 1957 to his brother David, Rowe wrote of the contempt their Grandmamma (Elizabeth Beaumont) had for Annie Hallett: "The Halletts, shall we say, signified to her in some area of the subconscious, a bourgeois milieu, cushioned, comfortable, and without style, which she could scarcely tolerate."

4 *allegrissima,* Italian: exuberant, very cheerful.

5 *apertura,* Italian: opening.

6 For a description of this house, see Brontë, Emily, *Wuthering Heights,* London: Newby, 1847.

7 See Harington, John RS, *Lynton Grange,* London: Pitman, 1866.

8 "Barberini" was Rowe's nickname for John O'Brien,* a PhD student at Cornell, living in Rowe's Renwick Place house at the time.

198 *To **David Rowe**, Buckingham Gate, London* *25 & 26 November 1991*

19 Renwick Place, Ithaca, N.Y.

Dearest David:

Very, very gently, it is beginning to snow; and I like to see it because, no longer, am I obliged to tolerate it. It's ten-thirty in the morning and, already I have had a very cheery guy to take away the things that I have given to Judy. "Oh, I like London, very friendly people in London"—so contrary to what myself thinks! So then we get to talk about New Orleans: "Great place." So I say I notice that you say "New Orleens" and I use the southern pronunciation "Noo Orleeans". And then we talk about the south; and I say what do you say for Lake Pontchartrain? And he says "Pontchautrein", and I say that I call it "Ponchotarain". Which is so much for nine-thirty. And now Allied Van Lines—Mark and Dan—have arrived to take away the rest of the stuff.

Nov 26, 1991

So Mark and Dan, as a pair, were *allegria con molto vivacita* and they did all the work by 5.00 p.m. with lots of questions and appreciations about provenance and all that stuff; and, had I written earlier today, I would now be in the mood to say all sorts of superlative things about the American workman.[1] Only, since one or two things were left behind, I had another visitation today from another member of the same outfit: and, by God, was it dour and lugubrious. It was the Upstate peasant at his worst and almost like having a disapproving Commie in the house! So, in other words, I now find it premature to indulge myself in dithyrambic about the U.S. workman.

Meanwhile, a phone call about a revolution!!!??? Some weeks ago a group of 180 students presented a petition to the faculty that everything should be done to persuade me not to leave; and, since the faculty never responded and, certainly I never heard about it, apparently they came in heavy today. Hence I began to receive phone calls asking me if I could help. But they've now gotten their comeuppance and little me ain't goin' to lift a finger.

A phone call from Matt in San Francisco the other day. He had come across the six Giovanni Maria Volpato pilasters which I bought from Plinio Nardechio in January '85 for $600.00.[2] And just guess how much they were being offered for in San Francisco? And I'd like to have you guessing because it's beyond belief. Without framing and my frames are superb, they are being offered for $21,600.00!

Amazing. Or don't you think?

My flight from Dulles to Heathrow is December 6, United Airlines Flight 902, arriving 9.00 a.m. December 7, Saturday.[3] I am so overjoyed and, of course, I am trusting that someone will be ready to extricate me.

Am so happy both with the student *emeute*[4] and with how much the engravings have risen in price. THESE BOTH MAKE ME FEEL JUSTIFIED.[5]

Unfathomable love,

    Colin

---

1 *allegria con molto vivacità*, Italian: cheerful with much liveliness.
2 Plinio Nardecchio: a print and engraving dealer in Rome.
3 Dulles International Airport, Washington, D.C., to Heathrow International Airport, London.
4 *émeute*, French: uprising, riot.
5 This sentence was handwritten in all capital letters.

Rowe with James Stirling at the wedding reception of Rosemary and James Rowe, Lincolnshire, England, 1990.

9
London

In July 1992, Rowe moved to central London, where he lived in an apartment that was prepared for him by his brother. Initially, he stayed for only two months.

In September he returned to the United States. He consulted with a surgeon in Boston regarding neurological problems resulting from the injury he suffered in 1943. Early in 1993, he underwent back surgery and then returned to Ithaca where he attempted, unsuccessfully, to sell his house. Later that summer, he negotiated with Academy Editions in London to publish *The Architecture of Good Intentions*. At the end of July, he wrote a long letter to Cynthia Davidson* regarding the first issue of her *ANY* magazine, *Seaside and the Real World: A Debate on American Urbanism*, July/August, 1993. In August he attended the wedding of Matt Bell* and Cheryl O'Neil* in Maine. He then returned to London in September.

Rowe lived in London from September 1993 to October 1994, where with his editor, Alex Caragonne,* he completed *As I Was Saying*, a three-volume collection of essays. But conditions in London did not agree with him. "As you probably guess", he wrote in 1993 to Margaret Webster* in Ithaca, "I find London hyper expensive and far less than exhilarating... it's just a bit a mess, a tragedy and a bore; and, quite often, I want to cry about it all." Several of his closest London friends—Alvin Boyarsky,* Jim Stirling,* Douglas Stephens—had recently died, and the proximity of his brother and sister-in-law, in Oxford, was of little help. "Just bland, bland", he wrote to Steve Peterson* and Barbara Littenberg.* "No mountains, no lakes, no rivers that I can perceive and, for the moment, no gratifying royal scandal." In October he left London for good, returning to the United States to live near several of his former Cornell students in Washington, DC.

---

*To **Matthew Bell** & **Cheryl O'Neil**,*   *1 March 1992*   **199**

Rome

Matt/Cheryl:

Thanks for the scoop on the Casa di Savoia—but what a degradation! [...][1]

So, since I can't' get out and walk around, I am finding Rome squalid and boring. I went to Roberto and Karin the other night and the staircase almost produced a heart attack.[2] But, genuinely, it did; and, as I sat around recuperating, I was able to think of my own version of that apt.—very different from theirs where they have nothing but nursery furniture. Then a dull dinner which was confused by the presence of Franco Purini and absence of Laura Thermes.[3] We were; Roberto and Karin, B. and J. McMinn,[4]* Friedrich and Livia St. Florian ([...] Judy seems to be addicted to his wife), a New Zealand guy and his wife, both linguistically very fluent (he works for R. and she, *molto Inglese* but O.K. just happened to be brought up in Firenze).[5] In other words ten people in all; but, what with Franco, it wasn't exactly stimulating.

And, otherwise, I never get further than Da Pancrazio, La Pollarola and Palazzo M[6]—where the new *portiere* conveys Pierina's love to all who might seem to require it.[7]

Needless to say I realise now that it was a mistake to come to Rome. I should have given these lectures in Ithaca in the Fall. They would have had better impact; but, then, <u>how</u> could I have known that Giovanni <u>could</u> have been so slow?[8] And the pic is now like this.

Here I am in Astra's curious apt., which <u>you</u> know well but which is a place where the inconsistencies are something of a problem for myself. For instance: a *batterie de cuisine* sufficient to support a fairly lavish villa but <u>no</u> surface for preparation; no drawers for disposing shirts and things; no bathtub though this could very easily have been provided; two entrance doors which more or less resemble the entrance to a safe deposit vault; a telephone in the remotest location from bed and any working surface.[9] But I am baffled by the whole scenario.

Grab it? Would prefer to be in London and putting things into order and I suppose that it was only the stuff at Bollinger which brought me here.[10] But I don't <u>want</u> to be here; and, short of being *a Londra*[11] or <u>in USA</u>, would prefer to be driving around the Marche with Our Man in Istanbul.[12]

However Goodill* will be appearing with Melissa in an hour or so and, just possibly, though A. and T. can't come to dinner, R. and M. might restore my happiness.[13]

Lurv an all,

> *Colin*

But <u>why</u> are artichokes <u>utterly</u> deprived of commonsense?[14]

Un abbraccio per tutti, basta Roma and tell Brian I'll write.[15]

> *C*

---

1 The House of Savoy, which ruled the Kingdom of Italy from 1861 until the end of the Second World War.
2 Roberto and Karin Einaudi.*
3 Laura Thermes, Italian architect, the partner of Italian architect Franco Purini (b 1941). Together, they designed "Five Squares" in Gibellina, Italy, 1982.
4 Bill and Jeanne McMinn.*
5 "R.": Roberto Einaudi;* *molto Inglese*, Italian: very English.
6 Da Pancrazio and La Pollarola are restaurants in Rome. Palazzo Massimo alle Colonne housed the Cornell Rome Program.
7 *portiere*, Italian: concierge. Pierina was the former *portiere* at the Palazzo Massimo.
8 "Giovanni" was one of Rowe's nicknames for John O'Brien.*
9 *batterie de cuisine,* French: cookware.
10 Rowe intended to move permanently to London. Bollinger Roma SpA was the international removals and storage company with whom he had stored his belongings in Rome.
11 *a Londra*, Italian: in London.
12 "Our Man in Istanbul": Robert Goodill,* a student in the Notre Dame Program in Rome and subsequently in the Urban Design Program at Cornell, so called because he had worked with Rowe and Bill McMinn* on a competition entry for Istanbul.
13 Melissa Weese, Goodill's* wife.
14 "Artichoke" was Rowe's nickname for "architect".
15 *Un abbraccio per tutti, basta Roma,* Italian: A hug for everyone, enough of Rome; Brian is Brian Kelly.*

65 Darwin Court, Gloucester Avenue, London

"Poppi, Poppi, why Poppi's in Pugllia isn't it and close to Castel del Monte; and, like everything in those parts, it's rather over built up."

"[...] Poppi is in Toscana, close to Bibbiena and not too far from the sources of the Arno."

Oh dear, oh dear, but Poppi is a very nice town, with a beautiful *giardino pubblico* for its approach and, when you get there, it's arcaded and you might swear that it was somewhere in the Veneto—perhaps somewhere just north of Possagno. However, I don't suppose that you will be going to see Dorothy in Poppi, even though Susie's hairdresser in Boston comes from there. [...][1]

Dearest Judy: a very strange way to begin a letter. But I enjoyed your phone calls this afternoon, and, also, let me have your report on the Cinque Terre which I always confuse with the Sette Commune just north of Vicenza.

Fred was going to come to dinner on Monday night preparatory to driving down to somewhere near Cortona to spend a couple of weeks with his *famiglia*.[2] However, he didn't stay to dinner because of the French who are so <u>very</u> helpful—lots of truck drivers outside Calais blocking all the roads so as to prevent importation of English lamb. Like Agincourt all over again, or don't you think? So he had to go to Dover-Ostend instead. But, apart from Fred, this place is getting to be a desolation and a charnel house. First Alvin B. croaks last year,[3] second Douglas Stephen in January, then Peter Murray shortly after you left, and then dearest Jim.[4] But it is like a lesson in *ars moriendi*; and I really begin to wonder why I was sufficiently deluded to come back here.[5] James is off on a trip around the world [...], Simon is jaunting around in Francia [...] David continues to be charming and I give rather good presents to Dorothy [...]. Then, of course, there is Ed Jones⋆ just around the corner, whom I <u>should</u> see, but I hardly know him, and Michael Wilford just up the street, whom I <u>must</u> see; but what about John Miller?⋆ Well, I greatly fear that Susan scarcely wishes the presence of any person who knew John before she did. [...]

[Jim's] funeral service was very well done, St Mary Woolnoth is good but very small Hawksmoor and, with organ, string quartet, choir, Mozart anthems, with a soprano to do the twiddly bits, occasionally it approached the sublime.[6] [...] With Jim there in a coffin and under a black pall, I could only weep, pray for the repose of his soul, and hope that he could have no cognisance, except for the Mozart, of anything that was going on.

Obituaries, on the whole, good; but some vicious—as the *Daily Telegraph*, unsigned, but the product of the odious Gavin Stamp. Then it was nice that Francesco Dal Co came from Venice just for the service. I had never expected such a devotion; and, afterwards, we sat, before he left again for Heathrow, and we ate—to calm our emotions—the most excellent smoked salmon sandwiches and we drank, as Jim would have approved, the most superior "Moët et Chandon". Not exactly an Irish wake, not exactly a wedding, but I hope that you grab the pic.

David, of course, ate nothing. He thinks it highly impolite to attempt to eat while attempting to talk (kinda tough? Since most of society seems to be based upon the possibility); and, afterwards both D. and D. came back here and Dorothy stayed the night.[7]

Strange reactions. *Bouleversee*[8] by the collection which even she has to admit is at least something.[9] But, looking at my Falda palaces; "Aren't they terribly dull?" They are now arranged in the bedroom corridor / mini galleria to make a *strada dei palazzo*: "But, perhaps, when displayed like this, with Caprarola in the middle, they do seem to become at least—interesting?"[10]

But my dearest, my dearest, at Oxford my acanthus garden furniture from Ithaca is displayed upon her terrace, [...] and, apart from admiring this ravishing trans-Atlantic gift, what does she say: "But, dear Colin, it's getting to be rather rusty isn't it?"[11]

An estimable, if hysterical, woman, an excellent mother, intelligent sometimes tragic, sometimes vivacious, always well meaning, but Dear God, the Calvinist curse, Geneva and John Knox, must lie terribly heavy upon Edinburgh. Though [...] there still survives the supreme *disinvoltura Scozzese*.[12] In my garden at Oxford, of which she is proud—false perspectives and all—she has recently entertained Gianni Agnelli, Buddy Boy Cossiga and all those.

And what do I say?

Unlike me, she has made herself Italian; and, [...] she has become a pre-eminent part of my life.

Whatever silly, inept things she says I just accept.

My dear, come back and let's talk.

    Colin

P.S. After Jim, whom I knew for fifty years, my greatest friend is, obviously Fred; and I have known Alfredo, I think, ever since 1964, again a long time. Again a long time, a very long time. All the same, in spite of the horrors, I AM, I remain ME.

    Colin

---

1   *giardino pubblico*, Italian: public garden.
2   *famiglia*, Italian: family.
3   "Alvin B.": Alvin Boyarsky.⋆
4   "Jim": James Stirling.⋆
5   *ars moriendi*, Italian: the art of dying.
6   James Stirling's⋆ funeral took place at the Anglican Church of St Mary Woolnoth in London, designed by Nicolas Hawksmoor.
7   "D. and D.": David⋆ and Dorothy Rowe.⋆
8   *bouleversée*, French: overwhelmed.
9   Rowe's collection of Italian prints displayed in his London apartment.
10   *strada dei palazzi*, Italian: palace street.
11   Rowe refers to the cast iron garden furniture he gave Dorothy Rowe⋆ for her St Margaret's Road house, Oxford.
12   *disinvoltura Scozzese*, Italian: Scottish ease.

201   *To Alan Colquhoun*   *11 November 1992*

19 Renwick Place, Ithaca, N.Y.

Dearest Alan:

So many thanks for *The Invention of Tradition* which I found waiting for me when I returned from New York.[1] So I am reading it and these are my opinions so far.

Naturally, I first of all read the Scotland part—because of you and because of Dorothy; and, of course, it confirmed all my intuitions.[2] For have I not always said that Scotland was invented by Sir Walter Scott?

Also I greatly enjoyed the Welsh part which I thought was the most serious of all; and I was delighted to find in it Iolo Magannoc, who—didn't you know it?—was some sort of ancestor of Elizabeth Williams. But the great hero of the Welsh nationalists whom I used to know.

On the other hand I found the British Monarchy part circumspect and dull—when it could have been amusing; and, as for the goings on of Lord Lytton in India, I have to say that they left me stone cold.

However I'm still readin' and gettin' kicks.

You were not, I imagine, happy at the Guggenheim the other day and neither was myself.[3] But, really, I had forgotten how trivial and indifferently detailed that triumph of American architecture just happens to be. And, also, I found the Century Club not much more than a shambles. But the eulogia and the quantity of persons trying to claim apostolic succession.... Well, just think about it.

Then, as for me, I am evidently an actor and an audience of about three hundred people will always turn me on in a flippant and slightly vulgar way. But it was tough because I had been told by Richard Meier★ to speak only for five minutes and had then been told, by P.D.E. that I _must_ speak for longer.[4] And, hence, my extempore which, though _they_ seemed to enjoy it, made _me_ less than happy.[5] [...]

[In moving to Gloucester Avenue in London] I came to live in a socialist wine and cheese belt—when I really belong to S.W.3[6]—for reasons of proximity to various people—Alvin, Douglas, Jim, among others.[7] But my relationship with my nearest neighbors in Regent's Park Road has not exactly been prominent. I went to dinner with J. and S. in January before I went to Roma: and I went to dinner there in April when I came back and Pat was paying a visit.[8] But that has been _tutto_; and nor have they responded to any invitations which I have presented.[9] And I was _really_ eager to show to _them_ my little collections.

But is this the result of ineptness and accident? Or is it a result of policy? [...] Anyway I have been shattered by this; but I am now, quite coldly recovered from my _bouleversement_.[10] Simply I am me, tolerably resilient, and I see few hopes of any further intimacy on that front.

Dear Alan, you are too proud and too intransigent to confess to emotions such as these which I disclose. However, no sweat and _un abbraccio affettuoso_.

    Colin

P.S. Now I have to clean up papers here and get myself ready for that little operation on one of my lower vertebrae—the one I damaged so many, ever so many, years ago.[11]

All of which means that my present mood is distinctly less than incandescent.

    Colin

---

1 Hobsbawm, Eric and Terence Ranger eds, _The Invention of Tradition_, Cambridge, England: Cambridge University Press, 1983.
2 Alan Colquhoun★ had studied at Edinburgh College of Art; Dorothy Rowe★ was born in Edinburgh.
3 A memorial service for James Stirling★ was held on 19 November 1992 at the Frank Lloyd Wright★ designed Guggenheim Museum in New York, followed by lunch at the Century Club. See Rowe's letter to Dorothy Rowe★ dated 27 November 1992 (p 387 in this volume).

4 "P.D.E.": Peter David Eisenman.*

5 For Rowe's eulogy, see Rowe, Colin, "Eulogy: Jim Stirling", in *As I Was Saying: Recollections and Miscellaneous Essays*, Alexander Caragonne ed, 3 vols, Cambridge, MA: MIT Press, 1996, vol 3, pp 341–352.

6 Rowe's Gloucester Avenue apartment was in the NW1 postal district of London. The SW3 district is Chelsea, an affluent area with high property values and a large concentration of expatriate Americans.

7 Alvin Boyarsky* (1928–1990), Douglas Stephen (d 1992), and James Stirling* (1924–1992), all of whom died shortly before Rowe moved to London.

8 "J. and S.": John and Su Miller.* Pat Miller,* John Miller's wife from 1957 to 1970.

9 *tutto,* Italian: all.

10 *bouleversement,* French: upheaval.

11 In early 1993 Rowe underwent surgery in Boston to correct damage to his lower vertebrae sustained in a parachute drop of 1943; regarding the parachute incident, see Rowe's letter to Ursula Mercer* dated 20 August 1943 (p 29 in this volume).

202   To *Alex Caragonne*, London   *12 July 1992*

65 Darwin Court, Gloucester Avenue, London

Alex:

It is completely amazing, to me, how all of Jim's obituarists, even those who are malicious and vicious, never even question the plausibility of the date which he established for his birth: April 22 1926.[1] They don't even begin to imagine the possibility of this chronology.

Now, as his sister said to me the other day after the funeral service: "But you and I know, don't we, that this type of dissimulation was one of Jim's most juvenile vanities?" And then she said: "And I don't know why it's not visible."

So I first met Jim in December 1942 (aged sixteen-and-a-half?) and, by this time, he has already spent a year at the Liverpool School of Art. Just possible. But, then, are we to imagine Jim, in less than eighteen months, acquiring a commission in The Black Watch followed by a commission in Paratroops and, then, at just over eighteen years—by a month or so—participating in the Normandy landings? No there is no way in which this is possible; but even the horrid obituarists who abound in this country, don't seem to grab any problem here.

All the same, myself gives Jim a date in 1923—at the latest 1924. However, no sweat. Because, surely, everyone is justified in the date they choose to assume.

And now a quote from Osbert Sitwell, *Winters of Content*, ed. of 1950, pp. 16-17:

I may add, since we talk of criticism and for the help of those in doubt, that when I write a long sentence, I do not write it by mistake, or because I have not given thought to the point of where and when to end it; but that to the contrary I compose it in this way, when I do so, because I believe in the continuing of a particular tradition of English prose as well as of others for I am not, as occasionally seems to be presumed, the first of English authors to employ for his purposes the long sentence—and I share with many of them, both of my own time and before it the conviction, gained through a lifetime of reading and writing, that certain descriptions are best achieved, and certain sentences of definition best obtained, by the use of a long sentence as that. Upon I am this very moment working; that in short (as Henry James* so frequently wrote at the end of some imposing array of phrases and qualifications), I have faith in the use of the long sentence when the long sentence is required, and of the short sentence, too, when that is needed. But I eschew neither. I think that the short sentence can possess a dramatic intensity that the long sentence can seldom rival, and I think that the long can support a sustained beauty and subtlety to which the short cannot lay claim.[2]

So GRAB it because it's surely true. Or dontcha think?

> *Colin*

1 "Jim": James Stirling* died in June 1992. Rowe was convinced that Stirling was born earlier than 1926, the year recorded in his many obituaries.
2 Sitwell, Osbert, *Winters of Content, and Other Discursions on Mediterranean Art and Travel*, London: George Duckworth, 1950, pp 16–17. The Rowe Library holds ten volumes of Osbert Sitwell.

[handwritten]

To **Dorothy Rowe**, *St. Margaret's Road, Oxford*   *15 September 1992*   **203**

19 Renwick Place, Ithaca, N. Y.

Dearest Dorothy:

M.R.I. is an anagram for "Magnetic Resonance Imaging" and this is what I experienced in Boston the other day.

They strapped me on to a stretcher, elevated it, slid me into a tube, bombarded me with whatnots for about 35 minutes; and—unlike X-ray—M.R.I. can deliver cross sections through the bone at any level required, science fiction! High tech! But, after the previous diagnosis—perfunctory to say the least—this is the first to convince me; and it is all the result of the influence of Susie's father, who taught at the Dartmouth Medical School, Hanover, N.H., a number of years ago.

So, although it seems improbable, the medical school at Dartmouth College dates from the early 1790's and antedates any teaching of medicine either at Harvard or Yale; and, as an assistant there, Susie's father had this guy Birkenfeld who was a product of Cornell. So get the pic!

So, at Dartmouth, there was a Doctor Sachs—London Jewish and brother of buddy boy Sachs who left so many Italian drawings to the Fogg Museum at Harvard. So you see how it all begins to fit.

Apparently, by origin, neuro-surgery is an English thing; but, for all that—as Birkenfeld told me—it would be extremely difficult in England to set up such an orthopaedic/neurological consultation as I had the other day.

Of course, if this is going to mean the end of pain and inept walking, I am entirely delighted; and, as a celebration, I have just bought by telephone a couple of Louis Seize pieces which I saw in Boston the other day.[1] They are two separate pieces with white marble tops, a commode and a sort of highboy, quite minor and—by English standards quite cheap; but they exhilarate me and, if I leave the Chippendale to James (*Le Rosbif*), I think that I shall leave the Louis Seize to Simon.

Lotsa lurv,

> *Colin*

P.S. They are costing me $6,300; in the Pimlico Road I would estimate $16,000; but in reality they are only costing me $4,000—since Susie owes me the rest![2]

---

1 Louis Seize: French Decorative style during the reign of Louis XVI (1774–1791).
2 Pimlico Road is an antique district in London.

204   *To **David Rowe**, Buckingham Gate, London*   *no date, c 16 October, 1992*

19 Renwick Place, Ithaca, New York

Dearest David:

Last night in bed I was reading a biography of Zachary Taylor, obit 1850 after a very short term in the White House; and I found it a terribly, terribly dull career. Plantations at Louisville, KY and Baton Rouge, LA, tours of 'duty' in the military, success in the Mexican campaign of 1846... and then the sudden ascent from obscurity. So this was after being obliged to listen to one of those televised 'debates' among the different candidates. Which was dreadful; but of course.

To be doubted whether Geo. Bush will make it and,[1] I think, to be hoped not, since his sniping at Clinton[2] (like his sniping at Dukakis) is altogether too low class.[3] And, then, Ross Perot![4] Well, to me his only virtue is that—Perrot/Perrault—I confuse him with the architect of the east front of the Louvre! And Bill Clinton? A trip to Moscow and peace demonstrations in Grosvenor Square? No sweat! Much more should he be impeached because, after a Rhodes Scholarship at Oxford, he and his wife baptized their daughter 'Chelsea'.[5] Oh please, oh Chelsea, oh please...! However, needless to say, 'Chelsea' receives not any reference whatsoever.

A dim look out? But more so because of the way these guys talk—as though the U.S. were not a huge, rich, disturbed and pullulating political society but as though it were a little, little, bitty town and they were running for mayor. But, also, no eloquence and no dignity or resonance of language.

So this is me—insomniac as usual—in bed; and, then (but not absolutely like Mrs. Baldwin contemplating sex with her husband).[6] I began to think about England. And, for the first time, I grabbed an obvious, the obvious, difference in political procedure.

You see, here, presidential candidates are dragged out of the *poché*, enjoy a few years of illumination, and then are condemned, once again, like so many political bugs, to retreat into the woodwork.[7] But you name it; and it's rather the rule than the exception: Jimmy Carter, Gerald Ford, Harry Truman (?), Warren Harding, Calvin Coolidge, William Howard Taft, Grover Cleveland, Chester Arthur, Millard Fillmore, Benjamin Harrison, James Buchanan, Martin Van Buren.

Like a list of the more ineffective Popes, elected for the convenience of the College of Cardinals, you can extend back—at least to c. 1832—the list of the *faineants* presidents; and curious to compare this with the longevity of English tenures of prominence—Ld. J. Russell, Ld. Palmerston, Gladstone,* Disraeli,* etc.[8] But, like very old used cars, the American political system seems to be unable to recycle old used presidents, nor even to be able to provide them with an adequate dumping ground. And now a quote from *Dear Bess*, letters from Harry Truman to his wife, New York 1983. It's dated 1911 and I think that it might amuse you.

I think one man is just as good as another so long as he's honest and decent and not a nigger or a Chinaman. Uncle Will says that the Lord made a white man from dust, a nigger from mud, then threw up what was left and it came down a Chinaman. He does hate Chinese and Japs. So do I. It is race prejudice I guess. But I am strongly of the opinion that negroes ought to be in Africa, yellow men in Asia, and white men in Europe and America.[9]

So this is Truman aged 27. So just grab it. Purest Missouri one can't help thinking.

Anyway, as you must guess, I am beginning to find American political biographies to be immensely interesting, to be absolutely alluring in their dullness. All those people in Boston and New York went to Europe every other year; and, if they didn't always succeed in marrying their daughters off to Roman princes or English peers, perhaps they always hoped to come back with appropriate trophies of 'culture'. But the world of the typical American president is far away from the fantasies of Henry James; and, as an antidote, it's quite rewarding to read about them. Not as rewarding as reading about the Popes; but still, in *gestalt* language, the world of the T.A.P.'s does just happen to be the ground which supports the activity of H.J.'s implausible figures.[10]

Or do I begin to seem improbably grass roots.

    Colin

P.S. A new expression not fully understood by the students. DWEM. Oh Michelangelo, Machiavelli, Mozart is just a DWEM. So DWEM means "Dead, White, European, Male"; and this is evidently an aspect of the pseudo grass roots.

    Colin

P.P.S. [...]

Another P.S.

Matt called me yesterday about a lec. at the U. of Maryland by Frampton.[11] Lecs about "The New York Five" of so many years back in which myself had refused to participate—make bad blood.[12] But not to withhold Ken. He had no reservations like mine and he, simply, charged. Michael Graves★ had ratted on the modern movement, *ergo, finis* Michael; John Hejduk★ simply tried to make bad poetry (I agree); Charlie Gwathmey had never learned how to make a big building (this is abundantly visible); Richard Meier★ (the only talent); and Peter Eisenman★ (who was invented by C.R. and never understood what it was all about).[13] Interesting and I am surprised. Apropos of Frampton it seems to me a *renversement des alliances*;[14] and, about this Matt said that he had gained the impression that so many English architects were still fighting about the Spanish Civil War, that it was all a matter of:

    ...old, unhappy, far-off things
    And battles long ago[15]

Profoundly true, perhaps a reason why Jim failed in England.[16] I will use it.

Best, best,

    Colin

Had Francoise Choay to lunch the other day.[17] She loathes Mitterrand and is ever so happy that she voted against Maastricht.[18]

1   In 1992 George Herbert Walker Bush was the forty-first president of the United States and, as the Republican candidate, he sought a second term in 1993.

2   William Jefferson "Bill" Clinton (b 1946) was the Democratic presidential candidate in 1992. He served as the forty-second president from 1993 to 2001.

3   Michael Dukakis (b 1933), Democratic presidential candidate in 1988, lost to George HW Bush.

4   Henry Ross Perot (b 1930), billionaire Texas businessman, Independent presidential candidate in 1992 and 1996.

5   Chelsea Victoria Clinton (b 1980); on the name "Chelsea", see Rowe's letter to Matthew Bell★ dated 21 October 1992 (p 384 in this volume).

6   Lucy Baldwin, Countess Baldwin of Bewdley (1869–1945), wife of Prime Minister Stanley Baldwin for 53 years.

7   *poche*, French: background fabric; literally "pocket".

8   *fainéants,* French: layabout, idler, slacker.

9   Harry Truman to Bess Wallace, Grandview, Missouri, 22 June 1911, in Ferrell, Robert H ed, *Dear Bess: The Letters from Harry to Bess Truman, 1910–1959*, New York: WW Norton and Co, 1983, p 39.

10 "T.A.P.": The American Presidents.

11 Kenneth Frampton (b 1930), British architect, critic, and historian.

12 "The New York Five" was comprised of architects Michael Graves,★ John Hejduk,★ Charles Gwathmey, Richard Meier,★ and Peter Eisenman.★ Their domestic architecture was the subject of an exhibition at the Museum of Modern Art, New York, in 1969, and of *Five Architects: Eisenman, Graves, Gwathmey, Hejduk, Meier*, New York: Wittenborn, 1972, introduced by Rowe, with an essay by Kenneth Frampton.

13 *ergo finis*, Latin: thus finished.

14 *renversement des alliances*, French: reversal of alliances.

15 Wordsworth, William, "The Solitary Reaper", 1815.

16 "Jim": James Stirling.★

17 Françoise Choay (b 1925), French urban theorist and art and architectural historian.

18 François Mitterrand (1916–1996), president of France from 1981 to 1995. The Maastricht Treaty, aka. the Treaty on European Union, established the European Union and led to a single European currency.

205   *To Matthew Bell*   *21 October 1992*

19 Renwick Place, Ithaca, N. Y.

Matt !, Matt !!, Matt !!!

This is just a *cri-de-cœur*;[1] but I'm thinking about Chelsea, Chelsea Clinton, the possible 'princess' CHELSEA.[2] But, poor child, and just why did her parents impose such cruel and unusual punishment? And can you not imagine Henry Adams sniggering about this and Alice Roosevelt Longworth snorting? And how, after her papa was at Oxford for two years (even though Geo Bush perceives Oxford to be a left wing university) was the papa so gauche as to connive at such cuteness?[3]

So what about Pimlico Clinton or Belgravia Clinton? "This is my daughter, Belgravia" really sounds much better. And Marylebone Clinton is really quite distinguished. But CHELSEA is, somehow, irremediably l.m.c. Paddington Clinton[4]—like Paddington Bear?[5] Bloomsbury Clinton—overtones of Virginia W.? Holborn Clinton—too masculine? Kensington Clinton—and you can go on piling them up. But CHELSEA !!!???[6]

However, let us not forget that Florence Nightingale was called Florence because she was born there and her sister was called Parthenope because she was born in Naples. But, being Italian, it sounds better, at least I think; and, if only they'd called the brat CELSI perhaps it might just have been O.K.

However, I can't help thinking that Chelsea and her father, the name and the proposed political program, involved a deep psycho-spiritual affinity; and, having heard his white trash voice (which is almost identical with Perrot's),[7] myself wishes to have <u>nothing</u> to do with it.

Of course, trouble is that the voices of none of the candidates is other than frightening. Their voices, none of them, have resonance, timbre, pitch, generosity, or power of projection. Mrs. Patrick Campbell, Edwardian actress, said about somebody: "he talks like a typewriter and moves across the stage like a chest of drawers"; and I am miserably afraid that this is true of all the present candidates.

But why? Woodrow Wilson had a voice to carry a gathering of 5,000 persons, Lincoln's voice must have had more than equal capacity, and the possession of a powerful voice was evidently some sort of political necessity down until as late as 1940.

So, for the present failure of the powerful voice, should one not think about the means of mechanical amplification which all these persons have been accustomed to use; and, for the equivalent absence of gesture which has caused them to behave like members of a Punch and Judy show—well isn't that an affair of T.V.?[8]

Dorothy, needless to say, is all for Clinton: "But, Colin, he's a graduate of OXFORD: and Bush isn't exactly out of the top drawer now is he?" "But, Dorothy, Yale and Andover...?" So, as you may well guess, that gets you nowhere.

In other words, dear Matt, I think that I am going to vote for Bush. Not that I approve and I voted Dukakis last time, but the thought of Arkansas curls me up around the edges.[9]

Best love to Cheryl,[10]

    Colin

P.S. It's too late for opera; but have decided to try to persuade you to enter politics. In the present circumstances [your] *basso profundo* voice should go far.[11] Try hard a bit and you could soon be Junior Senator from Maryland!

    Colin

---

1 *cri du cœur*, French: a passionate outcry; literally, cry from the heart.
2 Chelsea Clinton (b 1980), the daughter and only child of Hillary and Bill Clinton, the forty-second president of the US. Bill Clinton was the Democratic candidate for the president at the time this letter was written.
3 George Herbert Walker Bush (b 1924), the forty-first president of the United States and the incumbent president at the time this letter was written.
4 "l.m.c.": lower middle class.
5 Paddington Bear, introduced in 1958, was a fictional character in children's books written by Michael Bond.
6 Like Chelsea, Pimlico, Belgravia, Marylebone, Paddington, Bloomsbury, Holborn, and Kensington are areas of London.
7 Bill Clinton was born into a lower middle-class family in the Southern state of Arkansas. Ross Perrot, the Independent candidate for the US presidency at the time this letter was written, was from Texas.
8 "Punch and Judy" is a traditional popular puppet show featuring Mr Punch and his wife, Judy.
9 Michael S Dukakis (b 1933), Democratic presidential candidate who ran against George HW Bush in the 1988 election.
10 Cheryl O'Neil,* was a former student of Rowe's and a graduate of Cornell's Urban Design Program, married to Matthew Bell.*
11 *basso profondo*, Italian: deep bass.

19 Renwick Place, Ithaca, N. Y.

Dearest Dorothy:

A little bit of Robert Benchley which I came across the other day: "Yes, the Vatican is very splendid, very fine, only trouble is, the trouble is, I think, is that it really lacks a woman's touch."[1] Not quite up to Ogden Nash; but something of the same style.

Have been reading about Philadelphia in the 1790's, when it was briefly the capital of this country and absolutely crammed with French refugees—10,000 of them. So Talleyrand, 'the bishop', was emphatically <u>not</u> acceptable and the Orleans princes were living just above a barbershop a few doors away from Geo. Washington; and it seems that you could scarcely go out to dinner without tumbling over the Vicomte de Noailles (who, in 1789, had pleaded for the abolition of titles and whose wife, together with her mother and grandmother, had all been guillotined within minutes of each other), the Duc de Rochefoucauld-Liancourt, etc, etc. But these were all the guys who, on the Susquehanna about sixty miles from here, attempted to found a French colony to be called Azilum where all that remains is an ultra-red neck motel called the Queen Marie Antoinette. But it makes you think, you know, of how Louis-Philippe learned to carve ham when he was a waiter in Bardstown, Kentucky and of how he always carved and told the guests about how he acquired his proficiency, this when he was presiding at the Tuileries.[2] But, if you acquire crazy details in the way which myself does, it also makes you think about that earlier Duc de la Rochefoucauld who, when he was dying, was asked if he didn't wish to make a full confession: "No, no, that will be quite gratuitous. God will think twice before he turns down a La Rochefoucauld."

Trouble is here that nobody, absolutely either understands or is amused by this sort of stuff.

Instead, here, there is a new faculty member called Kay Walking Stick![3] Now <u>can</u> you believe it? Professor Walking Stick! But <u>what</u> can she be? And <u>what</u> can she look like? Sometimes I do think that while 'democracy' may render the Americani savagely witty, it can also make them curiously rabid: "Dear Dorothy, may I introduce you to Professor Walking Stick. She is, you must know, a great genius."

Dear Dorothy, when Kay Walking Stick walks my way, I really do begin to feel that I have outlasted my time.

Un abbraccio affettuoso.

    Colin

P.S. At Bardstown, Kentucky, there is a famous Trappist monastery where Thingummy Bob Merton, almost a saint, lived until very recently; and the Trappist monks bake a particularly delicious bread.[4] So, in the 1790's, Bardstown was the end of the stagecoach route from Philadelphia; and it was in the inn there that Louis-Phillipe, as he told Disraeli,★ learned how to carve with such elegance.

So, some years ago, Judy and I went to Bardstown; and there, on the menu in the very same building was: 'King Louis Phillippe gourmet special on toasted Trappist monk!'

So we ate it (shades of the 1790's?); and it was not so bad.

    Colin

P.P.S. I find myself—but rather too late—anxious to make a number of little American trips. For instance to Maine, where I have never been, and up the Kennebec and Penobscot rivers. Via the Kennebec you can reach the headwaters of the Chaudiere which flows down to the St. Lawrence and to Quebec (Geo. Bush at Kennebunkport and General Wolfe on the Heights of Abraham)—a rather secret route used by the Bostonians in 1775. But, then, I want to go there for other reasons too. In the north aisle of Bath Abbey is the monument to William Bingham erected by his son-in-law, Alexander Baring and, on this, a great deal depends. Bingham had acquired three million acres in Maine—as who would not? But that is a whole story in itself. The susceptible Alexander, marries Bingham's daughter, later becomes Lord Ashburton and, presumably to protect the Baring holdings in Maine, makes the treaty, with Daniel Webster about the American-Canadian border which Palmerston called the Ashburton Capitulation. And, hence another reason for visiting Maine—just to see, from the Baring point of view, what was at stake. Not all that very much I can't help thinking.

But, dearest Dorothy, it all takes you into the orbit of the second Lady Ashburton, the dreadful Harriet who was so excruciatingly rude to Jane Carlyle. And big problems here. Harriet Ashburton gave Mrs. Carlyle a dress as a Christmas present; but this was a Xmas present for servants and H.A. was well aware of what she was doing.

A long way from Philadelphia in the 1790's? But perhaps not so very far.

In any case, I begin to perceive that I missed my metier.

    Colin

1 Robert Benchley (1889–1945), American humorist and newspaper columnist.
2 The exiled Louis Phillippe I (1773–1850), French king from 1830 to 1848, is reported to have stayed at the Hynes Hotel, now the Old Talbott Tavern, in Bardstown, Kentucky, during his visit to the US between 1795 and 1798.
3 Kay Walking Stick (b 1935), professor of art at Cornell, 1988–2005.
4 The Abbey of Our Lady of Gethsemane, 1848.

---

*To **Dorothy Rowe**, St. Margaret's Road, Oxford*   *27 November 1992*   **207**

19 Renwick Place, Ithaca, N. Y.

Dearest Dorothy:

For Jim's affair at the Guggenheim on Thursday last week there spoke: Philip Johnson,⋆ Paul Rudolph, Harry Cobb, Cesar Pelli, Michael Graves,⋆ Charles Gwathmey, Richard Meier,⋆ Peter Eisenman,⋆ Robert Stern, Robert Maxwell,⋆ Michael Wilford, Robert Livesay, Craig Hodgetts, Jacquelin Robertson⋆ and Colin Rowe—with Philip first and myself last.[1]

So fifteen people altogether and I began to think that they would never end. So Rudolph and Pelli were evidently representing various phases of Yale and Wilford was representing the office; but, as to the rest of them I just don't know. Then, in the audience, there were Frampton and Colquhoun,⋆ Hejduk⋆ looking absolutely like death and, to me, the always improbable Isosaki (but how that man gets around).[2] Then the inevitable Barbara Jakobsen, the difficult Warren James (ex-Cornell, something to do with <u>those</u> J's, who has worked for Bofill in Barcelona, tagged around with an impoverished Spanish Habsburg and, finally, settled down in marriage with a P.R.R.P.—Puerto Rican Rum Princess). Then Mary and Kate and Sophie—Ben being scuba diving in the Red Sea—and Kate making a very, very distinguished little speech, which Mary, Judy and I rehearsed with her the night before.[3] And then a gang particularly related to me: Steve and Barbara Peterson,* Bill and Jane Ellis, Pat Miller,* Judy Wolin, of course Di Maio* and Kim,* Peter Szilagyi, Dan Shannon and others.[4]

In other words, I didn't know that I knew quite so many people; and, beginning and end and much to my embarrassment, it was quite a bit my own *ricevimento* rather than Mary's.[5]

Trouble was, for me, my talk. I had planned a talk for fifteen minutes and then been told, by Meier, that I could only speak for five. Therefore, I had left behind my script for fifteen minutes, only to be told, by Maxwell, that he intended to talk for that length of time and to be told, by Eisenman,* that I should go on for at least as long as Maxwell.

And that's the pic. After a lot of preparation, bereft of notes for the longer talk, I had to extemporise and lost a lot of my lines. But, apparently, it still went well and Mary and Kate—and even Philip—seemed to like it. But I have my own reservations.

Intrinsically, as you know, I am a ham actor. I can be in a condition of the most extreme depression; but, given a subject with which I am happy and an audience of at least five hundred persons, I can illuminate myself and charge ahead—which, remembering enough, here I proceeded to do.

And this means that, after all the religiosity and lack of astringency, all the unctuousness and sanctimoniousness, I began with citing a conversation of years ago with Jim's mother: "O Colin, there should be no surprise that Jim is infatuated with Manhattan. Of course, he wasn't born in New York. But it was the next best thing. He WAS conceived there—in a boat moored off the W. 46th St. Pier—the old Cunard pier—and I SHOULD know."

Well, naturally, vulgar though it might have been, apart from providing info (the sort that Jim would have liked) it brought down the house; and, after that—unfortunately—they became limp in my hands. So I produced Jim to James R. about the French clocks and their superb mechanism which didn't work.[6] And Jim says to James: "You ask me what I paid for these things. Well let me tell ya', a lot more than your bloody uncle would be prepared to pay."

And all this allowed me to continue. Just what an enormous pleasure it would be, for me, to be sitting with Jim and reading the obituaries—the more vicious the better.

But, particularly, the *London Times*, which recorded Jim's most influential readings as having been Saxl and Wittkower's* *British Art and the Mediterranean* and Colin Rowe's celebrated *Towards a New Architecture*. And, hearing this, the New York audience absolutely roars its astonishment. And, then, dearest Jim says to me: "Well you lousy bastard, you were less than two years old when you wrote this book. But why the hell did ya never tell me?"

But Dorothy I can only represent Jim in this way; it is my re-creation of Jim—Empire furniture and a shared conversation style of which, I think, that you disapprove; and as a consequence, I think that I'd better go on to lunch which followed.

The Century Club by Stanford White, which one is supposed to revere, turned out to be far less than splendid. Indifferent entrance foyer from which we are moved into a badly converted palm court with quite horrible portrait of (?) Cardinal Spellman, set out with a U-shaped table and utterly miserable collapsible chairs. So, at the head of the U, we are placed, with Mary in the middle, myself on her right, Philip on her left, Judy on my right and Susie on Philip's left. An interesting placement since both Judy and Susie had gate crashed, but a boring placement since, having nobody opposite, it did make conversation a little more difficult.

And to eat: a bowl of soup served in something about the size of a coffee cup to be consumed with something about the size of a teaspoon, badly cooked rack of lamb with etceteras, a stewed pear with chocolate sauce, and, after I have rung and banged to make a presence, with Mary to rise and make a thank you. And this was all.

But, on the whole, it was better done than I had expected. Pat, who is now a grandmother, succeeded in looking only about thirty-five years old and Peter, in the end, wasn't all that lousy.[7] Looking for the apostolic succession of course he was; but, all the same, he kept it fairly quiet and it wasn't as bad as I thought it might have been.

And then there was the weekend before in Boston with all the medical findings. But I think that you already know about this.

Meanwhile poor Susie is dreadfully distressed about her father's death—of Alzheimer's disease—and totally neglected; and I don't begin to understand it in any way because she loses control when she attempts to tell me.

There seem to have been seven brothers: two ambassadors, two high court judges, a secretary of state (foreign sec.), and Susie's father who was sent to Dartmouth for medicine. And that is just about as much as I can grab. So Papa returned to Dartmouth because Mamma was ill; and that is why she is buried in Hanover, New Hampshire; and this is why, I think, that the three daughters were sent to school in the U.S. [...]

I am amused by a conversation which, allegedly, you and Judy had in Poppi. Allegedly you said to Judy: "why don't you marry him?" So cheers to you and thanks a lot; and, maybe, we will <u>still</u> be able to bring it about. In spite of our always-constant recriminations you do know that she and I only remain happy when we are together. So I wish we could be; and, finally, I think she does too. In the end, we would be terribly, desperately happy together. But let's not hope for too much.

Best, best,

Colin

P.S. In fact, in the end let's not hope for <u>anything at all</u>. Though a charming idea— and nice of you to bring up, and though I was touched—just wouldn't work out you know.

Colin

---

1 Memorial service for James Stirling* held at the Guggenheim Museum in New York City on Thursday, 19 November 1992.
2 Kenneth Frampton,* Alan Colquhoun,* John Hejduk,* and Arata Isosaki (b 1931).
3 James Stirling's* widow, Mary, and the Stirling's daughters, Kate and Sophie, and son, Ben.
4 Judith DiMaio* and Susie Kim.*
5 *ricevemento,* Italian: reception.
6 "Jim to James R.": James Stirling* to James Rowe.*
7 Pat Miller* and Peter Eisenman.*

*To **Alex Caragonne**, Berkeley, California* *20 May 1993*

19 Renwick Place, Ithaca, N. Y.

Carissimo:

I have just read <u>all</u> of your stuff.[1] I have enjoyed it, admired it, made occasional emendations; and now, trying to be good, I am sending it back to you.

Comments

I didn't know that Hoesli* had made a lec. at the U. of T. in 1982.[2] Never have been asked to do so myself and this must illustrate where the real enemy is presumed to be located. But, as to 'old unhappy, far off things and battles long ago', neither was Jim asked back to Liverpool.[3] Nor have been either Robert Maxwell* or myself.[4]

I think that you give a <u>little</u> too much prominence to Michael and the *hotel particulier*.[5] Years ago, the h.p. was always prominent in the thought of Maxwell and myself; and, as Susie intimates, it was lying around at Cornell as an 'attractive' theme which Michael simply took over. But no? But in any case I gave M. lots of *materiel* for that book which <u>never</u> did he acknowledge.[6]

<u>You</u> may—but I don't think that you are—be carrying on to the point of obsession and you should begin to cease and desist.

But, dear Alex, would love to see you and, as Bernini used to say, I remain *il tuo devotissimo* and *umillissimo servitore.*[7]

Though <u>not</u> quite.

Best, best, and would love to see ya'.

Colin

P.S.

While you are talking about OMU[8] perhaps there should be a footnote to record that, apart from the firing of Chimacoff, Sherwood and Koetter* in 1973,[9] with reference to Jerry W's tenure in 1970, at that time there was an aborted attempt to fire him too.[10]

Hejduk* was at Cornell in the years '58 to '60.[11]

Don't know how you handle this—or whether you might or should—but I think that you should also give <u>some</u> credit for the Nine Square problem to Bernhard and myself. Likewise the Texas Houses—an attempt to Palladianise Mies*—would seem to indicate an obvious influence from You Know Whom.[12]

Think that you have handled B. very, very well.[13] When I introduced P.D.E. to B. in Zurich in 1961,[14] P.D.E. was, quite gratuitously, appalled [...][15]

---

1   A manuscript of Caragonne, Alexander, *The Texas Rangers: Notes from an Architectural Underground*, Cambridge, MA: MIT Press, 1995.
2   According to Caragonne* in *The Texas Rangers*, Bernhard Hoesli* lectured at the University of Texas-Arlington in 1982, not the University of Texas at Austin, where Rowe and Hoesli had taught together in the mid-1950s.
3   From William Wordsworth, "The Solitary Reaper", *Memorials of a Tour in Scotland*, 1803.
4   James Stirling* was a graduate of the University of Liverpool as were Rowe and Robert Maxwell.* In November 2013, Maxwell was "asked back to Liverpool".

5 Michael Dennis;* *hôtel particulier*, French: grand townhouse. On Michael Dennis and the *hôtel*, see Caragonne, *The Texas Rangers*, p 349.
6 *matériel*, French: equipment, hardware; In the preface of Dennis, Michael, *Court and Garden: From the French Hotel to the City of Modern Architecture*, Cambridge, MA: MIT Press, 1986, Michael Dennis* wrote of "an indefinable debt to Colin Rowe".
7 *il tuo devotissimo* and *umilissimo servitore*, Italian and English: your devoted and humble servant.
8 "OMU": Oswald Mathias Ungers* (1926–2007), chair of the Cornell School of Architecture from 1968 to 1973.
9 Alan Chimacoff, Roger Sherwood, and Fred Koetter.* See Caragonne, *The Texas Rangers*, p 356.
10 Jerry A Wells.*
11 John Hejduk.*
12 On the nine-square problem, see Rowe's letter to Alex Caragonne* dated 30 June 1995 (p 430 in this volume).
13 "B.": Bernhard Hoesli.*
14 "P.D.E.": Peter Eisenman.*
15 Final line not shown on copy; original lost.

To **Judith DiMaio**, *West 67th Street, New York, N.Y.*   *3 & 5 June 1993*   **209**

19 Renwick Place, Ithaca, N. Y.

Dearest Judy:

I enclose the piece that I did for Jungle Jim plus a covering letter for Cinzia Buddyboy; and hope that you like.[1] Possibly there is just a bit too much of *me* in it; and I am sure that Dorothy will say that. But it is substantially what I said back in November.

June 5

Got your phone call this morning while Candide and Brian were out for breakfast at the State Street Diner.[2] Ugh! I shudder at the ideas of both the breakfast <u>and</u> the diner!

But, yesterday, Brian and I went [on] a completely delicious and ravishing drive— Cazenovia, Skaneateles; and, my dear, it was almost like the Garden of Eden with everything just growin' like mad in a most profligate and profuse way.[3] Brian says that it is all more lush than anything until you get down in Virginia; and I believe that he must be right—Connecticut, Pennsylvania and Maryland, you know, just don't do it. Though, of course, if you like it's all a camouflage; and it doesn't quite disguise the austerity and the gauntness and the glaciation. However it's the land around Cayuga and Seneca that was most stripped down by the glacier; and, most everywhere else, you get the most charming little drumlins—and big ones too. But, as I try to overcome my prejudices, it makes me think that southern Sweden at this time of year must be a bit like this, with a geological severity overlaid by a vegetable benevolence/bountifulness—all highly piquant and un-Mediterranean.

Anyway we went to look for a wedding present for the future Mr and Mrs Bell in rather a good shop in New Woodstock which usually has good, though pricey, Chinese stuff, both export porcelain and blue and white; but some rich people from Palm Beach, Southampton and Park Ave., who have lately acquired a house in Cooperstown had, more or less, cleaned it out.[4] Rest was: tedious Hepplewhite, sentimental awful pics which she is trying to push, and not so good plates, bowls and teapots of generally Chinese provenance; but boring.

However I did buy from there, retrospectively and by telephone. She had a little <u>set of four American, repro, Regency chairs</u> with green silk damask cushions which cause them to look more French than English. A bit meager but still pretty nice, I bought them for $450.

So O.K. I succumb to your pressure. Yes. I <u>will</u> come to Como-Bellagio for two weeks in August.

Lotsa......

    Colin

P.S. Lookin' at a book the other day—forget what—discovered, in Naples, a mid-eighteenth century Palazzo Bartolomeo Di Maio? Know it? Or know anything about it? All I know that it has a subsidiary stair which is quite a good little Rococo effort.

    Colin

---

1 Now lost, the enclosure was a revised version of the eulogy Rowe delivered at the Guggenheim Memorial for James Stirling* in New York, as sent in Rowe's 31 May 1993 letter to Cynthia Davidson,* editor of *ANY*. Titled "J.S.F. 1923–1992", it was published as "A Tribute to James Stirling" in *ANY* 2, September/October 1993, Robert Maxwell,* consulting editor; republished in Rowe, Colin, *As I Was Saying: Recollections and Miscellaneous Essays*, Alexander Caragonne ed, 3 vols, Cambridge, MA: MIT Press, 1996, vol 3, pp 353–358.
2 "Candide" was one of Rowe's nicknames for John O'Brien;* "Brian": Brian Kelly.*
3 Cazenovia and Skaneateles are small towns in Central New York.
4 Matthew Bell* and Cheryl O'Neil* married in August 1993. See Rowe's letter to Steven Peterson* and Barbara Littenberg* dated 3 September 1993 (p 402 in this volume).

210   *To **Dorothy Rowe**, St. Margaret's Road, Oxford*   *4 & 5 June 1993*

19 Renwick Place, Ithaca, N. Y.

Dearest Dorothy:

On Tuesday, after Memorial Day weekend, I had to leave the house between 9.30 and 12.30 p.m. (early for me) so that the house could be shown; and, surprisingly, it was shown to no less than 24 realtors.[1] In other words, things are maybe looking up; and, then, a woman who came this morning displayed a lot of interest and was charmed by the library.

Then, for your diversion, I include the leader from Tuesday's *Times* but, as I told you before Christmas, they'd be eating up Clinton and demonizing him before the end of May.[2] And you must now see that I was right. But for the Democrats in the White House to have hired a man who served Nixon, Reagan and Bush is surely quite a bit more than a little mad! Pity that he did in Stephanopoulos because, in his *equipe* one is told that he has far more ingenuous persons than <u>that</u>.[3]

Then, for your edification, I enclose the Jim piece which I think that <u>you</u> may consider too flippant.[4] All the same Mary did like it quite a lot and such persons as heard or have read it have signified that they consider it appropriate and agree that one should attempt to <u>sell things as they were</u>.[5] And it will be published along with contributions from Colquhoun,* Maxwell* and Francesco dal Co.[6]

Brian Kelly* came last night from Saratoga where he had been staying with his parents; and, today, we have done a little drive around an extraordinarily lush countryside—this through those amazingly opulent and elegant little towns which are spread along Route 20, the east-west highway of emigration to the north of Ithaca. But Cazenovia, Skaneateles, Auburn, Seneca Falls, Waterloo and Geneva, which we visited, are entirely ravishing, pathetically ravishing, at this time of the year—though God help them in the winter; and we found wonderful landscapes which I had never, never seen. For instance, an extremely intimate little valley with a lot of black and white Holsteins (some little, little) from which we emerged into a completely primordial scene. The little valley was enclosed by a lot of big drumlins but, once we had reached the primordial scene, it was almost as though the glacier had retreated only yesterday—a mad display of little bonds, irrational rocks (glacial erratics) and not very successful trees, it was almost as though a dinosaur might appear at any minute.

But, apart from this episode which provided a sort of sinister relief, again and again, dearest Dorothy I was thinking what a great pleasure if you had been along also to absorb all this seductive environmental business—intense cultivation and provocatively elegant not-so-little houses. But I have always felt this about the absolute bounty of UpState during the summer and, driving through the rocky and forested dreariness of Massachusetts, all the way from Boston to Pittsfield, I have often known the utter ecstasy which persons from Massachusetts must have experienced two hundred years ago as they blazed a trail in this direction.

And Brian more or less said the same today: "how superior UpState really is to anywhere north of Virginia; and what a pity that the aura and the ethos of nineteenth century America could not have been protracted so as to defeat most of the twentieth century horrors. But it is all so vulnerable and fragile isn't it?"

Which is today's story; and, as you must know, myself exists—more or less—by the consumption of landscapes and artifacts within them; and this means that I have a problem ahead. I don't want the most heroic landscapes; I don't need Monte Amiata and Radicofani; I don't need the Big Bend of the Rio Grande and the Grand Canyon; and, my dearest, just what does this mean for me? Am I to become an addict of Ireland, Scotland and Wales?

With all this said, today we bought nothing. Indeed nothing to buy. Some rich people, with houses in Palm Beach, Southampton L.I. and N.Y.C., have recently bought a house in Cooperstown and have cleaned out the area.

So that is it.

P.S. But not completely. Have just bought, by telephone, four American repro Regency chairs which we did see. Surprisingly cheap—$400—and I am sure that you will like them quite a lot. Their cushions are a green silk brocade and they make the chairs look more French than English.

And another story. You know that Maryland song to the tune of Tannenbaum of the Civil War period which culminates in the lines:

> She is not blind, nor deaf nor dumb,
> Huzzah she spurns the northern scum
> She breathed, she burns, she'll come, she'll come
> Maryland, my Maryland.

Well, Brian tells me that, every year at the opening of business, the first motion put before the legislature is to delete these lines; and this is entirely traditional. But, each year and just as traditionally, the motion is always rejected:

> Avenge the patriotic gore
> That flecks the streets of Baltimore
> And be the battle queen of yore
> Maryland, my Maryland.[7]

P.P.S. Very strange. Although the vegetation here is almost as profligate as a poor man's Garden of Eden, there were three degrees of frost a couple of nights ago. So you are never allowed to be completely unaware that you are not in the south.

Saturday [June 5]

Judy rings this morning. She has found a place in the *dipendenze* of a villa, on the water on the east side of the lake north of Como, leading up to Bellagio and Villa Serbelloni.[8] Two bedrooms, kinda neo-classical and $350 a week. But, though it sounds enticing, I am reluctant to accept. Would need a car (to be hired in Zurich where it's cheaper than in Wopland); and I think about further expenses.

So I am beginning to sound like Arthur and Rosemary Mizener.[9] Their daughter married one of the Colts, the armaments people from Hartford, Ct. who used to own Villa Serbelloni. But, though it was always at their disposition, they always preferred S.W.3 and Pavilion Road![10]

---

1 Rowe was attempting to sell his house at 19 Renwick Place, Ithaca, New York.
2 Friedman, Thomas L, "Clinton, Saluting Vietnam Dead, Finds Old Wound Is Slow to Heal", *The New York Times,* 1 June 1993, A1. A report on President Clinton's address given at the Vietnam Veterans Memorial in Washington, DC on Memorial Day.
3 George R Stephanopoulos (b 1961) served briefly as Bill Clinton's *de facto* press secretary; *équipe,* French: team.
4 Rowe's November 1992 Guggenheim eulogy for James Stirling.★ See Rowe's letter to Judith DiMaio★ dated 3 and 5 June 1993, note 1 (p 391 in this volume).
5 Mary Stirling.
6 Rowe, Colin, "J.S.F. 1924–1992"; Colquhoun, Alan, "Architecture as a Continuous Text"; Maxwell, Robert, "Modern Architecture After Modernism"; Dal Co, Francesco, "The Melancholy Experience of Contemporaneity", *ANY* 2, September/October 1993, Robert Maxwell ed.
7 "Maryland, My Maryland", words by the poet James Ryder Randall, 1861.
8 *dipendenze,* Italian: Rowe's italianization of the French *dépendance.*
9 Arthur (1907–1988) and Rosemary (née Paris) Mizener. Arthur Mizener was the Mellon Foundation Professor of English at Cornell from 1951 to 1975.
10 In a letter dated 11 November 1992 to Alan Colquhoun,★ Rowe wrote of his own preference to live in "London, S.W.3." (see p 378 in this volume).

211   *To Vivian Constantinopoulos,*[1] *41 Glasslyn Road, London*   *10 June 1993*

19 Renwick Place, Ithaca, New York

Dearest Vivian:

I return to you your questionnaire, completed as well as I can do it; and I do hope that my tone doesn't sound too querulous. But some of the topics to which I was supposed to address myself did piss me off. However bureaucracies bungle and we all know that.

Anyway, conscientiously, I have attempted to respond to it; and, as a description of the book, I believe that my reply to 10, 11, 12 is the very best that I can do. There, *in noce*,[2] it all is; and I can't help thinking that it should be very useful for ad. purposes.[3]

But the 'going away' of Andreas <u>does</u> distress me; and I am wondering, if you could bear to be so indiscreet, will you tell me <u>why</u>.[4] But I <u>love</u> Andreas, the eternally evasive Greek, and, since he loved his mag, I am wondering what horrid collusions and monstrous machinations brought about this deplorable <u>debacle</u>.

So I read what I have just written and I think: Wow, wow. Am I <u>really</u> someone who has just escaped from a Winston Churchill speech or a late Henry James⋆ novel? And you must know that I am not.

Well there it is; and, if you feel unable to tell me about the dirt, I shall elicit the info from Andreas.

Best love,

Colin

COLIN ROWE

P.S. But, poor Andreas, without his mag, I just don't know what he will do.

Colin

But it's curious, or don't you think? But I had never thought of connecting W.C. and H.J. any time before writing this letter.

Colin

ACADEMY GROUP LIMITED
42 LEINSTER GARDENS LONDON W23AN FAX 071-723-9540 TELEPHONE 071-402-2141

EDITOR/AUTHOR QUESTIONNAIRE
for COLIN ROWE

Full name (Certain cumulative catalogues print authors names in full, and ask us to supply this information):
Colin Frederick Rowe

Series title (if any):
Don't know what this means. But, surely, there is no series involved.

If you are not the primary editor of the above work, please enter name of main editor:
There is no one else. All my own work.

The following information is needed for copyright and cataloguing purposes:
Think this is officious and irrelevant; but here we go.

Birthdate: March 27 1920. But Jim Stirling⋆ and Frank Lloyd Wright⋆ always lied about this. And, therefore, why should <u>myself</u> tell <u>you</u> the truth?

Citizenship: American

Your present affiliation (We normally print this under your name on the title page of your book in our seasonal lists, in prospectuses, etc.):
Don't quite know what this means.

Legalistically, for what this may be worth, I am Andrew Dickson Prof. of Architecture, Emeritus at Cornell University; but I would hate that kind of thing to be used.

Please give the full address (including post code/zip code) for correspondence with you:
Best have: 65 Darwin Court, Gloucester Avenue, London N.W.I. 7BQ

Please give office and home telephone numbers:
No office number. Res. 267-0399

Home:

Office:

Short autobiographical note (on the lines of Who's Who. *Please include academic and other distinctions, memberships in learned bodies, posts held, travel, other book, articles published in primary journals, and so on. Please do not be unduly modest: We are interested in any information which will help us market and promote your book):*
Difficult. Publications with M.I.T.: The Mathematics of The Ideal Villa, Collage City and very many casual essays. Hon F.R.I.B.A. Awards, in the U.S. from A.I.A and A.C.S.A.—"the most significant teacher of architecture in the latter half of the twentieth century". But how very silly. Has taught at U. of Liverpool, the U. of Texas, Cambridge, Cornell.

Have you established contacts that could help in the promotion of your work? Please give details:
I can only think this to be a profoundly irrelevant question. I have so very many contacts in the USA, in England, Italy, Switzerland, Germany, Japan, that I could not begin to list them; and Collage City is even translated into Serbo-Croat and, in Sarajevo, I am sure that it's selling like hotcakes.

We should appreciate a list that set your book from others in the field.
Please list in order of importance.
Answers to requests 10,11,12 are so interconnected that I do not see how they can be separated.

This book is a series of related essays written over a protracted period of time and parts of it have been delivered as lectures at a variety of institutions in Berlin, Barcelona, Rome, Zurich, Houston and primarily, at Cornell.

Addressed to architects and those with a general interest in architecture, it derives from mostly three presumptions: that, effectively, modern architecture—*The Architecture of Good Intentions*—is deceased; that this condition should be no good reason for any wild enthusiasm; and that, as yet, no comprehensive approach has emerged to occupy the vacancy.

The book and its readers: (Please give description of your book suitable for its intended audience. This will be used as the basis of advertising copy. Try to indicate what makes the book unique and useful).
Supposing architects to be neither more nor less rational than the rest of humanity, it is an attempt to articulate that complex of cultural fantasies and prejudices which, in the early years of the twentieth century elicited—for better or worse—something of a revolution in the art of building; and then, it is a further attempt to trace back these climates of opinion, characteristically so much in conflict, not to their origins but to their first highly visible adumbrations.

Please give a 150-word description of your book in simple non-technical language. Salespeople and booksellers in all countries should be able to use it to direct the book to the right buyers. Please say what the book is about, its main purpose and audience, and its importance as you see it. Don't be afraid to state what would be obvious to specialists.

It is something of a contention of this book that, for rather longer than one may care to think about, the architect's psychological constitution has, for all its overt rationalism, been far more intimately a product of the tumultuous tradition of Hebraic and Christian messianic speculation, politicized in the eighteenth century and aestheticised in the nineteenth.

The source of most of our splendours and miseries?

I really do think so.

For lack of space we sometimes need to describe your book in just a few words. Please provide a very short statement that summarizes your book and suggests its unique qualities in one sentence.
I note your 'summarizes' (with American spelling); but <u>what</u> am I to say the book is about: a belated critique of modern architecture from one of the faithful who has always disbelieved?

In order of importance, what are the three most important papers or articles in your collection, and briefly, why?
Am unable to reply

But see my response to 10,11,12. and I can't talk about three—Father, Son, and Holy Ghost and all <u>that</u>. However, if one <u>must</u> talk about <u>three</u> then <u>Epistemology</u> and <u>Eschatology</u> (the most important of the essays—theological underpinnings of mod. arch) comprise one statement (often suggested but never so clearly pronounced); While <u>Iconography</u> provided a bridge to <u>Mechanism</u> and <u>Organism</u>, contrary attitudes recognized by John Stuart Mill in the 1830's but still scarcely observed by modern architects and their devotees. Essential all this for a comprehension of the psychology of mod. arch.

Are these particularly distinguished contributors to your collection whose names will help sell your books? If yes and we can cite their names in promotion, please list them in order of importance.
There are no other contributors to what you choose to call my 'collection'.

What individual disciplines or professional categories may be expected to buy your book? (Please be very specific about the level and type of buyers).

Primary Market(s): Architects and architectural students

Secondary Market(s): May Be popular with cultural conservatives and the like. That is if we are lucky.

Was your book written specifically as a textbook?
Absolutely NOT.

Yes No Required Supplementary

If answer is yes, please describe the level of book, the type of institution where it would be used, and the name(s) of course(s) in which it would be used.

If answer is yes, are there any special pedagogical features (e.g. exercises, worked-through problems, bibliographies, appendices, tables) that should be mentioned when promoting your book?

If your book is not a textbook, are there any special features (e.g. graphics, tables, appendices, annotated bibliographies, references) that should be mentioned when promoting your book?
Am able to think of none.

Are there any countries in which your book will be of particular interest?
Suppose throughout the English speaking world, the principal countries of Europe (though latest the French), Latin America, Japan.

Please list similar or competing books. providing, if convenient, publication dates, publishers, prices and page lengths. In what respect is your book different?
I am unable to do this.

But perhaps might be compared with David Watkin, <u>Morality and Architecture</u> which Alvin Boyarsky* suggested to me was maybe dependent on lectures which I gave at Cambridge c. 1960 and which D.W. attended. However, Watkin writes from the point of view of the neo-orthodox and is altogether too bitter about his subject matter.

Please list, in order of importance, the names of scholarly or professional societies and associations, or industrial corporations, to whose members your book is likely to be of particular interest.
This should be obvious. See 19.

Please list in order of importance those conferences and professional meetings at which your book should be displayed.
You must know this better than me

Publications: (please list in order of importance those journals where your book should be advertised)
Again, you must know this better than me. But I recommend attention to the Milanese scene: *Casabella* and *Domus*

Please list those journals and newsletters that should receive a copy of your book for book review purposes.
The usual mags in the U.S., England, Italy, Switzerland and Germany. Also Barcelona and Lisboa,

Will you provide VCH with an personal mailing lists for promotion of your book
Yes No
To begin with I don't know what VCH means and, to continue, I don't like the idea of personal mailing lists.[5]

But suggest that you send copies to:

Charles Moore, University of Texas, Austin, Texas
Robert Stern, Columbia University
Fred Koetter,* Yale University
Vittorio Lampugnani, *Casabella*

---

1 Rowe was to publish *The Architecture of Good Intentions* with Academy Editions, London. On 15 April 1993 Vivian Constantinopoulos,* a freelance agent for Academy, sent Rowe a questionnaire that she noted "may seem a little detailed but it is a statutory requirement from Academy, and parent company VCH [...]." This letter and the completed questionnaire are Rowe's reply.
2 *in noce*, Italian: in essence, "in a nutshell".
3 "ad.": advertising.
4 Andreas Papadakis (1938–2008), Greek-born British publisher of architectural books who founded Academy Editions in 1968. See Rowe's letter dated 5 September 1993 to Matthew Bell* (p 405 in this volume).
5 VCH is the parent company of Academy Editions.

19 Renwick Place, Ithaca, N. Y.

Dearest Cynthia:

   Many thanks for the new copy of *Architecture New York* which I lately received from you.[1] I have read it with interest, amusement and, ever renewed amazement. In other words, I have been highly stimulated by it; but I am still left wondering why a small resort situation which is almost in Alabama should be able to elicit so bizarre a variety of passions.[2]

But why?

And you must understand that myself is baffled, that I fail to comprehend. Because surely, if we are a truly pluralist society, then how can there be any virtue in debate? And, if we are a *melange adultere du tout*, then, evidently, anything short of criminal activity must be equally valid.[3] And, if such may be the case, then what—what possibly—can there be wrong with Seaside? It possesses a respectable constituency (one presumes the combined resources of Atlanta, New Orleans and Birmingham minor money); it must represent a legitimate point of view; it may not be a complete success; but, in all common sense, can there be any very convincing reasons as to why future Seasides should not proliferate? Seaside may be as lamentably spurious as it is often declared to be. But what matter? By condemning high quality *kitsch* it will not be made to go away. And should seaside be adequate reason for the extremities of terror which it seems to inspire in the amassed community of late modernism? And is it not at least possible that good money will drive out bad?

Apparently, neither Duany* nor Plater-Zyberk* are architects of profound ability.[4] But I cannot understand that this need be an issue. Together, they are architectural entrepreneurs of great intelligence; and, in their quite minor way, they belong to the same theater and style as did John Nash—the spectacular good and the spectacular not so good. So *kitsch* they may produce; but what's the sweat? When there are so few entrepreneurs of their capacity around—and they are needed—just why the glaring hostility?

But we tolerate. Or do we not? And, if we tolerate, then may not the architects of Seaside be received with a decent understanding? And, if we are not able to tolerate (now said to be very un-American), might we be persuaded to compete?

Or, heaven forbid, will competition only result in another fatal compromise, a collusion with the powers of darkness—with bankers and developers, with a dreadful trampling upon the sentiments and the ambitions of the under-privileged?

Now, the 'doctoring' of pluralism has never engaged my own complete support. At it's best it seems to me to be a case of *tout comprendre c'est tout pardonner*—a patent impossibility—and, at its worst, to be a subversion of all plausible standards of judgment.[5] However, when so surreptitious a 'doctrine' is proclaimed from the housetops, decidedly it may be a little bit odd that Seaside be subjected to so intensive a discrimination. But, of course and as we know, secluded within the sociological ambiguities of the debate there always remains the secret agenda of style, tactfully evaded and almost denied by most participants.

So it's what the people want. Or, alternatively, it's what the people, did they but know it, should require. Not simply a case of Neo-Trad versus Mod Arch; and, as solution to this issue, one can only guess that, though the market may become flooded with allegedly sophisticated French theory, in the end this is unlikely to assist any comprehensible adjudication.

All the same, this is to make only a minor point and myself is more concerned with the cultural innocence and the ingenuous prejudices of so many of those persons who contributed to *ANY*'s debate; and, in this day and age, was it not supremely difficult to get so very many of the truly *naïfs* together assembled, to bring together so many intellectually disparate personalities between whom there could be little possibility of profitable interchange? And think particularly about the entirely delightful observations of Professor Neil Smith, urban geographer at Rutgers, who has lately (with the assists from a colleague in Paris) enjoyed the excitement of discovering space.[6] Or so it would seem.

So, with commendable candor, Professor Smith takes us on a quick trip into a *terra incognita* to which he has recently been exposed; and one may sense his pride of discovery:[7]

"The angle I want to take may seem strange to you but it is natural for an urban geographer. One thing that contemporary urban geography deals with is the politics of spatial difference, which I think lies at the center of a very wide ranging discussion that has been going on among social theorists, architects, cultural theorists, geographers, and many others. It is central to the arguments around what Ed Soja, in the subtitle of his book *Postmodern Geographies*, calls the "re-assertion of space" in social and (let me also add cultural) theory. Spatial difference has been rediscovered in the last decade as a means of beginning to inscribe a new politics founded on spatial rather than temporal difference, an antihistoricist politics. The question quickly arises, what is the language of spatial difference? Is there a parallel language for spatial difference that matches the somewhat more sophisticated language of historical difference?

The place to which many of us would go for guidance on this is Henri Lefebvre's work on the production of space. In the early 1970's, way ahead of any of us, Lefebvre produced an extraordinary book entitled *The Production of Space*, in which he argues—to summarize the aspect of this thesis—that around 1910 a dramatic historical shift occurred in what happened to space. This is an extraordinary insight, and how Lefebvre affirms this is rather odd. He talks about Picasso's painting."[8]

Now, Lord love a duck! One had scarcely imagined that in 1993, even at Rutgers N.J., a retarded message from a long vanished Paris, described as "an extraordinary insight" would still be conceived of as a vital *apercu* that more than eighty years after the eruption of Analytical Cubism, the citation of Picasso's painting of that date should still be designated as something "rather odd".[9]

And it is, at this stage, that I am frightfully embarrassed. Is Professor Smith a genuine red neck? In which case one would be delighted to have him to dinner. Or is he a reproduction red neck, his own, personal, version of Seaside? In which case one might be disinclined to enjoy his society.

But, apart from his supreme unawareness, almost equivalent to the "invincible ignorance" which used to be stigmatized by the Church (of Rome), genuinely I would like to come on with an attempt to alleviate his condition. For, horribly patronizing though I may be, surely, the evidently adorable Neil must require instruction—by somebody.

But can we, possibly, convey to him this very obvious information? Can we assure him that the "production" of positive space (and the recognition of such space) is nothing so very recent as he seems to assume? And should we not be allowed to tell him that the date 1910 has long been celebrated? That it was acknowledged even by Virginia Woolf some sixty years ago? That it represents no great revelation vouchsafed to the incredible acuity of Henri Lefebvre?

So, while I think about these questions, I become reduced to the status of some horrid little insect which bites and stings; and, hence and quite promptly, more questions ensue. For instance, is there any way that our dearest noble savage can be told that space-talk, related to 1910, has been one of the principal motifs of Anglo-American visual criticism for almost the last fifty years? That this is one of the leading motifs of so called urban design? That German talk about *raum* had already become a cliché of criticism long, long ago?[10] That Theodor Lipps was one of its great proponents? That Lipps was already published in New York as far back as 1907? That the declaration of space, as a positive value, probably derives from a lecture given by August Schmarsow in Dresden in 1894? That is: a good eighty years before the 'findings' of Henri Lefebvre to whom "we" are all so suddenly indebted.

But not to protract this disagreeable and peevish style of vituperation; and, instead, very briefly to direct attention to the way in which you—and presumably Peter—set up your little *conferenza*.[11] And didn't Liz and Andrés altogether receive too much undeserved flak?

In general, I receive the impression that people have thought so, that it was something of a lynch job, a kangaroo court; and, personally, I think that to have focused so completely on Seaside was an error, producing a scene very much too confrontational and inhibiting the possibility of any useful intermediary talk.

But just everybody was too uptight, too pro or con, and went to absurd lengths to be so. Like Peter attacking the American suburb. But too ridiculous! And just why? Like Andrés proclaiming his faith in architectural variety—the more architects the better, as though the Woods in Bath or John Nash in Regent's Park had ever thought in such terms.

Like the endless agonizing over the failure of Seaside to be politically representative community (no blacks and no white trash), as though any such development previously conceived, from Belgravia to Hampstead Garden suburb and all of their North American equivalents, had ever involved any notion of socio-political integration!

No. We got both the moans and the groans; and it is time to recognize that, both in Seaside and the attacks upon it, there is a painful element of hysteria, that in both cases good judgment plays very little part. Way back, Howard Van Doren Shaw could build a picturesque plaza in Lake Forest which is devoid of anything feverish; but, since the advent of modernism, it would be apparent that this can scarcely be done—and no need to say why.[12]

Anyway, instead of "Seaside", I can only suggest that, just perhaps, yourself might have used another title: like "Seaside, Siedlung Halen and Port Grimaud"? And I make this suggestion because I am sure that this title involves the topic, authenticity versus *kitsch*, which is what you really want to bring to the surface.

So the issue of Seaside versus Something Else, though scarcely arrived in the U.S., was already present in Europe in the late 1950's; and, ever since then, it has engaged my attention. So, along with Peter, I went both to Siedlung Halen and Port Grimaud in 1961-62 and I can still hear him screamin' and yellin'; and, of course, it is one of the classic confrontations.[13]

Outside Bern there is Siedlung Halen, a little pseudo city for the upwardly mobile of impeccably late Corbusian pretensions, and then, down on the coast of Provence, there is Port Grimaud, a Mediterranean debauch, another pseudo city which, in the end, has called the tunes with a much more overt allure; and these are two entirely different postures. A case of puritanism versus profligacy? Though the same sociological deficiencies apply to both, of course it must be this; but it must still be entertaining, or shocking that, in spite of the acceptability of Siedlung Halen, the success story belongs to Port Grimaud.

And, in the end, is not this a very important issue? In the end, is not Seaside very much more than a demure and sexually reduced descendant of Port Grimaud? And, in the trip from Port Grimaud to Seaside, has not the European harlot become the improbable American virgin?

  Colin

1 "Seaside and the Real World: A Debate on American Urbanism", *ANY* 1, July/August 1993, Cynthia Davidson ed, David Mohney guest ed.
2 The "small resort situation" is Seaside, Florida.
3 *mélange adultère du tout,* French: an adulterous mixture of everything.
4 Andrés Duany★ and Elizabeth Plater-Zyberk,★ urban planners of Seaside, Florida.
5 *tout comprendre c'est tout pardonner,* French: to understand everything is to forgive everything.
6 Neil Smith (1954–2012), geographer and academic.
7 *terra incognita,* Latin: unknown land.
8 Smith, Neil, "Reasserting Spatial Difference", *ANY* 1, July/August 1993; Lefebvre, Henri, *The Production of Space,* Donald Nicholson-Smith trans, Oxford: Blackwell, 1991.
9 *aperçu,* French: insight.
10 *raum,* German: space, realm.
11 Peter Eisenman,★ Cynthia Davidson's★ husband.
12 Howard Van Doren Shaw (1869–1926), Chicago architect who began a small Arts and Crafts development in Lake Shore, Illinois, in 1897.
13 Siedlung Halen, 1955–1961, a housing community near Bern, Switzerland, designed by Atelier 5; Port Grimaud, France: a 1960s seaside town of Venetian canals and fishermen's houses designed by François Spoerry on the Riviera near Saint Tropez.

213 To **Steven Peterson** & **Barbara Littenberg**, *East 66th Street, New York City* *3 September 1993*

65 Darwin Court, Gloucester Avenue, London

Steven-Barbara:

I went to Maine the other day, to Portland for the Matt-Cheryl wedding; and I was disappointed by Maine.[1] It was my first time there and, mostly, I found it a distinctly overcrowded, overrated coastal strip from which one could scarcely see the sea because of a lot of rather weedy trees. And, behind it, but no hinterland whatsoever—just an infinite extent of dreary forest.

Almost no Greek Revival and not so many good later houses either, I found myself comparing it, to its detriment, with Upstate and Vermont and wondering why. But, of course, one shouldn't say this and bad mouthing Maine must be a bit like bad mouthing the Declaration; but all the same. So Kennebunkport is charming and, also, Camden; and Penobscot Bay is a magnificent piece of water; and we didn't get to Bar Harbor but we got the general pic—dreadfully impoverished, and, as for Augusta, which one thought might just be a center of throbbing animation, well, just a mill town with a very, very mini State House. But, at least, I am glad to have been and to have seen the house of G.B., out on a peninsula and not unlike a station on the Via Dolorosa for the disappointed Republicans who were gazing at it with grief.[2]

A Newport for very early eco-freaks? Anyway that is what myself thinks. Anyway, on the way back, we—Brian Kelly★ and C.R.[3]—did drop in at Exeter and saw the Kahn★ library which, apart from the to be expected problems of entrance, is a demurely modest and an entirely convincing building—K. at his very best and absolutely to be respected.[4]

So E.R.I.M. or Here I Am in Limeyland and not wholly infatuated, appalled by the expense and not particularly gratified by the stimuli.[5] Just bland, bland. No mountains, no lakes, no rivers that I can perceive and, for the moment, no gratifying royal scandal. But I yearn for geology and glaciations and that is why I am thinking about Cambridge, New York.[6] Meaning that I positively require an accumulation of drumlins, glacial erratic and all that stuff.

Dorothy has sufficiently recovered that she is going to make a little trip to Puglia in the next couple of weeks or so.[7] This with James and wife and Simon. But, needless to say, no advice can be accepted. They are going to stay at Cisternino—between Martina Franca and Ostuni and they appear to have no conception of the topography. "But we must go to Otranto"—not knowing how far away it is; but Lecce and Trani are surely too remote. So I despair. "I am very interested in Frederick II Hohenstaufen but I don't want to see too many Romanesque churches!" Well, but why are you goin' there? Or is it just to see a few *trulli*?[8] However D's guide book, published in London, tells her that few English and absolutely no Americans ever go to Puglia; and, in spite of evidence, since she believes this, no doubt she still enjoys the thrills of traveling in *terra incognita*.[9]

I go to dinner with John★ and Su Miller★ this evening. Interesting? But, fundamentally, I am bored and can't help thinking that sometime soon you all should come and pay me a little visit. But please do think about it.

Un abbraccio and best best,

    Colin

P.S. This little apt has become *existenz maximum*.[10] Absolutely it crawls with detail—pics and rugs—and I deplore it. During the last year, having become accustomed to emptiness—which is also an acoustic scene—I find that I enjoy it. However, let not this prevent you from sending me the good Xeroxes of the Piranesi Campo Marzio. I need these in order to extract from D. things which I already possess![11] So please, please, please, try to send them quick.

    Colin

---

1 Matthew Bell★ and Cheryl O'Neil.★
2 "G. B.": George HW Bush (b 1924), former US president whose summer house was at Walker's Point in Kennebunkport, Maine.
3 "C.R.": Colin Rowe.
4 Architect Louis Kahn,★ Phillips Exeter Academy Library, Exeter, New Hampshire (1971).
5 "E.R.I.M.": "Eer I em", a play on the "Limey" pronunciation of "Here I am."
6 Peterson★ and Littenberg★ live in Cambridge, New York, at this time.
7 Dorothy Rowe★ was suffering from cancer at the time.
8 *trulli*: traditional Apulian dry stone dwellings, typically whitewashed and with conical roofs.
9 *terra incognita,* Latin: unknown lands.
10 *existenz maximum*: Rowe's phrase, meaning "maximal existence".
11 "D": David Rowe.★

65 Darwin Court, Gloucester Avenue, London

Dearest Margaret:

So all the time I was in Ithaca I never visited you in the Slide Library! But this was not because of antipathy or horror with either the S.L. or its denizens. No, it is rather because of my general distaste and misery with regard to the present constitution of East Sibley—with the exception of your particular outfit.[1]

But, you know that the place is rapidly going down the tubes and I don't wish to appear there as *un revenant*[2] or *une voix d'outre tombe* uttering maledictions[3]—like some old Italian horror and pronouncing: "But I told you so"—with which J.A.W. would altogether too strenuously agree.[4] Just, though the prospect of East Sibley continues to distress me, in the *personaggio* of a witch or a Jeremiah I have no wish to present myself; and, even though I have now confused my tenses, I am sure that you have always understood all that I am talking about.[5]

Simply, it is amusing or painful—and I don't know which—to have become retarded and *passé* at C.U.; and this at the same time when one is not so regarded anywhere else in the world!

However to forget all this and, instead, to concentrate upon what may be outstanding problems and your Lib.

There are two pics from Joseph, *Geschicte der Baukunst*,[6] two houses from Amsterdam, which I need for my book—to which, shortly, I shall be able to direct my undivided attention.[7] I believe that Irena brought them to you and I am wondering whether, quite soon, I could have the relevant pics and negatives.[8]

Before he left for Knoxville, Tennessee John, with his usual absence of clarity, told me that I was in debt to the Slide Library for pics made—again for my book.[9] Now most of the pics made were also for the school and for slides which the Lib must have in its possession. But could you let me know about this and bill me accordingly?

As you probably guess I find London hyper expensive and far less than exhilarating. For instance the prices of real estate are absurd. And, as an example, just around the corner from here English John Miller* told me the other night about his house. In 1972 they paid for it 50,000 Pounds and it is now valued at 750,000!!! And this is not at all exceptional! And then, about exhilaration, I begin to feel that I have approached a condition of wreckage: my friend Douglas Stephen—croaked on a trip to New Zealand: Alvin Boyarsky*—croaked; Jim Stirling*—croaked; Leon and Rita Krier*—split; Dominic and Nina Michaelis*—split, with she looking after a hundred cows in Oxfordshire and himself gone away (with multiple sclerosis) to Aix-en-Provence. Then, with my brother just a bit *difficile*—and the boys quite loudly saying so—it's just a bit a mess, a tragedy and a bore; and, quite often, I want to cry about it all.

Grab the scene? Grab the misery?

Much love,

    Colin

P.S. I have just been reading quite a lot of Turgenev and his evocations of Russian landscapes are quite extraordinary—but, reading him, you become immersed in a

Russian summer, the snows gone away, the delicacy, the lavishness of the air![10] All of this observations of the 1850's—before T. had gone to Paris. But so much of it like Upstate in the summer to this day. I am reading T, for both Russian and Upstate reasons.

    Colin

1 Cornell's Department of Architecture was housed in Sibley Hall, which was divided into East and West Sibley.
2 *un revenant*, French: ghost, creature returning from the dead.
3 *une voix d'outre tombe*, French: a voice from beyond the grave.
4 "J.A.W.": Jerry A Wells.★
5 *personaggio*, Italian: person, character.
6 Joseph, D, *Geschichte der Baukunst*, Leipzig: EA Seemann, 1904.
7 Rowe, Colin, *The Architecture of Good Intentions*, London: Academy Editions, 1994.
8 Irene Ayad, an architectural history student in the School of Architecture at Cornell.
9 John O'Brien.★
10 Ivan Turgenev (1818–1883), Russian novelist, poet, and dramatist.

To **Matthew Bell**   *5 September 1993*   **215**

65 Darwin Court, Gloucester Avenue, London

Dear Matt:

Everything continues to piss me off. Like driving on the wrong side of the street, like the wrong sort of electricity twice as strong as anywhere else, like this insane Germanic kitchen; but the most ludicrous of apparently normative local customs absolutely bent my mind when I came across it yesterday.[1] This was in a supermarket where, in order to get a cart, you had to put quite a considerable bit of money into a slot—just like in one of those bad airports—in order to release it!!!???? But CAN you believe anything so contrary to elementary common sense? And, just as in one of those horrible airports, then you had to surrender the cart within the building itself and lug the stuff over to the vehicle! And, amazingly, this is thought to be entirely reasonable! You see it doesn't clutter up the streets....

But I don't see how even Italian bureaucracy at its most bizarre could think up any procedure quite so mad as this. Talking about acting in restraint of trade, talking about this energy of self defeat; but, apparently the supermarket wants you to buy as little as possible and its docile clients happily concur. It's like mineral waters you know, and just like English mineral waters, this must be a system infinitely superior to any other to be found. But stubbornness, insanity and folly. However "we English like to do things in our own way". And that's about it and even the faintest (private) protest seems to be entirely in vain; and, instead, people condone it: "Oh, you see abandoned carts all over London and it's got to be stopped". But no awareness of the *non sequitur* when you can't take the carts outside anyway![2]

After that little outburst I now send you a few clippings for your amusement. The piece from last week's *Sunday Times*: "Americans Turn Nasty In A Bout of Brit Bashing" was a most extraordinary performance but, unfortunately, I didn't keep it. However, do read the reply from *The Independent*—with devastating quotes from Henry Adams; and, parenthetically, do notice that both the English right and left wings are absolutely united in their anti-Americanism.[3] From <u>that</u> unhappy country there can be no good which can <u>ever</u> <u>come</u>. <u>They</u> talk about dollars <u>all</u> the time (not true) but <u>we</u> are above such low concerns (emphatically <u>not</u> true); but that's the way *gli Inglese* try to understand things.[4]

Then I send you the revelation of a few real estate ads and I ask you how these people can contrive to afford it. Prices, but everywhere, are what you might expect to pay in Westchester or Bucks County; and look at the stuff that you get. John and Su Miller* (with whom I had dinner last night!) bought their house for Fifty Thousand—Pounds—in 1972 and it's now valued at Seven Hundred! So think of that now! And even Tom Muirhead* [...] has just paid Seventy for a very [...] little apt., two small rooms, just off the Euston Road; and then only think about Renwick P. where I can't get a seller even at $150—approximately the price of Tom's poor little rooms![5]

So Leon and Rita have split, with he in Provence and she in Belsize Avenue;[6] and likewise Dominic and Nina, she, with the cows, in Oxfordshire and he, on the sea, outside Toulon.[7] And, then, there is Andreas Papadakis and that is very, very odd indeed.[8]

One is told, you see, that he was forced out of *A.D.* for embezzlement![9] But that they won't prosecute because of the scandal! But, again, a real estate problem—hushed up in the English way. Had bought a rather horrid, Tudor kind of, house just off Windsor Great Park which had belonged to Ld. Hillingdon (?), a former viceroy of India, and was diverting funds to pay for it; and, therefore, one isn't supposed to talk to him any more. But everything just crumbles. Or don't you think?

Dorothy has sufficiently recovered that she is shortly going to make a little trip to Puglia with James and Mrs James and Simon. They are going to stay at Cisternino, midway between Martina Franca and Ostuni and this for a whole week. But no advice can be given: "I am not greatly preoccupied with Frederick II and I don't want to become a slave to Romanesque churches. Lecce? And what is there at Lecce? But I want to go to Otranto because of Horace Walpole. But Martina Franca? Well it isn't even in my book and I am sure that you must over-rate it. And Trani? Well isn't that just another Romanesque church?"

Grab the pic. They are supposed to sit in Cisternino the entire week, becoming more and more fractious, with herself resisting all trips further than Alberobello. A wonderful thought; but her guide book tells her that very few English and absolutely no Americans ever pay a visit to Puglia.

Best love to Cheryl and I know that I must make the St Lawrence trip some day.[10]

Best, best,

    Colin

P.S.: For reasons quite as inscrutable as Dorothy's, David is now proposing to buy something in Burgundy. "It's on a medieval trade route, there are a lot of Romanesque churches, and you can drive there very quickly. People will come to stay there in their way south. No it won't be a small chateau by a disciple of Serlio. Just a modest farmhouse with a reasonable amount of land and little more than habitable."

However, don't we know?

    Colin

---

1 Rowe had moved recently to London from Ithaca, New York.
2 *non sequitur*, Latin: a statement or thought that doesn't logically follow.
3 The enclosures are lost.
4 *gli Inglesi*, Italian: the English.
5 Rowe's home at 19 Renwick Place in Ithaca, New York, which he was attempting to sell at this time.
6 Léon and Rita Krier.*

7   Dominic and Nina Michaelis.*
8   Andreas Papadakis (1938–2008), Greek-born British publisher of architectural books who founded Academy Editions in 1968 and purchased *Architectural Design* magazine in 1975. In 1994 Rowe published *Architecture of Good Intentions* with Academy Editions.
9   "A.D.": *Architectural Design*.
10 Cheryl O'Neil,* Rowe's former student at Cornell and Matthew Bell's* wife. The "St. Lawrence trip" refers to Rowe's desire to visit the St Lawrence River Valley.

To *Matthew Bell*   *12 September 1993*   **216**

65 Darwin Court, Gloucester Avenue, London

Matt:

I was to have gone to Oxford for the weekend but I have not been able to do so because of raging altercations. It has been Dorothy's birthday and she has refused to have Him around; and, meanwhile, James has had two flaming rows with his papa in two successive days—over the phone I have to presume.[1]

So cheerful! Or doncha think? And, increasingly, I wonder why I ever came here. My brother insists on mumbling in a voice so low that he can scarcely be heard [...] ; and when people ask him to repeat himself, his temper becomes quite foul. But it really, really is most distressing—particularly as I don't want to become violent myself.

However, enough of this; and, for your entertainment / instruction I send you more news from the real estate front. So absorb it, compare it with D.C. and let me have your reactions. But it appears to me that one can't touch a mid-nineteenth century terrace house, four floors, in any moderately reasonable part of the world for less than approximately one million bucks; and, then, you've just got to look at the crap in the country. And then, and in terms of rental, you just have to think of One Hundred and Fifty Pounds a week, approximately One Thousand Dollars a month for what is, obviously, a completely wretched one bedroom walk up in Hammersmith or Chiswick. But Jesus Christ and it makes ya' think. In any case you perceive the general drift of a quasi-Argument? In this country 19 Renwick P., a desirable property in a university town with a landscape setting never to be found here, would surely be considered a spectacular item to be sold at $400,000 or upwards. And in Ithaca.....?[2]

As a relief from all this I have been reading Turgenev[3] and thinking about Russia which I believe must be a lot like Upstate[4]—with ravishing summers, appalling winters and a Greek Revival presence. A slovenly outfit one knows it must have been, like Mississippi, squalor—all those slaves and serfs—with a top dressing of elegance; but, reading T., still leaves me thinking about Upstate at the same date, forests and water, an interminable landscape and, somehow, an overwhelming perfume / fragrance / smell.

So why don't you and Cheryl read a bit of Turgenev?[5] So I know that you don't read novels. But nineteenth century novels can be very instructive—history, sociology and literature all in the same package—and why not begin with *Smoke* and *Fathers and Sons*.[6] And I am sure that you would find them very rewarding.

And now, 7. p.m, apparently, all problems are healed and I get lovey-dovey calls from Oxford—Dorothy telling me that she can't bear Turgenev and finds Lermontov a very great bore and David telling me that apart from Lampedusa's *Gattopardo*,[7] the only novel which he enjoys is Lermontov's *A Hero of Our Time!*[8]

God help me. But I've got to get out... out!

Best, best,

    Colin

P.S. Dorothy disdains to accept as a present my *Pianta di Milano* and my two maps of Italy.[9] "I don't find those things in the least bit interesting. But who needs such things on the wall?"

    C.

---

1 "Him": David Rowe.*
2 Rowe's house at 19 Renwick Place in Ithaca, New York, which he was attempting to sell at this time.
3 Ivan Sergeyevich Turgenev (1818–1883), Russian novelist, short story writer, and playwright.
4 "Upstate": Upstate New York, the region where Ithaca is located.
5 Cheryl O'Neil,* Rowe's former student at Cornell and Matthew Bell's* wife.
6 Turgenev, Ivan, *Smoke*, 1867, first published in *The Russian Messenger*, March 1867, and *Fathers and Sons* (1862).
7 Mikhail Yuryevich Lermontov (1814–1841), Russian Romantic writer, poet, and painter.
8 di Lampedusa, Giuseppe Tomasi, *The Leopard*, first published as *Il gattopardo,* Milan: Feltrinelli Editore, 1957; Lermontov, MY, *A Hero of Our Time*, Iliya Glazunov & Co, 1840.
9 *Pianta di Milano*, Italian: Plan of Milan, an Italian engraving that Rowe gave to Dorothy as a gift.

217   To *Alex Caragonne*, London   *7 November 1993*

65 Darwin Court, Gloucester Avenue, London

Alex, *il mio caro bene:*[1]

    I am using an Olivetti with an Italian keyboard and it seems to have a will of its own which despises English. For instance: it has a great distaste for the letter W which is balanced by a corresponding enthusiasm for the letter Z and this is already beginning to disclose itself.

So I received your letter of November 1 by special delivery on afternoon of November 5, celebrated for fireworks and the 1605 affair of Guy Fawkes and,[2] since I went down to Brighton yesterday, after some contemplation I am replying to it at the earliest opportunity and, to begin with I will charge ahead:

Just as Xtian history is intersected by the Incarnation and, thereby, becomes B.C. and A.D., I think that I might claim that my own personal history is intersected by the experience of Texas and, thereby, might become Pre-Texas and Post-Texas which might allow for a periodization P.T., T. and PoT.—or, better, Before Texas, B.T., to be followed by T; and A.T., otherwise After Texas.[3]

Thus, to imagine the first book: *Texas and Pre-Texas*—with a play on Texts and Pretexts.

"Introduction". Autobiographical remarks. A bit of Warburgismus; a meeting in Arezzo and Arthur Brown, Jr;[4] with Arthur Brown in Rome ("how well Borromini knew how to use his *hors d'echelles*[5] but in my day in Gromort's studio we all had a great *culte* for Carlo Rainaldi"),[6] the Beatification of the Blessed Maria Goretti; Jean Murray Bangs.[7]

"Mrs. H.H.H."[8]

"Lockhart, Texas". Although our relationship had ceased this was surely written under her influence.

"Memorandum of March 1954"

"Design Program, March 1954"

"Comments of Director, May 1954"

"City Planning Memo, April 1955"

A note to observe that, written under the influence of Texas, were "Chicago-Frame" and *vide* Howard Barnstone,⋆ "Neo-Classicism"[9]

"Program v. Paradigm", 1983. Fundamentally a rumination upon Austin, T.

And then: two pre-Texas pieces, "Forms and Functions" and "Roots." These to establish how much the experience of Texas had altered my state of mind. Also "Character and Composition" is a pre-Texas piece. Also "Transparency" is a piece written in Austin and "Transparency II" (published in *Perspecta* and recently republished by Columbia could—and perhaps should be incorporated in this section.)

After Texas

"Le Corbusier: Utopian Architect"

"Churchill College"

"Sidgewick Avenue"

These are all early Cambridge pieces, the latter two specimens of 'practical' criticism. They date from 1959 and, in spite of the lapse of time, as comparable critical performances they might be followed by

"Robert Venturi and the Yale Mathematics Building" and "Who, but Stirling?"⋆

Then, deriving from that fecund year (1959 when I still hoped to make an impact upon English architecture) there is also "The Architecture of Utopia" published in *Mathematics* but, within this section, there should also be included—The Provocative Façade—, whether in its short, published, version or the longer version which, almost exists. This because the P.F. was an item of Cambridge conception.

a dark forest.

I don't recollect enough of your items 10, 12, 13, 14, 15, 17, 21 to know what to do about them but I assume that LAT—*Long After Texas*—should give predominance to

"Talent and Ideas", Walter Gropius Lecture at Harvard, 1987 which it seems that, contrary to their practice, they didn't want to publish—though I <u>did</u> have an audience of 800 and standing ovations; and

"Classicism, Neo-Classicism, Neo-neo classicism", a piece which became lost; and

"Grid / Frame, Lattice / Web"

This seems to involve a distribution of casual pieces between AT and LAT and I await your intelligence and discretion about this. But think of the Yeats quote that Fred likes so much:

> Where the best lack all conviction
> And the worst are full of passionate intensity[10]

Also there are other eulogia: one for Alvin Boyarsky★ and another in a Madrid publication for Jim which some people (not me) think is better than the New York one.[11]

Well that is it. And I shall now now write to R.C. and attempt to settle the affair of *A.O.G.I.*[12]

Best, best,

   Colin

P.S. But not all. There is the historical spoof for the explanation of "Roma Interrotta;" and, surely, we should include—with appropriate illustrations?[13]

I have no immediate access to a Xerox machine. That is short of dropping in on the P.O.W. which I don't think would be appropriate. Therefore could you let me, in the course of time, have a repro of this memo.

   Colin

---

 1 *il mio caro bene*, Italian: my dear beloved.
 2 5 November is Guy Fawkes Night in Britain.
 3 "Xtian": Christian.
 4 Arthur Brown Jr (1874–1957), prominent San Francisco architect.
 5 *hors d'échelle*, French: in "Two Italian Encounters", in *As I Was Saying: Recollections and Miscellaneous Essays*, Alexander Caragonne ed, 3 vols, Cambridge, MA: MIT Press, 1996, vol 1, p 9, Rowe defines Brown's *hors d'échelle* as "the calculated intrusion of an out-of-scale element".
 6 Georges Gromort (1870–1961), French architect, design teacher at the École des Beaux Arts in Paris, and author of *The Elements of Classical Architecture*, New York: Norton & Co, 2001.
 7 Maria Goretti (1890–1902), Italian virgin-martyr, canonized saint of the Roman Catholic Church.
 8 "Mrs. H.H.H.": Jean Murray Bangs, Mrs. Harwell Hamilton Harris.★ Harwell Harris was chair of the School of Architecture at the University of Texas at Austin in the mid-50s, when Rowe taught there. See Rowe's letter to Lisa Germany★ dated 14 and 24 July 1995 (p 435 in this volume) and "Texas and Mrs. Harris", in Rowe, *As I Was Saying*, vol 1, pp 25–40.
 9 *vide*, Latin: see.
10 William Butler Yeats, "The Second Coming", 1919.
11 "Jim": James Stirling.★
12 "R.C.": Roger Conover,★ editor, MIT Press; "A.O.G.I.": *The Architecture of Good Intentions*.
13 See Rowe, "Roma Interrotta", in *As I Was Saying*, vol 3, pp 126–53.

218   *To **Blake Middleton**, San Francisco*   *18 April 1994*

65 Darwin Court, Gloucester Avenue, London

Dearest Blake:

   This is to wish you both immense fecundity and every extremity of happiness; and it is also to say, with many regrets, that I shall be unable to attend either your wedding or any of the subsequent celebrations.[1] The spirit may be extremely willing; but space, time, obligation and, I suppose, money, all of them are going to act to impede movement of the flesh.

You see I have just come back from the U.S., where I made four lectures at New Haven, spent a weekend in New York, another weekend in Providence, and several days in D.C., to return to a charette here with Alex Caragonne.★

So it won't, I think, be a very tough charette; but Alex will be here, acting under persuasion of Roger Conover★ of M.I.T., to help me put into production three volumes of collected bits and pieces, about 150,000 words in all, to be delivered to

M.I.T. by August.[2] So it <u>will</u> be done; and, then, with four books suddenly produced, won't this just be flooding the market? And I suppose it may be (the first book will be *The Architecture of Good Intentions* ready with Academy Edition); but, then, I wish that you were here so that I could describe the other three books to you.[3] But let's hold back on that until September when I hope to be living in Washington, D.C. and I hope to be having you all to come stay.

You see I have lately decided that I just can't bear to continue living in this very curious country; and, of course, the members of my family are utterly infuriated.[4] So, just when they thought they had me reliably pinned down and trapped, they are again to be frustrated by the lure of Amerika! So tough shit. But I just can't bear any longer to cope with the combined absence of animation and appalling expenses/ difficulties—laundry at Three Bucks a shirt, shopping, cleaning and all the rest which make the ineradicable problems of life here in London.

Or, in other words, I have decided to move in to one of those Classic Residences by Hyatt in Connecticut Ave.[5] So this will be a full service job, unobtainable in this country—twenty five foot living room, balcony and two bdrms, with cleaning, laundry and three meals a day, with swimming pool in the basement all included. And this, God being willing, is where I shall hope to see you.

But, dearest Blake, I look forward immensely and I just notice that, had I announced my intention to leave for Wopland, *la mia famiglia* would not, in any way, have been so appalled.[6] Best, best,

Colin

1 Middleton* had invited Rowe to attend both his wedding on Martha's Vineyard and the reception in New York City that followed.
2 Rowe, Colin, *As I Was Saying: Recollections and Miscellaneous Essays*, Alexander Caragonne ed, 3 vols, Cambridge, MA: MIT Press, 1996.
3 Rowe, Colin, *The Architecture of Good Intentions*, London: Academy Editions, 1994.
4 England.
5 In mid-October 1994 Rowe moved from London to Washington, DC's Classic Residence by Hyatt. In mid-December 1994 he moved from the Hyatt to the Kennedy-Warren, also on Connecticut Avenue in DC.
6 *la mia famiglia*: Italian, my family.

---

*To **Judith DiMaio**, West 67th St., New York, N.Y.*   *28 April 1994*   **219**

65 Darwin Court, Gloucester Avenue, London

Dearest Judy:

I thought that the enclosed might amuse you as I was amused by the little piece which you sent me about Harold Acton which, by the way, was not very accurate.[1] H.A. was not descended, as they said, from a long line of Neapolitan statesman and rather it was like this.

John Acton, 1736–1811, was born at Besançon, a member of an English Catholic family of which the younger branches had to find jobs abroad; so he served first in the navy of Tuscany and, after 1779, in the navy of Naples where he ultimately became both prime minister and lover of the Queen. Then, in 1791, he succeeded to the title and the estates of a remote cousin becoming Sir John Acton, 6th baronet of Aldenham Hall, Shropshire—though, apparently, never tempted to return there, preferring to be married to his niece whose father was also in the Neapolitan service.

So grab the pic. He is inevitably involved with Sir William Hamilton and, of course, Emma is also, more or less the lover of the Queen?

So he was followed by Sir Richard, 7ᵗʰ baronet, d. 1837, and succeeded by John Emerich Edward Dalberg Acton, born in Naples in 1834 and taken back to England at age 3, 8ᵗʰ baronet, the English historian who became Lord Acton in 1869. So some of his cousins stuck around in Naples—army, navy, etc.—becoming the Baroni Acton and, after 1860, continuing in the Italian / Piedmontese service. Then there was an uncle Charles Januarius, 1803–1847, created cardinal by Gregory XVI; but, on the whole, <u>Lord</u> Acton didn't really seem to <u>know</u> his Neapolitan cousins, that is with the exception of Laura, Princess of Camporeale by her first marriage, who was later married to Marco Minghetti—and see his statue outside Palazzo Braschi.

Sorry about all this; but it's just to indicate the absence of a long line of Neapolitan statesman.

Love, love,

    Colin x x x x x

---

1   The enclosure is lost; Sir Harold Acton* (1904–1994). See Rowe's letter to Alan Colquhoun*
     dated 3 February 1990 (p 342 in this volume).

220   *Memo to **Roger Conover**, MIT Press, Cambridge, Mass.*[1]   *2 August 1994*

From Colin Rowe

Re: *Third volume*[2]

Dear Roger:

I finished typing, yesterday, Tuesday at 3.00 p.m.; and I was flooded with recollections of how Gibbon felt after <u>he</u> had ceased from scribbling on, I believe, June 27, 1787 and went out to take a walk around the garden at Lausanne, when the moon was shining on the lake and all that....[3]

Anyway, I breathed a sigh of relief and, then, my brother came in and was also reminded of Gibbon. But enough for that. Alex will be sending you the package on Friday; and I am writing this memo to go with it.[4] And, principally, it concerns corrections of text.

First of all my spelling <u>may</u> be inconsistent. That is: it may oscillate between American and English usage—Harbor / harbour, favor / favour—I would prefer it to be completely Americanized.

Then, as to further emendations: I am unable to tolerate that extraordinary document called *The Chicago Manual of Style* which seems to reduce all prose to the status of an English World War II sausage—much more bread than meat. And so, I list names: Washington Irving, Fenimore Cooper, Mark Twain, Harriet Beecher Stowe, Henry James,* Edith Wharton, Scott Fitzgerald, Ernest Hemingway, Gertrude Stein, H.L. Mencken, Edmund Wilson, Mary McCarthy—and I can't suppose that any of these would have had—or did have—<u>any</u> respect for the editorial dictates of Chicago.

But what I particularly lament about *The C. M. of S.* is its determination to substitute the use of <u>that</u> for the use of <u>which</u> since, though English and American usage has never been clear about the difference and even Henry James was apt to screw up, there <u>still</u> is a difference. But have you noticed that <u>that</u> is now being substituted for <u>who</u> and <u>whom</u>? (*The New York Times* any day and, following its example, *The London Times*).

Then what is also regrettable about *The C. M. of S.* is its veto on single quotes.[5] It always has to be "...". But single quotes, '...', mean something else; and, to insist upon double quotes, on <u>all</u> occasions, is both misleading and destructive of <u>nuance</u> and the possibilities of irony.

Which is about as much as I have the capacity to say and which means that, if you have any editors recently graduated from Radcliffe, Oberlin, or Smith and determined to apply the deplorable dictates of *Chicago* then do prevail upon them to desist. Their efforts will only drive me frantic or intractable.[6]

But, apart from that, dear Roger <u>do</u> feel free. The Irish and eighteenth century 'myself' is otherwise completely relaxed. Expurgate, prune and manipulate at your own discretion and I shall not be thrown into appalling fits of hysterics.

    Colin Rowe

[handwritten]

P.S. The Irish usage: 'What did himself say and what did yourself reply?' though, perhaps, an affectation still betrays its eighteenth century origins as used by Samuel Johnson and Edmund Burke. 'I, you, he' are not <u>quite</u> the same as 'myself, yourself, himself,' yet I derive the practice from friends in Dublin, and, also, from, Osbert Sitwell, as, I think, it has a certain Celtic resonance. Should be used or, otherwise, likely to be lost. The language needs it. With the absence of this Dublin component, the language would be diminished.

---

1   Though without an address, this letter—titled "Memo" by Rowe—was almost certainly written in London, shortly before Rowe's return to the US to live in Washington, DC.

2   Volume 3 of Rowe, Colin, *As I Was Saying: Recollections and Miscellaneous Essays*, Alexander Caragonne ed, 3 vols, Cambridge, MA: MIT Press, 1996.

3   English historian Edward Gibbon (1737–1794). The sixth and final volume of his most important work, *The History of the Decline and Fall of the Roman Empire*, was published in 1788. "I will not dissemble the first emotions of joy on the recovery of my freedom, and perhaps the establishment of my fame", Gibbon wrote of his feelings on completing this series. "But my pride was soon humbled, and a sober melancholy was spread over my mind by the idea that I had taken my everlasting leave of an old and agreeable companion, and that, whatsoever might be the future date of my history, the life of the historian must be short and precarious." See Rowe's letter to Pat Miller⋆ dated 12 August 1963 (p 141 in this volume).

4   Alexander Caragonne.⋆

5   *The Chicago Manual of Style* is a guide for American English concerned with grammar, usage, and document preparation (16th ed; Chicago: The University of Chicago Press, 2010).

6   The "efforts" of *The Chicago Manual of Style* irritated Rowe until the end of his life. In a 27 November 1997 letter to Megan McFarland⋆ at *Rizzoli International Publications, Inc*, he wrote: "I had begun to think that I had reached such a stage of my development (four books and a great many articles over a very long period) as to be immune from the persecutions of the *Chicago Manual of Style*. But that was until I received the copy-edited version of my introduction of the Koetter⋆-Kim⋆ monograph."

Colin Rowe in London, 1993

10
Washington, DC

1995–1999

When Rowe moved to Washington, DC, in October 1994, initially he lived in the Classic Residence by Hyatt. Two months later he moved to the Kennedy-Warren, an "enormous late Deco building of c 1930, having all of the merits of the immediately pre-Modern", where he was looked after by a host of close friends.

In Washington, DC, Rowe collaborated with Leon Satkowski* on a book about sixteenth-century Italian architecture. He was awarded the Royal Institute of British Architects' Royal Gold Medal in London, June 1995, and in 1996, he published a highly autobiographical three-volume collection of essays, *As I Was Saying*, and negotiated with a Swiss publisher on new editions of *Collage City* and *Transparency*. At the end of April 1996, a *Festspiele* was staged in his honor at Cornell. Earlier that month, to his great sorrow and dismay, his sister-in-law Dorothy,* "an ideal product of eighteenth century Edinburgh", with whom he had shared so many letters for over a quarter of a century, died.

During this, the final five years of his life, Rowe writes to his family in England, to former students and old friends, to publishers and misguided bill collectors, and to William Safire* at *The New York Times*. The letters are lucid, humorous, and replete with wisdom and insight. Some are concerned with new writings that Rowe intended to publish. A few address the inevitable details of death and burial. One discusses the establishment of a Rowe archive in Austin of books and artifacts, an "'in the beginning is my end' affair... a little tribute to Texas which, after all is said and done, does remain my favorite state."

Rowe died in Washington, DC, on 5 November 1999. In spring 2000 his ashes were scattered at the Temple of the Four Winds at Castle Howard in Yorkshire, England. His last book, *Italian Architecture of the 16th Century*, co-authored by Leon Satkowski, was published posthumously in 2002. His library and a small collection of his papers were moved to the Charles Moore Foundation in Austin.

MEMORANDUM
*To **Cynthia Davidson**, ANY Offices / New York, N. Y.[1] no date,*   *ca. mid-October 1994*   **221**
Washington, D.C.

REACHING GALE FORCE LOCALLY

Was it one of Oscar Wilde's characters who said: *I don't like ghosts: their appearance is against them?* But, of course, there are ghosts <u>and</u> ghosts (not many ghosts in Italy, they belong to the Gothick North), there are ghosts in Henry James*—evil emanations which one sees, and experiences, from the other side of a lake, and there are ghosts in Walter Scott more condensed and malevolent, which gibber away at the end of the bed; but, on the whole—like the ghosts character in Oscar Wilde—I don't really very much care for them myself. Only very rarely does their <u>appearance</u> seem to be benign.

And, then, <u>what</u> is the difference between ghosts and spirits? Etymology appears to be indifferent. German Geist may be rendered, in English, fairly equally as 'ghost' <u>or</u> 'spirit' (or even, I suspect as 'jest'). Is it that 'ghosts' are apt to be Germanic and 'Spirits' Latin? That the English language waivers between the two? And the 'root' words German and the words of 'cultivation' Italo-French, one needn't be surprised. But, all the same, it <u>is</u> amusing that German *Heilige Geist* can, in English, become Holy Ghost and, also, (for those of more accomplished sensibility?) Holy Spirit.

Which may have directly to do with my own favorite Geist (Peter's domestic pet) the Zeitgeist.[2] Is <u>it</u> a ghost? Or is <u>it</u> a spirit?

And, to answer this question (if we must) as regards the English speaking world, I suppose that we should take some notice of the mood of Regency England where, in 'cultivated' circles, I think that 'the Spirit of the Age' made its first decisive appearance as an import from Germanic lands.

But dearest Cynthia, at dinner last night it was suggested to me that *Sturm und Drang* might have been an appropriate name for an umbrella shop in a long vanished Berlin.[3] *Storm and Stress*—with its implications that the umbrella has been blown inside out— would surely be altogether too explicit for New York or London, in <u>those</u> places, one has to think, in Madison Avenue of *Crouch & Fitzgerald* (do they continue to sell umbrellas?),[4] or, in Piccadilly of *Swayne, Adeney & Briggs*.[5] No *Sturm & Drang* just couldn't be an umbrella shop in London—<u>they</u> prefer more old time *Risorgimento* names like *Negetti & Zambra* (I like to imagine other London shops like this: *Verdi & Volta?*—combo of musicology and electronics, now dealing in very sophisticated hi-fi; or a hybrid; *Burlap & Bari / Brindisi*– a sort of early version of *L.L. Bean*).[6] But, in New York, as in a long vanished Berlin, I can only think that it might be very okay—but emphatically with-it, what Samuel Johnson called 'an effusion of wit' in, nowadays New York.

However, <u>we</u> do know that *Sturm und Drang* was <u>not</u> an umbrella shop; but a late eighteenth century, and very illustrious, German movement of the mind, a reaction against French formalism and rationalism to which 'we, all of us, owe so much'. Before *Sturm und Drang*—important names like Herder, Hamann, Schelling, Schlegel, whom I confess I have never read—I believe that 'the Spirit of the Age' was more a principle of poetry and prestige than a principle of historical exegesis. So, as a principle of poetry, I can smell it but know nothing about it; but as a principle of prestige, it is much more highly overt. Immanent in Vasari's conception of his own day and in his evaluation of Bramante (who made everything easy), it is obviously related to ideas of progress and culmination, *il modern si glorioso*; and, as soon, it figures in the French eighteenth century *querelle* between the ancients and the moderns.[7] Then, in England and with Christopher Wren, the *gust of the age* becomes a matter of institutional decorum. In prominent undertakings, a wise individual will accommodate himself to it; and interesting that he should speak of *gust* with its two connotations: Italian *gusto*, with its implications of food and drink, the more insipid English <u>taste</u>; and English <u>gust</u> (German *geist* yet again) with its implications of 'gust in the wind'.

And if Wren was scarcely a proto-Romantic, it is perhaps here that we begin to find the difference between 'spirits' and 'ghosts'. With the exception of the Holy Ghost, *invaluable creature*, critical invention of genius, ghosts just don't breath, their behavior is much more like that of mobile wax works, Oscar Wilde's character said: *their appearance is against them*. But 'spirits' are a different species. They breathe and they also fly. In the Bible the Holy Ghost/Holy Spirit makes quite a point of delivering important messages disguised as a bird. And 'spirits' must also be exponents of wit. For, though the Holy Spirit which presides in English speaking lands doesn't <u>seem</u> to be a highly coruscating creature, the *Saint Esprit*, as this entity exists in France, perhaps a more condensed hypostasis, probably makes quite a point, and a pleasure, of exhibiting what Samuel Johnson went on to call "the unexpected compilation of ideas", in both senses this entity must be *spirituel*. And the *Santo Spirito* in Italy? His (Her?) utterances, one guesses, not quite so pungent as in France. But, at least 'spirited' and, sometimes rather boisterous.

So the Holy Ghost was not always with us. A product of Hellenistic neo-Platonism, like so many other triads—faith, hope, and charity; commodity, firmness, and delight; goodness, truth, and beauty; beginning, middle, and end?; time, place and action; possibly three blind mice?—is, as one begins to think about it, something of an imperative for the thought of late Antiquity. But the Holy Ghost has also an important Jewish pedigree. After Yahweh has cooled down—though not time consuming, even for an omnipotent being that act of creation must have involved an awful lot of intellective hard work—and, after He has promised a Redeemer, and even if this Redeemer has not yet arrived—still, by a process of dialectic, the presence of Two must predicate the sometime arrival of number Three.

No matter: the definition of the Holy Ghost still took quite a time; and, as I read about it, I discover that, if even the divinity of Christ was not officially promulgated until the Council of Nicaea in 325, the Holy Spirit had to wait for a little longer. The 'final' recognition/articulation of this Third hypostasis of the Godhead was the work of: Athanasius, bishop of Alexandria "completed by the Cappadocian Fathers Basil the Great (d. 379), Gregory of Nazianzus (d. 389) and Gregory of Nyssa (d. 395)."

And a tough time they must all have had of it. The great problem seems to have been the consubstantiality of Father, Son, and Spirit—how the Spirit "was distinct from Father and Son while sharing the same essence"; and, this, so it seems, they "solved by differentiating their modes of origin"; the Son is generated (by the agency of the Spirit's annunciation to the Virgin Mary?); but the Spirit proceeds." [...][8]

'The Holy Spirit is the life and activity of God at work in the world of nature and also in and through people. The Hebrew word for 'spirit' is the same as that for 'breath' or 'wind', and can even imply 'life', just as the English word 'spirit' forms the root of others, such as 'inspire', 'expire', and 'respiration', meaning 'breath in life'.

Now, how about this? If for 'God' in the first sentence, we were to substitute 'History', it would then read:

"The Spirit of the Age is the life and activity of History in the world of nature and also in and through people."

And, then, as you add the rest and do you not find, quite suddenly, that you have produced a beautiful manifesto for the Zeitgeist boys, so far as I know far better than they've ever been able to dream up for themselves? And isn't this the logical and emotive expansion of Mies van der Rohe's* "the will of the epoch translated into space", a statement of 1923 which Mies, later, substantially qualified or retracted?[9]

In his "gust" of the age, Wren also invokes the wind, and at his time, almost in the same world as that of Racine and Poussin, this gust might be interpreted as a casual proto-Romantic exhibition of sentiment, the sort of hit and miss, somewhat amateur, which the English kind of strew around. But, like so many other things, it just had to be imported to the Germanic lands for an extensive/intensive critical construct to be erected on so fragmentary a base. And, hence, *Sturm und Drang*, an evolutionary concept of time, and, in spite of Napoleon, the overthrow of French formalism, in Germany, England, and most everywhere else. So I think you have to imagine the Zeitgeist as a notion vaguely floating around, not in full employment, partially articulated by the criticism of *Sturm und Drang*, but utterly unknown to their contemporaries or near contemporaries. And I think of Robert Adam, Ange-Jacques Gabriel, not to mention Claude-Nicolas Ledoux, and the rest of those 'revolutionary' guys. For, however *parlante*, with some of these, 'architecture' might have become, these still thought of a more or less static and eternally valid Antiquity; and, in a card game, this would be a losing hand. This in spite of the arrival of persons like Karl Friedrich Schinkel. This, and it does seem odd, because of the sophistication of so many German thinkers—who, at the same time, did not conceive of themselves to be sophisticated. Oh no! The artificial was a peculiar French prerogative. And the German thinkers? These were, for the most part *naturmenschen*—paradoxically expounding an evolutionary theory, a preference for 'becoming' over 'being', a corresponding 'theory' of creativity—sublime inspiration, and a new sense for organicity.[10]

In the context of these new values, the notion of the Zeitgeist—originally a drifter—before finding its equivalent to a Council of Nicaea, it was to find such formulation, perhaps and I guess, in Georg Friedrich Wilhelm Hegel's *Phenomenology of the Spirit*, Hamburg, 1807—from, whence, then flow so many blessings and so many causes for grief. Envisaged as a 'spiritual' and therefore, for him, a 'real' essence by Hegel, it was rendered a matter of 'fact' and 'force' by many later disciples (Marx? Lenin? Marinetti? Mussolini?), I believe that, in the psycho-life of the modern architect (an ideal type)?, it still retains some of Hegel's original 'spiritual' connotations—and, no doubt, very nice too!; but I continue to notice that Zeitgeist-ian devotees continue to presume that technology is their private property. And I further notice that, when an esthetic culture conceives of itself to be something else, which has been one of the leading characteristics of modernism, then there are certain horrors of Hegelian descent (the behavior of political cousins) which will go unnoticed.

Dearest Cynthia, I write so long and quickly, because I have just gotten around to reading that number of *ANY* almost exclusively, devoted to myself—I find the 'fashionable' overprinting to be too distracting for an easy read. So, meditating on what I have been able to absorb, I do feel compelled to utter. As regards their quasi-religious affiliation, your contributors seem to me mostly of the Zeitgeist-ian persuasion and, so far as I understand, I am being cited for something that good guys don't do. I am, patently—a-political, but of course; I am simultaneously Francophobe and formalist—surely an almost impossible act since one might have thought that all formalists are, *ipso facto*, Francophile; with approaching senility, I have sold out, I fail to understand the regenerative power of modern architecture—but, dearest God, how excruciatingly *passé* can *ANY*'s contributors become?; and, heinous offence, my consciousness of the 'Spirit of the Age' is deficient.

So, I will merely allude to other little items: that I now dote on the architecture of Edwin Lutyens, P.D.E., instead of that of Le Corbusier*—wrong: as an architect I find Lutyens disgustingly cute, but, in trying to overcome prejudice—and isn't this imposed upon us?—I do find most of his garden plans, though not the texture of his gardens, to be worth quite a bit of attention; and, that I habitually sit in a room lined no longer with books but with eighteenth century engravings and I grab the subliminal message: but how painfully *effete*. And, since this is Peter's particular contribution, I must make some response to it. And this is to question the ability of his eye. Just how can Peter sit in a room for, probably two hours, confronted with a wall of images and not recognize an Italian sixteenth century collection when he sees it?—a small Deposition, evidently from a private chapel in northern Lazio or southern Umbria; engravings after Primaticcio, Bandinelli, Giulio Romano, Parmigianino, Polidoro di Caravaggio, among architecture images several from Lafrery.[11] How can anyone of even average visual acuity, average culture and sensibility, sit with these things, positively glaring at him, and fail—within thirty seconds—to comprehend their chronological provenance? The work of a sixteenth century mind and hand, so entirely different from the eighteenth century, that this suspension of ocular observation really does call for explanation, Peter does have an eye, or so I have believed. Was it just me—so very forbidding, or was it the historical crap which he pre-conceived to be the signature of my *ambiente*.[12]

But this is *en passant*[13] and *il faut revenir a nos moutons* or,[14] in my case, my single little old sheep—that maltreated Zeitgeist, imagined to be an implacable agent of destiny, and not as the 'hypostasized essence' which, quite evidently, just happens to be its 'existential' predicament. But I protest: this is maltreatment of a perfectly innocent little old sheep. It is cruelty to a dumb animal; it is idolatrous and, of course, more concentrated protest against Zeitgeist adulation is not unknown. With Isaiah Berlin* it has been a constant theme; with Karl Popper,* one of two major themes; with Ernst Gombrich,* a theme which persistently recurs; but, since architects, on the whole, are hostile to the printed page—since they do not, they cannot, or will not read—given this incapacity, or obdurate resistance, it should go without saying that, for architects, on the whole, the effect of these quite celebrated critiques has been like so much water off a duck's back. They cling to their Zeitgeist—allegedly it tells them what to do and, then, since, in theory, they accepted dictation, it exonerates them from personal responsibility—they cling to their traditional Zeitgeist like so many fundamentalist Christians clinging to a traditionalist view of creation long after this antique proposition had been, to all intents and purposes, exploded from 1859 by the point of view of Charles Darwin, himself originally a creationist. So will the artichoke continue recalcitrant for quite as long as the 'religious right' and one is tempted to say: "God forbid."[15]

Because, dear Cynthia, I'm quite fond of the Zeitgeist—when it's in its proper place. It's an old sheep; I've drunk its milk; and I am accustomed to the, very limited, charms of its society. Unlike Isaiah Berlin and Karl Popper, my attitude towards it is not one of disdain. But, when it comes to super-Zeitgeist—or should I say the *Heilige* Zeitgeist, the conflation of the Holy Spirit and the 'Spirit of the Age',—then I become compelled to say something about critical irresponsibility. In a highly self-critical 'situation' this kind of stuff is simply 'not on'.

And it becomes all the more vicious when, to the Zeitgeist, is attributed an ethical content; for, then, this becomes a moral aberration, like the enormity of Alexander Pope's WHATEVER IS, IS RIGHT (and, in his *Essay on Man*, he capitalized this bizarre statement). But, in the end, is not this what Zeitgeist adulation is all about? WHATEVER IS is the product of the Zeitgeist, the product of historical necessity and, therefore, it IS RIGHT. And as for, WHATEVER IS TO BE, well that's just the same; and protest WILL BE of no avail. Indeed, it will be frivolous, a dereliction of duty, and, as *ANY*'s contributors have declared it to be in the case of Elizabeth Plater-Zyberk* and Andres Duany,* no more than opportunist playing to consumerism and the 'bourgeois' market. But who, really, is playing to the market? For does the adulation of the Zeitgeist involve any principle of resistance?; and, if so, myself fails entirely to see it. Instead, I see only collusion with accepted socio-political myth.

So you see, when I succumbed to reading it, that number of *ANY* really did piss me off—if such was *ANY*'s inscrutable objective; and I have typed all of this in one, long, unbroken session. Nor, so far as I am aware, have I said anything not to be discovered in pieces I've already published. *Collage City*, written with Fred Koetter,* is by no means an amoral or an a-political document; and, if your contributors could only have cut the hysteria in which they indulged themselves about formalism—so much, 'I am too holier than thou'—then the whole number would have been slightly less nauseating—for me and quite a few others. As it is, among your major contributors, the only one who talked sense, who offered definitions of formalism, both in the accepted, opprobrious sense and in the pre-Revolutionary sense was Peggy Deamer—and the rest of them simply <u>shuffled</u> the two sets of connotations with preference for the worst.

Dear Cynthia this is written for <u>you</u> and <u>will</u> constitute one of the components of my new book which is well underway to be called, *Footprints and Footnotes*; and, after that, *en retraite* as I now am, hopefully I will cease to disturb the deep sweet sleep of the architectural company.[16] But I should still send you two little *trouvailles* of which you may not be aware.[17]

The first is in that curious, but often entertaining, language, *Franglais* and it goes like this:

> *Il y'avait un jeun homme de Dijon*
> *Qui a dit: Je m'enfiche de religion,*
> *On effec, moi je crois*
> *Ils sont besto tous les trois*
> *Le Pere, et the Fils, et le Pigeon.*[18]

Then, the other one is just straight Limey; but it's almost as good as Ogden Nash at his most devastating:

> The girls who frequent picture palaces
> Have no use for a pyscho-analysis,
> And though Sigmund Freud
> Is profoundly annoyed,
> They cling to their old fashioned phalluses.

Last line surely too long? But those English, as I know only too well, are incapable of the full brilliance of American concision. And this <u>could</u> be transliterated as:

The architects who are averse to the printed word, though some of them are now displaying cognizance of French critical theory, have, only a few of them, exposed themselves to Lithuanian and German-Jewish critiques of Historical determinism but so it seems, unlike Sigmund Freud, these have not been 'profoundly annoyed' and perhaps most of them have the disdain of the erudite for the *naïfs*, and the scorn of the intelligent for intellectual provinciality. So like 'the girls who frequent picture palaces', these desperate architects, with touching, or abysmal, faith, still 'cling' to their old fashioned fetiches.

A sad story and I wish it were not as things, mostly happen to <u>be.</u>

P.P.S. But, as a last word, dearest Cynthia, may I implore you not to instigate any more of those ideological lynchings, or kangaroo courts in which your contributors, so wantonly, are prone to exercise themselves. Be assured by me, they can do no good to architecture. And, maybe worse than that, like old time 'white trash' in the former Confederate States, they are barren of legitimacy, whether intellectual or otherwise. And, even worse, they only appear to make ridiculous, both those who affect to judge and those who promote.

P.P.S. In giving this letter a title, "Reaching Gale Force Locally", I was thinking of 'the wind of destiny' and its possible vagaries and idiosyncrasies. A soft breeze in some locations? Reaching tornado and cyclone force in others? Producing funny little twisters moving across the deserts of Idaho? But I have written too much and too extravagantly to ask you to have patience with more....

1   The full address: "Anyone Corporation, 40 West 25th Street, 10th Floor, New York, N.Y."
2   Peter Eisenman,* Cynthia Davidson's* husband.
3   A mid-eighteenth century proto-Romantic movement in German music and literature.
4   Crouch & Fitzgerald, a now defunct Madison Avenue shop for leather bags and briefcases.
5   Swaine Adeney Brigg, London makers of equestrian and leather goods since 1750.
6   Negetti & Zambrat, British producers of scientific and optical instruments.
7   *querelle*, French: dispute, controversy.
8   An entire page is missing here.
9   van der Rohe, Mies, "Baukunst und Zeitwille", in *Der Querschnitt* 4, 1924. Translated into English in Johnson, Philip C, *Mies van der Rohe*, New York: Museum of Modern Art, 1978, third ed, p 191.
10 *naturmenschen*, German: natural men.
11 Rowe's "room" is lined with sixteenth- (not eighteenth-) century engravings.
12 *ambiente*, Italian: environment, ambience.
13 *en passant*, French: in passing, an aside.
14 *il faut revenir à nos moutons*, French: Let's get back to where we were, what we were doing or saying.
15 "Artichoke" is Rowe's name for "architect".
16 *en retraite*, French: retired.
17 *trouvailles*, French: finds.
18 There was a young man from Dijon
    Who said: I don't care for religion
    In effect, I think
    They are besto all three
    The Father, and the Son, and the Pigeon.

To **Michael Manfredi**, New York City   *26 November 1994*   **222**

Apt. 814, 3133 Connecticut Ave., Washington D.C.

Dear Michael:

Your letter of October 19 has been following me around. I left London on October 6—in every way it was really an expensive and exasperating dead loss—and I came here to D.C. which, on the whole, I quite like. So the place which I moved into[1]—a sort of Sunset Home for the Senile—was, emphatically, a wrong move and I am correcting it with the arrival of books and furn and things in the next day or so. So I am moving into the Kennedy-Warren, into a large apartment at the back with north, east and south exposures; and, from it, one can only <u>see</u> the tops of the trees of Rock Creek Park and one can only <u>hear</u> (or so I am told) the lions and the elephants in the Zoo. In other words, I shall be *entoure des arbres et des animaux* and I am very much looking forward to it.[2]

The *ANY* extravaganza myself found to be gruesome rather than excruciating;[3] but, all the same, distressingly patronizing about U.D.[4]

However we will talk about all this—and quite a bit more—when you pay the visit for which I am hoping.

LOTSA LURV?

    Colin

1   Classic Residence by Hyatt in Washington, DC.
2   *entouré d'arbres et d'animaux,* French: surrounded by trees and animals.
3   "Form Work: Colin Rowe", *ANY* 7/8, September 1994.
4   "U.D.": Urban Design.

3133 Connecticut Avenue, Apt. 814, Washington, D.C.

Dear Mary:

Another year, another empire gone! Wasn't it Wordsworth who said something like this—though I don't really care.[1]

Anyway, this apt. is beginning to look quite habitable—lots of adequate rugs, engravings, books almost arranged, and only awaiting a five foot diameter white marble slab as a dining table. But I think that five feet is right—will seat eight (?) and, in any case, can't be bigger. But what do you think—a bit too big?

So I am about to retrieve various bits of apparatus and objects from *Inghilterra*.[2] At St Maggie's Rd Dorothy has quite a lot of highly acceptable stuff of mine, mostly table stuff—late Georgian runners, Waterford finger bowls, Cantonese blue and white, bits of Bristol blue, a Worcester urn that looks as though it ought to be Paris, a couple of little terra cotta pre-Columbian jobs from Guadalajara.[3] In fact quite a trove and none of it either in use or very visible. So this shouldn't be exactly an act of depredation. And, then, *chez toi* I have that alabaster model of the Duomo in Florence which is very dear to me.[4] [...] I always had a fantasy about it: an apt. in Florence, a window with a view of the Duomo, and, on a plinth in front of the window, the Model!

So this would have been the View from Bellosguardo! And, now, I want it to be foreground for the View of Rock Creek Park![5] So grab the pic? I don't want to tear it away from you but I do regard it as an intrinsic part of my collection and, of course, it will be one more reason for you coming to visit.

But, at Belsize Avenue, I have always felt for it, found it uncomfortable, and commiserated with it on its predicament.[6]

Best love and I am sure that this will not be like pulling up a mandrake root,

Colin

P.S. I shall try to persuade David to make arrangements.[7]

P.P.S. I am hoping that Mark G. will be staying here sometime in Feb when he comes over to look at Jim's buildings (and project sites?) in the U.S.[8]

Tell him that I am working on the guest b.r.[9] It is to have—I hope—a vaguely Sienese *trecento* look with a big check blanket from L.L. Bean to suggest a painting by Pietro Lorenzetti as a setting for the Birth of the Virgin.[10]

But I didn't know that L.L. Bean was active in Toscana so very long ago.

Colin

---

1 From William Wordsworth's "November 1806".
2 *Inghilterra*, Italian: England.
3 "St. Maggie's Rd": St Margaret's Road, the Oxford house of Dorothy Rowe.*
4 *chez toi*, French: at your house; On the alabaster model, see Rowe's letter to Rosemary Rowe* dated 22 October 1996 (p 506 in this volume).
5 Rowe's apartment featured a view of Rock Creek Park in Washington, DC.
6 Belsize Avenue was the home of Mary Stirling.
7 Ultimately, David, James, and Simon took the model personally to Rowe in Washington, DC.
8 Mark Girouard;* On Girouard's February visit, see Rowe's letter to Dorothy Rowe* dated 4 March 1996 (p 464 in this volume).

9 "b.r.": bedroom.
10 LL Bean, an American mail-order, online retailer founded in 1912 by Mr LL Bean; Pietro
   Lorenzetti (1280–1348) was an Italian painter from Siena.

*To **Mary Stirling**, Belsize Avenue, London*   *8 January 1995*   **224**

3133 Connecticut Avenue, Apt. 814, Washington, D.C.

Dear Mary:

Did you know that St. John's Wood was originally the wood of the Knights of St John of Jerusalem, later the Knights of Rhodes and, still later—after 1523—the Knights of Malta? And I certainly didn't until I read about the Knights of Malta the other day.

But the later story, a bit involved, goes like this. The knights had been established in Clerkenwell not far from the Charterhouse and then, in the 1850's, there came along a Sir George Bowyer, 7th bart, one of the usual converts to the C. of R., becoming in 1858 himself a knight of Malta (And this, of course, is the department of useless information). But all of this would, no doubt, have amused Jim—it is so ironically saturated in Romanism. For it was Sir WhatNot who conceived the idea of a return to St John's Wood, an alliance with the Sisters of St Elizabeth, who were struggling for their insalubrious Holborn, and an establishment—for the greater glory of God—at the upper end of Grove End Road.[1] Incredible. But, if you look at the belligerently baroque and ultramontane church which he built, you will get the pic. Had Jim known he would have been entertained.[2] And, did the hospital know, perhaps it might be a little more thoughtful.[3]

Meanwhile I am here and very glad to be so. Because don't you see that, with Jim, Alvin, Douglas gone—and with Leon vanished to the vicinity of Cannes— London didn't really have very much more to offer me. That is apart from *la mia Famiglia*.[4]

So what do I have here? Well, this is a large apartment house of about 1930, with a restaurant, a shop, a laundry and all those services which were absent at Darwin Court.[5] And I am located at the back of it with north, east and south exposures and, except to the north (where there is a sort of ravine), nothing but a view of the trees of Rock Creek Park—but nothing. Then, immediately to the south is the Zoo; but, unfortunately, I don't hear the lions and the elephants. Then, for what it is worth, Lyndon Johnson lived here before becoming president; and, allegedly, Otto von Habsburg during W.W.II! Then, with high ceilings and hardwood floors, there are two b.r.'s, two baths, l.r., d.r., so called sun porch and so called foyer which is very ample.

But I begin to sound like a real estate advertisement; and all this is only a Three Dollar taxi ride away from the Nat. Gall.![6] And, therefore, should you be surprised that I don't really miss Darwin Court in the very least bit [...].

In other words, if and when you happen to be in this part of the world (perhaps a big if and when?), do feel free to pay a visit and do notice that there should be three spare beds.

Best, best love to all of you.

     Colin

P.S. Came across a piece of Hilaire Belloc the other day which I think must have been intended for Jim. It is about champagne:

Beneath an equatorial sky
You must consume it or you die;
And stern, indomitable men
Have told me, time and time again,
The nuisance of the tropic is
The sheer necessity of fizz.[7]

C

---

1 Presumably, Conventual Church of St John of Jerusalem, Grove End Rd.
2 "Jim": James Stirling.⋆
3 Presumably, Hospital of St John and St Elizabeth, Grove End Rd.
4 *la mia Famiglia*, Italian: my family; Rowe's London friends James Stirling,⋆ Alvin Boyarsky,⋆ and Douglas Stephens⋆ had recently died, and Léon Krier⋆ had moved to Provence, France.
5 Rowe is describing the apartment house into which he had recently moved, the Kennedy-Warren. See Rowe's letter to Michael Spens⋆ dated 14 February 1995 (p 425 in this volume).
6 "Nat. Gal.": The National Gallery of Art, Washington, DC.
7 From "The Modern Traveller" of 1898 by Hilaire Belloc (1870–1953), Anglo-French writer and historian.

---

225   *To **Dorothy Rowe**, St. Margaret's Road, Oxford*   *8 February 1995*

Apt. 814, 3133 Connecticut Ave., Washington D.C.

Dearest Dorothy:

The almost simultaneous deaths of your near neighbour, Nancy Lancaster, aged 96 at Hasely and Mrs. Parish at Dark Harbor, Maine, has produced a crop of comparative obituaries.[1] So I send you two: from *House Beautiful* and *Vanity Fair*;[2] and I like neither magazine—H.B. was never up to the level of *H. and G.*, which has now ceased publication in N.Y.C., and *V.F.* is a revival, would be clever, of what in the 1920's was a celebrated publication.[3]

So, I can't help thinking that Lancaster comes off better than Parish—but I can't help thinking that both of them were too much addicted to curtains; and, in the case of Lancaster, journalism—as usual—gets it wrong. Thus nothing about Geoffrey Alan Jellicoe at Ditchley and for his later work for the Trees at that house in Dorset which has been recorded by Michael Spens.[4]⋆ But <u>what</u> would you expect. However, I thought you might enjoy.

Here it snowed on Saturday morning and has not melted yet and, since the sidewalks are icy, I haven't been out since; but, in Ithaca, twelve inches of snow seems to have fallen and the temperature seems to be 30 below f.p.![5] But, here, in spite of the deadly white prospects the windows are open.

Alex Caragonne⋆ is coming next week (also a woman from M.I.T.) to address themselves to the three volumes of my collected essays which M.I.T. plans to publish in October and for which one must find a title before the end of Feb. But <u>what</u> is it to be?[6]

Then next week, I am also told that Peter Eisenman⋆ is to give a lecture at Syracuse—and I wish that he would stop it—which is announced as: "The Legacy of Colin Rowe." Ba, ba, ba, ba! And God help me!

Enough for the moment,

Love,   *Colin*

1 Nancy Lancaster, celebrated decorator whose work at Ditchley House (James Gibbs, 1722; purchased by Lancaster in 1933) earned her the reputation of having "the finest taste of almost anyone in the world".
2 "Sister Parish" (1910–1994), interior decorator from Maine, internationally renowned for having renovated the Kennedy White House.
3 *House and Garden*.
4 Spens, Michael, *The Complete Landscape Designs and Gardens of Geoffrey Jellicoe*, London: Thames and Hudson, 1994.
5 "f.p.": freezing point.
6 Rowe, Colin, *As I Was Saying: Recollections and Miscellaneous Essays*, Alexander Caragonne ed, 3 vols, Cambridge, MA: MIT Press, 1996.

To **Michael Spens**, *Wormiston-by-Crail, Fife, Scotland*   *14 February 1995*   **226**

Apt. 814, 3133 Connecticut Ave., Washington D.C.

Dear Michael,

I have several times begun to write but have been too confused to continue; and, by this, I mean at sixes and sevens.[1] You see The Sunset Home for the Senile, otherwise Classic Residence by Hyatt, just didn't work out.[2] There was the odd general or so—but what a sweat, and the usual collection of little old Jewish ladies—*gemutlich* but exhausting.[3] And then there was the food—obligatory but inedible.

So I quit Classic Residence on December 2 and, simultaneous with the arrival of my things from London, I moved into this place which is enormous late Deco building of c.1930, having all of the merits of the immediately pre-Modern.

Entrance foyer, enormous and pseudo-palatial with adjacent restaurant, shop and laundry; and, then, the interminable corridors which are typical of D.C. But this apt is a complete joy—two b.r.s, two baths, a large foyer, an adjacent l.r., a dining room and a so-called sun porch, it looks out over nothing but the trees of Rock Creek Park![4] But amazing! On the one side there is city and, on the other side, there is approximate wilderness.

And, then, the building is not without provenance. Apparently Harry Truman lived here (or so they say) and Lyndon Johnson (for what it is worth) and, also—but believe it—no less than Otto von Habsburg, either lobbying desperately or trying to escape his momma who was sitting the scene out in Tuxedo Park![5]

But, apart from Rock Creek, down below, though I can't see it, there is also the Zoo and I am told that, during the summer, I shall be able to hear the lions......

Trouble with the typewriter and I move on to another machine.

A displaced P.P.S.

Didn't G.A.J. also do things at Longleat for Ld Bath?[6] Would love to know about this too!

And what else to say?

*   Have been re-reading, and re-enjoying, your Jellicoe book and I don't think that he was too good at mod. arch.[7] On the other hand how about that house for Ronald Tree in Barbados which I think is superb? And why don't you publish it—that dining portico with the steps down into it!

*   But, about Ditchley, the Nancy Lancaster obituaries—in *Vanity Fair* and *House Beautiful*—have <u>nothing</u> to say about G.A.J.'s participation, which made me just a

little bit sad.[8] But, if I think that north Oxfordshire, around Ditchley, just happens to be the most deadly country, I suppose that Nancy Perkins Field Tree Lancaster just had to possess it—a case of the Virginia mystique of the Lee name. All the same I would like to have seen Hasely and Nina Michaelis was always going to take me there—only we left it rather too long.[9]

*   What about a book on Cecil Pinsent whom, I assume, must have been Geoffrey Scott's lover?[10] The gardens at I Tatti don't excite me but the very small Villa Le Balze, just below the Villa Medici at Fiesole, is a very brilliant little job and then there is Iris Origo's place, La Foce, just south of Montepulciano. And there must be many more.

So it would be a book about Anglo-American houses in early 20C Tuscany which I would like to know about. But who would put it together?

*   Meanwhile, Academy Editions have sent me four, just four, complementary copies of *A.O.G.I.* and I think that they must be mad.[11] But it's just so sniveling, cheap shit mean in a situation where MIT has the basic politeness and common sense to send twenty copies!

But I will write to them and scream and yell.

Then, about the degringolade of England (though not, I think, Scotland) just what is there to be said? Like the decay of the Venetian Republic it has been a long decline and it has been obscured by the accumulations of immense commercial opulence. But all of this was better understood a hundred years ago then, nowadays, it now is. However let me not get involved with what you think of as the warm beer, hovis and eccentricity syndrome since it now appears that I am going to be in London towards the end of June and will, there, be seeing you.

Best, love,

  Colin

P.S. I think the London affair is goin' to be a bit of a strain but you will shortly become aware of the dets.[12]

  Colin

---

1   "At sixes and sevens": British idiom, a state of confusion or disarray.
2   On 2 December 1994, Rowe moved from Hyatt's Classic Residence to 3133 Connecticut Avenue, both in Washington, DC.
3   *gemutlich*, German: comfortable, agreeable, friendly.
4   "b.r.s": bedrooms; "l.r.": living room; Rock Creek Park: a large natural area bisecting Washington, DC, administered by the National Park Service.
5   Otto von Habsburg (1912–2011), Archduke Otto of Austria, was the last Crown Prince of Austria-Hungary (1916–1918); Tuxedo Park, New York: an elite village in Orange County, near New York City.
6   "G.A.J": Sir Geoffrey Alan Jellicoe (1900–1996), English architect, urbanist, landscape architect, and garden designer; co-author with JC Shepherd of *Italian Gardens of the Renaissance*, London: Benn, 1925.
7   Spens, Michael, *The Complete Landscape Designs and Gardens of Geoffrey Jellicoe*, London: Thames and Hudson, 1994.
8   See Rowe's letter to Dorothy Rowe* on Lancaster and Ditchley, dated 8 February 1995 (p 424 in this volume).
9   Nina Michaelis, who lived in London from 1993 to 1994. See Rowe's letter to Mark Girouard* dated 12 December 1995 (p 457 in this volume).
10 Cecil Pinsent (1884–1963), British architect and garden designer of Berenson's Villa I Tatti (1909–1914) and Origo's La Foce (1927–1939).
11 Rowe, Colin, *Architecture of Good Intentions*, London: Academy Editions, 1994.
12 "London affair": 20 June 1995 ceremony in which Rowe received the RIBA Gold Medal Award.

3133 Connecticut Avenue, Apt. 814, Washington, D.C.

Dearest Mary:

Thank you so much and: But, of course![1]

I shall be traveling with Judy and, since Fred is acting as one of my sponsors, perhaps I may be more or less en suite with himself and Susie—though J. and S., when together, are apt to be rather like a pair of hostile pussy cats.

Then there is the question, or the problem of Bill McMinn,* and I don't want to overload you. But Bill is the dean of architecture at Cornell U. and, in a fit of love, protectiveness and pride, he is insisting on coming to London for The Occasion. He is not an intellect, rather he is a nice kind of Southern liberal, Mississippi style; and, since I have known him since 1954, I don't want to have him feeling neglected and out in the cold.

Of course he is quite likely to be traveling on Sunday and, hence, the issue will scarcely arise; but, just in case, I shall be overjoyed if you could send an invitation to: Dean William McMinn, College of Architecture, Cornell U., Ithaca, N.Y. 14853. [...]

Best love,

   Colin

P.S. Does one, in England, say 'travelling' or 'traveling'.[2] I have been so busy correcting proofs into American English that I have lost all sense. However I have refused to spell English 'judgement' as American 'judgment'. This is a monstrosity and people here generally agree with me.

   C   (NO PEN TO BE FOUND) [handwritten]

---

1   Mary Stirling had proposed to throw a party together with Robert and Celia Maxwell* in celebration of Rowe's having been awarded the Royal Gold Medal.
2   "Traveling", with one 'l', appears in the first sentence of this letter.

Apt. 814, 3133 Connecticut Ave., Washington D.C.

Dearest Dorothy,

This is the stuff which I mailed to Frank Duffy a day or so before I left for Oregon on April 22 and I assume that they <u>must</u> have received it.[1]

First of all a copy of a letter for which I kept no Xerox:

Dear Frank Duffy: I am very conscious of all the quasi-apotheositic ra-ra which the R.I.B.A. is preparing for me; but I know that I have to work with all of you to make the occasion a success and, therefore, there are here appended lists of invitations and guests.

I do hope that these will not appear to be intolerably officious and I can only implore you to accept them for what they are—a very rough guide from which one shouldn't try to deviate.

Sincerely,

And, second, a Xerox of my lists. And, since Steve Peterson⋆ and Barbara Littenberg⋆ propose to arrive on the Saturday from Firenze, I shall add them in for a possible dinner in a subsequent letter to F.D. as I shall also add Sarah Matheson.

Best, best love,

Colin

P.S. It rained a lot in Oregon with lots of rainbows. Oregon is like a little welfare state criss-crossed with remnants of Baden-Wurttemberg. Meaning all problems appear to be solved and the picture is of a benign and placid society which enjoys a modest prosperity. Predominant influences are New England and Boston and I believe that it was mostly settled from there—by land. So Los Angeles was mostly settled, by land, but from the Mid-West—Iowa, Nebraska, Oklahoma; and San Francisco was mostly settled from the sea as was also Seattle (related to Alaska), which all makes for decisive differences.

Thus, about Portland, Oregon, there is not a trace of anything Wild West or aberrational; and it really is a surprisingly decorous small city of about 800,000 persons with little ethnic diversity and a very grand site on the right bank of the Willamette River (pronounced Willamette) and at the confluence of the Willamette and the Columbia. Surrounded by low, forested semi-mountains—or extremely steep hills—to the east and the south and these act as terminals to most of the streets which is very gratifying. Then, from some thirty miles away—and again to the east—this is all presided over by the huge snow-covered and volcanic Mount Hood. Founded in 1847, blocks are two hundred feet square and streets are eighty feet wide between buildings surfaces. So it has a very acceptable scale, a surprising number of reasonably distinguished buildings, and—unlike so many American cities—it was not wrecked and torn down by the so called urban renewal in the 1960's and its general fabric remains surprisingly intact. So a tolerable place and an unexpected pleasure.

So I was the first Pietro Belluschi Distinguished Professor at the Univ. of O. in Eugene, O.; and Eugene is, in the end a bit of a bore. But to tell you about P.B. He was born, of all places, in Ancona in 1899, grew up in Rome and Bologna, was an officer in the Italian army in W.W.I, in the Italian retreat from Caporetto fought at the battle of Piave, graduated from the University of Rome in engineering and then, sponsored by a Contessa di Robilant, came to Cornell in 1923 to do a bit more engineering. And can't you see it all? This Ancona-Rome-Bologna boy under the auspices of Don Thingy Gaetano, of the Dukes of Sermoneta (then Italian ambassador in D.C.), gravitated west and finally ended up in Portland, where, being very astute, he became very rich.

A sufficient but not a great talent that is what he was; but, after removing to Boston as dean at M.I.T. in 1950, he became a conspicuous power and an inflated reputation, returning to Portland in 1973.

So that was the reason for my being in Oregon. He must have left at least $300,000 to the University of Oregon when he died, aged 94, last year. At my Portland lec, midday Friday, everything went very smooth and there were about 500 persons, including the survivors of the Belluschi family *in toto* and I was surprised that I knew so many people in Portland.[2] But about twelve people came up afterwards almost to throw themselves into my arms. So I was mildly astonished and (of course) pleased and the residue of the Belluschi family just had to say that Pietro would have enjoyed everything that I had to say—though I very much doubt it.

Anyway, that's the story.

> *Colin*

P.P.S. With what is threatening to happen, which is beyond my control, I don't understand <u>how</u> in London I am going to be able to meet Simon, James, and Rosie, whom I most want to see.[3]

So tell me, please-please, what to do.

> *Colin*

---

1 Frank Duffy (b 1940) was president of the RIBA from 1993 to 1995. The RIBA was awarding Rowe its Gold Medal at this time.
2 *in toto*, Latin: complete, in its entirety.
3 The 20 June 1995 RIBA Gold Medal Award ceremony and reception.

To **Michael Spens**, *Wormiston-by-Crail, Fife, Scotland* *29 May 1995* **229**

Apt. 814, 3133 Connecticut Ave., Washington D.C.

Dearest Michael,

I send you a present from Oregon.[1] James Tice took me here the other day and I became a convert: and I don't mean to the Order of St Benedict but to this particular Aalto library.[2]

But have you seen it?

It's on a butte which you approach through a forest with stations of the cross, all suggestively *Italiano*; and if, following this, the monastic buildings are nothing to write home about, the extreme reticence of the library suddenly becomes a consummation of the site.

Screened or veiled by dark existing trees you can scarcely see it; but, all the same, it's very modest and scarcely disclosed vertical surface collaborates with the horizontal surface of the butte to emphasise, without any exaggeration, the very powerful view westwards over the valley.

But you gotta go look. I never expected to be impressed. I never liked Aalto at M.I.T.,[3] but all this leaves me extremely *emotionné* and I look forward to your reactions.[4]

Best love and regards,

> COLIN ROWE *Colin*

P.S. Don't <u>think</u> about a speech or pseudo eulogy for me because <u>they</u> don't want it.[5] <u>They</u> are accustomed to <u>two</u> speeches, one before and one after the award; and the idea of a <u>third</u> speaker—to represent Cambridge—is not acceptable to <u>their</u> sense of tradition. Tough shit; but so it is and will see ya' *chez Maxwell*.[6]*

> *Colin*

1 A postcard of Alvar Aalto's Mt Angel Abbey Library in St Benedict, Oregon, 1964–1970.
2 James Tice, formerly a student in Rowe's Urban Design Studio at Cornell (MArch, 1970), taught in the University of Oregon's Department of Architecture in 1995 when Rowe was the inaugural Pietro Belluschi Distinguished Professor there.
3 Baker House (1947–1948) is a dormitory at MIT designed by Alvar Aalto.
4 *emotionné*, French: very moved.
5 Earlier Rowe had asked Michael Spens* to give a speech in his honor at the RIBA's June 1995 ceremony in which Rowe was awarded the Gold Medal. The RIBA later limited the speakers to two: Robert Maxwell* and Fred Koetter.*
6 *chez Maxwell*, French: at the Maxwell* house / home. Maxwell, his wife Celia Scott, and Mary Stirling hosted a reception following the RIBA award.

230 To **Mary Stirling**, *Belsize Avenue, London*   *24 June 1995*

3133 Connecticut Avenue, Apt. 814, Washington, D.C.

Dearest Mary:

I have returned exhausted and debilitated.[1] I am not accustomed to such hectic goings on. But all the people to whom I spoke—sometimes too briefly and sometimes not briefly enough—left me feeling a bit like little ole' Marcel Proust, returning to Paris in the final episode of *A La Recherche des Temps Perdus*—lots of people changed beyond any recognition![2]

But your party was a great pleasure and I thank you enormously; and, after you, the *ricevimento* at Lincoln's Inn Fields was the next best.[3]

Best regards and lots of love to all of you. Or should I say y'all?

It was a wonderful party.

> *Colin*

1 Rowe had just returned to Washington, DC from London, where he received the RIBA's Royal Gold Medal.
2 Proust, Marcel, *À la recherche du temps perdu* (translated as both *Remembrance of Things Past* and *In Search of Lost Time*), 1913.
3 Together with Robert Maxwell* and Celia Scott, Mary Stirling had held a reception party following Rowe's receiving the RIBA Gold Medal; *ricevimento*, Italian: reception.

231 To **Alex Caragonne**, *San Antonio, Texas*   *30 June 1995*

Apt. 814, 3133 Connecticut Ave., Washington D.C.

Alex:

This relates to *The Texas Rangers*.[1]

About the origins and provenance of The Nine Squares Problem: I believe that it came from Poland via Liverpool.

When the Polish School of Architecture came to Liverpool in 1942 (and it must have stayed there perhaps five years) people were much astonished by the Polish *panache*.[2] Particularly the Warsaw Poles were able to condense difficulties and to elevate vapid complexity to a poetical dimension; and they operated, for the most part, with a somewhat ruthless combination of Corbu* and the Ecole des Beaux Arts—so that Matthew Nowicki was scarcely the comet which Lewis Mumford found him to be but much more of a routine emanation of Warsaw pedagogics immediately prior to W.W.II.[3]

Anyway, it must have been about 1944 (it couldn't have been earlier) that Robert Maxwell* and myself looked with something like amazement at a product whose author I do not recollect. It showed a hall comprised of twelve highly attenuated columns, nine squares, with each square covered by a flattened saucer dome which, nowadays, would be thought to be in the manner of Sir John Soane; and that was absolutely all.

So it was a primary statement which has remained indelibly inscribed within my mind. It was magic; and I think that it is from this Polish source (and my talk about it) that John Hejduk* must have derived his Nine Square Problem which, of course, he radically elaborated.[4]

Essentially not a 'modern' idea. A 'modern' idea would surely have involved four squares, I.E. with a column in the middle; but John augmented this fundamentally Polish vision with intimations of Mies,* of Palladio,* and of Michelangelo at St Peter's.

*** I send you this just in case and because I shall forget it all when I make a phone call.

    Colin

P.S. There is a book about The Polish School of Architecture in England—both at Liverpool and after it went to London.[5]

    Colin

---

1 Alexander Caragonne's* recent book, *The Texas Rangers: Notes from an Architectural Underground*, Cambridge, MA: MIT Press, 1995.
2 The University of Liverpool hosted the Polish School of Architecture from 1942 to 1946, during the German occupation of Poland. Rowe was an undergraduate at Liverpool from 1938 to 1942 and from 1944 to 1945; *panache,* French: flamboyance.
3 Mumford, Lewis, "The Life, the Teaching, and the Architecture of Matthew Nowicki", *Architectural Record*, June / September 1954.
4 See "The Nine-Square Grid Exercise", in Caragonne, *The Texas Rangers*, pp 189–195.
5 Szmidt, Bolesław, *The Polish School of Architecture, 1942–1945: The University of Liverpool*, Liverpool: Charles Birchall & Sons Ltd, 1945.

---

*To **Judith DiMaio**, American Academy in Rome, Via Angelo Masina 5, Rome*   *1 July 1995*   **232**

Apt. 814, 3133 Connecticut Ave., Washington D.C.

Dearest Judy:

    I don't think that you will really like Montecatini—at least I don't.[1] Going north-south it is O.K.; but, moving east-west, it is part of that pretty awful and almost interminable strip which extends from Prato, through Pistoia, to Pescia. On the other hand, I think that you may not have been to Pescia, which is a little version of Firenze with its own little river and which is very well worth a few hours look around.

Then what about S. Miniato dei Tedeschi which is not so very far away. It is a Y-shaped town with its own little version of the Palazzo dei Cavalieri from Pisa. Then, of course, not far away from Massa and Carrara, there is Chiavari where the chairs are still made....?

Then how about leaving that part of the world via Bagni di Lucca which was an important *stazione di villeggiatura*[2] in the 1840's and 50's—at least for English and Americans. William Wetmore Story spent time there,[3] also Margaret Fuller (related to Buckie),[4] also Robert and Elizabeth Browning.[5] And, from there, you could continue over the mountains to Parma-Piacenza where, at Piacenza, you could briefly drop in, have a little refreshment, and take a look at Farnese horses in front of the Municipio.

Then, of course, the Vittoriale which, both outside and inside, you will be quite wild about. And, then, what to do and where to stay. The lake is very long and I don't really see the point of driving around it; but at Bogliaco, further north, there is a rather interesting palazzo (where Joseph II once stayed in the 1780's) which, a bit like Palazzo Colonna, has two bridges across the highway to connect it with its garden. And, knowing your tastes, I think that you might like it. Then, at Bogliaco, somewhere outside and to the south of town, there is to be found *un studioso tedesco*, in other words Max Bacher and his wife Nina, niece of Otto von Simson, brother-in-law of the English Prinzessin Margaret von Hessen und Bei Rhein.[6] They live in Darmstadt-Stuttgart and are *molto simpatico* and *gemutlich*.[7] Nice house too; but they may be *senza telefono* and, short of driving up and playing it by ear I don't know what to advise.[8]

Unfortunately what I believe to be the most *recherché* hotel on Garda is on the other side of the lake—though not too far up.[9] It is a place where, coming back from Venice, the Duff Cooper's used to stay, year in and year out; and it's on a bit of land that sticks out, but I don't have its name and I think that it might be too far away from you.[10] However, with a map I am sure that someone in the Academy must know what I am talking about.

Then, I disadvise the Lago d'Iseo—unless you are crazed for Lady Mary Stuart-Wortley-Montagu, who introduced vaccination from Turkey to England, and, therefore, to the world in general.[11]

But I would skip Iseo though I might look in on San Pellegrino Terme, another version of Montecatini.

Then I don't think that you are going to be rendered ecstatic by Lugano which is average-elegant. But, though you are *not* going to stay at the hotel Villa d'Este (called after the follies and the infamies of Queen Caroline of Brunswick, consort of Geo IV—"oh gracious queen, we thee implore, to go away and sin no more, or if that effort be too great, to go away at any rate")[12] but if, even you doesn't have enough clothes for the Villa d'Este in Cernobbio you will, I know it, be rendered almost delirious by Cesare Cattaneo's little apartment on the left hand side of the road as, driving north, you come into town.[13] My dear, I think that it's much the best and far more animated/vivacious than Terragni.

Then Varese. Of course go to the sacred mountain which, I think, must be the best. And, then, the next lake over from Maggiore (I forget its name) has a charming little sacred mountain sequence all of its own. It is subdued and it's quiet and it is just *un po'Inglese*; but I think that you might adore it in spite of all that.[14]

And then you come to Varallo where, at the bottom of the approach valley Grignasco, there is a little church by Guarini.[15] But Varallo is superb and in spite of your absurd prejudice against nuns (which I partly share). Varallo is only to be enjoyed by accepting these nuns. Their cooking is not good, their rooms are cheap, and their intentions are benevolent. But what is more they occupy the top of the hill (like nothing down town) and after dinner provided by the nuns, you can walk around with magnificent views and all of those *tempietti*.[16] So that is the squalid-magnificent way in which it works at Varallo. And CEASE howling about nuns as though the poor things were part of a Gothic horror.

Instead go to Casale-Monferrato, interesting but not agreeable town, Gonzaga and Savoia influences, brilliant staircases, terrible boredom, the *grandezza* and the failure of Italy, I quite love it—and tell me what you think.[17]

Also, reverting to Lugano, you might-could-should (yes Mr. Shaw) go up to Montagnola and inspect the big-grand Milanese villa which houses the American School in Switzerland. This, the school, was the creation of Jerry's *patronne*, Mary Crist Fleming from Philadelphia; and, in the general complex, you might find that traces of Jerry's activity still exist.[18] Most notably he added a rather Japanese entrance patio to Mrs. Fleming's house, containing a pool with stepping stones to get to the front door—pretty hazardous you might think; and, for good reasons, the Flemings used to call it The Bishop's Pool. This because the Bishop of Gibraltar, in full canonicals but perhaps rather short sighted, didn't quite see his way—and just fell into the water. *Tableau.*

But to get the complete pic, you've got to grab that the Anglican Bishop of Gibraltar possesses a diocese which includes the entire Mediterranean and one of the Popes (Leo X?) said to the B. of G. of his day: "Your lordship in whose diocese I have the honor to reside." So the B. had come to Montagnola for a confirmation service and a thoroughly wet prelate was what resulted from Jerry's manipulations!

Then, and if you go to Casale-Monferrato, you might remember that somewhere not too far away, and on a steep hill, there is a wonderful Neo-Classical villa which you so much admire and myself has never been able to find. It belonged to the Communist, publishing, Feltrinelli who got done in; and it descends the hill in a succession of colonnades, exedrae, covered *passerelles*, *tempietti*, and all the rest.[19] You should check it out in the Lib at the Ac and discover its exact location.[20] Fred K. once found it but he couldn't get in. However I don't think that this should faze your determination!

Then, at Parma, will you see the Bertoia room with the simulated crystal columns? Or was it you who sent me there? But, at Parma, go to Fontanellato and see the Parmigianino room in that little brick *castello*. And I don't think that you have seen this.

Then, not too far from Bergamo, there is a villa with a chapel frescoed by Lorenzo Lotto which I have never seen but which, I am sure, that you will find.[21]

All of which might seem to suggest that you will return from Piemonte via Genova and, hence, could take in Chiavari and the chairs *in viaggio*.[22]

Dearest Judy, I am so sorry that, in London, I was so difficult. But it was, all the time, so hectic and febrile that I could only be demented. But it was so good of you, on the Wednesday when I felt completely beat, to bring me *vino, salmon affumicato*, a lemon and white chocolate.[23]

So *un abbraccio appassionato* and I hope to hear that, in Chiavari, you have bought some chairs.

   Colin

P.S. Since I returned here, for the most part the weather—overcast and gloomy—has been more lugubrious than it was in London.[24]

P.P.S. Matt arranged a little tour of the British Embassy for U. of M. students and persuaded me to go along.[25] Am glad that I did. The B.E., part French *hotel particulier* and part Palladian villa, must be quite the best foreign diplomatic outfit in D.C.;[26] and it is only a pity, I think, that Lutyens chose to make it a concession to an imaginary Virginia, to make it brick and to dress a remarkably astute plan with all too rustic, quasi-Qu. Anne facades.[27] But you could do it all over Leo von Klenze and the results might be astonishing—*and* much more Washington.[28]

By the way, first recognition of *Architecture of Good Intentions* comes from *Casabella*;[29] and I wonder how long the, Scully* dominated *N.Y.T.* will be able to resist a review. A long time I think, what with Goldberger and Muschamp, before any salutations arrive![30]

Colin

1 Judith DiMaio,* then in Rome, intended to tour parts of Italy and in this letter Rowe advises her; Montecatini Terme, in the province of Pistoia in Tuscany, Italy, was one of the places she would visit.
2 *stazione di villeggiatura*, Italian: holiday resort.
3 William Wetmore Story (1819–1895), an American sculptor, art critic, poet, and editor.
4 Sarah Margaret Fuller Ossoli (1810–1850), an American journalist, critic, and women's rights advocate.
5 Robert (1812–1889) and Elizabeth (1806–1861) Browning, prominent British Victorian era poets.
6 *unstudioso tedesco*, Italian: a German scholar.
7 *molto simpatico*, Italian: *gemutlich*, German: very sympathetic and friendly.
8 *senza telefono*, Italian: without a telephone.
9 *recherché*, French: sought after.
10 Duff Cooper (1890–1954), British Conservative Party politician, diplomat, and author.
11 Lady Mary Wortley Montagu (1689–1762), English writer and diplomat, renowned for her letters from Turkey.
12 Thomas Denman, British lawyer, from his defense of Queen Caroline in the early nineteenth century.
13 Cesare Cattaneo (1912–1943), Italian Rationalist architect.
14 *un po'Inglese*, Italian: a bit English.
15 Varallo Sesia, a town in the province of Vercelli, in the Piedmont region of Italy.
16 The convent is part of the Basilica of Sacro Monte di Varallo complex; *tempietti*, Italian: plural of *tempietto*.
17 *grandezza*, Italian: greatness.
18 Jerry A Wells;* *patronne*, French: patroness.
19 *passerelles*, French: walkways.
20 "Lib at the Ac": Library at the Academy.
21 Lorenzo Lotto (1480–1557), Northern Italian painter and illustrator.
22 *in viaggio*, Italian: on the road.
23 *vino, salmon affumicato*, Italian: wine, smoked salmon.
24 Rowe had recently moved back to Washington, DC, from London.
25 Matthew Bell;* "U. of M.": University of Maryland.
26 *hôtel particulier*, French: mansion.
27 The British Embassy, designed by Sir Edwin Lutyens and built of brick resembles a Queen Anne style English country manor.
28 Leo von Klenze (1784–1864), German Neoclassic architect.
29 Rowe, Colin, *The Architecture of Good Intentions*, London: Academy Editions, 1994, was dedicated to Judith DiMaio.*
30 *The New York Times* architecture critics, Paul Goldberger and Herbert Muschamp, studied with Vincent Scully* (b 1920), distinguished architectural historian, at Yale.

---

233 *To **Edward Jones**, London*   *5 July 1995*

Apt. 814, 3133 Connecticut Ave., Washington D.C.

Dear Edward:

In Canada does one discover those painfully patronising Polish jokes which are so prevalent in this country? Like how many Polacks does it take to unscrew a light bulb? Apparently they presume that just everybody from Poland is stupid, stolid and plodding; and this does not concur with my own experience or with the myths which I have received. And, according to my estimation, the Poles are something quite different: lots of <u>brio</u>, lots of <u>panache</u>, self consciously nationalist with veneers from Paris, at least these were the Warsaw Poles whom I used to know. But this was in that long ago period when, at Liverpool, there was <u>that</u> Polish School of Architecture in exile.[1]

The Warsaw Poles had great style and great names—like Podwopinski, Boriseivitch, Pilsudska, Czerniowska—but they also had an incredible capacity to make difficulty go away. Almost they could reduce <u>any</u> problem to only <u>two</u> elements which, since then, I have always regarded as the criterion of great intelligence.

Well, in the late-Thirties, Warsaw must have been a brilliant school, one of those educational experiments which can <u>never</u> be re-assembled and its basics were very simple: it was a conservative Beaux Arts academy which had become radically modified by an enthusiasm for Le C.[2]

So the results <u>could</u> be crude; but, in general, they were apt to be remarkably good and Lewis Mumford's strange infatuation with Matthew Nowicki is really no more than a tribute to this particular style of Warsaw pedagogics.[3] And I once said this to Stanislawa Nowicki and, without pressing the argument, she was compelled to agree.[4] Yes, Warsaw was exactly what I said it was. It was knowledgeable, intelligent, flamboyant, nothing at all like the G.S.D. or like <u>anything</u> to be found in England.[5]

So in quite a lot of ways, Texas may have been a more <u>intellectual</u> attempt to recapitulate Warsaw 1939; and this is why I would like you to find me a copy of that Polish School of Architecture book which must have been published in London, <u>circa</u> 1950.[6]

It cannot be hard and, being wildly unfashionable, it cannot be expensive; but I plan a piece about Warsaw as some kind of historical restitution.

---

1 Due to the German occupation of Poland in 1942, the Polish School of Architecture moved to the University of Liverpool where Rowe was an undergraduate student. See Rowe's letter to Alexander Caragonne* dated 30 June 1995 (p 430 in this volume).
2 Le Corbusier* (1887–1965), Swiss-born French architect.
3 Matthew Nowicki (1910–1950), Polish-born architect and educator. See Rowe's letter to Alexander Caragonne* dated 30 June 1995 (p 430 in this volume).
4 Stanislawa (Siasia) Sandecka Nowicki, Matthew Nowicki's widow.
5 "G.S.D.": Harvard's Graduate School of Design.
6 Boles and Szmidt eds, *The Polish School of Architecture, 1942–1945: The University of Liverpool*, Liverpool: Charles Birchall & Sons Ltd., 1945.

---

*To **Lisa Germany**, Austin, Texas*　　　　　　　　　　*14 & 24 July 1995*　　**234**

Apt. 814, 3133 Connecticut Ave., Washington D.C.

Dear Lisa Germany:*

I wish that I knew you and, after reading your book on Harwell Harris, I feel that I almost do.[1] I bought your book in Portland, Oregon, the other day and, almost ever since, I have been reading it. So, by now, I think that I must have read it several times and, always, with entertainment and interest.

A pity that you don't exhibit the plan of the Dallas Pace Setter House of 1955 because, surely, that is one of the very best plans by H.H.H.—and I am thinking about the invisibility of the garage/car port from street and approach drive, with its pedestrian accessibility, through the cortile/patio, to the front door.[2] But I suppose that this is one of the classic twentieth century solutions—largely unnoticed—and that it deserves a sustained round of applause—the doors of garages and the rear ends of cars should, neither of them, be visible from the street.

So, did Harwell fully understand this dictate (always understood by John Staub in River Oaks) and I don't think that he did—this though his distribution of automobiles on residential properties was generally very elegant.[3]

But your display of plans and pics, an abundance to which I have not been previously exposed, encourages me to say more; and, some of this, you are not going to like:

Harwell's bathrooms, by the standards of the day and even in quite grand houses, are appallingly contracted and insufficient. They are skimpy and they do not sustain the tradition of the grand American bathroom which had been already established by 1910. Indeed, in spite of Jean's anti-European propensities, Harwell's bathrooms are hopelessly miniature and *existenz minimum*.

And the rest of my problems relate (they always have related) to Harwell's inability to handle furniture, books and pictures—a problem also with F.L.W.[4] But the absence of extended walls for pictures; the altogether too improvised look of bookshelves—in the West Havens houses the shelves in the living room look like something that a not too bright graduate student might have assembled for a very temporary residence; and then the furniture, which looks as though it has been brought in for a short term rental to very lower middle class tenants—no traces of any austere selective process, nor any evidence of any ideal apostolic poverty. If fact the kitsch of an extremely undesirable motel; and it has been very rewarding for me to have been made aware of all this because it carries me back to the Harris house in Austin in the year 1954, when I was compelled to think about everything which I saw (and did not see) as a product of financial misfortune or some other vicissitude. And, believe you me, I did know Jean Harris excessively well.[5]

About David Thurman's study of Texas during these years, to which Alex Caragonne★ also refers, I am inclined to be sceptical—just as I was sceptical of his questionnaire when I received it some years back.[6] Simply, no question can ever be neutral and David Thurman's questions, it seemed to me, assumed too much about Harris and some sort of decisive role which he was supposed to have played. But there was never any decisiveness about Harwell; and whatever emerged at Texas was a result of Jean's insistence that both Bernhard and myself should act as Harwell's speechwriters, which for a period of several months—February to May '54—both of us did.[7]

Now, to explain all this, after receiving Thurman's questionnaire, I wrote a little memo to myself entitled "Texas and Mrs. Harris." This was in 1988 and, for obvious reasons, it was only privately circulated. But, since it will shortly appear, among other memorabilia and essays, in a book (three vols) to be published by M.I.T. in late October, I am taking the liberty of sending you a copy; and meanwhile, let me iterate: Thurman did get things wrong.

First of all, I did not appear in Texas until January 1954.

Second of all, about Marcus Whiffen★ whom Jean positively loathed.[8] I don't know when Whiffen came to Texas (in 1953?); but I do know when he left, in the summer of '54. This because I haven't seen Marcus Whiffen (whom I found completely amiable) since having drinks with him in a Lexington Avenue bar in the August of that year. And so Whiffen in no way overlapped the arrival of Hejduk,⋆ Slutzky⋆ and Hirsche.[9]⋆ (your p. 144)

Third of all, and as to the appointments of Fall 1954: John Hejduk was introduced by Bernhard and there can be no doubt about that. But then I am a little baffled with reference to your remarks about Slutzky and Hirsche; and, again, I suspect info from Thurman. In any case, though with Harwell's guarded approval, the Yale appointments were made at my instigation (after all myself had been at Yale only a couple of years before); and, since Slutzky and Hirsche both appeared within the same few days of late August, I cannot understand your remarks, p. 142, that Harris was so excited by Hirsche that he asked for yet another Yalie. No this was just not the case and, whosoever Thurman may have consulted (possibly H.H.H. himself), he did get it wrong. It was Rubin who came later, as the result of a *demarche*[10] made by both Slutzky and Hirsche![11]

July 24, 1995

A big break because so much of your book I have greatly appreciated particularly your publication of Harwell's remarks about the Hollyhock House. But, dearest Lisa, if I may so address you, I know that out of a disgusting scene at Texas, you were hoping to discover a hero and so you went to Raleigh, North Carolina—to, as they say, the horse's mouth. An intelligent move, the intelligent move, so far as concerns Harwell's architecture; but, since horses are not exactly verbally articulate creatures and since their limited memory is scarcely other than personal, perhaps not such a good idea as an assumption of Harwell's pedagogics. For, as an educator, his credentials were, and remained, entirely without existence; and this, in the end, became the evaluation of all the faculty whom he appointed. And perhaps more significantly, it also became the ultimate opinion of Bernhard Hoesli.⋆ No, unlike Jean, this particular horse was not a thoroughbred; and, in spite of (or because of?) the uncharacteristic words which Bernhard and myself so injudiciously (?) put into his mouth, this horse just wouldn't run.

A slightly bitchy letter? But it is not intended to be so; and can only conclude with

My very best regards,

Colin Rowe

P.S. But, apparently, I haven't yet concluded.

From time to time Rudolf Wittkower⋆ would speak of Palladio's⋆ architecture as 'organic'; and, of course, so long as one assumes a Platonic cosmology so it must be regarded—as something intrinsic to the greater whole.[12]

However, to persons who confess a Wrightian, or post-Darwinian, allegiance, anything 'organic' must involve fantasies of mutation, emergence, and growth.

But, if both positions are comparatively harmless, it still might be better if the significance of these separate predicaments were to be spelled out *en clair*, which seems to be a proposal beyond the capacity of Bruno Zevi.[13]

And B.Z. might now lead to K.F.[14]

So there is a question, and an answer, which I was first exposed to the other day in Oregon:

Q. What is a rare book?
B. A rare book is a book which doesn't have an introduction by Kenneth Frampton.

But I do wish that K.F. had awarded you the complement of paying attention to your words and I refer to the extravagant claims made on p.xii to "the so-called Texas Rangers."[15] So Hejduk and Slutzky enjoyed almost no communication with Harris (the lines of communication were severed by Jean within approximately nine weeks) and, certainly, <u>myself</u> owed no 'autonomy' as a teacher to '<u>him</u>'. But, when it comes to Seligman, whom as <u>you</u> say, p.144, "came after Harris's resignation" (some fifteen months after to be precise), just <u>how</u> does dear Kenneth involve Werner in that little *galere*?[16] But do please tell me. But, on the other hand, don't tell me because I am sure that it also embarrassed you too.

And I think that really must be all. And the message? Read Germany for architecture: read Caragonne for pedagogics.[17] And the two together, should you wish it, will give you a balanced pic.[18]

Lots of the best,

    Colin

---

1 Germany, Lisa, *Harwell Hamilton Harris*, Austin: University of Texas Press, 1991, foreword by Kenneth Frampton, introduction by Bruno Zevi. Harris⋆ was chair of the Department of Architecture at the University of Texas at Austin from September 1953 to June 1955. Rowe taught there from January 1954 to June 1956.

2 Harris' *House Beautiful* Pace Setter house was exhibited at the State Fair of Texas in 1954.

3 John F Staub (1892–1981), American architect of large, period-style residences, many in the River Oaks neighborhood of Houston, Texas.

4 "F.L.W.": Frank Lloyd Wright.⋆

5 Mrs Harwell H Harris, Jean Murray Harris.⋆ See Rowe, "Texas and Mrs. Harris", in Rowe, Colin, *As I Was Saying: Recollections and Miscellaneous Essays*, Alexander Caragonne ed, 3 vols, Cambridge, MA: MIT Press, 1996, vol 1, pp 25–40.

6 David Thurman. See Caragonne, Alexander, *The Texas Rangers: Notes from an Architectural Underground*, Cambridge, MA: MIT Press, 1995, p xiv.

7 Bernhard Hoesli.⋆

8 Marcus Whiffen⋆ (1916–2002), English-born, Cambridge-educated architectural historian. Taught at the University of Texas at Austin, 1953–1954.

9 John Hejduk,⋆ Robert Slutzky,⋆ and Lee Hirsche⋆ (1927–1998).

10 *démarche*, French: move, maneuver.

11 Regarding Irwin Rubin, see note 6 above.

12 Rudolf Wittkower⋆ (1901–1971), legendary architectural historian with whom Rowe studied at the Warburg Institute, University of London, from 1946 to 1948.

13 *en clair*, French: clearly.

14 "B.Z. might now lead to K.F.": Bruno Zevi might now lead to Kenneth Frampton. Zevi wrote the introduction to Germany's book. Frampton wrote the foreword.

15 The "extravagant claims" are those made by Kenneth Frampton in his foreword.

16 Werner Seligmann;⋆ *galère*, French: a group of people having an attribute in common.

17 In her three-page reply to this letter dated 29 August 1996, Germany wrote Rowe that she was "interested in Harris' architecture and not much moved by the controversies surrounding his brief time at the University". She "knew the gossip from that era", she stated, and "waded through it to get to what was salient to anyone interested in his architectural ideas". Harris, she said, "was not a good director of a school of architecture and he did not take responsibility for the creation of the Texas Rangers. On these issues he couldn't have been [...] more forthcoming. He clearly forgot that you recommended the hirings of Slutzky⋆ and Hirsche⋆ [...] However, you are mistaken if you think that he wished to steal credit for their hirings away from you or anybody else. Their arrivals here just didn't matter as much to him as it does to you."

18 Earlier in this same letter, regarding the hirings and Rowe's insistence that he had written a notable speech for Harris, Germany wrote, "I realize the importance of these facts to you because after all they are the cues that brought you onto the stage, as it were, of this, my story of Harwell's life. By placing the hiring of the Yale faculty members in Harwell's hands instead of yours, by overlooking your writing of his speech regarding the school's curriculum I, in effect, took away your lines in the drama." Although Lisa Germany⋆ could not have known it in 1996, in a letter to Henry-Russell Hitchcock⋆ dated 23 September 1955 (p 97 in this volume), Rowe had written a satirical drama about the UT-Austin Department of Architecture, giving himself a lead role.

*To **Michael Spens**, Wormiston by Crail, Fife, Scotland*   *26 July 1995*   **235**

Apt. 814, 3133 Connecticut Ave., Washington D.C.

Dearest Michael:

Birkhäuser wants to do a German publication of *The Architecture of Good Intentions*; and I send you a copy of their letter to me and of my, mildly indiscreet, letter to them.[1]

So this is to ask for your advice. Is their complaint legitimate or imaginary; and, if legitimate, then what to do? And, if need be, can you bring any influence to bear?

You may show them the letter from Birkhäuser; but, of course, you will have conveniently mislaid mine.

Best love,

     Colin

P.S. Have just been reading a rather good biography of Samuel Johnson and, needless to say, I still find Jamie Boswell quite irresistible.[2] Apparently his first remark to S.J. was as follows: "I do come from Scotland but I can't help it." But bizarre.

P.P.S. Am I correct in supposing Sir Norman Foster to be a talent without taste and Sir Richard Rogers to be a highly superior used car salesman?[3] I derive this impression of Sir Richard from just having read his Reith Lectures, *Cities for a Small Planet*, a collection of self-serving banalities if ever there was one.[4] But, if you haven't read, do read; and I can't help thinking that Lloyd's recent troubles are some sort of product of that building.[5] Like St Peter's to the Reformation and Versailles to the French Revolution? And doesn't this relate to Parkinson's Law?[6]

     Colin

---

1   Both letters are lost. Michael Spens⋆ owned Academy Editions, the British publisher of Rowe's *The Architecture of Good Intentions*.
2   James Boswell wrote *The Life of Samuel Johnson, LL.D.,* London: Henry Baldwin, 1791, considered by many the greatest biography written in English.
3   Norman Foster (b 1935) and Richard Rogers (b 1933), prominent English architects.
4   Rogers, Richard, *Cities for a Small Planet*, The Reith Lectures, 1995, London: Faber and Faber, 1997.
5   Lloyd's of London, a renowned international insurance market, underwent the most traumatic period in its history from the late-1980s to the mid-1990s. Their corporate headquarters in London, Lloyd's Building, was designed by Richard Rogers and opened in 1987.
6   Parkinson's Law: work expands to fill the time available for its completion.

*To **Leon Satkowski**, Minneapolis*   *27 July 1995*   **236**

Apt. 814, 3133 Connecticut Ave., Washington D.C.

Dear Leon:

I am so glad that you like *Bramante to Scamozzi and Beyond* because I do too; and I am amused that you are relatively bored by the Quattrocento because also me. And thus far so good.[1]

In any case, as Vasari well knew, Roman Bramante initiated an era of great longevity; and I take it that the canonical works are Casa Caprini, the Tempietto, and the apse of S. Maria del Popolo—in that order.

Then I suppose that the resonance and the tragic *seriosita* of Roman Bramante might be best explained via a comparison of S. Maria delle Carceri at Prato and S. Biagio at Montepulciano.[2]

But Bramante eclipses the Quattrocento, as you more or less intimate, so that Brunelleschi and to a lesser extent Alberti scarcely re-enter the general repertory of practice until the time of Burckhardt.[3]

So a flashback to B. and A., with Michelozzo and particularly Giuliano da Sangallo (v. important domestic contributions).[4] Then "a long way around to the Tempietto" or "Bramante the great synthesis" with, I think, the latest date for the T.[5]

So Urbino, Padua—Mantegna/Squarcione, Milano/Filarete, etc., relations with Leonardo, leading thru to the Duomo of Pavia which was so beautifully displayed here at the Nat Gall the other day in the form of the contemporary model.[6] Then Rome and the paradigmatic performance with *chiaroscuro* gradually displacing contour.

I can see my way so far and then I should notice that I believe, on occasion, of making an argument with an array of slides not necessarily closely integrated with the text; and I mean by this that the role of Casa Caprini might be stipulated by a presentation of buildings affiliated to it, even including as late as Somerset House and that little job at Newport R.I. Also perhaps even the Tempietto might, just might, be presented with Hawksmoor's mausoleum at Castle Howard.

But, about Raphael, I am entirely at a loss and I wonder whether we should have a chapter to be called "The Rome of Leo X".

Then, with Giulio, Sanmicheli, Peruzzi, Serlio, I think that it all becomes fairly plain sailing; but what to do about the younger Antonio da Sangallo, prototype of the architect as bureaucrat, who can be very tedious but who also can be very good. So does one, must one intersperse him with Michelangelo?

But there should be another array of pictures surely for Palazzo Branconio, Palazzo Spada, Villa Pia, Villa Medici, and their many descendants in Italy and elsewhere.

And then the year 1550, Julius III del Monte, and the appearance of Vignola, Vasari, Ammannati. So this is absolutely your stuff and did Julius III suffer from gout? But surely, an excursion to Fontainebleau with Primaticcio and Serlio, Bolognesi all three! Cosimo! And have you ever thought that he was the great, great, great, great, grandfather of Queen Anne? But do we annex Buontalenti to Vasari/Ammannati? Or is he too much of another generation—which, of course he is.

Then I don't know where else to put Venice and so myself goes Venetian plan, Venetian facade, comparisons with Florence-Rome, Venetian obsession with columns, Cardinal Cornaro, Falconetto, Serlio and the Venetian palace, Sansovino (Pevsner* doesn't even list him in his index), Andy P. and his palaces, the Palazzo Thiene and Giulio, an array of miscellaneous Venetian villas, an array of Serlio villas which must have influenced Palladio,* Palladian villas, P's churches, Scamozzi............????????[7]

Strada Nuova, Genova.

Giacomo della Porta, Domenico Fontana, leading to the softened style of Carlo Maderno.

Gardens, the mid century v. Villa Aldobrandini at Frascati.

A new integration in Rome c. 1600—of course it is very visible. Resumption of Vincenzo Scamozzi.

But there is still so very much left out. Guido Guidetti, Antonio Labacco, and on and on.

However I think that the virtue of a book with a good arrangement of pics and intelligent captions may well exceed that of a lecture series, where once seen things are seen for good; and I also think that, if this a text book, then there should be an entirely separate annotation of dates and attributions for quick reference. For instance, Peter Murray once said to me: "so you think that the Collegio Romano is by Ammannati do you?"[8] But surely if there are doubts and rejected attributions these should be stipulated. Again for instance, in your *Giorgio Vasari*, at Citta di Castello there is a Capella Vitelleschi which Venturi gave to Giorgio and it is far from beneath contempt but perhaps a little too far south and too Papal States for Vasari's theater of operations.[9] But I would like to know just what you think about this attribution.

Dear Leon I have written far too much and become a little bit carried away. But let me have your reactions and I am very much looking forward to your arrival.

My phone number is: 202-462-7955.

Best, best,

    Colin

P.S. By the way you are entirely right in what you suspect. Mail, both in and out, in D.C. does seem to be slightly Italian in its retardation; and, if the Feds suffer in the same way (but I doubt they do!) then certain patterns of reaction might well be explained.

    Colin

P.P.S. Thinking about the incarnation and B.C. and A.D., this division of time could surely be applied to the succession *quattrocento-cinquecento* when the latter's become B.B. and A.B.— with B for Bramante!

And isn't this what, implicitly, Vasari recognized? But, and I am not proposing that we should labor this, did not Vasari perceive Brunelleschi and Alberti as 'pioneers' (almost in the Pevsner[10] sense but for the full revelation of *il moderno si glorioso*[11]— then that arrives with Pope Della Rovere and Donato B.).[12]

I suppose that, during the A.B. period, quotes from Brunelleschi are occasions of archaizing 'Toscanita'. And, as such, 'provocative'.

    Colin

---

1 *Bramante to Scamozzi and Beyond* was Rowe's proposed title for a book to be co-authored by Leon Satkowski.* The book *was* published, but after Rowe's death, and was titled *Italian Architecture of the 16th Century*, Princeton, NJ: Princeton Architectural Press, 2002.

2 *seriosita*, Italian: seriousness.

3 Jacob Burckhardt (1818–1897), Swiss historian of art and culture, author of *Die Kultur der Renaissance in Italien*, 1860.

4 "B. and A.": Brunelleschi and Alberti.

5 "T.": *Tempietto*, by Donato Bramante, Rome.

6 Italian Renaissance Architecture: Brunelleschi, Sangallo, Michelangelo: The Cathedrals of Florence and Pavia and Saint Peter's, Rome, exhibtion at The National Gallery of Art, Washington, DC, 18 December 1994–16 April 1995.

7 "Andy P.": Andrea Palladio* (1508–1580), Italian architect.

8 Peter Murray (1920–1992), British historian of Renaissance architecture.
9 Satkowski, Leon George and Ralph Lieberman, *Giorgio Vasari: Architect and Courtier*, Princeton, NJ: Princeton University Press, 1993.
10 Nikolaus Pevsner* (1902–1980), *Pioneers of the Modern Movement* (London: Faber, 1936); republished as *Pioneers of Modern Design* (New York: Museum of Modern Art, 1949).
11 *il moderno cosi glorioso*, Italian: the so-glorious modern.
12 "Donato B.": Donato Bramante.

237   *To **Robert Maxwell**, Tasker Road, London*   *7 September 1995*

Apt. 814, 3133 Connecticut Ave., Washington D.C.

Dearest Roberto:

My correct address is: 3133 Connecticut Avenue, Apt 814, Washington, D.C. 20008; and, since yourself seems to be determined to believe that I live in Chevy Chase, Maryland, it renders deliveries just a bit difficult and protracted.

I have just finished correcting proofs, both text and pics, for the forthcoming three volumes (!!!) which MIT expects to produce for the end of October; and let me tell you it's been a terrible, grueling sweat.[1] However I sent it off yesterday and now I am <u>almost</u> ready to begin my new <u>opus</u> which is to be called BRAMANTE TO SCAMOZZI AND BEYOND; but, for the moment, I am just taking a little time to breathe.[2]

The R.G.M. was delivered to me over the weekend by Judy DiMaio* and we were both in full agreement that it succeeds in looking like a piece of chocolate money wrapped up in gold foil. But it's a visual triviality, everything is terribly blurred, and the profile of H.B.M. is entirely without any <u>edge</u> or contour. But compare it with the clarity of almost any nineteenth century medal and you will see what an appalling job the Royal Mint now manages to do.

Then, I learn from a review in the *T.L.S.* that, apart from being a former student of Rudi Wittkower's,* I am also a student of Chas. Jencks!* But it's a favourable review and don't you think that this is quite charming?[3]

And what else?

Am quite excited about the sixteenth century Italian book and, since I don't want completely to exhaust myself with it, I am going to do it in collaboration with Leon Satkowski,* Cornell graduate of about 1970 who went on to study with Jim Ackerman* at Harvard. So, last week or so, we talked about it all for three excessively concentrated days and evolved a sequence of chapters like:

Bramante and Romanitas (with flash backs)
Interlude: Raphael and Peruzzi
Michelangelo, Giulio Romano, and the Revolution of Architectural Form
1546 and Michelangelo
Architecture at Court: Fontainebleau, Vignola, Vasari, Ammannati
The Most Serene Republic: Falconetto, Sanmichele, Sansovino
Palladio* and the Myth of Antiquity
Etc, etc.

So grab the idea? I have lots of lecture notes and Leon has just published a book on Vasari. Then Leon will also contribute references to all the most recent Italian and German publications—so people won't be able to catch us out. Then Leon thinks that it is high time for a new work from the point of view of Heinrich Wölfflin and he agrees with me that, to quote Focillon, our objects must be to trace *la ligne des hauteurs*.[4] And then just _what_ is the competition? Heydenreich and Lotz?[5] The late Peter Murray? Franz Metternich? My former Cambridge student, Howard Burns? Jim Ackerman who gets more sociological every day? No I don't think that we have anything to fear.

Apart from this my brother tells me that Patrick Hodgkinson is very distressed by *Good Intentions*.[6] Apparently it is (as Q.V. used to say) an inexcusably _shocking_ betrayal of mod. arch. But just where he been hidin' out for all these years.

Anyway I am feeling exhilarated and cheerful and, in this condition, I am sending my best love to you and Celia.[7]

Un abbraccio stravagante and I am _so_ happy not to be in the vicinity of Gloucester Gate.[8]

   Colin

1   Rowe, Colin, *As I Was Saying: Recollections and Miscellaneous Essays,* Alexander Caragonne ed, 3 vols, Cambridge, MA: MIT Press, 1996.
2   *Bramante to Scamozzi and Beyond* was written with Leon Satkowski* and published after Rowe's death as *Italian Architecture of the 16th Century*, New York: Princeton Architectural Press, 2002. See Rowe's letter to Satkowski dated 27 July 1995 (p 439 in this volume).
3   Ballantyne, Andrew, "What remains for those who meant well?", a review of *The Architecture of Good Intentions: Towards a Possible Retrospect*, London: Academy Editions, 1994, in the *Times Literary Supplement*, 28 July 1995, p 21.
4   *la ligne des hauteurs*, French: the high line.
5   Heydenreich, Ludwig and Wolfgang Lotz, *Architecture in Italy, 1400 to 1600*, Baltimore: Pelican, 1974.
6   Patrick Hodgkinson (b 1930), British architect best known for his Brutalist Brunswick Centre (1972) in London.
7   Celia Scott, architect and sculptor, Robert Maxwell's* wife.
8   In 1993 and 1994, Rowe had lived at 65 Darwin Court, Gloucester Avenue, in London, one-half mile north of the Gloucester Gate, Regent's Park.

To **Ernst Gombrich**, *Briardale Gardens, London*   *September, 1995*   **238**

Apt. 814, 3133 Connecticut Ave., Washington D.C.

Dear Ernst:

   It is a very long time ago that you allowed me to take a look at what must have been your Vienna dissertation. As a matter of fact it was very late in the year 1946! But, after almost half a century, my mind is still penetrated by what I believe that I saw—one of your visual images which I haven't seen from that day to this.

So let me tell you what I seem to remember. It is the sixteenth century engraving, a cross section of the duomo at Mantua which is projected backwards into perspective, completely explanatory of this wildest of cross sections.

But am I the victim of a hopeless illusion? Am I in the grip of a fantasy about something which never _was_ but _ought_ to be? And, if I am not deluded, then just how is it that this so important engraving has escaped any attention except your own?

Need I say that I do hope that I have not been the subject of an hallucination and that yourself will be able to tell me all about this engraving—which, so far as I know, is not in the Calcografia. Then, and supposing this engraving not to be the product of a too heated imagination, I think that you already know to what this letter must lead:

could you be so good as to supply me with a copy of it so that it might be published (with prominent expression of credit) in my new sixteenth century book?

I should be immensely grateful,

With very best regards,

COLIN ROWE   *Colin*

P.S. I think that I should tell you something about the book which is probably going to be called *Bramante to Scamozzi and Beyond* and which I plan to write in collaboration with Leon Satkowski,★ a former student of mine who went on to study with Jim Ackerman★ at Harvard.[1]

So we plan a sequence of chapters something like this:

The Year 1500 in Rome
Bramante and Romanita
Interlude: Raphael and Peruzzi
A revolution of architectural form: Michelangelo and Giulio Romano
The year 1546 and Michelangelo
Architecture at Court: Fontainebleau, Vignola, Vasari, Ammannati
The Most Serene Republic: Falconetto, Sanmicheli, Sansovino, Palladio★ and the Myth of Antiquity
Scamozzi and Other Sixteenth Century Archaïsers (though I am not sure about this)
The Year 1600 in Rome

Within which mesh we hope to be able to grab the Sangallo's, Serlio, Pyrrho Ligorio, Guido Guidetti, Domenico Fontana, Giacomo della Porta and, I suppose, miscellaneous others. Then there will be a chapter on "The City and the Garden" which, as yet, we don't quite know where to place; and Bramante will be attended by a flash back to Urbino, etc, etc.

Then we also plan a more prominent role for visuals than is the customary procedure. Thus, and almost at the beginning, Giuliano da Sangallo's church at Prato will be compared with his brother's at Montepulciano of forty years later (example, internals and weight of walls in plan) will be allowed to speak for the influence of Bramante and, ultimately, the influence of the Tragic Scene; thus Casa Caprini will make a first appearance with a display of its progeny; and thus, to conclude Bramante and to prelude Raphael, there will be a confrontation of the apse of Santa Maria del Popolo and, less than fifty years apart, obviously the Cappella Chigi. But this sort of thing which is incredibly informative you certainly don't get in Heydenreich and Lots![2]

And now I wanted to ask your opinion. We plan to end the next chapter with another confrontation between the Sala di Constantino and the Medici Chapel, both prefaces to so many later sixteenth century spaces but, again, a highly suggestive juxtaposition which one never sees.

So, in Sala di Constantino, the simulated architecture of the corners functions to separate the three big frescoes and it is patently Michelangelesque in origin. So, in Cappella Medici, the big scale architecture of doors and aedicules acts to articulate the small scale architecture of the tombs. So the two volumes, both involving a distension of wall surface via an accentuation of angle, share what is approximately a common spatial strategy; and there is no need to ask any question as to priority.

Do you attribute Sala di Constantino exclusively to Giulio? Or, for general distribution, do you postulate an initiatory involvement on the part of Raphael?

Was it Raphael who annexed details from the Sistine ceiling for the niches with their popes and allegories? Or is it Giulio all the way?

I don't recollect that Frederick Hartt even considers the issues;[3] but, in a conversation of some time back, I remember Sydney Freedberg as opting for Raphael.[4] But do you feel this element of doubt? And since—in the present state of knowledge—no one really knows, does it really matter?

I write to you, not expecting more than the briefest of replies—Giulio yes, Raphael No—just to give you some idea of what the proposed book will be about. It will be occupied with what Focillon called *la ligne des hauteurs* and,[5] to some extent, it will be a reintroduction of Wolflinnian strategies.[6] But I can't see either the late Peter Murray, or Jim Ackerman, or my former student Howard Burns, any of them being remotely concerned with bringing together Sala di Constantino and Cappella Medici, two works so very close together in time.[7]

    Colin

Which is all to say what we both know that carefully presented visuals may serve to propound very simple but very important questions.

---

1 The book was published posthumously as Rowe, Colin and Leon Satkowski, *Italian Architecture of the 16th Century*, New York: Princeton Architectural Press, 2002.

2 Heydenreich, Ludwig and Wolfgang Lotz, *Architecture in Italy: 1400–1600*, Baltimore: Pelican Books, 1974.

3 Frederick Hart (1914–1991), American Professor of the History of Art at the University of Virginia, historian of Italian Renaissance art and Michelangelo.

4 Sydney Freedberg (1914–1997), professor of Fine Arts at Harvard from 1953 to 1984, historian of Italian Renaissance art.

5 Henri Focillon (1881–1943), French historian of medieval art; *la ligne des hauteurs*, French: the high line.

6 Heinrich Wölfflin (1864–1945), Swiss art historian who developed classifying principles to aid in the formal analysis of works of art.

7 In his one-page, handwritten reply to Rowe from London dated 26 September 1995 regarding Mantua, Gombrich* wrote, "I don't think you remember correctly: I never had an old engraving of the duomo, only a postcard after [a long 14"] illustration showing the system of the 5 naves." Regarding the Sala di Constantino, Gombrich noted, "I don't think one should doubt that Raphael was planning it at the time of his death [...] and I think it is a nasty habit of art historians, always to think that one shows oneself superior by doubting the veracity of contemporaries. Moreover Philip Pouncey and John Gere [...] attribute some drawings for the battle of Constantine to Raphael, and I tend to trust their connoisseurship. How far he had got in planning the whole, we can of course never know, but he was a fierce worker!" In conclusion, Gombrich congratulates Rowe, stating, "The project of your book sounds exciting. Do you know the old little vol. by Paul Frankl 'ENTWICKLUNGSPHASEN DER NEUEREN BAUKUNST'? I found it useful."

---

*To **David Rowe**, Headington, Oxford*   *19 September 1995* **239**

Apt. 814, 3133 Connecticut Ave., Washington D.C.

David:

    I thought that you might be diverted by the enclosed.[1] It seems that dearest Sandy is about to enjoy an apotheosis.[2] But don't you perceive the picture which is about to emerge? A long neglect and persecution, no other work in the office for almost twenty years, a confounding of critics, and the triumph: not only Butterfield and Street but also large scale Aalto and joys of gradualist democracy[3]—revived Scandinavia—versus the horrors of a *dirigiste* and French and simplistic you know what![4]

But the poor victim—"Mr. Wilson* and another renowned architect, Sir Leslie Martin";[5]* and just think about it: Leslie going to spend W.W.II at Tring in a cottage provided by Victor Rothschild,[6] Leslie remaining at Tring after 1945, Sandy arriving at the L.C.C.[7] Sandy deciding that it might be a good idea to move to Tring too, and the inspiring little conversations to and from Baker Street. And then Leslie's, very gentle, megalomania:[8] Whitehall to be demolished[9]—or mostly so—and, with the street gone (no more views of Westminster from Trafalgar Square) a new era of rational bliss—a web of identical little brick courtyards on the model of Caius College, Cambridge![10]

But all of this, you know, was published; and, then, this very QUIET ambition was allowed to extend itself. And it came to settle in Bloomsbury. Leaving St. Martin's Lane, apparently, as a piece of townscape, imagining Brunswick Square as a pendent to the all brick Whitehall, the great theatre of operation now became a piazza in front of the B.M. with St. George's Bloomsbury to serve as a version of the campanile of San Marco.[11]

So this was the *entree* of both Patrick and Sandy![12] And such was Leslie's partiality for Sandy that the Library job wasn't enough.[13] Sandy <u>must</u> have another huge job in Liverpool—nothing more than a <u>very</u> large office building to the rear of St. George's Hall and over the entrance to the Mersey Tunnel![14]

Altogether a remarkable piece of patronage and, particularly so, considering Sandy's credentials—work for the L.C.C. on Benton Road (with Alan Colquhoun* and others) and his own house at Cambridge.

Strange that there was never any talk about a competition! One of the scandals of the late Welfare State? But why go on? However diminished they might be, Sandy's fees are still going to be very, very good; and this is not to mention the promotion of the St. Pancras Library to the detriment of the Bibliotheque Nationale. "Oh yes sir, you'll always find we do things better here sir...."

So <u>great</u> fun for everybody. But, in spite of Alvar Aalto, there was always the Foundling Hospital site, secluded, only cleared in the 1930's, and <u>not</u> sacred space of London. However, may be too monumental—and surely better by far to build a large hamburger joint in the sluttishness of the Euston Road than to provide symmetry between Brunswick and Mecklenburg Squares....[15]

And don't you think so?

Love,

    Colin

---

1   The enclosure is lost. Presumably it was a newspaper clipping concerning St John Wilson.*
2   Colin (Sandy) St John Wilson* (1922–2007), English architect with whom Rowe taught at Cambridge in the late 1950s and early 1960s. See Rowe's letter to Wilson dated 12 April 1958 (p 118 in this volume).
3   British architects William Butterfield (1814–1900) and George Edmund Street (1824–1881), and Finnish architect Alvar Aalto (1898–1976) influenced the work of Wilson,* whose principal work, The British Library, Rowe describes here as "large-scale Aalto".
4   *dirigiste,* French: one who revels in directing.
5   Sir Leslie Martin* (1908–1999), British architect and educator who became head of the Architecture School at Cambridge University in 1956.

6   Tring: a small market town in Hertfordshire, England, and the hometown of the fourth Baron Victor Rothschild (1910–1990), member of the famous banking dynasty.

7   London County Council.

8   In the early 1960s, Leslie Martin⋆ was commissioned by the British government to redevelop the area between St James' Park and the Thames Embankment in London. Martin's plans called for the destruction of many existing buildings. The plans were met by opposition and never executed.

9   Whitehall Palace (1619–1622), London masterpiece of the English Renaissance architect Inigo Jones⋆ (1573–1652).

10 The brick Harvey Court of Caius College, designed by Martin⋆ and Wilson⋆ in 1961.

11 "B.M.": British Museum.

12 *entrée*, French: introduction. Patrick Hodgkinson (b 1930) and Colin (Sandy) St John Wilson.⋆

13 Wilson⋆ designed the new British Library (1962–1990), the largest public building built in the United Kingdom in the twentieth century. Initially it was intended to be located opposite the British Museum, on a seven-acre site that required demolition of an essential part of Bloomsbury. After years of controversy, this decision was overturned and the library was built next to St. Pancras station on a site at Euston Road.

14 Liverpool Civic and Social Centre, proposed in 1965–1969 and in 1970–1973, the building was never finished.

15 Although the Foundling Hospital site *was* proposed, to Rowe's dismay the new British Library was built on Euston Road.

*To **John O'Brien**, Tennessee*   *25 & 28 October 1995*   **240**

Apt. 814, 3133 Connecticut Ave., Washington D.C.

Dearest John:

What a terrible, terrible mess and very much, very much, I <u>do</u> feel for you. And I know that I can't say just as easily as that: "Now do get better....."[1]

So, dearest John, obviously myself was very, very lucky. The fracture (although it was multiple) was very low in the spine; and the paraplegia (which was not complete because I could still feel my toes) began to go away after about five weeks.[2] And, since I was a prize exhibit, I also had a royal visit—though not specifically for <u>me</u>. The Duchess of Gloucester, face completely enamelled, asked me a sequence of not very intelligent questions which were intended to be sympathetic, and they culminated in: "Are you able to get about in bed?" And it reduced me to persiflage: "Oh mam, I'm getting so incredibly mobile you really would be surprised."

But, if it wasn't <u>quite</u> true, it was all that I <u>could</u> say; and, after that, of course she really had to move on and to leave me to the inquiries of the Duke who was also very heavily made up; and, in a very Hanoverian voice (one should say Hanovewian), he just contrived to utter: "Hef you been abwoard?" And this hospital meeting with The Illustrious House of Hanover with all of its intimations of the Protestant Succession was my only exposure to the Royal Animal until, years later, I met the *roi de Suede*,[3] the archeologist Gustav between Viterbo and La Quercia.[4]

So I have felt the effects of that little spinal disruption from that date to this; and so I know that one never really recovers. But, at least, neither you nor I are dead as, not so very long ago, we both would have been; and, whatever may be said to you, I am privately convinced that <u>you—with all your natural ebullience</u>—is going to make a significant recovery. So don't, don't surrender to the sin of despair. But it's tough, very tough, and I know it—but, all the same, I am reminded of a friend of mine whom I last saw in the Charing Cross Hospital when he was paralysed from the neck downwards. He had gone to Africa, been bitten by a bug, and <u>this</u> was the result, and it is one reason why I avoid Africa. But Harry Robinson did <u>not</u> believe that this was forever to be, and the paralysis slowly receded; and now he is living on Gozo, the next island to Malta, with a black servant to push the wheelchair. And this is a case of personal FAITH—though <u>not</u> of a religious order. So, you poor old thing, though I might begin to sound like a Christian Scientist, do try to remain convinced and do try to remain suffused with HOPE....

Which might lead us to the consideration of saintliness, and I have just discovered the most wonderful new one. She is Anglo-Saxon, <u>obit</u> 700, and she was abbess of Ely, and you won't believe her name. She is SAINT SEXBURGA![5] And are you not surprised that either of us, nor Matt, nor Brian, have <u>ever</u> heard of her?[6] But far better, I think, than St. Nicholas of Trani and a pity that there ain't a St Hamburga.... Her feast day is July 6 and, by then, I am trusting that you will, with God's help, be much better.

Then I think that I am going to make a recording for you and it will surely be better than watching T.V. I have lately learned the dates and the family names of <u>all</u> the Popes since Alexander VI Borgia; and you can imagine what a pleasure this is. But just to have a kind of chronological grid in which to slot otherwise random info. And this should give you useful employment. For instance, 16th C Popes did not enjoy long reigns and Paul III Farnese, 1534–1549, is the longest, with Gregory XIII Boncompagni, 1572–85, as a close follow up. Then Paul V Borghese, 1605–21, and Innocent Xl Odescalchi, 1676–89, are the two longest 17th C reigns; but, after 1700 things begin to change and, in the 18th century, you get Clement XI Albani, 1700–21, Benedict XV Lambertini, 1740–58, and Pius VI Braschi, 1775–1799, a length of tenure that appears to be a complete novelty.

So follow this with Pius Vll Chiaramonti, 1800–23, Pius IX Mastai-Ferretti, 1846–78, and Leo Xlll Pecci, 1878–1903, and—if you like-add Ratti, '22–39 and Pacelli, '39–58, and it begins to appear that, around 1700, things really did change. So what was it that caused the Popes to live longer while their power declined—until at least Leo XIII. Was it the incipience of the Enlightenment? And I give you this for the purposes of speculation.... And I think that it's your sort of topic.

Dear John, Dante's *lasciate ogni speranza voi che entrate* doesn't apply to you and to your rehab center and I think I shall send you a recorded Berlitz Italian course.[7] So, meanwhile, *un abbraccio appassionato e ti saluto con entusiasmo*.[8]

Lotsa lurv,

Colin

Colin

P.S. There seem always to have been those Popes so excited by the prospect which confronts them (or so dilapidated) that they expire almost immediately after election; and such have been: Pius III Piccolomini, 1503, Marcellus II Cervini, a charming guy, 1555, Urban VII Castagna, 1590, Gregory XIV Sfondrati, 1590–91, Innocent XI Facchinetti, 1591, Pius VII Castiglione, 1829–30, and, more recently, Papa Luciani, 1978.

But now I am showing off.

Colin

John:

I have just woke up after a most astonishing visual dream and I really do feel that I have seen a new world—and you were in it too!

You know that I have never been <u>inside</u> Blenheim P.[9] And I have never thought that I had missed much. But such was the impact of the dream that, until a few minutes, such was the strength of the illusion, that I was still wondering just <u>why</u> the photographers, the historians and the guidebooks had been so <u>very</u> blind or so <u>very</u> neglectful, or prejudiced! You see I entered <u>the</u> most wonderful world, sometimes outside, sometimes inside, which was compounded of Vanbrugh <u>and</u> Michelangelo <u>plus</u> contributions from Alberti and Piero della Francesca.

So it seemed to happen like this: my brother decided that, finally, I <u>should</u> see the inside of Blenheim—no more long views from across the lake.[10] So he drove off with Simon and me and, while he was parking the car, Simon and I forged ahead. And, then, I was all by myself and went through a quite conspicuous archway to the right. And that's when the shock came. I left the limestone behind and came into a courtyard which, mostly, seemed to be of marble—big, red marble Corinthian columns of the scale of Vanbrugh against a background of flat, marble surfaces, mostly white, and—as I now see them—somehow connected with the Alberti *tempietto* for Giovanni Rucellai—or, anyway, sort of *quattrocento* and a bit like one of those Urbino pictures. But it was at several levels and there were also bands of blackish-greenish marble. But more than this! All this was tied together by a minor architecture of white Carrara which was obviously—though not directly—connected with the Medici Mausoleum—though there was <u>no</u> sculpture—only very miniature groups of little, little *putti* which had been much caressed by the human hand and occurred on the top of pedestals at the end of balustrades.[11]

So I ran out to grab Simon who was charging ahead to get to the front entrance; and then we went on and, underneath—it must have been one of the terraces—there was a totally fabulous chapel, not tall and not big, where <u>you</u> were discovered in an apse—you went up white steps at the sides in order to get into it—which was obviously the seating of the D. and the Duchess of Marlborough—and there were four seats, two sort of thrones and two minor ones.[12]

So I ran out to grab David and I had to yell at him because he had almost reached the front door; and it was after that that I woke.

But absolutely vivid and, so far as I can construe it, not at all Freudian. And I thought that you might like to know.

Also, I think that you might like to know about the Royal Gold Medal.[13] But, dear John, it is really kinda frightful. There is a badly executed profile of the Q. of E. on the one side and some words on the other; and it doesn't look so much like gold as it looks like chocolate money wrapped up in gold foil, with H.B.M. absolutely lacking in contour and age, with traces of precision none, and—all in all—*molto Inglese* and not at all like the Revelation which I have just been vouchsafed.[14]

So Meditate upon All This because—if Auguries occur nowadays—then I think that it <u>must</u> be one.

Colin

---

1 A recent accident had left John O'Brien* paralyzed. O'Brien, a former PhD student at Cornell, lived with Rowe at 19 Renwick Place in Ithaca in 1991 and 1992.

2   Here Rowe is recounting injuries he himself sustained in a practice parachute jump in Britain in 1943. See Rowe's letter to Ursula Mercer★ dated 20 August 1943 (p 29 in this volume).

3   *roi de Suède*, French: king of Sweden.

4   In a letter dated 24 September 1969 to Pat Miller★ in London, Rowe wrote from the American Academy in Rome, "In Viterbo—a brief rencontre with the King of Sweden all mixed up with a hysterical female from N.Y.C.—*la fanciulla del West* or *la passa del Central Park*. Won't go on about the K. of S. except that he was a nice old thing and wasn't able to get any excavating done because it rained all the time [...]"

5   St Sexburga of Ely (d 699).

6   Brian Kelly.★

7   *lasciate ogni speranza, voi ch'entrate*, Italian: All hope abandon, ye who enter in. From Dante's *Divina Comedia*, Inferno, Canto III.

8   *Un abbraccio appassionato e ti saluto con entusiasmo*, Italian: a passionate embrace and enthusiastic greeting.

9   "Blenheim P.": Blenheim Palace (1705–24), Woodstock, Oxfordshire, England. An English Baroque palace of limestone designed by Sir John Vanbrugh, Blenheim was the home of the Churchill family for three hundred years.

10 Colin's brother, David Rowe,★ lived in Oxford very near Blenheim Palace.

11 *putti*, Italian: plural of *putto*, representations of naked children, often cupids or cherubs, in Renaissance art.

12 "the D.": the Duke.

13 Rowe was awarded the RIBA Royal Gold Medal on 20 June 1995.

14 *molto Inglese*, Italian: very English.

241   To *Alex Caragonne*, Ithaca, N.Y.   *1 November 1995*

Apt. 814, 3133 Connecticut Ave., Washington D.C.

Alex:

Just a few names you should think about:[1]

Gladys Margarita Diaz.★ Miami Cuban, ex-Cornell, a bit of a bomb and I used to call her—to her mother's displeasure—*La Pasionaria*. She is this year teaching somewhere in C.U. but not in Sibley.[2] Make contact with her and come to your own opinion.

Miriam Gusevich.★ Cuban Jewish, ex-Cornell, very intelligent and I believe to be found in Wisconsin/Minnesota.

Martha Pollak. Almost from Dracula country, Carpathian Jewish, ex-Cornell, husband French and they have an apartment in no less than the Rue de Varennes! To be found, I think, at Chicago Circle and has written a book (I think v.g.) on 17th and 18th century Turino.[3] I would grab her.

Leon Satkowski.★ v.v. tall: Martin Dominguez used to call him "that interminable person". Obviously of some sort of Polish origin and, not so obviously, Jewish. After Cornell did graduate work in the hist. of arch. at Harvard; taught at Syracuse; at present to be found at the U. of Minnesota. Has written a book on Giorgio Vasari and he and I are to collaborate on *Bramante to Scamozzi*.[4] I think that you must have him to speak. Werner S[5] holds in high regard.

Hector Arce. Old San Juan, P.R. (papa went to Harvard); a charmboat much regarded by Fred and Susie; an El Greco physique—he once sent me a Christmas card with the words "warmest tropical greetings from your mildly attenuated friend". Jerry would think a v. good idea.[6]

Esteban Sennyey.★ From Caracas, name is Hungarian, papa is an Hungarian *graf* serving as a pilot in VIASA, mother is Bavarian and they took him all the way to

Budapest to be confirmed, in the U.S. Embassy by Cardinal Mindszenty!!![8] Hyper exuberant, *naturaliter Americana*. Ex-Cornell U.D., taught Syracuse, was two years in Firenze, at present to be found in San Juan, P.R. Absolutely a must: the name elicits instant enthusiasm from Fred, Jerry, Michael, Matt Bell,* etc.[9] In Dublin terms 'a broth of a boy'.

Jorge Rigau. San Juan, P.R., Cornell grad and undergrad, much more reserved than Stefano, was a bit of a tough guy whom myself used to find a little intimidating. *La Pasionaria* tells me that he is now an authority on the architecture of the Caribbean. You and he would probably relate. I think between a maybe and a must but ask Jerry because I think that they were kind of *lié*.[10]

Paolo Berdini.* Roman; U. of P.,[11] Cornell, Columbia, a godson of Pope Pacelli, 1939–58!; and, like the Pacelli's, his family outfit has been handling legal affairs for the Holy See since about 1860. *Yerse, yerse, yerse;*[12] a savant, has translated me into Italian, is erudite about Mies van der Rohe,* is `going to teach at Stanford—or has already gone. Tom Schumacher* [speculates] a one-time involvement in terrorism; but this I just do not believe. Came from Rome for the R.G.M. affair in June in London. Think that you have to grab.

As Esteban would say *un abbraccio fervente*,

   Colin

P.S. The possibility of a conspicuous Jewish and Latino component kinda calms me down.

   Colin

P.P.S. Inadvertently, and before beginning *Bramante to Scamozzi*, I find that I have almost made yet another book! As they say, it will be a slim volume—three essays; and I hope that it will be my *envoi* to mod. arch., God being willing.[13] But will tell you about it later.

   Colin

---

1 A reply to Caragonne's* request for suggestions for speakers for the Rowe *Festspiele* to be held at Cornell the "last Friday, Saturday and Sunday morning in April" 1996. See Rowe's letter to David Rowe* dated 15 November 1995 (p 455 in this volume).
2 "C.U.": Cornell University. The College of Architecture, Art and Planning was housed in Sibley Hall where Caragonne* was teaching at the time.
3 Pollak, Martha, *Turin 1564–1680: Urban Design, Military Culture, and the Creation of the Absolutist Capital*, Chicago: The University of Chicago Press, 1991.
4 Satkowski, Leon and Ralph Lieberman, *Giorgio Vasari, Architect and Courtier*, Princeton: Princeton University Press, 1994.
5 "Werner S": Werner Seligmann.*
6 Jerry A Wells.*
7 *graf*, German: historical title of German nobility, the British equivalent of count or earl.
8 VIASA: Venezolana Internacional de Aviación Sociedad Anónima, referred to in English as the JSC Venezuelan International Airways.
9 Fred Koetter,* Jerry A Wells,* Michael Dennis,* Matthew Bell.*
10 *lié*, French: attached, connected. (This word is graphically obscured in the original letter.)
11 "U. of P.": University of Pennsylvania.
12 *yerse, yerse, yerse*, Turkish: eats, eats, eats.
13 *envoi*, French: explanatory concluding remarks; farewell. Rowe was planning a book tentatively titled *Footprints and Footnotes*. Initially conceived as "slim," it grew in size. See Rowe's letter to George Baird* dated 4 January 1996 (p 459 in this volume).

3133 Connecticut Avenue, Apt. 814, Washington, D.C.

Dearest Judy:

I hate anniversaries and I positively loathe anniversary presents and I have always found the celebration of anniversaries something just a bit morbid. There are those seventeenth century lines—are they Herrick or are they Marvell?—which begin something like this:

> At my back I hear
> Time's winged chariot ever drawing near

and which end:

> The grave's a fine and private place
> But none, I think, do there embrace[1]

So no pleasure in anniversaries—which interest you so passionately. So I am here warning you about a casual present which you are about to receive. It comes from Tiffany's and it's going to consist of <u>four</u> candlesticks like those <u>two</u> which are illustrated here.[2] So a mail order fantasy on my part. But I thought that you might like them because I think that they make a sort of seventeenth century impression and I hope that they are as good as they seem to look. And also because <u>two</u> are <u>no</u> good for a table. They establish neither a rhythm nor a space—and, hence, are only good for mantelpieces and marble topped commodes. So you can put four of them on a little table or, like Astra, you can play with them in a slightly obsessed way...

Sorry that I was not able to grab your interest in The Procession of the Holy Ghost; but, if the Pigeon is just more than you can cope with (like the possibility of nuns at Varallo?), then will you give me your opinion about angels. And just when, in the course of evolution did these monstrous creatures first put in an appearance? At Sodom Lot and his wife were warned by an angel to get the hell out of it quick; but, apparently, in the Old T. Jewish angels just didn't romp flapping their wings.[3] Instead, they just looked like everybody else and you had to take their hybrid predicament... well, with no feathers, I just don't understand <u>how</u> you were to know about it.... And then, although the ancient Greeks did have gods with wings, these were just little bitty attachments to the feet, decorative additions which couldn't have assisted them in getting around quick.... So, in the New T. there is the Angel of the Annunciation which brings the bad news to the B.V.M.[4] But <u>did</u> this guy have wings? Or was he-she-it just another Jewish guy who had walked in off the street. [...]

You've got to admit that the wings did contribute plausibility to the credentials—as also did the Pigeon which came along too. And <u>how</u> difficult to have a bird in the room—this apart from the Freudian connotations of the word *uccello!*[5]

I remember that Kaya has always found this whole business to be *molto difficile*; and it certainly is a big iconographical problem.[6] But, for those like me who can't stand birds—like me, it really would be nice to know just how these semi-birds came about and, also, why their heredity has received so little attention.

Suspect, like so much else, a late Byzantine composite of the Greek and the Hebraic given definitive form by the fantasies of the Italian *machismo*. But, perhaps, much more interesting than the Procession of the Pigeon....

Anyway, when you put candles into these jobs from Tiffany's, perhaps <u>all</u> will be illuminated....

Darling Judy, please do try and see if Revelation descends. 'Cos don't candles excite the Almighty quite a lot?

Lots lurv,

>   *Colin*
>   *XXXXXX*

P.S. Have just discovered that your Don Fulco Santo Stefano della Cerda, Duca della Verdura[7] (my next door neighbour in E. 82 Street, '67–69) was a friend of Nancy Mitford because I've been reading her letters and there he is.[8] So she quotes him in repeating that old New York joke about St. P.: "Gotta tell you folks something about the Boss. First of all she's a woman. And, then she's black...".[9]

So this was news to Mitford and it contributed to the charm of "darling Fulco"; but, all the same, she is rather delightful about Heaven, where residence is so interminable that it's best to make sure, once you have arrived, that you get into the 'right' set. This because there are likely to be a lot of people there whom you won't want to know....

From footnotes to Mitford I discovered that Don Fulco, S.S. della C., D. della V., Cavaliere di Malta, etc, etc. published an autobiography called *A Sicilian Childhood*.[10] This was in 1976 and, probably, it's still available.

>   *C*
>   *X X X*

P.P.S. The D. della V., so I also discover, once gave a dinner party in Paris for the D. and Dess. of Windsor and ex-king Umberto of Italy.[11] And Umberto di Savoia just happened—to the general misery and impatience—to arrive more than an hour late. So, according to Mitford, October 1950, what followed was scarcely an absolute joy; and it all began with the female Windsor saying to the ex-K. of I.: "My King went of his own accord but you were kicked out and I don't think you ought to make us wait for you."

This was on October 19 and what does one say? Poor Fulco, unfortunate Umberto, [...]? Or so much for The Bitch from Baltimore? Or does one say, as they said in that restaurant in the Prati: *Viva Pio Nono, viva Pio Nono e morte la Casa di Savoia*?[12]

My dearest [...] A big *abbraccio*,

>   *Colin*
>   *XXXXX*

But, after age seven, anniversaries surely do belong to the danse macabre and I only remember Simon's because it's St Valentine's Day.[13]

---

1   Marvell, Andrew, "To his Coy Mistress," c 1650.
2   The clipping is lost. The four candlesticks were given in honor of Judith DiMaio's* birthday.
3   "Old T.": Old Testament.
4   "B.V.M.": Blessed Virgin Mary.
5   *uccello*, Italian: bird; Sigmund Freud's *The Interpretations of Dreams* of 1899 associates birds with sex.
6   Kaya Arikoglu, a graduate student of Rowe's; *molto difficile*, Italian: very difficult.

7   Fulco Santo Stefano della Cerda, Duca della Verdura (1898–1978), Italian jewelry designer.
8   Nancy Mitford (1904–1973), English novelist and biographer. Presumably, the book Rowe was reading was Charlotte Mosley ed, *Love from Nancy: The Letters of Nancy Mitford*, London: Hodder & Stoughton, 1993.
9   "St. P.": St. Peter.
10 Republished as di Verdura, Fulco, *The Happy Summer Days: A Sicilian Childhood*, London: Phoenix, 2000.
11 "D. and Dess.": Duke and Duchess.
12 *Viva Pio Nono, viva Pio Nono e morte la Casa di Savoia*, Italian: Long live Puis IX, Long live Pius IX and death to the House of Savoy.
13 *danse macabre*, French: dance of death; Simon Rowe,* born 14 February 1970.

243   To **David Rowe**, Headington, Oxford   *10 November 1995*

3133 Connecticut Avenue, Apt. 814, Washington, D.C.

Dearest David:

A clipping from *The New York Times* today.[1]

So Harold Acton's bequest to N.Y.U.—to the department of art history—seems to exceed all private gifts to American universities since 1967; and I assume this means to exceed all private gifts which have ever been made!

And to think that N.Y.U. was only a second choice—after he was turned down by Christ Church![2] But, as an instance of academic silliness, this is beyond imagination! And what was Christ Church thinking about? That La Pietra would be too much of a problem to run?[3] That the endowment was insufficiently large! That it couldn't cope with the legalities? But, really, it was about the most inconsiderate negative since the British govt. turned down the offer of Corsica in 1768 when the Genoese Banco di San Giorgio tried, first of all, to sell it in London.

I was only once at La Pietra and this was in the time of Harold's papa. Arthur Brown, with his eclectic practice in San Francisco—Crockers and what not—did business with Arthur Acton years back when he also supplied objects for McKim, Mead and White *et al* (it was Arthur Brown who told me all this); and most of the profits of these dealings were ploughed into Florence real estate.[4] But the big money must have come from Chicago and mid-West railroads which was Mrs. A's contribution and it must have been this which paid for the La Pietra property c. 1900. But, about the collections and magnificent furniture, B. Berenson was persistently contemptuous.[5] And could this have affected Christ Church?

Or could they have been in the grip of some residual socialist fantasy? But I can scarcely think so.... But their terrible ignorance is very devastating to think about; and I am sure that, in the end, it is just a case of the a-visuality of Oxford.

However get three Oxford paperbacks—*Popes*, *Saints* and *A History of Heresy*. Though a-visual they are very entertaining to read. Best, best love and do tell James about this.[6]

   Colin

P.S. This clipping was attached to an article about Gordon Wu of Hong Kong who has just given $100,000,000 (one hundred million) to the Princeton engineering school. And, coming from H.K., this cannot be a matter of tax breaks.

But why is it that English institutions really make no effort to solicit gifts? Personally I think because they are too accustomed to govt support.

Colin

———————

For instance Cornell raised Fifty M. from alumni quite recently. But the Brit G. doesn't encourage that sort of thing.[7] Or does it? But v. short sighted? And, also for instance, I am constantly pestered by Yale but have never heard a word from Liverpool; and, while Yale keeps you supplied with lists of all graduates since the 1920's, L'pool makes no attempt....[8]

Colin

———————

1 The clipping shows a chart titled "A Closer Look. Helping Higher Education. Major private gifts to colleges since 1967, in millions of dollars". It lists donors and their donations to the American universities: Lousiana State University, University of Pennsylvania, University of Southern California, Emory, Rowan College of New Jersey, and Regent University Virginia Beach. It highlights a $100 million gift from Gordon Wu to Princeton (see Rowe's PS) and ends by noting—and this Rowe has circled—Sir Harold Acton's (1904–1994) bequest to New York University valued at between $125 million and $500 million.
2 Christ Church College, Oxford University.
3 "La Pietra" was the name of Harold Acton's villa and 57-acre estate in Florence bequeathed to New York University in 1994. According to the clipping noted above, the bequest included the house's renowned furniture and art collection as well as $25 million in cash.
4 Arthur Brown (1874–1957), American architect of San Francisco's Opera House, City Hall, Ferry Building, and Coit Tower.
5 "B. Berenson": Bernard Berenson (1865–1959), pre-eminent American art historian specializing in the Renaissance.
6 James Rowe* was a graduate of Oxford University.
7 "Brit G.": British Government.
8 A graduate of Liverpool's program in architecture, Rowe studied at Yale in the 1951–1952 academic year, but took no degree.

---

*To **David Rowe**, Headington, Oxford*   *15 November 1995*   **244**

3133 Connecticut Avenue, Apt. 814, Washington, D.C.

Dearest David:

The Headington place? Waldencot?[1] I don't know what you should call it; but I would call it Walden Cottage and accept the connotations of Concord, Emerson and Thoreau. These might even be a talking point. Or would Walden Place be too pretentious? And do you by now have an accurate measured plan?

I had Alex Caragonne* here for the weekend. For this semester he is operating as a visiting critic at Cornell U. and he told me dreadful stories about the present condition of the S. of A.[2] For instance, the fees at present are $30,000 p.a. (this excludes cost of living), and one semester in Rome is an extra: $25,000 for a few weeks of living not too far from Palazzo Cenci (?) in conditions of superlative squalor!

And the results of all this parental expenditure? A recent thesis—for graduation consisted of this: the principal gallery of Sibley was hung with long strips of paper and the windows were open so that they were able to blow in the wind![3] And that was it, with a jury sitting around to make affable commentary upon this demonstration!

But <u>nothing</u>, Alex finds, is taught. Because to teach <u>anything</u> would be a violation of the student's creativity....

However this is not the worst which Alex came down here to talk about and the worst is <u>this</u>: prompted by Lee Hodgden⋆ and retiring Dean Bill McMinn⋆ there is to be an Occasion, the last Friday, Saturday, Sunday morning, in April there is to be an Occasion—to celebrate Me! And there appears to be no way that I can escape it. It is to be a Recognition—of R.G.M., general activity, recent publications, etc.

Most of it is to take place simultaneously in two, separate, auditoria. It is to result in a *Festschrift*; and innumerable persons are to utter, to introduce the utterers, to comprise symposia—and <u>you</u> can grab it.

So principle *eulogia* will be delivered by (or so I am told); Henry Millon⋆—ex Wittkower⋆ student, curator of architecture at the Nat. Gall.; Kurt Forster⋆—E.T.H. Zurich and Getty Foundation; and Geo. Baird⋆—Toronto and Harvard U. Then there will be sessions chaired by Fred Koetter⋆ and Michael Dennis⋆ and Werner Seligmann,⋆ and delivery of papers and introductions of delivery of papers, and Peter Eisenman⋆ will reminisce, and no doubt the whole extravaganza is going to cost C.U. a bomb— what with travel and hotels and what not. And I <u>do</u> wish that they <u>would give me the money instead</u>.

But I expect a mess—with moments of light relief. For instance, Esteban Sennyey,⋆ very wild and woolly, will introduce what I have to say (this is at the very end and if I am <u>not</u> dead); Gladys Margarita, Miami-Cuba and <u>very</u> vivacious will introduce Eisenman⋆ (whom she will embarrass quite a bit); Judy will do <u>some</u> sort of intro at the very beginning (but dreading it); Michael Dennis will talk about the differences between French and English squares (don't know what he can say); Paolo Berdini⋆ will talk probably about M. v. d. R. in Berlin;[4] Leon Satkowski,⋆ interminably tall and correspondingly slow, will say something about Tuscan *maniera* (Vasari, Buontalenti, the Grand Duke Francesco, etc);[5] Johanna Doherty, Dorothy's *bete noire*,[6] will address herself to late eighteenth century French public gardens, with their Napoleonic *sequelae* in Italy;[7] Steve Peterson⋆ will do an analysis of *Roma Interrotta* and U.D. strategies—will be <u>good</u>.[8] But this is just a few of what I am going to be obliged to sit thru; and, for the benefit of expected overflow in the other auditorium (I doubt it), then there is the threat of closed circuit T.V.!!!!

Apotheositic? Or *pour encourager les autres*?[9] I must confess that I don't know; but, since more than half of the fac up there see me as the abomination of desolation, as a retarded monster, I think that it must be a <u>demonstration</u> on the part of the remainder. Or is it a case of "oh democracy what crimes are committed in thy name"?

Anyway, just thought I'd tell ya.

    Colin

P.S. In these parts <u>Thoreau</u> is pronounced as in <u>there</u> but I pronounce it in the French way. So Tom Schumacher⋆ took me up about this and I pointed out that <u>Thomas</u> is also pronounced in the French way and isn't that strange when <u>Tom</u> is diminutive <u>Tomaso</u>—as Tomaso d'Aquino.

---

1 David Rowe⋆ had recently purchased a house in Headington. Here Rowe speculates on what this house might be called.

2 "S. of A.": School of Architecture.

3 Sibley Hall, which housed Cornell's College of Architecture, Art and Planning.

4 "M. v. d. R.": Mies van der Rohe.*

5 Rowe himself had suggested Sennyey,* Margarita, Berdini,* and Satkowski* as possible speakers to the *Festspiele* organizer, Alexander Caragonne.* See Rowe's letter to Caragonne dated 1 November 1995 (p 450 in this volume).

6 *bête noire*, French: a disliked person or thing.

7 *sequelae*, Latin: followings, consequences.

8 *Roma Interrotta*, an urban design competition in 1978 staged in Rome in which 12 competitors were asked to redesign one section of Rome as described on Giambattista Nolli's 1748 map of that city. Steven Peterson* was a key member of the Cornell/Rowe team. See Rowe, Colin, "Roma Interrotta", *As I Was Saying: Recollections and Miscellaneous Essays*, Alexander Caragonne ed, 3 vols, Cambridge, MA: MIT Press, 1996, vol 3, pp 127–153.

9 *pour encourager les autres*, French: in order to encourage others.

To **Mark Girouard**, London   *12 December 1995*   **245**

3133 Connecticut Avenue, Apt. 814, Washington, D.C.

Dear Mark:

I agree with you that the use of Esq is completely appalling.[1] Matthew Arnold deplored it and Nancy Mitford said NO; and, therefore, judge my horror when the Midland Bank printed my cheques C.F. Rowe, Esq! Like printing Esq on a visiting card; but I couldn't get them to understand! Anyway, I never use it except with people who are dreadfully square like, sometimes, my brother.

But I will expect you late February or early March and I hope that you will come and stay here. The apt is quite good, two b.r.'s and two baths, so no confusions and probs. Also Lyndon Baines Johnson lived in this house—for what that is worth; and, I am told—but strange, strange, the Archduke Otto![2]

When you are here you should think about visiting the British Embassy and you should write ahead to fix this. It's worth a look. So, with ref to J., I suppose that you will visit Rice, Cornell and Harvard.[3] Or will you also visit sites of the unbuilt?

I am so sorry that Nina Quintus van Zuylen Michaelis is all alone except for all those cows.[4] Dominic is shacked up with some woman at Aix-en-P.—at the Jas de Bouffrant no less![5]

But, apropos of Nina, did you ever read Geoffrey Scott's *Portrait of Zelide*?[6] It's all about Belle van Zuylen whom Boswell wanted to marry and who ended up in Neuchatel. But what a ravishing creature Nina still continues to be.

Un abbraccio,

   Colin

1 Esq: Esquire. On the "use of Esq.," see Rowe's letter to James Rowe* dated 23 September 1996 and his letter to David Rowe* dated 22 May 1997 (pp 500 and 514 in this volume).

2 Lyndon Baines Johnson (1908–1973), vice president of the US from 1961–1963; President from 1963–1968; and Archduke Otto of Austria, Otto Habsburg (1912–2011).

3 "J.": James Stirling* (1926–1992). At the time, Stirling's US buildings were at Rice, Cornell and Harvard Universities; Girouard* planned to visit Rowe in Washington, DC, while conducting research for a book that would become *Big Jim: The Life and Work of James Stirling*, London: Chatto Windus, 1998. Regarding Girouard's visit, see Rowe's letter to Dorothy Rowe* dated 4 March 1996 (p 464 in this volume).

4 Nina Michaelis had been married to Dominic Michaelis,* a former student of Rowe's at Cornell. Rowe had been a friend to the couple since 1964.

5 Dominic Michaelis;* Aix-en-Provence, France; Jas de Bouffant was the country home

of Louis-Auguste Cézanne from 1859 until his death. His celebrated son, Paul Cézanne (1839–1906), painted his first works on the walls of house and continued to live in the house until 1899.

6   Geoffrey Scott, *Portrait of Zelide*, 1925.

246   *To **David Rowe**, Headington, Oxford*   *21 December 1995*

3133 Connecticut Avenue, Apt. 814, Washington, D.C.

Dearest David:

The merest note.

∗   I enclose a copy of an article from *The New Yorker* on cookbooks.[1] I hope that you find it incredibly amusing and that you will send a xerox to James and Rosie.

∗   I have made up a package of the recent book to send to Dorothy and will also send her a letter to go with it.[2]

∗   Mark Girouard∗ has wished himself here for a brief visit in February. So no sweat. He is equipped with a grant from the Graham Foundation to visit Jim's buildings at Rice, Harvard and Cornell.[3] He also says that he has completed visits to 250 *chateaux* in France. So God help us....

∗   M.G. and Jim lead to Mary S. and here I want you to do something.[4] I believe that she may be wrapping up all the objects at Belsize Avenue in some sort of legal conveyance and I <u>don't</u> want this to include <u>my</u> alabaster model of the duomo in Florence which Dorothy <u>loaned</u> to Jim.[5] So, obviously, it has become very valuable and, in any case, I do want to have it <u>here</u>.

Now Jim understood that it was <u>not</u> a gift, that I <u>wouldn't</u> make such a gift—to him, that it was <u>not</u> in Dorothy's capacity to dispose of it; and he regularly asked when I was going to take it away. But <u>Mary</u>......???

Anyway I will write to Mary very shortly—big explanation nicely sugar coated— and, then, I would like <u>you</u> to initiate removal.

Get the idea? It's got a lot of *cachet*.[7]

Colin

P.S.   *December 27*

Letters seem to become a little late in leaving this house—in this case to my surprise.

So I have had Richard Role∗ staying here—and his name always makes me think of the Hermit of Hampole who missed out on what he should have become.[8] But he took his things away and also helped me to put a lot of books into a condition approaching order. Also he left me with an <u>enormous</u> Vasi engraving—view of S. Maria Maggiore from the Quattro Fontane, mountains in the background, about 30" x 56"—which he bought in Syracuse, N.Y. for $250.00![9] So I pretend not to like Vasi—Astra's sort of thing—but this piece <u>is</u> rather grand and is useful in the D.R.[10]

Since you are so much preoccupied with Coleridge these days shouldn't this lead to Carlyle? Never read him myself but, after Coleridge, is he not the greatest English language proponent of German *Geist*?

And the *Heilige Geist*, or the *Saint Esprit*, reminds me of what I was told the other day.[11] Very interesting <u>and</u> judicious; but, when Wojtyla celebrated mass the other day with the Orthodox Patriarch, with reference to the H.G. he left out the *filioque* which the Greeks have never accepted.... Am amused.[12]

Colin

1 Lane, Anthony, "Look Back in Hunger: Cookbooks Old and New and the Perils of the Kitchen", *The New Yorker*, 18 December 1995, p 50. Across the top of this photocopy, Rowe printed: "THIS IS A LONG ARTICLE. I'VE ONLY COPIED FIRST PAGE TO GIVE YOU A FLAVOR."
2 "The recent book": Rowe, Colin, *The Architecture of Good Intentions*, London: Academy Editions, 1994.
3 James Stirling;* On Girouard's* visit, see Rowe's letter to Mark Girouard dated 12 December 1995 and to Dorothy Rowe* dated 4 March 1996 (pp 457 and 464 in this volume).
4 Rowe acquired the alabaster model of the Duomo while teaching at the University of Cambridge in 1960. For its history, see his 22 October 1996 letter to Rosemary Rowe* (p 506 in this volume).
5 Mary Stirling, James Stirling's* widow.
6 Belsize Avenue was the London home of James and Mary Stirling.*
7 *cachet*, French: distinction, character.
8 Richard Rolle (1290–1349) with two l's—an English writer and hermit known as the Hermit of Hampole.
9 Giuseppe Vasi (1710–1782), architect who, between 1746 and 1761, published ten books of etchings showing the monuments of Rome.
10 "D.R.": dining room.
11 *Heilige Geist*, German and French, *Saint Esprit*: Holy Spirit.
12 Wojtyla: Pope John Paul II (1920–2005); H.G.: Holy Ghost; *filioque*, Latin: "and (with) the Son", a phrase found in the Western Christian churches' Nicene Creed but not in the Greek Nicene Creed.

To **George Baird**, *Cambridge, Massachusetts*   *4 January 1996*   **247**

3133 Connecticut Avenue, Apt. 814, Washington, D.C.

Dear George:

This is going to be a rather long letter but, first of all, I <u>should</u> say something about Paulo Berca.[1] He came here just before Christmas, remained only a few hours, and left—for Torino—to get a plane from Kennedy for Milano-Linate—very convenient at both <u>this</u> end and <u>that</u>!

So I found nothing that wasn't engaging and I don't ask you to imagine our conversation. Of course, we talked Vittone, Cavour, Casa di Cavois, quite a bit (one always does with <u>Piemontese</u>), and I was amused that he had worked for Ignazio Gardella who, along with Franco Albini used to be one of my heroes; then we didn't look at too many pics (he was, maybe, a little intimidated or, perhaps, he isn't very visual?); but I was left with a general impression which has caused me to invite him back again. He is not at all a bore and I want him to meet friends of mine—Tom Schumacher,* Matt Bell,* Brian Kelly*—who would create a general conversation which I know that he would find stimulating.

So I sent him away with a copy of my new three volume opus—book of bits and pieces; and <u>this</u> is for <u>you</u>—or, if you already have it, it's for <u>himself</u>.[2] But a nice guy who is without tedious, tendentious, intellectualistic arguments—or so I found.

And now about *The Space of Appearance*—a <u>very</u> good title![3] And, as a beginning, your chapters, "Panopticism" and "Organicist Yearnings"... obviously grab me: this because your themes are both so close to/parallel with my own chapters, "Mechanism" and "Organism" in *Good Intentions*....[4]

So, about both of these, you do the direct plunge *in medias res*, while—perhaps by excessive circuitousness—I attempt to maintain some 'historical distance'.[5] And this is why, I suspect, that my book is to be read either as a preface or a sequel to yours. That is: most of my 'history' is a big scale cultural survey with, implicitly, the French Revolution center stage. Primarily I am based upon John Stuart Mill and his two essays on Bentham and Coleridge, representing the mechanist and organicist positions in very early—and symmetrical—deployment. And, then, I proceed to 'decorate' Mills intuitions with flashbacks: Benjamin Thompson, Count Rumford, and Edmund Burke most specifically. And it might seem that, in general, my interest is rather more in origins than *denouements*.[6]

And then you!?

Much more interested in the near present? Much more engaged, polemical? Much more political?—though I don't know about this! But much more concerned with recent physical manifestations which, quite patently, myself doesn't possess the patience to cope with....

Thus, your 'history' is mostly of happenings since 1968 which, most emphatically, I agree is a crucial date; and, beginning this way, necessarily it becomes highly specific and concrete. Also, it allows you to introduce some wonderful flashbacks. For instance, reading you, I kick myself (if that is possible) for having missed the not so inferential critique of Bentham produced by Chas Dickens!—perhaps because I don't like Dickens and don't like Raymond Williams either (?). But such is prejudice because, at the same time, I feel perfectly happy—when they are writing about the condition of the poor in Lancashire/Manchester—to observe the linkage between Benjamin Disraeli* and Friedrich Engels!

But Utilitarians and *Sturm und Drang*—thesis and antithesis waiting for the Marxian combo....[7] And the Benthamite descent is easiest to illustrate—can be linked with Saint-Simon and that socialist-Positivist stuff; but the descent—Herder, Burke, Hegel, Coleridge, Carlyle, Ruskin—is less visually accessible and more difficult to make convincing. And I get the idea that yourself has, also, encountered this problem — you stick much closer to 'architecture' in "Panopticism" than you do in "Organicist Yearnings"....!!!

But, to use the language of Aby Warburg and Fritz Saxl, the two books just do happen to be "good neighbours"; and I can imagine Saxl putting them on the shelves in close adjacency.

However, is myself—so far—the only person to understand the degree to which they amplify, corroborate and, in the end, sponsor each other?

Rhetorical question because I don't know!

All the same, I would like to know/read the reviews which you have received—or is this too early?—and this because, for *Good Intentions*, after sixteen months, all that I seem to have received is this: some rather dim reviews in England, some rather rabid reactions from Anglo-*retardataires* who, rather quaintly, still conceive of themselves as marching in the vanguard of 'progress', and, from the North American continent—but nothing....[8]

And I wonder to what extent something like this is going to be your fate—too *au courant*, too dense, too arcane (?), to be accessible to the dinosaurs of architectural education?[9]

Of course, we must neither of us expect a review from *The New York Times*. That is altogether too much the province of a highly specific New Haven patronage.[10] But how about an <u>intelligent</u>, well placed review <u>of both of us together</u> coming from London? You see, taking us together, <u>we do constitute an 'event'</u> of 1994–95; and this means that, though, divided, we may fall—or elicit little interest, possibly, together, we may at least seduce.

Charles Jencks*? Robert Maxwell*? James Madge*? But, in suggesting something like this, I don't want to impose a pseudo-gregariousness or to violate your privacy. However, do think about it, be as ruthless as ever you may be inclined, and try to let me have your opinion.

Un abbraccio,

　　Colin

P.S. P.D.E. seems to think that I have missed my *métier*.[11] Thinks that my remarks about Arthur Brown, Jr., H.R.H., Mrs. Harris, Martin Dominguez, Leon Krier,* Alvin B. and James S indicate a new career for me.[12] So I am thinking of making a little book to be called *Footprints and Footnotes*—a sort of inferior, contracted and architectural version of Wm. Hazlitt's *The Spirit of the Age,* 1825.[13]

　　COLIN ROWE　　*Colin*　　　　　　　　　　　　　　　　January 4 1996

P.P.S. I haven't yet checked out my little *apercu* about Disraeli and Engels;[14] haven't yet unpacked <u>that</u> part of my books; but the relevant text for Disraeli is *Sybil*, I think 1846, and I wouldn't be at all surprised if it were to turn out that he <u>did</u> know Engels.[15] Interesting if he did. For Disraeli and dukes, Young England, read Pugin, John Henry Newman and the Church of Rome, but don't look for an Enlightenment pedigree. Then, for Engels, take the antithesis Enlightenment—*Sturm and Drang* at its most extreme; and I imagine himself and his buddy seeing each other home, negotiating the Chalk Farm Station and <u>never</u> stopping for a drink at the Carisbrooke Castle.[16]

But Benjamin D., and English Conservatism following him, had very little use for the Enlightenment.

　　Colin

If you <u>don't</u> like my idea, if it seems to you to be presumptuous, <u>don't</u> hesitate to say so. But, after you get your reviews *tout seul*, I still think that it be <u>opportune</u> if there were to be a joint review ready to go.[17]

Find you very, very clever on p. 293: "Considered as a broad-based social phenomenon, neoconservatism wishes to be both politically traditionalist yet economically and technologically modern." But fascinating to imply (as I think you do) this linkage between Quinlan Terry and Richard Rogers!

1　Berka was Baird's* graduate student at Harvard.
2　Rowe, Colin, *As I Was Saying: Recollections and Miscellaneous Essays*, Alexander Caragonne ed, 3 vols, Cambridge, MA: MIT Press, 1996.
3　Baird, George, *The Space of Appearance*, Cambridge MA: MIT Press, 1995.

4   Rowe, Colin, *The Architecture of Good Intentions*, London: Academy Editions, 1994.

5   *in medias res*, Latin: into the middle of things.

6   *dénouements*, French: final resolutions.

7   *Sturm und Drang*, German: Storm and Stress, late eighteenth-century German literary movement that exalted nature, feeling, and human individualism over Enlightenment rationalism; here contrasted with the Utilitarians.

8   *retardataires*, French: latecomers. On Anglo-*retardataires* reactions, see Rowe's letter to Robert Maxwell★ dated 7 September 1995 (p 442 in this volume).

9   *au courant*, French: aware.

10 The architecture critics at *The New York Times* were former students of Vincent Scully,★ renowned architectural historian at Yale in New Haven, Connecticut.

11 "P.D.E.": Peter David Eisenman;★ *métier*, French: calling.

12 Remarks expressed by Rowe in volume 3 of *As I Was Saying*; "H.R.H.": Henry Russell Hitchcock;★ "Alvin B.": Alvin Boyarsky;★ "James S.": James Stirling.★

13 This book, for which Rowe wrote essays until 1999, was never published.

14 *aperçu*, French: insight.

15 Disraeli,Benjamin, *Sybil, or the Two Nations*, 1845.

16 That Benjamin Disraeli★ (1804–1881) might have known Friedrich Engels (1820–1895) is of persistent interest to Rowe at this time, elaborated in his letter dated 4 March 1996 to Dorothy Rowe★ (p 464 in this volume).

17 *tout seul*, French: entirely alone; no joint review of *Space of Appearance* and *Good Intentions* was published.

248   *To Mark Hinchman*   *21 January 1996*

MEMORANDUM
From: Colin Rowe
Re: IRRELEVANT BOOKS TO READ

Dear Mark:

The other day I suggested Consuelo Vanderbilt's *The Glitter And The Gold*.[1] I have never read it; but I would like to and, in any case, I thought you might enjoy.

Then, more recently, I recommended Lesley Blanch, *The Wilder Shores of Love*.[2]

You see I believe in the reading of memoirs, diaries, autobiographies, biographies and the like. That is because, like Disraeli,★ I conceive these to be the stuff out of which history is made. Then, also, it's because I *do* like a bit o' gossip.......

So, if apparently I am destined to write bibliographies I will begin with Americano pieces which might be amusing; and the first of them will relate to a generation born in the 1860's and disposed to an Italian drift.

So:

Tryphosa Bates Batcheller, *Italian Castles and Country Seats*.[3]

Tryphosa came from Boston and was socially ambitious. She is an absurdity and a joy. She sang; but I don't know how well; and, like so many Americans of her generation, she made her way in Italy. That is, her book is *very* liberally scattered with all the *best* names. She sings for Queen Margherita at Stupinigi, she sings for the Melzi d'Erils, she performs for the Ercolani in Bologna. Indeed, coming from Back Bay and devoted to what was obviously a decadent/corrupt society, Tryphosa explains both Marinetti and the rise of Futurism. Also I think that, in explaining Marinetti, she helps (just a bit) to explain Mussolini.

Francis Augustus McNutt, *Diary of a Papal Chamberlain*.[4]

Frank McNutt's family came from Virginia by way of Ohio. He was ultra conservative and became *plus Catholique que le Pape*.[5] He was a linguist of genius; and, marrying as he did, he acquired a <u>sufficient</u> income. He married into 'old New York', Margaret Van Cortlandt Ogden, and he thus became a connection of the Goelet's, which I am sure <u>must</u> have been useful.

In Rome (I don't know how much it excited <u>her</u>) the two of them lived in Palazzo Pamphili in Piazza Navona. They rented it, restored it and, for the jubilee of Leo XIII, they gave a party which, <u>probably</u>, was a catastrophe. Anyway it was, perhaps, a <u>little</u> beyond <u>their</u> size.

Meaning that, though they might have had Cardinal Rampolla, Cardinal Merry del Val, a host of German princes and the best part of Austria-Hungary, on the whole (and this is my reading of it) the Colonna's, the Orsini's, the Lancellotti's and all *that* sort of gang just didn't show.

So do read the book. The McNutt's seem to have oscillated their later existence between the Tyrol and Bar Harbor; but, all the same, while seeing no more Popes he still was able to make a quite extensive little collection of Habsburgs and Bourbon-Paramas.

Logan Pearsall Smith, *Unforgotten Years*.[6]

This is a story originating in Philadelphia and quickly transferring itself to London. L.P.S.'s parents owned a bottle factory in Camden N.J. and acquired considerable notoriety as revivalist preachers. Of his two sisters, Alys married Bertrand Russell (2nd Earl Russell) and Mary married Bernard Berenson. This is a very entertaining book and L.P.S. enjoyed <u>no</u> illusions. It is v. important to read in connection with Berenson and I think that it must have lately been augmented by another publication called *Remarkable Relations*.

You see Mary Berenson's first husband was an Anglo-Irish Lawyer, Frank (?) Costelloe; and the Costelloe girls married into Bloomsbury. So this book is written by Somebody Strachey.

George Santayana, *Persons and Places* and *The Middle Span*.[7]

Santayana's parents were Spanish; but his mother later married a Sturgis from Boston; and the Sturgis's were China Trade which later ramified into banking in London, I.E. connections with the Peabodys and the Barings. So, apart from the banking interest, I think of three rather important Sturgis's. Russell Sturgis was a Gothic Revival architect who wrote and also built; and I think that you should check him out. There are v. important R.S. buildings at Yale; and, up the lake at Aurora, there is a charming dining room which he added to the house of the Wells College president. Then Julian Sturgis got himself a house built by Voysey which is at Hog's Back in Surrey. Then Howard Sturgis, who lived mostly at Windsor at a house called Queen's Acre, wrote a novel, *Belchamber*, which I have never read—though I remain curious to do so.

So the letters of Santayana suggest that he much valued his Sturgis step-relations; but, of course, you might also read Santayana's own novel, *The Last Puritan* which is a pseudo-Bostonian recollection. But apart from being more or less a class mate of Berenson and Charles Loeser at Harvard, of course S. was a most important professor of philosophy at Harvard (though I don't think that William James approved) and, also a most important aesthetician.

So, for Berenson and as a beginning, I suggest the recent biography of Ernest Samuels, *B.B., The Making of a Connoisseur* which has elaborate bibliographies; and, maybe Louise Tharp, *Mrs Jack*, because Isabella Stewart Gardner did have so much to do with his early career. Also what about Whatnot's, *Duveen*, because Jo Duveen (someone once said: How perfectly Duveen) was the great tycoon art dealer who, for a long time, retained Berenson as a source of favorable attributions.[8]

When, if you want to go further, I suggest Iris Origo, *Shades and Shadows*.[9] The Marchesa Origo whom I met in Rome in '81 may be still alive; and, if she is, she must be almost the last link with that Italian-American-English world which is the concern of these notes. The background is New York and Anglo-Ireland. Papa was Bayard Cutting, the dreamboat of his class at Harvard whom Rufus Choate, when he became ambassador to London in 1900, took away with him as *attaché*. So there he met Sybil Cuffe, daughter of the mildly impoverished Lord Desart; and, hence, Iris. So Bayard rapidly croaked. He was spittin' blood and it was a case of T.B.; and, presumably, via the Cutting New York-Long Island money, Sybil equipped herself with the Villa Medici at Fiesole (it had been an English house since about 1750) and proceeded to a variety of other marital careers, of which the first was Geoffrey (*The Architecture of Humanism*) Scott.

---

1   Vanderbilt, Consuelo, *The Glitter and the Gold*, New York: Harper and Brothers, 1952, memoirs.
2   Blanch, Lesley, *The Wilder Shores of Love*, London: Murray, 1954; a biography of four British women.
3   Batcheller, Tryphosa Bates, *Italian Castles and Country Seats*, New York: Longmans, Green, and Co, 1911.
4   MacNutt, Francis Augustus, *Diary of a Papal Chamberlain*; a.k.a. *A Papal Chamberlain: The Personal Chronicle of Francis Augustus MacNutt,* Rev John J Donovan ed, New York: Longmans, Green, and Co, 1936.
5   *plus Catholique que le Pape*, French: more Catholic than the Pope.
6   Smith, Logan Pearsall, *Unforgotten Years*, Boston: Little, Brown, & Co, 1939.
7   Santayana, George, *Persons and Places*, vol 2, *The Middle Span*, New York: Charles Scribner's Sons, 1945.
8   Samuels, Ernest, *Bernard Berenson: The Making of a Connoisseur*, Cambridge, MA: Belknap Press, 1979; Tharp, Louise, *Mrs. Jack: A Biography of Isabella Stewart Gardner*, Boston: Little, Brown, & Co, 1965; Behrman, SN, *Duveen: The Story of the Most Spectacular Art Dealer of All Time*, New York: Random House, 1951, 1952.
9   Origo, Iris, *Shades and Shadows: Part of a Life*, London: John Murray, 1970; an autobiography.

249   To **Dorothy Rowe**, *St. Margaret's Road, Oxford*   *4 March 1996*

Apt. 814, 3133 Connecticut Ave., Washington D.C.

Dearest Dorothy:

Have just had Mark Girouard⋆ for a <u>long</u> weekend—Thursday to Sunday—and found it immensely entertaining. Very shy but—once relaxed—v. amusing. <u>Not</u> an intellectual![1]

For instance, I say: "Do you suppose that Benjamin Disraeli⋆ knew Friedrich Engels?" And there is <u>no</u> supercilious dismissal of the idea! Instead you get a kind of Agatha Christie mental action. "Well, just as Karl Friedrich Schinkel went to Manchester shortly after Waterloo, so Disraeli <u>did</u> go there in the early 1840's—background to *Sybil*. So Engels <u>was</u> a mill owner in Manchester, owner of one of those buildings that Schinkel raved about and which Disraeli talked about too. Why! I would even think that it was Engels who showed him around! And the whole social programme of Young England (I mean D's little party): Of course, basically Edmund Burke and Walter Scott but, otherwise, surely Engels, Engels, Engels. But of course! Engels on the conditions of the Manchester proletariat is almost exactly the same as Disraeli... But, yes, yes...."

But little old me found this sort of reaction to be immensely refreshing!

And another case.

Among the books here he found a biography of Lady Sackville, mother of Vita, by Susan Jay Alsop who lives in Georgetown. So she is the widow of the late Jo Alsop, journalist and cousin of the Roosevelts and, as Susan Jay, she is a descendant of that John Jay who, in Paris, was a signer of the treaty between G.B. and the U.S.—was it in 1784? But you know the place where it was signed—and so did Mark. Rue de l'Universite, then a hotel, still a hotel, with a plaque outside telling the story.[2]

So the future Lady Sackville—oldest of the very many illegitimate children of Lionel Sackville—became her father's hostess (he was married) at age 18, when he became British 'Minister' to the U.S., c. 1882. But no problem! For once, Qu.V. was highly amused—just as long as the 'ladies' here in D.C. were able to find the arrangement 'acceptable'. So the 'ladies' did and the future Lady S. enjoyed a *succes fou*.[3] But very much so! And, in her first season, she received an offer of marriage from no less than Chester B. Arthur, then a widower and later to be a rather inglorious President.

Then, of course, about 1900, she had to prove herself illegitimate—in a court of law—so that her husband (she had married her cousin) could retain the title of Lord Sackville. But, those Victorians were very strange.

Well, then, there was the second lawsuit. Sir John Murray Scott, private secretary to Sir Richard and Lady Wallace (Sir R.W., himself, was an illegitimate son of the Regency Ld. Hartford—the Ld. Steyne of Thackeray's *Vanity Fair*) anyway Sir J.M.S. had left Lady S. a tremendous lot of French furniture and bric-a-brac—about as much as the present Wallace Collection—and the Scott family brought a case against her: argument undue influence.[4] But their position was about as hopeful as the predicament of a snowball in hell: they were just an awful dowdy lot, Lady S. was still glamorous, and—in any case—all of it was John Murray Scott's entirely personal right (bequest of the Wallace's) to dispose of. So Lady S. emerged triumphant, sold the lot of it to Duveen who, then, got rid of it from coast to coast—all the way between New York and San Francisco!

So, at this state, Mark emerges from his bedroom: "Colin, it's completely clear to me that SHE did HIM in"—meaning that Lady S. murdered Sir J.M.S.!!! "But I don't know why nobody has ever seen it! HIS family had their suspicions but they didn't go beyond undue influence. But if only my father were alive; HE would agree."

So seems that Mark's papa was—through the De La Warr's—a some kind of cousin of Lady Sackville and could never be shaken from a fixed idea that she was a completely unscrupulous woman, almost a Lady McBeth, *capable de tout*.[5] "So it seems" (this is verbatim) "that you know—you say slightly—Susan Jay Alsop.[6] But we must ring her up immediately and find out what she thinks. But I think absolutely NO doubt."

So, I have never imagined such impulsiveness; and, unfortunately, Susan Alsop wasn't at home—otherwise she might have been over here, or we might have been over there, just in two shakes of a lamb's tail!

So, you grab the pic? It was all *un plaisir imprevu*—but completely.[7] No argument—thank God; but just an effervescence of social chit-chat—And what do I have to conceal from Mary about Jim?[8] With Margaret Geddes, Gross Herzogin von Hessen und bei Rhein, all mixed up in the same package as the horrors of Peter Reyner Banham!*

I think it was great fun for all and a pity that he knows nothing whatsoever about Italy!

Je t'embrasse,[9]

    Colin

It must be a visitation from the Holy Ghost (*Heilige Geist*) but of late, the gift of tongues—including French—suddenly seems to have descended upon me!

    Colin

P.S. We were talking about Edward Croft Murray, Prints and Drawings at the B.M., not v. good and now croaked.[10] So do you know the former Mrs. Croft Murray whom, I believe, now lives in Oxford under some other name.

She is *nata* Giovanna Saffi and I used to know her brother, Antonio who became *direttore* of the Accademia Santa Cecilia.[11] But a Risorgimento name and the first Saffi I have heard about—was he Aurelio?—along with Mazzini and Garibaldi was one of the *triumviri* of the Roman republic of 1848 (which, if we are not careful is going to lead us straight to Buckminster Fuller), and I believe that Aurelio Saffi (lots of streets called after him) also taught at Oxford—as some sort of mid-Victorian liberal refugee.[12]

Anyway, Giovanna Saffi married Edward C-M in the Tempietto of San Pietro in Montorio!

But was this a very clever thing to do?

    Colin

*** The route from the Roman Republic to Bucky Fuller travels like this: Margaret Fuller, early nineteenth century—sort of Biedermeier-Boston, a great *causeuse* (like Bucky), as she was getting pretty long in the tooth, embarked upon the grand tour.[13] In London she told Carlyle that she 'had decided to accept the universe' and he said something like: "Well, God, she'd better"; but she didn't stay in London very long and she arrived in Rome just in time for all the excitement—all those poor, nice, infatuated boys being slaughtered by the French, virtually in the garden of the present American Academy at Porta San Pancrazio. So she takes up nursing at Santa Trinita dei Pellegrini and the Principessa Belgioioso, rich Milanese liberal is among her associates (but, with the Principessa B. also note more architectural ramifications, The Firm B.B.P.R.—Banfi, Belgiojoso, Peressutti, Rogers—groan for the dreadful Richard and Lloyd's of London—is related to the P.B.); but, taking time out from all this melodramatic nursing, Margaret Fuller contrived to marry her little Roman aristo.[14] He was the Marchese Ossoli—Palazzo Ossoli and v. nice Peruzzi job just adjacent to Palazzo Spada. And she conceived, at her late age and just like St. Anne, a child. But calamity. As the French were about to enter Rome, they had to leave quick. So where did they go and with whom did they stay? But obvious, obvious: they went to Bagni di Lucca to stay with the Brownings; and then, as they were about to sail from Livorno to New York, Elizabeth B.B. gave Maggie F. a bible with emotive inscription.[15] Get it. So they were shipwrecked off Fire Island (could have been saved but insisted on being rescued *a trois*) and are all buried in Mount Auburn Cemetery, very pretty too, in Cambridge, Mass. [16]

x x x x x   Colin

P.S. I have just had lunch. It came out of the *surgelato*[17] department and it was that delicious and indispensable Italian delicacy, *bastoncini di pesce*.[18] I gave a plate of it to Mark G. on Friday and poor thing, with that advertisement, his appetite was aroused and, by no means, did he anticipate fish fingers!

But do tell David about Mark G. To him—it's so silly—you merely mention and name and there are a series of *frissions d'horreur*.[19] But he could have a perfectly amiable time with him.

His wife, you know, is Chicago Jewish! And we were talking about that kind of thing. And what about the term "Jewess"! I said, of course, George Eliot, in her very pro-Semite *Daniel Deronda*, had used the term but that it was no longer used in this country, that the female of the species was often a very difficult proposition in the English language—as also in Italian.[20] But, German *Englader-Engladerin*, and, French, *Americain-Americaine*—they work out very well. But, in English, except for "prince" and "princess", the "ess" suffix is a bit of a pain. So I lead through "lion" and "lioness", "tiger" and "tigress", to "jew" and "jewess", and he grabbed the pic. Said he'd be more careful in the future; said his father (he is fixated on his father, ex-colonial governor of Kenya) always used the term "jewess"—my son married a jewess—(but doesn't it sound odious?); said he thought the term was still frequently used in England; IS IT?; said that his daughter, age 20 might have reservations about it; but I think that the outcome is that my name will not be blessed at: 11 Colville Road, W.II.[21]

Bye,

Colin

★★★★

By the way, from reports in the *N.Y.T.*—quite neutral, I do think that the B.R.F. is about to be pretty silly about the former Diana Spencer—not to be H.R.H. not to be the Pcess of Wales.[22] But this has nothing to do with 'morality', or 'behaviour', or 'popularity', or anything like that. It's just that, according to strict protocol, she must become: H.R.H. Diana, Princess of Wales. There's no way around it—and Mark agreed that both Burke and Debrett would so argue;[23] thought she might become D.P. of W.,[24] Duchess of Whatever, you can't separate her from being H.R.H.D.P. of W. because this would be against all English (American for that matter) practice and principles of legitimacy.[25]

So they did it on Wallis Warfield Simpson (and no need to talk about that bordello in Hong Kong and that aborted child from her affair with Galeazzo Ciano); but this is a tougher little cookie and, in this case, just watch for what happens if the B.R.F. and B.P. attempt to push this line![26]

The precedent is Consuelo Vanderbilt. When she split from him, she remained H.G. Consuelo D. of M.[27]

IN LAW THIS IS HOW THINGS ARE![28]

---

1   Rowe made a distinction between "intellectual" and "intelligent". He regarded himself as the latter and expressed mild suspicion of the former.

2 The Treaty of Paris, ending the American Revolutionary War, was signed in the Hotel d'York on 3 September 1783 by John Jay, John Adams, and Benjamin Franklin.

3 *succès fou*, French: fantastic success.

4 Wallace Collection: London collection of over five hundred pieces of eighteenth-century French furniture.

5 *capable de tout*, French: capable of anything; unpredictable.

6 Susan Mary Alsop (1918–2004), the Grand Dame of Washington society.

7 *un plaisir imprevu*, French: an unforeseen pleasure.

8 From Mary Stirling about James Stirling.* Mark Girouard* was conducting research for a book on Stirling entitled *Big Jim: The Life and Work of James Stirling*, London: Chatto Windus, 1998.

9 *Je t'embrasse*, French: I hug you.

10 "B.M.": British Museum.

11 *nata*, Italian: née.

12 *triumviri*, Latin: triumvirate.

13 *causeuse*, French: talkative woman.

14 Richard Rogers designed the corporate headquarters of Lloyd's of London, a building that Rowe disliked.

15 "Elizabeth B.B.": Elizabeth Barrett Browning (1806–1861).

16 *à trois*, French: all three together.

17 *surgelato,* Italian: frozen, frozen foods.

18 *bastoncini di pesce*, Italian: fish sticks.

19 *frissons d'horreur*, French: quivers of horror.

20 Girouard, George, *Daniel Deronda*, Edinburgh: William Blackwood & Sons, 1876.

21 "11 Colville Road, W.II": Girouard's* London address.

22 "Not to be Her Royal Highness not to be the Princess of Wales": Prince Charles and Princess Diana were divorcing at this time. Rowe deliberates on the question of Diana's title after the divorce.

23 Burke's and Debrett's: directories of peerage and gentry.

24 "D.P. of W.": Diana Princess of Wales.

25 "H.R.H.D.P. of W.": Her Royal Highness Diana Princess of Wales.

26 Wallis Warfield Simpson was an American socialite twice divorced when Britain's King Edward VIII abdicated the throne in December 1936 to marry her. When Edward was made Duke of Windsor, Simpson became Duchess of Windsor, but the title "Her Royal Highness" was never applied to her.

27 Her Grace Consuelo Duchess of Marlborough (1877–1964), née Consuelo Vanderbilt, was married to Charles Spencer-Churchill from 1890 to 1921.

28 Printed by hand in left margin.

250   *To Tom **Schumacher**, Florence, Italy*   *8 March 1996*

3133 Connecticut Avenue, Apt. 814, Washington, D.C.

Tom, *il mio caro*:

A fabulous letter, a 'treasure' of observation, which I read, and re-read, with always increased pleasure!

So Clement XII Corsini, 1730–40, is exactly what I expected. Got the job when he was 78 years old, had been a protégé of Clement XI Albani, was stricken with gout when he assumed the Throne—that primitive wheelchair in that *salone* must be his— went blind after two years, and, though he instigated a papal lottery and other nice things, on the whole he didn't enjoy a very 'successful' reign.[1] Obviously, in the 18th century, the name Corsini is to Florence what the name Rezzonico is to Venice—and that explains those two over ambitious houses.

Did La Pietra originally belong to them and do they regret having gotten rid of it?[2] About a hundred years ago did I meet a Nicky Corsini? Maybe I did. But I have no recollection of him apart from the name.

So, here, life continues. There were two big snow falls; and one still wakes up in the morning, sometimes to a landscape powdered with white. At the Philip Johnson* affair,[3] MOMA and Columbia, I had a bit of *success fou*— wasn't hard because nobody had much to say, but I spoke, as I was supposed to do, for ninety minutes.[4] So Phil was captivated and, with Phyllis Lambert,* I have acquired a new friend. So, with all that Bronfman money, plus guilt about bootleg gin,[5] *ci vediamo*.[6]

Anyway, I have been violently stimulated by all this; and I am beginning to find that I have almost written a book. It's to be called *Footprints and Footnotes*; and it's gonna be good. A suite of connected essays culminating in "Calamities of Arch. Ed." But the *Heilige Geist* seems to have descended upon me.[7] Am suddenly equipped with the gift of tongue—'bout time—and I am driven and transported—jus' takin' time off to write to y'all—and I must have already written about 30,000 words. Ra, ra, ra!

And what else? Well, in 1988–'90, I 'wore' a mustachio; and it caused reactions. Like from the little old lady in the restaurant in Naples: *"Ma, lei, con gli occhi blu e les baffe lunghi,"* holding my hand, *"Lei e il vero tipo Normanno"*; and just think about that now.[8] Or the question from the waiter in the place in the Campo dei Fiore (I'm there with Astra): *"E lei, signor baffone?"*[9] Well to add a little terribilita to the world, I've just begun another *baffone*.[10] Won't be as protrusive-quasi-questioning as yours; but, in the interests of *il faut souffrir*,[11] draped over most of the lips, it is intended to render eating and drinking a little self conscious and *un po difficile*—though not as difficult as it must have been for Friedrich Nietzsche![12]

Choice of *parti* can't be hoped to be an issue before mid-April.[13] *Bufutissimo all natura?*[14] Or wax (?), twist, and twirl *all moda artificiale?*[15] But that's the general pic.

So, as a gesture of machismo and social protest, I am about to adopt a new iconography—very little on top a lot around the mouth; it will be a sort of compensation down below for a willed-and-chosen absence up above; and, if the black guys at the desk downstairs already find the new quarter inch crew cut kinda *chic*, I am sure that they will approve the combo. But have always thought mustache growing to be an engaging activity for wet afternoons...

Dear Tom, my best, best love to Patti and I do miss you both very much.[16]

Un abbraccio fervente and, dear Patti, *je t'embrasse chaleureusement*.[17]

   Colin   *x x x x x*

P.S. Tom! You borrowed a book of mine and didn't return it; but that doesn't matter. Problem is that I don't remember either the author or the title. So it's about modernity—in the general rather than the architectural sense; and it starts in the 18th century. Do please try to remember because I desperately need to consult it for a crucial footnote.

P.P.S. Tom! You, long ago, told me that it was desirable for me to be *baffuto*— permanent exhibit.[18] So, ever since, I've been doing pendulum swings, trials—with pleasure, and errors—with regret. Since your advice—it was in '67 God help up—as trials, I've sponsored at least six of these things, and—as errors, I've kept them for a few months (longest 23) and then caused them to go away. But, this time, it's for real. The exhibition will persist. After all this yin and yang, I have, finally, accepted your excellent suggestion.

   C.

1 *salone*, Italian: salon. Rowe's reference to "that primitive wheelchair in that *salone*" suggests he is replying to an image that Schumacher* had sent him of a painting of Pope Clement XII.

2 Villa La Pietra, fifteenth-century Renaissance villa in Florence. In 1994 the villa was given to New York University by Harold Acton. See Rowe's letter to David Rowe* dated 10 November 1995 (p 454 in this volume).

3 The symposium Autonomy and Ideology: Positioning the Avant-Garde in America was held 1–3 February, 1996, at Columbia University and the Museum of Modern Art in New York. For Rowe's talk, see "The Avant-Garde Revisited", in Somol, RE ed, *Autonomy and Ideology: Positioning the Avant-Garde in America*, NY: Monacelli Press, 1997, pp 48–67.

4 *succès fou*, French: fantastic success.

5 Phyllis Lambert* (b 1927), Canadian philanthropist and heir to the Bronfman fortune made in part by the sale of alcohol. Together with her father, Samuel Bronfman, she commissioned Mies van der Rohe* and Philip Johnson* to design the Seagram Building.

6 *ci vediamo*, Italian: until we meet again.

7 *Heilige Geist*, German: Holy Ghost.

8 *Ma, lei, con gli occhi blu e i baffi lunghi*, Italian: but you, with blue eyes and long mustache; and *lei e il vero tipo Normanno*, Italian: you are a true Norman type.

9 *"E lei, signor baffone?"*, Italian: "And you, Mr. Mustache?"

10 *baffone*, Italian: mustache.

11 *il faut souffrir*, French: one must suffer.

12 *un po difficile*, Italian: a bit difficult; Nietzsche wore an enormous mustache.

13 *parti*, French: type, disposition.

14 *Bufutissimo alla natura*, Italian: a very natural-looking mustache.

15 *alla moda artificiale*, Italian: in the artificial fashion/mode.

16 Pat Sachs, Tom Schumacher's* wife.

17 *je t'embrasse chaleureusement*, French: I embrace you warmly.

18 *baffuto*, Italian: mustached.

---

251 To **Dorothy Rowe**, *St. Margaret's Road, Oxford*   *19 March 1996*

3133 Connecticut Avenue, Apt. 814, Washington, D.C.

Dearest Dorothy:

Cara mia, I am sure that the enclosed will provide you with immense diversion.[1] It was left in my apt the other day by Mark Girouard* who, as part of his monograph on Jim, had just interviewed the author in Phoenix, Arizona.[2]

The author, when I first knew him, went by the name of Denis Owtram and this appeared to embarrass him enormously.[3] It too much suggested the saga of that empire upon which the sun never set. He is, in fact, the great grandson of that General Owtram who, I think, had something to do with the Indian Mutiny. But what? And I have to admit that I don't know. I suppose that the name is Scottish? Like General Sir Henry Havelock?[4] But all of this was a great grief to Denis.

At the beginning of December 1942 I went up with him by train from Liverpool to Glasgow, change and on to Perth—Queen's Barracks—where, of course, there was also Jim to be found—sweeping up the floor of that 600 ft long weaving shed; and Denis occupied a bunk above me.[5]

So it was difficult: Denis would have nightmares and begin to scream; it would wake everybody up within three or four hundred feet; and I would have to get up to pacify him—big *problema*.

It appeared that, during the 1920's and '30's, his papa had a coffee plantation in Kenya, and it was there that he had entertained Winston Churchill—apparently for quite some time; and that was the source of the traumata. Denis had wanted to go into the Air Force and was only put in to the Army by reason of some bureaucratic bungle; and his father had written to Churchill about it—and 'worse' than that: Churchill had signified interest, as a result of which Denis lived in constant fear. The prospect was too dreadful! Winston Churchill might arrive in Perth, Scotland; and, then, the occasion would be too terrible. It would be an exhibition of privilege not to be tolerated. It would be too ostentatious. Churchill would release him into the Air Force; and this would be an insufferable use of prerogative—and, hence, the nightmares.

So, before we all left Perth, Denis did receive the news that, if he wished, he would be transferred; but grab it!—as you might suppose he refused to avail himself of this 'dispensation'!

Then my next acquaintance with him is in Liverpool when I was teaching there, '48–'51, and he was, by now, very odd indeed. He had become incredibly reclusive and shy; and the most extravagant affirmation of this had become his addiction to taxis and his horror of lectures. So that these combined: to attend a lecture he had to arrive in a taxi; and to get away from the lecture—with minimum of social contact— he had to keep the taxi waiting, generally 60 minutes or so!

Then Jim and I were once allowed to breach his privacy—by the way, he had now changed his first name to Christopher—and he was living in a couple of upstairs rooms, rented from a typical Liverpool landlady, in a dismal red-pressed-brick house in, I think, the Aigburth Road—with, of course, curtains or blinds permanently drawn.[6] And the rooms were a spectacle. You could scarcely move in them. He was devoted to Frank Lloyd Wright* and everywhere—upon a double bed and all over the floor, top of the wardrobe, and you name it—there were big and exquisitely made architectural models of buildings in the style of Wright, the production of himself: and Christopher/Denis, needless to say, slept on a little narrow pad on the floor.

An unusually exotic escape from 'ancestral' memories of India and more direct recollections of Kenya? And combined with whiffs of incense and soupçons[7] of orientalia, it could remind you of Huysmans' A Rebours;[8] but it wasn't at all like that! Although, when Jim and I got downstairs, it did become rather odd. The landlady rushed out to open the door—which was barred—and she rushed out with a scent spray or, as they say, an atomizer; and this is really true, and Jim got the worst of it, and I remember her exact words—as she pressed the little thing that you squeeze: "I've had boys of my own and I KNOW what they like." So a slightly dazed and stinking Jim, with me less so—we emerge into the damp and foggy streets of Liverpool.

This is about the last I saw of him and, sometime later—I should think in the mid to late '50's—as Christopher Owtram, and presumably following his 'mana' (is that the word?)—he left for Vancouver, B.C., where the Liverpool performance seems to have been repeated—quantities of beautiful models and all the rest. But I get the impression that there was never any problem about money (that coffee plantation, even with the Mau Mau, must have paid off quite well)[9] and it must have been during this Vancouver period that he changed his name, yet again: Christopher had become too much and he now translated himself into "Crisstofa."

But the prospects of ultimate bliss were, in Vancouver, far too close to resist. It was to be Scottsdale, Arizona,—it was to be shades of F.L.W. and Mrs. Wright, Olgivanna from Montenegro, and Wright's sort of factotum, Wesley Peters, and his wife, no less than Svetlana Alliluyeva Stalin, who later left him to live next door to Steve Peterson* in Princeton![10] But how very small is the world.

So, for purposes of the new life—there was a further name change. Better get rid of the last shreds of that dreadful imperialism/colonialism, better discard every remnant of that dreadful baggage: the name Owtram must go—we will now become: "Crisstofa Saiaonne"! And, in the course of doing so, we will acquire a wife from Kyoto....

A rather protracted identity crisis! Yes mam, kind of reminds me of that book by Nigel Dennis—and is he not also from Kenya.[11] Anyway some place like that; and Mark G. tells me that, in Phoenix where he spent a long weekend, the *tout ensemble* is much the same as it was in Liverpool and, as—I am told—it was in Vancouver—the place is adrift with the most interesting/superb, big, architectural models![12]

Brian Kelly,* who spent a year at the Univ. of Ariz. at, of all places, Tempe, reacts rather splenetically, to all this: "Well, just what you'd expect in that Fascist state. If they're not rednecks, they're all kooks and krazies!"

So, read on with *Notes... of Numerical Interest.* The whole business is now absolutely Pythagorean....

P.S. Agostino Chigi was also into horoscopes and that's what the frescoes of the Farnesina are all about—the constellation of the heavens at his birth date.[13] Found a Mussolini horoscope the other day.[14] Made about 1910 and distressingly accurate???? A nice story about Mussolini. The prefect of Forlí was asked by the Ministry of the Interior, c. 1906, to send a report on his character. He wrote: "A young man of vivacious intelligence and modest culture"! The ultimate in letters of dis-recommendation?

1   Written by Crisstofa Saiaonne (aka Denis Owtram), the enclosure is titled *Some Notes of Numerical Interest to be Found in the Life of James Frazer Stirling—Architect—UK—1924–1990.*
2   Girouard, Mark, *Big Jim: The Life and Work of James Stirling,* London: Chatto & Windus, 1998.
3   Denis Owtram (1924–2004), was born "Outram" in Uganda, the great grandson of Lt General Sir James Outram (1803–1863), a distinguished British Indian Army officer during the Indian Rebellion of 1857. Rowe first met Owtram while an undergraduate at the University of Liverpool.
4   Major General Sir Henry Havelock (1795–1857), "The Hero of Lucknow", served with James Outram in 1857.
5   For Rowe's description of the weaving shed, see his *As I Was Saying: Recollections and Miscellaneous Essays,* Alexander Caragonne ed, 3 vols Cambridge, MA: MIT Press, 1996, vol 3, p 342.
6   "Jim": James Stirling.*
7   *soupçons,* French: suspicion.
8   Huysmans, Joris-Karl, *À rebours* (*Against nature*), 1884, a novel whose main character, an eccentric aesthete who disdains bourgeois society, retreats into a world of his own creation.
9   The Mau Mau Uprising was a military conflict in Kenya (1952–60) between anticolonial groups called the Mau Mau and the Kenya Regiment of the British Army.
10 Svetlana Alliluyeva Stalin (1926–2011), aka Lana Peters, was married to Wesley Peters from 1970 to 1973. Peters was a Taliesin architect and Frank Lloyd Wright's* son-in-law.
11 Dennis, Nigel, *Cards of Identity: British Literature,* New York: Vanguard Press, 1955, satire on class prejudice and identity theory. Born in Surrey, England, Dennis (1912–1989) moved to Southern Rhodesia in 1918.
12 *tout ensemble,* French: all of it taken together.
13 In his *La fede astrologica di Agostino Chigi* of 1934, Fritz Saxl maintains that Agostino Chigi (1456–1526) commissioned Baldassare Peruzzi to paint the ceiling of the Sala di Galatea in his Villa Farnesina to show the stars positioned in the heavens as they were at the time of Chigi's birth.
14 Benito Mussolini (1883–1945), leader of the National Fascist Party in Italy from 1922 to 1943.

3133 Connecticut Avenue, Apt. 814, Washington, D.C.

Dear Phyllis:

This Fed Ex communication concerns <u>two</u> copies both related to Vancouver, B.C.

I enclose a photocopy of the memo about Jim Stirling* which Mark Girouard* suggested that I send you.[1] I hope that you are startled and amused to receive, from Phoenix, Arizona, so wildly Pythagorean a disclosure. And I add to this a copy of a letter which I am sending to my sister-in-law in Oxford (she is dying of cancer and in great pain and I send a letter for her entertainment—with <u>no</u> mention about the horrors—once a week).[2]

So this is the relevant info re Denis-Christopher-Crisstoffa Owtram-Saiaonne which, because, in terms of Canadian history, must involve your interest, in the hope that it will stimulate.

Way back you asked me—like some Fabulous Agatha Christie detective: "<u>What</u> about <u>that</u> Seaman's Institute, 1952, in Vancouver B.C.?" Well, here it is and we did it in <u>three</u> weeks just to pick up a bit of cash so as to continue.[3] I'm rather entertained by it—sort of New Brutalism *avant la lettre*,[4] with bits of all sort of people: <u>no</u> Corbu,* some Adolf Loos in my perspectives, some Mies,* a lot of De Stijl, I think Terragni for the long slot beneath the cantilever, Neutra for the exposed beam ends[5]—I suspect the Tremaine House at Montecito outside Santa Barbara,[6] and <u>then</u> all that <u>black</u> concrete!!!; but <u>all</u> the crudeness entirely *voulu*....[7]

So, in the office, though I didn't know it, it seems to have been a little political hot potato; and, hence, the mirror imaging and all the rest—presumably the 'corrective' work of Ned Pratt. However, with the Terragniesque slot (though where you find it in Terragni I <u>don't</u> know), and, then, with the kinda pilasters—not structural—poised above the beam ends in the slot—very curious—in some way I can't help thinking that it comes on—just a bit—looking like an early work of Peter David Eisenman.*

But I had <u>genuinely</u> forgotten all this until you asked your question; and perhaps, I <u>wanted</u> to forget about it. So it isn't so much *une oeuvre supprime* as an *oeuvre oublie*.[8]

Proctor le Mare, whom Brian Richards* mentions in his letter was, more or less, in the same class at Liverpool as Jim S. and what I hope is going to be our friend in Phoenix.

Best, best wishes,

     COLIN R.

---

1 See note 2, Rowe's letter to Dorothy Rowe* dated 19 March 1996 (p 470 in this volume).
2 Rowe's letter to Dorothy Rowe* dated 19 March 1996 (p 470 in this volume).
3 In 1952, together with Brian Richards* and while in the service of Sharp Thompson Berwick & Platt, Rowe designed the Seamans Institute, Vancouver, BC. Rowe's enclosure included (1) a memo from Owtram (see Rowe's letter to Dorothy Rowe* dated 19 March 1996, p 470 in this volume); (2) a letter from Richards; and (3) photographs and drawings of the Seamans Institute. The latter two enclosures were later copied to Joan Ockman* in Rowe's letter to her dated 6 August 1998 (p 530 in this volume). The Richards' letter is copied there.
4 *avant la lettre*, French: before the term was coined; literally, "before the letter".
5 Le Corbusier* (1887–1965), Mies van der Rohe* (1886–1968), Giuseppe Terragni (1904–1943), and Richard Neutra (1892–1970) were famous Modern architects.
6 Warren Tremaine House, Montecito, California, 1947, designed by Richard Neutra.
7 *voulu*, French: deliberate.
8 *une œuvre supprimée* as an *œuvre oubliée*, French and English: a work lost as a work forgotten.

3133 Connecticut Avenue, Apt. 814, Washington, D.C.

Alex:

    This is the Fred-Susie Rizzoli piece—for <u>your</u> instruction and amusement.[1]

Seems I say very nice things about both of them—in <u>first</u> five pages: Fred is "an incandescent intelligence" and Susie's Chinatown is "almost the urbanistic equivalent of an adagio movement by Mozart". But, surely, <u>very</u> nice?

And, then, in <u>last</u> five pages: I mention Kodak, two Princeton buildings, and Chattanooga, Tennessee, not to mention a general salute to urbanistics, "quite exceptional in the repertory of modern architecture". So a slight qualification about <u>brick</u> and a <u>very acceptable</u> final para.

But, as I told you, I sent it to New Haven and I <u>did</u> look forward to a happy response—both over the phone <u>and</u> in writing.[2] So I waited; I got worried that maybe they hadn't got it; and I rang up four days later—Fred, bland, perfunctory, yeah, yeah; and Susie, "I don't think you like our buildings". But, God Almighty, in the opera I'd made them a present of the U.S. Constitution!

So, if a muted reaction can be bizarre, lemme tell ya', <u>this</u> reaction <u>is</u> bizarre. I have made a present of a highly eligible Neo-Conservative argument and it <u>should</u> attract attention at the front of a clean, big Rizzoli book. It's an intellectual position and a <u>line</u>. And it <u>should</u> go quite a ways towards contributing a bit of—badly lacking—political *chic*. Think that, whichever wins the election, this is a highly palatable argument which <u>someone</u> is going to notice. Then it grabs the eco lobby and all that! Also, it <u>should</u> grab the Yale Corporation. But don't you think?

Susie's reaction I expected. Both of us knew this some months ago—practically <u>astute</u> but, in terms of theory/apologetics, <u>dim</u>. But Fred's <u>lack</u> of reaction, for a time, <u>did</u> distress me. However, I have to suppose that he is exhausted by excessive work that his normal intelligence is suffering atrophy—and <u>this</u>, just as his physical presence <u>is</u> betraying fatigue.

Meanwhile, it has <u>slightly</u> chilled my affections—though I have no doubt that they will recuperate.

Ti saluto con un abbraccio affettuoso,[3]

    Colin

Anyway, it <u>will</u> be the third chapter in *Footprints and Footnotes*—C.I, "Thanks to the R.I.B.A."; C.II, "The Impossibility of the Avant Garde"; C.III, "At Home with the Genius Loci". Then, C.IV will be, "Washington, D.C, or Lockhart, Texas Revisited"—and for this I await your Farrakhan stuff. And Fred-Susie should fit very elegantly into this sequence.[4]

So following chapters will be—not entirely sure of order: "History of Futurism: Future of Historicism", "Intelligence and the Intelligentsia", "*Toutes les Gloires de la France*, Almost",[5] "An English Success: an English Anomaly (?)", "Structure and Event, or the Calamities of Architectural Education (Harvard)", "*Divertimento* (Cornell)"; and a few more just might become insinuated into this fabric.[6] But don't you see how K.K. fit into all this—critiques of scientism, historicism and French linguistics?[7] But <u>they</u> come out smelling like a rose!

"Divertimento" will be the terminal piece. Pietro Cortona ceiling from Palazzo Barberini. Tiepolo ceiling from Villa Pisani at Stra. Apotheosis. Sequence of American and English light verse and American wit. A good quote from Italo Calvino. A tour of the United States and Mexico with several excursions to Canada. Things seen. A job—three weeks—in Vancouver, very interesting, New Brut, *avant la lettre*.[8] Envoi.

Dedication to: Phyllis Lambert⋆ and to the Memory of Lilian Priuli-Bon. Excursus on Contessa Priuli.[9] Lots more long footnotes and excursus pieces. 25,000-30,000 words already written. Think that the *Heilige Geist* and not the *Heilige Zeitgeist* is breathing down my neck, things are going so quick.[10]

 Colin

[handwritten]

APRIL 10

 STILL NO COMMUNICATION FROM NEW HAVEN / BOSTON!!!???[11]

---

1 The definitive draft of Rowe's "Living with the Genius Loci", a review of the architectural and urban design work of Fred Koetter⋆ and Susie Kim,⋆ later published in Plattus, Alan J ed, *Koetter Kim and Associates: Place/Time*, New York: Rizzoli, 1997, pp 10–17.

2 At the time of this letter, Fred Koetter⋆ was dean of Yale's School of Architecture in New Haven, Connecticut.

3 *Ti saluto con un abbraccio affettuoso*, Italian: I greet you with a warm hug.

4 Incomplete on Rowe's death, *Footprints and Footnotes* was never published.

5 *Toutes les Gloires de la France*, French: All the Glories of France.

6 "*Divertimento* (Cornell)", Italian and English: "Fun (Cornell)"

7 "K.K.": Koetter-Kim.⋆

8 *avant la lettre*, French: before the term was coined (literally "before the letter"). For the three-week job in Vancouver, see Rowe's letter to Phyllis Lambert⋆ dated 21 March 1996 (p 473 in this volume).

9 Lilian Priuli-Bon was an elderly friend of Rowe when he studied at the University of London's Warburg.

10 The *Heilige Geist* and not the *Heilige Zeitgeist*, German and English: the Holy Spirit and not the Holy Spirit of the Times.

11 Koetter⋆ was in New Haven. Kim⋆ and the office of Koetter Kim & Associates were in Boston.

To **George Baird**, *Cambridge, Massachusetts*   *9 April 1996*   **254**

3133 Connecticut Avenue, Apt. 814, Washington, D.C.

Dear George:

 If you are not 'one of them' I get the ideas that the technophiles think you are a technophobe.

Anyways, with undue paranoia, it is to that I attribute the 'loss' of the taped transcript of my little talk on the occasion of my receiving the R.G.M. last June. The P.R. dept. of the R.I.B.A. just 'lost' it![1] Or should I presume incompetence!

But it's been quite a sweat to put the talk back together again for purposes of publication—you know that the R.I.B.A. has now set up another periodical publication in order to cope with its own Journal?[2] But it has become so absurd.

So I'm sending you a typescript of my version of what I did say—rather expanded in its latter part... and this <u>might</u> provide some clues for your review of the 3 vol job.[3]

The *Good Intentions* review in the Harvard mag, I had read before—they sent me a copy—but thanks; and, of course, it is the sort of thing that I expected, though more elaborate than anything which has appeared in London.[4]

As to reviews of *Space of Appearance*, didn't find them exactly 'penetrating'.[5] Apparently there is great difficulty in grasping the nineteenth century fusion of the mechanicist and organicist ideas—in spite of Karl Marx and all *that*. But I still think it would be 'intelligent' if we could elicit a joint review.[6] Perhaps Paolo Berdini* who was talking about me in Milano yesterday? Will see you at my neo-Baroque apotheosis in a few weeks time.[7]

Best, best,

    Colin

P.S. Think all that *Festspiele* stuff is kind of a bit 19C—Brahms Academic Festival sort of thing—<u>just a bit</u> that is no longer <u>very</u> apropos?

---

1   At their request, Rowe sent the public relations department of the Royal Institute of British Architects a tape recording of his June 1995 acceptance speech for the Royal Gold Medal.
2   The speech was published in two parts: "Thanks to the RIBA", parts 1 and 2, *The Journal of Architecture* 1, 1996, nos 1–2.
3   Baird's* review of Rowe's "3 vol. job", *As I Was Saying: Recollections and Miscellaneous Essays*, Alexander Caragonne ed, 3 vols, Cambridge, MA: MIT Press, 1996, appeared in *Harvard Design Magazine*, spring 1997.
4   Sommer, Richard, "Review of *The Architecture of Good Intentions: Toward a Possible Prospect*", *GSD News*, winter/spring 1996, pp 49–51.
5   Baird, George, *The Space of Appearance*, Cambridge, MA: MIT Press, 1995.
6   No joint review was written.
7   Rowe *Festspiele* at Cornell University on 26–28 April 1996, at which Baird was a principal speaker.

★   *Eulogy for Dorothy Rowe*[1]   *April 1996*

One of the most entertaining little trips which I made with my late sister-in-law, Dorothy, was in April 1988. It was from Rome to a country which I shall call eastern Farneseland and it was my nephew, James, who drove.

It is part of the world which, for me, begins at La Storta—last change of horses as you were driving down to Rome from Siena; and it is just after La Storta—with a side trip to Nepi, in itself rather dull—that certain great topographical themes make their preliminary announcement.

It is a territory to be examined, literally, at three levels: a great rolling plateau with distant presiding mountains—Monti Cimini and Soratte—and then, incised within it, intricate and secret little valleys, sometimes almost wholly private, sometimes admitting to the basic datum of plateau, and, sometimes, receiving the more remote mountain signals. It is the landscape of Nicolas Poussin; and it finally comes on quick—between Sutri and Capranica.

But, at Capranica, you know you are <u>there</u>; you have <u>arrived</u> within full Farnese orbit, the orbit of Alessandro, *il gran' cardinale*, with the emanations of his wild pink chateau already beginning to vibrate.[2] For, in English terms, Capranica is almost the estate village for Caprarola and the little church of the Madonna del Piano, to the right of the Via Cassia going north, is by the way of being a very quiet rehearsal for the triumph prepared by a succession of architects—Baldassare Peruzzi, Antonio da Sangallo il Giovane, and the hyper-cerebral Giacomo Barozzi da Vignola—for Alessandro Farnese.

To my regret I never made a trip with Dorothy to western Farneseland—to Gradoli, to Farnese itself, and to the site of Castro—*Qui fu Castro*; but, except for the tough little job provided by the *castella* at Gradoli, I think she would have been disappointed.[3] And, leaving behind us the five-sided extravagance of Caprarola, that day we went on to lunch at San Martino al Cimino, to La Quercia, and to the Villa Lante at Bagnaia.[4]

All in all a very orthodox little drive around? But, for Dorothy, who was already beginning to tire very easily, this was a major endeavor; and the exhausting return journey was purely her own invention. We just _had_ to go to Soriano nel Cimino—that villa with a waterfall in the cliff below it; we _had_ to return to the Via Cassia by the most savage of declivities—Calcata, Mazzano Romano—which, in a location so very close to Rome, I would not have thought possible.

And, a week later, there was a much more relaxed tour of the Colli Albani; and, after the Viterbo country, this was an anti-climax: "But these landscapes are Claude rather than Poussin"; and: "Was it, perhaps, always a little suburban down here?" And, after this, a dinner at La Costanza: Dorothy, James, and my friend, Paolo Berdini*—with Paolo being a little skeptical and his voice very weary:

Oh, _poor_ Italy—_everything_ north of Rome—that's _Austria_—and _everything_ south of Rome? That's _Africa_—

A devastating piece of *campanilismo* which seems always to deserve that remark of Porfirio Diaz:[5]

Oh, _poor_ Mexico—_so_ far from God and _so_ close to the United States.[6]

So this was the sort of thing Dorothy enjoyed in Italy; a day spent in exercising her excellent eye for landscape and for architecture, with an evening spent in generalizing the experience. But, now, to bring her to England.

Did she possess the gift of happiness? A difficult question: and I very much doubt if she allowed herself to ask it. For, inherently, she was too energetic to become depressed and too much anxious to participate in general activity to enjoy whatever the pleasures of solitary contemplation might be. And this was partly her sense of duty and obligation.

Thus, it might be the Slide Room at the Architectural Association which she felt compelled to serve;[7] or it might be Scottish dancing at Columba's, Pont Street, with which she felt obligated to involve herself; or, at Cheltenham Terrace where she lived for more than thirty years overlooking quasi-military goings-on at The Duke of York's Headquarters, it might be a general possessiveness. And it must have been her protection of Cheltenham Terrace—integral part of the Burton Court-Chelsea Hospital complex—which, apart from her role as mother, was Dorothy's greatest achievement.

The ground landlords were Ecclesiastical Commissioners and they—with their characteristic lack of intelligence—proposed to demolish. But, with extreme determination, _she_ put a stop to all _that_. She organized a resident's association, solicited external support, accumulated a portfolio of expert advice such as, I imagine, had never been put together before, <u>she became *femme forte et formidable*</u>, and the representatives of the Church of England's real estate could only surrender—with very advantageous options for the residents to buy.[8] But the best of all supporting letters, as I remember it, was Sir John Summerson's and it went something like this:

While Cheltenham Terrace is not a remarkable work of architecture it has what we call O.G.V.—outstanding group value—and it is for its O.G.V. that it must be preserved.[9]

Then, wherever she was, Dorothy was always a gardener and trees seemed to grow for her with a density and quickness otherwise quite unknown; and thus it <u>was</u> at Cheltenham Terrace, Ledwell, and St. Margaret's Road, Oxford: what for most people would take a growth of twenty years it seemed that she could have in less than ten.[10]

Then, with growth-continuity a very big thing with her, in the politic of her mind was she a conservative—of a Burkean cast, or was she a classic liberal? And it seems to me that she was a bit of both.

She <u>could</u> be almost Metternich-ian.[11] When the government of the Shah collapsed she was less than overjoyed; and, when I remonstrated with her, she told me—with the amazing common sense of Edinburgh—that, <u>now</u>, things could <u>only</u> become worse.[12] But, at the same time, she was also able to contemplate—and propose that I attend—a midnight mass at St Columba's, Pond Street; and, when I told her that this was a mish-mash which John Knox would <u>never</u> have tolerated, this was so much water off a duck's back. It seemed that St Columba's had its own, legitimate and autonomous, conventions.

And, to come nearer home, had Dorothy lived during the Risorgimento, just how would she have felt about it?[13]

Let's say that, with her predisposition towards Italy, in England she might have known the principal Italian exiles: Panizzi at the British Museum, the brothers Ruffini, later Aurelio Saffi in Oxford. But would she have known Mazzini, also living in Chelsea?[14] And, if so, what might she have thought?

I have read recently, since she died, about a conversation between Camillo Cavour and Charles Sumner, United States Senator from Massachusetts; and I immediately wanted to talk to her about it.[15] It took place in Turin in 1859—the time of Magenta and Solferino; Sumner had come up from a long time in Rome and Cavour's information service seems to have been very good: Had not Senator Sumner been seeing quite a lot of Lady William Russell? And had he not found Lady William to be *tres Autrichienne*?[16]

A curious conversation; and, apart from being no friend of Austria, nor of the pope himself for that matter, just how might Dorothy have reacted in the years 1859–60? Friend of Italy as she was, she would have been, I think, a level-headed federationist. As was the case with the Shah, she would have been effusive about nothing; and absolutely <u>not</u> for <u>her</u> the soft haze of English liberal sentiment which obscured Trevelyan's retrospect. Altogether she was too Edinburgh for <u>that</u>.

Let the Piedmontese remain in Piedmont; their record in Sardinia since 1720 was no recommendation for letting them into the Kingdom of Naples; let the Grand Duchy of Tuscany remain intact; let us avoid the patent absurdity of a centralized French bureaucracy; And, oh yes—in terms of high drama, in their different ways both Mazzini and Garibaldi were a very acceptable pair of picturesque heroes; but, then, what to say about Garibaldi's red shirts?[17]

In 1961, when there were all those signs around saying *Torino vi chiam*,[18] Dorothy had seen that centennial exhibition and it had confirmed her suspicions.[19] For there, in a vitrine, inside the collar of one of Garibaldi's shirts, she had noticed the label: "Thresher and Glenny, The Strand, London"; and, after that sighting, Garibaldi could never be exactly the same again.

For Dorothy it had all the value of a Lytton Strachey reprise on the life of Queen Victoria.[20] And Garibaldi was all the better for it. After the grand opera of the official story it allowed for ventilation and irony—the mythological Garibaldi couldn't quite survive it—; and this was all of a piece with what I think of as the astringency of her Edinburgh sensibility.

Like an ideal product of eighteenth century Edinburgh, she was—all at once— cosmopolitan, censorious and stoic. She had lived in Paris for several years before she lived in London; an enthusiast for architecture, she was never less than critical about the strange obsession from which architects so often suffer; and she accepted the horrible imminence of her own death with the most conscious decorum—when her voice was already very weak, over the phone she told me that it would do me no good to witness her "approaching demise".

As she grew older she became, more and more, an indefatigable traveler. One year it might be India—"yes I agree with you about Jaipur and Udaipur but I don't understand what it is that you see at Fatephur Sikri"; another year it might be Egypt—"but the camels at Aswan are so difficult"; and, in April 1995, it was a wedding in Houston, Texas. After which, in Washington, D.C., we paid a visit to that exhibition of Italian Renaissance models of domes which had come to the National Gallery after its earlier showing in Venice at Palazzo Grassi—"but what a pity this isn't being shown in London.[21] However, short of dismantling the V. and A. where would they put it?"

And, with this visit to the National Gallery, perhaps I might conclude these brief notes. We both of us went around in wheelchairs and Dorothy found this to be an exhilarating means of travel: we could swoop across a room to see whatever it might be. Nevertheless she didn't like the hanging of the Italian pictures. She found it too sparse and too spotty; and she preferred—as I do—a more crowded display. On the other hand, she found the exhibition itself—of the domes—to be immensely gratifying; and particularly the late *quattrocento* dome of Pavia only built during the course of this century: "Is this what it seems to be, the trial run for St Peter's?"

At which stage there is little more that I can say. No doubt I have made too prominent certain themes of Dorothy's character; but, for me, these still appear to be the leading themes: landscape and gardening, architecture and its protection, the Risorgimento as a myth of English liberalism, and, above all, a refreshing skepticism, always ready—as with Edward Gibbon[22]—to "cast a cold eye."[23]

Those who knew her are diminished by her death: in everything she did she was inventive, generous, proud, candid and clever. She "nothing common did nor mean."[24] She was an excellent, devoted mother. As I contemplate what I should probably call the dissolution of my late sister-in-law, King Lear's lament over the body of Cordelia seems to be horribly appropriate:

> Why should a dog, a horse, a rat, have life
> And thou no breath at all? Thou'lt come no more,
> Never, never, never, never, never![25]

But, as regards herself, I believe she would have found such sentiment to be reprehensible and selfish, for practical purpose melodramatic and useless. And, given her simultaneous taste for the grand and her disapprobation of it, I imagine that, to Shakespeare, she might well have preferred Edith Sitwell:

..... Are we not all of the same substance,
Men, planets and earth, born from the heart of darkness,
Returning to darkness, the consoling mother,
For the short winter sleep—o my calyx of the flower of the world,
you the spirit
Moving upon the waters, the light on the breast of the dove.[26]

Dorothy was displeased by such evasive circumlocutions as 'he passed away', 'she is no longer with us'. I almost hear her objections resound in my ears.

N.B.[27]

If you don't like "from an excellent, devoted mother" down to the end of E. Sitwell, it's very easy to miss it out—or to miss parts of it out.
e.g. delete "why should a dog, a horse, etc" *and* "o my calyx of the flower of the world"
Am v. diffident about these myself. But the "evasive circumlocutions" is surely <u>spot on</u>?

---

1 The definitive draft of a eulogy given by Rowe at the memorial service of his sister-in-law Dorothy Rowe⋆ (1924–1996), ex-wife of David Rowe⋆ and mother of Colin's two nephews, James and Simon Rowe.⋆ Of Rowe's eulogy, David Rowe wrote, "He has caught her exactly."

2 *il gran' cardinale,* Italian: the great cardinal, grandson of Pope Paul III and important patron of the arts.

3 *Qui fu Castro,* Latin: Here Stood Castro, an inscription on a solitary column marking the city's destruction in 1649.

4 Vignola's Villa Farnese at Caprarola, Italy, 1559–1573, a pentagon constructed around a circular, colonnaded courtyard.

5 *campanilismo,* Italian: parochialism or local patriotism.

6 Porfirio Díaz (1830–1915), president of Mexico for nearly thirty years, often credited for this saying although there is little evidence to sustain that he made it.

7 In the 1980s Dorothy Rowe⋆ was slide librarian at the Architectural Association in London.

8 *femme forte et formidable,* French: strong and formidable woman.

9 Sir John Summerson (1904–1992), renowned British architectural historian.

10 Ledwell refers to the small cottage purchased by David Rowe⋆ in 1967, located in the village of Ledwell, Oxfordshire, England.

11 Klemens Wenzel, Prince von Metternich (1773–1859), Austrian statesman, organizer of the Congress of Vienna of 1814, which determined the settlement of Europe after the Napoleonic Wars.

12 Dorothy was born in Edinburgh, Scotland.

13 The Risorgimento was a movement for the unification and independence of Italy, which was achieved in 1870.

14 Giuseppe Mazzini (1805–1872), Italian nationalist, and promoter of a republican state, whose writings spurred the Risorgimento.

15 Camillo Cavour (1810–1861), a leading figure in the Risorgimento; Charles Sumner (1811–1874).

16 *très Autrichienne,* French: very Austrian.

17 Giuseppe Garibaldi (1807–1889), Italian patriot whose conquest of Sicily and Naples led to the formation of the Italian state.

18 *Torino vi chiam,* Italian: Turin calls you.

19 The Italian Centennial of Unification Commemoration held in Turin, Italy, in 1961.

20 Giles Lytton Strachey (1880–1932), author of the irreverent, witty biography, *Queen Victoria,* London: Chatto & Windus, 1921.

21 Italian Renaissance Architecture: Brunelleschi, Sangallo, Michelangelo—The Cathedrals of Florence and Pavia, and St Peter's, Rome, National Gallery, Washington, DC, 18 December 1994–19 March 1995.

22 Edward Gibbon (1737–1794), English historian, author of the six-volume history, *The Decline and Fall of the Roman Empire,* London: Strahan and Cadell, 1776–1789.

23 Yeats, WB, "Under Ben Bulben", 1939.

24 Marvell, Andrew, "Horatian Ode Upon Cromwell's Return from Ireland", 1650.

25 Shakespeare, *King Lear,* 1608, act 5, scene 3.

26 Sitwell, Edith, "Green Song", 1944.

27 "N.B.": *Nota Bene,* Italian: Note Well. Meant for David Rowe,⋆ who reviewed the eulogy before Colin gave it.

3133 Connecticut Avenue, Apt. 814, Washington, D.C.

Dearest Miriam:

A mere note—which is also a short critique.[1]

I want you to think of yourself as a racehorse—Or, if that is too much, perhaps as a well pedigreed French poodle being entered for a competition at some sort of WASPY place—Mad. Squ. Garden?

So you have to go through your tricks—pacing, barking, begging, and all the rest. Or, if you don't like the animal analogy, you have to be a great tragic actress in the French tradition— and I think that Rachelle must have had <u>much</u> greater distinction than Sarah B....[2]

So this is about <u>presence</u> and <u>delivery</u> and <u>you</u> are <u>not</u> paying attention to it.

So, take a deep breath... and, with it, acquire a <u>range</u> of voice; practice histrionic whispers which could cut the biggest auditorium like a knife; become disingenuous; become carefully careless; ascend to rolling percrations: become mistress of the pregnant pause. <u>But</u> DO THINK ABOUT THIS: DO GRAB IT. Logic and rhetoric are <u>not</u> to be separated; and it's a <u>fatal error</u> ever to assume that the *Respublica*[3] can be appreciated via the strategies of the *Resprivata*.[4]

<u>And</u> this is also a terrible American propensity: to talk <u>loud</u> is to be <u>undemocratic</u> and equality insists that we should, all of us, mumble along together. But this is <u>really</u> an <u>insult</u> to democracy.... But is it not? Because though one might <u>pretend</u> one is sitting by a fireside—and very nice too (F.D.R.?)[5]—it's really La Scala in which you've been <u>called</u> to play...[6] artfully artless, *sans gene*, and all the rest.[7]

And N.B.[8]: Michael Dennis★ throws himself away—about as animated as a slice of Melba toast; and, likewise, Liz Plater-Zyberk;★ and, ever, so many more.

No, dearest Miriam, <u>practice</u>... and think of all those instructions in musical Italian— *allegro ma non troppo*, and what all.[9] Practice <u>speed</u> and <u>gradient</u>, <u>crescendo</u> and <u>decrescendo</u>. Practice AND and BUT; and Paolo Berdini★ knows this <u>not at all</u>. Also, introduce <u>yourself</u>, call attention to your <u>dilemma-predicament</u>...and then it all goes away—just like Leon Satkowski★ had quite gotten rid of an appalling stammer. But, dearest Miriam, I believe it used to be called ELOCUTION, and became lost because, no doubt, conceived to be painfully insincere. <u>But</u> there <u>is</u> the greater <u>sincerity</u>.... [...]

Un abbraccio,

   Colin

P.S. Say things like this—very deliberately—"AND I now intend to make a parenthesis; it is, of course, a risk, but, when it's finished, I shall <u>hope</u> to be <u>able</u> to recover my line of argument...."

And you will leave the audience looking forward to acrobatics. Don't think that even *le caractere noble* (Garibaldi?) can entirely dispense with this stuff; and, as for Winston Churchill (1 / 8 Iroquois was he) and his <u>pastiches</u> of Edmund Burke, well— perhaps—<u>he</u> rather overdid it.[10]

Loved to have talked without all of that crowd.

   Colin

1 Rowe is writing Miriam Gusevich,* his former student at Cornell from 1970 to 1979, in reference to a talk she gave at his Cornell *Festspiele* the weekend before.
2 Rachel Félix (1821–1858) and Sarah Bernhardt (1844–1923), both actresses.
3 *Respublica, res publica,* Latin: a public thing, ie public affairs; commonwealth.
4 *Resprivata, res privata,* Latin: a private thing, personal property.
5 "F.D.R.": Franklin Delano Roosevelt (1882–1945), when president of the US, gave 30 evening radio addresses—called "fireside chats"—between 1933 and 1944.
6 La Scala, the renowned Milan opera house.
7 *sans gêne,* French: without embarrassment or constraint; unabashed behavior.
8 "N.B.", *Nota Bene,* Italian: Note Well.
9 *allegro ma non troppo,* Italian: cheerful but not too much.
10 *le caractère noble,* French: the noble character.

256   *To **Werner Oechslin**, Zürich, Switzerland*   *n/d, c June, 1996*

3133 Connecticut Avenue, Apt. 814, Washington, D.C.

Dear Werner Oechslin:*

You must find me terribly remiss, rude, irresponsible: this because I have never replied to your letter of May 19, 1994. But the trouble is that I only found it two days ago.

You see in May 1994 I was involved in packing things. I hadn't found London too very gratifying or *simpatico* and I was getting ready to come back to the U.S. And this was when a copy of your French edition of *Transparency* arrived and became immediately absorbed into the general mess.[1]

So it resurfaced the other day because Birkhäuser is about to publish a paperback edition of *Collage City* and I opened some boxes of books which had languished undisturbed for more than two years.[2] So that is the story of my apparent delinquency!

So I like the French edition of *Transparency* quite a lot and, particularly the substance and the tone of your preface. And that is my immediate reason for writing—but again concerned with Birkhäuser. For their new paperback I have just finished a piece of Bernhard's editorial performance—very, very favourable—and I want to have your opinion on it—particularly as it, necessarily, invades the 'territory' of 'transparency'.[3]

Then, since Birkhäuser/Berlin wants to produce an anthology of my essays from the 3 vol M.I.T. publication (M.I.T. produced it very badly) I am suddenly excited/emboldened to think of you as contributing a preface. But it would be a great pleasure to me if you could.[4]

Birkhäuser proposes about 280 pages and 100 illustrations and I very much like the idea of this contracted version—the 3 vols are more than a bit exhausting....

Then I would like to correct a footnote of yours from *Transparence*, footnote 49, which you derived from Werner Seligman.* But dearest Werner knows <u>nothing</u> about this stuff. I.E. In the mid-'50's Ben Weinreb had scarcely <u>begun</u> to operate,[5] the architecture library at the U. of T.[6] was an old and a *retardataire* collection,[7] and—above all—there was matter of *richesses* to be derived from <u>petrodollars</u>![8] It was a collection <u>wholly</u> neglected—a product of provincial laziness and ignorance; and I can imagine its equivalent in some quasi-extinct theological college in a place like Macerata....

But American collections of that kind <u>did</u> possess the books which had been considered valid forty to fifty years earlier: Guadet, Owen Jones, and, of course, Letarouilly. And not only *Les Edifices de Rome Moderne* but also *La Basilique de Saint Pierre et le Vatican.*[9]

In other words, Seligman's information is quite, quite wrong!!!; and, had there been anyone in that school with the intelligence—or the influence—to buy from Weinreb, it must be obvious that the labours of Bernhard and myself would have been superfluous.

But, in any case, I don't think that you will find that Weinreb was an <u>active</u> dealer in the United States until quite a bit later. And, you know, he had the habit of buying in the U.S.—<u>cheap</u>, storing his purchases <u>in</u> the U.S., publishing a catalogue in London, and then selling in the U.S.—with minimum charges for shipping....

But I go on too much and this is just to re-establish contact.

Un abbraccio,

    Colin Rowe

P.S. You refer to letters from Pevsner* deploring the E.T.H.'s involvement with *Transparenz*.[10] Would love it if you could send me Xeroxes.[11]

---

1 Rowe, Colin and Robert Slutzky, *Transparence, réelle et virtuelle,* Paris: Editions du Demi-Cercle, 1992, introduction by Werner Oechslin.* In the English version of this book, *Transparency*, Basel: Birkhäuser, 1997, Oechslin's introduction was translated as "'Transparency': The Search for a Reliable Design Method in Accordance with the Principles of Modern Architecture", pp 9–20.

2 Rowe, Colin and Fred Koetter, *Collage City*, Basel: Birkäuser Verlag AG, 1997.

3 Bernhard Hoesli.*

4 Rowe, Colin, *As I Was Saying: Recollections and Miscellaneous Essays*, Alexander Caragonne ed, 3 vols, Cambridge, MA: MIT Press, 1996. Birkhäuser did not publish an anthology of these essays.

5 Ben Weinreb (1912–1999), London, world-famous antiquarian architectural bookseller.

6 University of Texas at Austin.

7 *retardataire*, French: out of date.

8 *richesses*, French: wealth.

9 Letarouilly, Paul, *Les Edifices de Rome Moderne*, Paris: Didot Frères, 1840; Letarouilly, Paul, *La Basilique de Saint Pierre et le Vatican*, Paris: Vve A Morel, 1882.

10 Nikolaus Pevsner* (1902–1983), German-born British architectural historian, editor of the London-based *The Architectural Review*; "E.T.H.": Eidegenössische Technische Hochschule (Swiss Federal Institute of Technology) in Zürich.

11 Oechslin* did not send photocopies of the letters to Rowe.

*To **Judith DiMaio**, ℅ Moroni, Via della Minerva, Rome*   *10 June 1996*   **257**

3133 Connecticut Avenue, Apt. 814, Washington, D.C.

Dearest Judy!

When you rang the other day I had just put an address on an envelope to send a letter to you; but I had David Roncayolo staying with me and—<u>until he left</u>—I just wasn't able to do anything.[1] But believe me, it was like that! Good, virtuous and infinitely exhausting....

So <u>now</u> there is your postcard and I see <u>where</u> you live.[2] You are just opposite—are you not?—a very popular pizzeria which has a basement with little views into model dungeons as you are going down the stairs; and your building, I think, is of the 1930's—and Carlo Massimo was to be found in the pizzeria often with the daughter of Ibi Amin....[3]

But what's new here? So the extra bookshelves finally arrived and primal chaos is beginning to diminish and I already know, at least, exactly where all the Italian books are... which is a relief. But you discover all sorts of things. For instance, the earliest parts of Palazzo-

Doria-P. are sixteenth century and Aldobrandini,[4] and the Pamphili only acquired it by marriage with Olimpia, *nata* Aldobrandini, a Borghese widow whom somebody married in 1647, and then *si estinta l'antica casata P* and, by another marriage, the whole outfit came to the Doria-Landi of Genova in 1671.[5] But, all the way thru, they never seem to have sold anything and only sustained—as regards objects—one major loss: and this was in 1655 when, for reasons of political convenience (!), they gave a Caravaggio, at present in the Louvre, to Louis XIV!!! In other words, let this be an <u>awful</u> lesson....

Made a trip the other day to Williamsburg and it was dreadful—an earlier America, completely sanitized, of a Rockefeller imagination.[6] But don't, any more, say I am <u>always</u> negative. I went there with the most utopian hopes of being able to buy a bit of their repro bric-a-brac; but, Judy, it's God awful—inexcusably bad French polish and all—and I had expected to find there (but WHY?) a tribe of little William Morris gnomes absolutely devoted to authenticity. So this was a case of <u>becoming</u> negative rather than the *a priori* condition of always <u>being</u> so.

Alex Caragonne* is coming here the day after tomorrow and then we go, the next week, for that mid-career-in-crisis summer school; and, after that, to spend a few days with Steve and Barbara at Cambridge, N.Y.[7] And then Paolo Berdini* will come and, since he wants to see the Cezanne exhibition in Philadelphia and Robert Slutzky* is determined that I should too, this might be a very opportune thing to do.

Anyway the Piranesi-Robert Adam Campo Marzio piece is framed and hung and that is why I want the Ampio e Magnifico Collegio and then this biblio-pranzo room might begin to look just a bit O.K.[8]

And what else?

Dearest Judy I have just come across an awful lot of stuff related to our German trip in 1983 and, in spite of the food, can't help but feeling that I would love to be there again. BUT NOW THERE HAS BEEN YOUR CALL....

---

1 David Roncayolo was a former student of Rowe's from Venezuela.
2 Judith DiMaio* sent Rowe a postcard from Rome depicting the area where she resided near the Pantheon.
3 Idi Amin (1925–2003), dictator of Uganda from 1971 to 1979. Rowe consistently refers to him as "Ibi". See his letter to Dorothy Rowe* dated 6 April 1989 (p 325 in this volume).
4 Palazzo Doria Pamphilj on Via del Corso, Rome.
5 *si estinta l'antica casata P,* Italian: the ancient lineage P (Pamphili).
6 Colonial Williamsburg, Virginia. Williamsburg was founded in 1620; restoration began in 1923, largely financed by John D Rockefeller Jr.
7 Steven Peterson* and Barbara Littenberg.*
8 Two eighteenth-century engravings intended for Rowe's apartment in Washington, DC.

258 *To **Mary Stirling**, Belsize Avenue, London* *13 June 1996*

3133 Connecticut Avenue, Apt. 814, Washington, D.C.

Dearest Mary:

Won't be able to come to your garden party. Instead I shall be at Harvard participating at what I think is really a mid-life-career-in-crisis summer school which I don't expect to enjoy.

I briefly met Kate in N.Y.C. at the beginning of February.[1] She was, sort of, swept up to me and then swepped away again—but not before giving me her address. And then, of course, I lost the address! So, if she is still there—since I am feeling slightly remiss—could you tell me where?

Then I had Mark Girouard* for five days or so at the beginning of March and had wonderful—and not at all intellectual—conversations. I hadn't before appreciated how very agreeable he is. And did you see the Jim horoscope that he was provided in Phoenix, Arizona?[2]

Then I received an honorary doctorate from the New Jersey Institute of Technology and the technology part of it makes me very amused. Also it was a bit like some kind of Edwardian epiphany. They had an organ playing Edward Elgar and that sort of stuff—more or less most of the time![3]

Will you be going to Dorothy's memorial service at Magdalen?[4] If you do, write me about it. And I do find myself missing her very, very much. But it must be quite the worse for Simon....

Best love,

    Colin

---

1 Kate Stirling, Mary Stirling's daughter.
2 For Girouard's * visit, see Rowe's letter to Dorothy Rowe* dated 4 March 1996 (p 464 in this volume). For "horoscope" see Rowe's letter to Phyllis Lambert* dated 21 March 1996 (p 473 in this volume).
3 Edward Elgar (1857–1923), English composer known especially for his *Pomp and Circumstance Marches*.
4 Dorothy Rowe,* who had died in April 1996.

To **Philip Handler**, *West Hartford, Connecticut*   *25 July 1996*   **259**

3133 Connecticut Avenue, Apt. 814, Washington, D.C.

Philip!

    I hate it when I send a letter asking questions and, then, I never get a reply. But it seems that I have placed you exactly in this position.

I.E. Have just been sorting out papers and have come across a letter of yours of January 2 which asks me questions and you haven't had a reply.

Anyway, the Chick Austin house:[1] it is a replica of Vincenzo Scamozzi, Villa Ferretti Angelo between Venice and Padua on the Brenta canal and it is published in Scamozzi, *L'Idea Dell'architettura Universale* of 1613 or so. But you will also find a pic of it in Giuseppe Mazzotti, *Palladian and other Venetian Villas*, London-Alec Tiranti, 1958.

After our dinner of about three weeks ago Alex and I went to Cambridge, N.Y. to spend a couple of nights with Barbara and Steven and we saw some superb things along the way.[2] We left the Mass Pike to go first to Northampton and then, by a back road to Williamstown, Hoosick Falls and Cambridge;[3] and I suggest that you and Maddy do it too.[4] Apart from the usual Greek Revival and assorted bits of Gingerbread there were superb mill buildings and also the occasional row of working class housing, each house two to three windows wide, often painted white, and just waiting to be gentrified. But make a reconnaissance, go, see, and take pics.

But Northampton could be several days and it's <u>amazing</u> that it isn't more talked about. And <u>you</u> are on top of it. So original settlement was obviously from Hartford and that town was, perhaps, a headwater of navigation with very little connection to Boston. And settlement must have been later 17th century—since Russell Hitchcock⋆ has a house there of 1691; and Northampton is really worth a bit of serious research. I mean it's a book and <u>you</u> have to do it—perhaps along with Steve!!![5]

So I <u>had</u> been there before—in the 1950's; but I hadn't seriously seen it. But, for some 300 years a continuous exhibition of quality, and to be judged by the most exacting standards!!!

Anyway, I raved about it in Cambridge, N.Y. And now I'm raving about it to you. So why don't <u>you all</u> make a rendezvous there with Steve and Barbara [...] And I think it will be a revelation—and an easy book.

Un abbraccio and best, best,

    Colin

P.S. <u>Do it and it will surprise the world</u>—it's far more than just an Americana thing.

    Colin

---

1   The A Everett "Chick" Austin house, Hartford Connecticut, 1930. The Handlers lived in West Hartford and asked Rowe about this house. Rowe first visited the house in 1952 with Henry-Russell Hitchcock.⋆ See "Henry-Russell Hitchcock", written 1988, in Rowe, Colin, *As I Was Saying: Recollections and Miscellaneous Essays*, Alexander Caragonne ed, 3 vols, Cambridge, MA: MIT Press, 1996, vol 1, p 18; and "The Avant-Garde Revisited", Somol, RE ed, *Autonomy and Ideology: Positioning an Avant-Garde in America*, New York: The Monacelli Press, 1997, pp 60–64. Also, see Rowe's letter to Eugene Gaddis⋆ dated 13 September 1985 (p 273 in this volume).
2   Alexander Caragonne;⋆ Barbara Littenberg⋆ and Steven Peterson.⋆
3   Northampton and Williamstown, Massachusetts; Hoosick Falls and Cambridge, New York.
4   Maddy Handler, Philip's⋆ wife.
5   Steven Peterson.⋆

260   *To **Wayne Copper**, McKeesport, Pennsylvania*   *12 August 1996*

3133 Connecticut Avenue, Apt. 814, Washington D.C.

Dear Wayne:

I know that I must sound like a voice from before Noah's Ark had gotten afloat; but it's 9:30 in the morning, I am thinking about you, and I have just enjoyed a nice and protracted telephone call at 1720 Fawcett Avenue.[1] So you grab that much of the pic and now to continue.

Birkhäuser Verlag A.G. in Basel and Stuttgart, which has published things of mine before, is now in the throes of producing three more items. These are: a new edition of Bernhard Hoesli's⋆ *Transparenz*—the Zurich version of Rowe and Slutzky⋆ *Transparency*; a paperback edition of Rowe and Koetter,⋆ *Collage City*—they did in hardcover some years ago, again edited by Bernhard Hoesli;[2] and a condensed version, edited by Kurt Forster,⋆ of my three volume books of collected essays which I am sending to you at Fawcett Avenue under separate cover.[3] And all of this has just <u>happened</u> to me—with no activity on my part!

So what about the figure-ground book of so long ago?[4]

I regard this as a genuine contribution to knowledge, as one of the best things ever done at Cornell, and—since it still languishes without publication—as still an incomplete project. Which causes me to ask whether you would permit a German publication?

In days gone by I think that it was too much to hope for any interest from English language publishers but I believe that things are now changed—and particularly as regards the Germanic lands. And then these German Swiss do produce with brilliant graphics. So the result could, now, be a very important atlas—and specifically important wherever the German language prevails because of plans of: Stuttgart, Wiesbaden, Munich, Vienna, Dusseldorf, Schwerin, and Schloss Hechingen.

So will you think about it? Suggest that it would be useful both for you and the public, that it wouldn't mean much work for you (some textual revision? I do not have the text to hand), with a brief, and hopefully cogent, introduction from me.

So think, think, and best, best,

> Colin Rowe

P.S. Ring me when you get back—(202) 462-7955—and think about driving over for a weekend.[5] Think this is the best way to fly and here in D.C. you will be able to compare notes with other old Istanbul hands, Matt Bell★ from Pittsburgh and Bob Goodill★ from Erie—ex-Cornell and, before that, ex-Notre Dame.

---

1 Wayne William Copper★ (1942–1999).
2 See bibliography.
3 The "condensed version" of *As I Was Saying* was never published.
4 In spring 1967 Copper★ had submitted a thesis title, "The Figure/Grounds", to the Graduate School of Cornell University for the degree of Master of Architecture.
5 Copper★ was departing for Istanbul when Rowe telephoned him. Here Rowe suggests he fly from Pittsburgh, near where he was living, through Washington, DC.

To *Judith DiMaio*, ℅ Moroni, Via della Minerva, Rome   *28 June 1996*   **261**

3133 Connecticut Avenue, Apt. 814, Washington, D.C.

Dearest Judy!

I have just come back from my little session—mid-career-in-crisis summer school at Harvard and am now engaged in recovery. Each session was for four hours! So that you can guess that it was slightly exhausting.

Stayed at Fac Club and have some new reactions to Quincy Street. Carpenter Center seemed to me—this time—to be a rather silly affair of much ado about nothing... but really![1] Fogg respectable but too demure. Jim, OK but so-so.[2] And Gund Hall trite and triste.[3] So, on the other side, Sever which absorbs too much light and doesn't refract any....[4] But Robinson Hall probably the best—very lucid, beautiful brickwork and exquisite-erudite play between brick and stone.[5] So fire station still a charmer and Memorial Hall, of course, great. But the excitement was for Robinson Hall.

Then, to my surprise but probably *not* yours, Harvard has no slides of Unity Temple *and* NO slides of Altes Museum, Akropolis Palast or Charlottenhof—nor any plans of bedroom floor at Garches!!! And, after this I was not greatly surprised that—in all that spacious ground floor—with auditorium, lib, etc—the men's johns consist of just two urinals and one W.C.!!! But truly astonishing.

Anyway, after these four-hour sessions, I found that I could just contrive to eat dinner and to keel over. So rang nobody and have to call now to apologize to Susie, Michael, Jorge, Rudolfo, etc.[6]

So, after that was all over (Alex C. was with me), we drove to *chez* Barbara-Steven at Cambridge, N.Y.[7] We drove through Northampton, Mass, which is superb and *should* be seen—I had forgotten it; and then, in Williamstown, to the Clark Institute—where their alleged Piero is not a Piero and both of the buildings are a heap of junk.[8] Then the next day to Bennington and Manchester. A bit *difficile* as Alex wanted to go to Saratoga and was reluctant to see antique shops.[9] But it was another case of my reputation for being negative. He thought I was exaggerating about the place; and it was only after we had gotten there that he, too, found that there was nothing.

So came back down to Susquehanna and it was after Lewisburg that there came a most terrible and immobilizing deluge.

Anyway there's a book that I want you to buy—and for me too—and also tell Brian and Matt.[10] It is Mario Gallarati, *Architettura Scala Urbana,* Alinea Editrice, Firenze 1944, and I found it among Steven's things. But it's one chapter which made me excited. There are four other Gonzaga towns of which we don't know anything.

West of Mantova and north of the river there are: Isola Devarane, Rivarolo Mantovano, Pomponesco; and south of the river—but I can't find it on the map—there is S. Martino dell'Argine. And these are all of the late 16th C, belonging to the sequence (or rather making up the sequence) Sabbioneta-Gualtieri.

So not mentioned in *Citta da Scoprire;* but, obviously, a must *and* Go See.[11] As it says in the book—and I believe it—it is the squares in these towns (and think of Gualtieri) which exerted influence in Torino and, hence, Paris-London (and possibly in Livorno?). So do drive up and take a look—and pics.

Otherwise I send you two clippings from *N.Y.T.*[12]

Dearest Judy, love, love, love,

    Colin x x x x x

P.S. Apparently they precede Gualtieri. Got your p.c.'s.[13] Please keep my clipping about Marc. T. C-i-c-e-r-o. I believe this is part of the information explosion....

    Colin

1   The Carpenter Center for the Visual Arts at Harvard, 1962, designed by Le Corbusier.★

2   "Jim": James Stirling,★ architect of the Sackler addition of 1985 to Harvard's Fogg Museum built in 1895.

3   Gund Hall, the Graduate School of Design at Harvard, 1972, designed by John Andrews.

4   Sever Hall, Harvard, 1878, designed by HH Richardson.

5   Charles McKim designed Robinson Hall, 1904, to house Harvard's School of Architecture.

6   Susie Kim,★ Michael Dennis,★ Jorge Silvetti,★ and Rodolfo Machado.★ Here, and elsewhere, I have kept in Rowe's text his incorrect spelling of 'Rodolfo'.

7   Alexander Caragonne;★ *Chez* (home of) Barbara Littenberg★ and Steven Peterson.★

8   The Sterling and Francine Clark Art Institute, Williamstown, New York, houses *Virgin and Child Enthroned with Four Angels,* c 1460–1470, alleged to be the work of Renaissance painter Piero della Francesca (c 1415–1492).

9   *difficile,* French: difficult.

10 Brian Kelly★ and Matthew Bell.★

11 *Citta da Scoprire*, a contemporary travel guide.
12 *"N.Y.T."*: *The New York Times*. The clippings are lost. Rowe's PS suggests that one of the clippings was concerned with "Marc T. C-i-c-e-r-o", Marcus Tullius Cicero (106–43 BC), Roman orator, statesman, and philosopher.
13 "p.c.'s": postcards.

To *James Madge*, London   *1 July 1996*   **262**

3133 Connecticut Avenue, Apt. 814, Washington, D.C.

Dearest James:

I have just come across a book, Mario Gallarati, *Architettura: Scala Urbana*, Alinea Editrice, Firenze 1994, of which the last chapter might interest you.[1] It's all about Gonzaga-Estense urban interventions in a territory which you and Victoria must know excessively well.[2] But, apart from Gualtieri, I didn't know a single one.

So do you know: Rivarolo Mantovano, Isola Dovarese, Pomponesco, and—I think that it's more remote—S. Martino dall'Argine? They seem to be remarkable and, so far as I can see, not to have penetrated any of the even faintly popular literature. Also they seem mostly to be foundations/developments of the 1580's—and, apart from Livorno, there doesn't seem to be anything like them of <u>that</u> date. But repeat: <u>not</u> noticed and <u>surely</u> models for Place des Vosges, Charleville, Piazza S. Carlo in Turin, Covent Garden, and Londonderry—which precedes Covent Garden and became a model for settlements in Connecticut.

In other words, I am wildly excited and I await your observations. This is, partly, because I am writing a book to be called *From Bramante to Scamozzi* (I am doing this with Leon Satkowski,★ a former student of mine who now knows all about Vasari-Ammannati-Buontalenti, and we are doing alternative chapters) and I think this sort of stuff will be kinda *chic* in the final remarks.[3]

My best love for Victoria and *un abbraccio affettuoso,*

    Colin

P.S. Think I <u>may</u> have a sort of haunting memory—sort of—of Rivarolo. This from driving all by myself from Pavia to Montagnana in '69. Also <u>have</u> you been to Cento? I <u>never</u> have. But, apart from being the birthplace of Guercino, as part of the Estense policy of accommodating the Sephardic diaspora from Spain, this is where the Disraeli's came from—though <u>the</u> Disraeli★ didn't seem to know this.[4]

    Colin

1 Gallarati, Mario, *Architettura: Scala Urbana*, Firenze: Alinea Editrice, 1994. Rowe "came across" the book in June 1996 at Steven Peterson's★ home in Cambridge, New York. See Rowe's letter to Judith DiMaio★ dated 28 June 1996 (p 487 in this volume).
2 Dr Victoria Watson (b 1959), architect, married to James Madge★ from 1993 until his death. Madge and Watson owned a vacation house in Northern Italy that they visited several times each year.
3 The book, co-authored by Leon Satkowski,★ was published posthumously as *Italian Architecture of the 16th Century* (New York: Princeton Architectural Press, 2002). For the Gonzaga towns, see pp 294–298.
4 Benjamin Disraeli★ (1804–1881), British writer, prime minister, and aristocrat of Jewish birth.

3133 Connecticut Avenue, Apt. 814, Washington, D.C.

Dearest Robert:

I am thinking, yet again, about the ambivalence to L.C.[1]

Open vol I of the *O.C.* at p. 103 and contemplate the pic of the *jardin suspendu* and note the proximity-intimacy of the trees outside....[2]

An excessively, wrenching, moving image? But eloquent? Or don't you think so? And wouldn't you like to be just there? With the leaves of the tree almost obscuring everything else?

Well, alter the immediate foreground rather for the worse and that's almost my location. So I'm ten floors up and it's still a case of *la ville verte*.[3] But literally, I can see nothing but leaves!.... "a green thought in a green shade"? With a long pointer I could almost touch the trees.... I almost feel like a noble savage.

Have you ever been to that Loudon landscape at Great Tew just northeast of Blenheim?[4] Well, the effect here is somewhat the same and, from April to October, any middle distance is not to be found.

In England, Victorians usually permitted the middle distance—a few trees close to the house and then a gap, and then the boundary of, let's say, pine trees and rhododendrons. But, in this country, they were much more extreme.

A precocious, bourgeois, version of the collective Corbu* had in mind. The foyer is described as "Art Deco Aztec"; and think of that now! But the black guys, who comprise the service, are highly stylish and not at all menial: "Well, and ha ya doin today?"; and, from an old black guy with a white beard—and I have just made a verbal mistake: "Well, perfeeor, THAT was a Freudian lapse!!!"

But, to return to the real *unité*—where I am not able to imagine such an agreeable society—and to consider only the topic of trees.[5]

"Great blocks of dwellings run through the town. What does it matter? They are behind the screen of trees."[6]

But what did happen to the trees in *ville radieuse* and *Zeilenbau* city?[7]

When, in theory, it was almost criminal to build anything, when the buildings were to be as pellucid/transparent as the landscape, neither the pics nor the project drawings any longer make any big deal of the trees.... But notice Corbu's drawings. The famous trees, "friends of man", become miniscule and weedy, the profusion of John Claudius Loudon is very far, far, away, and, on the whole, as a simple confrontation of the built and the arboreal, surely Eaton Square and the Avenue du Bois de Boulogne make a far better showing?

Very sad thoughts for a rather hot afternoon when I haven't yet turned on the air conditioning? And sadder still because, surely, things didn't have so to be.

Have just come down from Upstate N.Y. to the accompaniment of lots of Auden-ary sensations and lots of eco-empathy.[8] Not "a leisured drive through a land of farms" but a kind of drift through a forest, either authentic or simulated. It seems that, in the nineteenth century, nobody could build without planting. You built the house—this is Steve Peterson's* house at Cambridge, N.Y. in 1856—and immediately you planted four trees in front of it. But it's totemistic and almost idolatrous. And then you get the more extreme cases—out in more open country—where the house sits in the little <u>cube</u> of trees. But I know <u>nothing</u> like it elsewhere. The cute little white painted house—Ionic or gingerbread—is caressed by trees and the final impression is wildly animistic. The trees guarantee what was to be the prevailing *sfumato* of the Wrightian interior.[9]

Well, here I am in the sort of proto-*unité*, sort of *avant la lettre*, and the effect is much the same.[10] And what you have here, from 1929–30 programmatically is more or less what Corbu wanted to build—about two hundred apartments, foyer, restaurant, shops and services, a small library (?), what seems to be a music room (anyway it has a grand piano), and three levels of underground parking (an escarpment permits this) of which, even at Marseilles, Le C. never dared to dream. But it's all so very odd; and, being Southern, so affable / genial and, I believe, genuine.

But, increasingly, I despair of arch ed. Have just been at Harvard where I was involved in a crisis-in-mid-career summer school. Three sessions, lecture turning into seminar, of <u>four hours each</u>. And that's why I'm writing at such length—because I'm still feeling so flat. But Harvard U. and its slide collection!!!??? I thought that I might pick up a few more slides and, of course, they <u>didn't</u> have them. They didn't have a plan of the Altes Museum, nor of the Akropolis Palast. No plan either of Unity Temple and <u>no</u> plan of the bedroom floor at Garches....[11]

Which all causes me to think how perfectly sweet Garches might be if, as a preface, it was partly to be concealed by a Loudonesque accumulation of monkey puzzles and weeping willows.

My best love to Celia[12] and *affettuosamente*,[13]

    Colin

P.S. Had a phone call from Rome this morning when I learned that a Rosa di Tivoli was being offered in the Via Del Babuino for $30,000.00! This for just <u>one</u>; and I <u>gave</u> my pair to David![14]

    Colin

---

1 "L.C.", "Le C." and "Corbu" are Rowe's abbreviations for the Swiss-French architect Le Corbusier⋆ (Charles-Édouard Jeanneret-Gris, 1887–1965).

2 Le Corbusier and Pierre Jeanneret, *Œuvre complète, 1910–1929*, Willi Boesiger ed, vol 1, Zurich: Les Éditions d'Architecture Artemis, 1991. First published in 1929; *jardin suspendu*, French: suspended garden.

3 *la ville verte*, French: the green city.

4 John Claudius Loudon (1783–1843), Scottish garden designer of Great Tew in Oxfordshire, 1808–1811.

5 Proposed by Le Corbusier⋆ for diverse regions and climates, the *Unité d'habitation* was a large, singular housing block typically built of concrete with an internal shopping "street" and a cluster of small buildings on its rooftop. Its first and most famous manifestation was built in Marseille, France, 1946–1952.

6 Le Corbusier⋆ (see note 1) quoted by Rowe in the final paragraph of "On Conceptual Architecture", *Art Net*, 1975.

7 *Ville radieuse* (radiant city) and *Zeilenbau* city were urban design schemes proposed by Le Corbusier⋆ in the late 1920s and 1930s.

8 "Auden-ary": WH Auden⋆ (1907–1970), an Anglo-American poet born in York, England, who moved to the US in 1939.

9 *sfumato*, Italian: softness, mellowness.

10 *avant la lettre*, French: before the term was coined; literally, "before the letter"; Rowe is writing from the Kennedy-Warren (1930–31), a very large, premodern apartment building in which he lived the last five years of his life.

11 Le Corbusier's⋆ Villa Stein de Monzie at Garches, France, 1926–1928.

12 Celia Scott, Maxwell's⋆ wife.

13 *affettuosamente*, Italian: affectionately.
14 Rowe had given his brother, David, two paintings by Philipp Peter Roos, aka Rosa di Tivoli
   (1655–1706); see his letter to David Rowe* dated 17 August 1996 (p 497 in this volume).

264   *To James Madge*   *5 August 1996*

3133 Connecticut Avenue, Apt. 814, Washington, D.C.

My dear James:

You are the first victim of my new Xerox machine. I thought that they were enormous and, when I found out that nowadays they are quite small, I went out and bought one. So here are the relevant bits of the Mario Gallarati text and I hope that you will now be able to go to Isola Dovarese and Pomponesco.[1]

It would be a nice idea to join you and Victoria in those parts at the end of the month; but I think that I shall have to put it off for next year and I am looking forward to it.[2]

So poor Jane did die.[3] My brother sent me a copy of *The Times* obituary which I found slightly odd. "she met and made friends with such great names of Modernism as Henry Moore, Le Corbusier,* Elizabeth Lutyens...". But <u>what</u> has Elizabeth Lutyens to do with anything mod.?[4]

Un abbraccio,

   Colin

1 Gallarati, Mario, *Architettura a Scala Urbana*, Firenze: Alinea Editrice, 1994. See Rowe's
   letter to James Madge* dated 1 July 1996 (p 489 in this volume).
2 Victoria Watson, James Madge's* wife since 1993.
3 Jane Drew (1911–1996), celebrated modernist English architect and town planner. Madge*
   had been married to Drew's daughter, Jennifer Alliston (1937–1986).
4 (Agnes) Elisabeth Lutyens (1906–1983), an English composer.

265   *To David Rowe, Headington, Oxford*   *5 August 1996*

3133 Connecticut Avenue, Apt. 814, Washington, D.C.

Dearest David:

This is to introduce:

GEORGETOWN UNIVERSITY
VILLA LE BALZE
MARCELLO FANTONI
DIRECTOR OF STUDIES[1]

He and his wife, Cinzia, came to dinner last night and he left me surprisingly happy and impressed. Good presence, physique, voice, neither ra-ra nor supercilious, his age is about 40 and he is <u>not</u> the type of academic administrator. His speciality is <u>Mantova and the Iconography of the Gonzagas</u> and I believe that all of you would like him and I also believe that Dorothy would have been charmed—would have found both of them so sympathetic that she would have invited them to stay! So I am thinking of him as both an advisor and a performer and I am suggesting that you get in touch.[2]

Therefore, let me lay out the sequence of what might be the first Dorothy Rowe Memorial Lecture and you can begin to think about it.

The Gonzagas took over Mantova in 1382—see Domenico Morone, *Expulsion of the Bonacolsi in the Palazzo Ducale*—and by the mid quattrocento, they had acquired the habit of introducing star performers.[3] Hence Alberti, S. Andrea and S. Sebastiano, Mantegna, Giulio Romano and, in early 17C, Rubens. So S. Andrea has a vial of the blood of J.C.; but, after that, the dominant theme of iconography becomes Roman and Imperialist—Mantegna's *Triumphs of Caesar*, at Hampton Court and Palazzo del Te, which is a celebration of the special relationship of the Marchese Federigo with Charles V. And, therefore, imagine a protracted pictorial sequence of the different Giulio interiors leading to Sala dei Giganti, itself really a theatre of Imperial judgement. Then also remember that Federigo married Maria Paleologa, descendant of Byzantine emperors and heiress to Monferrato.

With all that, after Chas V, it is perhaps inevitable that the Gonzagas should slide into the service of Philip II and that some of them should even be brought up in Madrid—and there is, thus, a generation who find themselves—the younger ones— in the Spanish service as viceroys of Sicily and Milan. But note also, in France, the Gonzaga de Nevers—and, in Nevers, there is a Quai de Mantoue....

So then there are the minor cities—to be handed out to junior member of the family?—and, of these Guastalla and Sabinetta are the most famous; but, then, here comes the news (and see xerox), there are at least four more which are, to all intents and purposes, quite unknown.[4]

And these are: Rivarolo Mantovano, S. Martino dall'Argine, Isola Dovarese, and Pomponesco. (And, in this sequence, there is also Gualtieri—an Estense feud held by the Bentivoglio of Bologna and intervention dating from 1592.)

So these are, mostly, products of Gonzagas returned from the Spanish service and, if you annex them to Giulio and P. del Te, there is something of a revelation as to Gonzaga influence.[5]

So look at the xerox and grab the message. But just look at those squares and arcades—and all of them concentrated in a flatly rural—and now unvisited—part of the world. But, of course, Mantova was visited and, in those days, these places—all products of the 1580's were known..... So, then, move to Paris, 1605, Place de Vosges / Place Royale, and to the Place Ducale at Charleville in Lorraine, 1606, where the Duc just happened to be Charles de Gonzague-Nevers—Nevers again!

And the architects just happen to be, in Paris, Louis Metezeau, and, in Charleville, his brother, Clement Metezeau.

O.K. So, after an arcane beginning (all the iconography), the urbanistics would be the great public news. But doncha' think? In London, Covent Garden is 1631, in Torino Piazza S. Carlo begins as a project of 1637; and, if both of these are generally spoken of in connection with Henri IV and the P. des Vosges, then if Henrietta Maria is daughter of Henri IV and Q. of E., Maria Cristina di Francia, her sister, is the wife of Vittorio Amedeo di Savoia.....!!!!

But nice work, don't you think? And you tie it all up with Charles de Nevers becoming Duke of Mantova in 1627 and his selling the Gonzaga pics to Charles I—just before Il Sacco di Mantova by the Austrians in July 1630.......

But I think that this would make an elegant—and surprising—opening lecture—a trade between Mantova and England; and I am sure that it would be the sort of novelty for the Oxford Italians which you are thinking about—this apart from its being a genuine contribution to knowledge. And I add another xerox showing the location of all these little towns which are <u>now</u> to be considered <u>so</u> influential.[6]

However, I suggest other possibilities:

<u>Giuseppe Poggi</u>, the Piazzale Michelangelo and the Public Garden in 19th C Italy.

See French origins of public gardens: Nimes, Montpellier, Bordeaux, Toulouse, Avranches, Rennes, Nancy. In the later 18th C these were created by provincial intendants on the sites of obsolete fortifications. The public garden in Italy was a French-Napoleonic export. A foro Buonaparte was proposed for Firenze, also Torini; there are the not very good p.g.'s in Venice;[7] but the *beau ideal* of the type is Valadier's Piazza del Popolo and Pincio in Rome.[8] Before Nap. the only p.g. is Prato della Valle in Padova. A nice little 19th C specimen is to be found at Trani. A not so nice specimen is also in Rome, the Passeggiata del Gianicolo: a nationalist polemic against what became the papalist Pincio.

Problems of terrain: the approach to the sacred site—*sacro monte* at Varese, Monte Berico at Vicenza: the destination as a plateau-belvedere, the Piazzale Michelangelo.

The P.M. as a great 19th C urbanistic statement.[9] Approaches from the river and the Porta Romana. A superb *passeggiata*.[10] *Firenze capitale*.[11] <u>Parkway</u> and ramps.

But <u>note</u> that the parkway is supposed to be an American invention of Frederick Law Olmsted in the 1880's!!!

This could also be a very elegant lec. But who would do it? Giorgio Ciucci? He <u>did</u> write a very nice thing on P. del P. and P.[12] but <u>I don't</u> think that he would accept a prescribed topic. And, in this context, I <u>don't</u> think that Marcello would be appropriate—no use him for the Gonzagas. But how about Matthew Bell★ whose Italian is v. good? Or how about Michael Dennis,★ now at M.I.T., whose Italian is excellent and who would understand the topic perfectly?

Then I have lots of other ideas but won't let you have them until they are more articulate.

Best, best, *un abbraccio* and all that,

    Colin

P.S. I also send you the *N.Y.T.* obituary of Jessica M.[13]—The *T. of L.* doesn't call out the Romilly daughter who, apparently, lives in N.Y.C.[14]

Jane Drew died in Darlington.[15] This is info from James Madge★ who was the son-in-law and, about Gonzaga towns, you should contact James. He and his new wife have a *casa colonica* in the next village to Rinaldo Mantovano!!!![16]

Address: 70 Compton Street, EGIV 0515. Tel: 490-0515 ???

    Colin

"And honour as long as the waves shall break, To Nelson's peerless name."

But it was wicked and very shocking affair; and I once had a Mimi Caracciolo sitting next to me at dinner in New York who <u>still</u> felt it very badly. So, of course, Lord Holland was right and it <u>was</u> Emma Hamilton acting under the influence of Maria Carolina of Naples who, apart from being the sister of Marie Antoinette, was also the mistress of Sir John Acton, prime minister and grandfather of the historian. Then, about Poundbury,—it can look bleak on a bad day—how very much they miss the point!

OVER   OVER   OVER

**** The Villa Vizcaya is supposed to be a composite Venetian sort of job—mostly based on the Villa Rezzonico outside Bassano. Its real architect was mostly a Chilean guy, Diego Suarez, who got his training working for Arthur Acton at Villa La Pietra and then went on to do gardens for Charles Loeser at La Gattaia—just behind S Miniato al Monte. He ended up by living in Long Island married to a Marshall Field widow for whom he made gardens now disappeared......

---

1 A photocopy of Marcello Fantoni's business card. The address reads as follow: Via Vecchia Fiesolana, 26—50014 Fiesole (FI) Italy, tel. (055) 59.208, fax (055) 59.95.85.
2 Rowe is suggesting Fantoni as possible advisor and lecturer for the The Dorothy Rowe Memorial Lecture series, organized and sponsored by David Rowe.*
3 *Expulsion of the Bonacolsi in the Palazzo Ducale in 1328*, a painting by Domenico Morone, 1494.
4 The "Xerox" enclosure is lost.
5 Giulio Romano (1499–1543) and his best-known work, Palazzo del Te, Mantua.
6 The enclosure is a photocopy of a map of an area just north of Parma, Italy, on which eight small towns are circled.
7 "p.g.'s": public gardens.
8 *bel idéal*, French: idealized type or model.
9 "P.M.": Piazzale Michelangelo.
10 *passeggiata*, Italian: walk.
11 *Firenze capitale*, Italian: Florence capital. Florence was the capital of the kingdom of Italy prior to 1861.
12 Giorgio Ciucci, *La Piazza del Popolo: storia, architettura, urbanistica* (1974).
13 Jessica Mitford (1917–1996), English author, civil rights activist, and political campaigner.
14 "T. of L.": *Times of London*.
15 Jane Drew (1911–1996), English modernist architect and town planner.
16 See Rowe's letter to James Madge* dated 26 July 1997 (p 516 in this vol).

To **David Rowe**, *Headington, Oxford*   *11 August 1996*   **266**

3133 Connecticut Avenue, Apt. 814, Washington, D.C.

Dearest David:

Topics and persons:[1]

Anglo-Florentine Houses and Gardens c. 1900. Arthur Acton at La Pietra, Bernard Berenson at I Tatti, Charles Loeser at La Gattaia, Charles Augustus Strong at Le Balze, Iris Origo at La Foce, Sir George Sitwell at Montegufoni, Alice Keppel at L'Ombrellino, etc.

This is a very rich and engaging topic. Its pre-history would go back to the 18C—Zoffany, Tribuna of the Uffizi; Temple Leader at Vincigliata in the 1850's, etc. An Italian perspective to be desired. Who to do it?

The Cultural Politics of the Grand Duke Cosimo. A problem when a descendent of bankers becomes a territorial potentate: buildings, pictures, academies, and *trionfi*.[2] Who to do it? Franco Borsi?

The Enlightenment in Tuscany and the Grand Duke Pietro Leopoldo. P.L. of Habsburg-Lorraine, G.D. of T. 1765–1790, Emperor 1790–1792, is the central figure and from him the later Habsburgs descend.[3] Unfortunately, they didn't like Mozart but was otherwise terrific—abolished the death penalty, drained marshes, extended cities, and—all in all and in Toscana—seems to have been the brains of the family. Who to do it? Carlo Gresti?

Something Piedmontese and I agree with you: you would like Vittone and Alfieri. So Henry Millon at the Nat Gall here is really the person to do it;[4] but there was just arrived within the orbit of my attention H.A. Meek, *Guarino Guarini,* Y.U.P. 1988, and he is to be found at Queen's University, Belfast!!![5] So, maybe, you could smell him out?

London capital in the 19th C Italy??? Sounds shocking and might be v. interesting— particularly for railroad developments. For instance, see the following attached xeroxes: Lewis Cubitt, King's Cross, 1851–52, compared with I. K. Brunel and B. H. Babbage, the Leopolda and Maria Antonia stations, Firenze, 1847.[6] Interesting. Yes/no? But, at that date, where else would the money come from—and also the know-how—except from London? Then would also suspect London investment in Piedmont. But who financed the different Alpine tunnels and Mont Cenis was not completed as late as 1870.

The line from Naples to Caserta? Presumably Rothschilds of Naples who closed down, with the Borbone, in 1860?

The Galleria in Milano, after 1859? London and Zurich.

The bitching up the Florence by making that terrible piazza in the 1880's? London and Zurich.

But who would do this about Risorgimento and post-Risorgimento infrastructure. I think that is almost a Denis Mack Smith topic.[7] But, surely, he could suggest.

Papal Urbanism in Romagna, the Marche, Umbria, etc.

There are a surprising quantity of papal interventions but you are not likely to get an Italian v. interested in this—for obvious reasons. However, in about five years time, it could be Matt Bell*—when he has collected a few more specimens.

However, from this list you will see why I lead off with Marcello Fantoni and The Gonzaga: Iconography and Urbanism. Marcello would be a v. good P.R., advice and contact man.

> *Colin*

P.S. If you do decide on Marcello would suggest taking him on a little trip to Rousham and Hidcote particularly Hidcote—and, possibly Snowshill.[8]

P.P.S. Then, apropos of Rosa di T, I would suggest hanging those two animals and their attendants in the back of the drawing room at S.M.R., opposite the door to the dining room. Looking away from each other I think they'd spruce up the room no end and make it v. O.K. for potential Italian visitors—Piranesi front, Rosa da T. back!!![9]

> *Colin*

*Italian Gardens in the United States???

There are quite a few of them but would this be O.K.?

Anyway publications are like this:

American: Charles Platt, *Italian Gardens*, 1894
Edith Wharton, *Italian Villas and Their Gardens*, 1903

English: Charles Latham, *The Gardens of Italy*, 1905
H. Inigo Triggs, *The Art of Garden Design in Italy*, 1906
Sir Geo Sitwell, *On the Making of Gardens*, 1909

So, at least as regards publication, the American priority <u>seems</u> to be established and specimens are, usually, very <u>pure</u>.

Therefore, is it a thought? And, if so, could be done by Claudia Lazzaro (at last a woman) who teaches, in Art History, at Cornell and has a book, *The Italian Renaissance Garden*, Y.U.P., 1990.

Colin

---

1 David Rowe* had initiated an annual lecture at Oxford University on Italian topics in honor of Dorothy Rowe*. Here, Rowe advises him on possible "topics and persons" for that lecture.
2 *trionfi*, Italian: Italian triumphal processions.
3 "P.L. of Habsburg-Lorraine, G.D. of T.": Prince Leopold II of Habsburg-Lorraine, the Grand Duke of Tuscany.
4 "Nat Gall": National Gallery of Art, Washington, DC, where Henry A Millon (b 1927) was dean of the Center for Advanced Study of the Visual Arts from 1980 to 2000.
5 "Y.U.P.": Yale University Press.
6 The two enclosures are photocopies taken from two unidentified books (one Italian, one English) both showing mid-nineteenth-century train stations with prevalent double-arch structures. The Italian book shows two 1847 illustrations of Florence: E Presenti's Leopolda Railway Stations and one illustration of Isambard Kingdom Brunel and Charles Babbage's Maria Antonia railway station. The English book shows three illustrations of Lewis Cubitt's King's Cross railway station, 1851–1852, London, under which Rowe has typed, "Double arch also occurs at Gare du Nord in later '50's. But don't know any other cases."
7 Denis Mack Smith (b 1920), English historian specializing in Italian history from the Risorgimento onward.
8 Rousham House and Garden, Hidcote Manor Garden, and Snowshill Manor and Garden in Oxfordshire and Gloucestershire are not far from David Rowe's* house in Oxford.
9 Rowe is suggesting locations for David to hang two Rosa di Tivoli paintings and various Piranesi prints in "S.M.R.", St. Margaret's Road, Oxford. On these paintings, see note 15 to Rowe's letter to Robert Maxwell* dated 1 July 1996 (p 490 in this volume).

To **David Rowe**, *Headington, Oxford*   *17 August 1996*   **267**

3133 Connecticut Avenue, Apt. 814, Washington, D.C.

David!

Further names:[1]

Hugh Honour/John Fleming. They live in Lucca.

Francis Haskell? I would rather not.

Kurt Forster,* Zurich. Can prove very nicely that it was Giulio and <u>not</u> Palladio* who was responsible for Palazzo Thiene in Vicenza. And this was also Inigo J's idea....[2]

Clemente di Thiene? Nice guy. Good name. A saint in the family. Think about him.

Lisciseo Magagnato. Used to teach at U. of Redding. Director of Museo Castelvecchio in Verona. Strong possible.

Clare Robertson. U. of Reading. A book on Alessandro Farnese, cardinal.

Paolo Portoghesi. In spite of everything a possible.

David (Archbishop in partibus) Matthew? Like Ernst G. must, at least, be *molto vecchio*; but, otherwise, be O.K.[3]

But, if you leave it to the professor of Italian, obviously you will get a sequence: Dante, Petrarch, Boccaccio, Ficino, Pica della Marandola, etc. Though what about G.B. Vico in Naples?[4]

P.S. Things of mine at S.M.R.[5]

As regards furn there are: Piedmontese (?) Louis XVI mini-commode. Three Chippendale chairs (same as a set in Williamsburg), Hepplewhite chest of drawers, small Qu. Anne/Geo I "oystershell" mirror.

As regards pics and engravings there are: Peter Foldes oil, Peter Foldes gouache, Blondel Façade of Tuileries, Façade of Halle des Marchands Drapiers, St Stephen's Walbrook, Coleshill, small Poussin (we used it as an illustration in *Collage City*), Ben Nicholson litho (found it in a book and apparently the only one he ever did).

As regards glass, china, objects, etc., there are: two pre-Columbian (Tarascan) terra cotta figures; a hexagonal, Japanese cachepot; a Worcester urn, slightly damaged; 3 blue and white Cantonese plates; 4 Limoges cups and saucers; some blue Bristol; 6 late Georgian rummers; 6 ditto finger bowls; and miscellaneous.

And, about these three categories, I propose the following:

glass, china, objects, be sent to me here
pics and engravings remain in situ, with exception of small Poussin
Hepplewhite chest and Qu. Anne mirror be sent to me here (Louis Seize commode to be subject to further discussion.)

I would like to exchange it—it would be your gain—for the small mahogany, Gillows (?) escritoire job—originally mine—at the rear of the drawing room and, at that end of the room, the Louis XVI item would acquire visibility and be able to ally itself with the Dutch marquetry.

And, then, I transferred to James and Rosie: Chas Eames revolving chair and what is here called ottoman; brass bed; cantilever table; 3 oriental rugs; engravings, "Pianta di Milano" and "Fireworks at Frankfurt, 1740"; miscellaneous books—*History of Technology, 5 vols*, standard sets Racine, Corneille, Moliere, Voltaire, the duc d'Aumale's *Histoire des Princes de Conde*, etc.[6]

And, then, Simon didn't do so well. He got: pair Matthew Boulton candelabra; Turgot Plan of Paris; and a rag bag of clothes, shoes, books, including Encyclopedia Brit, 11th ed.

And, then, dear David:

c. 1770, architect's table; 1826, Library chair; Wm IV chair (the first piece I ever bought)

Rosa di Tivoli's

after Elsheimer (Goudt), "Flight into Egypt"; "Ceiling, Banqueting House"; "Palazzo Reale, Naples"; "Chas II Building, Greenwich"; Flemish *kermesse*—little people doing naughty things; three Poussins; Sebastien Bourdon, "Seven Acts of Mercy".[7]

Pair Geo IV wine coolers, coat of arms of Earls of Dartmouth

Oriental rugs. One mod and v. expensive (don't know why I bought it); one v. small

1 A continuation of the list that Rowe had begun in his letter of 11 August 1996 to David Rowe* of possible speakers for the Dorothy Rowe Memorial Lecture, Oxford University (see p 495 in this volume).
2 Giulio Romano (c 1499–1 November 1546), Andrea Palladio* (1508–1580), and Inigo Jones* (1573–1652). Rowe wrote his master's thesis on the drawings of Inigo Jones.
3 "Ernst G.": Ernst Gombrich* (1909–2001), Austrian-born British art historian. See Rowe's letter of September 1995 to Gombrich (see p 443 in this volume); *molto vecchio*, Italian: very old.
4 Giambattista Vico (1668–1744), Italian political philosopher, historian, and critic of modern rationalism.
5 "S.M.R.": St Margaret's Road, Oxford, David Rowe's* former residence and home of recently deceased Dorothy Rowe*.
6 singer, Charles et al, *A History of Technology, Five Volumes*, Oxford: Oxford University Press, 1954.
7 All nine are engravings.

To **Dr. Isabelle Rucki**, *Birkhäuser Verlag AG, Basel, Switzerland*   *18 September 1996*   **268**

3133 Connecticut Avenue, Apt. 814, Washington, D.C.

Dear Dr. Rucki:

Here are a few observations related to the paperback edition of *Collage City*; and page numbers refer to <u>Birkhauser's</u> hardcover edition.[1]

* P. 254, *Plan of Washington, D.C.* The plan which Bernhard published is a terrible pain and he would be the first to applaud the enclosed substitute.[2] It is a version of Pierre-Charles L'Enfant's *Plan of 1791* and was published by Andrew Ellicott, 1792–93.

I think the text—with the United States of America in the plural is rather charming. And should we try to print this as a readable caption underneath?

* P. 235, *Piazzale Michelangelo, Firenze.* Bernhard's <u>two</u> pictures of this I find to be singularly useless and the <u>one</u> which we published in the English edition provides very much more information. I enclose a Xerox of it—missing a bit of foreground. Apparently we got this from the Touring Club Italiano and I don't know why B. didn't use it.

* P. 93, *Plaza Mayor, Vitoria, Spain.* This is rather an important talking point but here it becomes very much lost. Suggest that it should surely be as big as the Place des Vosges, p. 74. But how to do this without messing up adjacent lay out?

* *Dust cover.* English dust cover was/is <u>green</u>—for ecological reasons?—and it carried that beautiful plan of Wiesbaden which is an intrinsic part of the polemic of the book. So how about this? Personally, I think that <u>green</u> is rather better than red—it is less aggressive?—and that Wiesbaden is an overt revelation of content……

So this is all that I have to suggest related to graphics; and I regard these observations as important in the order in which I have set them down.

And then my piece about Bernhard and I hope you like it.[3] It is mostly an appraisal of the book. And it is, quite a bit of it, about the superiority of Swiss graphics to English—though I don't say <u>quite</u> as much. Some of it was easy to write, some of it very hard; but I don't think it's too obscure. Anyways, I await your reactions. The terminal emphasis on the plan of Franzensbad is another argument for giving prominence to equally beautiful Wiesbaden. But we might need a representative Mondrian and Van D.[4]

    Sincerely,   COLIN ROWE

1 Birkhäuser had published a German translation of *Collage City* in hardcover and intended to publish a paperback edition of same. See Bibliography.

2 Bernhard Hoesli,* who had edited the hardcover edition.

3 Ultimately, this paperback edition featured a bright green dust cover which carried a small black and white plan of Wiesbaden. When Birkhäuser initially suggested a paperback edition of *Collage City*, Rowe asked only that he be permitted to "add a letter to Bernhard at the end". In the paperback, Hoesli's* letter, written in Zürich in 1984, follows the *Collage City* text and is titled "Kommentar zur deutschen Ausgage." Rowe's "piece about Bernhard", titled "Nachwort zur Neuasgabe" (pp 275–278), concludes the book. For the English original of this "Nachwort" see note 3 to Rowe's letter to Werner Seligman dated 3 October 1996 (p 504 in this volume).

4 Piet Mondrian (1872–1944) and Theo Van Doesburg (1883–1931), Dutch De Stijl artists.

269   *To James A. Rowe*   *23 September 1996*

3133 Connecticut Avenue, Apt. 814, Washington, D.C.

Giacomo-Alessandro:[1]

Way back—in 1880 or so—Matthew Arnold was already protesting against the English use of Esq; but I'd better not get on to that. When W.D. Howells was U.S. consul in Venice—this was in the 1860's—I am told that it said Esquire on his passport; and, when he arrived at Civitavecchia, the *dogana*[2] reacted like this: *"Esqui Re... Re degli Esqui—Sua Maesta!"*[3] But I've noticed that usage—both here and in England—is already deserting Mr.

However, I am now told that <u>Sir</u> Richard Rogers has now become the <u>Lord</u>;[4] and it leaves me wondering whether the advisors of H.B.M. are nowadays, <u>completely</u> demented.[5] Or do you think that being probably a God Almighty Bitch, she thought it up all <u>by herself</u> just to annoy the P. of W?[6] But, you know, <u>that</u> building, in spite of Karl Popper* and all the others, is almost <u>visible</u> proof that prediction <u>is</u> possible.[7] It was surely an intimation of catastrophe; and, if I'd been one of Lloyds <u>names</u>, once I'd seen the drawings I'd have <u>gotten</u> out quick.

And as for the <u>Lord's</u> living room which is in the book that you sent me......????[8] The two houses overlooking Burton Court were joined together by the previous tenant, I think Lord Onslow, but for what purpose join together two drawing rooms and then make them two stories high—and this when all you have to put in them is a few Corbu* chairs, an Andy Warhol, and a coffee table?

But thanks for the book—you shouldn't have bought it—and of course you are correct in what you suspect: I have been in quite a few of these funny rooms—generally to my discomfort and regret.

So by all means y'all think of coming here for Christmas. You will be able to meet Mary Fawkes, who always calls me Mistah Colin, and is my cleaning woman from North Carolina, and whose sister—equally very black but in a more elegant style—is also called <u>Mary Fawkes</u>! And this second Mary also comes along too, which, as you might guess, is a bit confusing.

 Colin

P.S. And how about Barcelona? Interesting but over-rated? Until the late 18C the Spanish crown discriminated against it in favor of Genoa—this because the Genoese banks (like Lloyds) persistently helped out when Madrid went bankrupt. And I think that this shows—before the 1890's the buildings are an exhibit of 'poor man's town'. But, after that, quite a bit to look at: Palau della Musica Catalau, Palacio Guell, Pueblo Espanol (for the expo of 1929), etc.

But Gaudi looks better in the old town than when he's standing around in that grid....[9]

Abbraccio per Rosie,

    Colin

---

1   "Giacomo-Alessandro" was one of Rowe's Italianized nicknames for his nephew James.
2   *dogana*, Italian: customs officer.
3   *"Esqui Re... Re degli Esqui—Sua Maesta!,"* Italian: "Esqui King... King of Esqui—His Majesty!"
4   Richard Rogers (b 1933), British architect.
5   "H.B.M.": Her Britannic Majesty.
6   "P. of W.": Prince of Wales.
7   Richard Rogers, Lloyd's Building, 1978–1986; a 14-storey tower in downtown London, the corporate headquarters for insurance group Lloyd's of London.
8   Presumably, Burdett, Richard, Richard Rogers and Peter Cook, *Richard Rogers Partnership Works and Projects: Works in Progress*, London: Monacelli Press, 1996.
9   Antonio Gaudí (1852–1926), Spanish Catalan architect, designer of Palacio Guell ("in the old town") and the basilica church, Sagrada Familia ("standing around in that grid").

To **Rosie & James Rowe**, *Bath, England*   *26 September 1996*   **270**

3133 Connecticut Avenue, Apt. 814, Washington, D.C.

Dear Rosina-Giacomone:[1]

    Sounds Mozartian doesn't it? But this p.s. to my last letter is deadly serious.

I enclose a pic made by my new xerox machine. It is from a Christies, London, catalogue for April 1991; and you may, or you may not, like the piece of English furniture which is advertised for sale.[2] Me? It's not exactly my style but that doesn't matter because I am interested in its provenance rather than its looks. So read down to: "PROVENANCE: The White House, Washington, U.S.A."—and <u>then</u> proceed to meditate......

What <u>does</u> this mean?

Myself, I can't think that it means that they are strapped for money; and, therefore, it leaves me (Hercule Poirot) only able to think about some terrible combo of wickedness and stupidity—with one of those little explosive scandals to follow.[3]

So what was <u>wrong</u> with this innocent little English piece out of the world of Jane Austen? Did it have bad vibrations simply because it was English? But they have <u>always</u> had both French and English furniture. And <u>why</u> did they choose to sell it in London instead of New York? But isn't this as though they didn't want to be known? Surely it would have fetched a higher price in N.Y.C.? But imagine what <u>might/would</u> have been said about it in the *N.Y.T.*: "White House selling National Heirlooms?" So there must have been something covert, secluded, clandestine about this operation which has succeeded in escaping attention until just now—when I write to you.

Looks to me like the sort of piece that Jackie K. might have acquired.[4] But Lady Bird Johnson, Patricia Nixon, Betty Ford, Rosalynn Carter, and Nancy Reagan don't seem to have had any problem with it.[5] And so: what <u>was</u> it about Barbara Bush?[6] Mrs

Reagan, who would have found it *chic*, might have wanted to take it with her, and the present Hillary just wouldn't understand.[7] And, therefore, why did Barbara B., as they say, 'de-accession' it? I think a serious and a disturbing problem here. Like the affair of Cardinal Rohan and the Diamond Necklace at Versailles?[8]

But another piece from the same sale is much more crudely to be explained. This is Mrs Thatcher, in a sudden access of economy and 'good housekeeping', selling off Pugin furniture from her part of the New Palace of Westminster![9] "No, no, let's get some formica instead." But it reeks of Pce Albert of Saxe-Coburg-Gotha and, therefore, why get rid? But it's all *en suite*[10] with the Goddam building as Sir W.C. would have told her.[11]

Incalculable lurv',

    Colin

Have you yet been to King's Weston and Blaise Hamlet?[12]

What about Poundsbury???[13]

Have just been reading the diary of Karl Friedrich Schinkel's English journey of 1826.[14] He was difficult to impress. It is generally said that he admired Manchester—warehouses and mills—but this seems to be based on a misconception. On the other hand he was impressed by woollen mills at Stroud and perhaps you should go take a look.

Then he didn't find Bath anything like good enough???[15] But he didn't like English townhouses much anyway. He found their doorways awful mean.

When he was in Liverpool—of which he approved—he received a letter from his wife in Berlin. It took just six days....

*How about Frampton Court?

*If you look up Stroud in that *History of Technology* you'll find it's the place where the lawn mower was invented—in the 1830's.[16]

    Colin

---

1. Rowe's Italianized names for Rosie* and James Rowe.* A handwritten line, with arrow pointing to "Rosina-Giacomone" reads: "OR SHOULD IT BE JACOPONE—LIKE JACOPONE DA TODI ! OR GIACOPONE?" Jacopone (Crazy Jim) da Todi (1230–1306) was an Italian Franciscan friar from Umbria. "Giacopone" is an alternative spelling.
2. The enclosure was a photocopy of p 124 of a Christies, London, catalogue with a picture captioned "A REGENCY BRASS-MOUNTED ROSEWOOD DISPLAY CABINET" followed by a description that includes the cabinet's dimensions (41" w x 61" h x 17" d) and concludes "Provenance: The White House, Washington, U.S.A., £7,000–10,000."
3. Hercule Poirot, a fictional Belgian detective created by English novelist Agatha Christie (1890–1976).
4. Jacqueline Kennedy (1929–1994), wife of US President John F Kennedy.
5. Wives of US presidents ("first ladies") from 1963 to 1988.
6. Barbara Bush, the wife of George HW Bush, first lady from 1989 to 1993.
7. Hillary Clinton was first Lady at the time of this letter.
8. Louis René Édouard de Rohan, known as Cardinal de Rohan (1704–1803) was implicated in "The Affair of the Diamond Necklace" involving Queen Marie Antoinette in the court of Louis XVI of France (1780s).
9. Margaret Thatcher (1925–2013), Prime Minister of the United Kingdom from 1979 to 1990.
10. *en suite*, French: part of a set.
11. Sir Winston Churchill (1874–1965).

12 The Kings Weston House (1712–1719) is a Baroque house in Bristol designed by Sir John Vanbrugh. Blaise Hamlet, a complex of small houses around a green, was designed by John Nash in the Picturesque style, built in northwest Bristol around 1811.

13 Poundbury (Rowe consistently spelled it with an "s"), a pioneering example of urban development near Dorset, England, featured a recently completed housing complex by Rowe's friend and protégé, Léon Krier.* See Rowe's letter to Robert Maxwell* dated 3 October 1996 (p 503 in this vol).

14 KF Schinkel, *Reise nach England, Schottland und Paris im Jahre 1826.* Republished in Germany in 1986.

15 James* and Rosie Rowe* had recently moved to Bath, England. Many of the sites that Rowe mentions are near that city.

16 Rowe had recently given James *A History of Technology, Five Volumes.* See his letter to David Rowe* dated 17 August 1996 (p 497 in this volume).

To **Robert Maxwell**, *Tasker Road, London*   *3 October 1996*   **271**

3133 Connecticut Avenue, Apt. 814, Washington, D.C.

Dearest Robert:

I wonder if you have seen pictures of Poundsbury; and, if you have, I wonder if—like me—you wonder what has happened to Leon.[1]

Which means that, as for me, I don't find the Plato content or the ideality factor to be absolutely palpitating. Townscape minus prettiness?; townscape toughened up?; or is it a rather glum and lugubrious little Irish eighteenth century town which has, inexplicably, escaped attention? But I <u>had</u> thought that Leon was a sort of mini-Mozart, a case of *jeunesse et quoi*; and <u>what</u> has happened?[2] Could it be association with the Gothic empirical fantasies of the B.R.F. and by extension, the P.O.W.?

Might be interesting, I think, to compare with that other Duchy of Cornwall estate across the river in Kennington and of nearly ninety years back. I mean that S.D. Adshead affair which, if you were to add a bit of syncopation is—in actual fact— much more Leon.[3]

But, at Poundsbury, that old Giorgio de Chirico component, seems to me is entirely absent.[4] Seems that we are to have neither good old mod. arch. (Siedlung Hallen?) nor *architettura razionale*; and I'm pissed.[5]

Love to Celia and I'm seein' quite a bit of Colquhoun,[6]*

Un abbraccio affettuoso,

   Colin

---

1 Regarding Poundbury, see note 13 to Rowe's letter dated 26 September 1996 (p 501 in this volume) to Rosie* and James Rowe.*

2 *jeunesse et quoi*, French: youth and such.

3 The Duchy of Cornwall Estate in Kennington, South London, 1913, designed by Stanley David Adshead (1868–1946), the first editor of the *Town Planning Review*.

4 Giorgio de Chirico (1888–1978), Greek-born Italian artist whose enigmatic paintings influenced Surrealism.

5 Siedlung Halen (1957–1961), a Modernist housing estate near Bern, Switzerland, designed by Atelier 5; *architettura razionale*, Italian: "rational architecture", a movement in Modern architecture in Italy from the 1920s to the 1940s.

6 Celia Scott, English sculptress married to Robert Maxwell*. At the time of this letter, Alan Colquhoun* was a research fellow at the National Gallery of Art, Washington, DC.

Apt. 814, 3133 Connecticut Ave., Washington D.C.

Dearest Werner:

I am missing you and would like to see you. But, meanwhile, a question.

Do you suppose that Le C. was rather more of a painter than he was an architect?[1]

This is rather a silly question but I don't think of it as a vulgar one. This because, at certain times in history, to be primarily a painter has not made that person a worse architect. Indeed I think rather the reverse. And, of course, this infers the argument that, if painting is the simulation of three dimensions in the reality of two, then very great architecture is—yes, yes—is the simulation of two dimensions in the reality of three....

So I can write to you about this because, immediately, you know that I am thinking about Garches, La Tourette, and Michelangelo's façade of San Lorenzo.[2]

I returned to all this the other day because Birkhauser is producing a paperback edition of Bernhard's translated version of *Collage City* and, some twelve years later, I have been looking at in detail in order to add a short piece about Bernhard to go with it—at the end. So I send you a copy of what I sent to them because it might amplify what I might be thinking about in writing to you.[3]

Well, as you guess, Corbu*-Mike is the primary exhibit—with, among other things, the verticality which Mike introduced in transforming the façade which he inherited from Antonio da Sangallo.[4]

Then, while you think about Mike and Antonio da S., you might also think about Vignola v. Palladio.* And, by comparison with V., you might just wonder whether Andy P., up in the Veneto, is not a little bit provincial.[5] (Perhaps a reason why he so much appealed to the English?). But V., as a perspectivist, is a façade man. He acts flatten. Whereas with P., except at the Redentore, the façade is never a big deal.

And think also about Alberti at Sant' Andrea and San Sebastiano.[6] But he is always primacy of the vertical surface stuff.

Anyway, I give you all this to play with and I await your reactions.

Un abbraccio affettuoso,

     Colin

P.S. I notice that you are going to appear at Carpenter Center—along with K.F.[7] And what is he going to say about Le C.?

And what about T.V. (Tony Vidler) at C.U.?[8]

P.P.S. Birkhauser also wants me to make an anthology from my three volume essay book (which M.I.T. produced so badly) and I think that this is quite a good idea—a crop and change, cut and paste job, [...].[9]

---

1   "Le C.": Le Corbusier.*

2   Villa Stein de Monzie at Garches, France, 1926–1928 and Sainte Marie de La Tourette, near Lyon, France, 1956–1960, both by Le Corbusier.*

3   Rowe, Colin and Fred Koetter, *Collage City*, Bernhard Hoesli ed and trans Basel: Birkhäuser

Verlag, 1984. The paperback edition to which Rowe refers and which carries the "short piece about Bernhard"—translated to German, titled *"Nachwort von Colin Rowe"* ("Afterword by Colin Rowe"), pp 275–278—was published as Rowe, Colin and Fred Koetter, *Collage City (Geschichte und Theorie der Architektur)*, Basel: Birkhäuser Verlag AG, 1997. Rowe's orginal English version of the "short piece about Bernhard" was enclosed with this letter. It reads: "At the time that Bernhard Hoesli suffered his fatal heart attack in the airport at Bangkok I was about to write to thank him for his German edition of *Collage City* and to add some comments about what I felt to be its superiority to the English original. On the whole I regard it as the *editio princeps*.

The English text was written, with Fred Koetter,* in a spasm of great excitement and concentration between late August and mid December of 1973. It was an exhilarating collaboration and a version of it, edited by myself, was first published by *The Architectural Review* in August 1974. The full text was then to appear in London—this was discussed with a publisher in July 1974—but great delays and unforeseen difficulties ensued; and, as the M.I.T. Press expressed interest, negotiations with them followed. M.I.T. agreed to take over a page and picture lay out which had already been assembled in London—this was possibly a mistake for everybody concerned—and, with this somewhat hybrid pre-history, the book ultimately appeared in 1978—with the text of 1973.

Now, one trouble with *Collage City* has always been its extreme 'cleverness', a state of mind which, in some popular judgements, can never be either 'true' or 'good' but which must always be either shallow or casuistical; and which, worse than that, to some persons, must be entirety devoid of ethical content. No, even if you bore your readers almost to extinction, you've just got to be 'serious'. You must avoid the *allegro vivace* like the plague....

And, then, there is the problem of conflict between visuals and verbals.

Thus, as a long essay, simply to read *Collage City* need not, I suspect, exhaust either the patience or the mind. Though the text is sometimes too elegant or rhetorical, it is fairly elementary and the discussion, I think, is conducted with both logic and compassion. But, when the eye becomes distracted by a continuous bombardment of illustrations (an effect of the page lay out?), from the disparity of stimulus, the duality of argument will likely dissipate concentrations and a low grade intellectual confusion will be the only-too-inevitable result.

But is not this a problem with the illustrated book—as a species? Certainly, I do find it so myself; and this is why I am now about to applaud the discretion, and the distinction, of Bernhard's editorial undertaking. Looking at content as well as surface, he has approached his problem seriously but with a lot of joy; and some of his graphic emendations—like the Palazzo Chiericati replicated three times over so that it really does become a version of the Stoa of Attalos—have an absolute knock-out charm. But, in general, his graphics, which very much amplify our own, display a lucidity which, for me, is still something of a Swiss revelation.

Thus, with Bernhard, his pictures are both generous in their spread and more succinct in the economy of their impact; their didactic content is more pristine; their dialectical purpose more visible; their collaboration with the text is close; they become argument rather than decoration; they are help both to reason and to understanding. Indeed, it may be an irony of the German edition that, while the text is critical of the notion of *Gesamtkunstwerk*, Bernhard—with a heavier symphonic orchestration—has made of the 'total-book' something of a *Gesamtkunstwerk* in itself!

Also, sometimes, he is more ruthless than Fred and I would ever have dared to be. And, thus, his superimposition of Townscape and Archigram images, page 45; and, thus, his publication, page 58, of Alison and Peter Smithson's utterly deplorable project, "Happstadt Berlin", of 1968. And, though we also found this monster to be a major source of pain, writing only five years after it had appeared in the world and not caring to offend certain English susceptibilities, we just wouldn't have touched it!

But Bernhard had also another range of perceptions. Apart from his having worked for Le Corbusier,* he shared with me a taste for Cezanne and Poussin. He liked to remind students—at least in Texas where the landscape assisted a discourse of this kind—of Cezanne's alleged ambition "to do Poussin over again on nature", or to make of Impressionism something 'solid', *comme l'art des musees*; and, if this was the area of our great agreement (not exactly an attempt to do Palladio* over again on architecture!!) it may serve to explain his rapid response to *Collage City*—as also to *Transparency*.

He saw the essay and the book as inter-connected; he had a prejudice, as do I, for an assertive frontality, for an emphatic presentation of picture plane; and I think he understood such an organization, with a predominant face—almost with eyes of its own—as both a product and a pre-condition of collage, with, of necessity, collage acting to flatten the space in which it appears.

Or does it?

For instance, a little experiment which has just occurred to me. You take a large reproduction of a painting, perhaps by Renoir; then you tear up a page of the *New York Times*, but any other newsprint would do; then you take a pretty large piece of the shreddings and you just paste it on. So, *presto*, you have not only made a collage (probably of dubious merit) but you have also acted to flatten out Renoir's space according to the later procedures of Cezanne and Synthetic Cubism.

Obvious, simple, frivolous (?), a bit philistine; but, when all the smoke clears, at the last analysis it is something like this that *Transparency* remains all about; and Bernhard's consciousness of this sort of thing—again like my own—became very highly developed from the influence of Robert Slutzky's* practice and conversation—themselves probably a particular aspect of the teaching of Josef Albers. And, with Robert, this whatever-it-might-have-been was, at that time, apt to become focused as a criticism of De Stijl—with exemplary quality attributed to Mondrian and subsidiary significance to Van Doesburg.

Thus, Mondrian was seen to present not a decorative flat pattern but a type of profoundly constructed space: a deep white space with, up front, a constellation of 'accidental' figures, red, blue, yellow, tied together by a fabric of black lines, which—though it connects the figures and is given tension by them—also acts (by this same elasticity) to drag forward the spatial concavity which it causes to become discharged, as some sort of animating tremor, into the vertical surface of the picture plane.

Now, either one sees this or one does not. And, as Le Corbusier* wrote, there are always *les yeux qui ne voient pas*. But, once perceived, this is a message—or even a part of knowledge—which will not go away; and, if this was the primary ingredient of the Slutzky teaching—a commerce between flatness and depth—then, once presented with it, one could only admit that the ever-so-fascinating Van Doesburg knew very little about it. So, by contrast to Mondrian: with Theo van Doesburg one finds atmospheric space and 'interesting' construction of red, blue, yellow planes which, because it is situated within a naturalistic matrix, can scarcely enjoy any valuable *rapport* with the two dimensional pictorial surface. An argument related to one point versus two point perspective, to a compact versus a diffuse apprehension of both object and context, to an intercourse between the three and the two dimensional, in the end this is an argument related to the pregnancy of picture plane, patently to be derived from the findings of Gestalt psychology; and it is something about this mode of interpretation, about the latency of depth in surface—the greatest potential of both façade and plan?—which underlies at least the idea of *Collage City* and which, hence, must have engaged Bernhard's interest.

So, had he lived, about this difficult topic—which is really the copulation of the spherical and the flat—I would have implored him to make some commentary—since, I myself find it impossible to discuss with any hope of conciseness. But, as it is, I can only take the opportunity of this new German edition to offer Bernhard my posthumous thanks.

To repeat: to find a visual apparatus organized with so much logic is an extreme pleasure; and, then, it is an intense joy to find the plan of a little town like Franzensbad (this was its name in Baedeker's day), p. 242, with a whole page to itself! But how unassuming, how quietly accomplished, and how elegantly simple it is: a few blocks of solid city—not enough to be wearisome, a surrounding park, and a random framing of mostly attenuated buildings. But how refreshing when, nowadays, so many people try so very hard...and is it not the perfect exhibition—casual splendors—of a double, and Germanic, sensibility? Compare, for its general posture, with Wiesbaden at the same date."

4 "Corbu-Mike": Le Corbusier*-Michelangelo.
5 "Andy P.": Andrea Palladio* (1508–1580), Venetian architect.
6 Leon Battista Alberti (1404–1472). His Basilica of Sant'Andrea and church of San Sebastiano are both in Mantua.
7 "K.F.": Kenneth Frampton.
8 "T.V. at C.U.": Tony (Anthony) Vidler at Cornell University. Vidler had recently been named dean of Cornell's College of Architecture, Art, and Planning.
9 No Birkhäuser edition of *As I Was Saying*, Rowe's "three volume essay book", was published.

273 *To **Rosemary Rowe**, Bath, England*   *22 October 1996*

3133 Connecticut Avenue, Apt. 814, Washington, D.C.

Rosina dearest-carissima:

Look forward to your arrival. And what do I crave, need, want?

When dearest Simon helped me pack books and I gave him lots of Agatha Christie, Dorothy Sayers, etc., I suspect there was some confusion which has only lately become visible. Anyway I am missing two things which I had in London and no longer have here.

These are:

★   Vol I of the three vols of the catalogue of the Mostra del Barocco Piemontese, 1960. This is on architecture and scenography, is *molto importante*, and its absence devalues the other two.[1] So get the pic: an expensive catalogue in 1960 and now much sought after.

★   *Complete Sherlock Holmes* in two vols.[2] One vol missing. And I can't believe that these went out with the garbage.

Then there is that alabaster model of the cathedral of Firenze—duomo campanile and baptistery, mid 19th C, and all under one of those big glass covers which they also used for clocks. And this is *chez* Mary Stirling....

So the history of this piece, in so far as I knew it, is amusing. At the beginning of 1960 it was standing on the floor just inside the front door of the architecture buildings at Cambridge U.—all by itself; and I went back to poor Miss Baldry—the secretary, shamefully overworked and underpaid—who had to do everything all by herself. And it appeared that it was a malign influence—"Sir Leslie had ordered that it be thrown out. As the Professor he knows that it is something which the students should not see. So by all means, do take it if it is something which you feel that you could use."[3] So I draped my raincoat over it, put my arms under it, and transported it back to my apt. An extraordinary story because it could have been sold, even at that time, in the vicinity of Pont Street or Lowndes Square for something like Pounds Stirling Seven Hundred and Fifty. However, though such a transaction would have provided money for quite a lot of books, any such simple, commercial, solution was not to be considered. No, Sir Leslie would prefer that the garbage men take it away....

So its subsequent history? Well, though I left it behind with furniture and *objets* when I left for Ithaca in 1962 and though Dorothy didn't include it with the furn which was sent in '65, in the course of time (though not I think for the same reasons as Leslie Martin★) she too lost patience with it. And then, one dreadful day, she handed it to Jim with words which must have been something like this: "This is Colin's you know but perhaps you could keep it at Belsize Avenue"!!!![4] So Jim understood that it was not her's to give and that it was mine and used to ask me when I was going to take it away. So grab the pic. I should have taken it to Gloucester Ave when I came there from Rome in March '92;[5] but I procrastinated, Jim croaked; and Mary became *la vedova inconsolabile*.[6] So time not exactly propish. But now she writes to me about selling the house—and this would suggest staking the claim and, at least, removing it.

Like pulling up the mandrake root? May be; may be not. But, of course, it's delicate and requires professional packing. But could you bear it? You shrink, I know; but I have initiated the process and should be only too happy to add further gas / steam / voltage to the diplomatic endeavor. So let's begin the *demarche* because,[7] with this piece at Bel Av, I continue to feel as though I have been raped.[8]

Oh Yes. And bring some bottles of that Robinson's Patent Barley concentrate so that I can have a change from iced tea.[9] Y'all will be able to consume Prosecco, Villa Antinori, Barbaresco, etc but a little bit of barley water will make a change.

Love, love,

    Colin x x x x x

P.S. David has sent me pics of Poundsbury and I wonder if he got them from you.[10] I find it—as I expected I would—a bit low on the ideality factor, a bit *morne, triste, et lugubre*.[11] And you?

    C

1   *molto importante*, Italian: very important.
2   Doyle, Arthur Conan, *Complete Sherlock Holmes*, Doubleday, 1930.
3   "Sir Leslie" Martin* (1908–2000) was head the Architecture School of Cambridge University where Rowe taught from 1957 to 1961.
4   Belsize Avenue ("Bel Av") was the home of Mary and James (Jim) Stirling.*
5   After spending several months in Rome, on his return Rowe moved from 19 Renwick Place in Ithaca to Gloucester Avenue in London in March 1992.
6   *la vedova inconsolabile*, Italian: the grieving widow.
7   *démarche*, French: line of action, maneuver.
8   The reacquisition of this alabaster model—approximately 12" w x 23" l x 16" h—was a persistent concern of Rowe's. Eventually, it was brought to him in Washington, DC, by David, James, and Simon Rowe.* He prominently displayed it in his apartment at the Kennedy-Warren, and ultimately left it in his will to Steven Peterson* and Barbara Littenberg.*
9   Rowe did not drink alcohol at this time.
10 Regarding Poundbury, a housing development designed by Léon Krier*, see Rowe's letter to Robert Maxwell* dated 3 October 1996 (p 503 in this volume).
11 *morne, triste, et lugubre*, French: dismal, sad, and gloomy.

To **Michael Spens**, *Wormiston-by-Crail, Fife, Scotland*   *9 December 1996*

274

Apt. 814, 3133 Connecticut Ave., Washington D.C.

Dear Michael:

A way of killing several birds with one stone. I seem to be giving dinner about once a week to Alan Colquhoun* and this is because he is some sort of Research Fellow at the National Gallery—here for the whole year. Now I was unaware that such situations/positions existed—either for shorter or longer periods; but it appears that they do and He Who Gives Them Out is Henry Millon...[1] and that, among others, he has Claudia Lazzaro 'working on' Italian gardens, somebody else on Marinetti, a German guy, etc; and it appears to be all quite charming: they're always having little parties and the lib. at the Nat. Gall. is most liberal in its policies.[2]

So how about it? And is not yourself most violently eligible? But do think about it because, then, could you not make *sortés* from here to a variety of places?[3] Henry is Dean of... Architectural Studies and, of course, he was Director of the Am Ac in Rome from, I think, 1972 to 1976.

When Christopher Cornford taught drawing at the S. of A. at Cambridge he was quite atrociously treated by Leslie[4]—very *de haut en bas*[5] in that patronizing liberal way and that's how I came to know both himself and Lucy and why I used to go around to Conduit Head which is really a very acceptable Voyseyesque house—nothing sensational but a nice blue and white Dutch lines.[6] But further impressions vague. However, I would guess that it must have been one of those good taste, Hepplewhite interiors, upper middle-class *détente* style of which there used to be so many—simple Chippendale too gutsy and simple Regency too loud; and you dined in the living room because the house had already been subdivided.[7]

So what did happen to this particular *ameublement*?[8] When Robin (?) Darwin (and Peter E.)[9] prevailed upon Christopher to move to the R.C.A. was all of it shifted to London?[10] And is that why all of the furn. at Spring House is so entirely foreign to me? Because the furn. in your pics is quite horrible and I can only think about Christopher on a shopping binge in the Tottenham Court Road and Lucy resolved to grin and bear it!!!

I gave my Farewell to Cambridge Party at Conduit Head—with music and fireworks in the garden (guests didn't know its purpose) and left the next day with Peter for Harwich and Antwerp; and this is why I have always regretted—and never seen—the new house which I now perceive was intended as a representation-residence, sort of quasi-embassy, rustic style, for a London academic and his family province.......[11]

But also about the furniture at Conduit Head I am reminded of a performance of Monteverdi's *L'incoronazion di Poppea* and what must have been the first appearance of Alfred Deller, with that voice which astonished the world.[12] So I was working for Joseph Emberton at the time and the next day I was telling him about it—though it didn't seem that he was very interested in it.[13] There was, I said, a difference between a counter-tenor voice and a *castrato* voice—with the *castrato* voice the result of artifice, like the great Farinelli who sang every night to the King of Spain.[14] And, I said, "They used to do the operation in Naples...."

So, surprising reaction: "MAPLES, MAPLES, I never did like that firm and NOW I understand the reason why"!!! But I love it; and, when adjacent to Maples and Heals, it pre-empts the idea of any shop around those parts: Wicked Italians, and Handel included with them, just mucking around with nature....

Un abbraccio,

    Colin

P.S. If you write to Henry Millon at the Nat. Gall. he is <u>Dean</u> Henry Millon, though I don't know what he is Dean of.

Dean Henry Millon
Center for Advanced Study Architecture and the Arts

or Henry Millon, Dean, etc.... which I rather prefer

So, as a replacement of Conduit Head, Spring House must be a transcendence of Cornford—proto Darwin gesture. And that must go for the furniture too.

    Colin

*Stanislaus von Moos also at Nat Gall—just to give you an idea.[15]

---

1 Henry Millon (b 1927), architectural historian of the Renaissance and Baroque, from 1980 to 2000 the first Dean of the Center for Advanced Studies of Visual Arts at the National Gallery of Art at Washington, DC.
2 "lib. at the Nat. Gall.": library at the National Gallery.
3 *sorties*, French: exits, departures.
4 Christopher Cornford (1917–1993) taught drawing at School of Architecture at Cambridge from 1951 to 1962. Professor Sir Leslie Martin* (1908–1999) became the head of that school in 1956.
5 *de haut en bas*, French: with condensation.
6 Conduit Head was the home of Cornford and his wife, Lucy Jameson (1941–1993), when Rowe taught with Cornford in the late 1950s.
7 *détente*, French: relaxed.
8 *ameublement*, French: furniture.
9 Sir Robert Vere "Robin" Darwin (1910–1974), British artist and rector at the Royal College of Art, and Peter Eisenman,* a graduate student at Cambridge at the time.
10 "R.C.A.": Royal College of Art, where Cornford was head of the Department of Humanities from 1962 to 1979.
11 Peter Eisenman.*
12 Alfred Deller (1912–1979), English singer known as "the Godfather of the Countertenor".

13 Joseph Emberton (1889–1956), English modernist architect.
14 *castrato*, Italian: a man whose sopranolike singing voice is often produced by castration of the singer before puberty.
15 Stanislaus von Moos (b 1940), Swiss art historian and architectural theorist.

275   *To **David Rowe**, Headington, Oxford*   *15 December 1996*

3133 Connecticut Avenue, Apt. 814, Washington, D.C.

David:

This pic—from James Madge*—is from Isola Dovarese, one of those Gonzaga towns which I told you about.[1] Kinda wild doncha think? And he says that this sort of *coronamento*, with brackets, is something of a repeat performance throughout these towns.[2] Affiliation? Presumably from Luca Fancelli, Alberti's executive architect in Mantova, and then through Giulio Romano? But terribly surreptitious sort of things going on. And the amazing thing is totally unknown!

The latest thing in these parts appears to be a split in the intellectual right wing which has, by now, even hit the *N.Y.T.*[3] So there are now the neo-cons and the theo-cons—both critical of the preset supreme court. So, to be neo-con is to take a stand upon the Declaration and related natural law theory but, to be theo-con, is to insist on no less than St Thomas Aquinas—all the way!! And it seems that this is now about to obsess schools of law and schools of divinity.

So, add this to the debate focused upon abortion, homosexuality and euthanasia, and I am sure that Bryony will have a nice little time at Harvard....[4] A case, I think, of too much theory and too little history.

But you see how it all ties up with that 1797–9 treaty between the U.S. and Tripoli and Clause XXI of that treaty: "the United States is no way founded upon the principles of the Christian religion"?[5]

So the present Supreme Court is completely wedded to this proposition but nobody else seems too much to like it. And then there are the anomalies: like the president swearing on the Bible and all that stuff.

But you never would have believed it. But, seriously, would you?

Lots of best wishes,

   Colin

Don't have the Headington address...Waldencot, etc....[6]

P.S. The items of furniture arrived today—December 16—so "thanx" and I've been struggling with the unpacking. But curious the etymology of *ameublement*,[7] It. *mobile* and the idea of mobility. Must be late medieval, don't you imagine?[8]

   Colin

1   The enclosure is lost. Isola Dovorese is a Gonzaga town in the Province of Cremona in Lombardy, Italy. See Rowe's letter to Judith DiMaio* dated 28 June 1996 (see p 487 in this volume) and his letter to James Madge* dated 1 July 1996 (p 489).
2   *coronamento*, Italian: crown.
3   "*N.Y.T.*": *The New York Times*.

4   Dr Bryony Soper, David Rowe's* second wife.
5   The Treaty of Tripoli, 1797, was a routine diplomatic agreement with the exception of the phrase on religion cited by Rowe above.
6   David's new address in Oxford, Headington. Here Rowe refers to the house as "Waldencot".
7   *ameublement*, French: furniture.
8   *mobile*, Italian: furniture.

To **James Madge**, London   *15 December 1996*   **276**

3133 Connecticut Avenue, Apt. 814, Washington, D.C.

Dearest James:

Am entirely devastated by the little palazzo job in Isola Dovarese.[1] But, more or less, I swoon—all of those em-ergent and di-vergent things.

I suppose that I shall <u>have</u> to be present at the first Dorothy Rowe Memorial Lecture at Magdalen C, Oxon, towards the end of May—no escape since now she's become a culture heroine and it's going to be Warburg Institute plus the Italian Ambassador... and, of course, verbal, verbal, all the way....

So, with <u>that</u> done, I expect to go to Potsdam, Dresden, Prague, Landshut (there is supposed to be more Giulio there), Bad Ischl, Bad Gastein, Klagenfurt, and Udene—a due south route from Berlin which, obviously, hasn't been travelled for years and, no doubt, will have its own revelations...but I've never been to Potsdam, Dresden, or Prague.

So that's the general story and, but of course, I <u>have</u> read Osbert Sitwell. But have <u>you</u> been to Crema? Much, much better than Cremona; and how lucky you all are to be all on top of that stuff—like the little room frescoed by Parmigianino in the pink chateau at Fontanellato. But I think that I owe all of this originally from O. Sitwell. But the Palazzo, very rustic, is a complete knockout!!!!

Lotsa lurv to you both,

Colin

---

1   Isola Dovorese, a Gonzaga town in the province of Cremona in Lombardy, Italy, near where Madge* kept a vacation house. See Rowe's letter to James Madge dated 1 July 1996 (p 489 in this volume).

To **Megan McFarland**, *Rizzoli International Publications, Inc.*   *22 February 1997*   **277**

3133 Connecticut Avenue, Apt. 814, Washington, D.C.

Dear Megan McFarland:*

I had begun to think that I had reached such a stage of my development (four books and a great many articles over a very long period) as to be immune from the persecutions of the *Chicago Manual of Style*. But that was until I received the copy-edited version of my introduction of the Koetter-Kim* monograph.[1] And, now, I don't know what to say, except that your proposed emendations are so many that, if I were to attempt to cope with them, the job could only be enormous.

However, let me first make some commentary upon the opening five or six pages of your text; and I will notice to begin with two errors which you—yourself—have introduced.

★ p.1. I say "a Mario Praz strategy" and you 'correct' this to a "Mario Pratz Strategy"; and I can't understand why you charge ahead to rectify what you are obviously ignorant about. Mario Praz is a well-known name. He was an eminent Italian literary man and a collector of genius whose furniture and objects are now installed at the Museo Napoleonico in Rome. But this is enough to suggest that it would be quite appalling if an outfit like Rizzoli were to publish his name as PRATZ!!! The name could be Piedmontese but he came from Umbria rather than Germany. Also, to capitalize "strategy" is completely unwarrantable.

★ p.4. I say "the Palace of Diocletian at Spalato/Split" and you render this as "the Palace of Diocletian in Spoleto/Split"!!! But this is ridiculous. Spalato is in Dalmatia (the Adriatic coast of former Jugo-Slavia, and Split is its Serbo-Croat name), while Spoleto is in Umbria, location of a fashionable musical festival!!! And, had you not assumed carelessness on my part, this could have been checked by a little carefulness on yours. Also, with reference to small towns like Spalato—or Spoleto—one doesn't say in but at.

Then, and still in these first pages, there are other—capricious and arbitrary? — editorial indulgences which violate both sound and sense. For instance:

★ At the bottom of p. 2 I say "But a close thing"; and you take it out;

★ On p. 4 I say "I have always recognized" and this becomes "I have already recognized";

★ On p. 6 I write "… it is all precipitated with the most persuasive liveliness… it is the reverse side of the medal to Storrow Drive" and this becomes "… it is precipitated with the most persuasive liveliness… the reverse side of Storrow Drive." And, at this stage, I begin to wonder just what is going on, what must be deliberate and what might be careless. The omission of a period or the omission of "the medal."

However, I am simply unable to go through the rest of the text in this way and I will notice, at random, just a few things which I find not acceptable, as for example:

★ p. 9. "While as for competition from an earth mother…"? You delete. But why?

★ p. 11. Reference to Kaiser Wilhelm II and *The Merry Wives of Saxe-Coburg*. Are you worried about the sensibilities of the British royal family? Otherwise why delete?

★ "Mechanicist and idealist" becomes "Mechanist and idealist" Why?

★ And, particularly with regard to the *Chicago Manual*, you display a tendency to substitute "that" for "which." Also, on p. 15, I write "As for you *traditore*,[2] retrograde and *retardataire*" and you introduce a comma between "retrograde" and "*retardataire*."[3] But this is *Chicago* at its worst and it is utterly destructive of any rhetorical pitch.

COMMENTARY UPON REVISED TEXT

★ 'American' versus 'English' usage.

I believe that I am conversant with both—only I remain sufficiently 'English' never to speak of a thing being 'British'—so long as it isn't an embassy or a former empire.

I always consult both Webster and O.E.D.[4] Also both Mencken and Fowler.

Generally speaking I find high level American journalism superior to English. But, on the other hand, much American academic writing is appalling (worse than English if that is possible); but take a bit of old style English *Belles-lettisme* and it <u>can</u> be extremely lucid and get you to the point quick...

*   "which" or "that"

Which is the man who/<u>that</u> bit the dog? That is the dog which bit the man. Too much use of that for which is sloppy and is equally prevalent on both sides of the Atlantic.

*   Quite a lot of people when answering the phone are apt to say: "Yes, this is he" (and this is v. American); but I can't do it: I say: "Yes, that's me"—but I don't know which *Chicago* prefers. However this leads to the exotic Anglo-Irish use of myself, yourself, himself, themselves—and it sounds more normative in the plural. However, it <u>can</u> strengthen a statement.

*   A review like *The New Republic* or *First Things* very often says "doesn't" for "does not"; but you don't seem to like. Not 'American'?

*   Asterisks. I twice use a series of asterisks. This is to break the text into sections— beginning, middle, end. Please use some equivalent.

Sincerely,

Colin Rowe

1   Plattus, Alan J, *Koetter Kim and Associates: Place/Time*, New York: Rizzoli, 1997 with essays by Colin Rowe and Fred Koetter.*
2   *traditore*, Italian: treacherous.
3   *retardataire*, French: latecomer.
4   "O.E.D.": *Oxford English Dictionary*

To **Simon Rowe**, *Lucknam Park, Colerne, Wiltshire, England*   *21 May 1997*   **278**

Apt. 814, 3133 Connecticut Ave., Washington D.C.

Caro il mio Simone:

Have you read Stella Gibbons, *Cold Comfort Farm*, a best seller of 1932 now republished by Penguin?[1] If not do. It's a spoof on Mary Webb, D.H. Lawrence and all that stuff—cotswoldery and throbbing heart of Shropshire and what all and I think that it might be desirable for James to read it too.

This, because—as I interpret it—he may have caught a curious dose of the William Morris Disease, endemic in your parts in Chipping Camden-Broadway and roughly equivalent to the Shaker Furniture Disease in this country. Or so I construe the evidence of that which he seems to be concerned in reproducing with his own hands!!![2]

Now Wm. Morris is very O.K.—for wall paper; but I do think that the form is apt to be a little bit too sincere unless it is painted black, then, when it tends to become an aspect of Japonaiserie and can be read as proto-Mackintosh and, as dining chairs, my grandmother Beaumont had a whole lot of that stuff.[3] But see the Max Beerbohm essay, "1880," when men and women hurled their mahagony into the streets.[4]

Anyway, I think that you should take the Giaco-Rosa to C.C./Broadway, visit the Gordon Russell fabrik and attempt to relieve the inflammation.[5]

It might, you know, be diverted by turning his attention to early 17C French models—like a simplified sort of Louis Treize.

Best Love,

Colin

1   Gibbons, Stella, *Cold Comfort Farm*, London: Longmans, 1932.
2   At the time, James Rowe* was making a set of William Morris-designed chairs by hand.
3   Charles Rennie Mackintosh (1868–1928), Scottish architect and furniture designer. Much of Mackintosh's furniture was painted black.
4   Max Beerbohm (1872-1956); Beerbohm, Max, "1800", *The Works of Max Beerbohm*, London: William Hieneman, 1922, a collection of essays originally published in notable periodicals.
5   "Take the Giaco-Rosa to C.C./Broadway": take James*-Rosie Rowe* to Chipping Camden/Broadway to visit the Gordon Russell Museum. Russell (1892–1980) was an English furniture designer and craftsman.

279   *To **David Rowe**, Headington, Oxford*   *22 May 1997*

Apt. 814, 3133 Connecticut Ave., Washington D.C.

Dearest David:

I am <u>very</u> pleased. This morning, at Sotheby's, N.Y., I have just bought a little painting, oil on vellum relined onto canvas, 11-1/8 by 8-¼. And it is <u>after</u> Giovanni Battista di Jacopo di Guasparre, called Il Rosso Fiorentino (1494–1540). Subject is *Saturn and Philyra*—Saturn has turned himself into a horse in order to make love to the nymph, Philyra (you would have thought <u>not</u> a good idea but <u>she</u> seems to like it a lot), and, bottom right, there is a rather excited little putto carrying Saturn's scythe. Supremely elegant—I think—proto School of Fontainebleau and all that. And the price: $2,000.00!!!

So Vasari says that, at that time (late Leo X) Rosso prepared drawings of all the Gods, for copper plates; these were afterwards engraved by Jacopo Caraglio: (and) among these drawings are Saturn turning himself into a horse, and Pluto carrying off Proserpine,[1] so what I have is a painting after the drawings, or engraving, which, probably, is not very much later; and the provenance is also quite good; it came from the estate of Perry Rathbone, who was one of people around Christies....[2]

But, apparently, nobody was interested... and Judy's friend, Jennifer—who dropped in from her department at Sotheby's to get it for me and was expecting Three to Five, when she told me was quite as elated as now I am.[3] She supposes that it would have gone for more in London; but she concludes that it was <u>those</u> people, American collectors who are frightened of mythical and religious subjects and buy impressionists because they are easy, who are responsible for my little bargain.

Anyway, she is going to send me the prices of the sale end, with the catalogue, I shall send these to you so that you can study the New York market. And, meanwhile, I am immensely happy.

Love,

Colin

They will buy—when they are not thinking Impressionist—still lives—fruit, flowers, oysters and dead animals—but the market for anything else—even minor Joshua Reynolds—doesn't seem to be exactly competitive. Though, very strangely, very big pieces by Luca Giordano seem to be a very big deal???!!![4]

    C

1 Giorgio Vasari (1511–1574); Vasari, Girorgio, *Lives of the Most Excellent Painters, Sculptors, Architects*, vol 3, Florence, 1550.
2 Perry T Rathbone (1911–2000), director of the St Louis Museum of Art from 1940 to 1955 and of the Museum of Fine Arts, Boston, from 1955 to 1972.
3 Jennifer Mitchell was curator of Sotheby's Pre-Columbian department at the time.
4 Luca Giordano (1634–1705), Late Italian Baroque painter and printmaker.

*To **James Rowe**, Bath, England*   *14 June 1997*   **280**

Apt. 814, 3133 Connecticut Ave., Washington D.C.

Dearest James:

I had a visual dream early this morning—though not sufficiently powerful to permit accurate recall. Anyway, I was visiting *la famiglia*—you, Rosie, Simon, David, Dorothy—in what seemed to be a converted mill house—with a rather free plan inside.[1] The site was perfectly flat but there were a lot of water courses and what you would expect running through the garden, which Dorothy, with evident enthusiasm, was beginning to take under control. So the inside was on two levels, with bedrooms on both floors and, apparently, you and Simon wrapped me up in an oriental rug (?) and carried me away to sleep in what must have been Simon's bedroom in which there was a quite beautiful black and gold lacquer chinoiserie cabinet!!!??? And it was at that interesting stage that I woke up....

However the purpose of this letter is not to give you an opportunity to conduct a Freudian analysis but it is to give you info about my movements in July.

So will start in Berlin and will drive down to Mantova with purpose of visiting those *piazze Gonzagesche* that I have told you about.[2] And it will be Berlin—Marienbad—Prague—Bad Ischl?—Ljubljana (how daring and what a surprise!)—Trieste—Bassano del Grappa—and Mantova, arriving there on July 13 and, probably staying at the Albergo San Lorenzo, more or less alongside Alberti's Sant' Andrea.

So will be driving down with J. Di M.[3] (she hasn't yet drowned herself in a bottle of Recoaro as Simon once proposed) and, after time in M., we shall be leaving for God's Own Country on July 17 from Milano-Malpensa which is very inconveniently located.[4]

Therefore, get the general pic. The night of July 16 we shall have to spend somewhere en route to Milano (Parma?, Piacenza?, Crema?) because the plane will be at 12.15 midday and there might be a bit of traffic on the autostrade (usually is) to the south of Milano. So do y'all come or do you not come? This because *rencontre* will, inevitably, be brief—though could be extended by a possible night in Parma.[5]

So do think seriously,

    Colin

P.S. Am told that, in Parma, they don't say *grazie* but that they say *merci* and I suppose this is a tribute to the Bourbon de Parme (?).[6] But you could always go on to Triente and maybe even Ljubljana....

---

1   *la famiglia,* Italian: the family.
2   *piazze Gonzagesche,* Italian: Gonzaga squares. The Gonzaga squares are in Isola Devarane, Rivarolo Mantovano, Pomponesco, and S. Martine dell'Argine. See Rowe's letter to Judith DiMaio★ dated 28 June 1996 (p 487 in this volume).
3   "J. Di M.": Judith DiMaio.★
4   "M.": Mantua.
5   *rencontre,* French: meeting.
6   *grazie,* Italian: thanks; *merci,* French: thanks.

281   *To **James Madge**, London*   *26 July 1997*

3133 Connecticut Avenue, Apt. 814, Washington, D.C.

Dear James,

Found your letter with all the info as to how to reach 17 Via Bignoli when I returned here a week ago. But three addresses!!! As Lady Bracknell said they always "inspire confidence, even with tradesman". And where is Thackholme Barn which sounds so Icelandic and almost W. H. Auden?[1]★

Anyway I enjoyed our dinner in Mantova, hope that you—both of you—did too and the restaurant at Torre Picenardi gave—rather surprisingly all things considered—great satisfaction to everybody.

Meanwhile, I have a little request that you might consider. The campanile of San Marco fell down in 1902 and a few days later, in—I believe—*The Morning Post,* there was an editorial about it. It must never be restored, a terrible loss to all humanity but no prefect of Venice must ever be inspired to rebuild it...You get the pic; it is a perfect piece of preservationist doctrine according to Ruskin and Morris: we should mourn but we must not fake, human hands cannot restore the patina of time....

Well I have lost my Xerox of this stuff and I wonder, since you are so close to it (the British Museum Library now, unfortunately The British Library) if you could drop in some day and retrieve it for me. I have asked my brother to do this but he seems to have no consciousness that time is involved and that I would like it for a little lec.

Hope that this isn't a deadly sweat and
A big *abbraccio* for you both,

    Colin Rowe   *Colin*

Decided that Prague is Zurich trying to be Salzburg but too picturesque to possess the authority.

---

1   James Madge★ and his wife Victoria Watson had three houses: a flat in Central London, a barn in the Yorkshire Dales, and a small terrace house in the town of San Giovanni in Croce, which is in the Po Valley on the border of the provinces of Cremona and Mantua.

Apt. 814, 3133 Connecticut Ave., Washington D.C.

Dearest David:

As regards an interesting symposium, etc, the few days in Zurich were—for an absence of interest—something quite by themselves and I am not quite convinced that, as regards ideas, the Swiss must—effectively—have been neutral ever since 1815![1] But they are surely beyond and outside politics and all of the issues of Mod Arch and Marxism and all that (historical determinism, free will, etc) are completely beyond their consciousness. Or, in other words, trying to introduce them to Popper* and what not went down like a ton of bricks and the career of somebody like Anthony Blunt (I didn't talk about it) must be entirely beyond their imagination.[2] Nevertheless I was well received—spoke from only two slides!—but it was a relief to leave on the Sunday for Potsdam.

So a drive to Potsdam didn't take place [...] it meant that we didn't drive via Stuttgart, Coburg, to Berlin but that I took a short flight to Tegel and then that I took a taxi ride (with an Indian driver!) to the Hotel Cecilienhof in Potsdam.

Now Potsdam is a MUST★★★★[3] and I advise that you and Bryony go there for a few days—perhaps to live—in September and you will find it (hire a car at Tegel) very rewarding.[4]

And, first of all, the hotel. It is a large piece of Stockbrokers Tudor, about four times the size of what you might expect to find in Surrey and Long Island, was built by Kaiser Wilhelm, in this preferred English Style during the years 1913–17 (?) for the Crown Prince and wife, Cecilie of Mecklenburg-Schwerin, and she remained there (apparently fully established) until just two days before the Russians arrived there in 1945! (Interesting that, after 1918, so many German royalties did not go into exile—Bavaria, Wurttemberg, Coburg, etc.) And that the Cecilienhof was therefore already for the Potsdam Conference just a few weeks later.[5]

So part of it is a hotel and the rest of it a museum which is positively infested by German and Japanese tourists; but, all the same, a nice place to stay since it is situated in the large park belonging to the Marmorpalais and one is not distracted by the site of ruins and indifferent urban renewal.[6]

But I think that you would be immensely gratified by Potsdam—even though it was bombed by the British on the night of April 14, 1945, very much of it, both urban and curiously rural, still survives and the general effect is modest, Italian, French, and Dutch—depending on where you happen to be.

From about 1820 onwards the prevalent domestic formula is English, picturesque and obviously derived from the more casual villas of John Nash. And this is something—the quantity or it—which I hadn't quite expected. But there are not only the different houses for the Prussian Princes—Charlottenhof, Glienicke, Babelsberg, Pfaueninsel, linked together by the landscapes of Peter Josef Lenne—but a whole lot more high bourgeois, aristocratic stuff, Italian villa stuff, which is put together far more assiduously than the English precedents. SO DO GO and, apart from Potsdam and its chain of lakes, you will find Mark Brandenburg to be a strangely 'new' country—sandy heath, very minor properties, indifferent villages, which might help to explain something of Kaiser Wilhelm's ambivalent anglophilia.[7] None of the richness of Western European landscapes here....

Afterwards we went on to Czechoslovakia—or whatever it is now called, dropped in at Franzensbad★★★;[8] spent a Night at Marienbad, in spite of its Edwardian reputation not all <u>that</u> hot; and dropped in at Karlsbad*** rolling plateau, deeply incised valleys, houses on precipitous cliffs, very much to be recommended; and then on to three nights in Prague.

So, as I expected it would, *Praha* left me quite cold.[9] But I always did find Czech nationalism just a bit revolting; and, after enduring the Place for three nights, I was only too glad to leave. [...]

And that's about all. En route from Mantua to Malpensa we <u>did</u> have a nice luncheon at Torre Picenardi*** though this did cut down several hours later on antique shops at Somma Lombardo. However, <u>this</u> restaurant was worth while and was advised by James Madge* who, with a house not too far away, I gave dinner to at Ai Garibaldini the night before and who <u>was</u> able fully to understand the problem of Mrs Robert. On the whole an interesting trip—in spite of everything and, I repeat, you MUST pay a visit to Potsdam and suggest the following:

Flight to Stuttgart, rent a car, drive to Wurzburg, Bamberg, Coburg.

Cross border to Karlsbad and Franzensbad, the best new small places which I saw (perhaps two nights) and then on to Berlin / Potsdam, which is a dull, flat, but fairly quick drive.

Saw a clever ad in Italy:

Tschiusami ai em an Eetalian giornalist.[10]

Lotsa lurve,

    Colin

P.S. The out of town campus of the ETH in Zurich is lugubrious and makes you see how silly are two doctrines: that a building should grow from the inside out and that all functions should be expressed. But this is quite mad *laissez-faire* and, if you are dealing with a coalition of buildings, it only results in jumble. Suppose that I always knew this but the horrors of the ETH just made it all that more clear.

Best thing, I thought, in Prague is this big Gothic hall of the 1490's. Their Nat. Gall is feeble but, as might be expected, they have good collections of engravings, though not available in shops to buy and I begin to realise that my own collection is really pretty good.[11] The Emperor Rudolf exhibition didn't seem to have too much to say.[12]

    Colin

---

1 Learning from Modern Architecture, an international symposium organized by Werner Oechslin* at the ETH (*Eidgenössische Technische Hochschule*) in Zurich.
2 Karl Popper* (1902–1994), Austrian-born British philosopher of science; Anthony Blunt (1907–1983), British art historian famously exposed as a Soviet spy.
3 Rowe rates the sights *, **, ***, or ****, the latter being the highest rating.
4 Dr Bryony Soper, David Rowe's* second wife.
5 In summer 1945 Truman, Churchill, and Stalin negotiated the Potsdam Agreement at the Cecilienhof.
6 Royal residence in Potsdam, designed in the late-eighteenth century by Carl von Gontard, and from 1789 by Carl Gotthard Langhans.
7 The Mark Brandenburg (Margraviate of Brandenburg), a major principality of the Holy Roman Empire from 1157 to 1806.
8 Rowe's star rating for the sights (see note 3).
9 *Praha*, Czech: Prague.
10 *Tschiusami ai em an Eetalian giornalist*: the phonetic replication of an appeal made with a heavy Italian accent: "Choose me, I am an Italian journalist".
11 "Nat. Gall.": National Gallery, Prague, *Palác Kinských*.
12 Exhibition Rudolf II and Prague, Prague Castle, 1997.

3133 Connecticut Avenue, Apt. 814, Washington, D.C.

Dear Werner:

Having just got back here three days ago I am now writing to thank you for the Zurich experience and all that.[1] But the new E.T.H. campus exceeds the possibility of belief. And just <u>how</u> are they to continue with such a project? It simply leaves me wondering about how very stubborn certain very stupid people can be....

I enjoyed particularly meeting Tobi Stockli[2] and your visiting critic from Berlin— my former student, Hans Kollhoff, and also Johannes Brunner whom I found *molto simpatico*.[3] But what I mostly learned in Zurich is what I already knew and is, again, related to the E.T.H. campus: that, if you plan a coalition of buildings, then each building <u>must</u> submit to the demands of the coalition, that the buildings cannot simply grow from the inside out according to the pious assumptions of modern architecture, that this is preposterous *laissez faire*....

Apart from that I found Potsdam—even after bombing and fifty years neglect—to be a revelation.[4] Charlottenhof, Glienicke, Babelsberg, Pfaueninsel, I had expected, but not the quantity of highly respectable Schinkelesque Italianate villas.[5] And these were quite remarkable.

Will let you have my text in a day or so and also the statement of my travel expenses.[6] Once again with many thanks and very best wishes,

sincerely,

Colin

Colin Rowe

P.S. Also saw the Bauhaus at Dessau!!!???[7] And I think that it ought to be properly photographed—searching details of inner angles and window reveals—because it really is much worse than I had expected it to be and certainly Erich Mendelsohn[8] would have rendered all such items far more laconic?[9]

Colin

---

1   Rowe had "just got back" from Zurich where he had given a lecture at the international symposium, Learning from Modern Architecture, organized by Werner Oechslin* at the ETH (*Eidgenössiche Technische Hochschule*) in Zürich.
2   Tobias Stöckli (b 1946), Hans Kollhoff (b 1946), and Johannes Brunner (b 1963).
3   *molto simpatico*, Italian: very nice, affable.
4   See Rowe's letter to David Rowe* dated 19 July 1997 (p 517 in this volume) for additional remarks on the symposium, Potsdam, and the ETH.
5   "Schinkelesque": refers to the Prussian architect and city planner, Karl Friedrich Schinkel (1781–1841).
6   Rowe sent no text. There was no publication.
7   Designed by Walter Gropius and completed in 1926, the Bauhaus Dessau housed the famed Bauhaus design school and was featured prominently in Rowe and Robert Slutzky,* "Transparency: Literal and Phenomenal". See bibliography.
8   Erich Mendelsohn (1887–1953), German architect whose renowned expressionist Einstein Tower was completed in Potsdam in 1924, two years before Gropius' Bauhaus at Dessau.
9   In his reply of 31 July 1997 to Rowe, Werner Oechslin* wrote, "Yes, the ETH campus is a tragedy—as are many things in architecture. <u>Modern</u> never did substitute 'Städtebau' as formed around 1900." He then noted that in Germany after 1945, whereas the DDR *did* subscribe to Städtebau, West Germany "installed ministries for traffic and housing only".

Dessau, he wrote, has importance now almost "exclusively as a (propagandist) icon". The academic world, he concluded, is "full of beliefs and ideologies with scarce capacities of looking at things with fresh mind and eyes...".

284   To *Alexander Caragonne*, *address unknown*   *1 August 1997*

Apt. 814, 3133 Connecticut Ave., Washington D.C.

Dear Alex:

I return your Zurich piece with my 'corrections' which, for the most part, are suggestions.[1]

The interview with Kevin Rhowbotham (whoever <u>he</u> may be)

I find distasteful and it surely does you <u>no</u> service. The "drive of critics, historians and other rag pickers of the miserable" is just <u>too</u> vulgar; and the *N.Y.T.* Obituary and the Bernhard piece does <u>all</u> that you need....

I would eliminate "another symptom of a latent, curmudgeonly 'old fogeyism'". "Private generation gap" is quite <u>enough</u> and a "curmudgeon" suggests that you are still using the language of Charles Dickens....

"Prescence" I assume is a spelling mistake and "presedence", when you <u>must</u> mean <u>precedents</u>, suggests either Emily Post or somebody arranging the order of guests for the Q. of E.

"It was recently, in 1944 I believe,"—<u>if</u> you are in doubt of the date.

You could relate "a quaint science fiction <u>tendency</u>" with Archigram and Plug-in City but *la tendenza*, to which you seem also to refer is something else.[2]

Lists of names should display analogous usage. I.E. in this [...].[3]

"*Le style* postmodern" gets you nowhere. It's not French usage and it's not English. Nor is it properly ironical...

"At the AA in London, in an entirely different cultural context/Alvin Boyarsky* brought forth" is my revision; but I still question "brought forth"... a bit too Abe Lincoln for present day purposes... "A.B. pursued"?

Don't know; but about "De" and "Von", doesn't it go like this? <u>Charles</u> de Selincourt or <u>Otto</u> von Habsburg, or, if no Xtian name <u>De</u> Selincourt or <u>Von</u> Ribbentrop? (obviously Otto v. H. is a bit too extreme); but e.g. Wilvan <u>van</u> Kampen or <u>Van</u> Kampen.

<u>Giles</u> Deleuze or <u>Gilles</u> Deleuze? I am too lazy to look; but <u>check it out</u>.

"Hejduk* had <u>labored mightily</u>". Surely <u>not</u>. This is like a not so eminent Victorian trying to be Old English....

<u>sometimes</u> best to say "the United States" rather than "the U.S."

Which is about all and I hope doesn't madden you too much.

best, best,

   Colin

1   Presumably, "Zurich piece" refers to the transcript of a paper Caragonne* presented at the July 1997 symposium Learning from Modern Architecture, ETH, Zurich. See Rowe's letter to Werner Oechslin* dated 21 July 1997 (see p 519 in this volume).

2   *la tendenza*, Italian neo-rationalist architectural movement that started in the early 1970s.

3   The last line of this page is not shown on the copy. The original is lost.

To **Arthur McDonald**, *Syracuse, N.Y.*   *2 August 1997*   **285**

Apt. 814, 3133 Connecticut Ave., Washington, D.C.

Arturo:

Surprised that Isaiah Berlin* is new to you—*The Hedgehog and the Fox* and all that.[1] He is now my brother's next door neighbour in Headington, Oxford; but, in that part of the world, I don't know what that means. I.E. though the houses are not very far apart, Sir Isaiah's driveway is about half a mile long....[2]

Anyway, he is ultimately a critic of Hegelian and Marxist mythology and, as such, is to be related to Sir Karl Popper* and Sir Ernst Gombrich*—only he is much more Establishment than they are. Thus, although they are all Jewish—Popper and Gombrich from Vienna and Berlin from Lithuania—P. and G. came to England as mature adults, while B. came as a child—to receive a very proper English education, including Oxford, where, apart from some time spent at the British Embassy in D.C., he has been ever since—Fellow of All Soul's and so on.

So, his language is more 'decorated' than theirs and—I've heard him at Cornell—he speaks as he writes, in long, elaborate, 'constructed' passages. But he must now be awful old—if Sir Ernst is now 87, and Sir K. has croaked, Isaiah Berlin must be 90 at least![3]

But he is part of a block of Jewish criticism, anti-determinist and pro free will, to which I subscribe; and he may be the most attractive member of that block which, implicitly must be hostile to most of the pretensions of modern architecture's apologetic.

So that is the general pic. I've read so much of him that, nowadays, I find him predictable; but, emphatically, he is someone who should be read. However, if you want to read this sort of stuff in a more simple language—but still within the tradition of English *belles lettres*—suggest Peter Medawar, *The Art of The Soluble*.[4] Medawar is an important biologist who puts this position from the point of view of an elegant sceptic.

Good to hear from you and think of spending a weekend here when you are next in these parts.

Un abbraccio

    Colin

    Colin Rowe

P.S. Saw, and heard, Werner in Zurich the other day![5]

1 Isaiah Berlin* (1909–1997), Latvian-born British philosopher, political theorist, essayist; Berlin, Isaiah, *The Hedgehog and the Fox: An Essay on Tolstoy's View of History,* London: Weidenfeld & Nicolson, 1953.

2 David Rowe* had recently purchased a house adjacent to, albeit distant from, Berlin's* house in Headington, Oxford.

3 Sir Ernst Gombrich* (1909–2001) and Sir Karl Popper* (1902–1994). Isaiah Berlin* (1909–1997) died at the age of 88, three months after this letter was written.

4 Medawar, Peter, *The Art of the Soluble,* London: Methuen, 1967.

5 Werner Seligmann,* who Rowe "saw and heard" at the Learning from Modern Architecture symposium at the ETH in Zurich in July 1997.

286 *To **Bruce Abbey**, School of Architecture Syracuse University* *12 October 1997*

Apt. 814, 3133 Connecticut Ave., Washington D.C.

Dear Bruce:

I have just been away at the Univ of Fla at Gainesville—45,000 students, scruffy live oaks and plums mixed with a few palms and no very noticeable declivities/acclivities. So this is the reason that your letter of September 12 has been so long neglected: it was waiting for me on my return last week.

So what to say?

Robert Maxwell's* lecture is, of course, pregnant with intelligence and you gotta' publish it?[1] But of course. However, to make a more amusing little book to be published under the auspices of Syracuse with Rizzoli/Monacelli?—in my possession since 1944 I have a *cahier*[2] of very witty Maxwell drawings (he gave it to me when he was leaving for India) and to give you an idea of its contents I send you xeroxes of a few sheets.[3]

So 'nuff implied? Along with "Functionalism and the Avant Garde"—with prefatory remarks by me?—should not this make a highly diverting publication? There seem to be 56 drawings altogether, bound in a University of Liverpool notebook, and I remember them as derived from sketches made by Robert as he was sitting next to me in dreadful, sadistic, lectures on Structural Mechanics; and I still find them something of a graphic revelation—all of them worthy of the *New Yorker* at a <u>much</u> later date....

Then, as to my little lecture of ten years ago:[4] I will let you have my own reactions as I decipher the typescript. But, as for you, I want you to think about the <u>two</u> Maxwell pieces—both very *chic*—as standing together—with an interval between them of half a century!!!

I look forward to your reactions.

Colin

1 Maxwell, Robert, "Functionalism and the Avant Garde", Dillenback Lecture, Syracuse University, April 1997. Published in Maxwell, Robert, *Ancient Wisdom and Modern Knowhow*, London: Artifice books on architecture, 2013, pp 82–103.

2 *cahier*, French: notebook.

3 The book was never published. Photocopies of five of Maxwell's* drawings sent to Abbey by Rowe survive. The original 56 drawings are lost.

4 Rowe's ACSA (Association of Collegiate Schools of Architecture) Lecture given at Syracuse, c 1987. The transcript is lost.

*To **Stanford Anderson**,*
Department of Architecture, MIT, Cambridge, Massachusetts   *7 November 1997*   **287**

Apt. 814, 3133 Connecticut Ave., Washington D.C.

Dear Stanford:

Excuse me for infringing your remoteness—and after such a long time; but today has been one of the most lugubrious House of Usher days. It has been of a positively Merovingian blackness and, for most of it, I have been feeling like *une voix d'outre tombe*,[1] a depression which was ultimately relieved by a UPS package sent by Suzanne Frank.[2] So she was here a few days ago and, in the package, was a copy of the dust cover of *Collage City* of which I had no recollection. So, Stanford, what you had to say has been positively therapeutic;[3] I am left feeling like the BVM after being impregnated by the Holy Pigeon; you have recharged my batteries; I have experienced a renaissance—and it's all through the gratification of your words.[4]

Now, obviously, this is an appeal for something else from you—but it's no more than an act of memory. Enclosed there is the xerox of a letter from me to Bill Saunders★ at Harvard and look at ps. 2, 3, 4. So do you know—I can't think of anybody more likely to know—the sources of the Hudnut quote and anything else that you can tell me about Hudnut?[5]

If without straining your powers of recollection, do let me know.

   Colin Rowe

1   *une voix d'outre tombe*, French: a voice from beyond the grave.
2   Suzanne Frank, former classmate of Stanford Anderson★ at Columbia; owner of House VI, designed by American architect Peter Eisenman★ (b 1932) and completed in 1975.
3   A quote from Anderson on the dust jacket of Rowe and Fred Koetter's★ *Collage City*, Cambridge, MA: MIT Press, 1978, reads: "The most brilliant essayist in the field of modern architecture is Colin Rowe, Professor of Architecture at Cornell University. His writings are passionately followed by a sizable number of people on both sides of the Atlantic and are a myth among many more architects and historians—a myth because a curious reticence has kept many of his essays from wide circulation."
4   "BVM": Blessed Virgin Mary.
5   Joseph Hudnut (1886–1968), architect, scholar, and educator; dean of Harvard Graduate School of Design from 1936 to 1953.

*To **Bill Saunders**,*
Assistant Dean, Harvard Graduate School of Design, Cambridge, Mass.   *18 October 1997*   **288**

Apt. 814, 3133 Connecticut Ave., Washington D.C.

Dear Bill:

"The Tyranny of the Coffee Table": a possible title for a contribution to your conference on interior design, furniture, etc....[1] What do you say???

Synopsis of story.... and I believe that it's true:

Coffee table unknown before 1925. A product of the Paris exhibition of that year. Jean-Michel Frank? As the Barcelona table adopted by Mies van der Rohe★ in 1929. Not adopted by Le Corbusier★ and Charlotte Perriand. It's career over the last sixty years both in 'modern' and 'traditional' interiors. An un-criticized cliche of the twentieth century....

An 'oriental' import. Previous 'occidental' furniture distributions. The coffee table and the conversation pit. Defects: the arrangement inhibits movement of people and, in fact, acts to nullify conversation which depends on the interchange of eyes rather than the proximity of knees. Produces divergence of persons. Divergence versus convergence. You have to lean forward rather than to lean back? Hannah Arendt and Le Corbusier on the role of the table.

So, with adequate visual documentation, etc, how does that grab you? It involves questions like physical mobility and the height of the settee, the 'obligation' to examine the overlooked, furniture as an index—and sponsor—of social change. In 1929 the King and Queen of Spain did not sit down in the Barcelona chairs which Mies,* presumably provided for that purpose. Apparently they saw at once that to do so would be self-defeating: the height above the floor, the inclination of the back, and the absence of arms all must have acted to dissuade them; they could see that they wouldn't be able to get out without an un-regal effort.

So that is the substance of "The Tyranny of the Coffee Table". Its prevalence is to be compared with the decline of the American bathtub—now too low, too shallow, too short, too narrow, and rarely provided with an inclined surface to support the head.

Hoping that all this might both edify and amuse, I now wonder if you could help me in a matter which concerns the Harvard dean of way back, Joseph Hudnut.

Bruce Abbey* recently sent me a transcript of the tape recording of a lecture which I gave at Syracuse in 1987 and, as of now, I know neither the date nor the place where I found this Hudnut stuff, but I would suspect it is of the earlier fifties; and it is all scrambled but the essential quote is Hudnut himself.

So he appears to deplore "grand compositions which corset the body of a live and unpredictable creature" and he concludes that "In every instance the live creature has refused the mold." But the substance of his remarks is like this:

> Every attempt by universities to establish a pattern laid out in advance has failed and ought to have failed. We must be free to develop the environment.... The task and the methods constantly change and no more than nature can tomorrow be predicted. No program is possible which extends beyond a dozen years. Let's imagine the university as city planners have imagined the city as a growing organism which formed life in the past as it will in the future. Our university will never be completed. If we make a master plan then, it must be in such general terms as will admit new interpretations and unexpected developments. We can take nothing for granted. Those facilities which have endured the longest may be the first to disappear.

> Let no building depend for its character upon its relationship to another nor let any of the open spaces be of such absolute proportions that new construction built into them will destroy them.[2]

Now some of this is true but much of it is late New Deal platitude; but, within forty years, how very much the terms of architectural discourse have changed! And what about Thomas Jefferson and the University of Virginia, which is here implicitly condemned? Or was there here a jab at MIT, with the old building to be compared with Aalto's Baker Dorm and Saarinen's Auditorium and Chapel?

In any case I would like to know more about Hudnut whom I once met in 1952. He did bring Walter Gropius to Harvard in 1937, did he not; and, perhaps more importantly, his influence must have been responsible for the appointment of Sigfried Giedion⋆ as Charles Eliot Norton Professor in 1938–39. Also was responsible for a change of name or title, from School or Architecture to G.S.D.; and, if so, when?

I would have written in reply to your letter of September 27 but I have been away at the Univ. of Fla.; and let me tell you that Gainesville is, almost, a fate worse than death—45,000 students on one campus!!!

Best wishes and hope that you can help.

> *Colin*
>
> Colin Rowe

P.S. I plan to use the Hudnut quote for a lecture at the U. of Miami towards the end of November; and, when it's once in shape I would be amused to give this lec again *chez vous*.[3]

---

1   The Design Arts and Architecture: A Colloquium conference given by the Harvard Department of Architecture in fall 1997.
2   Joseph Hudnut (1886–1968), architect, scholar, and educator, was dean of Harvard Graduate School of Design from 1936 to 1953. The source of the Hudnut quote is unknown.
3   *chez vous*, French: at your house; In November 1997 Rowe gave the lecture, "The Tyranny of the Coffee Table" at the University of Miami. He never gave the lecture at Harvard.

To **James and Rosie Rowe**, Bath, England   *7 December 1997*   **289**

Apt. 814, 3133 Connecticut Ave., Washington D.C.

Dearest James and Rosie:

A few notes of Miami and Dade County, Florida: population, c, 1910, 10,000, c. 1995, 2,000,000...!!!... A tenuous hispanophile fantasy which—thanks to Castro—has become a solid reality.[1]

A rich WASP society wanted, in the winter, to appear to be living in an Old Spanish colony;[2] and now a great many Cubans feel completely at home in it: De Tocqueville would have found it to be very interesting indeed.[3]

Miami Beach always old style Jewish New York and, until recently, much decayed, but, thanks to the Art Deco Revival, is now becoming very fashionable. So, if it were not for the old and rather sleazy Lubavich[4]—or rabbis slinking around the streets in black, you'd swear it was a setting for Babar and the Elephants—with Arthur and the other little elephants charging around on roller skates.[5]

Then Coral Gables, which more approaches the style of Palm Beach...

Food: a doubtful and mostly liquid Cuban mish-mash. But climate: rather promising it seems to me... that is if they'd only let it be so. But they seem to want it to be Arctic and result is that it is easy to get a very bad cold.

Anyway, I am telling you all this because it's a sort of colony of mine—Gwladys Margarita Diaz,[6]⋆ Miriam Gusevich,[7]⋆ José Gelabert, Jorge and Luis Trelles, not to mention Hector and Esteban from San Juan, P.R.,—all as astonished by it as I am—make it all seem very old time and, perhaps, in the not so distant future you all might find a brief visit would amuse.

Away from the sea, fumes of petroleum something awful; and one wonders how the palm trees survive....

Love, love, love,

Colin

1 Fidel Castro (b 1926) seized power in Cuba in 1959; at this time, many Cubans emigrated to Miami.
2 "WASP": White Anglo-Saxon Protestant.
3 Alexis de Tocqueville (1805–1859), French political thinker and historian.
4 Lubavich: Hasidic Jew.
5 Reference is to the fictional world of Babar the Elephant in de Brunhoff, Jean, *Histoire de Babar le petit éléphant*, Paris: Hachette, 1931, first ed.
6 Regarding Diaz,* Arce, and Sennyey,* see Rowe's letter to Alexander Caragonne* dated 1 November 1995 (p 450 in this volume).
7 Regarding Gusevich,* see Rowe's letter to her dated 2 May 1996 (p 481 in this volume).

290   *To **James Rowe**, Bath, England*   *31 January 1998*

Apt. 814, 3133 Connecticut Ave., Washington D.C.

James:

Did I ever send you a copy of *La Matematica della Villa Ideale*?[1]

I don't think that I did; but, since I found a lot of them the other day as I was sorting out some books, I am sending you one just in case. Translated by Paolo Berdini,* god son of Pope Pacelli, Pius XII, the white typewriter pope, who, for reasons that I don't understand, has such a bad reputation in this country.

Anyway, Paolo is now teaching at Stanford U, which must be very nice for him, though Tom Schumacher* thinks that he is really living there because, so Tom says, he was once a terrorist. However this is more than a bit malicious and I don't believe it; and you met Paolo in '88 at that dinner party that I gave in that restaurant where you can ask to go down into the basement and roam around under the seating of whatever the *teatro* used to be called....[2]

But what long effusive intros these wop types do write and how very intellectual it all sounds.

Lotsa lurv,

Colin

P.S. Paolo's family have been lawyers to the Holy See since the 1860's. But don't you imagine that the H.S. must have a very great many lawyers?

Colin

1 Rowe, Colin, *La matematica della villa ideale e altri scritti*, Paulo Berdini trans, Bologna: Zanechelli editore, 1993.
2 The restaurant was La Costanza in Rome. See Rowe's letter to Dorothy Rowe* 27 November 1988 (p 315 in this volume); *teatro*, Italian: theatre.

Apt. 814, 3133 Connecticut Ave., Washington D.C.

Dearest Judy:

My excitements over the past few days have consisted in getting my toe nails cut (Tuesday) and getting my hair cut, for the first time since December (Wednesday). So, since Frank and Dino have retreated to Acireale, or somewhere near Taormina, for the haircut I had to go to Supercuts across the street (I was confused for a time as to whether this meant haircuts or *filet mignons* and I shall never go there again....[1] It was done by a Japanese girl who didn't seem to understand English and is, probably, shockingly underpaid....)

But, of course, the great excitement was the shower of things arriving from you and, particularly, "Casa Caprini" which I want to hang underneath the "Battle of Constantine" with, on either side, the two Polidoro urns that you gave me way back—and then I've got to find somewhere for the inscrutable little Poussin which, I think, must be in your bedroom. AND then the "Villa Kerylos" which continues to give me a new angle (several new angles!) on what it is that you really like....[2]

Je reste a l'ombre de tes ailes

Colin *x x x x x x x*

---

1 Frank and Dino were Rowe's barbers. Acireale and Taormina are on the east coast of Sicily.
2 *Casa Caprini, Battle of Constantine,* and *Villa Kerylos* are engravings; the "little Poussin" an etching; and the *Villa Kerylos* was taken from a book.

Apt. 814, 3133 Connecticut Ave., Washington D.C.

Dearest Werner:

They tell me that you are in a hospital and this letter is to cheer you up. And it's about Le C.[1]

So, lately, I rediscovered a pregnant utterance from *Precisions* and it's about Garches.[2] And, French, it reads as follows:

Pour s'imposer a l'attention, pour occupier puissant l'espace, il fallait d'abord une surface premiere de forme parfait, puis une exaltation de la platitude de cetter surface par 'apport de quelques saillies ou de trous faisant intervener un movement avant-arriere.

Which, I suppose, may (just) be translated like this:

To absorb attention, to occupy space with power, the first necessity is a primary surface of perfect form (and there follows) an exaltation of the platitude of this surface by various juttings out (*saillies*) or cutting away (so as) to make a movement intervening from front to back.

But I love the exaltation of the platitude of the surface and think that you might too. And I do hope that the mere thought of it will invigorate you. And, feller, this quote is a terrific exegetic instrument.

And think—it also applies to La Tourette!³

So get well and continue to deliver the message!!!

Lotsa love and regards. And best wishes to Jeanie.⁴

    Colin

P.S. It's about time but later this year Birkhauser is publishing a German translation of *Mathematics of the I. V.*⁵ So you will be able to read it as you recuperate.

    Colin

---

1   "Le C.": Le Corbusier.*
2   Le Corbusier, *Précisions sur un état présent de l'architecture et de l'urbanisme*, Paris: Éditions Crès, Collection de "L'Esprit Nouveau", 1930). Translated to English by Edith Schreiber Aujame, *Precisions: On the Present State of Architecture and Planning*, Cambridge, MA: MIT Press, 1991; Garches: Villa Stein de Monzie at Garches, France, designed by Le Corbusier,* 1926–1928.
3   La Tourette: Sainte Marie de La Tourette, a Dominican priory near Lyon, France, designed by Le Corbusier,* 1956–1960.
4   Jeanie Seligmann, Werner's* wife.
5   Rowe, Colin, *The Mathematics of the Ideal Villa and Other Essays*, Cambridge, MA: MIT Press, 1976. Reprinted in German as *Die Mathematik der idealen Villa und andere Essays* with a new *"Vorwort"* by Colin Rowe, Christoph Schnoor trans, Basel: Birkhäuser, 1998.

293   *To **Irving Phillips**, Houston, Texas*   *20 May 1998*

Apt. 814, 3133 Connecticut Ave., Washington D.C.

Dear Irving:

Have enjoyed looking through your brochure—and thinking about it: and I still suppose that the most amazing thing that Corbu* ever said (to be placed along side the Maison Domino): "Have respect for walls—there is nothing there but the walls and the floor, which is really a horizontal wall..."!!!¹

Am at the moment in the grip of a little fantasy about Austin, T. which has been promoted, overtly, by Caragonne* and, perhaps covertly by Kevin Keim;² and this relates to some sort of annex to the Charles Moore House which would be to contain the collection of my things—and perhaps even (if I don't croak before then) myself.³

So things comprise furn and effects—oriental rugs, a quite good collection of sixteenth century Italian engravings, miscellaneous bric-a-brac, etc., and would require to be sympathetically housed in a series of rooms, *enfilade* and *promenade architecturale*, both studio and party house. In other words, it would be an 'in my beginning is my end' affair—and I think you get the pic.—a little tribute to Texas which, after all is said and done, does remain my favorite state.⁴

Now I shall shortly have a visit from Kevin who, I am pretty sure wants to talk about something like this—though where the money comes from I don't know; and, then, how about a visit from you?

Best, best, *Colin*

1. "Corbu": Le Corbusier*(1887–1965), Swiss-born, French architect. The source of the quote is not known.
2. Kevin Keim, director of the Charles Moore Foundation, Austin, Texas.
3. The "annex": Charles Moore's former studio in Austin, part of a complex of buildings that once constituted Moore's house and are now part of the Charles Moore Foundation.
4. Ultimately, Rowe's library, a few artifacts, and six boxes of Rowe's papers were housed in a single large room at the Moore Foundation without *enfilade* or *promenade architecturale* and together with a few models of Charles Moore's work and a series of Moore's polychromed moosehead columns. "In my beginning is my end" is the opening line of the poem "East Coker" (1940) in TS Eliot, *Four Quartets*, New York: Harcourt, 1943.

*To **Judith DiMaio**, West 67th Street, New York, N.Y.*   *4 July 1998*   **294**

Apt. 814, 3133 Connecticut Ave., Washington D.C.

Dearest Judy:

The Palazzo Barbaro was acquired, some time in the 1870's I should think, by Daniel and Ariana Curtis of Boston.[1] Dan Curtis had punched a little guy on the nose in a street car—didn't like his looks or something; and, after remarks by the judge, decided that he couldn't live in the U.S. anymore, and so with his wife, Ariana, who was English, removed himself to Venice where they bought the P.B. which became a famous American house. See John Singer Sargent, *The Curtis Family at the Palazzo Barbaro*. It shows Daniel and Ariana, plus son, Ralph, and daughter-in-law who was Lisa Colt from Hartford, Ct.[2]

But the Curtis's (who still own the place) could never quite afford it, so they rented it every other year to Isabella Stewart Gardner, who there entertained Henry James,* etc.—and, I imagine, Whistler, Berenson and on and on. So also think about Paul Curtis...!!! And, also Ralph and Lisa went to live at Villa Balbianello....[3]

Useful info for conversation at Palazzo B?

Then also Katherine de Kay Bronson from Prov., R.I. might be another useful topic because she was a friend of Robert Browning who wrote poetry for her and of H.J. who just wrote about her. And, if you use just a bit more, Mrs. B. went on to become the grandmother of the late Bernardo Rucellai!!!

July 4 1983 we were in Lindau, Bavaria.....

Love, love,

   Colin *x x x x x x x x x*

P.S. Mrs. B. lived in Asolo (won't you go there to lunch?) and so somewhere near the future Harry's Bar.[4]

1. Judith DiMaio* was to attend a party at the Palazzo Barbaro, Venice. Here Rowe writes her of its social and historical context.
2. Daniel Sargent Curtis was remotely related to John Singer Sargent, whose 1898 painting, *An Interior in Venice*, also depicts the Curtis family in the Palazzo Barbaro.
3. The Villa Balbianello was built in 1787 for the Cardinal Angelo Maria Durini at the tip of a peninsula and overlooking Lake Como.
4. Asolo is a town in the Veneto Region of Northern Italy. The original Harry's Bar, "the preferred destination of European aristocracy", opened in Venice in 1931.

Apt. 814, 3133 Connecticut Ave., Washington D.C.

Joan!

Here are the pics with a covering letter from Brian Richards⋆ who worked with me.[1]

⋆   Apparently the two inside perspectives are mine—or so Brian seems to think; and I think that they are both very nice.

⋆   He finds that "The ground floor plan is still classic"; but N.B. he means European and English "ground floor", or American "first floor".[2] So, when he says that the "first floor plan is missing", he means American second floor.

⋆   Our work on this dates from mid-July to mid August 1952; and building from 1953; and note the difference in execution. Our long horizontal slot (Richard Neutra?) prevails; but it seems that it acutely loses sense. I.E. it loses sense as a cantilever and to introduce what are pilasters upstairs—standing on top of beam ends!—when our upstairs was just simply concrete block. Also <u>our</u> windows do get terribly screwed up, or don't you think? And, as for the rest; notice the difference in the end elevations...

⋆   Ingredients? Presumably Neutra and De Stijl—me;[3] and Markelius[4]—Brian.[5]

Hope you can use...

Love and all,

Colin

P.S. Brian married Sandra Lousada, Anglo-Portuguese-Jewish; and her father had something to do with the R.C.A. and they had a house in Oxfordshire with part of living room floor of plate glass so that you can look down to a waterfall.[6]

Her maternal grandfather was A.P. Herbert, M.P., either independent or for the University of Oxford (seat which no longer exists); and he wrote books about divorce law with names like *Holy Deadlock*.[7] Brian subsequently worked in Paris and Morocco, before he returned to London where he lived for a time with Mary Shand, daughter of Morton Shand, *Arch. Rev.* and, subsequently Mrs James Stirling (now <u>Lady</u> Stirling and *vedova inconsolabile*.)[8] Took up with Peter Smithson—a conversion trauma?—and remains attached to all sorts of moving sidewalks, 'travelators' and things.[9] He once went with my brother to Rome; but David complains that he <u>wouldn't</u> look at anything.

    Colin

P.P.S. Think this project is very New Brutalist. But N.B. *avant la lettre*.[10]

    Colin

---

1 Enclosed with Rowe's reply to Ockman's⋆ request for information on the Seamans Institute—a building that he and Brian Richards⋆ designed while temporarily employed by the Vancouver architectural firm of Sharp, Thompson, Berwick, and Platt—were photocopies of photographs and drawings of the building and a letter of explanation from Brian Richards dated 16 January 1996 that Rowe had sent to Phyllis Lambert⋆ earlier. See Rowe's letter to Lambert dated 21 March 1996 (p 473 in this volume). The letter reads:

Brian Richards
Architect B.Arch (Lpool) RIBA
86 Elgin Crescent, London W11 2JL
Phone 0171-7277 484 Fax: 0171-7922306

January 16, 1996

Dear Colin

Good to hear that the Seamans Institute has become legendary. Bit late, I heard several years ago that they had pulled it down but then it was not built as we planned it—being mirror imaged and so everything was back to front.

I am sure there is scope for an essay on how left-handed architects plan differently from right-handed ones.

I enclose some of the original drawings. Alas the first floor plan—which was rather good, with a central core, is missing but I am sure the plan could be obtained with some better photos from Sharp Thompson Berwick & Platt. The enclosed copies were sent by Proctor Le Mare and are badly printed. The later pictures show the concrete painted brown. We wanted to paint it black—which comes from a building I had worked on in Markelius' office in Stockholm.

The ground floor plan is still a classic, I think, shades of Van Doesburg—you may remember we were very into De Stijl at the time. The elevators were of course wrecked by the panels below the windows. Your perspectives, particularly of the grand piano were masterly. You may remember we met the old admiral to show him the scheme before we sailed off to the south. Also that Ned Pratt was away on holiday when we were given the project and was very miffed on returning to find we had done the scheme?

Perhaps some research is needed into what happened to the Bakersfield Junior College and what was actually built.

Do let me know what Phyllis Lambert* makes of it and if there is to be a catalogue.

All the best, from Sandra and me

Yours

Brian

2 "N.B.": *Nota Bene*, Italian: Note Well.
3 Richard Neutra (1892–1970), Austrian-born, American modern architect.
4 Sven Markelius (1889–1972), modernist Swedish architect and post-war urban planner.
5 Brian Richards* (1928–2004), architect, studied at the University of Liverpool and at Yale before traveling with Rowe in North America in 1952 and 1953.
6 "R.C.A.": Royal College of Art.
7 AP Herbert (1890–1971), author of the satirical novel *Holy Deadlock*, London: Methuen, 1934, and independent Member of Parliament who campaigned for reforms in marriage and divorce laws.
8 P Morton Shand (1888–1960); "*Arch. Rev.*": *The Architectural Review*; *vedova inconsolabile*, Italian: grieving widow.
9 Peter Smithson (1923–2003), English architect.
10 *avant la lettre*, French: before the name existed; literally, "before the letter". Regarding 'New Brutalism' nomenclature, see Rowe's letter to Louis I Kahn* dated 7 February 1956 (p 107 this volume).

To **James Rowe**, *Bath, England*   *October 21, 1998* **296**

Apt. 814, 3133 Connecticut Ave., Washington D.C.

Dearest James:

Two related misunderstandings and the first is quoted in a Catholic magazine called *First Things,* and it relates to Malta.[1]

On one side of the door of a church is a sign in English calling for silence and decency in dress and forbidding shorts mini-skirts and animals. But, on the other side it says, in Maltese, "GHAJJAT JEW DISKORS BLABZONN... MINI SKIRTS JEW HOT PANTS".

So an American tourist was shocked and communicated with the magazine, which communicated with the Vatican—only to receive back an extended dictionary entry explaining that, in Maltese, the word "jew" is a conjunction meaning "or" and has nothing to do with the Jewish people....!!!!!

A bit like, don't you think?, the American student in Rome who complained that the Italians were very anti-Semitic. And, when Tom Schumacher* asked him why, he obtained the rather charming reply that, in relation to excited dogs, the Italians were always pointing to the floor and loudly saying "Jew". But, even with the explanation that the Italians were really saying "giu" (down) the student still seemed to be scarcely satisfied.

Thought that you and Rosie might be amused.

Best, best,

    Colin *x x x*

---

1 *First Things*, an interdenominational ecumenical journal published in New York, was founded in 1990.

297   *To **Judith DiMaio**, West 67th Street, New York, N.Y.*   *17 November 1998*

Apt. 814, 3133 Connecticut Ave., Washington D.C.

Dearest Judy:

I enclose that excerpt from the Sunday *N.Y.T.* and note the ref to Asplund.[1] Then I also enclose xeroxes of <u>three</u> Asplund tombs; Prince Oscar Bernadotte, Secretary of State Hjalmar Retting, and Admiral Ankarcrona.[2] And these, to my surprise, seem to be all that Asplund ever did in this line.

How about yourself looking up Sigurd Lewerentz?[3]

Anyway, I think your idea is charming and perhaps <u>we</u> could have a lot of Paris plates embedded in the inside walls.[4]

Love you for the project and I am sure that it will cause me to die happy....

Addio and I will write a will,[5]

    Colin

Sorry that it has taken so long to mail this letter but the Asplund book has been hard to find.

Dearest Judy, insist on the project. (November 23)

    Colin

---

1 Spindler, Amy, "Getting In", *The New York Times*, Sunday, 15 November 1998. Concerning Hollywood Memorial Park Cemetery, the article states: "There will be rooms for crypts open to the sky on top of mausoleums, and a cylindrical building suggested by Erik Gunnar Asplund's public library in Stockholm will be lined with book-shaped urns." Asplund (1885–1940) was a Swedish architect.
2 The "Xeroxes" are from Holmdahl, Gustav, Sven Ivar Lind and Kjell Odeen, eds, *Gunnar Asplund Architect, 1885–1940: Plans, Sketches, and Photographs*, Stockholm: AB Tidskriften Byggmästaren, 1950, pp 124–25. See below.
3 Sigurd Lewerentz (1885–1975), Swedish architect known for his designs for crematoria and cemetery building in Stockholm and Malmö.

4 Judith DiMaio★ had proposed a small temple for both Rowe's remains and hers with neoclassical Paris porcelain tea-cups embedded in the walls. Ultimately, Rowe's body was cremated and, in early 2000, the ashes scattered at Sir John Vanbrugh's Temple of the Four Winds, Castle Howard, North Yorkshire, England.

5 *Addio*, Italian: Goodbye.

*To **William Safire**, The New York Times, New York, N.Y* — *1998 (not sent)* — **298**

Apt. 814, 3133 Connecticut Ave., Washington D.C.

Dear William Safire:[1]★

About bimbos?

As one might expect the O.E.D. does not list the category; but, if one takes a look at the average Italian-English dictionary, one finds the following:[2]

"Bimbo, diminutive for baby or infant, masculine, with a plural of bimbi;"

And this is paralleled by the feminine,

"Bimba, with a plural of bimbe."

So there ensue my questions: just when did the word "bimbo" enter the language? And when did it change its gender?

I am prompted to ask for this info by a re-reading of several books by P.G. Wodehouse, 1938, 1947, and 1953, in which "bimbo", as a slang word, gives the impression of being well established; but, as in Italian, is always presented as a masculine term.[3] And so I will quote my sources:

The Code of the Woosters, 1938, p.48
"If I ever saw a 'bimbo' engaged in putting two and two together, that 'bimbo' was Sir Watyn Bassett" —Sir R.W. is an eminent medical practitioner.

Joy in the Morning, 1947, p.16
"When the details began to come in—I discovered that the 'bimbo' who had drawn the short straw was the Lord Worpleson"—Lord Worplesdon is a very rich shipowner.

The Mating Season, 1949, p. 42
"In the circles in which I move it is generally recognized that I am a resilient sort of 'bimbo'"—this is the young Bertie Wooster talking about himself.

Ring for Jeeves, 1953, p. 33
"Or could it be that he's blackmailing somebody? ...Very profitable I believe. You look around for some wealthy 'bimbo' and nose out his secrets."

p. 133
"He came sidling up to me said, addressing me (was) "Hallo 'Bimbo' old boy...and I hadn't been called 'Bimbo' since I was at school."

p. 134
"I suppose that you wouldn't care to buy this, 'Bimbo', old boy".

Now, for all I know, Wodehouse may have persisted in this usage after 1953 and it may have been his practice before 1938; and, personally, I suspect this word of having migrated into English during the 1920's. But did it first appear in the United States or in Britain? And I suspect the instrumentality of Wodehouse, a sort of 'mid-

Atlantic' person who, living in the U.S., paraded a mostly English caste of characters. But, though from Wodehouse there probably proceed both Monica Lewinsky and Christine Keeler (Profumo scandal of 1963), I don't see that he can give us any clue as to the change of sex![4]

I am writing to you because I enjoy your etymological enthusiasm and because I believe that this topic is just as likely to entertain you as it might have diverted the late Logan Pearsall Smith.

Sincerely,

    Colin Rowe, Cornell University, Emeritus

P.S. I find one exception to masculine 'bimbo' in Wodehouse, *Ring for Jeeves*, p. 15

"old Tembo the elephant doing this and that in the 'bimbo' or tall grass."

And here, where—perhaps for local color—fauna become flora, it must be noted that in his own text Wodehouse italicizes 'bimbo'.

Sincerely,

    COLIN ROWE

---

1 William Safire* (1929–2009), American author, syndicated political columnist for the *New York Times* and author of "On Language", a column on popular etymology in the *The New York Times Magazine*.
2 "O.E.D.": *Oxford English Dictionary*.
3 Pelham Grenville Wodehouse (1881–1975).
4 Monica Lewinsky (b 1973), an American woman with whom US President Bill Clinton admitted to having had an "improper relationship" in 1995–1996, resulting in the Lewinsky Scandal; Christine Keeler (b 1942), a former English model and showgirl with whom a British government minister became sexually involved in 1963, resulting in the Profumo Affair.

299   *To **Michael Spens**, Wormiston-by-Crail, Fife, Scotland*   *December, 1998*

Apt. 814, 3133 Connecticut Ave., Washington D.C.

Dear Michael:

    Just a thought apropos of James Frazer Stirling.*

The presence of the Polish School of Architecture at Liverpool was very important and I think that you should try to get hold of the book about it—called *The Polish School of Architecture*.[1] It occurs to me, for instance, that much of late Jim's unaccountable without some remote Polish influence. There were Poles from Warsaw and also, in those days, from Vilna but the metropolitan, Warsaw, Poles had much more panache and were almost flashy in their capacity to condense—an expressionist rather than dialectical version of Corbu.*

I mentioned this to Mark Girouard*; but, though Mark has many merits, he is too *Country Life*, too close to Hardwick and Chatsworth, to be able to grab such an idea.[2] However, think about the Staatsgallerie in Stuttgart and I believe that you might discover that something of this building's pedigree is related to Poland.[3]

So did Jim's career at Liverpool 'overlap' the Polish presence?; and I don't quite know when they left.[4] But no matter, I am suggesting an indirect influence rather than any personal contact; and Jim's gradual shift from Butterfieldian terribilita towards an expansive flamboyance seems to be in line with my implications.[5]

Best, best,

Colin

P.S. As a result of the misfortunes of their *pays natal* the Liverpool Poles never had opportunity to practice or develop;[6] but they were 'well connected' and there was even an Helena Pilsudska, daughter of the general.[7] They were a case of preponderant *style Corbu* deriving from a well concealed Beaux Arts background; and, some years ago, one was apt to find a decayed Polack persisting as an indigent fencing master in places like Phoenix, Arizona....[8]

Colin

1 Szmidt, Boleslaw ed, *The Polish School of Architecture, 1942–1945*, Liverpool: Charles Birchall and Sons, Ltd, 1945.
2 Mark Girouard* (b 1931), an English architectural historian and an authority on country houses. See Rowe's letters to Dorothy Rowe* dated 4 March 1996 and 19 March 1996 (pp 464 and 470 in this volume); his letter to David Rowe* dated 15 December 1996 (p 510); and his letter to Mark Girouard dated 12 December 1995 (p 457).
3 Neue Staatsgalerie, Stuttgart, Germany, by James Stirling,* Michael Wilford & Associates, 1979–1984.
4 The Poles left Liverpool in 1945. Stirling* studied architecture at the University of Liverpool from 1945 to 1950.
5 Refers to the architectural style of William Butterfield (1814–1900).
6 *pays natal*, French: native country.
7 Jadwiga (Helena) Palsudska-Jaraczewska (b 1920), Polish architect and aviator, daughter of two-time Polish Prime Minister Józef Klemens ('the General') Pilsudski (1867–1935).
8 *style Corbu*, French: Le Corbusier* Style.

*To **Michael Manfredi**, New York City*   *1 January 1999*   **300**
Apt. 814, 3133 Connecticut Ave., Washington D.C.

Dear Michael:

I woke this morning at one o'clock and thought what an odd combination of numbers: one a.m. on January one, 1999. And then I thought how remarkable was the combination 1.00 a.m., Jan 1, 1111—a combo which won't occur again until 2.00 a.m., January 2, 2222 which is quite a long time ahead!

But, apropos of the lecture in April, would love it if we could get some time to talk and whether you and Marion would think about spending some time here—two beds, two baths, etc.[1] But perhaps not convenient for the night of the lecture, when there is sure to be so much confusion. However, what about the following night?; and might that be at all possible? Because then, perhaps, we could all drive around and show ourselves things which, no doubt, we should all of us enjoy.

So think about it and the best of best wishes for the pre-millennial years

Colin

P.S. And even now I haven't seen Marion and your contribution to the Memorial Bridge / Arlington scenery....???[2]

Colin

---

1 Manfredi* and Marion Weiss were to give a lecture at the University of Maryland in April 1999.
2 Weiss / Manfredi* had won a national design competition for the Women's Memorial and Education Center at the ceremonial entrance to Arlington National Cemetery, opened in October 1997.

301 *To **James & Rosie Rowe**, Bath, England*   *5 January 1999*

3133 Connecticut Avenue, Apt. 814, Washington, D.C.

Dearest Rosalinda-Rosamonda and Jacopone:[1]

Received your pic of events on October 2; and, meanwhile, think of your Papa, Himself and Bryony, gone off to Nice to organize an invasion of Provence next summer.[2]

But, of course, I still remain the victim of Normanitas; I still remember the little old lady in Naples about ten years ago, who laid her hand upon my wrist, rubbed it a bit, and said: "*Ma lei, con gli occhi blu e le baffe lunghi* (at that time I had a *mustachio*) *e il vero tipo Normanno, il vero tipo Boemondo.*"[3]

And, needless to say, this perception left me devastated because, according to *Burke* and *Debrett*,[4] Bohemond Prince of Antioch, the greatest of the Crusaders, was/ is (through the Comtes de Brienne) the supposed ancestor of the Beaumonts, your paternal grandmother's family, and the immortal Bohemond, croaked 1111, is buried in a particularly ravishing little proto-Renaissance, semi-Islamic, mausoleum attached to the *duomo* at an otherwise disgusting little town, Canosa di Puglia.[5] So, this is my incipient argument about Italian *meridionale* versus Provence.[6] And I will go on to make another: In my alleged Norman background Romanesque architecture excites in me *un delire de touche* I have experienced at Ely (just want to caress those columns) and I have experienced it, to greater extravagance, at Troia and Trani and, hence, my involvement with those funny old Normans, who were so belligerent, capable, eclectic, and clever.[7]

So, we could see Monte San Michele d'Arcangelo on the Gargano peninsula and the whole of that coast southwards, including Otranto (where the Turks were responsible for a famous massacre) and all the way down to Santa Maria di Leuca on the heel of Italy, where it's beautifully cool because the wind blows from all directions.[8] We would, I think, skip Bari, Brindisi and Taranto, and perhaps take in Trulliland instead—Alberobello, Locorotondo, Martina Franca—all very much nicer than perpetually driving around in the, rather dreary, suburbs of Nice and Cannes. And we would return up the valley of the Agri river (spectacular scenery with snow mountains in Calabria to the S) and take in the Certosa of LaPadula (I've never seen it, but is said to be terrific) and then thru some precipitous stuff to all those Greek temples at Paestum.[9] And then Ravello, Amalfi, Castellammare di Stabia, before returning, via Montecassino, Anagni, etc, to Rome.

And, incidentally, we'd probably begin in Rome and go south through Ascoli Piceno.

But this would be a wonderful trip and Norman? But all the way! And much better than hanging around in the dreary adjacencies of the Cote d'Azur. And shouldn't be too difficult—start early and find a hotel early; and I'm sending you, with this, a little book on the Normans which I have found disappointing and not illuminating. For some reason there is no index in this edition and it leaves you with the idea that, simultaneously the author is over-generalizing or, like a hen, persistently pecking at the nitty gritty....

However, as Paolo Berdini* is apt to say: "Poor Italy, everything north of Rome is Austria, and everything south of Rome? that's Africa"!! And that, I imagine, is the reason why it's so easy to travel in the former Kingdom of the Two Sicilies without all the sweat of hotel reservations: people just don't go there (except for a few places) and, rarely in the summer.

So, think about it! And say nothing to David to whom I shall write separately....

Best of the best,

    Colin

P.S. Where, in the first decade of the century, Sir George Sitwell used to go; and where Osbert and Sacheverell picked up a lot of their info.[10] And also read Norman Douglas, *In Old Calabria* (travels before 1914)[11] and, possibly John Julius Norwich.[12] And, another year—who knows?—one might even go to Antioch!!! And much more stimulating than Leon Krier's* backyard at Claviers in the *departement* of Var....[13]

    Colin

P.P.S. The Normans must have been very good at the business of getting horses on to boats—apparently still difficult at the time of the Crimean War; but completely shocking when you think about these dreadful creatures rearing, and stumbling, and kicking in those very little and completely open boats which is all that the poor guys had available.

It is just heroic—and squalid—even to think about it and much more amusing (even instructive) to think about Scandinavian sex life in those long, dark winter months in Odense, Copenhagen, or wherever. But, to produce such an excess of population as to require so massive an emigration of younger sons! What perpetual screwing and fucking there must have been going on in Denmark *circa* 800–900!

It exceeds the imagination, all those horny monsters! And even to consider that the descendants of those who stayed at home are now settled down and pleating lampshades in a highly demure version of the welfare state....

A bientot and GRH*H*H.[14] But it does make ya' think, y'know.

---

1   "Rosalinda-Rosamonda and Jacopone": Rowe's Italianized names for Rosemary* and James Rowe.*

2   David Rowe* and his wife, Dr Bryony Soper.

3   *"Ma lei, con gli occhi blu e i baffi lunghi* (at that time I had a mustachio) *e il vero tipo Normanno, il vero tipo Boemondo"*, Italian and English: But you, with the blue eyes and long whiskers (at that time I had a mustache) and the true Norman type, the true Bohemond type. See note 4 below.

4   Townend, Peter ed, *Burke's Genealogical and Heraldic History of the Peerage, Baronetage, and Knightage*, 105th ed, London: Burke's Peerage Ltd, 1970 and *Debrett's Peerage and Baronetage*, 148th ed, London: Debrett, 2011.

5   Bohemond I of Antioch (c 1058–1111), leader in the First Crusade, nicknamed "Bohemond" after the legendary giant, *Buamundus gigas*. Canosa di Puglia is a town in Apulia, southern Italy.

6   *meridonale*, Italian: southern.

7   *un délire de touche*, French: an irresistible urge to touch objects.

8   On 12 August 1480 eight hundred Christian citizens of Otranto who refused to convert to Islam allegedly were taken to the Hill of the Minerva and beheaded by Turkish invaders.

9   "S": South.

10 George Reresby Sacheverell Sitwell (1860–1943), British antiquarian writer and Conservative politician, was father to authors Edith Sitwell (1887–1964), Francis Osbert Sitwell (1892–1969), and Sacheverell Sitwell (1897–1988).

11 George Norman Douglas (1868–1952), Austrian-born, British writer of insightful travel books including *Old Calabria*, London: Martin Becker, 1915 and *Fountains in the Sand: Rambles among the Oases of Tunisia*, New York: James Pott and Company, 1912.

12 John Julius Norwich (b 1929), English historian and travel writer.

13 Claviers is a French village west of Cannes in Provence, near the Department of Var, France, where the Rowes' friend, Léon Krier,* made his home at the time of this letter.

14 *À bientôt*, French: see you soon; so long.

302   *To **Joan Ockman**, Elkins Park, Pennsylvania*   *7 January 1999*

3133 Connecticut Avenue, Apt. 814, Washington, D.C.

Dearest Joan:

Thanks an awful lot for your very flattering article.[1] Of course I disagree with occasional interpretations; but no serious matter and, here, I only want to point out statements that are erroneous, most notably that I was not at Cambridge for the two years which you allege but for the four years, 1958–62—the great folly of my life!

Also, I am very curious about Clement Greenberg because I have never read him.[2] And do you think that I should?

But, on the whole, thanks a lot and—you done me proud and with elegant language.

Meanwhile I am still desperately looking forward to a visit from—Freudian laps to—Elkins Park and tell Robert that I will, will, absolutely WILL arrive just as soon as I can assemble Tom Schumacher* and Patti Sachs to make a, mostly, Jewish assembly *chez vous*.[3]

Admire your energy and assiduity, and look forward.

Best, best and *a bientot*[4]

> *Colin*
>
> Colin Rowe

1   Ockman, Joan, "Form without Utopia: Contextualizing Colin Rowe", *The Journal of the Society of Architectural Historians* (Society of Architectural Historians) 57, 1998, vol 4, pp 448–456.

2   In the article cited above, Ockman* referred to the American essayist and art critic Clement Greenberg (1909–1994).

3   At the time Schumacher* and Sachs lived near Rowe in Washington, DC; *chez vous,* French: at your house.

4   *à bientôt*, French: see you soon; so long.

303   *To **Robert Maxwell**, Tasker Road, London*   *2 March 1999*

Apt. 814, 3133 Connecticut Ave., Washington D.C.

Caro il mio Roberto:

I send you a xerox copy of a letter of yours that I found inside a dilapidated copy of Byron's works when I opened it the other day.[1] Dated 11/12/44, by now it is surely a historic item and I hope that you will treasure it as such. It is almost fifty-five years old and just think of that!!!

The book was given to me by Arthur Sprigg, was sent from Ruthin Castle, North Wales—surely a most laconic address—and was, apparently dispatched on December 29, 1941 with best wishes for 1942. But do you remember Arthur?—naive medical student who came to Liverpool after Winchester and New College, Oxon—and ever so much naiver than the alternative medicos, John Shepeard and Richard Welbourne, with their equally Anglican buddy Leonard Tyler....

Have also been enjoying a, rather expensive, course of physical therapy.

Ti saluto con un abbraccio fervente,[2]

    Colin

---

1 George Gordon (Lord) Byron (1788–1824). Presumably the book Rowe opened was *The Poetical Works of Lord Byron*, London: Ward Lock, 1879.
2 *Ti saluto con un abbraccio fervente*, Italian: I say goodbye to you with a fervent embrace.

Rowe on Rowe II
written by Colin Rowe, c 1995[1]

Rowe appears <u>not</u> to have believed in the Zeitgeist, <u>not</u> to have liked over-stuffed furniture and coffee tables, to have been addicted to American small towns and nineteenth century specimens of Americana, and to have been easily excited by Italian topography and buildings. He didn't like the word 'taste' but, since he was willing to accept its use, his own 'taste' in architecture was for 'the carefully careless'—what he called a Hadrianic disarray assembled out of highly punctilious bits and pieces.

Evidently he enjoyed poetry—both English and French; and he was prone to admire French poetry for the qualities he admired in the best French architecture—a very French cerebrality which he tended to prefer to Italian *bella figura*. Though a bit of a cerebral type himself, he rather disdained intellectuality. To intellectuality he preferred intelligence; but, when he found the two combined, this was something of an epiphany.

For all his obvious happiness in the United States, he remained very English. Like that archetypal English personality (and psycho-problem, <u>Hamlet Prince of Denmark</u>), he always <u>thought</u> too much about <u>thinking</u>; but he was, generally, too resilient to be depressive.

For purposes best known to himself, he occasionally affected 'red neck' disguise and his many friends felt obliged to tolerate a highly inept performance. Friends of his from Texas note that, while he was exhilarated when he found himself in the former Confederate States, he also shrank from them with some degree of dismay. He was a collector but not acutely possessive; he was apt to tire of things and give them away—and, only then, to regret the gift....

He was an architect *manqué*.[2] He is often said to have exerted great influence; but, in the opinion of at least this obituarist, this supposition is much to be doubted.

---

1 Written by Rowe, without a date, this "auto-obituary" was found among Rowe's papers in the Washington, DC house of Matthew Bell* in August, 2012.
2 *manqué*, French: unfulfilled; frustrated in the realization of one's ambitions.

With his father, Rowe riding a bicycle, Bolton-on-Dearne, England, c 1925.

Biographical Notes

Bruce Abbey (b 1943)
BArch, Cornell, 1966. MArch, Princeton, 1971. Architect and educator. Peace Corps architect, Tunisia between 1966 and 1969. Taught architecture at University of Virginia from 1974 to 1990, and at Syracuse University since 1990, where he served as dean from 1990 to 2002.

James Ackerman (b 1919)
Distinguished American scholar of Italian Renaissance architecture, notably of Michelangelo and Palladio. Studied under Henri Focillon at Yale from 1938 to 1941 and later with Richard Krautheimer (1897–1994) and Erwin Panofsky (1892–1968) at the Institute of Fine Arts at New York University. Taught at Berkeley in the 1950s and at Harvard from 1960 to 1990.

Harold Acton (1904–1994)
British writer and scholar born into a prominent Anglo-Italian-American family at Villa La Pietra, a Florentine estate that he willed to New York University on his death. Author of *The Last Medici*, 1932, and *Memoirs of an Aesthete*, 1948.

Stanford Anderson (b 1934)
BA, University of Minnesota, 1957. MA, University of California, Berkeley, 1958. PhD, Columbia, 1968. American architectural historian, theorist, critic, and educator. Taught at Massachusetts Institute of Technology (MIT) since 1963, where he was head of the Department of Architecture from 1991 to 2004, and director of the PhD program in History, Theory, and Criticism of Architecture from 1974 to 1991 and again from 1995 to 1996.

Wystan Hugh Auden (1907–1973)
Attended Christ Church College, Oxford. Pre-eminent British-American poet. Born in York, England; moved to the United States in 1939.

A Everett "Chick" Austin (1900–1957)
BA, Harvard, 1924. Museum curator and educator. From 1927 to 1944 Austin was director of the Wadsworth Atheneum in Hartford, Connecticut, where, in the early 1930s, he initiated exhibitions of Italian Baroque art, Surrealism, and the first American retrospective of Picasso. Later, he served as director of the John and Mabel Ringling Museum of Art in Sarasota Florida. From 1927 to 1944, he taught at Trinity College, Hartford, where he founded the Fine Arts Department.

George Baird (b 1939)
BArch, University of Toronto, 1962. Honorary degrees from Harvard, 1994, and Waterloo, 2012. Canadian architect, educator, writer and architectural critic. He taught at the University of Toronto from 1967 to 1993; and at Harvard's Graduate School of Design from 1993 to 2004; and was Dean of Architecture, Landscape, and Design at the University of Toronto from 2004 to 2005. Awarded Topaz Medallion for Excellence in Architectural Education in 2012. Author of *The Space of Appearance*, 1995.

Reyner Banham (1922–1988)
Distinguished English architectural critic, theorist, writer and educator. Beginning in 1949, he studied architectural history under Nicolas Pevsner at the Courtauld Institute. Editor of *The Architectural Review* in the 1950s. From the late 1960s until his death in 1988, he worked in London while living and teaching in the United States. Author of *Theory and Design in the First Machine Age*, 1960 and *The New Brutalism: Ethic or Aesthetic?*, 1966.

Howard Barnstone (1923–1987)
Attended Amherst College from 1940 to 1942. BA, Yale, 1944. BArch, Yale, 1948. Houston architect and educator. Taught at the University of Houston. Early residences influenced by the contemporary residential designs of Philip Johnson and Mies van der Rohe. Designed Rothko Chapel in Dallas in 1971. Suffered from manic-depressive psychosis. Author of *The Galveston That Was*, 1966.

Richard Becherer (b 1950)
BA and BArch, Rice University, 1974. MA and PhD, Cornell, 1978 and 1981. American architect and educator. Taught at the University of Virginia, Auburn University, Carnegie Mellon, and elsewhere.

Matthew Bell (b 1959)
BArch, University of Notre Dame, 1983. MArch, Cornell, 1989. American architect, planner and educator. Taught at Cornell in 1987, and was assistant to Rowe in the Cornell Rome Urban Design Program at the Palazzo Massimo in 1988. Since 1989, taught at the University of Maryland.

Pietro Belluschi (1889–1994)
Italian-born, American architect who, with a degree in Civil Engineering from Rome, studied at Cornell in 1923 before moving to Portland, where he practiced architecture. A leader in the Modern Movement in architecture, Belluschi was dean of the School of Architecture at MIT from 1951 to 1965.

Paolo Berdini (1951–2015)
School of Architecture, "La Sapienza", Rome. MS (history of architecture), Pennsylvania State University. MA (History of Architecture and Urban Design) Cornell, 1990. PhD (history of art), Columbia, 1994. Art and architectural historian. Taught art history at Stanford University beginning in the mid-1990s and as visiting professor at Harvard. Author of *Painting as Visual Exegesis: The Religious Art of Jacopo Bassano*, 1997.

Isaiah Berlin (1909–1997)
Russian-born British social and political theorist. Pre-eminent philosopher and historian of ideas. Among his many books are *The Hedgehog and the Fox: An Essay on Tolstoy's View of History*, 1953 and *Against the Current: Essays in the History of Ideas*, 1979.

Alvin Boyarsky (1928–1990)
BArch, McGill University, 1951; MA Regional Planning, Cornell, 1959. Canadian-born architect and educator. Taught architecture at the University of Oregon from 1959 to1962, in London at the Architectural Association and at Bartlett School, University College between 1962 and 1965. Associate dean of architecture at the University of Illinois at Chicago Circle from 1965 to 1971. Chairman of the Architectural Association from 1971 until his death in 1990.

Elizabeth Boyarsky (b 1927)
Born near London, the first female Verbatim Reporter in the United Kingdom.

Albert Bush-Brown (1926–1994)
American architectural historian and educator. Taught art history at Princeton, Harvard, and MIT. President of Rhode Island School of Design from 1962 to 1968, and of Long Island University from 1971 to 1985. Author of *Louis Sullivan*, 1960 and *The Architecture of America: A Social Interpretation*, 1961.

Alexander Caragonne (1935–2012)
BArch, University of Texas at Austin, 1958. MArch, Cornell, 1969. American architect, writer and editor. Practiced architecture and planning in California and Texas. Taught at Cornell, University of California, Berkeley, and elsewhere. Author of *The Texas Rangers: Notes from an Architectural Underground*, 1995. Editor of Rowe's three-volume book *As I Was Saying*, 1996.

Javier Cenicacelaya (b 1951)
BArch, Universidad de Navarra (Spain), 1975. MA (Urban Design), School of Architecture of Oxford, England, 1978. Spanish architect and educator. Dean of the School of Architecture of the University of Miami, late 1980s to 1991.

Alan Colquhoun (1921–2012)
AA Dipl Hons Architectural Association, 1949. Architect. Pre-eminent architectural critic, theoretician, historian and educator. Taught at the Architectural Association from 1957 to 1964; Cornell, 1968 and 1971; Dublin and Lausanne; and Princeton, 1981 to 1991 (Emeritus after 1991). In 1961, with John Miller, he co-founded the architectural firm of Colquhoun and Miller (1961–1989).

Roger Conover (b 1950)
BA, Bowdoin College, 1972. MA, University of Minnesota, 1976. Writer, curator and editor at MIT Press.

Vivian Constantinopoulos
MA (French Literature), University College London. Commissioning editor, Reaktion Books. Formerly editor of architecture and design books at Phaidon and Academy Editions.

Wayne Copper (1942–1999)
BArch, Cornell, 1965. MArch, Cornell, 1967. Architect. McKeesport, Pennsylvania. Wrote his Cornell thesis, "The Figure / Grounds" in spring 1967.

Cynthia Davidson (b 1952)
BA, Ohio Wesleyan University, 1974. Loeb Fellow, Harvard, 1990. Married Peter Eisenman in 1990. Founder and editor of *ANY* magazine.

Michael Dennis (b 1937)
BArch, University of Oregon, 1962. Architect, educator and planner. Private practice since 1981. Taught architecture and planning at Cornell from 1968 to 1981, then at the University of Virginia in 1986, and Yale, 1988, and since 1992, at MIT. Author of *From the French Hôtel to the City of Modern Architecture,* 1988.

Gladys M Diaz (b 1956)
BArch, Cornell, 1981. MArch, Cornell, 1982. Architect and urban designer specializing in project financing, real estate investment, adaptive reuse, and historic preservation in Miami.

Judith DiMaio
BFA, Bennington College, 1972. BArch, Cornell, 1974. MArch, Harvard, 1976. Architect and educator. Winner of Rome Prize in Architecture in 1977. Awarded Fulbright-Hayes Scholarship

in 1979. Taught at Notre Dame, the University of Kentucky, and, from 1988 to 2001, at Yale. Dean of Architecture, New York Institute of Technology since 2001. In 2009, she was invited to be the first Colin Rowe Resident in Design at the American Academy.

Benjamin Disraeli (1804–1881)
British parliamentarian, Conservative statesman and literary figure. Twice Prime Minister of the United Kingdom (1868 and 1874–1880). From as early as 1979, Rowe had intended to write a book on Disraeli, but never did.

Andrés Duany (b 1949)
BArch (architecture and urban planning), Princeton, 1971. MArch, Yale, 1974. American architect, urban planner, and writer. Co-founder of Miami firm Arquitectonica in 1977 and of Duany Plater Zyberk & Co, architects of Seaside, Florida, and promoters of New Urbanism in 1980.

Roberto Einaudi (b 1938)
BArch, Cornell, 1961. MArch, MIT, 1962. Architect and educator. Born in the United States, the son of Mario Einaudi, who taught at Cornell, and grandson of Luigi Einaudi, second president of Italy, he belonged to one of Italy's most important families in government, publishing and education. Practiced architecture in Rome. Founder of Cornell's Rome Program and, from 1986 to 1992, its first director, locating the program in the Perruzzi's Palazzo Massimo alla Colonne.

Peter Eisenman (b 1932)
BArch, Cornell, 1955. MS Arch, Columbia, 1960. MA and PhD, University of Cambridge, 1962 and 1963. Eminent American architect, theorist, educator and writer. One of the New York Five in 1972. Taught at Cooper Union, Princeton, Harvard, and Yale. First executive director of the Institute for Architecture and Urban Planning, from 1967 to 1982.

Kurt Forster (b 1935)
PhD, University of Zurich. Swiss-born architectural historian, educator, writer. Taught at Stanford, MIT, ETH in Zurich, the Bauhaus University in Weimar, and since 2005, at Yale where he directs the doctoral program in architecture. From 1984 to 1993 he founded and directed research institutes at the Getty Research Center in Los Angeles and the Canadian Centre for Architecture in Montreal. Fellow at the Whitney Humanities Institute.

Eugene Gaddis (b 1947)
Amherst College, 1969. PhD (History), University of Pennsylvania, 1979. Since 1981, curator at the Wadsworth Antheneum. Author of *Magic Façade: The Austin House,* 2007.

Lisa Germany (b 1954)
MA (art History), University of Texas at Austin, 1981. Loeb Fellow, Harvard, 1996 to 1997. Architectural historian, editor, writer, and journalist who covered architecture for many years. Received Flowers Award for Media Excellence in 1995. Author of *Harwell Hamilton Harris,* 1992.

Mark Girouard (b 1931)
British architectural historian, writer, and educator. Authority on English and French country houses. Writer and editor for *Country Life* magazine between 1958 and 1967. Slade Professor of Fine Art from 1975 to 1976. Author of *Big Jim: The Life and Work of James Stirling,* 1998.

William Gladstone (1809–1898)
British politician. Liberal statesman. Prime Minister of Great Britain four times during his 60-year career. Renowned for his oratory skills and for his rivalry with Benjamin Disraeli.

Ernst Gombrich (1909–2001)
Austrian-born, British art historian. A Senior Research Fellow at the Warburg Institute in London in 1946 and director of the Institute from 1959 to 1972. Knighted in 1972. Awarded the Goethe Prize in 1994. Instrumental in bringing to publication the early work of his close friend, Karl Popper. Author of *The Story of Art,* 1950 and *Art and Illusion: A Study in the Psychology of Pictorial Representation,* 1960.

Robert Goodill (b 1960)
BArch, University of Notre Dame, 1983. MArch, Cornell, 1995 (class of 1987). Architect. Taught architecture at Syracuse from 1989 to 1994.

Charles P Graves Sr (1927–2001)
BArch, Georgia Institute of Technology, 1954. MArch, University of Pennsylvania, 1958. Taught architecture at the University of Kentucky from 1958 to 2000. First dean of the University of Kentucky College of Architecture from 1960 to 1971.

Michael Graves (1934–2015)
BArch, University of Cincinnati, 1958. MArch, Harvard, 1959. Eminent American architect, educator and product designer. Winner of the Rome Prize in 1960. Taught at Princeton from

1962. One of the New York Five in 1972. Awarded National Medal of the Arts in 1999, the AIA Gold Medal 2001; and the Topaz Medallion in 2010.

Miriam Gusevich (b 1953)
BArch, Cornell, 1975. MArch, Cornell, 1979. Loeb Fellow, Harvard, 1996 to 97. Cuban-born American architect and educator. Taught at Washington University in St Louis, the University of Wisconsin-Milwaukee, and since 2000, at the Catholic University of America in Washington, DC.

Philip Handler (b 1940)
BArch, Cornell, 1964. MArch, Cornell, 1965. Architect, photographer and, together with his wife Maddy (BS, Cornell, 1965), a documentary filmmaker. In 1985, Rowe wrote to the Handlers' son, Michael (b 1968).

Harwell Hamilton Harris (1903–1990)
Pomona College, Otis Art Institute. Architect and educator. Apprenticed with Richard Neutra. In the 1930s and 1940s he was nationally renowned for his residential design. Director of the School of Architecture, University of Texas at Austin from 1952 to 1955. Practiced architecture in Dallas from 1955 to 1962. Taught architecture at North Carolina State University from 1962 to 1973.

Jean Murray Bangs Harris (1894–1985)
BS (Economics), University of California, Berkeley. Secretary of Labor, curator and writer. Canadian-born, grew up in Pasadena, California. The first woman Secretary of Labor in the United States. Married Harwell Hamilton Harris in 1937. In the 1940s she curated exhibitions on the work of California architects Bernard Maybeck and Greene and Greene. In the mid-1950s, assisted her husband, Harwell Harris, in directing the University of Texas at Austin's Department of Architecture. Moved with Harris to North Carolina in 1962, where she wrote articles on architecture and a food column for *House Beautiful*.

John Hartell (1902–1995)
BArch, Cornell, 1925. Artist and professor of architecture and art at Cornell, from 1930 to 1968. Chairman of Cornell's Department of Art from 1939 to 1959 and director of its graduate program in fine arts until his retirement in 1968.

John Hejduk (1929–2000)
BArch, University of Cincinnati, 1952 (after three years study at Cooper

Union). MArch, Harvard, 1953. Architect, educator, and poet. Fulbright Fellow to Rome, 1954. Instructor in Architectural Design, University of Texas at Austin from 1954 to 1956. One of the New York Five in 1972. Taught at Cornell from 1958 to 1960, Yale from 1961 to 1964 and Cooper Union from 1964 to 2000, where he was Professor of Architecture and Chairman of Department of Architecture from 1965 to 1975 and Dean, 1975 to 2000.

Klaus Herdeg (1937–2009)
BArch, Cornell, 1963. MAUD Harvard, 1964. Swiss-American architect, scholar, and teacher. Traveled extensively in India, China, and Iran. Taught at Cornell from 1966 to 1973 and at Columbia from 1973 to 1995, where he was appointed department chair in 1984. Illness forced his early retirement. Author of *The Decorated Diagram: Harvard Architecture and the Failure of the Bauhaus Legacy*, 1983, which Rowe reviewed for MIT Press.

Anthony (Tony) Heywood (b 1938)
BArch, Georgia Institute of Technology, 1960. Architect and educator. Lives and works in Italy since 1984. With wife Astra Zarina, he co-founded the University of Washington's Architecture in Rome and Italian hilltowns programs and the Northwest Institute for Architecture and Urban Studies in Italy (NIAUSI). Beginning in the late 1960s, worked with Zarina to restore the hillside town of Civita di Bagnoregio, Italy.

Mark Hinchman (b 1960)
BArch, University of Notre Dame, 1983. MArch, Cornell, 1987 (class of 1983–1985). MA, University of Chicago, 1995. PhD (Art History), University of Chicago, 2000. Interior designer and educator. Taught Interior Design at the University of Nebraska since 1998.

H Lee Hirsche (1927–1998)
American artist and educator. Studied painting under Josef Albers at Yale before teaching basic design in the department of architecture at the University of Texas at Austin from 1954 to 1956. Founded the studio art department at Williams College, Massachusetts, where he taught art for more than three decades.

Henry-Russell Hitchcock Jr (1903–1987)
BA, Harvard, 1924. MA, Harvard, 1927. Distinguished American architectural historian, educator, and curator. Wrote

Modern Architecture: Romanticism and Reintegration, 1929 and curated the MoMA exhibition of 1932, The International Style: Architecture Since 1922, with Philip Johnson. Taught at Vassar, Wesleyan, Smith, MIT, Harvard, NYU's Institute of Fine Arts, and at Yale, where Rowe studied with him in 1951–1952. Among his many books are *Early Victorian Architecture in Britain,* 1954, and monographs on HH Richardson, 1936, and Frank Lloyd Wright, 1942.

Lee Hodgden (1924–2004)
BArch, University of Kansas, 1946. MArch, MIT, 1949. Architect and educator. Studied with Alvar Aalto at MIT, then taught at North Carolina State before teaching at University of Texas at Austin with Rowe in the mid-1950s. In the late 1950s, Hodgden taught at the University of Oregon and, from 1961 until his retirement, at Cornell.

Bernhard Hoesli (1923–1984)
Swiss architect, collage artist, and educator. Worked in Paris in 1947 first with Fernand Léger and then for Le Corbusier from 1947 to 1951. In 1951 he moved to the United States, where he taught with Rowe at the University of Texas at Austin. From 1959, he taught at the ETH Zürich, and in 1969, he was appointed chairman of its architecture school. In 1979, with Paul Hofer and Adolph Max Vogt, he founded the Institute for the History and Theory of Architecture within the ETH.

Judith E Holliday (1938–2008)
BA, College of Wooster, Ohio. MLibSci, Columbia. From the late 1960s until retirement in 1996, she served as the principal librarian at Cornell's College of Architecture, Art, and Planning, with expertise in books on Italian art and architecture.

Thomas Howarth (1914–2000)
University of Manchester. PhD, University of Glasgow. Educator and collector. Emigrated to Canada in 1958. Director of the School of Architecture at the University of Toronto from 1958 to 1974. Amassed the world's largest collection of the work of Scottish architect Charles Rennie Mackintosh. Author of *Charles Rennie Mackintosh and the Modern Movement,* 1952.

George Howe (1886–1955)
BArch, Harvard, 1908. École des Beaux-Arts, 1912. American architect and educator. From 1913 to 1946, he practiced architecture in Philadelphia in various firms and in partnerships and

collaborations with William Lescaze, Louis Kahn, and Oscar Stonorov. Architect in residence at the American Academy in Rome from 1947 to 1949. Chairman of Yale's Department of Architecture from 1950 to 1954.

Steven Hurtt (b 1941)
BA, Princeton, 1963. MFA, Princeton, 1965. MArch, Cornell, 1967. Architect and educator. Taught at Cornell from 1969 to 1970, the University of Notre Dame. From 1973 to 1990, he was professor and dean of University of Maryland, School of Architecture, Planning, and Preservation.

Henry James (1843–1916)
American-born writer of fiction, biography, autobiography, literary criticism and books on travel, who spent much of his life abroad, especially in England, eventually becoming a British citizen. Seminal figure in nineteenth-century literary experiments in psychological portraiture, known particularly for his novels depicting Americans encountering the cultural and moral complex of 'the old Europe'.

Charles Jencks (b 1939)
BA (English Literature), Harvard University, 1961. MA (Architecture), Harvard Graduate School of Design, 1965. PhD (Architectural History), University College London, 1970. American-born architectural theorist, critic and educator. Landscape architect and designer. Studied under Reyner Banham and Sigfried Giedion. Taught at the University of Southern California and at the Architectural Association, London. Author of *The Language of Post-Modern Architecture*, 1977.

Michael Jencks (b 1962)
BArch, University of Notre Dame, 1986. PhD, Deakin University, 2000. Architect and educator. Practiced with Cooper Robertson & Partners. Taught architecture at the Institut Française d'Architecture, the University of Canberra, and elsewhere.

Philip Johnson (1906–2005)
BA, Harvard, 1930. BArch, Harvard, 1943. Distinguished architect, museum director, and curator. Founded the Department of Architecture and Design at New York's Museum of Modern Art, and, with Henry-Russell Hitchcock, curated the exhibition of 1932, International Style: Architecture Since 1922. Studied architecture with Walter Gropius at Harvard University. Collaborated with Mies van der Rohe

and, from 1967 to 1991, with John Burgee designing large-scale corporate and institutional buildings.

Edward Jones (b 1939)
DiplHons, Architectural Association, 1963. British architect and educator. At the invitation of OM Ungers, taught at Cornell in 1973, 1976 and 1987. Taught at the Architectural Association, the Royal College of Art, Princeton, Harvard, and elsewhere. In 1989 he co-founded Dixon Jones with Jeremy Dixon in London. Member of the RIBA Gold Medal Committee, he encouraged Rowe's nomination.

Inigo Jones (1573–1652)
Distinguished British architect instrumental in introducing Italian Renaissance architecture in England. In 1947, Rowe wrote his Warburg thesis on the theoretical drawings of Inigo Jones and his student, John Webb.

Louis I Kahn (1901–1974)
BArch, University of Pennsylvania, 1924. Eminent American architect and educator. Practiced with Paul Cret; collaborated with George Howe and Oscar Stonorov. Taught at Yale beginning in 1947, and from 1957 at the University of Pennsylvania. Fellow at the American Academy in Rome in 1951. Awarded the American Institute of Architects Gold Medal in 1971 and the Royal Institute of British Architects Gold Medal in 1972.

Brian Kelly (b 1957)
BArch, University of Notre Dame, 1981. MArch, Cornell, 1987 (class of 1983–1985). Architect and educator. Taught at Syracuse and Arizona State University, and since 1987, at the University of Maryland.

Burnham Kelly (1912–1999)
Williams College, 1933. Harvard (Law), 1936. MCityPlanning, MIT, 1941. Honorary Doctor of Humane Letters, Williams College, 1963. City planner and educator. Taught City and Regional Planning at MIT from 1945 to 1960 and at Cornell from 1960 to 1987. Dean of Cornell's College of Architecture, Art, and Planning from 1960 to 1971. Initiated a New York City program for Cornell architecture and planning students.

Sydney J Key (1918–1956)
BA (Art History), University of Toronto, 1941. Art historian and curator. Curator, Art Gallery of Toronto from 1948 to 1956. Lecturer at the Courtauld Institute, London from 1946 to 1947. Toured Italy with Rowe in summer 1947.

Susie Kim (b 1948)
BArch, Cornell, 1971. MArch, Harvard, 1977. Architect, urban planner. Together with husband Fred Koetter, founder and principal of Koetter, Kim, and Associates, Architecture and Urban Design, Boston, 1978.

Josef Kleihues (1933–2004)
University of Stuttgart, 1957. Berlin Institute of Technology, 1959. German architect and educator. From 1973, taught at Dortmund University of Technology. Director of the International Building Exhibition Berlin IBA from 1979 to 1987. Promoted urban critical reconstruction for the restoration of old Berlin.

Fred Koetter (b 1938)
BArch, University of Oregon, 1962. MArch, Cornell, 1967. Educator, architect and planner. Taught at Cornell between 1967 and 1973, and later at the University of Kentucky, Yale and Harvard. In 1978 with Susie Kim, he co-founded the Boston firm Koetter, Kim, and Associates, Architecture and Urban Design. Co-authored *Collage City* with Rowe, 1978. Dean of the Yale School of Architecture from 1993 to 1998.

Léon Krier (b 1946)
Studied architecture at the University of Stuttgart. Neo-traditional architect, architectural theorist, urban designer and educator. Worked for James Stirling in London from 1968 to 1971. Taught architecture at the Architectural Association and Royal College of Art between 1972 and 1992, at Princepton, the University of Virginia and more recently at Yale. First director of the SOM Architectural Institute, Chicago from 1987 to 1990. Critic of architectural modernism and suburbanism, and advocate of new urban developments. Author of *Architecture: Choice or Fate*, 1988.

Phyllis Lambert (b 1927)
BA, Vassar College, 1948. MArch, Illinois Institute of Technology, 1963. Canadian architect, philanthropist, and founder and director of the Canadian Centre for Architecture since 1947.

Le Corbusier (1887–1965)
Pre-eminent Swiss-born French architect, writer. Widely regarded as the most influential architect of the twentieth century. Rowe wrote extensively about Le Corbusier, specifically about his Villa Schwob (1917), Villa Stein at Garches (1926), Villa Savoye (1928), Unité d'habitation

(1946), and La Tourette (1957). Author of *Vers une architecture*, 1923 and *La Ville Radieuse*, 1933.

Barbara Littenberg (b 1949)
BArch, Cornell, 1971. Architect, urban designer, and educator. Worked for Richard Meier and James Stirling. Taught at Princeton from 1974 to 1978, Columbia, and Yale. Co-founder in 1979 of Peterson Littenberg Architecture & Urban Design.

Rodolfo Machado (b 1942)
Diploma and License of Architect, Universidad de Buenos Aires, 1967. MArch, University of California at Berkeley, 1971. Architect and educator. Taught at Yale, Rice, the University of Virginia, and Princeton, and from 1976 to 1986 at Rhode Island School of Design where he was chair of the Department of Architecture. From 1986 to 2010 he taught at Harvard, where he chaired the Department of Urban Design from 2004 to 2009. Since 1974, he worked in partnership with Jorge Silvetti with whom he co-founded Machado and Silvetti in 1985.

James Madge (1933–2006)
BA, University of Cambridge, 1959. Architect, writer and educator. Taught at the Architectural Association and the Polytechnic of Central London. Author of *Sabbioneta: Cryptic City*, 2011.

James O Mahoney (1907–1987)
BFA, Southern Methodist University, 1928. MFA Yale, 1931. Winner of the Rome Prize, 1932. Renowned muralist and painter. Professor of Art at Cornell from 1939 and chairman of the Department of Art from 1963 to 1968.

Michael Manfredi (b 1953)
BArch, University of Notre Dame, 1975. MArch, Cornell, 1980. Architect and educator. Worked for Richard Meier and Romaldo Giurgola before founding Weiss/Manfredi with Marion Weiss in 1989. A Cornell Fellow and Winner of the Paris Prize. Taught architecture studios at Yale, Harvard, Princeton, and the University of Pennsylvania.

Leslie Martin (1908–2000)
BArch, Manchester, 1929. PhD, 1934. Architect and educator. Member of the MARS group. Editor of *Circle*. Head of the New School of Architecture at Hull, 1934. Chief Architect of the London County Council in 1953 and in 1956, professor and chair of architecture at the University of Cambridge. Designed numerous university buildings in England. Knighted in 1957. Awarded Royal Gold Medal in 1973.

Robert Maxwell (b 1922)
BArch, University of Liverpool, 1948. Dip CD, University of Liverpool, 1949. Architect, educator, theorist and writer. Taught architecture at the Architectural Association from 1958 to 1962, and from 1962 to 1982 at the Bartlett School, University College, London (reader, 1970 and professor, 1979). Partner in Douglas Stephen & Partners, London from 1971 to 1980. Dean of Architecture, Princeton between 1982 and 1989. Professor of Architecture, Princeton from 1989 to 1993, now Emeritus.

Arthur McDonald (b 1939)
BArch, Pratt Institute, 1963. MArch, Cornell, 1973. Architect and educator. In private practice since 1978. Since 1974, he has taught architecture at Syracuse.

Megan McFarland
BA (Print Journalism), University of Southern California, 1985. MA (English), University of California, Berkeley. Editor at Rizzoli from 1994 to 1998 and senior editor at Phaidon from 1998 to 2006.

William G McMinn (b 1931)
BA, Rice University, 1952. BArch, Rice, 1953. MArch, University of Texas at Austin, 1954. Educator. Dean of the College of Architecture, Art and Planning at Cornell from 1984 to 1996. Founding dean at Florida International University and the School of Architecture at Mississippi State University. Head of the departments of architecture at both Louisiana State and Auburn University. Awarded the Topaz Medallion, 2006.

Richard Meier (b 1934)
BArch, Cornell, 1957. Pre-eminent American architect. One of the New York Five in 1972. Awarded the Pritzker Architecture Prize in 1984.

Ursula Margaret Mercer (b 1923)
BAHons, University of Liverpool, 1945. In the year behind Rowe at the University of Liverpool, for most of her professional life Mercer was an architect with the National Health Service in London.

Dominic Michaelis (b 1938)
MA Cantab, University of Cambridge, 1962. MArch Cantab, University of Cambridge, 1963. MS (architectural structures), Cornell, 1965. French-born British architect specializing in solar energy. In 1964 he married Nina Michaelis (b 1941).

Blake Middleton (b 1956)
BArch, Cornell, 1978. MArch, Cornell, 1981. Architect and educator, fellow,

American Academy in Rome, 1982. Taught in Syracuse Florence Program from 1982 to 1983, and later as a visiting professor at Harvard, University of Virginia, Yale, and Cornell. Worked for James Stewart Polshek from 1984 to 1997. Has been a partner at Handel Architects since 1997.

Ludwig Mies van der Rohe (1886–1969)
German-born American architect and educator. Pioneering master of Modern architecture. Director of the Bauhaus from 1930 to 1933 and of the Department of Architecture at Illinois Institute of Technology beginning in 1938.

John Miller (b 1930)
AA Dipl Hons, Architectural Association, 1956. Distinguished architect, theorist, and educator. In 1961 he was a founding partner of Colquhoun and Miller (1961 to 1989). In 1990 he founded John Miller & Partners, 1990 to 2008. A visiting critic at Cornell in the mid-1960s and early 1970s. Head of the Department of Environmental Design, Royal College of Art, London, between 1975 and 1985.

Pat Miller (1933–2015)
Journalist and editor. Married to John Miller from 1957 to 1970. Moved to Sydney, Australia, in 1970, and then to New York City in the mid-1970s. Editor and publisher of *New Woman* magazine beginning in 1984.

Thomas Muirhead (b 1946)
Dott in Arch, University of Florence, 1982. Irish architect, educator and writer. Taught at Syracuse University in Florence, SCI-ARC in Switzerland, and at the Architectural Association in London. Worked for Fry and Drew. From 1977 to 1992, he was a consultant to James Stirling. In private practice in London since 1983. With Robert Maxwell he edited *James Stirling Michael Wilford & Associates: Buildings and Projects, 1975–1992*, 1994.

Daniel Naegele (b 1953)
BArch, University of Cincinnati, 1977. Grd Dip, Architectural Association, 1987. MED, Yale, 1990. PhD, University of Pennsylvania, 1996. Architect, educator, writer and editor. Has taught at Iowa State University since 2001.

John O'Brien (1955–2010)
BA, University of Memphis. BA, University of Tennessee. BArch, University of Tennessee. MA, Cornell, 1989. PhD, Cornell, 2009. Art and architectural historian and educator.

Taught at the University of Tennessee beginning in 1993. Between 1991 and 1992, O'Brien lived in Rowe's Ithaca house while studying at Cornell. In 1995 an accident left him a quadriplegic.

Joan Ockman (b 1952)
BA, Harvard, 1974. BArch, Cooper Union, 1980. Architectural historian and critic; teacher, writer, and editor. Married Robert Slutzky in 1985. Taught at Columbia from 1985 to 2008, where she directed the Buell Center for the Study of American Architecture from 1994 to 2008. Author of *Architecture Culture, 1943–1968*, 1993.

Werner Oechslin (b 1944)
PhD, University Zürich, 1970. *Habilitation*, Freie Universität Berlin, 1980. Swiss educator, architectural historian, critic, and writer. Founder of the Bibliothek Werner Oechslin in Einsiedeln, Switzerland. From 1985 to 2010, taught at the ETH Zürich as head of the Institute for History and Theory of Architecture.

Cheryl O'Neil (b 1956)
BArch, Cornell, 1980. Studied with Rowe in Cornell's Urban Design Program between 1985 and 1987. Architect. Married Matthew Bell in 1993. Worked for Torti Gallas since 1993, principal since 1998.

Franz Oswald (b 1938)
BArch, ETH Zürich. MArch (Urban Design), Cornell, 1967. Studied philosophy, literature, and art history at the University of Zürich and the University of Bern. Architect, urban planner, and educator. From 1972 to 2003, taught at the ETH Zürich, where he was chairman of the Architectural Division from 1986 to 1989, and dean of the Faculty of Architecture from 1989 to 1993. Visiting professor at Cornell, Columbia, and Syracuse. In private practice since 1976.

Andrea Palladio (1508–1580)
Venetian architect of unsurpassed influence. Author of *Il quattro libri dell'architettura* (*The Four Books of Architecture*), 1570.

William Pedersen (b 1938)
BArch, University of Minnesota, 1961. MArch, MIT, 1963. Architect. Winner of the Rome Prize in 1965. In 1976, founding partner of Kohn, Pedersen, Fox Associates, architects in New York City.

Steven K Peterson (b 1940)
BArch, Cornell, 1965. MArch, Cornell, 1970. Architect, urban designer, and educator. Worked in London between

1972 and 1973. Taught at Princeton and Columbia. Directed the Syracuse Program in Florence from 1994 to 1995. Executive Director of the Institute for Architecture and Urban Studies in New York. Co-founded Peterson Littenberg Architecture and Urban Design in 1979.

Nikolaus Pevsner (1902–1983)
Distinguished German-born British art and architectural historian, writer, and editor. Moved to England in 1933. Edited *The Architectural Review* from 1945 to 1970. Author of *Pioneers of Modern Design*, 1936 and *The Buildings of England*, 1951–1974.

Irving Phillips (b 1936)
BArch, University of Texas at Austin, 1959. MArch, Cornell, 1964. Architect and educator. Taught at the University of Houston between 1975 and 1981, and at the University of Texas-Arlington in 1991. In private practice in Houston since 1969.

Elizabeth Plater-Zyberk (b 1950)
BA (Architecture and Urban Planning), Princeton, 1972. MArch, Yale, 1974. Architect, urban planner, and educator. Since 1979 taught at the University of Miami School of Architecture, and as dean from 1995 to 2013. In 1977 she co-founded the Miami firm Arquitectonica and in 1980, Duany Plater Zyberk & Co, designers of Seaside, Florida, and promoters of New Urbanism.

Karl Raimund Popper (1902–1994)
Austrian-born British philosopher and professor at the London School of Economics. Among his many books are *The Open Society and Its Enemies*, 1957 and *The Poverty of Historicism*, 1957.

Brian Richards (1928–2004)
Trinity College, 1942–1945. BArch Hons, University of Liverpool, 1950. Yale, 1951–52. Architect, writer and educator. Taught at the Architectural Association between 1964 and 1970 and again between 1976 and 1978. Worked for Sven Markelius in Stockholm, Wallace Harrison in New York City, and ATBAT in Paris, before establishing an architectural office in London in 1966 with expertise in urban movement systems. Author of *Future Transport in Cities*, 2001.

Jaquelin Robertson (b 1933)
BA, Yale, 1955. BArch, Yale, 1961. Architect and educator. Rhodes scholar at Oxford University from 1955 to 1957. Founder of the New York City Urban Design Group. Dean of the University of Virginia School of Architecture from 1980

to 1988. Partner in the New York firm of Eisenman / Robertson Architects between 1982 and 1988, and in 1989, co-founder of Cooper, Robertson, & Partners.

Su Rogers (b 1939)
BSc (Sociology), London School of Economics, 1961. Married John Miller in 1972. Taught at the Architectural Association and, from 1972 to 1977, at the Royal College of Art, School of Environmental Design. Director of the Project Office from 1976 to 1986. From 1986 to 2008, she was a partner in the architecture firm of John Miller and Partners.

Richard B Role (1958–2005)
BArch, Notre Dame, 1982. MArch, Cornell, 1990. Architect and educator. Taught in Florence, Italy, with Syracuse from 1989 to 1996, and with Kent State University from 1996 to 2005.

David Rowe (b 1928)
Degree in Law from University College, Oxford, 1950. Solicitor. Colin Rowe's brother and only sibling.

Dorothy Rowe (née Adams) (1924–1996)
BA Honors (Modern History), University of Edinburgh, 1945. Worked in Paris for the European Recovery Programme until the mid-1950s. Married David Rowe in December 1957. In the mid-1970s, joined the staff of the Architectural Association where, under the direction of Alvin Boyarsky, she managed the post-graduate practical training program and was slide librarian. Founding Secretary of the Oxford Italian Association. Colin Rowe's sister-in-law.

James Rowe (b 1965)
MA (Physics), University of Oxford, 1987. MA (Engineering), University of Cambridge, 1992. Structural Engineer. Colin Rowe's nephew.

Frederick W Rowe (1880–1964)
Schoolmaster in Bolton-on-Dearne, Yorkshire. Born Pixton, Derbyshire, England to Elizabeth J Jenkins (b c 1855) and John F Rowe (schoolmaster, b c 1846). Colin Rowe's father.

Helena Rowe (née Beaumont) (1887–1957)
Born Wath-upon-Dearne, Yorkshire, England to Elizabeth Rodgers (b c 1858) and Frederick Beaumont (farmer and innkeeper, b c 1852). Married Frederick W Rowe in 1917. Colin Rowe's mother.

Rosemary Rowe
MA (Modern History), University of Oxford, 1987. MS (Health Economics)

London School of Hygiene and Tropical Medicine, 1999. PhD, University of Bristol, 2004. Health Services Management. Married James Rowe in 1990.

Simon Rowe (b 1970)
BA (Psychology), University of Sussex, 1994. MS (Educational Psychology), University of Cardiff, 2003. Educational psychologist. Colin Rowe's nephew.

William Safire (1929–2009)
Attended Syracuse University. Writer, columnist, journalist and presidential speechwriter. Syndicated political columnist for *The New York Times* from 1973 to 2005. Author of *"On Language"* in *The New York Times Magazine* between 1979 and 2009. Awarded the Pulitzer Prize in 1978.

Leon Satkowski (b 1947)
BArch, Cornell, 1970. MA, Harvard, 1972. PhD, Harvard, 1977. Architectural historian, educator and writer. Studied Renaissance and Baroque architecture and painting at Harvard with James Ackerman and Sydney Freedberg, and at MIT with Henry Millon. Taught at Syracuse University between 1977 and 1986. Since 1986, he has taught at the University of Minnesota. Author of *Giorgio Vasari: Architect and Courtier*, 1993. Co-author with Rowe of *Italian Architecture of the 16th Century*, 2002.

William Saunders (b 1946)
BA, Denison University, 1968. MA, University of Iowa, 1973. PhD, University of Iowa, 1975. Educator, writer, and editor. Taught English at the University of Florence, Italy, and at Tufts, Boston, and Wittenberg universities. From 1982 to 1992, he was director of the Professional Development summer program at Harvard's Graduate School of Design, where he was Assistant Dean for External Relations from 1997 to 2012, and founding editor of *Harvard Design Magazine* in 1997.

Thomas Schumacher (1941–2009)
BArch, Cornell, 1963. MArch, Cornell, 1966. Winner of the Rome Prize in 1967. Taught architecture at Princeton and the University of Virginia, and since 1984 at the University of Maryland. Author of *Surface and Symbol: Giuseppe Terragni and the Architecture of Italian Rationalism*, 1991.

Vincent Scully (b 1920)
BA, Yale, 1940. MA, Yale, 1947. PhD, Yale, 1949. Distinguished architectural historian, critic, educator and writer. Professor of the History of Art in Architecture at Yale between 1947 and 1990, and since 1990 at the University

of Miami. Author of *The Shingle Style Today: Or the Historian's Revenge*, 1974.

Werner Seligmann (1930–1998)
BArch, Cornell, 1955. Graduate Studies, Technische Hochsschule, Braunschwieg, Germany, 1958–1959. Architect and educator. Taught at the University of Texas at Austin between 1956 and 1958; at ETH Zürich from 1959 to 1961 and 1990 to 1993; at Cornell from 1961 to 1974; Harvard, 1974 to 1976; and was professor and dean of Architecture at Syracuse University from 1976 to 1998. Fellow of the American Academy in Rome in 1981. Founded Werner Seligmann and Associates in 1961. Awarded the Topaz Medallion in 1998.

Esteban Sennyey (b 1956)
BArch, Universidad Central de Venezuela, 1979. MArch, Cornell, 1982. Venezuelan architect and educator. Taught architecture at the University of Puerto Rico since 1981.

John Shearman (1931–2003)
BA, Courtauld Institute, 1955. PhD, Courtauld Institute, 1957. Historian of Italian Renaissance Art and educator. Chairman of the Art History Department, Princeton from 1979 to 1985. Professor of Art History, Harvard between 1987 and 2002, and chairman of Harvard's Department of Art History from 1990 to 1993. Author of *Mannerism*, 1967.

Jorge Silvetti (b 1942)
Diploma and License of Architect, Universidad de Buenos Aires, 1966. MArch, University of California at Berkeley, 1969. Architect, architectural historian, theorist, critic, and educator. In 1985 he co-founded Machado and Silvetti Associates, renowned for their museums, public spaces, and university buildings. Taught at Harvard since 1975 and was chairman of Harvard's Department of Architecture from 1995 to 2002. Winner of the Rome Prize in 1986.

Robert Slutzky (1929–2005)
Certificate of Graduation, Cooper Union, 1951. BFA, Yale, 1952. MFA, Yale, 1954. Painter, teacher, and writer. Paintings in the collections of the Whitney and Metropolitan Museums, New York. Taught at the University of Texas at Austin from 1954 to 1956; at the Pratt Institute from 1960 to 1968; Cooper Union, 1968 to 1990; and the University of Pennsylvania, 1990 to 2002, where he was chairman of the Department of Fine Arts from 1990 to 1992. Co-author with Rowe of *"Transparency: Literal and Phenomenal"*.

James Thrall Soby (1906–1979)
Attended Williams College between 1924 and 1926. Author, critic, collector and patron of the arts. Curator (under AE Austin), Wadsworth Atheneum from 1929 to 1939. Trustee of the Museum of Modern Art in New York between 1942 and 1979 and advisor to its Committee on the Museum Collections, from 1940 to 1967. Editor of the *Magazine of Art*. Wrote numerous monographs on twentieth-century artists.

Michael Spens (1939–2014)
MA and Dip Arch, Cambridge University. Dip Regional Planning: Architectural Association. British architect, educator, publisher, writer, and editor. Research Fellow and Director of Architectural History and Theory at the University of Dundee. Beginning in 1982, he worked at Studio International publications. Published Academy Editions in London between 1993 and 1997, and Ernst and Sohn in Berlin from 1997 to 1998. Established an international committee to restore Alvar Aalto's Viipuri Library in Russia. Wrote and edited numerous books on landscape architecture, including *The Complete Landscape Designs and Gardens of Geoffrey Jellicoe*, 1994.

James Stirling (1926–1992)
BA Hons, University of Liverpool, 1950. Distinguished Glasgow-born British architect and educator whom Rowe tutored at Liverpool in 1950. In the late 1950s and 1960s, designed buildings for Leicester, Cambridge, and Oxford universities, in 1984 the Straatsgalerie in Stuttgart, from 1985 to 1992, three university buildings in the USA. Pritzker Architectural Prize Laureate, 1981. Taught at Yale. Married Mary Shand in 1964.

Christopher Tunnard (1910–1979)
Dip, Royal Horticultural Society, 1930. Canadian-born landscape architect, city planner and writer. Garden designer in the United Kingdom and the United States. He taught landscape architecture and regional planning at Harvard Graduate School of Design from 1939 to 1943 and from 1953 to 1978 taught city planning at Yale where he wrote numerous books. Author of *Gardens in the Modern Landscape*, 1938.

Oswald Matthias Ungers (1926–2007)
University of Karlsruhe, 1947, where he studied under Egon Eiermann. German architect and educator. Taught at the Technical University of Berlin between 1963 and 1967, dean of the Faculty from 1965 to 1967. Established offices

in Cologne, Berlin, Frankfurt, and Karlsruhe. Chairman of the Cornell School of Architecture from 1969 to 1975. After 1986, he taught as a professor at Kunstakademie Düsseldorf.

Margaret Webster (b 1944)

BA, University of Tennessee, 1966. Fulbright scholar in Vienna between 1966 and 1967. Director of the Knight Visual Resource Facility at Cornell's College of Architecture, Art and Planning from 1972 to 2002.

Frederick Morris Wells (1902–1983)

BArch, Cornell University, 1927. Architect and educator. Taught architecture at Cornell beginning in 1945. Head of Architectural Design from 1950 to 1968. Chairman of newly formed School of Architecture from 1968 to 1969.

Jerry A Wells (b 1935)

BArch, University of Texas, 1959. ETH Zürich, 1960 to 1962. Architect and educator. Taught at Cornell since 1965 and was department chair from 1980 to 1989. Married to Adele Wells from 1962 to 1975.

Marcus Whiffen (1916–2002)

BA, University of Cambridge, 1937. MA, University of Cambridge, 1946. Architectural historian, educator, and editor. Assistant editor for *The Architectural Review,* London between 1946 and 1952. Taught at MIT, at the University of Texas at Austin between 1953 to 1954, and from 1954 to 1959 was Architectural Historian at Colonial Williamsburg. Taught at Arizona State University from 1959 to 2000. Editor of the *Journal of Architectural Education,* between 1962 and 1967, and *Triglyph*, 1984 to 1990. Wrote extensively on English and American architecture.

Colin St John "Sandy" Wilson (1922–2007)

Attended Cambridge University between 1940 and 1942. Bartlett School, University College, London, 1949. Architect, teacher and author. Architect at the London County Council from 1950 to 1955. Taught at Cambridge between 1956 and 1969 and again from 1975 to 1989. Architect of The British Library, London from 1962 until 1997. Renowned collector of British modern art.

Rudolf Wittkower (1901–1971)

German-born British educator, distinguished historian of Italian Renaissance and Baroque architecture. Studied art history in Munich with Heinrich Wölfflin. Resident at the Herziana in Rome between 1923 and 1927. Director of the Warburg Institute, London from 1933 to 1956. Founder and co-editor of *The Journal of the Warburg and Courtauld Institutes*. In 1946 to 1947 he supervised Rowe's Warburg thesis on the drawings of Inigo Jones. From 1956 to 1969, he was chair of the Department of Art History and Archaeology at Columbia University in New York. Among his many books are *Architectural Principles in the Age of Humanism*, 1949.

Frank Lloyd Wright (1867–1959)

Eminent American architect, educator and writer. After 20 years of designing for suburban Chicago, in 1911 he designed a house and studio for himself in Spring Green Wisconsin and in 1932 founded the Taliesin Fellowship, a school of architecture. In the late 1930s, he built Fallingwater; Taliesin West, a winter home for himself and the Fellowship near Scottsdale Arizona; and the Johnson Wax Administration Building. His renowned Guggenheim Museum in NYC was completed in October, 1959, six months after his death.

Astra Zarina (1929–2008)

BArch, University of Washington, 1953. MArch, MIT, 1955. Latvian-born American architect, educator, and writer. Worked for Minoru Yamasaki in the late 1950s. Awarded Fulbright Scholarship and American Academy in Rome Fellowship in Architecture in 1960. With her second husband, Tony Heywood, she co-founded the University of Washington in Seattle Italian Studies program in 1970 and its summer program on Italian Hill Towns in 1976. Established University of Washington's Rome Center in 1984, and served as its first director from 1984 to 1994. From the late 1960s, she worked with Heywood to restore the ancient hillside town of Civita di Bagnoregio, Italy. With photographer Balthazar Korab, she co-authored *I tetti di Roma: Le terrazze, le altane, i belvedere*, 1976.

Kestutis Paul Zygas (b 1942)

AB, Harvard, 1964. MArch, Harvard, 1968. PhD, Cornell, 1978. Architectural historian, educator and writer. Taught at University of Southern California, from 1977 to 1984, and since 1984, at Arizona State University.

Chronology

27 March 1920. Born in Rotherham, South Yorkshire, England.

1920–1938. Lives at 37 Highgate Lane, Bolton-on-Dearne, South Yorkshire, England; attended Wath-upon-Dearne Grammar School.

October 1928. Colin's only sibling, David Rowe, is born.

October 1938. Begins architecture studies at the University of Liverpool.

March–December 1942. "Called up" 12 March 1942. Serves in basic military training.

December 1942. Elects to be a paratrooper in Britain's Royal Air Force.

June 1943. Fractures spine in practice parachute jump near Manchester, England. Hospitalized for more than six months.

January 1944. Honorable discharge from military service.

1944–1945. Completes architecture studies at the University of Liverpool; thesis: "Pump Rooms and Baths in Cheltenham"; awarded B Arch (II) on 7 July 1945.

1946–1947. Lives in basement apartment at 43 Paulton's Square in Chelsea, London while studying with Rudolf Wittkower at the Warburg Institute, University of London.

March 1947. Publishes "The Mathematics of the Ideal Villa" in *The Architectural Review*.

November 1947. Completes thesis for the Warburg Institute: "Theoretical Drawings of Inigo Jones: Their Sources and Scope". Awarded MA (Art History).

October 1947–1951. Design Critic and Fifth-year Master at the University of Liverpool.

October 1951–June 1952. Studies at Yale on Smith-Mundt Fellowship & Fulbright Scholarship.

June 1952–April 1953. Travels in North America with Brian Richards; works in Vancouver (summer 1952) and Bakersfield, CA (fall 1952).

Spring/summer 1953. Hired by Harwell Hamilton Harris to teach at the University of Texas-Austin beginning in January 1954.

May 1953. Visits Houston, Texas.

June–September 1953. Lives in New York City, 190 East End Ave.

September 1953–January 1954. Visits parents in Bolton-on-Dearne, England. Visits Paris and London.

January 1954–June 1956. Assistant Professor at the University of Texas-Austin for five semesters. Writes "Transparency: Literal and Phenomenal" with Robert Slutzky.

1956–1957. Teaches at Cooper Union in New York City where he lives on E 9th near Madison. Writes "Neo-'Classicism' and Modern Architecture".

January 1957. Rowe's mother dies.

1957–1958. Teaches at Cornell.

1958–1962. Teaches at the University of Cambridge, England. Writes "The Architecture of Utopia", 1959 and "La Tourette", 1961.

September 1962. Appointed Associate Professor of Architecture at Cornell for a period of three years.

1964. Rowe's father dies.

1966. Appointed Full Professor of Architecture at Cornell.

1965–1966. Leads Cornell Urban Design students in Buffalo Waterfront Project.

1967. Leads Cornell Urban Design students in Harlem redevelopment design competition.

1968. Bernhard Hoesli publishes Rowe and Slutzky's "Transparency: Literal and Phenomenal" as *Transparenz* in Switzerland.

Fall 1969 and fall 1970. Resides at the American Academy in Rome.

1972. Purchases house at 19 Renwick Place, Ithaca, NY.

August–December 1973. Writes *Collage City* with Fred Koetter in Ithaca.

1976. Publishes *The Mathematics of the Ideal Villa and Other Essays*.

June 1976. Undergoes operation in NYC to repair fracture to right hip sustained in 1973.

1976. Project for Nicollet Island, Minneapolis with Judith DiMaio.

1977–1978. Leads Cornell Urban Design Studio in *Roma Interrotta* competition.

1978. Publishes *Collage City*, co-authored by Fred Koetter.

1980–1981 academic year. Teaches in Rome for Notre Dame.

March–May 1984. Teaches at the University of Virginia as Thomas Jefferson Professor.

1984. Bernhard Hoesli dies in Bangkok.

1985. Named Andrew Dixon White Professor of Architecture at Cornell. Awarded AIA/ACSA Topaz Medallion for Excellence in Architectural Education.

October 1985. Undergoes second hip operation in Boston.

January–June 1986. Teaches in Florence for Syracuse.

January–June 1987. Teaches in Florence for Syracuse.

October 1987. Becomes a US citizen.

January–June 1988. Teaches in Rome for Cornell.

January–October 1989. Teaches in Rome for Cornell.

October 1989–February 1990. Teaches in Houston for Rice; injures back in February.

March–May 1990. Convalesces with Steven Peterson and Barbara Littenburg in NYC.

1990. Appointed Professor Emeritus.

September 1990–December 1991. Lives in Ithaca, NY.

January–June 1992. Teaches in Rome for Cornell for the last time.

June 1992. James Stirling dies.

July–August 1992. Lives in London at 65 Darwin Court, Gloucester Avenue.

September 1992–August 1993. Lives in Ithaca, NY.

1993. Undergoes surgery in Boston to correct damage to lower vertebrae.

September 1993–October 1994. Lives in London at 65 Darwin Court, Gloucester Avenue.

1994. Publishes *The Architecture of Good Intentions* in England.

October–November 1994. Lives in Washington, DC at 'Classic Residences by Hyatt'.

1995–1999. Lives in Washington, DC at the Kennedy-Warren, Connecticut Avenue.

June 1995. Awarded RIBA Royal Gold Medal.

1995. Sells house at 19 Renwick Place, Ithaca, NY.

April 1996. Dorothy Rowe dies. *Festspiele* held in Colin Rowe's honor at Cornell.

1996. Publishes *As I Was Saying*, edited by Alexander Caragonne.

5 November 1999. Dies in Washington, DC.

Spring 2000. Ashes scattered at Temple of the Four Winds, Castle Howard, Yorkshire, England.

2002. *Italian Architecture of the 16th Century*, co-authored by Leon Satkowski, published posthumously.

Select Bibliography

1947 . "The Mathematics of the Ideal Villa: Palladio and Le Corbusier Compared", *The Architectural Review* 101, March 1947, pp 101–104.
. "Theoretical Drawings of Inigo Jones: Their Sources and Scope", MA thesis, University of London, November 1947.

1950 . "Mannerism and Modern Architecture", *The Architectural Review* 107, May 1950, pp 289–299.

1953 . "Reply to Talbot Hamlyn's Recent Book", *The Art Bulletin* 35, no 2, June 1953, pp 169–174.

1954 . "Roots of American Architecture: An Answer to Mumford's Analysis", *The Architectural Review* 116, August 1954, pp 75–78.

1956 . "Chicago Frame: Chicago's Place in the Modern Movement", *The Architectural Review* 120, November 1956, pp 285–189. Reprinted in *Architectural Design*, December 1970, pp 641–647.

1957 . Colin Rowe and John Hejduk, "Lockhart, Texas", *The Architectural Record* 121, March 1957, pp 201–206.

1959 . "The Architecture of Utopia", *Granta*, 24 January 1959, pp 20–26.
. "Le Corbusier: Utopian Architect", *The Listener*, February 12, 1959, pp 287–289.
. "Criticism of the Annual Exhibition of AA School Work", *Architectural Association Journal*, September/October 1959.
. "The Blenheim of the Welfare State" (criticism of Churchill College design), *Cambridge Review*, 31 October 1959, pp 89–90.

1960 . "Sidgwick Avenue", *Cambridge Review*, 8 October 1960, pp 2–5.

1961 . "Dominican Monastery of LaTourette, Eveux-sur-Arbresle, Lyons", *The Architectural Review* 129, June 1961, pp 401–410.

1963 . With Robert Slutzky, "Transparency: Literal and Phenomenal", part 1, *Perspecta*, no 8, 1963, pp 45–54. Reprinted as *Transparenz*, Bernhard Hoesli ed, Basel: Birkhäuser, 1968.

1967 . *The New City: Architecture and Urban Renewal*, New York: Museum of Modern Art, 1967, pp 24–29.
. "Harlem Plan, New York", *World Architecture* 4, 1967, pp 10–15.
. "Museum of Modern Art Discovers Harlem", *Architectural Forum*, March 1967, pp 42–43.
. "Waiting for Utopia" (review of Robert Venturi, *Complexity and Contradiction in Architecture*, and Reyner Banham, *The New Brutalism*), *The New York Times Book Review*, 10 September 1967, p 351.

1971 . Colin Rowe and Robert Slutzky, "Transparency: Literal and Phenomenal", part 2, *Perspecta*, no 13/14, 1971, pp 287–301. Reprinted in *Parametro*, November 1985, pp 38–43 and pp 60–61; *Arquitectura*, September/October 1978, pp 34–42; and *A & U: Architecture & Urbanism*, no 2, February 2001, pp 21–46.

1972 . Introduction to Museum of Modern Art (New York, NY), *Five Architects: Eisenman, Graves, Gwathmey, Hejduk, Meier*, New York: Wittenborn, 1972, pp 3–7.

1973 . "Neo-'Classicism' and Modern Architecture", parts 1 and 2. *Oppositions*, no 1, September 1973, pp 1–26.

1974 . "Character and Composition; or Some Vicissitudes of Architectural Vocabulary in the Nineteenth Century", *Oppositions*, no 2, January 1974, pp 41–60.

1975 . "Collage City", *The Architectural Review* 158, August 1975, pp 64–91.
. "Colin Rowe on Conceptual Architecture", Artnet, October 1975, pp 6–9.

1976 . *The Mathematics of the Ideal Villa and Other Essays*, Cambridge, MA: MIT Press, 1976. Reprinted in Italian as *La matematica della villa ideale e altri scritti*, Paulo Berdini trans, Bologna: Zanichelli editore, 1993. Reprinted in German as *Die Mathematik der idealen Villa und andere Essays* with a new "Vorwort" by Colin Rowe, Christoph Schnoor trans, Basel: Birkhäuser, 1998.
. "Robert Venturi and the Yale Mathematics Building", *Oppositions*, no 6, fall 1976, pp 1–23.

1978 . With Fred Koetter, *Collage City*, Cambridge, Massachusetts: MIT Press, 1978. Reprinted in German as *Collage City*, Bernhard Hoesli ed and trans, Basel: Birkhauser Verlag, 1984. *Collage City* was subsequently translated into many languages.

1979 . "Rome Interrotta: Sector 8", *Architectural Design*, March/April 1979, pp 68–75.
. Foreword to Rob Krier, *Urban Space*, London: Academy Editions, 1979, pp 7–12.
. "Roma lnterrota: Sector 8", *Modulus*, 1979, pp 76–88.
. "The Present Urban Predicament": lecture presented to the Royal Institution, London, England, 18 June, 1979, as part of the Cubitt Lecture Series. Published in *Architectural Association Quarterly* 11, no 4, 1979, pp 40–48 and 63–64.

1980 . "Architectural Education in the USA": paper presented at a conference at the Museum of Moderm Art, 1971. Published in *Lotus International*, no 27, 1980, 42–46.
. Colin Rowe and Fred Koetter, "The Crisis of the Object: The Predicament of Texture", *Perspecta*, no 16, 1980, pp 109–40.

1981 . "The Present Urban Predicament", *The Cornell Journal of Architecture*, no 1, fall 1981, pp 16–33, 136.

1983 . "Program Versus Paradigm", *The Cornell Journal of Architecture*, no 2, fall 1983, pp 8–19.
. "Comments on the IBA Proposals", *Architectural Design*, January 1983, pp 121–27.
. "IBA Berlino: Passeggiate Berlinesi", *Casabella*, January/February 1983, pp 50–51.

1984 . "The Revolt of the Senses", *Architectural Design* 54, nos 7–8, July/August 1984, pp 7–9.
. "IBA: Rowe Reflects", *The Architectural Review*, September 1984, pp 92–95.
. "Zur Verschwundenen Offentlichkeit" (Vanished Public Life), *Baumeister*, September 1984, pp 46–52.
. "James Stirling: A Highly Personal and Very Disjointed Memoir", *James Stirling: Buildings and Projects*. New York: Rizzoli, 1984, pp 10–27.

1985 . "I Stood in Venice on the Bridge of Sighs", *Design Quarterly*, no 129, 1985, pp 17–31.

."Address to the 1985 ACSA Annual Meeting in Vancouver", (ACSA/AIA Award for Excellence in Architectural Education), *Journal of Architectural Education,* fall 1985, pp 2–6.

."Who but Stirling?", (Criticism of Sackler Museum), *Architectural Record,* March 1986, pp 122–123. Reprinted in *Architecture+Urbanism* 194, no 11, November 1986, pp 71–90.

1987 ."The Provocative Facade: Frontality and Contrapposto", *Le Corbusier Architect of the Century,* Great Britain: Arts Council of Great Britain, 1987, pp 24–28.

1989 ."Talento e idee: una conferenza = Talent and Ideas: A Conference", *Lotus International,* no 62, 1989, pp 7–17.
."Postmodern Urbanism", *Design Book Review,* no 17, Winter 1989, pp 11–30.

1990 ."Una historia ininterrumpida: sobre el Clasicismo, el Neoclasicismo, el Neoneoclasicismo", Arquitectura y Vivienda, no 21, 1990, pp 81–83. For English summary, see pp 81–83.
."Giulio Romano, Andrea Palladio: A Sixteenth Century Diversion—The Prescott H. Thomas Memorial lecture series, Fall 1986", *Cornell Journal of Architecture,* no 4, fall 1990, pp 198–205.

1991 ."Grid/Frame/Lattice/Web: Giulio Romano's Palazzo Maccarani and the Sixteenth Century", *Cornell Journal of Architecture* 4, 1991, pp 6–21, 206.

1993 ."J.F.S. 1924–1992", *ANY,* no 2, September/October 1993, pp 8–11.
."Las cenizas del genio", Arquitectura y Vivienda, no 42, July/August 1993, pp 2–6.

1994 .*The Architecture of Good Intentions,* London: Academy Editions, 1994.
."On Architectural Education", *ANY,* no 7–8, 1994, pp 48–51.
."Bibliotheca Alexandrina: An Also Ran?", *ANY,* no 7–8, 1994, pp 52–57.

1995 ."The Gospel According to Rowe", *Architects' Journal* 201, no 9, March 2, 1995, pp 20–21.

1996 .*As I Was Saying: Recollections and Miscellaneous Essays,* Alexander Caragonne ed, 3 vols, Cambridge, Massachusetts: MIT Press, 1996.
."Thanks to the RIBA—Part 1", *Journal of Architecture* 1, no 1, Spring 1996, pp 3–17.
."Thanks to the RIBA—Part 2", *Journal of Architecture* 1, no 2, Summer 1996, 105–114.

1997 .Colin Rowe and Robert Slutzky, *Transparency,* Introduction by Werner Oechslin, commentary by Bernhard Hoesli, Basel: Birkhäuser Verlag, 1997.
."A Modest Proposal for a New Suburbanism: On Continental Prototypes", *Harvard Design Magazine,* Winter/Spring 1997, pp 64–67.
."The Avant-Garde Revisited", RE Somol ed, *Autonomy and Ideology: Positioning the Avant-Garde in America,* New York: Monacelli Press, 1997, pp 48–67.

1999 ."Werner Seligman, 1930–1998", *Parametro,* no 228, March/April 1999, p 3.

2002 .Colin Rowe and Leon Satkowski, *Italian Architecture of the Sixteenth Century,* New York: Princeton Architectural Press, 2002.

2005 ."Urban Dilemmas: Prussian Rationalism, French 'folies de grandeur,' Catalonian Civility, Norwegian Urbanity", *The Architectural Review* 217, no 1297, March 2005, pp 58–71.
."Architectural Education, USA", *ZAPP Urbanism,* no 4, 2005, pp 24–37. Reprint of a paper given in November 1971 at the Museum of Modern Art in New York.

2012 ."Five Hundredth Issue: Word and Image", *Architecture and Urbanism* 500, no 5, May 2012. Excerpts from "The Mathematics of the Ideal Villa".

Letter and Illustration Credits
Letter Credits

David Rowe, Colin Rowe's Literary Executor. Permission to publish letters written by Colin Rowe, and excerpts from letters written to Rowe by his parents and David Rowe.

Lisa Germany. Permission to publish excerpts from her letter to Rowe in footnotes.

Werner Oeschlin. Permission to publish excerpts from his letter to Rowe in footnotes.

Courtesy of the Archives of American Art, Smithsonian Institution, Henry-Russell Hitchcock papers, 1919–1987. Permission to publish letters to Henry-Russell Hitchcock and excerpts from Hitchcock's letters to Rowe in footnotes.

Courtesy of the Alan Colquhoun Collection, Avery Architectural and Fine Arts Library, Columbia University. Permission to publish letters to Alan Colquhoun and footnotes related to these letters.

Courtesy of the Canadian Centre for Architecture, Montréal. Permission to publish letters to Peter Eisenman and Phyllis Lambert.

Courtesy of the Charles Moore Foundation, Austin, Texas, Colin Rowe Library. Permission to publish letters to Burnham Kelly, LN Haywood, Dorothy Rowe and Michael Spens.

Courtesy of The Louis I Kahn Collection, the University of Pennsylvania and the Pennsylvania Historical and Museum Commission, 030.II.A.65.22. Permission to publish letters to Louis I Kahn and footnotes related to these letters.

Courtesy of the Marcus Whiffen Collection, Archives and Special Collections, Architectural and Environmental Design Library, Arizona State University Libraries: Folder 27, Box 5. Permission to publish letter to Marcus Whiffen.

Illustration Credits

cover Colin Rowe by Valerie Bennet, 1992, © Valerie Bennett/National Portrait Gallery, London.
p 9 Photo courtesy of David Rowe.
p 28 Photo courtesy of David Rowe and Tony Eardley.
p 33 Photo by Bob Slutzky, courtesy of Joan Ockman.
p 122 Photo © Sandra Lousada.
p 137 Photo courtesy of Judith DiMaio.
p 174 Photo courtesy of Judith DiMaio.
p 193 Courtesy of Judith Wolin and the Rhode Island School of Design.
p 213 Photo courtesy of staff, University of Notre Dame-Rome Yearbook, 1980–1981.
p 278 Photo courtesy of David Rowe.
p 374 Photo courtesy of David Rowe.
p 414 Photo © Valerie Bennett/National Portrait Gallery, London.
p 542 Photo courtesy of David Rowe.
p 553 Photo courtesy of David Rowe.

Rowe at his grandfather's Springwell Farm, Bolton-on-Dearne, Yorkshire, c 1938.

Index

Rowe commonly used abbreviations and more obscure nicknames. These are present in the index under the formal name.

© 2016 Artifice books on architecture, the architects and the authors. All rights reserved.

Artifice books on architecture
10A Acton Street
London
WC1X 9NG

t. +44 (0)207 713 5097
f. +44 (0)207 713 8682
sales@artificebooksonline.com
www.artificebooksonline.com

All opinions expressed within this publication are those of the authors and not necessarily of the publisher.

Designed by Rachel Pfleger at Artifice books on architecture.
British Library Cataloguing-in-Publication Data.
A CIP record for this book is available from the British Library.

ISBN 978 1 908967 53 4

Artifice books on architecture is an environmentally responsible company. *The Letters of Colin Rowe: Five Decades of Correspondence* is printed on sustainably sourced paper.